What They Said in 1972

What They Said® In 1972

The Yearbook of Spoken Opinion

•

Compiled and Edited by

ALAN F. PATER

and

JASON R. PATER

MONITOR BOOK COMPANY, INC.

FOURTH ANNUAL EDITION

Printed in the United States of America

Library of Congress catalogue card number: 74-111080

ISBN number: 0-9600252-5-1

WHAT THEY SAID is published annually by
Monitor Book Company, Inc.
Beverly Hills, Calif.

To

The Newsmakers of the World . . .

May they never be at a loss for words

Preface to the First Edition (1969)

Words can be powerful or subtle, humorous or maddening. They can be vigorous or feeble, lucid or obscure, inspiring or despairing, wise or foolish, hopeful or pessimistic . . . they can be fearful or confident, timid or articulate, persuasive or perverse, honest or deceitful. As tools at a speaker's command, words can be used to reason, argue, discuss, cajole, plead, debate, declaim, threaten, infuriate, or appease; they can harangue, flourish, recite, preach, discourse, stab to the quick, or gently sermonize.

When casually spoken by a stage or film star, words can go beyond the press-agentry and make-up facade and reveal the inner man or woman. When purposefully uttered in the considered phrasing of a head of state, words can determine the destiny of millions of people, resolve peace or war, or chart the course of a nation on whose direction the fate of the entire world may depend.

Until now, the *copia verborum* of well-known and renowned public figures—the doctors and diplomats, the governors and generals, the potentates and presidents, the entertainers and educators, the bishops and baseball players, the jurists and journalists, the authors and attorneys, the congressmen and chairmen-of-the-board—whether enunciated in speeches, lectures, interviews, radio and television addresses, news conferences, forums, symposiums, town meetings, committee hearings, random remarks to the press, or delivered on the floors of the United States Senate and House of Representatives or in the parliaments and palaces of the world—have been dutifully reported in the media, then filed away and, for the most part, forgotten.

The editors of *WHAT THEY SAID* believe that consigning such a wealth of thoughts, ideas, doctrines, opinions and philosophies to interment in the morgues and archives of the Fourth Estate is lamentable and unnecessary. Yet the media, in all their forms, are constantly engulfing us in a profusion of endless and increasingly voluminous news reports. One is easily disposed to disregard or forget the stimulating discussion of critical issues embodied in so many of the utterances of those who make the news and, in their respective fields, shape the events throughout the world. The conclusion is therefore a natural and compelling one: the educator, the public official, the business executive, the statesman, the philosopher—everyone who has a stake in the complex, often confusing trends of our times—should have material of this kind readily available.

These, then, are the circumstances under which *WHAT THEY SAID* was conceived. It is the culmination of a year of listening to the people in the public eye; a year of scrutinizing, monitoring, reviewing, judging, deciding—a year during which the editors resurrected from almost certain oblivion those quintessential elements of the year's *spoken* opinion which, in their judgment, demanded preservation in book form.

WHAT THEY SAID is a pioneer in its field. Its *raison d'etre* is the firm conviction that presenting, each year, the highlights of vital and interesting views from the lips of prominent people on virtually every aspect of contemporary civilization fulfills the need to give the *spoken* word the permanence and lasting value of the *written* word. For, if it is true that a picture is worth 10,000 words, it is equally true that a verbal conclusion, an apt quote or a candid comment by a person of fame or influence can have more significance and can provide more understanding than an entire page of summary in a standard work of reference.

The editors of *WHAT THEY SAID* did not, however, design their book for researchers and scholars alone. One of the failings of the conventional reference work is that it is blandly written and referred to primarily for facts and figures, lacking inherent "interest value." *WHAT THEY SAID*, on the other hand, was planned for sheer enjoyment and pleasure, for searching glimpses into the lives and thoughts of the world's celebrities, as well as for serious study, intellectual reflection and the philosophical contemplation of our multifaceted life and mores. Furthermore, those pressed for time, yet anxious to know what the newsmakers have been saying, will welcome the short excerpts which will make for quick, intermittent reading—and rereading. And, of course, the topical classifications, the speakers' index, the subject index, the place and date information—documented and authenticated and easily located—will supply a rich fund of hitherto not readily obtainable reference and statistical material.

Finally, the reader will find that the editors have eschewed trite comments and cliches, tedious and boring. The selected quotations, each standing on its own, are pertinent, significant, stimulating—above all, relevant to today's world, expressed in the speakers' own words. And they will, the editors feel, be even more relevant tomorrow. They will be re-examined and reflected upon in the future by men and women eager to learn from the past. The prophecies, the promises, the "golden dreams," the boastings and rantings, the bluster, the bravado, the pleadings and representations of those whose voices echo in these pages (and in those to come) should provide a rare and unique history lesson. The positions held by these luminaries, in their respective callings, are such that what they say today may profoundly affect the future as well as the present, and so will be of lasting importance and meaning.

Beverly Hills, California

ALAN F. PATER
JASON R. PATER

Table of Contents

About the 1972 Edition . . .

The 1969 edition of *WHAT THEY SAID* inaugurated a new and different kind of reference series—one that had never before been attempted: a serious, in-depth record of the year in the words of the people who were most instrumental in shaping it.

Since that time, the passing parade of personalities and events has been continuously recorded in the pages of *WHAT THEY SAID*, in thousands of quotations expressing countless ideas and opinions on the myriad issues that make each year unique.

The 1972 edition is no exception. In fact, 1972 was a very fertile and productive year for events of national and international scope. Unprecedented state visits by a U.S. President to ostensibly hostile adversaries, the apparent winding down of a protracted and controversial conflict in Southeast Asia, one of the most hotly-contested U.S. Presidential elections in history—these were happenings that seemed to overshadow the on-going, year-to-year workings of the world.

Yet, all aspects of modern civilization have their own significance and demand attention—from the environment to industry, from journalism to motion pictures and the arts, from sports to education; all of these phases of contemporary life make up the whole of a year and are the seeds of a history which will flourish for the civilizations of the future.

We believe the 1972 edition of *WHAT THEY SAID* captures this year, as previous editions have for their respective years, in a manner that is singular and distinctive; and we hope it will provide many and varied uses now and in the future.

The Editors again this year wish to thank those educators, librarians and others who have given encouragement and offered suggestions on improving the series. All comments are of course welcomed, and any ideas deemed practical and worthy will be considered for forthcoming volumes of *WHAT THEY SAID.*

Readers who have used earlier editions will note some changes in the 1972 volume. Reflecting the increased significance of the women's liberation movement, a separate category, "Women's Liberation," has been added. Also, several new sections have been included in the "Editorial Treatment" pages: "Selection of Categories," "Selection of Speakers" and "Selection of Quotations"; these descriptive elements explain some of the standards and methods used in compiling *WHAT THEY SAID.*

Since *WHAT THEY SAID* is a reflection of the constantly-changing world scene, the issues and voices raised from year to year are bound to vary in interest and importance. Thus, by comparing each year's edition with those before it, the reader will find some topics receiving either more or less attention, according to their relevance in a given year, and some individuals, more than others, speaking out on the issues.

With no intention of being a news summary of 1972, following are some of the happenings reflected in many of this year's quotations . . .

ABOUT THE 1972 EDITION . . .

Civil Rights:

By far the most controversial issue in the civil rights field in 1972 was that of the busing of school children for racial balance. Also of note were the discussion of minimum quotas for minorities in college admission and employment as well as political party membership, and the possibility of a future black political party distinct from the Democrats and Republicans.

Commerce/Industry/Finance:

Consumerism remained a much-discussed national subject, along with counter-advertising, multinational corporations and the social responsibilities of business. Protectionism in the foreign-trade area was advocated by those who feel that the U.S. has been getting a bad deal from other countries in regard to trade quotas and restrictions, and condemned by those who feel protectionism would only worsen the U.S. trade position because of possible retaliation from abroad. U.S. industry's productivity decline was lamented widely, conglomerates were criticized with claims of monopolization and undue influence in national affairs, and a controversial sale of U.S. grain to the Soviet Union made big news. One of Senator George McGovern's stands in his Presidential campaign was his criticism of big business in general and what he called its unfair tax advantages and influences in the country.

Crime:

The California and U.S. Supreme Courts ruled against capital punishment, gun-control remained a very-much debated issue, and prison conditions came in for criticism. Revelations of corruption in police departments created headlines, and FBI Director J. Edgar Hoover died.

Education:

Financing of schools was an important subject in 1972, with alternatives to the property-tax sought. There was concern for the future of non-public schools, faculty labor unions loomed on the horizon, and vocation-and-career education received a good deal of support.

The Environment:

Some observers saw a decline of public interest in the environment in 1972, but such matters as the Alaska pipeline, nuclear power plants, solar energy, warnings of blackouts and brownouts and the United Nations Conference on the Human Environment, in Stockholm, provided much impetus to the general debate on conservation and pollution.

Foreign Affairs:

White House responsibility in foreign affairs was hotly debated in and out of Congress. Especially controversial were the limits of Presidential war-making authority and the policy responsibilities of Secretary of State William P. Rogers and National Security Affairs Adviser Henry Kissinger. Also of note were the subjects of U.S. bases overseas, the question of continuing such services as *Radio Free Europe*, *Radio Liberty* and *The Voice of America*—and the persistent debate on isolationism.

Africa:

The expulsion of Asian residents from Uganda occupied the spotlight in Africa this year. Other events included the attempted assassination of Morocco's King Hassan and the British-Rhodesian return to normal relations.

Americas:

Exiled former President Juan Peron returned to Argentina, remained a while, then departed. There were increasing moves by countries in the area to de-isolate Cuba; the U.S. and Cuba initiated talks to limit future use of Cuba as a haven for airliner hijackers; Chile accused the U.S. of interference in its internal affairs.

Asia:

Probably the number one international news story of 1972 was U.S. President Nixon's unprecedented visit to Communist China and his talks with Premier Chou En-lai. Also of note in this region were the reversion to Japan of Okinawa, the declaration of martial law in the Philippines, the apparent easing of tension between North and South Korea, and Prime Minister Mujibur Rahman's return to the new nation of Bangladesh.

Indochina:

The war dragged on in 1972. Late in the year, a peace treaty seemed to be at hand; but, by December 31, no agreement had been signed. The United States increased bombing in North Vietnam, including areas of Hanoi and Haiphong, and planted mines in the North's harbors. Charges of U.S. bombing of North Vietnamese dikes stirred criticism from around the world and brought denials by U.S. authorities. Former U.S. Attorney General Ramsey Clark visited Hanoi, and the issue of amnesty for U.S. draft-dodgers and deserters created much discussion.

Europe:

U.S. President Nixon's summit meeting in Moscow was a major event, as was the finalization of preliminaries for Britain's entry into the European Common Market. Northern Ireland continued as Europe's major trouble spot; Britain assumed direct rule of Ulster.

Mideast:

Arab terrorist attacks at Lod Airport (Tel Aviv) and at the Munich Olympic Games were two tragic headlines in 1972. Also making news was Egypt's ouster of Soviet military personnel.

Journalism:

The jailing of several newsmen for failure to reveal their news sources as ordered in legal proceedings brought to a head the confrontation between government and the news media. Criticism of alleged bias in journalism by the Nixon Administration, especially in the person of White House Director of Telecommunications Policy Clay Whitehead, prompted the media's retaliation and warnings of government censorship and manipulation of the news. *Life* magazine ceased publication after 36 years.

Government:

Public confidence in government was widely discussed in 1972, as were Federal revenue-sharing with the states and cities, and the growth and concentration of government (with President Nixon calling for reform of government and a decentralized approach with more decision power at local levels). The impounding by the President of funds already allocated for spending by the Congress became a heated issue, and criticism of secrecy and classification in government gained momentum.

Labor/The Economy:

Inflation remained the key subject in this category in 1972, with wage-price controls somewhat slackened. Tax reform was a big issue, including criticism of tax loopholes and calls for minimum income taxes, as well as the possibility of a value-added or national sales tax. Unemployment was either on its way down or continuing at too high a level, depending on who was doing the talking, and food prices continued to be a subject of consumer lament.

National Defense/The Military:

A strategic arms limitation agreement was signed by the U.S. and the Soviet Union during President Nixon's summit meeting in Moscow. Democratic Presidential nominee George McGovern's proposal to cut military spending was one of the year's most talked-about issues.

Politics:

Being a Presidential election year, 1972 was highly vocal in the field of politics. Some of the issues and events: the election itself, with President Nixon winning a landslide victory over Senator McGovern; the alleged Republican Party espionage and break-in at the Democratic headquarters at the Watergate building in Washington; Democratic charges of Justice Department rulings favorable to International Telephone and Telegraph Corporation in return for ITT political contributions to the Republican Party; the Vice-Presidential nomination and subsequent withdrawal of Democratic Senator Thomas Eagleton because of the revelations of past health problems; and the assassination attempt on Alabama Governor and Presidential candidate George Wallace.

Social Welfare:

Many proposals for welfare reform were presented in 1972, including the controversial $1,000 government grant suggestion by Democratic Presidential nominee George McGovern. A Social Security increase was approved by Congress over President Nixon's objection.

Transportation:

Airliner hijacking remained an international problem, with airport security programs beginning to be implemented on a major scale.

Literature:

Author Clifford Irving submitted to his publisher a reputedly authorized biography of Howard Hughes, which was thereafter repudiated by Hughes and later admitted by Irving to be a fraud. The suppression in the U.S.S.R. of writings by Soviet author Alexander Solzhenitsyn became a much-discussed topic in 1972.

Medicine:

The drug-abuse problem continued, as did the debate on abortion. Chinese acupuncture invited much interest.

Space/Science/Technology:

1972 witnessed two successful U.S. moon landings—*Apollos* 16 and 17—the latter marking the suspension of the *Apollo* program itself. A forthcoming joint U.S./Soviet space venture was being put together, and a controversial, proposed U.S. space-shuttle program received widespread criticism in Congress.

Sports:

Two events focused world attention on sports on 1972. One, the Olympiad in Munich, was marred by an Arab terrorist attack on the Israeli team. The other, the world chess championship match, held in Reykjavik, Iceland, was won by American Bobby Fischer, who defeated Soviet world champion Boris Spassky. In baseball, there was a pre-season player strike.

Editorial Treatment

ORGANIZATION OF MATERIAL

Special attention was given to the arrangement of the book—from the major divisions down to the individual categories and speakers—the objective being a logical progression of related material, as follows:

(A) The categories are arranged alphabetically within each of three major sections—

Part One:	"National Affairs"
Part Two:	"International Affairs"
Part Three:	"General"

In this manner, the reader can quickly locate quotations pertaining to particular fields of interest (see *Indexing*, next page). It should be noted that some quotations contain a number of thoughts or ideas—sometimes on different subjects—while some are vague as to exact subject matter and thus do not fit clearly into a specific topic classification. In such cases, the judgment of the Editors has determined the most appropriate category.

(B) Within each category, the speakers are in alphabetical order.

(C) Where there are two or more entries by one speaker within the same category, they appear chronologically, by date spoken or date of source.

SPEAKER IDENTIFICATION

The rank, position, occupation, profession or title of the speaker is given as it was *at the time the statement was made.* Thus, due to possible changes in status during the year, a speaker may be shown with different identifications in various portions of the book, or even within the same category. In the case of speakers who hold more than one position or occupation simultaneously, the judgment of the Editors has determined the most appropriate identification to use with a specific quotation.

THE QUOTATIONS

All quotations are printed verbatim, as reported by the source, except in cases where the Editors of *WHAT THEY SAID* have eliminated extraneous or overly-long portions. In such cases, *ellipses* are always inserted—and in no instance has the meaning or intention of any quotation been altered. (Material enclosed in parentheses is by the Editors, or by the source, and is used to explain or clarify.) Special care has been exercized to make certain that each quotation stands on its own merits and is not taken "out of context." The Editors, however, cannot be responsible for mistakes made by the original newspaper, periodical or other source, i.e., incorrect reporting, mis-quotations or errors in interpretation.

DOCUMENTATION AND SOURCES

Documentation (circumstance, place, date) of each quotation is provided as fully as could be obtained, and the sources are furnished with all quotations. In some instances, no documentation details were available, and in those cases only the sources are given. Following are the sequence and style for this information–

Circumstance of quotation, place, date/Name of source, date: section (if applicable), page number.

Example: *Before the Senate, Washington, Dec. 4/The Washington Post, 12-6:(A)13.*

The above example indicates that the quotation was delivered before the Senate in Washington on December 4. It was taken from *The Washington Post,* issue of December 6, section A, page 13. (When a newspaper publishes more than one edition on the same date, it should be noted that page numbers may vary from edition to edition.)

INDEXING

(A) To find all quotations by a particular person, regardless of subject, use the *Index to Speakers.*

(B) To find all quotations on a particular subject, regardless of speaker, turn to the appropriate category (see *Table of Contents*) or use the detailed *Index to Subjects.*

(C) To find all quotations by a particular person on a particular subject, turn to the appropriate category and then to that person's quotations within that category.

The reader will find that the basic categorization format of *WHAT THEY SAID* is itself a useful subject index, inasmuch as all related quotations are grouped together by their respective categories and can be read, compared and studied with ease. All aspects of journalism, for example, are relevant to each other; thus, the section on Journalism embraces all aspects of the news media. Likewise, all quotations on Vietnam are together in the section on Indochina; so a particular speaker's views on any phase of the war can be found in that section under his name.

SELECTION OF CATEGORIES

The selected categories reflect, in the Editors' opinion, the most widely-discussed public-interest subjects, those which readily fall into the overall sphere of "current events." They represent topics continuously covered by the mass media because of their inherent relevance to the changing world scene. Most of the categories are permanent; they appear in each annual edition of *WHAT THEY SAID*. However, because of the transient importance of some subjects, there may be categories which appear one year and are not repeated.

SELECTION OF SPEAKERS

The criteria employed in deciding whether a particular person will be included in *WHAT THEY SAID* are based on the Editors' judgment as to who is "prominent" or "influential" enough to be considered.

The following persons are *always* considered eligible: top-level officials of all branches of national, state and major local governments (both U.S. and foreign), including all United States Senators and Representatives; top-echelon military officers; college and university presidents, chancellors and professors; chairmen and presidents of major corporations; heads of national public-oriented organizations and associations; national and internationally known diplomats; recognized celebrities from the entertainment and literary spheres and the arts generally; professional sports figures of national stature; and commentators on the world scene who are recognized as such and who command the attention of the mass media.

The determination of what and who are "major" and "recognized" must, necessarily, be made by the Editors of *WHAT THEY SAID* based on personal judgment and on the attention paid to these people by the media, as well as from consulting directories of the world's notable personages in various fields.

Also, some persons, while not recognized as prominent in a particular professional area, have nevertheless garnered an unusual amount of news coverage and attention in connection with a specific issue or event. These people, too, are considered for inclusion depending upon the circumstances involved.

SELECTION OF QUOTATIONS

The quotations selected for inclusion in *WHAT THEY SAID* obviously represent a decided minority of the seemingly endless volume of quoted material appearing in the media each year. The process of selection is scrupulously objective insofar as the partisan views of the Editors are concerned (see *About Fairness*, below). However, it is clear that the Editors must decide which quotations *per se* are suitable for inclusion, and in doing so look for comments that are aptly stated, offer insight into the subject being discussed, or into the speaker, and provide—for today as well as for future reference—a thought which readers will find useful for understanding the issues and the personalities that make up a year on this planet.

ABOUT FAIRNESS

The Editors of *WHAT THEY SAID* understand the necessity of being impartial when compiling a book of this kind. As a result, there has been no editorial bias in the selection of the quotations, the choice of speakers or the manner of editing. Relevance of the statements and the status of the speakers remain the exclusive criteria for inclusion, without any regard whatsoever to the personal beliefs and views of the Editors.

Furthermore, every effort has been made to include a multiplicity of opinions and ideas from a wide cross-section of speakers on each topic. Nevertheless, should there appear to be, on some controversial issues, a majority of material favoring one point of view over another, it is simply the result of there having been more of those views expressed during the year, reported by the media and objectively considered suitable by the Editors of *WHAT THEY SAID* (see *Selection of Quotations*, preceding page).

Also, since persons in politics and government account for a large percentage of the speakers in *WHAT THEY SAID*, there may exist a heavier weight of opinion favoring the political philosophy of those in office at the time, whether in the United States Congress, the Administration, or in foreign capitals. This is natural and to be expected and should not be construed as a reflection of agreement or disagreement with that philosophy on the part of the Editors of *WHAT THEY SAID*.

Abbreviations

The following are abbreviations used by the speakers in this volume. Rather than defining them each time they appear in the quotations, this list will facilitate reading and avoid unnecessary repetition.

ABA: American Basketball Association
ABC: American Broadcasting Companies
ABM: antiballistic missile
ADA: Americans for Democratic Action
AFL-CIO: American Federation of Labor-Congress of Industrial Organizations
AIP: American International Pictures
AMA: American Medical Association
AMTRAK: American National Railroad Passenger Corporation
ARVN: Army of the Republic of (South) Vietnam
AT&T: American Telephone & Telegraph Company
CATV: community antenna (cable) television
CBS: Columbia Broadcasting System
CED: Committee for Economic Development
CIA: Central Intelligence Agency
DMZ: Demilitarized Zone
EPA: Environmental Protection Agency
FBI: Federal Bureau of Investigation
FCC: Federal Communications Commission
FDA: Food and Drug Administration
F.D.R.: Franklin Delano Roosevelt
FHA: Federal Housing Administration
GAO: General Accounting Office
GATT: General Agreement on Tariffs and Trade
GM: General Motors
GNP: gross national product
HEW: Department of Health, Education and Welfare
ICBM: intercontinental ballistic missile
IOC: International Olympic Committee
IRA: Irish Republican Army
ITT: International Telephone & Telegraph Corporation
JCS: Joint Chiefs of Staff
KO: knock-out
KP: kitchen police
MGM: Metro-Goldwyn-Mayer
MIRV: multiple individually-targetable re-entry vehicle (missile)

MP:	Member of Parliament
NAACP:	National Association for the Advancement of Colored People
NASA:	National Aeronautics and Space Administration
NATO:	North Atlantic Treaty Organization
NBA:	National Basketball Association
NBC:	National Broadcasting Company
NFL:	National Football League
NLF:	National Liberation Front
OAS:	Organization of American States
OPA:	Office of Price Administration
OTB:	Offtrack Betting Corporation
POW:	prisoner of war
PR:	public relations
ROTC:	Reserve Officers Training Corps
SALT:	strategic arms limitation talks
SEATO:	Southeast Asia Treaty Organization
SEC:	Securities and Exchange Commission
SMU:	Southern Methodist University
SST:	supersonic transport
TV:	television
UAW:	United Automobile Workers of America
ULMS:	undersea-launched missile system
UN:	United Nations
U.S./U.S.A.:	United States/United States of America
USIA:	United States Information Agency
U.S.S.R.:	Union of Soviet Socialist Republics

Party affiliation of United States Senators and Representatives—

C:	Conservative-Republican
D:	Democrat
I:	Independent
R:	Republican

The Quote of the Year

"Throughout history, it has been the inaction of those who could have acted, the indifference of those who should have known better, the silence of the voice of justice when it mattered most, that has made it possible for evil to triumph."

–HAILE SELASSIE

Emperor of Ethiopia; at United Nations Security Council meeting, Addis Ababa, Ethiopia, January 28.

PART ONE

National Affairs

The State of the Union Address

Delivered by Richard M. Nixon, President of the United States, in the House of Representatives, Washington, January 20, 1972.

Mr. Speaker, Mr. President, my colleagues in the Congress, our distinguished guests, my fellow Americans:

Twenty-five years ago, I sat here as a freshman Congressman—along with Speaker Albert—and listened for the first time to the President address the State of the Union.

I shall never forget that moment. The Senate, the Diplomatic Corps, the Supreme Court, the Cabinet entered the chamber, and then the President of the United States. As all of you are aware, I had some differences with President Truman. He had some with me. But I remember that on that day, the day he addressed that joint session of the newly-elected Republican 80th Congress, he spoke not as a partisan, but as President of all the people—calling upon the Congress to put aside partisan considerations in the national interest.

The Greek-Turkish aid program, the Marshall Plan, the great foreign-policy initiatives which have been responsible for avoiding a world war for over 25 years were approved by the 80th Congress, by a bipartisan majority of which I was proud to be a part.

Nineteen-seventy-two is now before us. It holds precious time in which to accomplish good for the nation. We must not waste it. I know the political pressures in this session of the Congress will be great. There are more candidates for the Presidency in this chamber today than there probably have been at any one time in the whole history of the Republic. And there is an honest difference of opinion, not only between the parties, but within each party, on some foreign-policy issues and on some domestic-policy issues.

However, there are great national problems that are so vital that they transcend partisanship. And so let us have our debates. Let us have our honest differences. But let us join in keeping the national interest first. Let us join in making sure that legislation the nation needs does not become hostage to the political interests of any party or any person.

There is ample precedent, in this election year, for me to present you with a huge list of new proposals, knowing full well that there wouldn't be any possibility of your passing them if you worked night and day.

I shall not do that.

I presented to the leaders of the Congress today a message of 15,000 words discussing in some detail where the nation stands and setting forth specific legislative items on which I have asked the Congress to act. Much of this is legislation which I proposed in 1969 and 1970, and also in the First Session of this 92nd Congress, and on which I feel it is essential that action be completed this year.

I am not presenting proposals which have attractive labels but no hope of passage. I am presenting only vital programs which are within the capacity of this Congress to enact, within the capacity of the budget to finance, and which I believe should be above partisanship—programs which deal with urgent priorities for the nation, which should and must be the subject of bipartisan action by this Congress in the interests of the country in 1972.

RICHARD M. NIXON

Progress Since the Sixties

When I took the oath of office on the steps of this building just three years ago today, the nation was ending one of the most tortured decades in its history.

The 1960s were a time of great progress in many areas. But as we all know, they were also times of great agony—the agonies of war, of inflation, of rapidly-rising crime, of deteriorating cities—of hopes raised and disappointed, and of anger and frustration that led finally to violence and to the worst civil disorder in a century.

I recall these troubles not to point any finger of blame. The nation was so torn in those final years of the '60s that many in both parties questioned whether America could be governed at all.

The nation has made significant progress in these first years of the '70s.

Our cities are no longer engulfed by civil disorders.

Our colleges and universities have again become places of learning instead of battlegrounds.

A beginning has been made on preserving and protecting our environment.

The rate of increase in crime has been slowed. And here in the District of Columbia—the one city where the Federal government has direct jurisdiction—serious crime in 1971 was actually reduced by 13 per cent from the year before.

Most important—because of the beginnings that have been made—we can say today that this year, 1972, can be the year in which America may make the greatest progress in 25 years toward achieving our goal of being at peace with all the nations of the world.

As our involvement in the war in Vietnam comes to an end, we must now go on to build a generation of peace.

To achieve that goal, we must first face realistically the need to maintain our defense.

Strong Defense Needed

In the past three years, we have reduced the burden of arms. For the first time in 20 years, spending on defense has been brought below spending on human resources.

As we look to the future, we find encouraging progress in our negotiations with the Soviet Union on limitation of strategic arms. And looking further into the future, we hope there can eventually be agreement on the mutual reduction of arms. But until there is such a mutual agreement, we must maintain the strength necessary to deter war.

And that is why, because of rising research-and-development costs, because of increases in military and civilian pay, because of the need to proceed with new weapons systems, my budget for the coming fiscal year will provide for an increase in defense spending.

Strong military defenses are not the enemy of peace. They are the guardians of peace.

And there could be no more misguided set of priorities than one which would tempt others by weakening America, and thereby endanger the peace of the world.

Foreign Policy

In our foreign policy, we have entered a new era. The world has changed greatly in the 11 years since President John Kennedy said in his Inaugural Address, "We shall pay any price, bear any burden, meet any hardship, support any friend, oppose any foe, to assure the survival and the success of liberty."

Our policy has been carefully and deliberately adjusted to meet the new realities of the new world we live in. We make today only those commitments we are able and prepared to meet.

Our commitment to freedom remains strong and unshakable. But others must bear their share of the burden of defending freedom around the world.

And so this, then, is our policy:

- We will maintain a nuclear deterrent adequate to meet any threat to the security of the United States or of our allies.
- We will help other nations develop the capability of defending themselves.
- We will faithfully honor all of our treaty commitments.
- We will act to defend our interests, whenever and wherever they are threatened any place in the world.
- But where our interests or our treaty commitments are not involved, our role will be limited.
- We will not intervene militarily.
- But we will use our influence to prevent war.
- If war comes, we will use our influence to stop it.
- And once it is over, we will do our share in helping to bind up the wounds of those who have participated in it.

As you know, I will soon be visiting the People's Republic of China and the Soviet Union. I go there with no illusions. We have great differences with both powers. We shall continue to have great differences. But peace depends on the ability of great powers to live together on the same planet despite their differences.

We would not be true to our obligation to generations yet unborn if we failed to seize this moment to do everything in our power to insure that we will be able to talk about those differences, rather than to fight about them, in the future.

And as we look back over this century, let us, in the highest spirit of bipartisanship, recognize that we can be proud of our nation's record in foreign affairs.

America has given more generously of itself toward maintaining freedom, preserving peace, alleviating human suffering around the globe, than any nation has ever done in the history of man.

We have fought four wars in this century, but our power has never been used to break the peace, only to keep it; never been used to destroy freedom, only to defend it. We now have within our reach the goal of insuring that the next generation can be the first generation in this century to be spared the scourges of war.

Economic Progress

Turning to our problems at home, we are making progress toward our goal of a new prosperity without war.

Industrial production, consumer spending, retail sales, personal income, all have been rising. Total employment, real income, are the highest in history. New home-building starts this past year reached the highest level ever. Business and consumer confidence have both been rising. Interest rates are down. The rate of inflation is down. We can look with confidence to 1972 as the year when the back of inflation will be broken.

Now, this is a good record, but it is not good enough—not when we still have an unemployment rate of 6 per cent. It's not enough to point out that this was the rate of the early peacetime years of the '60s, or that if the more than 2 million men released from the armed forces and defense-related industries were still in their wartime jobs, then unemployment would be far lower.

Our goal in this country is full employment in peacetime. We intend to meet that goal, and we can.

The Congress has helped to meet that goal by passing our job-creating tax program last month.

The historic monetary agreements—agreements that we have reached with the major European nations, Canada and Japan—will help meet it by providing new markets for American products, new jobs for American workers.

Our budget will help meet it by being

expansionary without being inflationary—a job-producing budget that will help take up the gap as the economy expands to full employment.

Our program to raise farm income will help meet it by helping to revitalize rural America, by giving up to America's farmers their fair share of America's increasing productivity.

And we also will help meet our goal of full employment in peacetime with a set of major initiatives to stimulate more imaginative use of America's great capacity for technological advance, and direct it toward improving the quality of life for every American.

Technology

In reaching the moon, we demonstrated what miracles American technology is capable of achieving. And now the time has come to move more deliberately toward making full use of that technology here on earth, of harnessing the wonders of science to the service of men.

I shall soon send to the Congress a special message proposing a new program of Federal partnership in technological research and development—with Federal incentives to increase private research, Federally-supported research and projects designed to improve our everyday lives in ways that will range from improving mass transit to developing new systems of emergency health-care that could save thousands of lives annually.

Historically, our superior technology and high productivity have made it possible for American workers to be the highest paid in the world by far, and yet for our goods still to compete in world markets.

Now we face a new situation. As other nations move rapidly forward in technology, the answer to the new competition is not to build a wall around America, but rather to remain competitive by improving our own technology still further and by increasing productivity in American industry.

Our new monetary and trade agreements will make it possible for American goods to compete thoroughly in the world's markets—but they still must compete. The new technology program will put to use the skills of many highly-trained Americans—skills that might otherwise be wasted. It will also meet the growing technological challenge from abroad, and it will thus help to create new industries, as well as creating more jobs for America's workers in producing for the world's markets.

Administration Proposals

This Second Session of the 92nd Congress already has before it more than 90 major Administration proposals which still await action. I have discussed these in the extensive written message that I have presented to the Congress today.

They include, among others, our programs to improve life for the aging; to combat crime and drug abuse; to improve health services; to insure that no one will be denied needed health care because of inability to pay; to protect workers' pensions rights; to promote equal opportunity for members of minorities and others who have been left behind; to expand consumer protection; to improve the environment; to revitalize rural America; to help the cities; to launch new initiatives in education; to improve transportation and to put an end to costly labor tie-ups in transportation.

The West Coast dock strike is a case in point. This nation cannot and will not tolerate that kind of irresponsible labor tie-up in the future.

The messages also include basic reforms which are essential if our structure of government is to be adequate in the decades ahead.

They include reform of our wasteful

and outmoded welfare system, substitution of a new system that provides work requirements and work incentives for those who can help themselves, income support for those who cannot help themselves, and fairness to the working poor.

They include a $17 billion program of Federal revenue-sharing with the states and localities—as an investment in their renewal, and an investment also of faith in the American people.

They also include a sweeping reorganization of the Executive Branch of the Federal government so that it will be more efficient, more responsive and able to meet the challenges of the decades ahead.

One year ago, standing in this place, I laid before the opening session of this Congress six great goals. One of these was welfare reform. That proposal has been before the Congress now for nearly two-and-a-half years.

My proposals on revenue-sharing, government reorganization, health care and the environment have now been before the Congress for nearly a year. Many of the other major proposals that I have referred to have been here that long or longer.

Now, 1971, we can say, was a year of consideration of these measures. Now let us join in making 1972 a year of action on them—action by the Congress, for the nation and for the people of America.

Now, in addition, there is one pressing need which I have not previously covered, but which must be placed on the national agenda.

School Financing

We have long looked in this nation to the local property tax as the main source of financing for public primary and secondary education.

As a result, soaring school costs, soaring property-tax rates now threaten both our communities and our schools. They threaten communities because property taxes—which more than doubled in the years from 1960 to 1970—have become one of the most oppressive and discriminatory of all taxes, hitting most cruelly at the elderly and the retired; and they threaten schools, as hard-pressed voters understandably reject new bond issues at the polls.

The problem has been given even greater urgency by four recent court decisions, which have held that the conventional method of financing schools through local property taxes is discriminatory and unconstitutional.

Nearly two years ago, I named a special Presidential commission to study the problems of school finance, and I also directed the Federal departments to look into the same problems. We are developing comprehensive proposals to meet these problems.

This issue involves two complex and inter-related sets of problems: support of the schools and the basic relationships of Federal, state and local governments in any tax reforms.

Under the leadership of the Secretary of the Treasury, we are carefully reviewing all of the tax aspects; and I have this week enlisted the Advisory Committee on Intergovernmental Relations in addressing the intergovernmental-relations aspects.

I have asked this bipartisan commission to review our proposal for Federal action to cope with the gathering crisis of school finance and property taxes. Later in the year, when both commissions have completed their studies, I shall make my final recommendations for relieving the burden of property taxes and providing both fair and adequate financing for our children's education.

These recommendations will be revolutionary. But all these recommendations, however, will be rooted in one fundamental principle with which there can be no compromise: Local school boards must have control over local schools.

Changing World

As we look ahead over the coming decades, vast new growth and change are not only certainties—they will be the dominant reality of this world, and particularly of our life in America. Surveying the certainty of rapid change, we can be like a fallen rider caught in the stirrups—or we can sit high in the saddle, the masters of change, directing it on a course we choose.

The secret of mastering change in today's world is to reach back to old and proven principles, and to adapt them with imagination and intelligence to the new realities of a new age.

And that's what we have done in the proposals that I've laid before the Congress. They are rooted in basic principles that are as enduring as human nature, as robust as the American experience; and they are responsive to new conditions. Thus, they represent a spirit of change that is truly renewal.

As we look back at those old principles, we find them as timely as they are timeless.

We believe in independence, and self-reliance, and the creative value of the competitive spirit.

We believe in full and equal opportunity for all Americans, and in the protection of individual rights and liberties.

We believe in the family as the keystone of the community, and the community as the keystone of the nation.

We believe in compassion for those in need.

We believe in a system of law, justice and order as the basis of a genuinely free society.

We believe that a person should get what he works for—and that those who can should work for what they get.

We believe in the capacity of people to make their own decisions in their own lives, in their own communities—and we believe in their right to make those decisions.

Quality of Life

In applying these principles, we have done so with the full understanding that what we seek in the '70s, what our quest is, is not merely for more, but for better—for a better quality of life for all Americans.

Thus, for example, we are giving a new measure of attention to cleaning up our air and water, making our surroundings more attractive. We're providing broader support for the arts, helping to stimulate a deeper appreciation of what they can contribute to the nation's activities and to our individual lives.

But nothing really matters more to the quality of our lives than the way we treat one another—than our capacity to live respectfully together as a unified society, with a full, generous regard for the rights of others and also for the feelings of others.

As we recover from the turmoil and violence of recent years, as we learn once again to speak with one another instead of shouting at one another, we are regaining that capacity.

As is customary here, on this occasion, I've been talking about programs. Programs are important. But even more important than programs is what we are as a nation—what we mean as a nation, to ourselves and to the world.

In New York Harbor stands one of the most famous statues in the world—the Statue of Liberty, the gift in 1886 of the people of France to the people of the United States. This statue is more than a landmark; it is a symbol—a symbol of what America has meant to the world.

It reminds us that what America has meant is not its wealth and not its power, but its spirit and purpose—a land that enshrines liberty and opportunity, and that has held out a hand of welcome to millions in search of a better and fuller and, above all, a freer life.

The world's hopes poured into America, along with its people. And those hopes, those dreams, that have been brought here from every corner of the world, have become a part of the hope that we now hold out to the world.

Spirit of '76

Four years from now, America will celebrate the 200th anniversary of its founding as a nation. And there are those who say that the old spirit of '76 is dead—that we no longer have the strength of character, the idealism, the faith in our founding purposes that that spirit represents.

Those who say this do not know America.

We have been undergoing self-doubts, self-criticism. But these are only the other side of our growing sensitivity to the persistence of want in the midst of plenty, of our impatience with the slowness with which age-old ills are being overcome.

If we were indifferent to the shortcomings of our society, or complacent about our institutions, or blind to the lingering inequities—then we would have lost our way.

But the fact that we have those concerns is evidence that our ideals, deep down, are still strong. Indeed, they remind us that what is really best about America is its compassion. They remind us that, in the final analysis, America is great not because it is strong, not because it is rich, but because this is a good country.

Let us reject the narrow visions of those who would tell us that we are evil because we are not yet perfect, that we are corrupt because we are not yet pure, that all the sweat and toil and sacrifice that have gone into the building of America were for naught because the building is not yet done.

Let us see that the path we are traveling is wide, with room in it for all of us, and that its direction is toward a better nation in a more peaceful world.

And never has it mattered more that we go forward together.

Look at this chamber. The leadership of America is here today—the Supreme Court, the Cabinet, the Senate and the House of Representatives.

Together, we hold the future of the nation, and the conscience of the nation, in our hands.

Because this year is an election year, it will be a time of great pressure.

If we yield to that pressure and fail to deal seriously with the historic challenges that we face, we will have failed the trust of millions of Americans and shaken the confidence they have a right to place in us, in their government.

Never has a Congress had a greater opportunity to leave a legacy of a profound and constructive reform for the nation than this Congress.

If we succeed in these tasks, there will be credit enough for all—not only for doing what is right, but doing it in the right way, by rising above partisan interest to serve the national interest.

And if we fail, more than any one of us, America will be the loser.

And that is why my call upon the Congress today is for a high statesmanship—so that in the years to come Americans will look back and say, because it withstood the intense pressures of a political year and achieved such great good for the American people and for the future of this nation, this was truly a great Congress.

The American Scene

Spiro T. Agnew
Vice President of the United States

We now live in a curious era when the national spotlight is forever focused on the paranoid and the masochist and the smear-America cheap-shot artist. We live in an era that panders to those darlings of the left who delight in denouncing this country . . . It isn't just the hard-core left that shrills the refrain. You find condemnations of America on the editorial pages of some of our most influential newspapers and magazines. You hear diatribes against America on nationally-broadcast TV and radio programs. You encounter anti-American philippics in our classrooms and our churches and our corporate board rooms—even in the halls of Congress.

At Maine Republican Convention, Augusta, April 28/ Los Angeles Herald-Examiner, 4-28:(A)3.

I sometimes think we Americans are too close to America to appreciate it, to realize what a truly wonderful country this is. We do not love America enough because we take it for granted, because we have basked for so long in the freedom and the luxury and the security of our great country.

Quote, 5-28:506.

I think that sometimes we forget, when we hear our nation denigrated, that America is *not* some anonymous ogre bent on perpetrating fiendish horrors in the faceless guise of a military-industrial complex or an affluent society or even a silent majority. America is living, breathing, flesh-and-blood people. America, ladies and gentlemen, is *you.* It is you and your parents and your children and your friends and your neighbors. And, as representative Americans, you are not racists, not violent, not dishonest. Americans, for the most part, are good, decent people; and this, your country and mine, is a good, decent country.

At Washington State Republican dinner, Spokane/ The Wall Street Journal, 8-18:4.

At this time, when some people seem determined to fasten group labels on people, and in the process to turn American against American, it would be well to remember that this kind of behavior is not progressive but regressive. It is not reform but recidivism. If it succeeds, it will most assuredly push America backward—into the failures of a bygone era of narrow-minded prejudices and internecine conflicts—an era in which people were judged not by their ability and energy but by their skin pigmentation and their ancestry and the church or synagogue they attended. Yet, in the name of reform, the practice of pitting the most publicized minorities against the least publicized minorities continues. In truth, each of us belongs to some minority group that has special interests. We are a nation of many religions, a people descended from many heritages. We are a nation of businessmen and laborers, of thinkers and doers, of disabled and hearty, of scientists and mystics. These differentiations should be important to us—but never so important that they overshadow our common identity. We are Americans—and that which unites us is infinitely stronger than our individual differences.

Accepting the Vice-Presidential nomination of the Republican Party, Miami Beach, Aug. 23/ The Washington Post, 8-24:(A)18.

John J. Akar
Former Ambassador to the United States from Sierra Leone

America is a multi-racial and multi-ethnic society. Neither militancy nor revolution, nor backlashism, nor isolationism will affect the inevitability of a great, glorious American future built on the solid rock of multi-racialism and multi-ethnicism.

At Boy Scouts banquet, San Francisco/ San Francisco Examiner, 2-10:42.

Saul Alinsky
Sociologist

If you took the American way of life and made a musical show out of it, the major theme would be dissonant.

Interview/The National Observer, 1-29:8.

Reubin Askew
Governor of Florida

Our region, after substantial prodding, is now freeing itself of fear, hate, ignorance and of the insecurity and isolation prompted by a hundred years of playing the role of the nation's political stepchild. A South is emerging which belongs not to the whites and not to the blacks, not to the rich and not to the poor . . . but to the people . . . all of them.

At University of South Florida/ The New York Times Magazine, 3-5:56.

Americans dream of a day when they're at peace in the world, and at peace with themselves. They dream of a day when all the fathers and all the sons, in all the prisons and jungles of Asia, not only come home again, but come home to stay; a day when we spread democracy abroad by making it work in our own country; a day when we place more value on human happiness than on the gross national product; a day when the work of the average man is a fascinating chapter in the story of his life, and not merely a price to pay for existing; a day when less work is spread among more people . . . so that all of us can share in the bounty of our land, as well as the blessing of our self-respect. They dream of a day when they're free to walk through any park on any night without fear or danger or harm; a day when the secrets of their private lives are not a matter for reports and files and photographs and computer cards; a day when they can trust and believe in what their leaders and countrymen tell them; a day when they've mastered at last the two greatest problems of 20th-century man—the problems of learning to live together, and learning to live with nature.

At Democratic National Convention, Miami Beach, July 11/ Vital Speeches, 8-1:614.

Russell Baker
Newspaper columnist

Those who say humor is dying are talking about the old humor of gaiety, a limited humor, when the country was more isolated than it is today. Now we have a sophisticated humor, a worldly humor that comes out of an awareness that ours is a country with global responsibilities.

Interview/Publishers' Weekly, 1-24:28.

Frank E. Barnett
Chairman, Union Pacific Corporation

. . . there is a danger that an inadequately-informed but emotionally-aroused public will move the government into efforts to accomplish too much too soon. Our resources as a nation are vast enough to inspire optimism concerning our problems, but they are not unlimited. Even the most optimistic view of our gross national product for the next five years falls far short of the cost estimated for full realization of all our social gains. Social problems, by their very nature, tend to produce emotional responses in the effort to find an immediate and complete solution. Hasty action based on emotion can actually delay improvements by diverting resources into marginal efforts or down blind alleys. The natural desire for

(FRANK E. BARNETT)

immediate results is the cause of much of the dissension between students and business. Both groups share many common concerns, but the difference is one of experience—an experience which teaches that immediate action often is not the best approach to take in solving a problem. The indirect, sometimes slow, and more complex route is often the straightest line in a lasting solution. Idealism and concern alone have never fed a hungry man. Our society has grown so complex it is beyond the easy solution to any problem. But I am confident that we are on the way to solving our pressing problems. I am confident that the institutions which have enabled America to achieve greatness will not fail us now.

At Texas Christian University/ The Wall Street Journal, 4-14:6.

Daniel J. Boorstin
Director, National Museum of History and Technology

One of the most effective weapons that can be used against a nation is to persuade it that it is suffering from incurable illness of some kind. I have been dismayed in talking recently to some politicians in Washington who refer casually to the "national decadence." I suggest that the best way to make a nation decadent is to persuade people to talk about its decadence.

Interview/U.S. News & World Report, 5-29:18.

Warren E. Burger
Chief Justice of the United States

We continue to live in a period when all our institutions are being challenged, often in a mindless way to be sure, but sometimes in a sober and constructive sense. Criticism can be useful, but constant, negative and carping criticism can distort our perspective and our sense of values. Whatever may be the shortcomings of our society—and they are numerous, no doubt—the fact is that the world still beats a path to our door; and the poor, the oppressed and the dispossessed continue to pour into this country from everywhere on the globe—if they are free to do so. This has been going on, as we know, for more than a century; and it suggests that, whatever our flaws, American opportunity, American freedom and American institutions continue to commend themselves to others.

Before American Bar Association, San Francisco, Aug. 14/ Vital Speeches, 10-1:740.

Arthur F. Burns
Chairman, Federal Reserve Board

I think that something has happened to the American people, something has happened to our system of responses, to both consumers and business people. They are not reacting to classical remedies the way they did, because they are living in a disturbed world and they themselves are disturbed and are, to a large degree, confused. These have been very troubled times and they have left their mark on the psychology of people, on the thinking of people, and that inevitably spills over into the economic realm. We have had a very long and most unhappy war which has divided this country and confused the people. Not very long ago we had riots in the streets and riots in the colleges; and now we have the busing of school children and we have all sorts of tax changes . . . Now we have youngsters who are going to vote, and now women are also marching in the streets, and we have unbalanced budgets. If only life would quiet down for a while. If only both the Administration and Congress became just a little less active in pushing new reforms for a while, if some of my academic colleagues would just keep quiet for a while, I think this country might absorb a little better all of these tumultuous changes around us and we might find that old-fashioned economic policies are working better . . .

Before Joint Congressional Economic Committee, Washington/San Francisco Examiner & Chronicle, 2-13:(B)5.

Earl L. Butz
Secretary of Agriculture of the United States

Somehow I have a deep-down feeling that the degree of good, old-fashioned patriotism that you have among people of rural America is a notch or two higher than among people in "downtown America." There are too many people in our country today who have lost those virtues of patriotism, of industry, of integrity, of production. There are too many people who don't know that if you want more you must produce more. I think rural people understand that. Congress could pass a law tomorrow that would guarantee every American a free loaf of bread every day, and sometimes I think they are about to pass such a law. But that law wouldn't amount to a cuss unless somebody between now and six o'clock tomorrow morning baked 200 million loaves of bread—and only men who work do that and not those who sit on their duff waiting for a nice handout.

The New York Times Magazine, 4-16:89.

Taylor Caldwell
Author

America is no longer a constitutional republic. (Rather) we are a degenerate democracy; and we all know that democracy decays into despotism.

At Rally for Conservative Americans, Boston/The Christian Science Monitor, 7-7:12.

John B. Connally, Jr.
Secretary of the Treasury of the United States

I personally believe that there is a growing lack of confidence in government in the United States—at the state level, the local level and the national level—not because of any one man or because of any one party. What's the inevitable result of it? A democracy unsustained and unsupported by a high degree of public confidence cannot long survive. And what is the alternative to a democracy? The alternative to a democracy in this land is a dictatorship—that's the alternative. So it behooves each of us—in politics and in the press and in public service—to give some of our thought and some of our time to try to objectively portray what this nation is and what it has been and what it hopes to be. And have we been so neglectful? Have we failed so miserably? How have we? Let's ask ourselves: Is there anywhere in the world where people are better fed, or better housed, or better clothed? Is there anywhere in the world where there are more freedoms? How many countries in the world have the freedom of assemblage, such as you have here? And even more than that, how many countries in the world have the freedom of the press which you enjoy? How many? How many have the freedoms that we consider inalienable rights—and they are in the language of our Constitution and our Bill of Rights. But they're as fragile as the political stability of the system under which they operate, and no more. And when that political system begins to totter and to weaken, then you can be sure that your rights and your privileges and your immunities—your rights as free men and women—begin to weaken and begin to totter. No nation as complex as this can survive without rules under which we all live and abide; and if we tend to destroy those institutions of government, we are, in essence, destroying the very fabric of this society. Improve them? Yes. Demolish them? No. And it is with that thought that I leave you—that each of us, it seems to me, has a very great duty and very great obligation. To criticize? Yes. To disagree? Yes. But also we have as leaders—if indeed we want to be

(JOHN B. CONNALLY, JR.)

leaders in our community or in our nation—we have a solemn obligation to be fair, to be objective and to keep in perspective what we are and what we hope to be and what we've accomplished. And I submit to you that, for all our frailties, there is no region of this planet, there is no nation on this earth, that has done as well in as short a time for as many people in as many ways as has this democracy of the United States of America.

Before American Society of Newspaper Editors, Washington, April 19/ U.S. News & World Report, 5-1:89.

Frank Corner
Ambassador to the United States from New Zealand

(On his leaving the Ambassadorship to return to New Zealand): The main thing I go back with now is a sense of the enormous creativity, adaptability and energy of Americans. At times I wondered if the United States was a country on the decline. But now, on balance, I think it is a country that is bursting into something new; rather noisily and argumentatively, but something new.

The New York Times, 9-7:49.

Allan Dershowitz
Professor of Law, Harvard University

It is widely felt by lawyers and civil libertarians that the Bill of Rights is in greater danger today than it has been in decades. And this feeling is correct, for three related reasons. First, this (Nixon) Administration has consciously set out to weaken the power of the other branches of government to protect our fundamental liberties. It has demeaned the Supreme Court by nominating justices whose only apparent qualifications have been a thorough distaste for the provisions of the Bill of Rights. Second, this Administration, more than any other in recent history, has adopted and encouraged the rhetoric of repression. The Vice President (Agnew) promiscuously lumps together for condemnation "the whole damned zoo of dissenters, malcontents, radicals, incendiaries, and civil and uncivil disobedients." Equating dissenters with incendiaries constitutes an unthinking and contagious attack on the very essence of the Bill of Rights. Finally, and most important, there seems to be a mood of repression, of intolerance, in the air. We, the American people, seem to have lost some of the vigilance that we have traditionally exercised in defense of our sacred rights. It is as if we all believed that we have become permanent members of the majority whose rights will never need safeguarding; as if the Bill of Rights was designed, not to protect us, but to protect some vague group called "them." But "we" are "them." If not today, then perhaps tomorrow. If not ourselves, then perhaps our children. We owe it to ourselves to see that our noble experiment with liberty, our Bill of Rights, is kept strong as we enter into our third century of nationhood.

Television broadcast/"Comment!", National Broadcasting Company, 6-18.

Milovan Djilas
Author; Former Vice President of Yugoslavia

The New Left and those influenced by it think the U.S. is wracked by crisis, but the so-called crisis in American society is largely imaginary. Race and class and generation gaps do exist, but there is no fundamental crisis. The crises you (the U.S.) have are aspects of the difficulty of adjusting to the electronic and technological revolutions of our time.

Interview, Belgrade/ The New York Times, 8-18:29.

Barry M. Goldwater
United States Senator, R–Ariz.

My complaint . . . rests not only with

that small, small handful who would destroy our institutions, but more I believe with the vast majority who just can't believe that anything could ever happen to the dream that for nearly 200 years has been America's, that for nearly 200 years has been the finest, most perfect, most fully-realized dream any people in the history of the world have ever put together or lived through. The overwhelming majority of Americans, the forgotten American as I have often called him—the man who works . . . prays, tends to his family duties, goes to church, pays his taxes, who participates in a small way or in a large way in government—unfortunately doesn't do enough to quiet the coyotes among us.

At Los Angeles Philanthropic Foundation dinner, Beverly Hills, Calif./ Los Angeles Herald-Examiner, 6-26:(A)12.

Billy Graham
Evangelist

The devil is at work in America. Everywhere you turn you see violence, pornography, hatred, crime, killing. Good is getting better, but evil is getting worse.

Dallas, June 11/The Dallas Times Herald, 6-12:(A)6.

L. Patrick Gray III
Acting Director, Federal Bureau of Investigation

I believe that the United States of America and her people have developed over the years the finest form of government and the best standard of living of any nation in the world, and that we—our nation and our people—represent a prize that any group having a form of government or a belief or an ideology different from ours might like to take over. I feel that we've got to be on the alert for that at all times, and I'm not prepared to state at this point of time that the Communist ideology has changed so that we can relax completely and be assured that our way of life is safe from anyone who might like to change it by force and violence. However, to say that I foresee an increasing threat from the Communist ideology as such—no. I view it as an existing threat, among many others, to our way of life—and one not to be taken lightly at all.

Interview/U.S. News & World Report, 7-10:60.

Roman Gribbs
Mayor of Detroit

If one word could be chosen to describe our country today, that word might be "caution." As a nation, we are resting and recuperating from a decade of unprecedented social and political change. The major challenge we face in the '70s is to accommodate a people's caution to a nation's needs. It would be tragic if, in our desire to rest, we closed our eyes to critical needs that must be met if we are to achieve the stability we so fervently seek. The very old, the very young, the very poor have a claim on the American conscience that cannot be ignored. There are national problems—crime, unemployment, drug abuse, deteriorating housing, pollution, school finance—that we must solve collectively if we are to solve them at all.

Before National League of Cities, Indianapolis/ San Francisco Examiner, 12-1:2.

James M. Hester
President, New York University

With each passing year, more and more of the private institutions that provide public services in America find themselves in financial jeopardy. In New York City the situation is extreme. When the New York Public Library, the Metropolitan Museum, the Museum of Modern Art, Columbia University, as well as New York University, are all in serious financial condition, the problem has reached critical proportions. Part of the tragedy is that relatively few people understand what is at stake. In fact, not many people care very deeply about the preservation of private institutions. With the expansion of government-operated services, many wonder why we need private

(JAMES M. HESTER)

institutions at all . . . the issue of the alteration of the character of our society, of the elimination of opportunities for private initiative and of the growing domination of our lives by large bureaucracies does not compel the kind of concern that civil rights, war and pollution have commanded. The reason is obvious: It is difficult to pinpoint the pain. The effects are too gradual to be widely perceived and to arouse vigilant action. And yet, for many of us there is little doubt that elimination of privately-organized public services would severely damage the vitality of life in this country.

Commencement address/ The Washington Post, 6-24:(A)14.

Walter J. Hickel
Former Secretary of the Interior of the United States

The mood of America is not as noisy as it was a few short years ago. But there is the frustration; there is a feeling of listlessness. People *want* to make things work. That is a great thing.

San Francisco Examiner, 1-21:34.

Hubert H. Humphrey
United States Senator, D–Minn.

America needs renewed faith in itself. The fabric of America is strong and resilient. Our nation has withstood civil war. We received into our midst wave after wave of immigrants who ultimately added their richness of cultural diversity. We have weathered economic depression and vast natural disasters. And while the threads of our civilization and national unity are often stretched taut, they have held—and are stronger for their testing. A nation that could build arsenals of awesome weapons in the pursuit of military objectives can build the schools and the hospitals and the nurseries and the libraries necessary to enrich our lives. A nation that developed a Marshall Plan to rebuild Europe can develop another to rebuild our neighborhoods and crime-ridden cities. A country that could reconcile its differences with wartime enemies and longtime rivals can summon the decency and justice necessary to reconcile the differences among our people. Our task is reconciliation, rebuilding and rebirth. Our nation was founded on the principle of faith and trust in the people. The "We, the people" of our Constitution's Preamble has too often been forgotten by those who govern. But it is in the people that our strength . . . lies.

Announcing his candidacy for the Democratic Presidential nomination, Philadelphia, Jan. 10/ U.S. News & World Report, 1-24:50.

Lyndon B. Johnson
Former President of the United States

I have never been convinced for a moment that, because of the Vietnam war or any other excuse we want to use, we have deprived the education program—or any other program. This country has the money to do anything it's got the guts to do.

Austin, Tex./The Dallas Times Herald, 2-2:(A)22.

Day after day, month after month, the portrayal of America as unclean, unjust and unworthy has been ground into the consciousness of our people. We no longer celebrate the many fresh triumphs of justice, for we linger over the residue of yesterday's shortcomings. We no longer measure the miles we have come toward a more humane, civil and peaceful world, for we are too busy calibrating the remaining inches of times we are trying to escape and leave behind. When we permit these dark perceptions to dominate us, we allow our future to be shaped by visions that are small and mean and diminishing to our potential. We are, in simple terms, dooming those who come after us to know what could only be a second-rate America . . . Whatever may be your own perception of where we are and where we may be heading, let me say for myself that I see little today suggesting that our system is failing; but I see all too much which convincingly argues that, by our doubts and hesitation, we may be failing the promise and potential of our system. We are not living in times of collapse. The old is not coming down. Rather, the troubling and torment of these days stem from the new trying to rise into place. With our nation's past efforts, with our long and faithfully-kept commitments, with our infinite successes in so many fields, we have brought into being the materials, as it were, with which to construct a new America. Faced with a task of such great dimensions, we have no time for melancholy. We have no cause for moroseness. We have work to be done—the greatest work any generation of Americans has ever faced. Believing that, I say: Let's be on with our labors.

Temple, Tex., Sept. 16/The Reader's Digest, January ('73):124.

Herman Kahn
Director, Hudson Institute

The average American is extremely concerned about the future of the country. He also feels that something is going wrong, but what's going wrong is the upper-middle-class. The average American is asking why the Harvard graduate wants to burn down the school; why doesn't anybody understand that being against busing (of school children for racial balance) does not mean being against Negroes; why don't newspapers and television and the movies reflect the world as it is? Americans are bothered by a credibility gap. Not the gap between the hippies and the President, not the gap between (Vice President) Spiro Agnew and the press, but between the average American and the prestige newspapers and the documentary on television. That's where the credibility gap is. There's an enormous hostility toward the upper-middle-class. People like (Alabama Governor George) Wallace talk about a guy with a briefcase, the professor with the pointed head. That's me he's talking about . . . And he's sort of correct. We're part of the class that has failed. We gave them the space program and the war in Vietnam. We gave them the wrong programs and then didn't answer when they questioned us. We didn't defend the programs, and that is a tragedy. So now they don't trust us, and everything in the media looks silly to them. The situations the average American understands perfectly, the media presents in a crazy way.

Interview/Human Events, 11-18:18.

Henry A. Kissinger
Assistant to the President of the United States for National Security Affairs

We are clearly living through one of the most difficult periods of our history. Some say we are divided over Vietnam. Others blame domestic discord. But I believe the cause of our anguish is deeper. Throughout our history we have believed that effort was its own reward. Partly because so much has been achieved here in America, we have tended to suppose that every problem must have a solution and that good intentions should somehow guarantee good results . . . Our generation is the first to have found that the road is endless; that in traveling it, we will find not Utopia, but only ourselves.

At "Salute to Congress" dinner, Washington, Jan. 26/The Washington Post, 1-28:(D)2.

I'm concerned about American civilization. We live in a world in which some countries pursue ruthless policies. We are in a period which someday may be compared to one of the religious ages, when whole values change. We are a warm-hearted people, concerning ourselves with a lot that is superficial, not willing to believe that we can make irrevocable errors, not willing to trust the judgment of the leaders until all the facts are in and it is usually too late, absorbed in bureaucratic infighting and indulging in various forms of debilitating nostalgia.

Interview, Washington/Life, 2-11:41.

Richard G. Kleindienst
Attorney General of the United States

The process of defining freedom of speech, of the press and of assembly has come alive again. Today, inflammatory public statements that would have been prohibited under the legal processes of a generation ago are freely tolerated. Massive peaceful demonstrations are not only permitted but are accommodated by extraordinary leeway in the use of public property, even to the inconvenience of others.

Before American Bar Association, San Francisco, Aug. 15/ San Francisco Examiner, 8-15:8.

Victor H. Krulak
Lieutenant General (Ret.) and former Pacific Commander, United States Marine Corps

Karl Marx designed what he reckoned was a fool-proof scheme for defeating capitalism. It has since been tried—in a score of places and a hundred ways—for the better part of a century. But it has never been able to meet the challenge of freedom, where man has the opportunity to succeed and the right to fail; where there is equity in government, participation by little people in important affairs, and where the events of the market-place govern the economy. The fact is, Marxism and its totalitarian trappings have failed. Certainly the cold aggression in Budapest, where Soviet tanks confronted Hungarian flesh and blood, was not a manifestation of success. The brutal aggression by the Soviet Army in Czechoslovakia four years ago—seen on millions of television screens—was not a manifestation of triumph. The erection of the Berlin Wall—a living monument to frustration—was not an example of Communist progress. The cold murder of untold thousands—perhaps millions—of Chinese, the rampant raging of the Red Guards, the forcible seizure of peasants' grain by Red Army troops, the related high-level bloodbaths, are not suggestions that Marxism is succeeding in China. And the propaganda drum-fire regarding Vietnam that we hear coming from every Communist source around the world, and parroted by our own Leftists, political opportunists and misguided activists—a drum-fire that seeks to shake our own convictions in the ability of our nation to solve its problems—is not a manifestation of strength. All of these symptoms—plain for any thinking American to see and analyze on his own —sound a note which should resound from one end of our country to the other. It is this: While the American system has made tremendous strides, our enemy is in trouble all over the world, and what he is doing, by every means possible, is to try to divert our attention from that tragic plight—to create doubts and apprehensions and cynicism in our own minds so that we will not make capital of their weakness. What is needed—and desperately today—is for the great mass of silent Americans to come out of their shells, acknowledge publicly and openly what they already know—that ours is a great, a dynamic and a successful country, that the ragings of those here at home who condemn our system are false, dishonorable and intolerable.

At Honor the Armed Forces program, La Jolla, Calif., July 7/ Vital Speeches, 9-1:685.

Walter Laqueur
Director, Institute of Contemporary History, London

Political power, like justice, must be made manifest to be appreciated. In this respect, the image of America, as far as the outside world is concerned, is more and more that of a nation unwilling to exercise power, a nation beset by a mood of pervasive defeatism and ridden with internal dissent.

The Sacramento (Calif.) Bee, 10-12:(A)20.

Archibald MacLeish
Poet, Playwright

When the great Depression of the '30s brought Marxism and the American Proposition face to face, on a battlefield made to Marxist specifications, there was every theoretical reason to suppose that Marxism would triumph. It did not. It failed even to scratch out a foothold in the United States. And why? Because the American Proposition, unimpressed with the mystique of economic determinism, fought its way out of economic disaster and adapted itself to the new century . . . The truth is that, far from being dead, the belief in man, which is the ground of the American Proposition, is now stronger in the United States than it has ever been, and potentially stronger in the world, for it is now the one great positive affirmation left. The history of Russia over this same period leaves no doubt that, whatever the military and industrial success of the Communist regime, it stands upon a negation of the human spirit; a suppression of human freedom; a censorship and regulation of the arts; and the universal tyranny of the State Police, at least as brutal as anything the Communists overthrew. And what we are learning, little by little, about the Great Cultural Revolution in (Communist) China suggests that, although the Chinese are doubtless more humane than the Russians, there's no great human affirmation in the Thoughts of Chairman Mao. It is still here (in the U.S.), in this Republic, still here after almost 200 years, that the last, best hope of man survives. And not only survives —grows.

Television broadcast/"Comment!", National Broadcasting Company, 4-9.

(The Republic) is no longer a visible force in the lives of most of us, as it was to our ancestors (in the 19th century)—I mean, the Republic as a sense of living in a community that has a common bond, that is essentially human in character and quality. We rarely even say we live in the United States; we live in New York or Boston or Chicago. We don't live together as a people with a common vision of ourselves and our destiny.

Interview, Conway, Mass./The New York Times, 5-7:(1)79.

David Mathews
President, University of Alabama

. . . Southerners have a unique sense of time and place, of belonging, of community. Southerners have roots. They have an identity. A Southerner—whatever his station, whatever his color—has a home. The Southern experience, for that reason, suggests to all of us the great value of being committed to some place and to some people, not merely by accident of birth but by design. In a society that is highly mobile, industrialized, urban and too often impersonal, people experience what may well be termed an identity crisis. To what and to whom do we owe our consideration and our allegiance? Many serious thinkers are concerned that such a society breaks down individual creativity and resiliency. The lesson of the South is that our allegiance to some home is one available antidote to that malaise . . . People of the South know that they were born of the trials of their ancestors; and that realization, used intelligently, should be a source of strength in troubled times.

Before Huntsville (Ala.) Chamber of Commerce/The National Observer, 3-4:13.

Frank McGee
Television commentator, "Today" Show, National Broadcasting Company

It seems to me that a good many Americans feel that they have been ignored for too long and that institutions, while not responding perhaps as well as they should to the needs of minority groups in the United States, are not responding to *their* needs, either. And they are rather weary—saddle-sore is an expression we used to use in the part of the country where I grew up—with being told that so many of the social evils are attributable to them. They are the middle class. There was a time, I can recall, when we said that . . . one of the redeeming graces of our society was that we did have a large and stable middle class. It's become rather more fashionable in recent years to sneer at the middle class and to say that all of the country's ills, or many of them, are attributable to them. And yet they look at themselves and they see that "We are, after all, those who work; we are, after all,

(FRANK McGEE)

those who pay the taxes. We send our children to school; we are patriotic. We may agree . . . that the (Vietnam) war is wrong or we may not; but it is our sons, after all, who are fighting and dying there." And they don't feel that their point of view, that their sense of moral values, that their sense of the rightness and wrongness of government directions are being taken into account.

Television broadcast/"Today" Show, National Broadcasting Company, 5-17.

George S. McGovern
United States Senator, D–S.D.

I want America to come home from the alien world of power politics, militarism, deception, racism and special privilege to the blunt truth that "all men are created equal; that they are endowed by their creator with certain inalienable rights, and among these are life, liberty and the pursuit of happiness." I want this nation we all love to turn away from cursing and hatred and war to the blessings of hope and brotherhood and love. Let us choose life, that we and our children may live. Then our children will love America, not simply because it is theirs but because of the great and good land all of us together have made it.

At Jefferson-Jackson Day dinner, Detroit/ The New York Times, 4-25:41.

There are elements in Southern life which can liberate the nation. The South, more strongly than any section, clings to a belief which values people more than their goods or bank accounts, and labors to preserve the bonds of community and family and place which tie us to our fellow mortals.

Before South Carolina Legislature, Columbia, June 28/Los Angeles Times, 6-29:(1)6.

Our people are alert to threats abroad. But they are equally concerned with the deterioration of our society from within. They see decaying cities, wasted air and water, rampant crime, crumbling housing and failing transportation. They see a government which is more preoccupied with its image abroad than with its failures at home. And they are tired of seeing their needs starved to underwrite corrupt governments overseas, to pay more than our share of alliances with the rich nations of Europe and to buy shiny new airplanes that don't fly, guns that don't fire and missiles that only increase the terror. I suggest that the most serious national-security questions today involve such questions as the health of our people, the quality of our schools, the safety of our streets, the condition of our environment, the vitality of our economic system and, most of all, the confidence of our society that this nation cares about its own.

Before the Senate, Washington, Aug. 1/ The New York Times, 8-2:14.

Vincent E. McKelvey
Director, United States Geological Survey

In the next 28 years we will create a "second America" in the very real sense that we will mine, pump, manufacture and build as much by the year 2000 as we did in all previous American history.

Plainview (Tex.) Daily Herald, 11-10:6.

Patsy T. Mink
United States Representative, D–Hawaii

We self-righteously expect all others to admire us for our democracy and our traditions. We are so smug about our superiority, we fail to see our own glaring faults, such as prejudice and poverty amidst affluence.

Before National Association for Foreign Student Affairs, Atlanta, May 2/ The New York Times, 5-5:6.

Thomas H. Moorer
Admiral, United States Navy; Chairman, Joint Chiefs of Staff

I think that, in some areas, the (American) people are willing to stand back and let someone else compete. But I also think that—and I think this is particularly pertinent with respect to the young people—that it's mandatory for countries such as ours—that has all the blessings and all of the resources and all of the know-how—to move forward and compete and be number one . . . Number one in every area: number one in sports, number one in industry, number one militarily, number one across the board.

Television interview/ The Wall Street Journal, 6-7:12.

Bill Moyers
Former Press Secretary to the President of the United States

We have, as Americans, an incomparable tradition of commitment to the human quest, to the ideals of government and democracy, and to the imperative of faith that exalts the work of every son of God born to earth.

Quote, 7-9:26.

Ralph Nader
Lawyer; Consumer rights advocate

(Addressing high school students): I want to level with you. This country's in trouble and we all know it. We have a society in America that treats teen-agers as children. Everything emphasizes this juvenile nature; it's a psychological climate . . . Don't be lulled into thinking that you can't seize power through citizenship. On the athletic field you never give up. You've got to do the same in the citizen-action arena. You shouldn't throw in the towel on the field of life itself. So what if you have these little teen-age problems? You should ignore them and concentrate on what's important. This is not the time to fool around, wasting countless hours watching television or chit-chatting—not when the future of civilization is at stake. Don't waste your time on these ridiculous problems. You can make a whale of a difference right where you are. You have numbers, brains and now the vote. We need your sensitivity. Special-interest groups have their team. We must field our team.

Cleveland/Life, 1-21:51.

Richard M. Nixon
President of the United States

It is kind of fashionable these days to say, "What difference does it make whether the United States is Number 1 in air transport or Number 1 in the merchant marine?" It makes a good deal of difference. We don't have to be Number 1 in everything; but we have to try to be. Whenever a nation or a person quits trying to be Number 1, he ceases or that nation ceases to be a great nation.

San Diego, Jan. 4/ Los Angeles Times, 1-5:(1)3.

Four years from now, America will celebrate the 200th anniversary of its founding as a nation. And there are those who say that the old spirit of '76 is dead—that we no longer have the strength of character, the idealism, the faith in our founding purposes that that spirit represents. Those who say this do not know America. We have been undergoing self-doubts, self-criticism. But these are only the other side of our growing sensitivity to the persistence of want in the midst of plenty, of our impatience with the slowness with which age-old ills are being overcome . . . Let us reject the narrow visions of those who would tell us that we are evil because we are not yet perfect, that we are corrupt because we are not yet pure, that all the sweat and toil and sacrifice that have gone into the building of America were for naught because the building is not yet done.

State of the Union address, Washington, Jan. 20/The New York Times, 1-21:18.

(Addressing the Soviet people): Most of you know our country only through what you read in your newspapers and what you hear and see on radio and television and motion pictures. This is only a part of the real America. I would like to take this opportunity to try to convey to you something of what America is really like—not in terms of its scenic beauty, its great cities, its factories, its farms or its highways, but in terms of its people. In many ways, the people of our two countries are very much alike. Like the Soviet Union, ours is a large and diverse nation. Our people, like yours, are hard-working. Like you, we Americans have a strong spirit of competition. But we also have a great love of music and poetry, of sports and of humor. Above all, we, like you, are an open, natural and friendly people. We love our country. We love our children. And we want for you, and for your children, the same peace and abundance that we want for ourselves and for our children. We Americans are idealists. We believe deeply in our system of government. We cherish our personal liberty. We would fight to defend it, if necessary, as we have done before.

Broadcast address, Moscow, May 28/ The New York Times, 5-29:3.

Our bicentennial era is a time for Americans to say to the world: "You helped to make us what we are. Come and see what wonders your countrymen have worked in this new country of ours. Come and let us say, 'Thank you.' Come and join in our celebration of a proud past. Come and share our dreams for a brighter future."

Broadcast address, San Clemente, Calif., July 4/Los Angeles Times, 7-5:(1)17.

It is time that good, decent people stopped letting themselves be bulldozed by anybody who presumes to be the self-righteous moral judge of our society. There is no reason to feel guilty about wanting to enjoy what you get and get what you earn; about wanting your children in good schools close to home; or wanting to be judged fairly on your ability. Those are not values to be ashamed of; those are values to be proud of; those are values that I shall always stand up for when they come under attack. Fortunately, what the new majority wants for America and what I want for this nation basically are the same . . . On matters affecting basic human values—on the way Americans live their lives and bring up their children—I am going to respect and reflect the opinion of the people themselves. That is what democracy is all about.

Radio address, Oct. 21/ The Washington Post, 11-12:(B)1.

Norman Vincent Peale
Clergyman; Pastor, Marble Collegiate Church, New York

I have had the privilege of traveling in many countries of the world, and some countries I love very much. I love the snows of the Alps and the quaint little villages of Switzerland. But every time I land once again at Kennedy Airport (in New York) and feel the throb and surge of this land, I know I am in the greatest country that God ever made . . . People come up to me in many places and say, "But don't you realize that this country has a lot of problems?" And I say to them, "I certainly do; and I am glad of it. When any country comes to the point where it no longer has problems, that country is on the way out." The only people I have ever met in my life who have no problems—I know right where they are—they are in Woodlawn Cemetery! They have no problems, no problems at all. But they are dead. It follows, therefore, I believe, in logical sequence, that problems constitute a sign of life. Indeed, I would go so far as to say that the more problems you have, the more alive you are. The person who has, let us say, 10 good old tough, man-sized problems is twice as alive as the poor, miserable, apathetic character who only has five problems. And any nation that does not have problems is in the cemetery of history.

Sermon at Marble Collegiate Church, New York/The National Observer, 12-23:11.

Lewis F. Powell, Jr.
Associate Justice, Supreme Court of the United States

America, its institutions and the values of our people, deserve a better billing than they often receive . . . It is said that religion is irrelevant, our democracy is a sham, the free-enterprise system has failed and that somehow America has become a wholly selfish, materialistic, racist society—with unworthy goals and warped priorities. It is also persistently said—and this is directed to lawyers and judges—that our system of criminal justice is repressive. If these criticisms are accepted, there is little wonder that our institutions and inherited values are no longer respected . . . It would be irrational to say that all of the criticisms of America and its institutions are unfounded. Yet, excessive preoccupation with our faults can weaken—or even destroy—the ties that bind a people together.

At American Bar Association annual meeting, San Francisco, Aug.13/ Los Angeles Times, 8-14:(1)17.

George W. Romney
Secretary of Housing and Urban Development of the United States

The principal lesson I've learned in my years in government is that we don't get fundamental reform in this country except as the result of crisis.

Interview, Washington, Aug. 30/ The Washington Post, 8-31:(A)14.

R. Sargent Shriver
Democratic Vice-Presidential nominee

I think we've lost a real sense of purpose, almost a sense of nationhood. I think we are floundering around trying to find a purpose for our country; and that's a very bad situation to be in. One of the deep tragedies that has overtaken many people in America is that some of them have no reason or desire to fight for their country. There is nothing that the United States seems to stand for which they would be willing to die for tomorrow. Let me draw a comparison with a little country like Israel. A large proportion of its people would rather die than give up the idea of that nation. That was the kind of spirit that existed in this country under General (George) Washington. It was a sense of national purpose that made people willing to die for that objective. I don't mean there's no one in the United States who feels like that today, but I think a large number don't feel that way.

Interview, Rockville, Md./ Newsweek, 8-21:13.

Herman E. Talmadge
United States Senator, D–Ga.

There are still some points worth making about this country. America still seems to be an attractive enough place so that we have to limit the number of people who can come in every year—and that is not true in all parts of the world. Our leaders are accused of being politically motivated, but what that really means is that they are accountable to the people of this country for what they do—and that is not true in all parts of the world. We are a country deeply torn by dissension, and different points of view are freely expressed—and that is not true in all parts of the world.

Quote, 10-8:348.

Maxwell D. Taylor
General, United States Army (Ret.); Former Chairman, Joint Chiefs of Staff

It has been a dismal revelation that we are no longer the American melting pot. We are tending to polarize into minority groups, each thinking and speaking in terms of the minority interest and competing for group advantage with little regard for the national interest. This is an internal weakness which could be very dangerous if we are ever again tested in a national emergency, such as the Cuban missile crisis, for example. Along with this tendency to polarization, we see a loss of national pride, a loss of respect for ourselves and for our institutions, starting with the Presidency and going down to the Mayor of the small town. We seem to enjoy denigrating our national institutions and our Constitutional practices. These are some of the things I have in mind when I talk about the weaknesses exposed by the war in Vietnam. The war did not cause them; it revealed them.

Interview, Washington/ U.S. News & World Report, 11-27:22.

Spiro T. Agnew
Vice President of the United States

I do believe when we look at much of the black leadership . . . they are not reflecting the real opinion of the black community, and they are more or less caught up in a situation where they are constantly looking at inadequacies, real or imagined, and very seldom able to articulate any approval of change that has been salutary and constructive.

TV-radio interview/"Meet the Press," National Broadcasting Company, 8-27.

(Arguing against forced busing of school children for racial balance and forced integration of housing): The artificial moves that people claim are necessary to break the halters often form new chains against integration because they put people together who are basically incompatible, but worse than being racially incompatible, are incompatible in tens of other ways. And that I find is inhibiting the natural melding of the country that should be taking place. In some ways, I think that the focus on the extreme and forced methods of racial mixing are counter-productive to the effort. This doesn't mean that I don't feel that where (there) has been a governmental restraint that prevents the (integration) result from taking place, that restraint shouldn't be removed. That's why I'm for open housing. That's the kind of restraint that nobody can break through. But once you have an open-housing law, the contrived forcing of people into contacts and neighborhoods where they don't have the same identity of interest, where they just don't fit or they don't mix, causes exacerbations that raise simplistic bars to the actual result coming about. We have a lot of the best and most successful mixing of the races taking place in areas where nobody notices it.

Interview, Washington/ The Washington Post, 9-30:(A)8.

John J. Akar
Former Ambassador to the United States from Sierra Leone

(It is sad that it requires) Malcolm X to flex, Rap Brown to rap and Stokely Carmichael to stoke before American blacks . . . (gain) instant respectability, recognition and other dramatic victories. The fault lies with our white brothers and sisters, for they fail to respond to poignant and eloquent words of a Dr. Martin Luther King.

San Francisco Examiner & Chronicle, 2-13:(This World)2.

Muhammad Ali (Cassius Clay)
Former heavyweight Boxing Champion of the World

No, I can't say blacks have no chance in America. We're free. We're doctors, lawyers, teachers and Senators . . . Look at me. I'm outspoken . . . I talk more than anybody. Nobody bothers me. There's opportunity . . . We can do anything. If somebody can't make it, it's his own fault.

Inglewood, Calif., June 19/ Los Angeles Times, 6-21:(3)3.

John M. Ashbrook
United States Representative, R–Ohio

(President Nixon) could have done three things which, together or possibly even separately, would have ended busing once and for all: he could have endorsed a Constitutional amendment banning all forced busing (of school children) for racial balance; he could have backed the Griffin amendment, removing jurisdiction on busing matters from the Federal courts; or he could have called on the House-Senate Conference Committee to approve my own House-passed amendment, which prohibits the use of Federal funds in behalf of busing. The President has done none of these things. Instead, he has contributed to the problem he says he wants to solve. The effect of his ambivalent proposals will be to prolong, not shorten, the busing controversy—and to support the practice of busing in the many areas where it is already taking place.

Human Events, 3-25:1.

Reubin Askew
Governor of Florida

I strongly oppose a Constitutional amendment to outlaw (school) busing (for racial balance)—not because I particularly like it or think it's a panacea for our problems . . . Busing is an artificial and inadequate instrument of change. It should be abandoned just as soon as we can afford to do so. Yet, by the use of busing and other methods, we've made real progress in dismantling a dual system of public schools in Florida. And I submit that, until we find alternative ways of providing an equal opportunity for quality education for all . . . until we can be sure that an end to busing won't lead to a return of segregated public schools . . . until we have those assurances, we must not unduly limit ourselves, and certainly not Constitutionally. We must not take the risk of seriously undermining the spirit of the Constitution, one of the noblest documents ever produced by man. And we must not take the risk of returning to the kind of segregation, fear and misunderstanding which produced the very problem that led to busing in the first place.

At Central Florida State Fair, Orlando, Feb. 21/The Wall Street Journal, 2-25:10.

Howard H. Baker, Jr.
United States Senator, R–Tenn.

(On the busing of school children for racial balance): Nashville is the most liberal town in Tennessee, and now 75 per cent of the people there are vehement on the subject. I have a hunch that everybody will end up against busing before it's over. If I ever saw an issue in my whole career where everyone is trying to find a way to decently oppose it, this is it. It's really ferocious.

San Francisco Examiner & Chronicle, 3-5:(A)6.

Alan Bible
United States Senator, D–Nev.

(On busing of school children for racial balance): Children who learn together and play together will be less likely to acquire the old racial fears and hatreds. But should our schools and our children bear the brunt of this problem? If it is wrong to tell a child he must go to a certain school because he is black, is it right to tell a child he cannot attend a certain school because he is white? Must the school bus become the principal vehicle for erasing racial boundaries? I think not. Forced busing, under court order, is not the solution. Two wrongs don't make a right. I disagree with the courts even over the Constitutionality of racial busing.

Human Events, 4-29:15.

Jack Brinkley
United States Representative, D–Ga.

Just as busing (of school children) was

wrong to enforce segregation, so is busing wrong to achieve integration.

Before House Judiciary Subcommittee, Washington, Feb. 28/ The Washington Post, 2-29:(A)6.

Louis R. Bruce
Commissioner, Bureau of Indian Affairs, Department of the Interior of the United States

I want to see Indian economies where dollars move from Indian hand to Indian hand and are not drained out by those non-Indian cities that develop and grow and feed upon Indian reservations.

News conference, Washington, Jan. 12/ The Washington Post, 1-13:(A)1.

Robert C. Byrd
United States Senator, D–W.Va.

The overwhelming majority of Americans, black as well as white, are strongly united in their opposition to this kind of social experimentation with our children (school busing for racial balance). In fact, opposition to massive school busing may be doing more to unite Americans of all races than any other issue in recent years.

Feb. 16/The Washington Post, 2-17:(A)12.

Emanuel Celler
United States Representative, D–N.Y.

To favor or oppose the busing of school children (for racial balance) as an abstract matter serves no useful purpose. As the Supreme Court said in the Swann case, "Bus transportation has been an integral part of the public education system for years." Today, approximately 40 per cent of all public school pupils in all parts of the country are transported to their schools by bus.

At House-Judiciary Committee hearing, Washington, Feb. 28/The New York Times, 2-29:18.

Shirley Chisholm
United States Representative, D–N.Y.

(On school busing for racial balance): My heart bleeds this evening for all of those who are addressing themselves to the fact that we must not and cannot have young children being carted from one district to another in order to be able to give them the kind of education that is necessary . . . Where have you been for these many years? The black and Spanish-speaking children in the Southern and Western parts of the United States have been bused right past the white schools in your communities in order to go to the dilapidated buildings reserved for them . . .

Los Angeles Times, 3-5:(J)5.

(On President Nixon's call for a stop to court-ordered school busing for racial balance): If Mr. Nixon ever claimed that he was entitled to the support of the black Americans, he lost that claim by calling, in effect, for a return to a plantation society for the entire nation.

San Francisco Examiner, 3-18:2.

Angela Davis
Political activist

A black revolutionary realizes that we cannot begin to combat racism and we cannot begin to effectively destroy racism until we've destroyed the whole system . . . Because I have a very strong love for oppressed people, for my people, I want to see them free and I want to see all oppressed people throughout the world free. And I realize that the only way that we can do this is by moving toward a revolutionary society where the needs and the interests and the wishes of all people can be respected.

Television interview, San Jose, Calif., Feb. 7/San Francisco Examiner, 2-8:18.

Thomas F. Eagleton
United States Senator, D–Mo.

(On busing of school children for racial balance): One, it's improper to bus solely for the purpose of racial balance. Two, it is improper to bus where the quality of the education at the receiving school dist-

(THOMAS F. EAGLETON)

rict—the end of the bus ride—would be inferior to that which the student would receive in his neighborhood school. And three, it's improper to bus where, for reasons of time or distance, you would affect the health of the student being bused. I think those are three pretty good guidelines that should not be violated in busing. I take the position that busing may well be necessary and still is a useful tool in breaking down the barriers of de jure segregation. Finally, I take the position that, from a legal point of view, the courts and Department of Health, Education and Welfare do not have authority to bus in situations of de facto segregation. And I agree with the finding of the Fifth Circuit Court of Appeals in the Richmond case that the courts do not have the authority to order busing across non-gerrymandered county lines. I underscore the word "non-gerrymandered," because if they are gerrymandered, obviously that would be de jure segregation and busing would apply.

Interview, Washington, June 30/ The Washington Post, 7-14:(A)13.

Edwin W. Edwards
Governor of Louisiana

To the . . . thousands of black Louisianans who have not yet enjoyed the full bounty of the American dream, we extend not a palm with alms, but the hand of friendship. We understand your plight. We shall lighten your burdens and open wide the doors of community. Artificial barriers which have kept black people from most policy-making positions and job opportunities at all levels of state government are going to come tumbling down.

Inaugural address, Baton Rouge/ Los Angeles Times, 5-12:(2)8.

Billy Graham
Evangelist

We (the current U.S. generation) have done more to bring dignity, equality and opportunity to minority groups than any other generation has ever done in the history of the world. We have hundreds of black millionaires in America. The American dream has come true for more millions in our generation than any that has ever lived.

San Francisco Examiner & Chronicle, 6-25:(This World)2.

Edith Green
United States Representative, D-Ore.

(Arguing against busing of school children to achieve racial balance): I don't think the evidence supports the conclusions that, if we just mix youngsters so that there are so many blacks and so many whites in a schoolroom, then they will get a better education. In fact, I think a careful reading of the evidence shows that a child's education and his ability to be educated, as a matter of fact, depend more upon the environment in which he lives than on the six hours a day in which he is transported to a school outside his neighborhood. I also think that it's a very patronizing way for the whites to view this—that a youngster who is black has to sit beside a youngster who is white in order to be educated. I do not think that in six hours a day you can offset the disadvantages which a child—black or white—may have because of the disadvantaged home in which he lives and the disadvantaged neighborhood. I think that the task is much greater than we have assumed. We're going to have to change homes, and we're going to have to change neighborhoods.

Interview/U.S. News & World Report, 4-3:20.

(On busing of school children to achieve racial balance): A lot of the so-called "limousine liberals," and some of my friends in the House who have plenty of funds to send their youngsters to private schools, have been great on busing as long as it was black children into white schools. But now, when they talk about busing white children into a black "ghetto" area, this is when they really ran into a buzz saw. There really isn't any equality of opportunity if you just say that the people who cannot afford to move to the suburbs, the people who cannot afford to put their youngsters in private schools, the people who cannot afford–as one Presidential candidate does–to pay $1,400 to allow his daughter to go to another school so she'd be with her friends–the ones who can't afford this are the ones who remain and are bused.

Interview/U.S. News & World Report, 4-3:21.

Robert P. Griffin
United States Senator, R–Mich.

Forced busing (of school children to achieve racial balance) not only has proven ineffective, it is counterproductive. It is a wasteful diversion of tax dollars which should be used to improve the quality of education. It increases racial tensions. It accelerates the flight from the cities to the suburbs and beyond. It runs counter to the desire of most parents who are primarily interested in seeing their children educated in a quality school–close to home.

Before the Senate, Washington/ U.S. News & World Report, 3-13:32.

Richard G. Hatcher
Mayor of Gary, Ind.

We (black people) are through believing. We are through hoping. We are through trusting in the two major white American political parties. Hereafter, we shall rely on the power of our own black unity . . . If we form a third political movement, we shall take with us the Chicanos, Puerto Ricans, the Indians, the Orientals, and that is not all. We shall also take with us the best of white America.

At National Black Political Convention, Gary, Ind./ The Washington Post, 3-12:(A)2.

Augustus F. Hawkins
United States Representative, D–Calif.

(On President Nixon's proposals against busing of school children for racial balance): The Administration seems to be retreating to a separate-but-equal school system. This is a sad day in the nation. It will brutalize the black children and return us to conditions that existed in the last part of the past century.

Before House Education and Labor Committee, Washington, March 27/ San Francisco Examiner, 3-28:2.

Arthur Hertzberg
President, American Jewish Congress

For the past half-century, the attitude of the Jewish community has been that what is good for society is good for the Jews. When the civil rights movement died and Jewish interests began to come into conflict with those of other groups, we over-reacted and turned inward, sacrificing our traditional concern for universal values in favor of the programs that would emphasize specifically Jewish problems. The time has come to redress this new imbalance, to take the middle position which says affirmatively and proudly: We are universalists and particularists; we care for all men and we care for ourselves; we work for what is good for the community and what is good for us; we strive for racial justice to the black man and support Soviet Jewry's struggle to be free.

Before American Jewish Congress, Cleveland, May 12/ The New York Times, 5-13:24.

Theodore M. Hesburgh
President, University of Notre Dame

Students, parents, teachers and administrators are calmly proving to the world that desegregation can work. Decent behavior on the part of our young people is not only possible but almost certain if their elders do not provide them with too many disgraceful examples to follow.

Newsweek, 3-13:23.

Herbert Hill
National labor director, National Association for the Advancement of Colored People

Not since the early years of this country has an American President so openly and deliberately joined with the enemies of black people (as has President Nixon). Today, the vast power of the United States government has been placed on the side of those institutions—huge industrial corporations, banks, public utility and insurance companies, the building contractors' associations and some segments of organized labor—that are perpetuating racist job patterns throughout the American economy.

At NAACP convention, Detroit, July 6/ The Washington Post, 7-7:(A)2.

Harold Howe II
Vice president, education and research division, Ford Foundation; Former Commissioner of Education of the United States

It is not surprising that, since the mid-'60s, some blacks have rejected integration as the solution to anything and sought black identification, togetherness and power. If those of us who are pushing so hard for integration had been sensitive enough, we would have been aware long before we were that it can be damaging to blacks both psychologically and economically. Early moves toward integration went too far in the direction of asking blacks and other minorities to join American society solely on white terms, to forget any pride or interest in their own heritage, or, if you will, to become white men. Now we know that integration has to be a two-way street, that it is not just a simple matter of mixing people in some judicially- or administratively-determined proportion, that non-whites as well as whites must help to set the terms, and that these terms must include as a matter of dignity and right the opportunity for non-whites to lead and control some of the institutions in our pluralistic society.

The New York Times, 12-10:(4)11.

Hubert H. Humphrey
United States Senator, D-Minn.

I am opposed to massive compulsory busing (of school children) that has as its sole objective racial balance based on a mathematical formula. I believe in integrated education. I am opposed to segregated education. I think it is fit, right and proper that you bus a child from an inferior school to a good school. I think it is wrong and doesn't make a bit of sense to bus a child from a good school to a poor school, and I think black parents and white parents both feel the same. Busing, when it is used to improve the quality of education, has its justification. When it is used to settle every racial problem in this country, it becomes divisive and it doesn't help.

TV-radio interview, Washington/ "Meet the Press," National Broadcasting Company, 3-12.

People come to me, time after time, as they become angry with me sometimes, and say, "Mr. Humphrey, what is it that you want for black people?" I'll tell you what I want for black people—it's what I want for me; no more, no less. That isn't special privilege; that isn't special consideration. It's just what the Constitution says. The Constitution doesn't say, "we, the white people" or "we, the black people" or "we, the rich people" or "we, the poor people." It says, "we, the people"!

The Washington Post, 5-28:(B)5.

I'm deeply interested in how we're going to implement the new era of civil rights; not just the laws that we have, but how we're going to open career opportunities in professional and technical schools. It isn't good enough just to have the blacks and others sleep in the same hotel you do or have no discrimination in employment. You've got to have a bigger trust that goes into open neighborhoods, that goes into reconstruction of the whole social environment so they begin to feel they're part of the social structure.

The Washington Post, 6-18:(B)2.

The Democratic Party got into trouble when its internal reforms came to be perceived as establishing specific quotas that favored young people, women and blacks over the more traditional elements of the Party, particularly ethnic Americans, blue-collar workers, the elderly and elected Democratic officials. By the same token, I would argue that the civil rights movements got into trouble when more and more people came to see it as an effort to give blacks a special break that was not afforded to other groups in the American society. We know this perception was wrong. But it exists, whether we like it or not.

At civil rights symposium, Austin, Tex., Dec. 11/The New York Times, 12-12:28.

Just as he confounded his critics with his dramatic trips to (Communist) China and the Soviet Union or his adoption of wage and price controls, (President) Nixon could just as easily seize the initiative on the civil rights front. A second-term President must begin to think seriously about the historical judgments of his Administration. And I can imagine no more harsh indictment than his having failed to lead the United States in the most critical and urgent area of domestic concern.

At civil rights symposium, Austin, Tex., Dec.11/The New York Times, 12-12:28.

Henry M. Jackson
United States Senator, D–Wash.

If it's public (education), it should be equal . . . But forced busing (of school children) based on race does not achieve this objective. On the contrary, it singles out a child because of the color of his skin and sends him off to school in a strange, sometimes distant, neighborhood. And with all that, there is no guarantee of a better school at the end of the bus ride . . .

The Washington Post, 2-15:(A)8.

(On Senator George McGovern's accusing Jackson of racism because of his opposition to school busing for racial balance in the Florida Democratic Presidential primary): I have supported every piece of civil-rights legislation to come before the Congress in the past three decades. If my opposition to forced busing solely to achieve a racial balance means I am a racist, then Senator McGovern is accusing 75 per cent of the voters in Florida, and indeed the majority of all Americans, of racism.

News conference, Madison, Wis., March 20/The New York Times, 3-21:32.

Jesse L. Jackson
Civil rights leader; Former director, Operation Breadbasket, Southern Christian Leadership Conference

Without the option of a black political party, we (black people) are doomed to remain in the hip pocket of the Democratic Party and the rumble seat of the Republican Party.

At National Black Political Convention, Gary, Ind., March 11/ San Francisco Examiner & Chronicle, 3-12:(A)1.

(Saying black votes will decide the 1972 Presidential election): Hands that once picked cotton can now pick Presidents; and that's a revolution.

Before Howard University alumni, San Francisco, May 14/ San Francisco Examiner, 5-15:5.

Daniel James, Jr.
Brigadier General, United States Air Force; Deputy Assistant Secretary for Public Affairs, Department of Defense

My young life was filled with orders, advice and encouragement. I was told to eliminate one by one all the reasons some bigot might say I (as a black) was not capable of standing beside him or deserving of equal opportunity. If he says you are dirty, make sure you are clean. If he says you steal, make sure you don't. If he says you are dumb, make sure you learn. If he says you are scared, make sure you are brave, my son. And if there ever comes a time to fight for your country, don't you run away and hide. And don't you ever, no matter what the provocation or the invitation, turn your back on your God or your country or that flag. Remember, they said, you are not African. You are an American, and this is your land. Many of those who will suggest you go back to Africa cannot trace their ancestors in this country as far back as you can trace yours. This is your nation, and don't you get so busy practicing your right to dissent that you forget your responsibility to contribute. If she has ills, you hold her hand until she is well, and then work for constructive change within the system. Let your own contribution to the problems of your race be a by-product of your achievement in your chosen field. You will prosper in proportion to your contribution to the nation. Remember that with the heritage of being an American goes the responsibility for developing that heritage and passing it on to your kids in better shape than you got it. Don't stop to argue with the ignoramous on the street who calls you nigger. You don't have the time. Press on. Perform. Perform. Excel. Excel. And when you drive back by in the limousine of success, that ignoramous will still be standing there on the corner wrapped in his hate. The power of excellence is overwhelming. It is always in demand, and nobody cares about its color.

Before National Association of Secondary School Principals/The Wall Street Journal, 7-25:14.

Jacob K. Javits
United States Senator, R–N.Y.

(On busing of school children for racial balance): . . . busing is a useful tool, a necessary tool, in desegregation. And desegregation is a necessary and essential tool –and the great majority of experts agree on this–in equal educational opportunity . . . Now, this tool should not be overused. But I believe the issue has become very emotional. Therefore, in order to advance, not retard, the whole progress of better education and school desegregation, we have to define reasonable limits on busing.

Interview/U.S. News & World Report, 4-3:22.

Lyndon B. Johnson
Former President of the United States

We know there is (racial) injustice. We know there is intolerance. We know there is discrimination and suspicion and division among us. But there is a larger truth. We have proved that great progress is possible. We know that much remains to be done. And if our efforts continue, if our will is strong, if our hearts are right and courage remains our constant companion, then, my fellow Americans, I am convinced we shall overcome.

At civil rights symposium, Austin, Tex., Dec. 12/The New York Times, 12-13:45.

To be black–to one who is black–is to be proud, to be worthy, to be honorable. But to be black in a white society is not to stand on level ground. While the races may stand side by side, whites stand on history's mountain and blacks stand in history's hollow.

At civil rights symposium, Austin, Tex., Dec. 12/Los Angeles Herald-Examiner, 12-13:(A)10.

Vernon E. Jordan, Jr.
Executive director,
National Urban League

It is increasingly clear that, to the extent that there is among the citizenry hope and faith in the American ideals, they are held by those who suffered most and benefited least. Black people today—for all our righteous anger and forceful dissent—still believe in the American dream. We believe today as we once believed in the dungeons of slavery; we believe as we once believed in the struggles of Reconstruction . . . and as we held our faith through the dismal days of separation and segregation. We believe because this is our land, too. And we must—in this year of doubt and confusion—remind a forgetting nation that this land is ours; that we have lived here since before the Pilgrims landed . . . and we are here to stay. This nation too often forgets that this land—this America, this Southern soil—is sprinkled with our sweat . . . watered with our tears . . . and fertilized with our blood. It too often forgets that we black people helped to build America's power and glory . . . that we dug taters . . . toted cotton . . . lofted bales . . . sank the canals . . . and lay the railroad tracks that linked ocean to ocean. Black people, too, sing *God Bless America*; we, too, sing "O beautiful for spacious skies, for amber waves of grain . . . " We, too, pledge allegiance to the flag—and for what America is supposed to represent. We've died in America's every war, even in segregated armies—and black boys are dying today in disproportionate numbers in the rice paddies in Indochina. Yes—this land is our land . . . and America will work for black people, too, or it will not work for anyone!

At Duke University, March 28/
Vital Speeches, 5-1:437.

The psychological effect of a moratorium on busing (of school children for racial balance) is to instill among many white citizens and among school boards the conviction that they need never desegregate. Busing is not an end in itself. It is but one of several mechanisms which can be used to desegregate illegal and unconstitutionally racially segregated schools. Forty per cent of all school children are bused, the vast majority for reasons that have nothing to do with desegregation. Only about three per cent of children are bused for purposes of desegregation; and it has been estimated that, even today, more children are bused to maintain segregation than to overcome it . . . Nationally, there is very little more busing now than there was five years ago, and, in some Southern states, court-ordered busing to desegregate the schools has actually resulted in less busing than previously.

Before Commonwealth Club,
San Francisco, April 7/
San Francisco Examiner, 4-8:6.

The debate over busing is reminiscent of the debate in the early '60s over the desegregation of public places. Then, as now, the basic issue was one of access. There is no inherent virtue in sitting next to a white child in school, just as there was no inherent virtue in sitting next to a white person at a lunch counter. But there is considerable inherent virtue in equal access to the rights and privileges of this society—and that is what the civil rights struggle today, as in the '60s, is all about. So long as this society has pretensions of being democratic and open, and so long as the resources of public education are concentrated in the hands of the majority white population, the public school system must be desegregated.

Before Phoenix Urban League, May 16/
Vital Speeches, 7-1:552.

I believe that white Americans must understand that busing (of school children for racial balance) is a phony issue and that the real issue is the Constitutional rights of black people. The passions of an election year can only compound the irrationality surrounding the busing controversy, which is so lethal that it is bound to seep outwards and poison the moral climate of the nation. Busing constitutes a "domestic Vietnam," and it is the responsibility of white Americans to act now or face the probability of looking back a decade hence at a nation embracing full apartheid and asking, "how did this happen?"

At National Urban League annual conference, St. Louis, July 30/Vital Speeches, 9-15:727.

. . . Black America lies becalmed today, halfway between hope and desperation. And unless the (Nixon) Administration acts more positively now, it would be a wiser man than I who could predict the direction we shall move when the wind begins to blow again.

Before Washington Press Club, Jan.17/ San Francisco Examiner, 1-18:2.

Herman Kahn
Director, Hudson Institute

This country has the most successful reversing of discrimination of any country in history. It's just coming out now in the scholarly literature, but it's been obvious for the last five years. Racism has been in a steadily sharp decline in the United States from 1960 to the present. There is no backlash against Negroes in any kind of a poll. I don't care who asked the questions, where they were asked or how they were asked. Basically, feelings toward Negroes have gotten more positive over the last 10 years. Even the most outraged ethnics turn out to have more positive feelings than they used to have. It's not necessarily true toward low-income Negroes, but that's a class issue and class is a much less serious problem than race. Class can be handled by money. Race cannot. The backlash that people talk about is a backlash against the upper-middle-class, not the Negro. The society was mobilized to reverse discrimination. The attempt was successful.

Interview/Human Events, 11-18:19.

Edward M. Kennedy
United States Senator, D–Mass.

In American history, you have to go back to the era of Reconstruction to find a comparable abdication by the Federal government of its responsibility for civil rights

. . . the cause of justice in America has not yet triumphed. It has not triumphed for Mexican-Americans. It has not triumphed for black Americans. It has not triumphed for poor Americans. So long as these Americans do not share equally in the benefits of law, the nation remains flawed, its promise unfulfilled.

Campaigning for Democratic Presidential nominee Senator George McGovern, Los Angeles, Sept. 10/Los Angeles Times, 9-11:(1)3.

Richard G. Kleindienst
Deputy Attorney General, and Attorney General-designate, of the United States

We (the Nixon Administration) have a better civil-rights record than any previous Administration. The civil-rights organizations won't recognize it–they are too tied in with the opposition party. We have appointed more Negroes as Federal judges than anyone else. We have given more government jobs to blacks than anyone else. We have accomplished massive desegregation of schools in the South, without untoward trouble. We are moving for open housing in the suburbs. We have put in racial hiring quotas under the Philadelphia Plan. We have brought more equal-hiring cases, and everything else. But we are not getting credit from the "liberals," and we are incurring displeasure of the "conservatives." We aren't winning points from either side.

Interview/U.S. News & World Report, 2-28:31.

Richard G. Kleindienst
Attorney General of the United States

It should be noted . . . that the dual-education school systems in the South have now been eliminated. And in every other area of civil-rights enforcement—employment, housing, public accommodations, voting—the Department (of Justice) has filed more suits and engaged in more litigation in the past three years than in the comparable period from 1966 to 1968.

The Dallas Times Herald, 8-6:(A)8.

Despite partisan claims to the contrary, I am pleased to note that in virtually every civil-rights category—education, employment, housing, voting and public accommodations—we (the Nixon Administration) have brought actions against more defendants in the same period of time than any previous Administration. We are forging a whole new spectrum of rights—women's equal opportunity rights, prisoners' rights, the right of indigent defendants to paid legal counsel—rights that were glossed over by a less sensitive society a generation ago.

Before American Bar Association, San Francisco, Aug. 15/ The Washington Post, 8-16:(A)14.

Jewel Lafontant
United States Representative to the United Nations

I have noticed the detailed specificity with which representatives of my country have in the past met accusations of discrimination, by parading endless statistics tending to show how well the minorities are performing in my country—in all areas—including but not limited to employment, education, business and housing. It is not the progress of minorities which should justify my elation in my country. Certainly, there has been some progress—indeed great, dramatic progress—but the remaining problems are infinitely complex and are not yet systematically approached. But we can be proud, maybe I should say we should be grateful, that the American system has evolved a dynamic, if not dialectical, interplay of forces—social, political and legal—which pushes all the ugliness and inhumanness of discrimination to the surface for all to see and which thereby demands a solution.

Before a UN committee/The National Observer, 12-23:11.

John V. Lindsay
Mayor of New York

Dammit, it's time for people to stand up (on the issue of school busing for racial balance). I realize no one likes busing. Busing has become a code word. But you can't waffle around on the issue . . . I am for busing because it is often the only way to integrate our schools. I am for busing because the alternative of perpetuated racial segregation is worse, far worse. I am for busing because if the choice is between inconvenience and the repudiation of the Constitution, I stand with the Constitution.

Television interview, Los Angeles, Feb. 23/ Los Angeles Times, 2-24:(1)33.

Sidney P. Marland, Jr.
Commissioner of Education of the United States

One of the very large social responsibilities of the schools is to bring about racial justice and racial accord—to get over the very abysmal record we have over the last 150 years as a nation.

Interview, Washington/ The Washington Post, 4-3:(A)4.

George S. McGovern
United States Senator, D–S.D.

(On busing of school children for racial balance): For more than a generation, black children were bused to avoid integrated schools. One of the more cynical aspects of our present debate is that President Nixon (who is against busing), seeking to make political capital of this difficult situation, is ignoring history and asking the nation to

(GEORGE S. McGOVERN)

believe that the (busing) problem began yesterday.

San Francisco Examiner & Chronicle, 2-20:(This World)2.

I believe that school busing and redistricting (to achieve racial balance), as ordered by the Federal courts, are among the prices we are paying for a century of segregation in our housing patterns . . . For 50 years, we have been busing white and black children out of their neighborhoods to attend other schools in order to preserve the principle of segregation. Now the court has said we're going to use busing for a different purpose. We're going to use it to try to break down the walls of segregation . . . And I think that is a concept worthy of our support.

U.S. News & World Report, 2-28:28.

(On President Nixon's broadcast address calling for an end to further busing of school children for racial balance): What we have just witnessed is a collapse of moral and political leadership by the President—a total surrender to (George) Wallace-ism and the demagoguery it represents. He has talked for years about law and order. What he has asked Congress to do now is to defy the courts and defy the Constitution. This course will doubtless be welcomed by many frightened people, but it represents a backdoor sneak attack on the Constitution of the United States.

At University of Illinois, Urbana/ The New York Times, 3-20:37.

I do not believe in a rigid quota system (of hiring people according to racial percentages). I've never committed myself to saying that we have to have exactly 11 per cent or 10½ per cent or whatever the percentage of a particular group is . . . I can and will (if elected President) see that there are black people in the Cabinet of the United States and on the Supreme Court. But I'm going to do the same thing for other groups. You've got to remember that never have we had a Polish-American on the Supreme Court. Never have we had an Italo-American on the Supreme Court. We've never had a Greek-American on the Supreme Court.

Campaigning for the forthcoming Presidential election, Buffalo, N.Y., Oct. 4/ The New York Times, 10-5:52.

Floyd B. McKissick
Former director, Congress of Racial Equality

More blacks need to be in decision-making positions. President Nixon will probably appoint a black Commissioner to the Federal Communications Commission within 30 days. We need blacks in the customs courts, on high-up policy-making boards, in financial circles like Wall Street and on the stock exchange boards. There are few blacks in government, except in agencies that relate to black people.

News conference, Dallas, March 24/ The Dallas Times Herald, 3-25:(B)1.

George Meany
President, American Federation of Labor-Congress of Industrial Organizations

The AFL-CIO wholeheartedly supports the busing of (school) children (to achieve racial balance) when it will improve the educational opportunities of the children. We deplore the actions of individuals or groups who are creating divisive political issues out of America's vital need to quality, integrated education.

Before Democratic Party Platform Committee, Washington, May 15/ San Francisco Examiner, 5-15:9.

Clarence Mitchell
Director, Washington, D.C., bureau, National Association for the Advancement of Colored People

(On the opposition to busing of school children for racial balance): . . . politically-motivated demagogues have somehow duped otherwise reasonable people into believing that sending children to school on a bus is the equivalent of serving cocktails in the school cafeteria . . . It is my opinion that the current busing controversy is really only the tip of the iceberg. The most massive problem is a social sickness that divides us by race, by class, by religion and even by intellect . . . Again and again, the purveyors of fear have aroused suburban communities or all-white city neighborhoods by picturing the little black children who arrive on a school bus from a ghetto neighborhood as the forerunners of muggers, dope peddlers and slum dwellers who are content to cram a family of nine into a one-bedroom apartment.

Before National School Board Association, San Francisco, April 15/San Francisco Examiner & Chronicle, 4-16:(A)23.

Walter F. Mondale
United States Senator, D–Minn.

Black children, and their parents, know that the real issue is not "massive busing (of school children) to achieve an arbitrary racial balance." They know that the real issue is our willingness to accept integrated schools. White children know this, too. And the health and stability of our society over the next 50 years will reflect the lessons which we teach our children today. This country is at a crossroads. School desegregation in the South is largely completed. But we from the North are now beginning to feel the pressure—which our colleagues from the South have felt for so many years—to abandon the course set by the 14th Amendment. If we do, we will deal a blow to public education, in the North and in the South, from which it may never recover. We will prove true those who have said the North favors racial equality only below the Mason-Dixon Line—and those who have said that the South cares more about winning the battle over school desegregation than it cares for the future of its children.

Before the Senate, Washington, Feb. 18/The New York Times, 2-19:20.

Edmund S. Muskie
United States Senator, D–Maine

(Regarding his 1971 statement that a 1972 Democratic Presidential ticket could not win with a black Vice-Presidential nominee): My statement was not an expression of preference; it was a statement of judgment as to what I thought were the political realities . . . I happen to resent the fact that those are the realities; and I commit myself to eliminate, insofar as I can and insofar as it is in my power, the discrimination which results in that kind of reality.

Miami, Jan. 8/San Francisco Examiner & Chronicle, 1-9:(A)1.

(On school busing for racial balance): If you're ready to put in the money necessary to bring quality education within the reach of every child, you're going to see the pressure for moving school populations reduced. I mean, every poll we take where we ask this question indicates that blacks as well as whites are not happy about moving their children miles and hours away from home to get good schools. And the pressure of blacks is this: They say to me over and over again that "we won't get money for our schools unless there are some white children in them."

Interview/The Washington Post, 2-27:(C)4.

Richard M. Nixon
President of the United States

(The) courts have gone too far—in some cases beyond the requirements laid down by the Supreme Court—in ordering massive busing (of school children) to achieve racial balance. The decisions have left in their wake confusion and contradiction in the law, anger, fear and turmoil in local communities and, worst of all, agonized concern among hundreds of thousands of parents for the education and safety of their children who have been forced by court order to be bused miles away from their neighborhood schools . . . The purpose of such busing is to help end segregation. But ex-

(RICHARD M. NIXON)

perience in case after case has shown that busing is a bad means to a good end. The frank recognition of that fact does not reduce our commitment to desegregation; it simply tells us that we have to come up with a better means to that good end. The great majority of Americans, black and white, feel strongly that the busing of school children away from their own neighborhoods for the purpose of achieving racial balance is wrong.

Broadcast address to the nation, Washington, March 16/ San Francisco Examiner, 3-17:40.

There is no escaping the fact that some people oppose busing (of school children for racial balance) because of racial prejudice. But to go on from this to conclude that "anti-busing" is simply a code word for prejudice is a vicious libel on millions of concerned parents who oppose busing not because they are against desegregation but because they are for better education for their children. They want their children educated in their own neighborhoods.

Broadcast address to the nation, Washington, March 16/ San Francisco Examiner, 3-17:40.

Heavy reliance on cross-city busing of school children (for racial balance) has failed to meet either of its intended purposes: to promote quality education for all and to end the racial isolation which we all agree must be ended. Instead, busing has disrupted and divided increasing numbers of schools and communities. Even the strongest proponents of busing recognize one fact: It would be physically impossible to transport pupils on a scale large enough to solve the most pressing problem of all, for even the most massive busing imaginable would still leave the vast majority of black and poor children in the inferior schools of the inner city—a lost generation deprived of the educational opportunity to which they, like all Americans, are entitled. It was for these reasons that I asked the Congress three weeks ago to declare a temporary national moratorium on new busing decrees, and then to enact new legislation to accomplish three things: 1) To establish in the law of the land the right of every American child to equal educational opportunity—more clearly and strongly than it has ever been established before; 2) To curb excessive busing by putting its usefulness into perspective with other, more workable, school-desegregation remedies: and 3) To redirect billions of dollars in effective aid into the inferior schools of this nation, where such aid is so urgently needed.

Before National Catholic Education Association, Philadelphia, April 6/ U.S. News & World Report, 4-17:97.

(The use of racial quotas in hiring is) a dangerous detour away from the traditional value of measuring a person on the basis of ability. In employment and in politics, we are confronted with the rise of the fixed quota system—as artificial and unfair a yardstick as has ever been used to deny opportunity to anyone.

Labor Day message, San Clemente, Calif., Sept. 3/ The Washington Post, 9-4:(A)2.

James G. O'Hara
United States Representative, D–Mich.

When I came to Congress 14 years ago, children in many parts of the country were being bused to certain schools (to maintain segregation) because of the color of their skin. I played a small part in correcting that situation. Now, once again (through the busing of school children to achieve racial balance), children are being assigned to schools on the basis of their color. I oppose it today just as I opposed it then. The Constitution demands that our institutions be color-blind.

Before the House, Washington/ The National Observer, 8-26:2.

J. Stanley Pottinger
Director, Office for Civil Rights, Department of Health, Education and Welfare of the United States

Two million black pupils were in 100 per cent minority schools in the 11 states of the South in 1968, and those children represented 68 per cent of the total Negro pupils in the region. For the current school year, the projection shows that this number of totally isolated children has dropped from 68 per cent to only 9 per cent. There was virtually no change in this figure in the rest of the country. What this means is that, by looking at the number of black children in majority-white schools, or the number who are totally isolated, or by any other standard, no matter how you measure it, today there are fewer black children in segregated schools—or, conversely, there are more minority children in integrated schools—in the South than in any other part of the country.

U.S. News & World Report, 1-24:31.

(Arguing against government-enforced racial quotas in employment and college admissions): Quotas, on the one hand, are numerical levels of employment that must be met if the employer is not to be found in violation of the law. They are rigid requirements, and their effect is to compel employment decisions to fulfill them regardless of qualifications, regardless of good-faith effort to fulfill them and regardless of the availability of capable applicants . . . Goals, on the other hand, are projected levels of hiring that say what an employer can do if he really tries. By establishing goals, the employer commits himself to a good-faith effort that is most likely to produce results. If a university falls short of its goals, that in itself does not result in non-compliance; a good-faith effort to achieve those goals remains the test.

The New York Times Magazine, 9-10:114.

Muammar el Qaddafi
Premier of Libya

We stand today with 25 million black Americans. We stand with 5 million black American Moslems who are suffering from racism. For in America they have the Bill of Rights and the Statue of Liberty; but under it is written, "entry is forbidden to blacks and dogs." What sort of freedom is that?

Tripoli, Libya, June 11/ Los Angeles Herald-Examiner, 6-12:(A)4.

Henry M. Ramirez
Chairman, President's Cabinet Committee on Opportunities for Spanish-speaking People

No other Administration has placed such a heavy emphasis on solutions to the problems of the Spanish-speaking . . . Next to the American Indian, Spanish-speaking rank lower than any other single group in such areas as educational attainment, housing conditions, employment, etc. Under the present (Nixon) Administration, we have witnessed a new awareness of the problem and a willingness to take steps to alleviate these conditions within the Spanish-speaking community.

News conference, Houston, Jan. 29/ The Washington Post, 1-31:(A)2.

Elliot L. Richardson
Secretary of Health, Education and Welfare of the United States

The only measure of desegregation enforcement is results. It cannot be measured by the level of rhetoric or the amount of money cut off from financially distressed school systems. It can be measured only by the persistent fulfillment of our legal and educational mandate—the elimination of dual schools based on race. And on that score, this (Nixon) Administration has a documented record of solid performance.

U.S. News & World Report, 1-24:31.

Hugh Scott
United States Senator, R–Pa.

I am on record and the Congress is on record against busing solely for the purpose of achieving racial balance in schools. I'm against the arbitrary quota system, because I don't think that children learn best by being constantly aware of the fact that, say, 47 per cent are of one race, 47 per cent of another race, and 6 per cent of still another. It is arbitrary and it works injustices. What we want is quality education, and, in my opinion, the courts are stumbling toward that goal.

Interview/U.S. News & World Report, 2-28:32.

Stephen G. Spottswood
Chairman, National Association for the Advancement of Colored People

Every year since 1619 has been a crucial year for the black people of America; and we (the NAACP) have been so busy for the past 63 of those years that we haven't had time for make-believe and pretense. There has been work to do; there have been sacrifices to make; there has been suffering to bear; there have been defeats to absorb; there have been victories—yes, glorious, hard-won NAACP victories—to build on. We've been busy, and whatever hope this nation has of ever reaching the Promised Land of democracy, it owes to us. It owes us for the men and women and children who have toiled and bled under our banner through the years. It owes us for the money we have put to work—pennies and dollars adding up to millions—drawn from the hard work of hundreds of thousands of people, mostly black, who gave in order to advance themselves and their country. It owes us for never allowing the rulers of this land to forget, for as much as a moment, the depth of their moral failures and the urgency of the need, and the certainty of disaster if they fail us. So when we in the NAACP say that 1972 is a fateful year in an age of crisis, let the people listen! When we raise our voice in determined prophecy, it will be ignored at the nation's peril. We shall declare ourselves now, so that there will be no ground for confusion, so that no man and no woman from one end of the country to the other can have any uncertainty about where the National Association for the Advancement of Colored People stands on the most important single issue facing the American people—the full equality of opportunity and attainment by 26 million Americans of African descent.

At NAACP convention, Detroit, July 3/Vital Speeches, 8-15:656.

(On the busing of school children to achieve racial balance): Nothing is a better measure of the seriousness of today's peril than the so-called busing issue. Who could ever have supposed that the question of how children ride to school would become the test of candidates for the Presidency, for the U.S. Senate, for seats in Congress and in Governors' mansions?

At NAACP convention, Detroit, July 3/ San Francisco Examiner, 7-4:2.

Leon H. Sullivan
Member, board of directors, General Motors Corporation

(Speaking from his position as first black member of the board of GM): Millions of black children are in the pipeline (for jobs); little black kids by the millions are in the pipeline and are coming along. We haven't even seen the wave of blacks that are coming on the job market in this country. They are going to be more demanding; they are going to be educated; they are going to be desirous that democracy work for them. Either America must Americanize for everyone, or there will be America for no one . . . The black community was more subservient when it was uneducated 30 years ago. Up to about 1930, the vast majority of the black community was functionally illiterate. It was only two generations out of slavery. But education now is beginning to produce a better-informed black American. He reads. He learns. He inquires and demands equality—equality of treatment, equality of opportunity, equality within the framework of the American system . . . It is becoming more and more realized, certainly in General Motors. One-half of the time of a GM directors' meeting is now devoted not to profits but to social problems—pollution, auto safety, minority employment.

Interview, Philadelphia/ The Washington Post, 5-27:(A)16.

George C. Wallace
Governor of Alabama

Several years ago, I told the politicians they had better stop this Federal takeover of the schools. Every one of these Senators here campaigning (for the March 14 Florida Presidential primary) has voted over and over again to take your children away from you. All six Senators who are in this race—and I have the Congressional record to prove it—have voted either to bus little children (for racial balance) or announced for it . . . When I win on March 14, the present (Federal) Administration is going to sit up and take action, because you are going to tell them they had better sit up and fly right, because we're sick of it and we're through busing our children to kingdom come.

At political rally, Jacksonville, Fla., Feb. 18/Los Angeles Herald-Examiner, 2-19:(A)4.

I never was a racist. I just never was against black folks. I was unfairly labeled by the Eastern press and the liberals who don't know the difference between a racist and a man who believes in states' rights.

Interview/ The New York Times, 2-26:14.

Busing (of school children for racial balance) . . . it's the most atrocious, callous, cruel, asinine thing you can do for little children. Fifty years from now, the American people will look back and say, "how cold and callous were those in our government that brought it about." And those that bring it about—where do they live? They don't live in Washington; they live over in Maryland or Virginia and they've got their children in a private school. They're more pluperfect hypocrites . . .

The National Observer, 3-25:5.

We've accepted nondiscrimination and freedom of choice in Alabama. But there has not been enough for the social schemers. They want ratios and balances, and they're busing our (school) children hither and thither into kingdom come to get it—and that's what I'm against. I'm for quality education for everybody, regardless of race, creed or color. I'm against the Federal government interfering in local matters.

Campaigning for the Democratic Presidential nomination, Cumberland. Md., May 6/The New York Times, 5-7:(1)53.

Earl Warren
Former Chief Justice of the United States

If there is one lesson to be learned from our tragic experience in the Civil War, it is that the question of racial discrimination is never settled until it is settled right. It is not yet rightly settled.

Quote, 6-11:553.

We will either go forward to our announced goal of providing that all men are created equal and as such are entitled to life, liberty and the pursuit of happiness, or we will denigrate the plural society we envisioned and developed and revert to a "house divided," which the prophetic Lincoln said cannot stand. We have suffered greatly from such divisiveness, and it would be well for those who are obstinate or timid or thoughtless to remember the admonition that those who fail to learn the lessons of history are destined to relive them.

At civil rights symposium, Austin, Tex., Dec. 11/The New York Times, 12-12:28.

Lowell P. Weicker, Jr.
United States Senator, R–Conn.

What we can't have (in the controversy over busing of school children for racial balance) is liberty and justice for all with our prejudices and wallets intact.

San Francisco Examiner & Chronicle, 4-2:(This World)2.

Louis J. West
Chairman, Department of Psychiatry, University of California, Los Angeles

Racism is rooted, I think, in a universal presumption of difference. Every individual who grows up normally needs a group to which he can attribute all the negative human qualities he denies in himself. I call this the Universal Stranger, whose initials, like Pogo's enemy, are Us. He is the alien group—hostile, destructive, dangerous.

San Francisco Examiner & Chronicle, 5-28:(This World)2.

Roy Wilkins
Executive director, National Association for the Advancement of Colored People

(On President Nixon's views against busing of school children for racial balance): We frankly didn't expect the President to use his office of President to come down and choose a partisan side. We thought he'd be President of all the people. Instead of that, he is along with the enemies of little black children. He can believe in busing or not believe, as he chooses; but for him to say so signals to the world that even the President of the United States is against us.

News conference, New York, May 25/ The New York Times, 5-25:10.

Hysteria over school busing (for racial balance) is sweeping the nation. Our people are reacting to exaggerated fears based on totally inadequate, and often distorted, information. Many of our politicians are pandering to these fears. They are appealing to all that is fearful, mean and callous in the American spirit . . .

News conference, New York, May 25/ The Washington Post, 5-26:(A)2.

Anyone who is against busing (of school children for racial balance) and says he is for equal education is a liar or a fool.

Washington, Dec. 17/ The Washington Post, 12-18:(C)7.

Commerce • Industry • Finance

James Abourezk
United States Representative, D–S.D.

Not only do conglomerates threaten the existence of small-unit farmers and ranchers who produce food solely for a living, but if they are allowed to become a significant factor in food production nationally, they will certainly adversely affect consumer prices. It's in the interest of people living in New York City, as well as in South Dakota, to keep family farms economically healthy.

The Washington Post, 2-26:(A)15.

(Federal Cost of Living Council Director Donald) Rumsfeld and (U.S. Secretary of Agriculture Earl) Butz are waving red flags in the consumer's eyes by talking about high beef prices. One condemns high prices; the other praises them. It reduces to that old ploy of pitting consumers against farmers in hopes that the mutual anger engendered will stop both farmer and consumer from focusing on the real inflators—the food processors and distributors, or so-called middlemen.

Before House Democratic Study Group Consumer Task Force, Washington/ The Washington Post, 3-18:(B)6.

Spiro T. Agnew
Vice President of the United States

(Urging business to give the public the facts about themselves): . . . if they (the public) don't understand you, they will dislike you. And if they dislike you, they will fight you. And if they fight you, as many are doing now, you will find yourself in all kinds of trouble—not only with the government but with the consumer groups, civic groups and your own employees . . . So why blame your workers or your customers or the public in general for their reservations about big business? They are guilty of nothing more than believing your own blue-sky press releases. They think you are raking in profits in prodigious amounts. They are convinced that you haven't a care in the world.

Before Harvard Business Club, New York, April 12/ Los Angeles Herald-Examiner, 4-13:(A)5.

Roger S. Ahlbrandt
Chairman, Allegheny Ludlum Industries, Inc.

The American steel industry is a resource of essential importance to the American society—a resource that cannot easily be duplicated; a resource that the nation cannot do without. It is vital to the national interest, basic to every other business and industry, and essential to the national security. Despite that, it continues to be assailed on many sides.

At steel industry economics seminar, Detroit/San Francisco Examiner & Chronicle, 4-16:(C)9.

Salvador Allende (Gossens)
President of Chile

The (giant international) corporations have gone as far as seeking to upset the normal functioning of the government and institutions of other nations, to start worldwide campaigns against the prestige of a government, to make it the victim of an international boycott and to sabotage its economic relations with the rest of the world.

At United Nations Conference on Trade and Development, Santiago, April 13/ Los Angeles Times, 4-14:(1)20.

Charles A. Anderson
President, Stanford Research Institute

In the past several years too much of our attention has been taken up with negative problems. Business leadership has been on the defensive with environmental issues, consumerism, civil rights and community involvement problems. Efforts to keep inflation under control have put business in the suppressor role—and so on. I would like to see the business leadership of our country challenged to use some added resources imaginatively and constructively in developing new economic strength for us. And I am convinced it can be done. We have a great amount of technology that is not being utilized. On the one hand, we have problems that need to be solved, markets to be served, products to be developed. On the other hand, we have tremendous technological and scientific capabilities—a priceless resource. And the way to bring them together is through U.S. industry.

Before Financial Executives Institute, San Francisco, Jan. 20/ Vital Speeches, 3-1:295.

Jack Anderson
Political columnist

The incestual relationship between government and big business thrives in the dark. When those responsible for it get caught in the sunlight, they are like fish out of water. They flip and they flop. They backtrack. They trip over their tongues. Are we going to tolerate this? Are we going to let them corrupt us? They are not your masters. They are your servants. *You* (the public) have the final decision. *You* have the final vote.

Newsweek, 4-3:53.

Erma Angevine
Executive director, Consumer Federation of America

Consumers need an independent (government) agency to handle the safety of food, drugs and other products. We have only to look at (the U.S.) Food and Drug Administration's dreary record on consumer protection to see why . . . Consumers need an agency with a commitment to the public's welfare. FDA has not shown that commitment. From where we sit, the (Nixon) Adminstration wants to keep consumer product safety in HEW not for our protection, but to be sure it can continue to protect the business community—at our expense.

The Christian Science Monitor, 3-23:10.

Lloyd M. Bentsen
United States Senator, D-Tex.

(Criticizing American diplomats for failing to press U.S. commercial interests abroad): Our State Department has too often been too quick to represent the interest of other nations over ours. Too frequently, our foreign-service representatives are more interested in the social season than American trade. If they aren't acclaimed as most-popular by their hosts and wreathed in garlands of flowers, they think they're failures. Most of these people still subscribe to the theory that American "dollar diplomacy" and "economic imperialism" are the bugaboos that make America disliked abroad. They look on businessmen seeking trade as an affront to their host countries' sensibilities. The goal of our foreign-service corps should not be to achieve personal popularity in the countries where they operate, but to win respect for the U.S.

Before American Petroleum Institute, Chicago, Nov. 14/ San Francisco Examiner, 11-14:58.

Secor D. Browne
Chairman, Civil Aeronautics Board of the United States

(Advocating a strong domestic aircraft industry): If you're going to support programs for health, education and welfare, you need wealth. And the aircraft industry is a principal source of wealth to this country . . . You remove the aircraft exports, and we're not looking so good. And if we keep on the way we're going, we may become a nation of service industries taking in each other's laundry.

Interview, Washington/ Los Angeles Times, 2-24:(3)12.

Yale Brozen
Professor of Business Economics, University of Chicago

It is through advertising, in whatever form that consumers come to know of the availability of a product and the specific advantages it offers. Without advertising, a consumer would have to spend time and sometimes money to get information on which to base a purchasing decision; either that or make decisions on a less-informed basis. Advertising reduces the consumer's cost of search.

Before Commonwealth Club of California, Feb. 24/Vital Speeches, 4-1:359.

Arthur F. Burns
Chairman, Federal Reserve Board

I firmly believe that a new and stronger international monetary system can and must be built. Indeed, I feel it is an urgent necessity to start the rebuilding process quite promptly. It is not pleasant to contemplate the kind of world that may evolve if cooperative efforts to rebuild the monetary system are long postponed. We might then find the world economy divided into restrictive and inward-looking blocs, with rules of international monetary conduct concerning exchange rates and monetary reserves altogether absent. As we learned last fall, a world of financial manipulations, economic restrictions and political friction bears no promise for the future. It is the responsibility of financial leaders to make sure that such a world will never come to pass.

At International Monetary Conference of American Bankers Association, Montreal, May 12/ The New York Times, 5-13:43.

Earl L. Butz
Secretary of Agriculture of the United States

I don't fear the invasion of the corporation into American agriculture in any substantial measure. As a matter of fact, there's evidence that corporations have been withdrawing from farm production in recent years. I can point to a number of corporations that were in the agriculture business and they are getting out. They can apply their capital more profitably elsewhere. I think there's a good reason for that, which is that agriculture will always remain a fairly personal business. The old Scotsman summed this up centuries ago when he said, "The eye of the master fatteneth the cattle." The hired man who works for the corporation punches his clock on a 40-hour week—and the seasons, the rainfall, the sun don't operate that way; the crops don't operate that way. In livestock farming, it's not the hired man who works for some distant corporation who will get up at 3 o'clock on a cold February morning to go out in the hog house and help the corporation sow have the corporation's pigs. Only the man who owns the sow and owns the pigs will do that. When you take the individual entrepreneurial interest out of agriculture, efficiency declines, costs go up and you're not competitive. Now, a family farm does not mean a small farm these days. Dad and son in a typical corn-belt farm now may well have $200,000 invested in the business. They may have 800 to 1,000 acres. Out in Montana in the wheat area, 2,000 acres may be the average family farm. Farming is now a very capital-intensive industry.

Interview, Washington/ U.S. News & World Report, 4-10:56.

A market-dominated agriculture lets production shift and adjust as consumer preferences change and as export demand grows. It is forward-looking. It lets farmers make production decisions based on crop profita-

(EARL L. BUTZ)

bility; and it tends to let farm production shift and adjust to farmers who can produce each crop best. A government-dominated agriculture is, almost by definition, backward-looking. Production becomes based on historical patterns and crop histories—yesterday's rotations and yesterday's yields.

Before National Association of Farm Broadcasters, Orlando, Fla./ The Wall Street Journal, 7-28:6.

John W. Byrnes
United States Representative, R–Wis.

(Regarding the results of a recent Congressional mission to Europe): I think we got the idea across to people in decision-making posts of the European community that we simply can't afford to be patsies any longer . . . We pointed out that a mood of protectionism is developing in this country, and unless something can be done about expanding our foreign trade, that feeling will grow and predominate.

Interview, Washington/ The Dallas Times Herald, 1-18:(B)21.

William J. Casey
Chairman, Securities and Exchange Commission of the United States

As to brokerage commissions, the negotiated rates that have been in effect for trades of $300,000 or more in value presently allow institutions to trade at less cost per share of stock traded than the cost to individuals on a per-share basis. These economies of scale are also built into the fixed-fee schedule for large orders—and rightly so. After all, it doesn't cost 10 times as much to execute a 1,000-share as a 100-share order . . . But commissions should also reflect the fact that large orders cannot be satisfactorily handled without a far greater degree of skill, responsibility and risk. The more realistic commission rates are, the better the securities markets will be for institutions and individual investors. There is no reason why both kinds of business cannot be economically profitable for brokerage firms and that comparable professional service cannot be provided in both areas . . . In dealing with commission rates, we have to consider all parts of the brokerage business. It is my view that, as much as possible, commission rates should reflect the cost of transactions and provide potential for a reasonable profit. This should be so whether rates are fixed or not.

Interview/ The Dallas Times Herald, 12-27:(D)9.

A. W. Clausen
President, Bank of America

Conscientious executives involved in international business desire to find ways in which their firms can not only be valuable and therefore welcome in the nation-states in which they operate, but also will be forces for the general good and peaceful existence of the world community. Indeed, the idea that this kind of business enterprise can be a strong force toward world peace is not so far-fetched.

The Sacramento (Calif.) Bee, 11-4:(A)18.

Don Conlan
First vice president and chief economist, Dean Witter & Company

It is utterly ridiculous to believe that war is a plus for the stock market. If we have learned anything at all from the Vietnam war, we should have learned that. The truth is that, ever since 1965, when the Vietnam troop buildup began in earnest, neither the economy nor corporate profits nor the stock market has performed as well as it would have if there had been no Vietnam. If the Vietnam situation blows up in our faces now, it will be disastrous for the stock market. Presuming that most of us survived an all-out war, the economy would be put in a strait-jacket. We'd have an excess-profits tax almost immediately.

We'd have tough price controls, rationing and all sorts of other interferences with our free-market system. No, there's not a stump of an excuse for claiming that war is a bullish development for stock prices.

New York/Los Angeles Times, 5-30:(3)10.

John B. Connally, Jr.
Secretary of the Treasury of the United States

During these recent months, I have sometimes heard the accusation that I have become a sort of bully boy on the manicured playing fields of international finance. You will not expect me to accept that characterization. But I will plead guilty of speaking in plain words as directly as I can. I do so because nuances and ambiguous phrases can only mislead the American people as to urgency of the problems we face (in the international financial arena). Equally, our friends abroad should know of our determination to solve those problems, with good will but with firm resolve. With that determination and resolve, I am convinced that the dollar will again be a currency sought after throughout the world, fully capable of carrying its share of the burdens of international finance. Indeed, I believe there is a truly unique opportunity for all nations to begin building a durable trade and payments structure based on equity and realism.

Before Council on Foreign Relations, New York/The National Observer, 3-25:14.

John T. Connor
Chairman, Allied Chemical Corporation

. . . it is essential, for the good of the country, that they (business and government) work more closely together. I don't think we can accomplish our national objectives or meet our national goals without this kind of cooperation and understanding. It is very difficult to bring this about. In our system, for political reasons, business and government are often political adversaries. But I think men of good-will on both sides will have to work toward a closer partnership. Otherwise, our system just isn't going to work.

Interview/Nation's Business, October:48.

Silvio O. Conte
United States Representative, R–Mass.

The oil industry is the most powerful lobby and the most powerful unit we have in the United States.

Before Joint Congressional Economic Subcommittee, Washington, Jan. 12/ The Washington Post, 1-13:(A)3.

Stewart S. Cort
Chairman, Bethlehem Steel Corporation

The failure is our nation's failure—the failure to realize what every other nation on this earth knows, that a strong steel industry is indispensable to the vitality of any modern industrial economy. And the incredible beauty of it is that this country wouldn't have to pay a heavy price to strengthen the steel industry. No need to bail us out, or nationalize, or subsidize. How can it be done? Well, give us tax policies that effectively encourage investments. Give us anti-trust policies that allow us to operate more efficiently. Give us trade policies that allow us to compete on something approaching equal terms. Give us rational and realistic pollution-abatement standards and tax policies that can help us meet them. And help us give the public a sharper realization that a healthy domestic steel industry is vital to their own interests. Give us this and we'll give you a great, a truly great, industry—a steel industry that can help drive our nation's economy to heights you and I can hardly comprehend. We can do it. We must do it. And I say we damn well better do it!

Before Executives' Club, Chicago, April 14/Vital Speeches, 5-15:461.

Severe criticism of business is fashionable. It'll get votes from the ideological

(STEWART S. CORT)

extremes, from those who are disillusioned, frustrated and fearful. It'll get votes from people who don't have that one commodity that has always sustained the American people of the past—hope.

San Francisco Examiner, 9-11:64.

E. M. de Windt
Chairman, Eaton Corporation

In this country we still have anti-trust laws passed to meet conditions of 60 years ago. If a couple of sick companies try to get together to try to survive, the government tells them they can't do it.

Nation's Business, February:40.

John Diebold
Management consultant

Private business is the most effective resource-allocator man has ever invented. For society to benefit from its dynamics and innovation, it is the social responsibility of business to make a profit; and it is the responsibility—and opportunity—of society to invent ways of applying business methods to meet the needs of man and of society. It must set incentives and constraints in such a way that profit is made doing the tasks society most needs in a manner society finds acceptable . . .

At French government symposium on An Economic Society for Man, Paris, June 21/ The New York Times, 6-25:(3)16.

Don Durgin
President, National Broadcasting Company Television

(Criticizing the proposal of "counter-commercials" in broadcasting): All advertising is advocacy, and we are being told that it justifies counter-advocacy. Advertising for large cars is said to warrant counter-ads warning that big cars pollute the air. Advertising for small cars is said to justify counter claims that small cars are fragile in accidents. Life-insurance ads could invite counter life-insurance ads. Foods with preservatives could bring the organic-food advocates into action. Confections could bring dental-health counter-ads. (Counter-ads) don't need to offer an alternative product. They don't necessarily sell anything. Their purpose is to un-sell something. And that something in the long run will be advertising itself.

At American Association of Advertising Agencies Western Regional Convention, Phoenix, Oct. 17/ Los Angeles Times, 10-18:(3)13.

Cyrus S. Eaton
Industrialist

Capitalism needs reforms. I have a great stake in this country; I have 14 grandchildren here. I believe that we must have much more contact between management and workers. We must have workers as stockholders and workers on boards. We have a long way to go.

Interview, Northfield, Ohio/ New York Post, 2-2:36.

Henry Ford II
Chairman, Ford Motor Company

All nations must respond to an overriding need for trade liberalization. We (in the U.S.) may aggressively resist unfair advantages and bargain equality of treatment, but we must adhere to the broader principle of trade liberalization.

Before Montreal (Canada) Chamber of Commerce, March 14/ The New York Times, 3-15:76.

I believe that the social responsibility of the corporation today is fundamentally the same as it has always been: to earn profits for shareholders by serving consumer wants with maximum efficiency. This is not the whole of the matter, but it is the heart of the matter.

At Ford stockholders' meeting, Detroit, May 11/ The New York Times, 5-12:55.

Roger A. Freeman
Senior fellow, Hoover Institution, Stanford University; Former Special Assistant to the President of the United States

The real harm of the corporate profits tax is that it punishes the efficient producer, restricts industrial expansion, penalizes capital formation and adversely affects our competitiveness in international trade. Immensely appealing politically, it is in economic terms the most detrimental tax in our system. Therefore, the value-added tax should, in my opinion, be used as at least a partial replacement of the corporate profits tax.

Before National School Boards Association, San Francisco, April 14/Vital Speeches, 5-15:468.

Betty Furness
Former Special Assistant to the President of the United States for Consumer Affairs

Today, the consumer still often wanders around in Wonderland, without a rabbit to guide him. We were brought up to believe in products. It is hard to be wary and to give up that faith. However, manufacturers are out to sell anyone foolish enough to buy. It's hard to accept, but that's how we play the Consumer Game.

San Francisco, March 24/ San Francisco Examiner, 3-27:26.

Weldon B. Gibson
President, Stanford Research Institute

In spite of problems within the private-enterprise system, the basic structure is sound and viable. It offers great promise to all mankind in the continuing search for greater economic and social progress. The system is responsive to change and is a powerful agent of change in line with (the) values and aspirations of the American system.

At White House conference on "The Industrial World Ahead"/ San Francisco Examiner, 1-26:55.

Wayne E. Glenn
President, Western Hemisphere Petroleum Division, Continental Oil Company

How much of our increasing domestic demand (for oil) we can hope to produce in the U.S. is very much a debatable point. As you know, the predictions and projections range all over the ballpark. The National Petroleum Council has indicated that oil imports could amount to 14.8 million barrels a day by 1985—or 57 per cent of total demand for petroleum in the U.S. . . . Many people may not realize the extent of the dollar drain this nation would be facing in 1985 if we are, in reality, importing 57 per cent of our petroleum by that date. Our balance-of-payments deficit at that time due to imported petroleum could be astronomical; and frankly, I don't see how the nation will be able to put up with that kind of increasing deficit.

San Francisco Examiner & Chronicle, 3-12:(C)11.

Edwin H. Gott
Chairman, United States Steel Corporation

The near-term outlook for steel is improving, with orders picking up as customers complete their inventory reductions. It is estimated that, with the expected pick-up in the economy, steel consumption in the United States in 1972 should increase about 5 per cent above the 1971 level. However, the ability of American steel producers to share in the future growth of domestic steel markets is highly dependent upon the government's success in controlling steel mill product imports to levels that are economically realistic and in line with the long-term growth of steel consumption in this nation.

Jan. 25/ The New York Times, 1-26:45.

The roots of this nation's foreign-trade dilemma run much deeper than the specific import-export problems of steel, or autos, or any other single American industry. They are the result of an approach to

(EDWIN H. GOTT)

foreign trade that, for too many years, catered to foreign economies at the expense of our own. And if chickens ever came home to roost, they did so last year with regard to this nation's past philosophy on international trade.

Before American Iron and Steel Institute, New York, May 24/ The New York Times, 5-25:67.

Robert W. Haack
President, New York Stock Exchange

Trading by institutions such as mutual funds, pension funds, insurance companies and banks has transformed an American securities industry which was built on the business of the individual investor.

The Dallas Times Herald, 5-7:(AA)15.

C. Howard Hardesty
Senior vice president, Continental Oil Company

I have a new name for the muckraker of the 1970s. If you accept "entrepreneur" as the generic term for "businessman," perhaps we can refer to these single-minded, persistent and totally myopic critics of businessmen as "antipreneurs." The negative prefix in antipreneurs is quite appropriate since those who hammer away at the business community are for the most part a negative lot. They reject, and they rebuke, and they reproach, and they frequently view with alarm, but hardly ever do they come up with anything constructive. The enemies of private industry are active today as never before, they are influential today as never before and—most disconcerting of all—they are succeeding today as never before. In what ways are they succeeding? Well, for one thing, they are changing some basic attitudes in this country. They are converting the United States of America from a nation that once respected initiative and economic achievement, that honored the rags-to-riches hero, to a nation that imputes to its businessmen the most venal motives and most despicable conduct, that is coming to idolize the reverse-twist, riches-to-rags antihero . . . Regardless of how much has been done to transfer control of American industry from private hands to government hands, the antipreneurs cry out for more. Could it be that our antipreneurs will be satisfied with nothing less than *de facto* nationalization of industry through a system of comprehensive rules disassociating all phases of production and distribution?

Before American Mining Congress, Washington/The National Observer, 4-22:10.

David K. Hardin
President, Market Facts, Inc.; President-designate, American Marketing Association

. . . advertising is the best and least-expensive way of bringing buyer and product together. If there were a better way, corporations would have long since switched to that better way. This is one of the things that is lost sight of today. As the restrictions on advertising increase, there is a tendency to switch corporate money into other less-effective and more-costly methods of merchandising. In the end, this is only going to make the product the consumer buys more expensive.

San Francisco Examiner, 6-16:65.

Philip A. Hart
United States Senator, D–Mich.

(On the influence of giant corporations): Have we reached the point in our society where there have been permitted to develop private concentrations of power, which, because of the enormity of their reach, make impossible the applications of public power to them? What do you do about them?

The Christian Science Monitor, 3-10:1.

S. I. Hayakawa
President, San Francisco State College

Mr. American executive! Mr. American (labor) union member! As you enjoy the music on your symphonic Sony, as you take snaps of your family picnic with your Nikon or Yashica camera, as you bop along the highways in your Toyota, please think about the rigidities in American business and labor practice that cripple our ability to compete in world markets. Tonight's paper tells me that Nissan Motors is sending representatives to pick a site around Los Angeles or Seattle to assemble Datsun trucks. Toyota Motors is also studying the possibility of opening an American assembly plant. Doesn't that scare you? It scares me!

San Francisco Examiner & Chronicle, 5-7:(B)2.

Henry J. Heinz II
Chairman, H. J. Heinz Company

The protectionist forces . . . are trying to reduce the problem to the simple equation of imports-plus-overseas-investment means less jobs for U.S. workers. This is a false equation. It assumes that only the other fellow benefits from our overseas purchases and foreign investments. In reality, trade and investment are two-way streets, with benefits to both parties to a transaction. Imports provide the foreign exchange that other countries need to buy our products. They help finance, in other words, our exports. Exports, in turn, are powerful generators of employment. Approximately 60,000 jobs are created by every $1 billion we export. Imports also help the consumer. They give him a wider choice of products at competitive prices. Tariffs and quotas tend to restrict choice, increase prices and feed inflation. In the longer term, they also lower exports. Protective legislation, in short, rewards the few it protects while penalizing everyone else.

At H. J. Heinz Company shareholders meeting/The Wall Street Journal, 10-30:10.

Harry Heltzer
Chairman, Minnesota Mining and Manufacturing Company

The multinational corporation's prime allegiance is to an orderly marketplace in which growing numbers of customers are served with goods and services, employees are provided with jobs, taxes are paid and shareholders receive dividends. Far more often than not, these interests coincide rather than conflict with those of the nation-state.

The New York Times, 11-9:72.

John W. Hill
Chairman, executive committee, Hill & Knowlton, Inc., public relations

The businessman who thinks of, and treats, consumerism and environmentalism as passing fads is only kidding himself. He may not like (consumer advocate) Ralph Nader, but he cannot overlook all the (consumer advocate) Bess Myersons who have been structured into the government at local, state and Federal levels. He cannot fail to recognize that these environmental and consumer-protection agencies and all the other regulation bureaus will keep seeking out new targets and creating new controversies. Whether or not this will be done wholly to serve the public interest or partly to justify the continuance of the bureaucratic existence, business will need to stay on the alert in these areas for a long time to come. And staying on the alert will mean keeping its house in order. It certainly doesn't mean evasive statements which are beside the point and fail to come to grips with the real problem. The great need today is for a new concept in corporate communications based on the proposition that a better-educated, better-informed, more-sophisticated public is sick and tired of being fed pablum. Straightforward, down-to-earth, man-to-man talk is necessary if the effort to win credibility for industry's communications is to succeed. It is difficult to get people to listen to business, let alone to believe it.

At Virginia Public Relations Conference, Williamsburg/The Wall Street Journal, 4-26:14.

Hubert H. Humphrey
United States Senator, D–Minn.

American agriculture and the family farmer are getting the short end of the stick. (President) Richard Nixon could wear overalls to his Cabinet meetings. He could sell his limousine and drive around Washington on a tractor. He could milk a cow on TV. But the farmers of Wisconsin still won't forget Richard Nixon's betrayal of the family farmer.

Campaigning for the Democratic Presidential nomination, La Crosse, Wis., April 1/ San Francisco Examiner & Chronicle, 4-2:(A)7.

Jack B. Jackson
President, J. C. Penney Company

I know this is a competitive business (general merchandising). It is not just buying and selling. You have to do it better. You have to have better merchandise and a better environment in the stores. People like to shop in a fashion atmosphere. I like to do business. It is like being in a sport. If you enjoy it, it's a lot more fun. I like to make a business pay, and I like to be a winner.

Interview, New York/ The Washington Post, 4-8:(H)5.

Jacob K. Javits
United States Senator, R–N.Y.

I think the tradition in Europe (toward foreign trade) is protectionist. Europe still has the psychological trauma of thinking that it's behind the eight-ball as it was 25 years ago, and that the United States is the rich surviving partner of the alliance and owes the European allies economic opportunities. It's psychological. They know it isn't so, but still persist in the belief we can afford it a lot better than they can. We do have 6 per cent unemployment. We have a $30 billion deficit. And we do have an enormous tax burden. Our people just won't take it.

Interview, Rome/ San Francisco Examiner, 1-6:20.

Thomas A. Kauper
Assistant Attorney General, Antitrust Division, Department of Justice of the United States

I suppose traditionally the frontiers (of antitrust enforcement) have altered because of changes in conduct. If you'd asked (former Antitrust Division head) Dick McLaren that question when he came in, I suppose he'd have said that conglomerate mergers were the frontier. I do think we're going to be a good deal involved with regulated industries. Also, I don't know just what to expect from the fact that more and more of our companies are more and more involved abroad. In a way, a frontier of antitrust enforcement is going to evolve because a geographical frontier is going to disappear. Any time you are trying to decide whether conduct is anti-competitive, you are making judgments based on how you believe firms react to each other. As we get firms that are reacting on an international basis, our precept as to what competition really is may change. It tends to be more the conduct that changes than the rules you apply to it. So I'm not altogether sure where the frontiers are going to be.

Interview, Washington/ The New York Times, 11-12:(3)7.

Henry Kearns
President and Chairman, Export-Import Bank of the United States

I personally just reject this philosophy that we (the U.S.) are priced out of the market. People call me and say, "You mean to tell me that you think we can compete with $4.50-an-hour labor against 50-cent labor some place else?" I just ignore them. Of course, if you take something like lace-work or even some electronic components—articles that require the intensive work of labor—that is a different matter. There we are at a disadvantage. But where massive cheap labor isn't important—where technology and machinery and tooling and the base market are important—then we do very well . . . We can tool up to produce in mass production through the use of machinery and tools better than any other country in the world. We also have the advantage of having the biggest pool of money, both to finance our international operations and to finance our exports. All I'm saying is that we have not priced ourselves out of the market in a wide range of exportable goods today. We could. We shouldn't if we can use a little restraint. Of course, if we go on and just absolutely disregard the possibility of pricing ourselves out, we will do it.

Interview, Washington/ Los Angeles Times, 1-26:(2)7.

The need to get U.S. businessmen off their domestic seats and into world trade is tied in with our well-known balance-of-payments problem, and thus with the strength of the dollar, the stability of the world monetary system, and with America's continuing ability to maintain its international commitments on which the free world so heavily relies.

Before U.S. Chamber of Commerce, Sao Paulo, Brazil, Sept. 1/ San Francisco Examiner, 9-1:66.

Virginia H. Knauer
Special Assistant to the President of the United States for Consumer Affairs

(People) expect that the media carrying an advertisement will share the responsibility for an ad's truthfulness. The public relies on the integrity of its newspapers . . . If your readers are stung by an advertisement, they don't just blame the advertiser—they blame you.

Before newspaper publishers, Lancaster, Pa., Feb. 25/ The Washington Post, 2-26:(E)1.

Consumer confidence in an industry (such as the building industry) can be a very fragile thing. It only takes a few builders who promise but don't deliver, who cheat rather than perform, who delay until the warranty expires rather than repair, to damage the reputation of your entire industry.

At Pacific Coast Builders Conference, San Francisco, June 8/ Los Angeles Times, 6-9:(3)19.

S. E. Knudsen
Chairman, White Motor Corporation

The plain truth is that our country is in trouble. We can no longer console ourselves by saying our productivity is better than it was 10 years ago. We must face the fact that our productivity is improving at a very slow and unsatisfactory rate in comparison with other countries. We have lost what was once a distinct competitive edge over the rest of the world. Now we need to do whatever is necessary to get it back. This problem, in my opinion, rates priority over all the many others confronting our country in the 1970s. Unless we make progress with this one, we can do very little about the rest. I suggest we consider going back to an approach that helped in solving a problem of equal difficulty nearly 30 years ago. In 1942, when industry was tooling up for World War II, the American business community realized that after the war there would be an enormous problem of conversion to peacetime production and employment so as to prevent a postwar collapse. For this purpose, it organized and supported a private group of thinkers and leaders who devoted most of their time to this problem of nearly 10 years. This group was known as the Committee for Economic Development (CED). It was a focus of thinking and planning for the postwar period. It gave direction to legislation and government planning. It provided strong and distinguished intellectual leadership . . . Now we are facing a new and different crisis, the crisis of productivity; and it has occurred to me that, to meet this crisis, we may need another group like that original CED—a new group organized for the single purpose of finding ways to improve the efficiency of American industry and to regain its competitive leadership. We might

(S. E. KNUDSEN)

call it the Committee for American Productivity. The name is unimportant. The important thing is to generate some new attitudes, chart some new courses, get some fresh breezes stirring.

Detroit/The National Observer, 4-15:13.

Olivier Long
Director general, General Agreement on Tariffs and Trade (GATT)

(International) trade negotiations have a knack of not being exactly what one at first imagines. Trade negotiations represent a very dynamic and fluid field. In the monetary field, you are dealing with one commodity: money. Nothing is easy in monetary matters, but it concerns *one* thing. In the trade field, you are dealing with things that go from sardines to textiles and computers, and which are all loaded with domestic political implications and emotions. Therefore, it is very difficult to try and forecast. One has to be able to adapt. It's like downhill skiing: You must always be ready to be on one ski and then the other, to take a bump and a curve and a sudden dip. That's why it's fascinating.

Interview, Geneva/The New York Times, 12-24:(3)12.

William S. Lowe
President, Chamber of Commerce of the United States

Anyone who has been in sports cannot help feeling the thrill of competition. In business, there is a carry-over. You should at least respond to competition. When you get an order that your competitor might have received, you should enjoy a feeling of accomplishment. Our competitive free-enterprise system is built on this spirit, and this is the spirit that is being so abused today. Some claim we are losing it. Some claim we have lost it.

Interview, Mexico, Mo.,/Nation's Business, May:39.

H. E. Markley
President, The Timken Company

In the 1950s, teams of foreign officials and management representatives visited the United States to learn about productivity. We were their envy. They were astonished by the productivity performance records we were able to achieve. So they learned from us—everything they could. And they put it to work. While we in the United States have let our productivity growth rate drop, our foreign competitors have pushed theirs higher than ever . . . What does this mean to the American consumer? Our share of the world's automobile production has been cut in half in less than 20 years. For decades we were the world's leading producer of machine tools; we are now in fourth place. Last year we produced only 20 per cent of the world's steel. Nine out of 10 home radios that Americans buy are imported. One of every six new cars are imported. One of every two black-and-white television sets bought is imported. Hundreds of other examples could be mentioned. What all of this amounts to, however, is quite clear. We are being out-produced. And we have no one to blame but ourselves.

At Mount Union College, Alliance, Ohio, Jan. 18/Vital Speeches, 3-15:345.

Paul N. McCloskey, Jr.
United States Representative, R–Calif.

(On last year's Federal loan guarantee for Lockheed Aircraft Corp.): It's a bad precedent when you bail out a company solely because it's big and does business with the government. I believe in the free-enterprise system, and that includes the right to succeed if you're good and fail if you're mismanaged.

The Washington Post, 6-3:(A)4.

Charles B. McCoy
Chairman and president, E. I. du Pont de Nemours & Company

(On the social responsibility of business): Certainly the economic side is the number one responsibility—to maintain an economic performance that provides jobs and opportunities for people. And that is one area where business hasn't been able to do as well as it would like to. No business likes to go through periods of laying people off, because that is really a breakdown in the system. But it's not a perfect world. There are rises and falls. So there have to be ways to provide for the dips better than we've done in the past. Overall, I think business should see that its' strengths are applied, where they can do a job, to the general problems of society. We have certain resources of people, certain talents, certain financial resources, that we have to make sure not only are used to produce products but also are made available to help solve some of those problems.

Interview, Wilmington, Del./ Nation's Business, December:38.

George S. McGovern
United States Senator, D–S.D.

The accumulation of corporate power is among the most critical issues to be addressed in 1972 . . . As a practical matter, the decisions made in the board rooms of these (top 200) companies can have as much influence on the country's directions, and perhaps more, than the decisions made in the United States Congress or in the White House.

The Christian Science Monitor, 4-, :8.

(If elected President), I will move to stop the takeover of American agriculture by absentee corporations and Fifth Avenue farmers. Unless we act quickly, the names on the mailboxes of rural America in 1980 will no longer be Smith and Jones but Tenneco and Ralston-Purina and Dow Chemical. Not since (former Agriculture Secretary) Ezra Taft Benson occupied an overstuffed chair in the Department of Agriculture has there been an Administration that has been so closely aligned with agribusiness and so fundamentally antagonistic to the interests of working farmers as the present Administration. The new faces of the Nixon Administration are the old faces of the Benson Administration. They have returned to complete the job they so efficiently started 20 years ago: to preside over the extinction of the independent farmer in America. Unfortunately, they are doing a pretty good job of it.

At National Plowing Contest, Vernon Center, Minn., Sept. 11/ San Francisco Examiner, 9-11:2.

George Meany
President, American Federation of Labor-Congress of Industrial Organizations

I think a lot of our troubles abroad in trade could be ended, or to some degree minimized, if our government would take an entirely different posture in their dealings with these other countries. And the formula, as far as I am concerned, is very simple: Any time any country locks a door on us, we lock one on them. In other words, complete *quid pro quo*, all the way down the line.

Interview, Washington/ U.S. News & World Report, 2-21:32.

Helen Meyer
President, Dell Publishing Company, Inc.

Decision-making is one of the most important components for an executive—to make a decision, not to have a cliffhanger. You have to say either yes or no, even though a yes or no may be wrong at the time. You can't leave people in a vacuum. Be definitive, that's important. I can say yes or no. I'm sure I've been wrong a great many times; but in the overall average, it's worked out.

Interview/Publishers' Weekly, 3-6:24.

J. Irwin Miller
Chairman, Cummins Engine Company

(Business) will only retain its present relative freedom by voluntarily aligning its internal policies with clearly-expressed national goals. If business everywhere will pursue the spirit as well as the letter of

(J. IRWIN MILLER)

equal opportunity, there is apt to be less restraining legislation on the subject, and, in the long run, greater respect for business. If business voluntarily involves itself in the urgent problems of the communities in which it is located, those problems may yield to more effective and less expensive solutions. If business voluntarily identifies with the consumer and leads in the design of quality and safer products, there will be less pressure for restrictive laws. Business will retain its freedom of action by voluntarily doing always more than the law requires, voluntarily doing always less than the law permits.

Before Business Council, Hot Springs, Va./ The Christian Science Monitor, 10-26:7.

Lee L. Morgan
Executive vice president, Caterpillar Tractor Company

In every case where we have established manufacturing plants overseas, our exports from the U.S. have risen. Some of the increase is attributable to parts and components for machines manufactured abroad. But most of it has been in entire machines not made overseas. In other words, producing part of our product line in a foreign marketing area has strengthened that market's demand for other Caterpillar products manufactured in this country.

Nation's Business, February:34.

Frank E. Moss
United States Senator, D–Utah

Advertising has a capacity for enriching the imagery of our lives, nourishing our senses, sharpening our wits, honing competition, innovation, creativity. Let me say it: Advertising can be beautiful. And advertising can be flat and tedious, dull our wits, deaden our senses, distort our values, blunt the edge of competition, veil truth, overreach and underachieve.

Before American Advertising Federation, Washington, May 15/ The New York Times, 5-16:69.

Ralph Nader
Lawyer; Consumer rights advocate

To what extent, at the present time, are bankers being subsidized by having a monopoly of interest-free deposits in checking accounts? The Hunt report (by the President's Commission on Financial Structure and Regulation) figures show that some 51.4 per cent of bank deposits are demand deposits. This is quite a drop from the 76.2 per cent of 1950, and indicates that the value of this subsidy to total operation is declining; but still it is a powerful one. There is, of course, some cost incurred in obtaining these funds, for checking-account operations do generate costs. However, if this is a cost of the use of the money by the banking system, it seems more right and proper that it should be paid for by the users of that money, the borrowers, and not by the depositor-providers of that money. In other words, the prime rate should absorb the cost of checking-account operations, not the depositor in so-called "service charges," where the depositor is, in effect, subsidizing the corporate borrower.

Before American Bankers Association/ The National Observer, 8-12:11.

Richard M. Nixon
President of the United States

Our advantage has always been that we have given our workers the best technology. This is no longer the case. One of the reasons the Japanese and the Germans do so much better in certain fields is that everything they have now—all their equipment—is new. They didn't have any plant at the end of World War II, so, with our help, they completely rebuilt. The United States must devote much of its resources to the development of its technical capacities. Much of America's plant is old. We can't expect the highest-paid workingmen in the world to compete with old machinery against new machinery.

Interview/The Readers Digest, February:68.

These are the principles I profoundly believe should and will guide the United States in its international economic conduct: We shall press for a more equitable and open world of trade. We shall meet competition rather than run away from it. We shall be a stimulating trading partner and a straight-forward bargainer. We shall not turn inward and isolationist. In turn, we shall look to our friends for evidence of similar rejection of isolationism in economic and political affairs. Let us resolve to look at the ledgers of international commerce with new eyes—to see that there is no heroism in a temporary surplus nor villainy in a temporary deficit, but to see that progress is possible only in the framework of equilibrium. In this regard, we must take bold action toward a more equitable and open world trading order.

Before International Monetary Fund, Washington, Sept. 25/ The New York Times, 9-26:70.

Robert M. Norris
President, National Foreign Trade Council

Growth of our foreign investments goes hand in hand with the growth of our domestic economy. These investments have a long-range favorable impact on our exports, jobs and prosperity at home . . . Regrettably, however, those who would advocate even more restrictive measures continue to level their criticisms on foreign direct investments, claiming, for example, that such investments result in the so-called "export of jobs" rather than the preservation of job opportunities. Despite certain isolated instances of hardship, we reject as unfounded the generalized claims by some labor groups and members of government and academic circles that overseas manufacturing investments adversely affect U.S. exports and curtail American employment.

New York, Jan. 3/ The Washington Post, 1-4:(D)6.

Don Paarlberg
Director, Agricultural Economics, Department of Agriculture of the United States.

We now supply ourselves with food—the best diet ever, anywhere—with something less than 17 per cent of our income. If we stay with the family farm (as opposed to conglomerate-operated farms) and improve its efficiency, the percentage of income spent for food will go still lower . . . Should we sacrifice a form of agricultural production that has served us well, that has produced good people as well as good crops? I believe this to be the major farm-policy issue of the decade ahead.

The Washington Post, 2-26:(A)15.

H. Bruce Palmer
National president, Council of Better Business Bureaus

I am afraid that consumerism has become the vent-pipe for the frustration of an entire generation—(for) the individual's inability to change his environment, to protect the ecology, to overcome social imbalances, to uplift the less-privileged, to stamp out hunger . . . to find dignity within oneself.

San Francisco Examiner & Chronicle, 2-13:(This World)2.

We've got to let the consumer know that business is listening; let him let off steam and say what's on his mind. "Business is listening" is going to be a long-term theme. We've got to ask, "What's on your mind?"; because, when the consumer is complaining, you're in trouble. The business community is in trouble . . .

Interview, New York/ The New York Times, 5-7:(3)15.

Wright Patman
United States Representative, D–Tex.

I feel that the time has come to coordinate all aspects of regulation of institutional investors and to upgrade the role of the Securities and Exchange Commission for this purpose. I would give the SEC original jurisdiction over all elements of the institutional investment community–foundations, pension funds, bank trust departments, and all the others–the entire range. Obviously, such an approach–to have meaning–would have to go beyond the traditional SEC regulatory role. It is my intention to give them broad supervisory powers and–when necessary–to control and direct investment. I would do this not only to protect the money being invested, but also to protect the broader public interest in maintaining a competitive enterprise system. To accomplish this, the SEC would have to establish a special division with expertise–and a public interest character–going beyond the nuts and bolts of the securities business.

At First Trust Management Conference, New York, June 20/ Los Angeles Times, 6-21:(3)12.

Charles H. Percy
United States Senator, R–Ill.

. . . the question inevitably arises: Why do we need a Consumer Protection Agency? The answer–and it is a sad one to face up to–is that the consumer has been neglected and kicked around too often by the very regulatory agencies of government that we have set up to protect him . . .

The Sacramento (Calif.) Bee, 10-12:(A)20.

H. Ross Perot
Industrialist

(On the securities industry): This is an industry where, for many years, the broker's mentality was that he existed to make commissions. Now, that's the basic thing you've got to change. You've got to, more than anything else, protect your client's principle . . . Teaching a person technically how the market operates, how you operate as a broker, is not the hard part. It's showing him how to build a base of customers, teaching him to prospect and how to serve those customers. These are the things that we have to teach in our schools. The stockbroker has been a very narrow guy, historically.

The Dallas Times Herald, 12-27:(D)9.

Peter G. Peterson
Secretary of Commerce of the United States

(On business' responsibility to minority business enterprise): Most businessmen in leading positions, including banks, are beginning to understand, perhaps in a deeper way than they have before, that their success as businesses depends ultimately on the viability and success of the entire society, that is to say, the entire market. If you have nearly 20 per cent of the American population that is not part of that mainstream, that feel alienated, that are angry, that are not part of it, this could have an important effect on the total viability of the American society and, therefore, the total viability of the American market.

The Washington Post, 5-11:(K)5.

While it may be more than we can do to make the businessman a folk hero, it is at the very least essential that people see and feel the crucial link between the output of our industries and the kind of life we can enjoy.

Before American Chamber of Commerce of Mexico, Mexico City/ The Wall Street Journal, 6-14:14.

(Among the public's misconceptions are) some astounding notions about the amount of profits which corporations have at their disposal. Today there are almost as many people who believe that the key to improving their standard of living is to grab a larger share of what corporations earn, as there are people who believe that the answer lies in producing more. The fact, of course, is that as you (keep) on grabbing, you reach a point where the more you grab, the less you get. This is a mistake Senator (and Democratic Presidential nominee George) McGovern has made repeatedly. He wants free eggs for everybody and apparently feels that all he has to do to get them is to whip the hen. It won't work. The hen won't lay. His most recent proposals seem to rest on a confidence, perhaps well placed, unfortunately, that the public does not know or appreciate the importance of incentives for business to invest, incentives to grow and incentives to provide more jobs. (A recent survey shows) the public's median estimate of the manufacturing profits in the United States was 28 cents on a dollar of sales, after taxes. This estimate was seven times the actual 1970 experience.

At Securities Industry Association conference, New York, Sept. 6/ The Dallas Times Herald, 9-7:(E)4.

Business today is so unpopular in this country that it may have become dangerous even for the Secretary of Commerce to venture a word in its defense.

San Francisco Examiner & Chronicle, 9-17:(This World)2.

What do we mean by "trade policy"? Is it as neat and compartmentalized as the technical world of tariffs, quotas, non-tariff barriers, export subsidies and the like? . . . I believe we shall increasingly find that trade policy is foreign policy, trade policy is security policy, trade policy is domestic policy, trade policy is energy policy—indeed, trade policy will fall at the intersection of all of these policies—to be only integrated at the highest kind of strategy, that thing we call our national interest.

At National Foreign Trade Convention, New York, Nov. 13/ Vital Speeches, 12-15:130.

Samuel Pisar
Authority on international trade

. . . we cannot any longer afford the luxury of restricting trade with the Soviet Union at a time when such a policy is not even effective. Our allies are trading many of the things we refuse to trade. Our balance of payments no longer is in shape to afford this kind of policy. Our business community doesn't like it, and neither do our labor unions. Our interest is to let the American businessman do his thing—to sell where he thinks he can sell—as long as it doesn't undermine the security of the country. Now, the President (Nixon) is on record as saying that it's all right to trade with the Russians. We should go back to our old image of a nation of Yankee traders willing to trade with anyone.

Interview, Paris/ U.S. News & World Report, 7-31:27.

Donald T. Regan
Chairman, Merrill Lynch, Pierce, Fenner & Smith, Inc.

1971 was the year Wall Street thought about itself. This year, we will begin to see changes in the physical structure of Wall Street. Rapid change will come in late 1972 and 1973. I can see the day, three to five years away, when we won't meet on any floor (like the major exchanges).

At Irving Trust Company seminar, New York/The Dallas Times Herald, 1-30:(B)1.

Being number one in our business (stock brokerage) means you've got to learn from the foolish mistakes others made. So you won't find Merrill Lynch taking foolish positions in cockeyed stocks. You learn to keep down costs. And you control greed. A lot of (brokerage) firms that went under were guilty of greed, blinded by it. Maybe it's too easy to get greedy on Wall Street.

The New York Times Magazine, 5-21:76.

(DONALD T. REGAN)

The growing and blind prejudice against bigness (in business) may cripple our ability to compete internationally in the country's best interest. Big is coming to equal bad in the public mind. Too many politicians are running on the platform of more taxation of big corporations—claiming, in effect, that if they can raise corporate taxes they will then have enough money to buy ointment for every social ill. This may appear to us to be seminal lunacy.

At Fortune 500 dinner, New York, May 25/The New York Times, 5-26:44.

Ed Reinecke
Lieutenant Governor of California

Whatever American businessmen have done to bring us out of that paradise of the "good old days," they deserve a grateful pat on the back and not a knife in it.

Quote, 8-6:121.

Henry S. Reuss
United States Representative, D–Wis.

(On the Treasury Department's delay on international monetary reform): Like a patient suffering with fever, the Treasury's attitude toward reform comes in fits and starts, interspersed with periods of profound coma.

Before the House, Washington, March 23/The New York Times, 3-24:65.

James M. Roche
Former chairman, General Motors Corporation

One of the gravest threats to our objectives of peace and prosperity is the rise in protectionist sentiment in both the advanced and the developing nations. In my country (the U.S.), pressure is growing for quotas on a long list of imported goods, as well as for new penalties to limit the free flow of investment. Japan has had wide-ranging barriers to trade and investment . . . Europe, too, has significant barriers to the flow of goods. These include non-tariff barriers which, while often difficult to detect, have increasingly impeded trade . . . Protectionism has also become a fact of life in many developing areas. So-called "local content laws" specify those portions of a product which may be imported and those which must be supplied from a local source.

At international business-economic cooperation symposium, Tokyo, April 12/ Los Angeles Herald-Examiner, 4-12:(B)5.

David Rockefeller
Chairman, Chase Manhattan Bank, New York

It is scarcely an exaggeration to say that right now American business is facing its most severe public disfavor since the 1930s. We are assailed for demeaning the worker, deceiving the consumer, destroying the environment and disillusioning the younger generation. It is tempting for businessmen to react by striking back at their critics, matching them invective for invective. Tempting, but hardly very fruitful if the rebuttal stops there. The essence of developing a favorable reputation lies not in trying to tell a good story when the performance does not justify it, but in upgrading the performance so there will be a good story to tell . . . Many of today's critics—not all, to be sure, but many—appear to feel that the system is beyond reform, and that the only solution is to destroy the capitalist framework and start all over again. Considering the seriousness and growing prevalence in some quarters of this attitude, it seems to me that businessmen have no choice but to become reformers themselves, making a conscious effort to adapt the operation of the market system to our changing social, political and technological environment. Because of the growing pressure for greater corporate accountability, I can foresee the day when, in addition to the annual financial statement, certified by independent accountants, corporations may be required to publish a "social audit" similarly certified.

Before Advertising Council/ Los Angeles Times, 1-3:(2)7.

William P. Rogers
Secretary of State of the United States

Robert Frost once wrote: "Before I built a wall, I'd ask to know what I was walling in or walling out." In "walling out" imports we would run the grave risk of "walling in" the very U.S. exports that we want to encourage. Building protectionist walls may seem tempting, but it can lead to retaliation and counter-retaliation. Today, no single country, no matter how powerful, can succeed in a unilateral policy of beggaring its neighbors or of exporting its domestic adjustment problems. It could be disastrous to our national interests to abandon our commitment to a more open world in which our economy, above all others, has flourished . . . The world of the future will not flourish behind walls—no matter who builds them and no matter what their purpose. A world divided economically must inevitably be a world divided politically. As Secretary of State, I cannot contemplate that prospect with anything but deep disquiet.

Before Chamber of Commerce of the United States, May 1/ The Washington Post, 5-22:(A)20.

Charles R. Ross
Former Commissioner, Federal Power Commission

(On corporate influence in government): The larger the corporation, the greater the political leverage. The greater the diversity in interests of the corporation, the larger the number of prospective appointments to regulatory commissions that must be influenced . . . Once on the scene, the regulator is confronted by sweet-talking executives, tough, hard-hitting lawyers and experts, even including experts in bugging. The doors of exclusive clubs are opened . . . The lure of life in the lap of luxury . . . becomes not just a dream but an actuality if one does not get too smart. On the other hand, if one gets too smart, it is back to the farm for our country bumpkin. The flattery, the press releases, the respect afforded an official regardless of performance, the cocktail parties, the utility and regulatory conventions at which comradeship between regulator and regulated is the number one business . . . the prospect of important legal clients, the thoughts of large political donations—all of these things work to insure the "right decision" or, if not, at the very least, the industry lawyer starts off with the dice loaded in his favor.

Before Senate Antitrust Subcommitte, Washington, January/ The Washington Post, 4-9:(H)1.

Paul A. Samuelson
Professor of Economics, Massachusetts Institute of Technology

(Advocating competitive stock brokerage rates): The Securities and Exchange Commission should long ago have acted to promote equitable and efficient competition, and control private monopoly. It is a sad, if not scandalous, fact that it was not until the Antitrust Division of the Department of Justice intervened to question the legality and propriety of the New York Stock Exchange's setting up a minimum commission schedule that our small progress in fighting monopoly in this regard was registered.

Before Senate Banking Subcommittee, Washington, March 23/ The Washington Post, 3-24:(D)7.

R. Sargent Shriver
Democratic Vice-Presidential nominee

(On why business is reportedly fearful of a McGovern-Shriver Administration): This is a theory I have; maybe it's not right. But I think that businessmen are accustomed in business to be making deals with each other, and that's what they understand . . . And they want to have a government that they

(R. SARGENT SHRIVER)

can make deals with, because that's the way they live.

Television interview/ The Wall Street Journal, 10-24:20.

Robert F. Six
Chairman and president, Continental Airlines

It has been my observation that a desperate management, in a frantic effort to implement employee communication, frequently treats its people like spoiled brats. The use of brain-storming sessions, of management chats, of this endless search for a two-way street whereby employer and employee may vent their souls and fall in love with each other misuses work time and shows depressingly small success. So, too, does the ancient plea that "My door is always open—bring me your problems." This is guaranteed to turn on every whiner, lackey and neurotic on the property. If you enjoy playing priest or psychiatrist, this is great fun, but it has nothing to do with the motivation of the employees. May I suggest that there are many millions of workers who actually, honest-to-God, like their jobs and are proud of their skills? Accepted doctrine seems to insist that employees hate work, hate the boss and have to be cuddled and cajoled into punching a clock because they would much rather be down at the library improving their minds or out on the beach playing in the sand. Ladies and gentlemen, despite what you hear, most people enjoy going to work in the morning. Honest! They find their tasks interesting—even challenging—their fellow workers like-minded people with whom they can share occupational concerns; many grow to be their best friends. The cadence of the job has a healthy rhythm. Their rewards are tangible and satisfying.

Accepting University of California, Los Angeles, Executive Program Association's Man of the Year award/ The Wall Street Journal, 9-7:16.

Olcott D. Smith
Chairman, Aetna Life & Casualty Company

Some critics in the United States fear the development of international corporations because of their size, their immunity from United States laws and the diminishment of national allegiance. But while critics in my country fear de-Americanization, critics here (in Europe) are apprehensive about United States corporate dominance of European economies. There is also fear of losing technological independence, particularly in such capital-intensive fields as aircraft or computer manufacture. It is a fear of a new colonialism. These are understandable fears, but I think they betray lack of vision . . . the increasingly global nature of business is carrying us forward. International commerce depends on at least rudimentary international law and commonly-recognized rules of business conduct. The very size and diminishing allegiance of multinational corporations that is feared on both sides of the Atlantic demands that governments work more closely together to regulate these corporate giants as well as to provide the world order that such corporations must have in order to function. Even now we see multinational corporations bringing people together in shared tasks, promoting better understanding. Business may set the stage for helping us achieve the goal that eluded the 19th century socialists—the goal of lifting mankind above narrow nationalism into world citizenship and all that promises for the more orderly governance of human affairs.

At opening of Aetna marketing office, Brussels/ The Wall Street Journal, 4-25:18.

Saul P. Steinberg
Chairman, Leasco Corporation

The fundamental alienation between business and government in the United States becomes more evident when you look at businessmen in Europe, in Japan or in Australia and their relationship and attitude toward their government. There is probably no one in England who runs a big business who does not feel he can sit down with the minister involved and discuss his problems openly and frankly; and there is probably no major businessman in America who feels he can. What we must develop is not just an easier working relationship for responsible businessmen and public officials, but the recognition that business works through incentives and that, given the right incentives, it can help accomplish the government's and society's purposes as well as its own.

Before Town Hall, Los Angeles, Aug. 1/ Vital Speeches, 10-1:746.

Allen P. Stults
President, American Bankers Association

There is no way profits can be too high. Profits are the fuel cells that energize our economy . . . Profits are the barometer of our economic climate, the standard by which we measure our economic well-being and the sole source of funding all civic, social, cultural and educational activities. To understand this is to recognize that the higher the profits, the more financial support for the better life.

Before American Bankers Association, Dallas, Oct. 9/ Los Angeles Times, 10-10:(3)8.

Edward M. Thiele
Vice chairman, Leo Burnett Company, advertising; Chairman, American Association of Advertising Agencies

(Charging the media with unfair coverage of the advertising industry and criticism of the business world): If business suffers as a result of unjustified harassment from government and consumer pressures, does this not affect the media to the same degree? Is not the stake the media has in advertising revenues all-important to them? Where, we can ask, will freedom of the press be if there is no press? So, if pure, objective reporting for its own sake is not sufficient motivation, certainly their own future existence should be . . . Certainly, we have all recognized the obvious unfairness of the press in giving treatment to a major complaint against business or perhaps the product of one of our clients, whether justified or not—only to have it disclaimed or answered several days later. But the complaint appears on page one while the disclaimer is buried among the obituaries.

Before American Association of Advertising Agencies, Boca Raton, Fla., March 18/ The New York Times, 3-20:57.

Dean F. Thomas
Vice president, Pillsbury Company

Perhaps one of the major maladies of American business is its inability to listen, or better yet, hear. Deafness to our kids, our customers and, perhaps worst of all, to ourselves. We don't really hear what we are saying, yet we spend 60 per cent of our time talking. A generation of babble—words, endless volumes of everyone trying to say something. But who's listening; who really gives a damn?

At United Grocers, Ltd., convention, San Francisco, March 13/ San Francisco Examiner, 3-14:59.

John G. Tower
United States Senator, D–Tex.

A profit merely shows that a firm is providing goods or services that people want and in sufficient quantity to cover the firm's costs and to provide a profit reward for doing so. The primary driving force of our economy is the motivation for business firms to make a reasonable profit. What so few people realize is that when business and commerce is good, the whole economy and all of the citizens are benefitting through increasing employment, higher incomes, more housing, better schools, better medical care, improved pollution control technology; in short, all the improvements in the quality of life that Americans should have.

Before Dallas-Fort Worth chapter, American Institute of Banking, Arlington, Tex., April 3/ The Dallas Times Herald, 4-4:(A)21.

Lynn A. Townsend
Chairman, Chrysler Corporation

. . . the requirements for making a profit and the requirements for a socially-responsible corporation are really interdependent and inseparable. The corporation's first duty is to gain the public's confidence in its products and services. When we act responsibly in areas outside the normal course of doing business, we reinforce the public's confidence in our company and its products. And that, in our judgment, is good business.

The New York Times, 4-2:(1A)8.

Al Ullman
United States Representative, D–Ore.

This is a very crucial time for the free world. There are divergencies among us; and we have got to get back to the basic fact that the free world can grow and prosper only if we have free movement of trade. If the rules governing this trade are obsolete, then we must devise new rules.

Brussels/ The Christian Science Monitor, 1-18:7.

The problems of world trade have expanded far beyond the scope of the very limited contractual relationships involved in the GATT proceedings. Nor is the mere alignment of currencies going to solve U.S. and world trade problems. We must establish a new trade policy based upon the total realities of all the elements that go into trade, including the currency problem, the Eurodollar and the cost of environmental protection.

Before American Paper Institute, New York, March 14/ The New York Times, 3-15:69.

Charles A. Vanik
United States Representative, D–Ohio

The free-enterprise system in America has become one large chicken factory, where little chicks—the small companies—are grown to maturity and made marketable to satisfy the unending appetite of conglomerate corporate America.

The Christian Science Monitor, 7-26:4.

Charls E. Walker
Under Secretary of the Treasury of the United States

You could buy a (Japanese) Toyota or a (Ford) Pinto here in San Francisco for about the same price. (The) Toyota in Tokyo would also cost you about $2,000, less transportation. But the Pinto in Tokyo, because of protective tariffs, costs you up to $5,000. The answer to this is not to block Toyotas from coming into the United States, but to get fair treatment in Japan for our products. It's a matter of hard-nosed negotiations which we really haven't done. For over a quarter of a century we've said we're too strong, we're too rich, we're too good—we don't consider economics. That day is gone. We do consider economics, and we've got to consider it more and more.

San Francisco, March 10/ San Francisco Examiner, 3-11:6.

Henry A. Walker, Jr.
President, Amfac, Inc.

We're the least-managed company in the world. My colleagues have as much say as I do, and sometimes more. I make marvelous decisions that are promptly overriden by them, and they do it without bashfulness or shame, but with reason. Seventy-five per cent of the time they are right. That's a high batting average, and it comes from having good people who are participating and having fun. As a result, we've got a hell-on-wheels management.

Interview, Honolulu/Time, 7-31:57.

William L. Wearly
Chairman, Ingersoll-Rand Company

Let's remind ourselves of what consumer freedom means. It means free trade. We believe in free trade because we know that only by free trade do most consumers benefit most . . . Free trade, permitting each area of the world to provide what it can most efficiently, lowers costs for all consumers and enlarges their satisfaction the world over. Do you want to forbid our consumers to buy German or Japanese cameras or automobiles, Guatemalan bananas or Brazilian coffee, French wine, Swiss watches or Italian gloves and shoes? Do you want them to forego importation of oil and pay higher prices for meat? Do you want to imprison them in the U.S. and forbid them to travel and spend money abroad? . . . The American consumer is a multinational consumer. He needs, wants and deserves freedom of markets in which to buy. The American producer is a multinational producer. He needs, wants and deserves freedom of markets in which to sell.

At Ingersoll-Rand annual meeting/ The Wall Street Journal, 8-8:10.

Ronald L. Ziegler
Press Secretary to the President of the United States

(On a just-signed agreement by which the Soviet Union will buy $750 million worth of U.S. grain over a three-year period): It will provide grain farmers with a boost in income. It will also provide jobs for Americans involved in shipping the grain, including longshoremen, seamen, exporters, railroad and barge line workers. It will reduce the cost to taxpayers of storage, handling and other charges associated with maintaining commodity stocks. The President (Nixon) also feels that the agreement is a tribute to the immense productivity of America's farmers which makes possible export sales of this magnitude. Finally, in terms of foreign policy, the President considers this agreement a very important concrete forward step in the commercial relations between the United States and the Soviet Union which benefits both countries. As such, it builds on the accomplishments of the summit meeting in Moscow last month.

July 8/ San Francisco Examiner & Chronicle, 7-9:(A)4.

Crime • Law Enforcement

Spiro T. Agnew
Vice President of the United States

When it comes to the point of whether this (Nixon) Administration or particularly myself, as an individual, is going to prefer the kind of diligent and strict law enforcement that is necessary to protect this country of ours, or whether we're going to agonize over the root causes and conditions of crime that's used as an excuse for some people to commit crimes, I'll stick with law enforcement every time. I know the agonizers are going to say I'm not particularly sensitive or concerned, but I want to be alive and I want my wife and family to be alive.

Before Police Department Holy Name Society, New York, March 19/ Los Angeles Herald-Examiner, 3-20:(A)7.

The tendency to look to society for individual fault all the time is distressing. Why should we worry about what is wrong with a system when a group of individuals have clearly performed in an aberrational fashion? The Attica (prison riot of 1971) thing, for example. Why shouldn't we always bear in mind that we were dealing with two- and three-time losers who committed serious felonies and who had already demonstrated their inability to be socially compatible with a normal society, rather than simply report what their criticisms of our society were? That has never been emphasized. You go get the records of the people who led the Attica revolt and you'll find out they've been malcontents and criminals for considerable time. I don't think those people's opinions should . . . be presented in the same manner as the opinions of people who try to serve society. So we've got to get away from this basic masochism of looking for any kind of dissident opinion and dignifying it.

Interview, Washington/ The Washington Post, 9-30:(A)1.

James Ahern
Director, Insurance Crime Prevention Institute; Former Police Commissioner of New Haven, Conn.

We do have a double standard for crime. Crime in the suites, as Ralph Nader calls it, gets completely different treatment from crime in the streets. Of course, some of this difference is legitimate. It's much more dangerous to rob people with a gun than to rob them with a fountain pen. But it's robbery, just the same. In fact, there are even ways in which white-collar crime is worse for society than street crime. White-collár crime is committed by our so-called leading citizens—by accountants and doctors, businessmen and lawyers—by the educated elite of this nation. When they disrespect the law, our whole system of values is threatened with collapse. So the first thing we must do about white-collar crime is to understand that it is crime; that it is just as dangerous and just as costly as the kind we read about in the headlines.

Television broadcast/"Comment!" National Broadcasting Company, 6-18.

Myles J. Ambrose
Special Assistant Attorney General of the United States and Special Consultant to the President on Drug Abuse Enforcement

In enforcing the drug laws, we are initially confronted with a virtually limitless supply of opium, the raw material of heroin. It is necessary to understand that a very small portion—perhaps five per cent—of the world's opium production is required to supply our addict population. As a matter of fact, all of the opium needed to supply the addict population of the United States can probably be grown in a 10-square-mile area almost anywhere in the world. The illicit American market is also the most lucrative, so that, as one source is eliminated, other potential sources are quickly developed. Those who smuggle heroin into this country are among the most sophisticated and inventive criminals in the world, and their ability to alter their delivery systems and methods of operation when discovered are unquestioned. Add to this the staggering logistics of trying to keep heroin from crossing our borders–225 million persons entered the U.S. last year; we have some 20,000 miles of coast and land borders–and you begin to appreciate the magnitude of the interdiction problem. This isn't to say the Federal government is throwing up its collective arms and saying, "What's the use?" Far from it. The President's (Nixon) programs have been carefully planned to mount a comprehensive assault to disrupt and abort the heroin traffic.

Before Town Hall,
Los Angeles, Sept. 12/
Vital Speeches, 10-1:738.

Jack Anderson
Political columnist

(On the death of FBI Director J. Edgar Hoover): J. Edgar Hoover transformed the FBI from a collection of hacks, misfits and courthouse hangers-on into one of the world's most effective and formidable law-enforcement organizations. Under his reign, not a single FBI man ever tried to fix a case, defraud the taxpayers or sell out his country. Hoover also was scrupulous at first not to step beyond the bounds of a policeman. But I would be hypocritical not to point out that, in his fading years, he sometimes stepped across those bounds.

May 2/The Washington Post, 5-3:(1)11.

Melvin Belli
Lawyer

The line between criminality and business is very, very thin. If a guy milks a big corporation, the courts just put him through bankruptcy. But if he does something funny with the books in his little Greek restaurant, they throw him in the slammer. If you commit a big crime, society forgives you because you've already stolen enough to belong to the country club, have clean clothes and well-shined shoes. A poor person who commits the same act is a "criminal type."

Interview, San Francisco/
Los Angeles Times, 4-9:(West)37.

Lloyd M. Bentsen
United States Senator, D–Tex.

(In 1968, Richard Nixon made) huge promises designed to make Americans believe that all of the answers could come from the White House–that the crime problem would be solved if only he became President. It has not been solved, of course. Crime rates have continued to rise under this Administration. The empty promises of the past have become the failures of the present.

Television broadcast, Washington, Jan. 21/
Los Angeles Herald-Examiner, 1-21:(A)2.

Philip Berrigan
Activist Catholic priest

(On prisons, after serving 39 months for destroying draft records): One can get very subjective about them, having felt their destructiveness in one's bones. Their time has passed . . . they are an obsolescent, bankrupt loss . . . laboratories of waste, injustice and desperation, outstanding examples of reciprocal revenge between society and the prisoner.

The New York Times, 12-24:(4)2.

George Beto
Director, Texas Department of Corrections

(Arguing against prison terms for marijuana users): An increasing number of middle-class marijuana offenders are not convinced they have done anything wrong. They don't propose to change their manner

(GEORGE BETO)

of living when they get out. And to think we can change them (in prison) is a vain hope.

Before State Senate Interim Drug Abuse Committee, Houston, April 10/ Los Angeles Times, 4-14:(1)32.

George Beto
Professor of Criminology, Sam Houston State University; Former Director, Texas Department of Corrections

Any prison program should be three-pronged in nature. There should be an emphasis on discipline, because the majority of prisoners come from highly permissive environments and have never been subjected to discipline, either internally or externally. Secondly, there should be an emphasis on constructive work, since 50 per cent of all inmates have no sustained record of employment prior to incarceration. Thirdly, there should be an extraordinarily high emphasis on education, since 90 per cent are school drop-outs, and you can do more with them now that they are confined.

Hunstville, Tex., Oct. 26/ The Dallas Times Herald, 10-26:(A)9.

John O. Boone
Massachusetts Commissioner of Corrections

Prisons now are schools for crime. To change this, we must get over wanting to do something bad to a person who has committed a crime. Society only feels the pain of crime, but it doesn't see the process that causes it to flourish. A lot of repeaters in prison are used by the syndicate. Why should we feed the syndicate? For 90 per cent of the inmates, crime is either a question of social conflict or distorted values. Counseling and practical help can change these men.

Interview, Boston/ The Christian Science Monitor, 4-1:10.

Bertram S. Brown
Director, National Institute of Mental Health

. . . I have personally felt for a long time that the penalties for the use and possession of marijuana are much too severe and much out of keeping with knowledge about its harmfulness. I have been strongly in favor of decriminalization, but not for the total removal of penalties.

Washington, Feb. 11/ The Washington Post, 2-12:(A)1.

Edmund G. Brown
Former Governor of California

(On the California Supreme Court ruling against capital punishment): (The decision) will do more to reduce homicides in California than anything that has been done in the last 100 years. Quickness of punishment, rather than severity of punishment, deters serious crime. The end of the death penalty will speed trials, because we will not have these delays by the courts which want to be sure that the execution of a person was right and just. It will be a deterrent because people who commit crimes will know they will be punished with dispatch and will not have the Roman-holiday atmosphere of some recent trials.

Feb. 18/ Los Angeles Herald-Examiner, 2-18:(A)2.

Warren E. Burger
Chief Justice of the United States

If we try to solve all the problems of prison reform, we will solve none. We must be content with modest progress and small victories.

San Francisco Examiner, 1-6:32.

It should not surprise us (that) when a young man from a dismal environment in the first place is found guilty and sentenced for two, three or five years in an institution, he leaves it a worse, not a better, human being. The deadly monotony of a confinement with no constructive or productive activity apart from ordinary daily work is bound to be devastating. It is axiomatic that inmates of these institutions are people who, for one reason or another, have not been adequately motivated and self-disciplined in life. The guidance and the standards that make most human beings willing to study, to work and to improve themselves are absent in such people. It would be an optimism approaching folly to rely on the assumption that every person convicted of serious criminal activity can be rehabilitated and restored to a useful life. Nevertheless, this is a near-universal human aspiration, and we must proceed on the assumption that most people can be improved. But to achieve that, we must begin with highly-trained (correctional) staffs of people who understand something of the problems of human motivation. Beyond that, there must be people qualified to train others in the useful arts and labor that Thomas Jefferson regarded as basic to American democracy.

Before National Conference of Christians and Jews/ The New York Times, 12-20:43.

Joseph P. Busch
District Attorney,
Los Angeles County, Calif.

(On the California Supreme Court ruling against capital punishment): I disagree with the criteria adopted by the court to determine that the death penalty is "impermissively cruel" when judged by "contemporary standards of decency." The court's rejection of public acceptance of capital punishment as an index to contemporary standards involves most curious logic.

Los Angeles, March 1/ Los Angeles Times, 3-2:(1)3.

(On the report of the National Commission on Marijuana and Drug Abuse): As a prosecutor, I believe that decriminalization (of marijuana use) would establish an unacceptable and schizophrenic legal situation in which the use is legal and the sale is illegal. Apparently it was the opinion of the Commission that research into marijuana is not sufficient to allow legalization, but is sufficient to permit decriminalization.

Before National Commission on Marijuana and Drug Abuse, Los Angeles, April 10/ Los Angeles Herald-Examiner, 4-10:(A)2.

Norman A. Carlson
Director, Bureau of Prisons, Department of Justice of the United States

Anyone not a criminal will be when he gets out of jail.

The Washington Post, 1-30:(A)1.

Frank G. Carrington
Executive director,
Americans for Effective Law Enforcement

(On capital punishment): Our concern for the victims of murderers leads inevitably to the abolitionist response that the execution of the death penalty upon killer "A" will not bring his victim, "B", back to life. This is, of course, true; but the question goes deeper than that. The fact that "A" is executed will not, concededly, bring "B" back to life; however, such arguments ignore the fact that, although "B" is beyond resurrecting, the fact that "A" has been executed for the crime, 1) may well deter "C," "D" and "E" from following "A"'s example of killing and 2) *will* make absolutely certain that "A" will never kill again.

Before House Judiciary Committee, Washington, March 16/ Human Events, 4-22:12.

Alan Cranston
United States Senator, D–Calif.

(Attorney General-designate Richard) Kleindienst has evidenced a high tolerance for wiretapping, mass arrests and preventive detention. His thinking is fuzzy when it comes to distinguishing between people who threaten our nation's security and people who merely disagree with him politically.

Before the Senate, Washington, June 1/ San Francisco Examiner, 6-1:4.

Richard J. Daley
Mayor of Chicago

(There is) no reason for handguns being manufactured . . . or imported. Handguns are used to kill one another. You can't hunt with them. A handgun is an encouragement for you to shoot someone else or for him to shoot you.

News conference, Chicago, May 17/ The Washington Post, 5-18:(A)16.

Edward M. Davis
Chief of Police of Los Angeles

It's far past the time for the courts to re-establish their priorities and to once again consider the rights of the community to be protected from those who either have no values or do not fear the consequences of their acts . . . Society is calling for protection, and few are willing to answer the call.

San Francisco Examiner & Chronicle, 2-20:(This World)2.

James E. Doyle
Judge, United States District Court for the Western District of Wisconsin

I am persuaded that the institution of prison probably must end. In many respects it is as intolerable as slavery—equally brutalizing to all involved, equally toxic to the social system, equally subversive of the brotherhood of man, even more costly by some standards, and probably less rational.

Madison, Wis., April 6/ Los Angeles Times, 4-7:(1)7.

Myron DuBain
Senior vice president, Fireman's Fund American Insurance Companies

. . . the most disturbing aspect of the crime problem—for the insurance industry and for society—is the statistical proof that arrests for persons under the age of 18 increased by 100 per cent during the past decade. In fact, nearly the entire rise in arrests for commission of serious crimes during the 1960s was accounted for by minors. Youngsters between 11 and 17 were convicted in over half of the prosecutions for burglary, larceny and car theft. These were not all inner-city youth. A doubling of suburban crime took place in the '60s, and two-fifths of those arrested in the suburbs were young people. Even more ominous: of all offenders under the age of 20 who were released in 1965, 74 per cent were *re*arrested by the end of 1969. These trends naturally presage a turbulent time for the law and for society. As for insurance, its basic underpinnings have received a severe shock, and will probably receive more of the same. The insurance industry depends upon a reasonable maintenance of order in society.

Before American Bar Association, San Francisco, Aug. 16/ Vital Speeches, 10-1:760.

Clinton T. Duffy
Former warden, San Quentin (Calif.) State Prison

(Arguing against capital punishment): Having . . . served for 10 years on the Adult Authority, I know that they aren't letting people loose to kill again. Michigan abolished the death penalty more than a century ago, and they have had a lower homicide rate—including the killing of police and prison guards—than adjoining states. I've never known a wealthy man to be executed. And regarding price, I can document the fact that it costs a good $20,000 more to execute than it does to carry out a life sentence.

San Francisco, Feb. 28/ San Francisco Examiner, 2-29:3.

Thomas F. Eagleton
United States Senator, D–Mo.

Crime is going to be controlled only when two things occur: one, when you get to some of the root causes of crime, which goes into the whole question of poverty, education, lack of job opportunity and the like; and secondly, when the system of criminal justice, as a system, can function quickly, efficiently and effectively. We haven't been doing very well in the first area, insofar as alleviating root-cause problems of crime. Poverty is still very much with us, and in many instances in a very abject way. And . . . secondly, we haven't done much with the entire criminal-justice system. The system itself bogs down from its own ponderous weight.

Interview, Washington, June 30/
The Washington Post, 7-14:(A)13.

. . . I am not in favor of further gun-control legislation. The simple reason is that I don't think it will be effective. I think the ones we've put on the books haven't worked, and I would not favor further meaningless forays into the gun-control field . . . I think the laws that are on the books that prohibit sales of weapons to felons or ex-felons and the like are about as far as we can go, and they have not been very meaningfully enforced. I'm very much of a pessimist insofar as the efficacy of further gun-control legislation is concerned.

Interview, Washington, June 30/
The Washington Post, 7-14:(A)13.

Sam J. Ervin, Jr.
United States Senator, D–N.C.

Nobody has ever brought me any hard evidence that would indicate the FBI has ever exceeded its legal authority. Now, mind you, its legal authority is very broad. It has full authority to investigate people—the conduct of people who it believes have committed crimes. It also has the full legal authority to investigate the conduct of people who it has reason to believe are about to commit crimes. It also has authority to exercise surveillance over domestic subversion—whatever that is. I have never been quite sure what subversion is. I think some people think at times I'm a subversive since I don't like some government tyranny. So I think it's very difficult for the FBI to exceed its authority. I do think that some of the trivia they collect . . . would indicate that they were really collecting information about political activities and political thoughts of people. But they may have had full authority to do that on the theory that those people were subversive—or about to get subversive.

Interview/
U.S. News & World Report, 3-6:44.

Current arguments for the abolition of capital punishment mark a new high in sentimentalism and disregard for the meaning of the law. The present complaint against the death penalty is that it constitutes "cruel and unusual punishment" and is thus prohibited under the Eighth Amendment to the Federal Constitution . . . For anyone who can read the English language, such arguments are manifest nonsense. The Constitution itself recognizes the validity of capital punishment, more than once. The Fifth Amendment says trial for capital crimes shall be initiated by a grand jury and conducted under due process of law. It should be obvious that the Constitution writers who made explicit provision for the death penalty in this fashion did not intend to outlaw the death penalty in the contemporaneous Eighth Amendment. If the argument against the death penalty ignores the clear meaning of the Constitution, it also ignores the brute facts of modern-day criminality. As capital punishment has been *de facto* abandoned in recent years, death through violent crime has increased dramatically . . . Under the Federal Constitution, the death penalty is a legitimate punishment. Under any standard of common prudence, it is a needed protection against the rising tide of violence in American society.

Television broadcast, "Spectrum,"
Columbia Broadcasting System/
The National Observer, 6-10:17.

John H. Finlator
Former Deputy Director, Bureau of Narcotics and Dangerous Drugs, Department of Justice of the United States

I know I'm the first lawman of my stature to speak out, but it's about time

(JOHN H. FINLATOR)

. . . The ineffectiveness of the criminal laws as a deterrent to use (of marijuana) is astounding. Meanwhile, we have ruined the careers and lives of hundreds of thousands of otherwise law-abiding citizens by needlessly subjecting them to the ramifications of being defined "criminal."

Interview/The Washington Post, 2-10:(A)3.

Charles R. Gain
Chief of Police of Oakland, Calif.

Policemen must reject the role of guardian of the status quo and rather become community leaders who provide social services unheard of 15 years ago . . . We are engaged in several social service-oriented projects like the new consumer fraud unit and a landlord-tenant dispute intervention program where more referrals to other public agencies are issued than citations . . . We send new officers out in the street with no money so they can see how it feels to be on the bottom. Core cities are clamoring for this kind of a social service-oriented police department.

Before Alameda County Bar Association, Oakland, June 20/ San Francisco Examiner, 6-21:12.

L. Patrick Gray III
Acting Director, Federal Bureau of Investigation

I believe in the FBI as a vital American institution. When it is criticized, I will look into the charges to determine whether they have any validity. If so, I will make the changes necessary to maintain the FBI's posture as the finest investigatory agency in the world. If they are not valid, I will defend the FBI with all the personal energies and capabilities at my command.

Before Thomas More Society, Washington/ The Christian Science Monitor, 5-19:12.

(On the differences in the running of the FBI between him and late Director J. Edgar Hoover): It's not a question of secrecy, but rather a difference of style. Gray is Gray, and Hoover is Hoover. There's not going to be any change in substance. It's a question of style.

San Francisco Examiner & Chronicle, 5-21:(This World)2.

(On FBI use of wiretapping and electronic surveillance): . . . in this tightly limited and controlled use of electronic equipment, the FBI conforms strictly with a law which has the sanction not only of Congress, but of our courts. This technique is employed only with the approval of the Attorney General and with the specific authority and order, in each instance, of a Federal court. FBI surveillances are instituted and maintained in a manner designed to afford the fullest protection of individual liberties while, at the same time, upholding society's right to protect itself against the ravage of organized crime. The fundamental right of any society is to preserve itself and to maintain its government as a functioning and effective entity . . . I believe that the record reveals that electronic surveillance conducted in accordance with law has proven to be a most successful weapon in the battle our society is waging against organized crime. We must not lose that weapon.

At crime-control conference, Biloxi, Miss., May 25/ The Christian Science Monitor, 6-5:2.

To equate law enforcement with repression is one of the most dangerous threats to a free society. Those who equate enforcement with repression are hurling a ghastly insult at the very people they purport to defend. Their inference is that crime is simply an expression of discontent, and they attempt to legitimize this expression by discrediting our efforts to curb it. I simply cannot overstate the outrage with which I reject these monstrous allegations.

San Diego, Calif./ The Dallas Times Herald, 7-5:(A)8.

I don't really know whether or not the enactment of tighter gun controls would produce a lessening in the number of assaults by handguns. I think of how many additional police would be required to enforce such laws, and I really don't know the answer; I haven't studied it out yet. But I do have the personal belief that the people of our nation should be willing to license and register their firearms. We should take at least that first step to see if we can't possibly then be in a position to screen out some of the undesirables who should not have weapons. I do not view this as a violation of the Constitutional right of the people to keep and bear arms. I view this as a way of regulating the keeping and bearing of arms.

Interview/
U.S. News & World Report, 7-10:61.

. . . any man who is elected President will probably have first and foremost in his mind a determination not to let that (a national police force) happen. So will the man who sits in my chair, and so will the members of Congress. I think all Americans are very much aware that this is a possibility in our country when you see so many other powers being given to a strong, centralized government. But a national police force is really not in keeping with our Federal system. I would be one of the very first to say that, so long as I'm the head of the FBI, we will not take the first small step toward the creation of a national police force.

Interview/
U.S. News & World Report, 7-10:62.

Let us not think that our government of laws is in danger only from those who openly proclaim their goal to set aside the whole of the legal structure. There is another enemy as well, less visible perhaps, but just as insidious—persons who in their own way weaken our society, damage our leadership principles and completely ignore the responsibilities of good citizenship. Officeholders who occasionally compromise principle or a public trust in exchange for gifts and favors, businessmen who pad their expense accounts and deflate their income-tax returns, would be stunned if anyone said they were not responsible and law-abiding citizens. They are—most of the time. The workingman who patronizes after-hour bars and neighborhood bookmakers, those who buy merchandise at prices and under circumstances that clearly suggest it is stolen, contribute to the survival of crime in our society—though they would be aghast at being called criminals. The president of a corporation who conspires to break the anti-trust laws because it assures a certain profit, the procurement agent who deals in secret kickback agreements, may give the appearance of being model members of society, and each undoubtedly seeks to retain that image. Yet each of these persons, and myriad others like them who have a cavalier attitude toward the law when it suits their purpose, attack the society of law from within . . . Man is said to be destroying his own physical environment—almost through careless disregard. And it should be obvious that man can destroy the social environment in the same way—by his failure to appreciate the individuality of freedom and the law. To be "law abiding" is no sometime thing!

Before City Club, Cleveland/
The National Observer, 9-9:15.

Occasionally, I hear rumors to the effect that the Acting Director is determined to convert the FBI to the communal life-style—that badges are "out" and love beads are "in"—and that discipline is one of the archaic concepts that have been relegated to the archives. Don't believe it. I know—and every man and woman in the FBI knows—that the Bureau would self-destruct without discipline.

Before Backstoppers, St. Louis/
Fresno (Calif.) Bee, 11-16:(A)15.

Lord Hailsham
Lord High Chancellor of the United Kingdom

An idea has got abroad that there is something respectable about civil disobedience. I have no doubt that cases exist in some countries where this may be so. But the trouble is that all civil disobedience is morally neutral. Once you appeal to force, and not to law, force will determine your claim without regard to the merits of it.

Before magistrates, Exeter, England/ Los Angeles Times, 4-23:(G)6.

James R. Hoffa
Former president, International Brotherhood of Teamsters

(On his experience while a prison inmate): Many ex-convicts revert to a life of crime because they have not received job training (in prison) that would assist them in obtaining employment in the outside world. License plate and mop bucket manufacturing are two examples of prison vocations that bear little resemblance to potential jobs in private industry. Eighty-five per cent of the inmates in Federal prisons lack any marketable skill when they leave prison. It is not for humanitarian reasons alone that we must reform the system. It is for our own safety. We have never faced up to the fact that most convicts will some day be released from the hell holes we call correctional institutions. They come out . . . more bitter, more disturbed, more antisocial and more skilled in crime than when they went in.

Before Senate National Penitentiaries Subcommittee, Washington, June 13/ Los Angeles Herald-Examiner, 6-14:(A)2.

Frank S. Hogan
District Attorney, New York County, N.Y.

I think the press, movies and book writers have overplayed organized crime. You hear statements to the effect that overlords possess hundreds of millions of dollars. The damnedest statements are made. Our experience is that some person who is supposed to be a big figure in the underworld is arrested for participating in hijacking, or attempting to burglarize a place, or dealing in a small amount of narcotics, or engaging in loan-sharking on a low level. Hell, if they have all these millions, it just does not square that they would be engaged in these things. I think there is a tremendous amount of exaggeration.

Interview, New York/ Los Angeles Times, 8-14:(2)7.

Richard Hongisto
Sheriff, San Francisco County, Calif.

. . . a prison fit for rats breeds rats and crime.

Upon taking office, San Francisco, Jan. 8/ San Francisco Examiner & Chronicle, 1-9:(A)6.

J. Edgar Hoover
Director, Federal Bureau of Investigation

Many hoodlums, unfortunately, have acquired a facade of semi-respectability in their communities. People find it hard to believe that these so-called "businessmen" can possibly be involved in illegal activities. Even more disturbing, from a law-enforcement view, is the seeming indifference of otherwise responsible citizens to the acknowledged existence of specific phases of organized crime in their communities. What they are overlooking, of course, is that hoodlum-connected major thefts increase their insurance rates, that labor racketeering increases consumer costs, that gambling and narcotics corrupt youth and that bribery of civic and police officials undermines good government and deprives the public of the protection to which it is entitled.

Interview, Washington/ Nation's Business, January:44.

Assertions that FBI wiretapping is widespread are absurd. If the FBI engaged in wiretapping to just a fraction of what its critics suggest, it would have no time for anything else. These critics who accuse the FBI of this practice can never produce any proof. Congressman (Hale) Boggs made a wild statement that his telephone had been tapped. That charge was simply not true. No telephone of any Congressman has ever been tapped since I became Bureau Director in 1924. He was put in the position of having to "put up or shut up" on that charge, and he shut up.

Interview, Washington/
Nation's Business, January:44.

Youths should be tried as adults when they commit a serious crime. I would like to see the juvenile age reduced to 15.

Before House Appropriations Committee, Washington, March 2/
The Dallas Times Herald, 4-28:(A)18.

To my mind, there are certain verities of life, such as personal integrity, character and dedication to duty which must continue to guide the FBI for years to come if it is to remain a responsible agency of government. These principles mean that the FBI is the servant of the people, is dedicated at all times to a search for truth, is guided by the highest ethical standards. It is this tradition of honesty, integrity and service I would want the FBI to symbolize in years to come.

Interview, Washington, May 1/
San Francisco Examiner & Chronicle, 5-7:(B)7.

Sarah T. Hughes
Judge, United States District Court for the Northern District of Texas

Most people don't understand what a correctional institution is. Many think it is just for punishment . . . Unless society subordinates all of the correctional purposes to the goal of rehabilitation, it faces the paradox of promoting the production rather than the reduction of crime.

Interview/
The Dallas Times Herald, 6-8:(A)1.

John E. Ingersoll
Director, Bureau of Narcotics and Dangerous Drugs, Department of Justice of the United States

(On recommendation that criminal penalties be removed for personal possession and use of marijuana): Any hopes of drying up the traffic and restoring the situation to its former level would be forever lost. We would simply have to learn to live with this abuse, much in the same calloused fashion that we have been taught to live with the problems of alcohol or automobile accidents.

Before California Peace Officers Association, Anaheim, Calif., May 24/
Los Angeles Times, 5-25:(1)31.

I guess we are going to have to resign ourselves to the fact that we are going to live with a drug problem in this country, and we are going to have to cope with it the best we can . . . Each year some 210 million people come across our borders or through our ports of entry. The number of ships that call at our ports are numbered in the hundreds of thousands, and we also have this number of aircraft flights that come in through international ports of entry, let alone the number of automobiles that come across borders . . . Unless we are going to call out the Army and the Marine Corps and the Navy, even then I doubt that we would be able to totally exclude the smuggling of drugs into the country.

The Washington Post, 8-14:(B)11.

Henry M. Jackson
United States Senator, D–Wash.

Some affluent white liberals who denounce "law and order" as a racist issue seem to be saying that it's perfectly all right for crime to thrive in the ghetto—as if black Americans don't deserve any better. Well, I think *this* is a racist attitude.

Before Professional Policemen's Protective Association, Milwaukee, Feb. 4/
Los Angeles Times, 2-5:(1)5.

Jerome H. Jaffe
Director, White House Special Action Office for Drug Abuse Prevention

It is possible that at least half of all street crime in this nation is drug related.

Washington, April 14/
The Washington Post, 4-15:(A)6.

Jacob K. Javits
United States Senator, R–N.Y.

(On last year's prison riot at Attica, N.Y.): The history of the Attica tragedy did not begin one year ago when the inmates took hostages and seized control of the prison. It began many years ago with the deplorable state of affairs which was allowed to exist in American prisons. It developed while inmates were often subjected to barbarous and inhuman living conditions which existed in the name of correction. The seeds of the tragedy were nourished by the incipient racism which exists to some degree in almost all prisons. It grew as many turned a seemingly deaf ear to efforts to abolish arbitrary and unreasonable disciplinary procedures, to improve food and medical services, to permit greater contact with family and friends, to establish a prison grievance procedure and to reform the entire sluggish criminal-justice system . . . The 200,000 inmates in our state and Federal prisons can no longer be locked up and forgotten. It is possible that Attica will merely become only a tragic historical footnote. It is equally possible that Attica will become the catalyst for public action. Which course we choose will depend in some measure upon how well we understand what happened a year ago.

New York, Sept. 25/
Los Angeles Times, 9-26:(1)22.

Edward M. Kennedy
United States Senator, D–Mass.

Critics of gun control have insisted that laws cannot control access to guns. Yet the record shows that even the limited provisions of the 1968 Gun Control Act have severely altered the flow of one kind of weapon—the imported handgun. There are others who believe the Constitution protects their right to have guns and that there is some derived right to pursuit of happiness with guns, free of government limits. But the courts have said time and time again that the Constitution does not interfere with the power of government to regulate deadly firearms. And those who find happiness in guns will just have to subordinate that pleasure to the right of all Americans to live free from the death and violence that the American gun mania has brought us.

Before House Judiciary Committee,
Washington/U.S. News & World Report,
7-10:69.

Richard G. Kleindienst
Deputy Attorney General, and Attorney General-designate, of the United States

(On capital punishment): Generally, I don't favor it. In most crimes it's not a deterrent . . . Then there are such cold-blooded, premeditated, rational acts where heinous crimes are committed—kidnapping, assassination, bombings. I think it should be used in isolated cases.

At his confirmation hearing before
Senate Judiciary Committee, Washington,
Feb. 22/Los Angeles Times, 2-23:(1)22.

I not only believe I would have the power but I would have the duty to use electronic surveillance. I don't believe the President, through the Attorney General, has the duty to snoop, to pry into the lives of people with political differences, but I do believe he has the duty to gain intelligence about people who use violence and try to overthrow the government by force.

At his confirmation hearing before
Senate Judiciary Committee,
Washington, Feb. 22/
Los Angeles Times, 2-23:(1)22.

Richard G. Kleindienst
Attorney General of the United States

I am shocked that the Democratic (Party) national platform makes charges of "unequal law enforcement by police, prosecutors and judges." I am shocked when it charges that in this country we have a "turnstile system of injustice, where most of those who commit crime are not arrested, most of those arrested are not prosecuted and many of those prosecuted are not convicted" . . . With President Nixon in office, the crime increase began to falter. In the first year (1969) it was 12 per cent. It was 11 per cent in 1970, and down to 7 per cent in 1971. And the trend has more than continued into 1972 . . . The truth is that we are seeing the rebirth of respect for law in this country; and this has been accomplished while assuring the defendant his rights under the law.

At meeting of police chiefs, Rhinelander, Wis., Aug. 29/ Los Angeles Herald-Examiner, 8-30:(A)9.

I think the social problem emanating from the prisons in this country is one of the most serious we have. When you look at the fact that 75 per cent of those persons who are convicted of felonies are rearrested within four years of their release from prison, then—whether you look at it from a humanitarian standpoint or as a matter of just strictly dollars and cents—you've got to say to yourself that we are doing something wrong in our penitentiaries. Instead of sending offenders to institutions of rehabilitation, so that when they come out they have a better chance of being a useful part of society, what you're really doing is sending them to places that almost guarantee they will be worse when they come out than they were when they went in.

Interview, Washington/ U.S. News & World Report, 9-11:82.

William M. Kunstler
Lawyer

(Praising revolutionary prison inmates): We're all in prison. It's just a question of whether you can see the walls and bars of the prison or not . . . We are not governed by sanity or by sane people. Our system is corrupt and rotten. Behind those bars and walls are people who are trying to understand the nature of our society and preparing themselves to do something about it.

At University of California, Berkeley, Aug. 4/San Francisco Examiner, 8-5:5.

(On last year's Attica, N.Y., prison riot which resulted in 43 people killed): There could be more Atticas and there should be more Atticas. Hostages should be taken (by prisoners). Hostages are a political weapon these days. Out of those hostages has come a wave of prison reforms throughout this country.

News conference, Attica, N.Y., Sept. 13/ Los Angeles Times, 9-14:(1)28.

Jerris Leonard
Administrator, Law Enforcement Assistance Administration, Department of Justice of the United States

In this age of fanatic confrontation and frenzied polarization of political thought, we are apt to neglect or even forget our traditions of a legal system based upon rational lawmaking. However, we continue to do so at our peril . . . (There) are irrational forces loose in this land. Unfortunately, law-abiding citizens are forced to live among others who do not live within the rules and who wish to destroy society itself. In the United States, there are forces at work which are alien to our constitutional system. Moreover, societies are often destroyed by internal enemies as they are overrun by foreign powers. Hence, the test for this nation is its ability to make itself secure without at the same time destroying its liberty and freedom . . . Crime must be reduced if society is to be protected.

Before Citizens for Law Enforcement Needs, Beverly Hills, Calif./ Los Angeles Herald-Examiner, 5-28:(D)3.

John V. Lindsay
Mayor of New York

Punitive and criminal measures with respect to marijuana make no sense whatsoever. (The) criminal-justice system is overcrowded enough.

At University of South Florida, Jan. 8/ The New York Times, 1-9:(1)60.

(The) United States is the most violent nation on the earth today. In the United States, it is a daily event for a person to be killed by a handgun. It is open season. You can buy a handgun as easily as a package of chewing gum.

Television interview/ "A.M. Show," WPLG, Miami, 1-28.

Lester G. Maddox
Lieutenant Governor, and former Governor, of Georgia

We see it in print, hear it from the pulpit, from Marxist socialist professors, that people commit crime because they're underprivileged. I went to school barefoot in the snow and ice, (but) I didn't shoot a policeman; I didn't hold up any store. You commit (crime) because of sin in your life.

Time, 8-21:44.

Benjamin J. Malcolm
New York City Commissioner of Correction

All men (in prison) are redeemable. Every man can be rehabilitated; and it's up to us in the community and in the field of criminal justice to see that this is done.

At his appointment, New York, Jan. 19/ The New York Times, 1-20:1.

Marshall McComb
Associate Justice, Supreme Court of California

I happen to believe that the death penalty is a deterrent to crime. My opponents claim it is a single, cruel punishment. I don't agree with them. Swift justice for murderers—including a speedy and public trial, followed by quick appellate review and execution—will help curb the climbing crime rate.

Feb. 19/Los Angeles Herald-Examiner, 2-19:(A)2.

George S. McGovern
United States Senator, D–S.D.

The 50 states will inevitably establish their own definition of dangerous drugs. They should do so in the knowledge that the prison terms which have often been imposed upon youthful experimenters with marijuana are many times more destructive than the substance itself. They should recognize that laws which define 20 million Americans (who smoke marijuana), and perhaps more, as criminals create a crushing burden for law-enforcement agencies, and that such laws inevitably divert law-enforcement resources from more productive activities. Some 45.4 per cent of all drug-law arrests in 1970 were related to marijuana; only 31.3 per cent were related to heroin and cocaine. Had the resources expended on marijuana control been applied to hard drugs, few would dispute the premise that they would have produced an immensely greater benefit to society even if they had produced only a slight rise in arrests.

Before the Senate, Washington, Feb. 15/Vital Speeches, 3-15:326.

. . . we must cut to an absolute minimum the flow of illegal drugs in this country. We should impose strict diplomatic sanctions against countries which permit opium production and which do nothing to halt its exportation. And at home we must search out and prosecute far more relentlessly than we are now the criminal network that controls the drug traffic and is condemning hundreds of thousands of Americans to a modern form of slavery.

Campaigning for the Democratic Presidential nomination, Los Angeles, May 31/ Los Angeles Times, 6-1:(1)28.

George S. McGovern
United States Senator, D–S.D.; Democratic Presidential nominee

I do not believe in sending anyone to prison or the penitentiary for the use of marijuana. But neither do I believe in the legalization of marijuana. I think it ought to be treated as a misdemeanor rather than a felony. And I think that's the position that most Americans take on it. I don't think we know enough about this substance to permit its legalization. I don't recommend its use to anyone.

Campaigning for the forthcoming Presidential election, Providence, R.I., Aug. 11/ The Washington Post, 8-12:(A)4.

It is imperative that our correctional system begin to impart some humane values to those it seeks to rehabilitate . . . some genuine belief in the humaneness of society . . . if we are to break the vicious cycle of crime.

U.S. News & World Report, 11-6:30.

W. Walter Menninger
Psychiatrist, Menninger Institute

(The report of the President's Commission on Marijuana and Drug Abuse) simply stated that smoking marijuana in the privacy of your home should be perfectly legal—as long as no one gave it to you, sold it to you and you didn't grow it yourself. Beautiful doublethink! It should be legal and yet it can't be legal.

San Francisco Examiner & Chronicle, 4-23:(This World)2.

Andrew P. Miller
Attorney General of Virginia

(The police officer today) must be as wise as Solomon, as honest as the man Diogenes is still looking for, as strong as Hercules, as intelligent as a college president and as tireless as an electric clock.

At police memorial exercises, Norfolk, May 15/ The Washington Post, 5-16:(C)6.

John N. Mitchell
Attorney General of the United States

The state of America's prisons comes close to a national shame. No civilized society should allow it to continue.

The Washington Post, 1-30:(A)1.

Hartland Molson
Member, Canadian Parliament

(Opposing the elimination of corporal punishment in prison): We have all known cases where people have not been influenced by correctional efforts—efforts to straighten them out and put them on the right path. There comes a time when there is only one lesson which seems to get across. I do not mean brutality, but a good, old-fashioned beating. They will remember their beating . . . I feel this is the best weapon we can use against this sort of person who is becoming more common every day. Motorcycle gangs who use chains are not gentle people. It is all very well to slap them on the wrist and send them to prison for three months because they have caused a disturbance. However, they understand one thing—what they like to give out they do not like to receive.

Before Parliament, Ottawa/ The National Observer, 7-22:17.

Patrick V. Murphy
Police Commissioner of New York City

We do no more for the criminal in jail than we do for animals in the zoo. We cage them and feed them . . . The average citizen has seen prison purely and simply as retribution. The uglier and grimier and older the prison, the more it has seemed to the average citizen to be a fine and splendid prison. (This system of) vengeance dehumanizes both the convicted prisoners and society. Our major problem is to change men's minds about what prison is and should be . . . We are the mightiest nation in the world; but despite all our energy and intelligence, all our science and technology, we have shown ourselves totally unable to cope with the problem of anti-

(PATRICK V. MURPHY)

social behavior. It is time for someone to shout: "Stop! This is crazy. It does not work. It is a disaster. It is a scandal!"

Before Columbia University Law School Alumni, New York, Jan. 28/ The New York Times, 1-29:33.

Crime has been increasing for many years. And let us not delude ourselves—it will continue to rise. The criminal mind will not repent. Criminal activities will not abate. Crime is woven into the fabric of our society. Crime will not abate when housing and education are inadequate, when there is widespread unemployment, when there is inequality of opportunity, when there is a woeful lack of full citizenship rights, when affluence and poverty live side by side. Why has our crime problem reached such proportions? The public does not always understand that the amelioration of social and economic injustice is a battle which must be fought together with the battle against crime. There can be no war on crime without a war on poverty, a war on racial discrimination, a war on inadequate housing, a war on underemployment.

At University of Oklahoma, June 2/ Vital Speeches, 8-15:663.

Aryeh Neier
Executive director, American Civil Liberties Union

(On the Supreme Court's curbing of Justice Department power to wiretap suspected radicals): The Supreme Court has rejected the government's boldest claim of powers to intrude upon individual liberties. The government had claimed that in the undefined interests of "national security" it could engage in a vast, lengthy, unsupervised and unchecked invasion of the privacy of people having only the remotest link with anything in any way criminal or even wrong. If this claim had been upheld, there would have been virtually no limits to the range of governmental intrusion on liberty that would have been implicitly authorized once the government invoked the talisman of "national security." In rejecting the government's claims, the Court has vindicated the Constitutional liberties of all Americans.

New York, June 19/ The New York Times, 6-20:23.

Louis S. Nelson
Warden, San Quentin (Calif.) State Prison

There's a different breed of prisoners today from five or ten years ago . . . In those days, prisoners came to us with a feeling they had done something wrong. They knew it wasn't right to steal, kill or rape. But in the past few years, many who have come to us have been led to believe that the only reason they came to prison was because of the defects of society. They believe they are prisoners of the political system, and thus many call themselves "political prisoners." As we get more and more of people who feel they are political prisoners, it may become necessary to devote all of our time to merely controlling the people in our midst, rather than correcting them.

Interview/ San Francisco Examiner, 5-11:22.

Richard M. Nixon
President of the United States

No institution within our society has a record which presents such a conclusive case of failure as does our prison system.

The Washington Post, 1-30:(A)1.

For those who traffic in drugs, for those who, for example, make hundreds of thousands of dollars—and sometimes millions of dollars—and thereby destroy the lives of our young people throughout this country, there should be no sympathy whatsoever and no limit insofar as the criminal penalty is concerned.

New York, March 20/ The New York Times, 3-21:1.

(On a Presidential commission report advocating the legalization of the use of marijuana but continuation of the illegality of selling it): I oppose the legalization of marijuana, and that includes sale, possession and use. I do not believe you can have effective criminal justice based on a philosophy that something is half-legal and half-illegal.

News conference, Washington, March 24/ The Washington Post, 3-25:(A)7.

All Americans today mourn the death of J. Edgar Hoover. He served his nation as Director of the FBI for 48 years under eight American Presidents with total loyalty, unparalleled ability and supreme dedication . . . His magnificent contribution to making this a great and good nation will be remembered by the American people long after the petty carpings and vicious criticisms of his detractors are forgotten. The FBI he literally created and built is today universally regarded as the finest law-enforcement agency in the world. The FBI is the eternal monument honoring this great American.

Washington, May 2/ The New York Times, 5-3:53.

The American people today are tired of disorder, disruption and disrespect for law. America wants to come back to the law as a way of life . . . In times past, in the days of the American frontier, the brave men who wore the badge and enforced the law were called by a name we do not often hear today. They were called Peace Officers. Today, though that term has passed out of style, the truth it expressed still endures. All the world yearns for peace—peace among nations, peace within nations. But without Peace Officers, we can never have peace.

Eulogy for FBI Director J. Edgar Hoover, Washington, May 4/ U.S. News & World Report, 5-15:112.

Government must never become so preoccupied with catering to the way-out wants of those who reject all respect for moral and legal values that it forgets the citizen's first civil right, the right to be free from domestic violence. Government must never mistake license for liberty, amorality for tolerance, indulgence for charity, or weakness for compassion.

Radio address campaigning for the forthcoming Presidential election, Camp David, Md., Oct. 15/The Washington Post, 10-16:(A)8.

Henry E. Petersen

Assistant Attorney General, Criminal Division, Department of Justice of the United States.

Generically, organized crime will never be eliminated. But organized crime in a syndicate sense I think we can do something about . . . Basically, what we're trying to do is to remove the experts; reduce organized crime to the garden variety of crime. We want to get away from the corruption and the fear of reprisal against witnesses and the obstruction of justice. If we can get it out of being a business and down to the basis of individual crimes committed by individual persons, then we can handle it much better.

Interview, Washington/ U.S. News & World Report, 6-5:68.

(Saying incarceration for possession of marijuana has not been a failure): Because there continue to be robberies it does not mean we should abandon the laws for robberies. Without sanctions, I see a greater move toward the drug culture. There is no reason to eliminate the legal sanctions. We must think in terms of regulating the family, implementing an educational program and assure ourselves that our medical data is valid before we talk about eliminating the one aspect of balance. The people of the U.S., by their legislatures, enacted those laws. I see no indication that they would permit the repeal of those laws. The alcohol problem is perhaps a worse problem than marijuana; but it does not follow that

(HENRY E. PETERSEN)

we should let the lesser problem reach those proportions.

At American Bar Association discussion on drug offenses and decriminalization, San Francisco, Aug. 14/ San Francisco Examiner, 8-15:8.

Peter J. Pitchess
Sheriff, Los Angeles County, Calif.

All handguns must be banned except for law enforcement and the military. For many years, my colleagues and I have steadfastly resisted any attempt to regulate or outlaw the possession of firearms. But times are changing. Our society is experiencing catastrophic upheaval. Our attitudes must change to conform to the demands of contemporary culture.

Before House Judiciary Subcommittee, Washington, June 28/ Los Angeles Times, 6-29:(1)15.

Lewis F. Powell, Jr.
Associate Justice,
Supreme Court of the United States

(On Justice Department wiretapping of suspected radicals): The price of lawful public dissent must not be a dread of subjection to an unchecked surveillance power. Nor must the fear of unauthorized official eavesdropping deter vigorous citizen dissent and discussion of government action in private conversation. For private dissent, no less than open public discourse, is essential to our free society. Fourth Amendment freedoms cannot properly be guaranteed if domestic security surveillances may be conducted solely within the discretion of the Executive Branch. The Fourth Amendment does not contemplate the Executive offices of government as neutral and disinterested magistrates. Their duty and responsibility is to enforce the laws, to investigate and to prosecute. But those charged with this investigative and prosecutional duty should not be the sole judges of when to utilize Constitutionally sensitive means in pursuing their tasks. The historical judgment, which the Fourth Amendment accepts, is that unreviewed Executive discretion may yield too readily to pressures to obtain incriminating evidence and overlook potential invasions of privacy and protected speech.

Supreme Court ruling, Washington, June 19/ The New York Times, 6-20:23.

Raymond Procunier
Director, California State Department of Corrections

We're doing everything that's available in corrections. But a prison system—no matter how good—is not going to solve the crime problem in this country . . . Prisons should be used for punishment for two kinds of criminal: the guy who is a physical menace or the big-time thief who is simply stealing too much to be allowed to stay on the outside. There is a percentage of guys in prison who should never get out. The problem is that, right now, we really have no sure way to determine who these guys are.

Interview, Sacramento, Feb. 29/ Los Angeles Herald-Examiner, 3-5:(A)3.

John R. Rarick
United States Representative, D–La.

(Arguing against proposed legislation that would ban handguns from private use): The crime escalation and the manipulated assassination syndrome are not reasons or justifications for the American to forfeit his guns; rather, they are all the more reason to keep them . . . The right to defend one's person, those loved ones dependent upon him, his state and country, are certainly the first order of priority in any civilized society. The unfettered right of the people to keep and bear arms in defense of themselves and their country is every bit as vital to the maintenance of their individual freedom as is the right of free speech and free press to the right of the people to be informed. If the proposed legislation is allowed to become law without any consideration of the serious Constitutional question involved, how long will it be before free speech and free press are no longer considered necessary as individual liberties? Controlling the people rather than informing them requires neither free speech nor free press.

Before House Judiciary Committee, Washington/

U.S. News & World Report, 7-10:69

Ronald Reagan
Governor of California

(On the California Supreme Court's ruling against capital punishment): This decision makes a mockery of the Constitution involved in establishing the laws of California. If it goes unchallenged, the judicial philosophy inherent in this ruling could be an almost lethal blow to society's right to protect law-abiding citizens and their families against violence and crime. It reinforces the widespread concern of our people that some members of the judiciary inject their own philosophy into their decisions rather than carrying out their constitutional duty to interpret and enforce the law . . . As one who has personally agonized over this issue, I understand and appreciate the humanitarian instincts of those who oppose capital punishment. Yet I find it most ironic that those who benefit from this decision–convicted murderers and assassins–do not share any respect for the sanctity of human life; nor did they display–in the violent acts that caused their convictions–the slightest degree of humanitarian concern or mercy for their victims. As an elected official deeply concerned about lawlessness, I can only view the Court's decision as one more step toward totally disarming society in its fight against violence and crime.

News conference, San Francisco, Feb. 18/ Los Angeles Herald-Examiner, 3-9:(A)14.

We will not reduce crime by legalizing a lot of things that have always been against the law. All the rules and efficient court procedures will not assure justice unless our people, a massive majority of them, are willing to accept the rule of law as a necessary alternative to the rule of the mob. Respect for law . . . for the ideal of justice for all . . . for equality . . . these things must come from within society itself.

Before State Bar of California, Monterey, Sept. 27/ Vital Speeches, 11-15:68.

Albert J. Reiss
Sociologist, Yale University

It is my conviction that there is extensive corruption in almost every major and many medium-sized police departments in the United States. Because of the way our vice laws are enforced and because of the way most police departments are organized and led, I am convinced that investigations are a poor index of the size of the corruption problem.

Interview/ The New York Times, 1-28:12.

Maxwell E. Rich
Executive vice president, National Rifle Association

The 24 million handguns estimated to be in private possession and the annual sales increases are indicative of the widespread anxiety for personal security. To ignore this concern by prohibiting the possession of handguns, to ban from the homeowner and businessman in a high-crime area the firearm which provides self-defense, is a disservice to the law-abiding citizen . . . There is no problem caused by the handgun in the hands of 99 per cent of the people; but to eliminate the handgun . . . in a hope of eliminating it from that 1 per cent criminal element–which is already prohibited from possession of any firearms under existing laws–is punishing the wrong party.

Before House Judiciary Committee, Washington/U.S. News & World Report, 7-10:69.

H. L. Richardson
California State Senator

(Many prison reforms are) making the prisons infinitely more comfortable than

(H. L. RICHARDSON)

they already are and so destroy a man's fear of going back. By giving broader rights within the confines of the institutions . . . we'll have none of the punishment aspect. The punitive aspect of prisons is totally forgotten . . . They're just nibbling away with these reforms. After a number of years, they'll see "success"—and there's going to be a helluva lot more people hurt.

Los Angeles Times, 3-27:(1)3.

Frank L. Rizzo
Mayor of Philadelphia

I don't know if it (capital punishment) will stop this type of activity (murder) by taking the life of the individual who commits this vicious crime, but I'm certain of one thing: He won't be around to commit another one.

Television broadcast, Philadelphia/ Newsweek, 1-24:18.

We've got to . . . stand our ground against lawlessness. Let the criminals know we are not going to tolerate crime, and the judge will put them in jail—which isn't happening. It's a merry-go-round. We catch them and arrest them, and nothing happens.

Interview, Philadelphia/ Los Angeles Times, 9-5:(2)7.

Nelson A. Rockefeller
Governor of New York

One of the most recent and widely-used techniques of modern-day revolutionaries has been the taking of political hostages and using the threat to kill them as blackmail to achieve unconditional demands and to gain wide public attention to further their revolutionary ends. I have followed these developments with great interest and considered that, if tolerated, they pose a serious threat to the ability of free government to preserve order and to protect the security of the individual citizen. Therefore, I firmly believe that a duly-elected official, sworn to defend the Constitution and the laws of the state and the nation, would be betraying his trust to the people he serves if he were to sanction or condone such criminal acts by negotiating under such circumstances.

Before McKay Commission, New York, April 5/The New York Times, 5-1:54.

George W. Romney
Secretary of Housing and Urban Development of the United States

We are asking a great deal of our police institutions, especially in our declining central-city areas, when we ask them to reduce crime by enforcement methods alone. We must recognize the major forces of social pathology that must be turned around before the police can have much chance of success.

Before International Association of Chiefs of Police, Salt Lake City/ Los Angeles Times, 10-24:(2)6.

John P. Saylor
United States Representative, R–Pa.

(On the U.S. Supreme Court's ruling against capital punishment): The decision places the law-abiding citizen at the mercy of the criminal. Five members of the Court have decided to coddle criminals; four believe death is a necessary deterrent to crime. The decision represents a free pass for murder, rape, burglary and other serious crimes. What has become of the concept of punishment for breaking the law? More and more criminals will engage in more and more serious crimes now that the Court has ended capital punishment. If anything is needed, it is harsher penalties for those convicted of felonies, not lesser penalties. Five men in America have saved the lives of 600 convicted felons. If their ruling were no broader than that, it could be applauded. Unfortunately, the ruling of the Court's simple majority will increase the likelihood of more serious crimes being perpetrated. The Supreme Court must be curbed or the criminal will rule supreme in our land.

Human Events, 7-29:15.

Whitney N. Seymour, Jr.
United States Attorney for the Southern District of New York

For too many years, those of us in law enforcement have politely requested businessmen to come to us when they encounter problems of fraud or corruption. We have offered our hand in friendship and promised to help business clean up its own house. Except in the rarest case, that invitation has been totally rejected. Businessmen seldom come to us with information about stock manipulations, mail frauds, kickbacks, bid rigging, labor racketeering, bribe-taking by public officials or other crimes that frequently occur in the business world . . . Businessmen too often tend to smile understandingly at illegal conduct by their colleagues while loudly complaining about "crime in the streets." We must set these things right.

Before Rotary Club of New York, July 20/The New York Times, 7-21:35.

There's a traditional difference in sentences for different types of crimes, and it tends to discriminate against the uneducated, unloved social reject. The guy who steals packages from the back of the truck is going to get four years. And the guy who steals $45,000 is going to get three months.

San Francisco Examiner & Chronicle, 10-29:(This World)21.

Raymond P. Shafer
Chairman, National Commission on Marijuana and Drug Abuse

We no longer look at a person who is an alcoholic as a criminal; we tend to give him medical care. We don't look at a heroin addict as a criminal anymore; we want to give him treatment; we want to make sure that he does not stay in that state. The same attitude should be in the use of any drug, including marijuana. We should talk in terms of educating them against the use rather than criminalizing them if they happen to experiment.

TV-radio interview, Washington/ "Meet the Press," National Broadcasting Company, 4-9.

R. Sargent Shriver
Democratic Vice-Presidential nominee

Crime is not only a problem for racial minorities. Millions of citizens of every race live every day under the silent oppression of violence. The new life within our cities is not the dream we saved and worked for: triple-locked doors, a dread of empty and dark streets and fumbling noises at the door.

Accepting the nomination, Washington, Aug. 8/The New York Times, 8-9:18.

Howard K. Smith
News commentator, American Broadcasting Company

One feels hopeless protesting the gun cult that prevails in this nation, but one has to. Between four and six thousand Americans are murdered a year by guns . . . compared to fewer than a hundred in European countries. The average American is 80 times more likely to be killed by a gun than the average Briton, German or Swede—because of their good gun laws and our bad ones. The FBI wants controls, the police want them, Presidents have begged for them, the Gallup Poll shows the people want them. Why can't we have them? Because the gun lobby will wreck any politician who tries to get them by campaigns of what can only be called lies. It says the Constitution guarantees uncontrolled ownership of guns. Not true, the courts have repeatedly ruled. It says controls will keep the law-abiding from owning guns to protect themselves. Untrue—laws would only require registration. The untruths are endless, and also endlessly believed.

News broadcast, American Broadcasting Company, 5-15.

Richmond A. Sprague
First Assistant District Attorney, Philadelphia County, Pa.

Today, we don't really decide whether a man is innocent or guilty. We spend more time worrying about how the government, how the police, got the evidence. Law enforcement must return to the basics: Is a man innocent or guilty? And if he is guilty, let him face his punishment.

Interview, Philadelphia/ The Dallas Times Herald, 4-19:(A)25.

Adlai E. Stevenson III
United States Senator, D–Ill.

(Advocating gun-control legislation): To those who believe the slogan that criminals —not handguns—commit crimes, this can be said: Criminals cause crimes, and handguns are the principal instruments of the death and injury they cause. Other instruments of possible injury which have legitimate uses—cars, even dogs—are licensed. There is no instrument more sinister than the lethal, concealable pistol. If a gun is not used in a crime, the chance of death is five times less. Any policeman knows that a suspect who must rely upon a knife, a bottle or his fists is not so bold and so dangerous as one armed with a gun.

Quote, 5-28:514.

Quinn Tamm
Executive director, International Association of Chiefs of Police

Legislators are still trying to find gun-control measures that won't infringe upon some sportsman's right to plink at beer bottles and empty cans.

The Fresno (Calif.) Bee, 11-17:(A)20.

Harold H. Titus, Jr.
United States Attorney-designate for the District of Columbia

I believe in free will. I believe there is such a thing as an evil, bad man. There are people who want money, who don't want to work.

Interview/The Washington Post, 4-10:(A)1.

James Vorenberg
Professor of Law, Harvard University

. . . the FBI does very little today to help with the nation's main crime problem, which is the problem of predatory crime: robbery, burglary, rape in the big cities. If they have the know-how, if they have the training capacity, they should disclose it, use it and make it available. If they do not have, they should make that clear and get out of the business of offering so-called training at the FBI Academy for local police. In the last 10 to 20 years, the FBI has lost its position as the most-respected police agency in this country among leading police officials. There is a strong sense that it has simply fallen behind—to some extent because of problems of ideology, to some extent because of secrecy, but mostly so because of rigidity and unwillingness to learn and consider new methods.

Interview, Washington/ Los Angeles Times, 5-23:(2)7.

John Waldron
Former Commissioner, London Metropolitan Police

The reputation of the police force depends on the bearing and efficiency of what we (in Britain) call the constable or the bobby—what you (in America) call the patrolman. He's the one who has contact with the man on the street, with the public. He must comfort the widow in the murder case, must tell parents their child has been killed in an accident. He has to deal with armed criminals, dangerous drugs, domestic disputes, endless stupid questions . . . the whole gamut of life.

Interview, Miami/ Los Angeles Times, 10-18:(6)14.

George C. Wallace
Governor of Alabama

I will oppose Federal legislation to enforce the registration of guns by our citizens, feeling that this measure could do little or nothing to deter criminal activity, but rather would prove restrictive to our decent law-abiding citizens, and could well encourage further activity by the criminal.

The Christian Science Monitor, 5-17:4.

If you are knocked on the head after this meeting, the criminal will be out of jail before you're even in the hospital. And on Monday they'll blame the policeman for it all.

Asheville, N.C., April/ The Christian Science Monitor, 5-17:4.

Edward Bennett Williams
Lawyer

(On the Supreme Court's curbing of Justice Department power to wiretap suspected radicals): Theoretically, (Justice Lewis) Powell's decision is great. But practically, it's worthless. The government will keep on tapping like it always has, only now they won't admit it. They'll just do it.

The National Observer, 7-1:2.

Jerry V. Wilson
Chief of Police of Washington, D.C.

Upwards of half of those arrested on major charges are using hard drugs of some sort. It is an oversimplification to say that drug abuse automatically leads to serious crimes of another nature, because the conditions that cause drug habits also cause crime. Still, it's definitely true that reducing dependence on drugs lessens reliance on crime to support a drug habit. There is no question that narcotics treatment and prevention programs are necessary to reduce street crimes.

U.S. News & World Report, 4-10:24.

Donald R. Wright
Chief Justice,
California Supreme Court

We have concluded that capital punishment is impermissibly cruel. It degrades and dehumanizes all who participate in its processes. It is unnecessary to any legitimate goal of the state and is incompatible with the dignity of man and the judicial process.

Delivering court ruling, Sacramento, Feb. 18/The Washington Post, 2-19:(A)1.

Samuel W. Yorty
Mayor of Los Angeles

Law enforcement can be brought back to its proper perspective only by a growing concern and respect for law and order by the public . . . The United States Supreme Court interprets the Constitution, but the citizen's immediate right to be secure in his person and property is protected by our policemen. You don't call the Supreme Court when your physical safety is jeopardized—you call the police.

At St. Anselm's College, Manchester, N.H., Feb. 8/Los Angeles Herald-Examiner, 2-9:(A)10.

Evelle J. Younger
Attorney General of California

The system of criminal justice is no longer effective. It is safer for astronauts to walk on the moon than on the streets of some of our cities at night.

San Francisco Examiner & Chronicle, 1-23:(This World)2.

It used to be that the favorite recreational activity of prisoners was playing baseball. Now it's filing lawsuits.

The Washington Post, 2-5:(A)1.

(On the just-concluded California election in which a proposition to re-instate capital punishment was overwhelmingly approved, even though the State Supreme Court earlier in the year outlawed the death penalty): Maybe our State Supreme Court will have

(EVELLE J. YOUNGER)

some second thoughts and consider the vote of the people as significant and realize they (the Court) over-reached. I'm not one who believes the Court should take a vote of the people before they decide on an issue. But don't forget, they blamed this on the people. They said this (capital punishment) offends contemporary standards of decency. When they say that, all you're saying is most people don't approve of it. Well, the people of California spoke on the question of contemporary standards of decency, and the Supreme Court of California was just plain wrong.

Los Angeles Times, 11-9:(1)26.

Jack H. Adamson
Professor of English, University of Utah

I find that some of my colleagues and many of my students equate academic freedom with the right to dissent. If they are correct in this equation, if that is really the essence of academic freedom, then surely there is more of it now than there once was. Here at Utah, the right is firmly established to question or attack the national Administration, the Mormon Church, the social institution of marriage, the Vietnam war or whatever. This is evident to anyone, and while I occasionally wince at the manners or even the cruelty of the dissenters, I consider their function valuable and I support it. But for me academic freedom is more than this . . . For me, academic freedom is not so much something I think as something I feel. And so the question is, with all this dissent and protest around me, do I feel free? No, not as free as I once did. If, after thoughtful consideration, I were to decide that the Nixon policy for the Vietnam war was the best policy for the nation, I would seek a forum off-campus to say it. On campus, I might not be assaulted, but I would certainly be harassed and intimidated. Sadly enough, even the classroom, at least for me, has been infected with this general atmosphere of threat. Perhaps I am an overly timid person, but in classes now I always feel some constraint, some intimidation that I never knew in the old days; and I ask myself how many small evasions and surrenders I am guilty of in presenting my views because I don't wish to risk unpleasantness, don't wish to confront the threat. If academic freedom includes not only the right to dissent but also a general atmosphere conducive to thoughtful consideration of issues, if it means a scholarly climate, a situation in which the human mind works at its best, then I think there is no question that we have lost some of our freedom, and I think we desperately need to regain it.

At Utah Conference on Higher Education, Sept. 15/Vital Speeches, 11-1:61.

Spiro T. Agnew
Vice President of the United States

(The) threat of dogmatism and intolerance of diverse opinion in the academic community is a matter of concern to every American. For history has demonstrated that there can be no more dangerous form of anti-intellectualism than that kind practiced by highly-educated, self-righteous intellectuals who consider themselves superior to the point of infallibility. Indeed, we know that the worst excesses of the mob during the French Terror were carried out under the leadership of "men of learning" who thought themselves the ultimate products of the Age of Reason and Science; that the ideological precursor of Mussolini's Fascism was a poet-philosopher; and that the minister of propaganda and enlightenment of Hitler's Germany held a Ph.D. from one of his country's most respected universities.

Before Capitol Hill Club, Washington, April 11/Human Events, 4-29:9.

If biased segments of the news media can distort the view of the world in which we live, it necessarily falls to the educational community, in pursuit of truth and fact, to assure that today's distortion is not perpetrated in tomorrow's history books. (Nevertheless) politicized material is getting into standard works that teachers and

(SPIRO T. AGNEW)

parents rely on as general reference books for today's students.

The Dallas Times Herald, 4-12:(A)23.

Too many of us view a college education as the sole measure of significant reward. Too often this has led to a lack of workers who combine art and thought to produce the magnificent buildings, highways and other works that grace our country. Youth of today deserves a better break than to be encumbered by white-collar values which have made a college education a byword for achievement. Finding ways to accord high prestige and acclaim to skilled labor is a most important goal for the decade ahead.

Before International Union of Bricklayers, Masons and Plasterers, Las Vegas, Nev., Sept. 11/Los Angeles Times, 9-12:(1)19.

Lloyd M. Bentsen
United States Senator, D–Tex.

In years past, the term "vocational education" has unfairly invoked a negative image. Too often, vocational schools were regarded as the dumping ground for the under-privileged, the under-achievers, the academic failures. But they were not the failures. The failure was in the school that did not offer suitable alternatives. The failure was in promoting college as the ideal and ultimate goal for all. At home and at school, children were presumed to prepare for college as a prerequisite for earning a living–like it or not–and regardless of the fact that only 20 per cent of the occupations in this decade and the next will require a college degree. When Ph.D.s are driving taxis, sociologists are filling gas tanks, bright young English majors have retired to their organic gardens and political science graduates are selling underground newspapers on street corners, there ought to be growing doubt about the value of a college degree.

At Texas Vocational Education Convocation, Dallas, Aug. 1/The Dallas Times Herald, 8-2:(B)3.

Derek C. Bok
President, Harvard University

Private universities are facing a real crisis of financing. I think we're going to have to provide new forms of aid from government, scholarship assistance, ways of enabling the college to assist students. We have students at Harvard who are so poor they can't afford to go to community colleges. The private university does relieve the public of much of the burden of higher education, and it must have help. There's an increasing blurring of lines between public and private; more and more colleges are getting substantial assistance from government, Federal and state.

Interview, Beverly Hills, Calif./Los Angeles Times, 1-17:(4)8.

Forbes Bottomly
Seattle Superintendent of Public Schools

Career education is one of the few change efforts in school programs that has seemingly had almost universal acceptance by parents and teachers. It is one of the few noncontroversial change efforts in education today. Parents view it as an effort to relate education to the real world and frequently find an enhanced interest in education on the part of their children as a result of participation in an occupational education program. Likewise, career education enables school systems to use business, industry and professional people as resources on a planned basis, thereby establishing a closer tie with the business community. It may also be that today's youth, in their search for "relevance," may come to view career education as one of the more relevant elements of public education today. This could lead to a reduction in absenteeism and the development of a more positive attitude toward education, and perhaps even toward the role of the individual in society.

The Christian Science Monitor, 4-22:8.

Albert H. Bowker
Chancellor, University of California, Berkeley

(On dealing with faculty labor unions): I think the problem with it is that in any university, unlike almost any other institution, there is very little distinction between workers and bosses. Faculty hire themselves, by and large set the standards for their work, recommend promotions and salary increases for themselves and set many of the conditions of work that in other areas of employment are really set by management. The problem of how to bargain with employee organizations under these circumstances has never been resolved very well.

Interview, Berkeley/ San Francisco Examiner & Chronicle, 3-26:(A)8.

Change was easy when universities were expanding. Now the only way we can change is to take resources from one place and put them in another.

Newsweek, 11-6:114.

Ernest L. Boyer
Chancellor, State University of New York

There will be a significant change in the kinds of people who want to go to college during the next decade. There'll be many more working adults and older persons engaged in study; and the reasons for this are clear. First, the birth rate is flattening out, and the big demographic bulges will occur at the middle or later years. The workweek is breaking up, becoming more flexible, shorter—which provides more leisure time. The retirement years are earlier and life expectancy is longer. The need to retrain workers is greater if we're to avoid early obsolescence. At the other end of the spectrum, many 18-year-olds who used to be pushed along to college are now taking time off to work and travel and get a better fix on their own life goals. I think this is a healthy trend, and in New York we're talking about a "step out" arrangement which encourages students to leave college—to "step out"—for a while and then return later when they're more ready for continued study. All of this suggests strongly that the old notion of getting one's education "out of the way" during the early years, and then drawing on that intellectual capital for 40 years, presuming all along that you're an "educated person," is a bankrupt notion . . . colleges can no longer be thought of as isolated islands for the young. They must serve not just young people but all people; and increasingly they'll be involved with many agencies and institutions beyond the university, including business and industry.

Interview, Washington/ U.S. News & World Report, 10-2:69.

Kingman Brewster, Jr.
President, Yale University

A university, in a very real sense, is caught in the middle of the generation gap. The younger generation and the educational institution are bound to be identified with social changes which the elders wish would go away. And I'm not about to disagree with them in some cases.

Interview, Yale University/ The Dallas Times Herald, 6-15:(B)16.

William E. Brock III
United States Senator, R–Tenn.

The Office of Education estimates that 24 million Americans 18 years and over are "functionally illiterate"—they cannot read, write or count at a fifth-grade level. Yet only 6.4 million Americans 14 years and over have not had at least 5 years of school. This does not say much for the quality of education received by 17.6 million of those Americans.

Quote, 5-21:486.

McGeorge Bundy
President, Ford Foundation

The American educational system would be better today, I think, if in the ordinary case the period between 6th grade and college were a year, even two years, shorter than it is now . . . The whole formal apparatus of the four-year degree could be scrapped if people were brave enough to do it.

U.S. News & World Report, 1-17:23.

William T. Cahill
Governor of New Jersey

I was particularly gratified recently to hear the President of the United States say what we have been saying for a long time in New Jersey, that the burden of financing education has fallen with increasing heaviness on the property owners and that the property tax today is becoming one of the most inequitable and regressive of all public taxes.

Trenton, March 18/ The New York Times, 3-19:(1)56.

Shirley Chisholm
United States Representative, D–N.Y.

(Advocating "learning centers" for commuting and working students who would advance at their own pace): What I am proposing is that we abolish the campus, the degree, the classroom and the course, as generations of students have known them. Let the "Old Ivy" continue to operate for those students who want a degree for the old-fashioned reasons–culture, prestige and even, in rare cases, the simple love of learning. It is clear now that if 60, 70 or 80 per cent of our young people are to continue their education after high school, which is a reasonable and probably necessary goal, new kinds of institutions must be created.

Before North Carolina Education Association, Greensboro, April 7/ The New York Times, 4-9:(1)27.

Robert L. Ebel
President, American Educational Research Association

School attendance can be made compulsory but learning cannot be; so some of our classrooms are loaded with youths whose only aim is to escape from learning.

U.S. News & World Report, 5-8:61.

Milton S. Eisenhower
President, Johns Hopkins University

The university is not a political institution. A university as such stands for nothing but education and research, and the only things it advocates in the field of public policy are those things which affect education and research.

Interview, Baltimore/ The Washington Post, 1-2:(D)4.

W. D. Elroy
Chancellor, University of California, San Diego

Few universities are acknowledged great without the environment of a great city; few cities are great without a strong university. We need each other.

San Francisco Examiner, 4-21:38.

Harold L. Enarson
President, Ohio State University

Faculty should not be expected to rival Bob Hope or Billy Graham. Teachers have a contagious enthusiasm for their subject. They have much to offer. But they cannot make learning easy, painless, effortless or self-evidently relevant to the moment.

At Kent (Ohio) State University/ The Wall Street Journal, 10-31:14.

Robert L. Ewigleben
President, Ferris State College, Big Rapids, Mich.

I think there's nothing more tragic in education than turning out students who understand all about their culture but nothing about making a living . . . Our university is dedicated to the idea that all work is dignified. Being an auto mechanic is just as dignified as being a college president. The main thing is that a man does work and is productive and gets satisfaction from that work . . . The post-*Sputnik* era was really a ridiculous era. We got a big hangup in our society on (college) degrees. We produced a situation where now, for example, there isn't one plumber in the city of Big Rapids. But there are a lot of unemployed physicists running around the country looking for jobs.

Interview, Big Rapids, Mich./ The Washington Post, 2-12:(A)10.

Marvin Feldman
Former Executive Director, Planning and Review Committee, Federal Office of Economic Opportunity

It would help to redefine vocational education, at least in part, as that aspect of an educational experience which helps a person discover, define and refine his talents, and to use them in working toward a career. This definition sees vocational education embracing, but not confined to, development of manual skills; it sees such skills used not merely to prepare for tasks, but as alternatives or supplements to verbal skills in the entire learning process. The definition requires, regardless of the educational level, an opportunity to learn and demonstrate learning in non-verbal ways, learning the relations between the educational program and the purpose and nature of work, developing a faculty for continuing growth, and the ability to work with, not merely alongside, others.

Interview/ The Wall Street Journal, 1-18:14.

Burton C. Hallowell
President, Tufts University

A university cannot afford to allow finances to so dominate its decisions that the quality of its education is diminished. At the same time, it cannot afford to pursue education without regard to cost effectiveness.

The New York Times, 1-10:(E)31.

Oscar Handlin
Professor of History, Harvard University

In the 1970s, we sentence more of our youth to more years in school than ever before in history, so that never have Americans been so poorly educated as now. I read the letters of unschooled Yankee farmers of the 18th century, who could not spell but who had something to say, and wonder whether their capacity to think would have survived the 16 years of schooling to which we subject their descendants. The victims, of course, have no idea of what is wrong with them; but since they thrash about so, everyone solicitously asks their opinion. More time is spent in talking about learning than in learning.

At Brooklyn (N.Y.) College commencement, May 31/ The Wall Street Journal, 8-2:8.

Zenon C. R. Hansen
Chairman and president, Mack Trucks, Inc.

We have discontinued support of schools where it appeared that the students were not appreciative of the opportunity being given to them, and where there were indications that the faculty was far-out. I get sick and tired of hearing that industry hasn't done a good job of selling our educators and students on the benefits of the free-enterprise system. If these college professors are so damned smart, they ought to know that in many instances the endowment for the buildings they are in, the very campuses they are on, have been created by the blood and sweat of people who never had a college education. If they are so dumb that they can't figure that out, we ought to get rid of them.

Interview/ Nation's Business, January:57.

Paul Hardin III
President-elect,
Southern Methodist University

I believe every college or university must do only those things which it can do exceedingly well, and not try to be all things to all people. The necessary corollary of that is that my ambition for SMU is that it achieve true excellence in every academic or extracurricular undertaking. It is better to omit a program or abolish a school than to muddle through.

Before Southern Methodist University board of trustees, May 12/ The Dallas Times Herald, 5-13:(B)1.

There's a tendency lately to downgrade the importance of higher education, what with the campus turbulence of the '60s, the over-production of Ph.D. degrees in some fields, the depression in the science and engineering fields and the current trend of anti-intellectualism. But we must be up to date, and I argue in favor of a broad general education . . . The most practical is the liberal-arts education, where you learn to learn and lay the foundation so you can roll with the economic picture. The day of the multiple career is permanently with us. Even people in the technical trades, such as plumbers, electricians, carpenters, etc., need exposure to the humanities and sciences or you run the danger of raising a generation of Archie Bunkers; and we don't want that, do we?

At Dallas Woman's Club, Nov. 1/ The Dallas Times Herald, 11-2:(E)7.

J. Archie Hargraves
President, Shaw University,
Raleigh, N.C.

College has got to be available to the guy on the job who wants to get his degree on weekends and in the evening. And we have to extend our curriculum to the community by going to them. Why shouldn't we provide training for prison inmates and farm workers?

The Washington Post, 4-23:(G)10.

S. I. Hayakawa
President,
San Francisco State College

(On student dissent that used to disrupt many colleges): The trouble with so many academic liberals and media people was they would take literally the idealistic rhetoric of some of the worst gangsters in the movement and accept it with all seriousness. Damn it, they were hoodlums. I never did believe the causes of violence were the stated causes. Actually, the strike (of students against S.F. State in 1969-70) was, in my opinion, generated by the intoxication of extremist students when they found the administration keeling over for any number of demands.

Interview, San Francisco/ The New York Times, 1-9:(1)49.

. . . this is one of our great problems in the United States: Are we going to continue to model our universities on the European idea of a university, which is to produce aristocracy? Or are we going to produce universities in this country that really have a basis in the popular will? Now, American universities have two very basic models to follow: One is the aristocratic center, like Oxford or Cambridge or Heidelberg. The other model is the American land-grant college, set up by the Morrell Act of 1878. The land-grant colleges used to be called agricultural and mechanical colleges. You'd get a bunch of farmers in Oklahoma who wanted to make money by farming; they wanted to know what made their pigs die. So the land-grant colleges were set up by the Federal government to meet the needs of all the people at the basic level of job training. I believe that the future of American education should lie in the direction of the 1970s or 1980s version of the land-grant colleges, with emphasis on urban problems rather than rural. That enormous concern with the welfare of all the people that the Morrell Act represents is something that we ought to have as a model in education. Damn it,

I don't think a democratic society should be trying to turn out aristocrats.

Interview, San Francisco/ Los Angeles Times, 2-6:(West)26.

(On violent student dissent which flourished in the 1960s): The steam has run out of the movement all over the country. The students who are in the universities now were in high school at the height of the uproar from 1962 to '68. Most of those students were exposed to the propaganda of violence and dissidence and rebellion while they were still high-school kids. By the time they saw the results of all this on television, by the time they heard all the arguments, by the time they graduated, they'd been through that kind of thought. They came to us already having matured beyond that point.

News conference/Newsweek, 10-23:67.

George W. Hazzard
President, Worcester (Mass.) Polytechnic Institute

We seek to educate people, not just train or inform them. Education is not measured solely by facts learned and data stored. In our view, an educated person is able to cope with changes in his environment. He is able to learn by himself, to think for himself, to analyze and deal with problems in a realistic and feasible manner. He recognizes his personal capabilities and limitations, and he is aware of the rewards and possible disappointments involved if he makes a maximum effort. Finally, he is sensitive to people, to personal interactions, and he is able to communicate with the society around him.

Interview, Worcester, Mass./ The Christian Science Monitor, 9-23:6.

Roger W. Heyns
President, American Council on Education; Former chancellor, University of California, Berkeley

(On campus disturbances during the 1960s): A number of things were cited as the reason for the disturbances here (in the U.S.)–alienation, the generation gap, inadequate discipline of the young, breakdown of the American family, failure of America to live up to its aspirations. All of these contained elements of the truth. But many of these factors are still with us, even though the disturbances have subsided. The trouble of the 1960s had its personal casualties. There is no question in my mind also that, wherever these things went on for any length of time, it was very hard for even the nonparticipant to keep on working and do constructive things. A lot of tension is not conducive to contemplation. Accusations hurled back and forth across the campus create distrust, and that is hard on learning. There was abrasion: faculty against faculty, faculty against students. Those are some of the harmful effects.

Interview, Washington/ Los Angeles Times, 4-5:(2)7.

John A. Howard
President, Rockford College

(Criticizing inappropriate government intrusion into college policy): We cannot believe that it is the wish of the citizens that all of higher education should be homogenized to conform to the ebb and flow of social theory. One of the great strengths of this nation has been a system of higher education characterized by a very great diversity, with different colleges operating on different assumptions and serving different objectives. Such a system not only supports and enhances a pluralistic society, but provides protection against over-response to the clamors of the day.

The Wall Street Journal, 8-30:8.

Harold Howe II
Vice president, education and research division, Ford Foundation; Former Commissioner of Education of the United States

. . . consider the fact that American youngsters today have by age 18 expended

(HAROLD HOWE II)

more time in front of the TV tube than they have in school. What should schools do about this? Ignore it? There is room for an alliance between formal education and the dual influences of communications and community, an alliance that formal education is entirely too reluctant to explore and that some of the prophets of openness are espousing. If you have read Ivan Illich, you are aware of his argument that most of formal schooling is unproductive if not destructive and that other agencies in society can perform better than schools the tasks in which schools arrogantly claim a monopoly. While I am not about to buy all that Illich has to say, I'd be willing to agree that, unless we educators join our institutions with the other agencies that clearly have major educational roles, we may find that the people who pay our bills are increasingly attracted to Illich.

Lecture, Yale University, Feb. 7/ Vital Speeches, 4-1:380.

John G. Kemeny
President, Dartmouth College

I think something has happened to our school system which can best be likened to a pendulum which has swung over too far to the other side. And I feel guilty, because I was one of the people pushing very hard a decade ago for greater freedom, flexibility and individual study in secondary school. But I think that, from an overly-rigid and overly-required curriculum in our school system, we have swung to the opposite extreme. Perhaps the schools are now too permissive with too much freedom of choice; with the result that, when students come to colleges, they really don't have the motivation.

Television interview, Boston/ The Christian Science Monitor, 4-1:(B)9.

Edward M. Kennedy
United States Senator, D–Mass.

(On the decrease in dissent on campus): The experience of the last year was not encouraging. The mood on most campuses was reminiscent of the silent generation of the 1950s. Those of us who visited and saw you returning to your books and guitars were puzzled.

Before Harvard Law School Forum/ Los Angeles Herald-Examiner, 1-7:(A)8.

C. Albert Koob
President, National Catholic Education Association

(On President Nixon's support of tax credits for parents of children attending non-public schools): Supporters of non-public education—battered but unbowed through a difficult and strenuous struggle for survival—now have the satisfaction of knowing that their efforts have not been in vain and that the nation's most influential voice is backing what skeptics charged to be mere rhetoric with the cold, hard facts of meaningful action.

June 26/The Washington Post, 6-27:(A)2.

Charles A. LeMaistre
Chancellor, University of Texas

Our universities are unfinished, they are incomplete and, most of all, they are imperfect . . . In that lies the strength and the ability to change. Change is never easy —but often it is a requisite for survival. This is the posture that higher education finds itself in today.

At Executives' Secretaries, Inc., convention, Dallas, May 18/ The Dallas Times Herald, 5-19:(B)5.

Richard W. Lyman
President, Stanford University

There have been doubters . . . who profess to believe that, in an era of expansion for public (educational) institutions, the private institutions will have a steadily-diminishing role to play. We would argue that they will have a bigger role, because there are certain valued qualities which flourish in the privately-controlled institutions. I am thinking of such things as variety of academic focus; the quality that comes from having to search out your own funds; student bodies that are smaller but which are national and international in composition; political autonomy; capacity for experimentation; and, as is so well exemplified here today, opportunity for citizen service in a philanthropic enterprise.

Launching a $300 million fund drive for the University, April 11/ Los Angeles Times, 4-12:(2)1.

Sidney P. Marland, Jr.
Commissioner of Education of the United States

Of all the problems and failings of modern education, the most devastating has been the failure to prepare students to enter a career . . . Boring young people throughout nine months of the year at elementary and secondary or post-secondary levels is wasteful. It is also impolite. But launching them into the world after 10 or 12 or 16 years unprepared for future study or for gainful employment is inexcusable. The career-oriented theme will help the reform movement focus on practicality and relevance as well as abstract knowledge . . . The idea behind career education is to make school of some use, and thereby to establish an intrinsic motivation not now present in elementary and secondary schools for many of our young.

The Christian Science Monitor, 4-22:8.

J. C. Matthews
President emeritus, North Texas State University

Universities in the past tended to be conservative, isolated from the community and pleased to refer to themselves as "a community of scholars." In the last 25 years, there has been a new concept in the making. "Who is in charge here? What is the proper role of the university?" are typical of the basic questions which are being asked. And politicalization of the faculty and students and a reduction of public confidence are the most obvious results to date.

At North Texas State University commencement, May 16/ The Dallas Times Herald, 5-17:(AA)30.

Charles J. McCann
President, Evergreen State College, Olympia, Wash.

(On the reasons for his college's elimination of "majors" and institution of an interdisciplinary curriculum): There were certain nubs that seemed to be the roots of all the evils (in the traditional college)—courses, departments, people tied to one kind of activity for the wrong reasons. Professors were teaching courses because they were listed in the catalog. Students were taking courses because they happened to be in the curriculum . . . Society's valid concern to have trained people has been pushed to the extreme . . . A college catalog has become a list of job titles, and this is being done at heavy cost to individuals. (Evergreen College's goal is) not to have a curriculum, to face up to the fact that there is no way, past a certain age, to legislate what a person needs to know.

Interview/Los Angeles Times, 4-17:(2)1.

Pauline Mills McGibbon
Chancellor, University of Toronto

The university president is the equivalent to a Prime Minister and makes policy. I walk a tight-rope of neutrality with faculty, students and alumni.

Interview, San Francisco, Feb.14/ San Francisco Examiner, 2-15:26.

William J. McGill
President, Columbia University

There is no law written on tablets of stone saying that a college education must be four years long for each and every student.

U.S. News & World Report, 1-17:23.

George S. McGovern
United States Senator, D–S.D.

Education deserves a more prominent place in the structure of the Federal government. Currently there are dozens of Federal education programs scattered throughout the Federal government. Both considerations suggest the establishment of a Cabinet-level Department of Education.

Before the Senate, Washington, Feb. 15/Quote, 2-15:248.

(Saying teachers should have the right to strike): Teachers belong in school—or on a picket line, if necessary—but not in jail . . . You should never have to face the choice between a jail term if you strike and educational deterioration if you don't.

Before American Federation of Teachers, St. Paul, Minn., Aug. 24/ The Dallas Times Herald, 8-24:(A)1.

He (President Nixon) has stood back and watched classrooms become so overcrowded that children have to share desks and teachers have no time to teach; and he has done nothing about it. He has stood back and watched school buildings—especially in our cities—turn into run-down warehouses for young people; and he has done nothing about that. He has watched school systems go virtually bankrupt and homeowners go into debt trying to pay their taxes on their property; and he has done nothing about that. He has watched school corridors and grounds become armed fortresses lined with policemen to protect our children from violence inside those corridors; and he has done nothing about that.

Campaigning for the forthcoming Presidential election, Detroit, Sept. 22/The New York Times, 9-23:14.

Thomas C. Mendenhall
President, Smith College

(On student protest on his campus): The civil-rights movement demonstrated the effectiveness of certain tactics, and there was a coming together of certain issues. Kent State and the Yale student protest of the Black Panther trials triggered three days of mass meetings. They were not unruly meetings; they were constructive. The difficulty was where do you go from here? Back to business as usual for the students seemed a terrible failure. Is the campus quiet today? The term one uses is "relatively quiet."

San Francisco Examiner, 3-10:24.

Maurice B. Mitchell
Chancellor, University of Denver

(On academic tenure): To me, coming out of the business world, tenure is one of the great curiosities of American working life. Essentially, it's a life contract in which the employer agrees to retain the professor for the balance of his career, but the professor is not obligated to remain should he get a better offer elsewhere . . . Tenure guarantees the right to teach, advise and write without interference. Once an individual has tenure, he cannot be penalized for holding or expressing unpopular views, for poor teaching, for failure to contribute to the intellectual life of the university, or even for an apparent lack of ordinary intelligence or moral responsibility that might be inferred from . . . views or actions.

U.S. News & World Report, 12-11:56.

Steven Muller
President, Johns Hopkins University

A university . . . is a deeply human organization in which reason and nature strive together as in mankind itself. Sometimes the flesh is martyred by reason; sometimes reason is martyred by human passion. Passion in the service of reason can lead to the utmost in human achievement. Reason in the service of passion can lead to the torment of men and women by each other. At universities, reason has a special priority. My own conclusion . . . is that we can survive each other only if we deal with each other fully and always as human beings, not as categories, hierarchies or abstractions. We cannot escape judging each other's performance. We are not equally gifted in a community that puts a premium on intellectual achievement. But we are all bright enough, in this unique community of the university, to tear each other apart if we choose. Let us refrain from that—collectively and singly. We are all so vulnerable to each other, let us at least treat one another with kindness. Finally, let us rejoice in our humanity and in the special opportunities that the university offers. Humor and laughter are also uniquely human. A human community without them is cursed . . . Let us resolve to strive, not only for achievement, but for the grace of laughter and kindness. We are here and now and able—and insecure and fragile—and alive—let us together make the utmost of what we are and what we have!

Address at his installation as president/ The Wall Street Journal, 3-24:8.

Frederic W. Ness
President,
American Association of Colleges

. . . there is present in this college generation a desire, almost unique in my years of experience, to reassert the value of values, to put into practice what older generations were content to preach. There is, in short, a new spirituality. Our problem as custodians of society's most evolved institution—the nation's liberal-arts college and university—is somehow or other to marshall this new creative spirituality and to focus it for the welfare of mankind. To do this is perhaps the most important of the things we have not as yet learned. Not to do it, and soon, may well mean the ultimate thrust into bankruptcy of liberal learning and the liberal-arts college.

At Newberry (S.C.) College, April 21/Vital Speeches, 8-1:638.

Richard M. Nixon
President of the United States

We all know that within the central cities of our nation there are schools so inferior that it is hypocrisy even to suggest that the poor children who go there are getting a decent education, let alone an education comparable to that of children who go to school in the suburbs. Even the most extreme proponents of busing admit that it would be years before programs could be set up and financed which would bus a majority of these children out of these central-city areas to better schools in the suburbs. That means that putting primary emphasis on more busing rather than on better education inevitably will leave a lost generation of poor children in the central cities doomed to inferior education. It is time for us to make a national commitment to see that the schools in the central cities be upgraded so that the children who go there will have just as good chance to get quality education as do the children who go to schools in the suburbs.

Broadcast address to the nation, Washington, March 16/ San Francisco Examiner, 3-17:40.

The disappearance of all nonpublic schools in this country would saddle the American taxpayer with an additional $3 billion annually in school operating costs, plus as much as $10 billion in new school construction . . . In short, if the nonpublic schools were ever permitted to go under in the major cities of America, many public schools might very well go with them because they simply couldn't undertake the burden. The fiscal catastrophe would be far from the only consequence. For many Americans, allegiance to their nonpublic community schools is their strongest single tie to city life. If their schools should close, many of these families would abandon the cities for the suburbs. This, in turn, would further worsen the racial isolation of our central cities—a development we must not permit . . . No single system, whether public or private, must ever gain absolute monopoly over the education of our children. For such a system would

(RICHARD M. NIXON)

never reflect the diversity and richness of our national heritage and character.

Before National Catholic Education Association, Philadelphia, April 6/ The New York Times, 4-7:14.

(Saying nonpublic schools should have some form of economic assistance from the government): Nonpublic schools have served this nation and people faithfully and well by maintaining and continuing the religious traditions and beliefs that are so integral a part of our American heritage. I believe that parents of school-age children should be provided the freedom to choose a religious-centered education for their children, if they desire—and I am determined to help guarantee that freedom of choice.

Radio address campaigning for the forthcoming Presidential election, Washington, Oct. 25/ The Washington Post, 10-26:(A)2.

Glen Olds
President, Kent (Ohio) State University

Our purpose (as educators) is to maladjust you to the status quo so you can lead us to new directions. You have made our campuses better with your discontent.

Before Akron University graduates/ Los Angeles Herald-Examiner, 1-7:(A)8.

Allan W. Ostar
Executive director, American Association of State Colleges and Universities

In public schools (of higher learning), budgets are based on enrollments—so fewer students mean smaller budgets. Yet costs tend to remain the same. When a student stays away, you lose not only his tuition but the substantial amount the state would otherwise contribute toward the cost of his education. Dormitories and dining halls are emptier, but debt-service payments must be met on the space the student would occupy, whether he shows or not. This is what is giving the college presidents nightmares.

U.S. News & World Report, 9-4:36.

Paul VI
Pope

Present-day youths are terribly allergic to whatever presents a repressive character, to any unjustified limitation of freedom. Therefore, the reference to moral rules, if it is to be accepted, must always appear, not as a negative element, a limitation, but as a promotion, an elevation, a step forward. Moral optimism must be the climate of these youths, and this undoubtedly is the most difficult task educators are facing today.

At conference of "The School in the Technological Society," Rome, Jan. 8/ The Washington Post, 1-9:(A)30.

Wendell H. Pierce
Executive director, Education Commission of the States

(The U.S. education system), known as the world's finest, is having troubles. We are pouring billions of dollars into education each year, and yet we are not satisfied that our schools are providing the kind of education needed by our students. We call for quality and equality, excellence, accountability and reform in education, but these calls will be merely cries in the wilderness unless both political and educational leaders work in harmony to improve education in every state.

Before Education Commission of the States, Los Angeles, May 17/ Los Angeles Herald-Examiner, 5-17:(A)6.

Alan Pifer
President, Carnegie Corporation

The traditional four-year degree is no longer sacrosanct. Today's students are more sophisticated and better prepared than they used to be, requiring some fundamental rethinking about the content and purposes of higher education.

Los Angeles Times, 2-14:(1)1.

Edwin A. Quain
Former chairman of the board, Georgetown University

Very often in the past six years, universities have been told that they must change to become relevant to the times. Apart from the fact that the word "relevant" has as many meanings as its users have moods, I would like to suggest that any change that is a surrender to force is bound to work harm before very long. To university administrators, I should commend the ideal of the Athenian relay racers who, on horseback, carried torches in a festival of the god, Pan: We must, in universities, make progress, but we must not run so fast that we put out the light!

At Georgetown University commencement/ The Wall Street Journal, 9-14:14.

Ronald Reagan
Governor of California

Frankly, I am not sure that the (teaching) profession has been paying enough attention to the need to get a dollar's worth of value out of every dollar spent on our schools.

Before National Association of Professional Educators, Los Angeles, Feb. 2/ Los Angeles Times, 3-3:(2)3.

Abraham A. Ribicoff
United States Senator, D–Conn.

Unless some government aid is forthcoming, most of our nonpublic schools will eventually disappear. Those that survive will do so by requiring tuitions which only the very wealthy can afford. The result will be that private and parochial schools, rather than being educational options for all, will be sanctuaries for the rich.

June 19/Quote, 8-20:182.

Wilson Riles
California State Superintendent of Public Instruction

If youngsters know that you care and believe they can do the job, and if you expect them to do it, they'll follow. Some teachers don't believe the child can learn, and then the ball game is over. Others think the children can learn but are just to be loved and understood, so they tolerate all kinds of behavior. The best teachers are those who believe children can learn, set standards and then help them reach the standards.

U.S. News & World Report, 5-8:62.

Frank L. Rizzo
Mayor of Philadelphia

. . . school boards are going to have to economize, just as the Mayors' offices have had to economize, and cut the fat. Let's get back to the three Rs. There has been too much fancy stuff that costs a lot of money. When you talk about high-school seniors who can't read or write, you wonder what all this money has accomplished. We moved ahead so fast. They had this new teaching philosophy: We had to do this and this; this is the way it has to be; let the 4-year-old kid tell his father there has to be an exchange of ideas. What there has to be is some old-fashioned virtue, (family) ties, respect for people. We got sidetracked because we had some eggheads who said if you did that, you were a conservative or a racist. Well, their methods don't work. We tried them for 25 years—that is a fair try. Let's go back to some of the old systems that were proven.

Interview, Philadelphia/ Los Angeles Times, 9-5:(2)7.

David Selden
President, American Federation of Teachers

We will not be able to establish an honest and effective national strategy for education until we have set up (a) United

States Office of Education as a quasi-autonomous arm of the government.

At education conference, Washington, April 5/ The New York Times, 4-6:25.

Sidney B. Simon
Professor of Education, University of Massachusetts

The grading system is the most destructive, demeaning and pointless thing in American education. It allows certain administrative conveniences—permitting assistant principals to decide who goes on probation and who can take an honors course—but it doesn't help learning.

Time, 11-27:49.

Page Smith
Author, Historian

The notion that a university is made "great" by squeezing books out of scholars and dismissing those out of whom books have not been squeezed has always seemed to me to be preposterous.

San Francisco Examiner & Chronicle, 9-17:(This World)2.

Samuel R. Spencer, Jr.
President, Davidson (N.C.) College

This country has been blessed with an almost unique dual system of higher education which includes both public and private institutions. The Dartmouth College case of 1819, in which Justice John Marshall upheld the autonomy of the college and refused to allow the Legislature of New Hampshire to take it under state control, guaranteed that strong private institutions, independent of political domination and influence, would grow alongside America's developing state universities. The importance of this dual system runs deep. The existence, side by side, of state and private institutions has contributed a healthy competition and diversity which has raised the level of both. But the fundamental importance of the dual system has to do with freedom itself. The colleges and universities of this country will never be shaped to the mold of any special interest or exploited for political purposes so long as some of them remain truly independent. Do not take their independence for granted. The preservation of it will not be easy.

Before Dilworth Rotary Club, Charlotte, N.C., Aug. 4/ Vital Speeches, 10-1:756.

Edward Stainbrook
Chairman, Department of Human Behavior, University of Southern California School of Medicine

Schools should be concerned with teaching how to get along with people, not just instruction in subjects and skills. And that includes medical schools. I was a psychiatrist for a while, until I got impatient with specialization and convinced of the need for all medical students to learn something about human beings.

Before wives of members attending American Medical Association convention, San Francisco, June 20/ San Francisco Examiner, 6-21:23.

Robert E. Stoltz
Southern regional director, College Entrance Examination Board

Education is in trouble, as much trouble as I have seen since I have been in education; and I don't think this trouble is a short-term affair. The general public distrusts educators and manifests declining confidence in those who administer its educational institutions, both secondary and higher. This lack of confidence will not disappear in the near future and will probably increase.

Before American Association of Collegiate Registrars and Admissions Officers, Durham, N.C./ The Wall Street Journal, 2-17:12.

Daniel Taylor
West Virginia
Superintendent of Education

We're on the verge of more significant movement in educational reform than at any time in this century. A demand for alternatives to the present system is growing. There has been an awful lot of rhetoric about change, but now we're accepting the fact that there *has* to be change.

U.S. News & World Report, 5-8:59.

Margaret Thatcher
Minister of Education of the United Kingdom

I have sometimes thought that some extreme advocates of equality (in education) would be happy even if all the children were in bad schools so long as they were all equally bad. I believe there is still a place for select schools of excellence.

Time, 2-28:48.

Charles W. Toth
Associate Professor of History, University of Puerto Rico

A distinguished professor remarked a few years ago that the campus (of the University of California) at Berkeley was now a more dangerous place, but at least it was more interesting. This is nonsense. A university campus should always be interesting, but it should never be a dangerous place . . . The university should always remain essentially a house of studies, and the suggestion by some critics that this is a respectable but archaic vision is nothing less than the product of an ill-concieved view of the function of higher education. To think, to write, to teach—not preach; to talk—not yell, are all major elements of a university atmosphere. When controlled activism is allowed to escalate to agitation and violence, then the expression of a point of view can no longer manifest itself. At this point, the ordinary processes of democratic institutions are by-passed and finally discredited.

Before National Honor Society chapters of the Caribbean Consolidated Schools, San Juan, May 30/ Vital Speeches, 7-15:605.

Stephen Trachenberg
Dean of university affairs, Boston University

(On firms that sell ghost-written term papers to students): Perhaps a crude justice will come when a term-paper executive looks up from the operating table to see one of his better customers approaching dressed in surgeon's gown, scalpel in hand.

Plainview (Tex.) Daily Herald, 6-11:(A)6.

Arnold Weber
Professor of Urban and Labor Economics, University of Chicago; Former Executive Director, Federal Cost of Living Council; Former Associate Director, Federal Office of Management and Budget

A good day in government goes like this: You get to your office at 7 or 7:30—no later than 8. You have 30 phone calls, eight meetings, seven decisions—involving millions of dollars—one emergency, where you think you react with at least minimal confidence. Then you go home and look forward to the next day when there will be a Congressional hearing. A good day for a professor, however, goes like this: You come in no earlier than 9, read *The New York Times* and have coffee. There are no classes scheduled, you see one student, and write five pages of an article. Then you go home and read a book you've always wanted to read—"to broaden yourself"—and you know that tomorrow you can do the same thing again if you want to.

The National Observer, 10-28:13.

William C. Westmoreland
General and Chief of Staff, United States Army

It is unfortunate but true that the ROTC, its programs and facilities, have in

(WILLIAM C. WESTMORELAND)

recent years been a lightning rod, a proxy target, for campus dissent. In the name of peace and harmony, its buildings have been burned, its classrooms destroyed, its drills interrupted. There is no doubt that those bent on destruction or removal of the ROTC from our campuses misunderstood its true contribution to American university education. In their efforts to show their dissatisfaction with U.S. foreign policy, ROTC has provided them with a convenient scapegoat.

At Norwich University commencement, Northfield, Vt., May 20/ The Dallas Times Herald, 5-21:(A)29.

Jack K. Williams
President,
Texas A&M University

We must give our students the mental equipment with which they may think clearly as well as feel deeply.

The Dallas Times Herald, 3-26:(Education)1.

The Environment

Spiro T. Agnew
Vice President of the United States

(Supporting the trans-Alaska oil pipeline): Here in Alaska, men still deal with nature on a day-to-day basis; and although you live with the kind of natural beauty the rest of us only dream about, you are constantly aware that nature is not necessarily benign. And you disagree with the notion that nearly all Alaska should remain one huge untouched natural park, its resources undeveloped, its treasures untapped. That is a pleasant romantic dream without reference to reality. That would result in stagnation; and stagnation is the antithesis of the frontier spirit. There is a spirit directly opposed to your pioneer spirit (in the states to the south). It is a spirit of anti-progress; a feeling that, instead of continuing to push toward new frontiers, we should stand pat or even retreat. Today many Americans seem preoccupied with the possible negative results of our actions instead of the actual positive results.

At Republican luncheon, Fairbanks, Alaska, July 24/ The New York Times, 7-25:18.

Wayne N. Aspinall
United States Representative, D–Colo.

(People) want to have their cake and eat it too. They want their three automobiles, their all-electric kitchen, their jet planes; but they don't want to pay the price (of possible harm to the environment). They want the energy, but they want it to come from "out there somewhere."

The New York Times, 3-19:(4)9.

Carl E. Bagge
President, National Coal Association

. . . I believe the nation must reshape its energy policies to meet the demands of both the environment and the marketplace. But I am convinced that neither the government nor the public can be pressured into wisdom. The rational way to achieve a balance between energy use and environmental protection is through colloquy, not controversy. No real national purpose will be served by hardening opposing views into sporadic confrontations where points are scored not so much against the other side as against the public spectators. The extremes in this issue are separated not only by philosophy but time. Energy producers who would claim baronial rights to develop resources with no regard for the environment are living in the dead past; and environmental enthusiasts who think the way back to Eden is to bypass energy expansion are living in an illusory future. I am not about to justify the bad old ways of energy pioneering, except to say that they must have seemed to many people a good idea at the time—and hindsight is a function of the future. But neither can I agree with the new dictum of the prominent environmentalist who told a Congressional hearing last year, "At every stage of energy production and use, unacceptable environmental degradation occurs." That statement is a clear challenge for the public to choose sides—energy or the environment, the tiger or the lady. But in less-dramatic terms, others keep pointing out that the essential force in improving the natural environment—not to mention the quality of human existence—is progressive technology based on adequate energy. Without that we cannot remove our own or nature's litter, recycle our resources or rebuild our cities.

Lecture, Colby College, Waterville, Maine, March 2/ Vital Speeches, 4-1:374.

Howard H. Baker, Jr.
United States Senator, R–Tenn.

If we cannot swim in our lakes and rivers, if we cannot breathe the air God has given us, what other comforts can life offer us?

Before the Senate, Washington, Oct. 18/ Los Angeles Times, 10-19:(1)12.

V. W. Bearinger
Vice president, science and engineering, Honeywell, Inc.

All of our current approaches to solving our energy problems either spend irreplaceable resources at an alarming rate or produce increasingly intolerable amounts of pollution. Yet there is a source of pollution-free power available today in solar energy. If one per cent of the solar energy falling on the Sahara Desert were converted to electrical power, it would supply the tremendous amount of energy we estimate the world will need in the year 2000. Put another way, the solar energy falling on the state of New York is double the energy being obtained today from the world's present production of fossil fuel—that is, coal and oil. Technical breakthroughs are not needed to solve this problem—the means to convert solar energy to electrical power is here today. The problem is an economic one. We must be willing to invest the capital required for energy-conversion equipment if we are to obtain pollution-free power . . . How much and how soon will we be willing to pay the cost for the better health and the aesthetic values to be obtained from a cleaner atmosphere? The point here is that technology alone will not overcome our basic problems of energy consumption—or the problems of mass transportation, housing, pollution control, medical care, crime prevention and public health. We must concern ourselves not so much with technology as with problem-solving.

Before the Washington Forum/ The Wall Street Journal, 6-6:20.

Phillip Berry
Former president, Sierra Club

Some of the most important decisions affecting the environment are not made by the government or by the people, but rather by the men who wield corporate power.

Before Democratic National Convention Platform subcommittee, San Francisco, June 12/San Francisco Examiner, 6-13:8.

Georg Borgstrom
Professor of Food Science and Geography, Michigan State University

. . . there is a dynamic relationship between food and population. Bringing more food to undernourished people means more people; it means acceleration of growth because it reduces infant mortality. The classic example is China, which trebled its population in the 18th century largely on the basis of the introduction of corn and the potato. To increase food production without trying very strictly to control population is catastrophic.

Interview/Los Angeles Times, 4-23:(G)3.

Phillip Burton
United States Representative, D–Calif.

(Advocating the establishment of a Golden Gate National Recreation Area in Marin County, Calif., near San Francisco): If we in the Congress do not act, the majestic area where sea and bay and land meet in a glorious symphony of nature will be doomed . . . What we are seeking to preserve is the dramatic coastal seashore of Marin County, with its grassy valleys and steep cliffs where the ocean thunders in its first meeting with the land after a (5,000-mile) journey from Asia. Here the sky is clear, the wind clean and the fog comes in the evening in gray clouds reflecting the orange sun setting across the Pacific Ocean. Here a man can walk and be lost in peace, hearing the sea, feeling the wind and touching the land.

Before House Subcommittee on Parks and Recreation, Washington, May 11/ San Francisco Examiner, 5-11:11.

Arthur W. Busch
Southwest Regional Director, Environmental Protection Agency of the United States

Pollution comes from people working, but we have to keep them working to get money to fight pollution.

At Southern Methodist University, Jan. 26/ The Dallas Times Herald, 1-27:(A)6.

Earl L. Butz
Secretary of Agriculture of the United States

(Arguing against the banning of farm chemicals): We can go to organic agriculture if we must, and there are those in this country that would like to drive us back. But before we do that, somebody must decide which 50 million Americans we'll let starve.

San Francisco Examiner, 2-22:32.

(On those who want to eliminate pesticides from agriculture): When . . . people talk about returning to nature, I want to know how far back they want to return. The reason for much of that attitude is that two-thirds of us in America are so young we never had the experience of biting into a wormy apple, looking at the worm hole and wondering, "Is it in there yet, or did I get him?" We think the God of Nature made a nice, red, plump, appetizing apple. God puts the worm in the apple, and man takes it out; two-thirds are so young that we do not appreciate it. He puts the termite in the timber and parasite in the pig, and man takes them out. The problem of agriculture is to convince the two-thirds of us who are under 30 that we get a nice, plump, juicy apple only because we disturb the ecology of nature.

Before Appropriations Subcommittee, Washington, Feb. 22/ The Washington Post, 5-28:(E)6.

Frederick J. Clarke
Lieutenant General and Chief of Engineers, United States Army

I don't see any way to stop population growth and economic growth, and I don't consider it our job to try to stop them; I think they're inevitable for the foreseeable future. The real conflict is the fact that we accept that growth places legitimate demands on resources, whereas there are a good many in the environment movement who question the validity of these demands and of growth itself.

The New York Times, 2-20:(1)1.

Barry Commoner
Professor of Biology, Washington University, St. Louis

The root cause of the (pollution) crisis is not to be found in how men interact with nature, but in how they interact with each other. In sum, a peace among men must precede the peace with nature.

News conference, Beverly Hills, Calif., Nov. 29/ Los Angeles Herald-Examiner, 11-30:(A)11.

Jacques-Yves Cousteau
Oceanographer

We are alone around the sun. Our water, our fragile blood, is contaminated . . . There is no other planet to retreat to in an emergency . . . We must stop and reverse the destruction of the earth by ignorance, selfishness and contempt.

Charter Day address, University of California, Berkeley, April 6/ San Francisco Examiner, 4-7:3.

If the governments of the various (world) states do not intervene in an adequate way, the oceans in the next 50 years will . . . be a sea without life, and humanity will not be able to survive the death of

(JACQUES-YVES COUSTEAU)

the ocean. Today there is not a single sea which is not affected by pollution . . . and it becomes increasingly difficult to stop the slow but inexorable end toward which we are heading.

News conference, Rome/ The Christian Science Monitor, 7-17:3.

Philip M. Crane
United States Representative, R–Ill.

To listen to some of the more paranoid allegations against the business community, one would almost suppose that the businessman lives in another world than our own. The theatre of the absurd produced by some of our crisis-mongers accuses the businessman of a calloused unconcern for the air we breathe, the water we drink and recreate in, our wildlife, our purple mountains and our fruited plains. Worse than the businessman's alleged unconcern is the suggestion that he actively promotes pollution of the environment in a reckless pursuit of self. The self-righteous have ever been guilty of overlooking human imperfection. Base motives are substituted for ignorance and human frailty. Presumably, such businessmen have found another environment for themselves and their children to live in.

Before the House, Washington/ The Wall Street Journal, 8-2:8.

While a legitimate concern, our environment will not be saved by the Water Quality Control Act of 1972 passed by the House, nor by the same version of this legislation unanimously passed by the Senate. In the House, there were only 14 nay votes. The stated objective of the bill is to give the country 100 per cent clean water by 1985. Yet, according to expert testimony before Committee, the estimated cost of achieving 100 per cent clean water by 1985 is $2.3 trillion. This $2.3 trillion just happens to be more than the entire world's gross national product. So quite obviously we are not going to be spending that amount of money to get 100 per cent clean water by 1985. Yet no one can fault the objective of the bill; we would all like to have 100 per cent clean water tomorrow. When a bill comes up for final passage, you are given the option of voting yes, or no. In this case, you are presumably for dirty water if you vote against "clean water" legislation. But these questions are never either/or. To believe they are is a logical fallacy; other alternatives do exist. Yet, I talked to many responsible Congressmen who were writhing in anguish over this dilemma. They were fearful of "national opinion," the Friends of the Earth and those sitting in the press gallery all looking down to see who was in favor of dirty water. In passing this kind of legislation, the politicians have called their own integrity and credibility into question. In response to a certain amount of public clamor and high-minded goals, they have plowed ahead and passed laws that cannot be realized. There is not a member in that House who is prepared to consider the economic consequences of a $2.3 trillion price tag by 1985. Can you imagine the necessary increase in taxes for a bill even approaching such a price tag?

At Hillsdale (Mich.) College/ The Wall Street Journal, 9-27:18.

Earl of Cromer
British Ambassador to the United States

The most serious problems which are going to face us (the world) over the next decade will be such things as how to bring explosive population growth under control; how to cope with the rapid depletion of the total stock of natural resources; how to cope with the problems of the pollution of the environment. We shall need to know how to apply new technological advances to the greater benefit of mankind. I believe human resourcefulness is such that we shall be able to find solutions. Perhaps we have made too much an ideal of growth; and in the process, we have not paid enough attention to the quality of life and the improvement of societies.

At dinner of Dallas Council on World Affairs, Dallas Chamber of Commerce and Dallas branch, English Speaking Union, March 23/ The Dallas Times Herald, 3-24:(A)13.

Paul R. Ehrlich
Professor of Biology, Stanford University

The overdeveloped countries are destroying the world, and they are also setting a model for the rest of the world . . . We have leaders in underdeveloped countries now feeling that, if they can get smoggy cities, it is a great sign of success.

At University of San Francisco, Feb. 20/ San Francisco Examiner, 2-21:22.

You can't solve the world's environment with biting the bullet and without facing very, very tough things like the redistribution of wealth, how the world's trade system operates, the things the United States is doing to the ecology of Vietnam, the activities of the predator nations—the U.S., Western Europe, the Soviet Union—trying to extract high-grade resources from underdeveloped countries. If we're going to save the globe, we're going to have to have international policy planning.

Interview, Palo Alto, Calif./ Los Angeles Herald-Examiner, 6-18:(A)15.

Elizabeth II
Queen of England

(Warning against neglecting the environment in a technological age): You cannot feed the beauty of the countryside into a computer, and statistics cannot by themselves make clean air, sparkling rivers or a contented community.

Yugoslavia/Los Angeles Times, 10-19:(1)2.

James C. Fletcher
Administrator, National Aeronautics and Space Administration

I don't think we would have had quite so much concern for earth's environment without the *Apollo* (space mission) pictures showing our world isolated in space. You can't help but be a little concerned when you see earth from space. It's a beautiful planet, all blue, standing out in space. There's nothing else like it in the solar system. It's the only one we've got, and we'd better take care of it.

Interview, Washington/ The Christian Science Monitor, 1-22:7.

Indira Gandhi
Prime Minister of India

The inherent conflict is not between conservation and development but between environment and the reckless exploitation of man and earth in the name of efficiency. Industrial civilization has promoted the concept of the efficient man, he whose entire energies are concentrated on producing more in a given unit of time from a given unit of manpower. Groups who are less competitive and less efficient are regarded as lesser breeds—for example, the older civilizations, the black and brown peoples, women . . . Obsolescence is built into production, and efficiency is based on the creation of goods which are not really needed and cannot be disposed of when discarded.

At United Nations Conference on the Human Environment, Stockholm, June 14/The Washington Post, 6-15:(A)22.

Carl A. Gerstacker
Chairman, Dow Chemical Company

I do believe with a passion in the profit motive. And I really believe that, if we hitch the profit motive to some of our problems, we will get them solved. Pollution-control will continue on forever if we see it simply as a drag on earnings, as a necessary nuisance, classified as overhead. If we see the *opportunity* in pollution and exploit that opportunity to the hilt, then we will help our earnings and we will solve our pollution problems, and we will solve

(CARL A. GERSTACKER)

the nation's pollution problems. But we need that profit incentive. Doing something simply because it's good citizenship is not enough. It doesn't really motivate.

Before Economic Club of Detroit, Feb. 22/Vital Speeches, 4-1:370.

Richard C. Gerstenberg
Chairman,
General Motors Corporation

•

As for air pollution, the myth-spinners continue to contend that more than 60 per cent of the nation's air-pollution problem is caused by automotive emissions. Estimates vary on this: The industry's scientists put the role of the automobile, based on the relative health effects of pollutants in the atmosphere, at about 10 per cent; and governmental estimates range from 15 per cent to 30 per cent for the nation as a whole. The Federal Environmental Quality Council has reported to Congress that automotive air pollution is declining, even though air pollution as a whole—with the exception of municipal incineration—is still increasing. We in the industry have acknowledged our moral as well as our practical obligation to make cars as safe and clean as possible. We are, however, deeply concerned about "regulatory overkill," about the billions that must be spent annually to achieve at best only very small percentages of improvements in highway safety and air quality.

Before Industrial Executives Club, Flint, Mich., March 29/ Vital Speeches, 5-1:431.

Eugene Guccione
Metallurgical editor, "The Engineering and Mining Journal"

According to certain misinformed environmentalists, construction of power-generating plants must be stopped in view of the air pollution crisis. But there is no such thing as an air pollution crisis—as thousands of air-quality tests done for the past 40 years by government and private institutions indicate. Concentration of particulates has gone down more than 80 per cent during the past 40 years. And, in this century, no increase has been found in the global atmospheric concentration of such pollutants as carbon monoxide, sulphur dioxide, nitrogen dioxide, hydrocarbons and lead.

Before Graduate School of Business Administration, Brigham Young University, April 10/The New York Times, 5-7:(3)14.

Frederick Gutheim
Architectural historian

In a way, they (urban parks) are the victims of their success. They mirror such national problems as crime, delinquency, overcrowding, drugs, traffic and environmental pollution. The result is an extensive invasion of chain-link fences, black-topped play areas, bright illumination, highways and parking. These piecemeal responses by hard-driven park administrators can eventually destroy the original creations of a century ago.

Los Angeles Times, 3-23:(8)8.

C. Howard Hardesty
Executive vice president,
Continental Oil Company

The simple fact is that we are spoiled rotten. Except for our family, sacrifices don't come easy to any of us. We want low-cost, low-sulphur fuel oil, but we don't want ships, pipelines, terminals or refineries on our shores. We want adequate supplies of domestic oil and gas, but we don't want to explore the potentiality of off-shore areas. We want more imports of crude oil, but we don't want to give foreign nations a stranglehold on our economy. We want more natural gas, but we will not let market forces set real values. We want more coal but don't want surface mining and prohibit coal's use by sulphur restrictions. We demand adequate supplies of electricty but resist setting of nuclear plants. We want to use more oil more efficiently but rush out to buy 8-mile-per-gallon automobile monsters . . . At this point in time, our environmental concerns are more deeply rooted than our energy concerns. So far, we are not willing to accept the fact that some trade-offs, some compromises will be needed to keep these inconsistencies from destroying our way of life.

Chicago, Nov. 13/
The New York Times, 11-14:65

Fred L. Hartley
President, Union Oil Company

I don't know who's behind the Sierra Club, but it obviously isn't people of good-will, not sincere environmentalists. Those same people use energy. You show me an environmentalist who walks—really walks, doesn't just put on a sweat-suit on Sunday morning—and I'll recognize this man as a contributor to the elimination of pollution. But they're all hypocrites. Saying you're against the problem isn't the solution. The solution is finding the science and technology and then implementing it . . . Now, if we weren't doing anything about pollution, the environmentalists would have a perfect right to challenge us for just sitting on our hands. But we are. We've improved in so many ways, you wouldn't believe the list.

Interview, Los Angeles/
Los Angeles Times, 2-20:(West)30.

Ken Hechler
United States Representative, D–W.Va.

I have seen what havoc and obliteration is left in the wake of strip mining. It has ripped the guts out of our mountains, polluted our streams with acid and silt, uprooted our trees and forests, devastated the land, seriously disturbed or destroyed wildlife habitat, left miles of ugly highwalls, ruined the water supply in many areas and left a trail of utter despair for many honest and hard-working people.

Before the House, Washington,
Oct. 11/The New York Times, 10-15:(1)34.

Chet Holifield
United States Representative, D–Calif.

What this country needs to dramatize our energy crisis is a good twenty-four-hour blackout.

The Washington Post, 11-30:(A)1.

Frank N. Ikard
President,
American Petroleum Institute

Today, in the United States alone, demand for energy is growing at tremendous speed. Look at what our energy supports: 120 million cars and trucks on the road, 3,000 jet aircraft in the skies daily, 12 million factories and office buildings, 60 million homes. Last year we used almost 6 billion barrels of oil, 500 million tons of coal, 22 trillion cubic feet of natural gas and 1,600 tons of fissionable uranium to fuel this nation. The days of cheap energy —when fuel was a bargain and taken for granted in every household and in every factory—are gone forever. And perhaps fortunately so, in the interest of our future discipline as a nation. Also, the air and water are no longer free channels for the dispersal of wastes. There is a great need in America for a carefully worked out set of rules to guide all industries and all citizens in the uses of energy, which becomes more valuable to us every day.

At Economic Education Workshop,
Arkansas State University,
July 24/Vital Speeches, 9-15:730.

James J. Kilpatrick
Political columnist

I often have thought that one day the accumulating madness of man will be manifested in one ultimate blow-up destroying the whole earth and reducing our planet to a cinder spinning through space. Then, after 10,000 years, archeologists from a distant galaxy will stumble across this curious planet and pause to explore a dead civilization that plainly had once contained great cities linked by broad highways.

(JAMES J. KILPATRICK)

Poking amid the ruins along these roads, they would find millions of small glass totems still bearing what the visitors would assume to be a religious or philosophical statement of man's transitory existence upon this earth: "No deposit, no return." Surely we can do better.

Television commentary, "Spectrum," Columbia Broadcasting System/ The National Observer, 8-26:13.

Jerome Kretchmer
Environmental Protection Administrator, City of New York

I took them (a class he teaches) out to the (garbage) landfill, and there was nothing so overwhelming as standing there a couple of hours and watching 650-ton barges loaded with New York City's refuse being unloaded at the rate of 14,000 tons a day and watch it get carried out a mile, two miles, to the landfill site and see it get dumped and watch these wagons come back . . . you have the feeling it is never-ending; you have the sense you are never going to get rid of it and that no systems are being designed to create less of it.

San Francisco Examiner & Chronicle, 5-21:(This World)27.

Manfred Kroger
Food scientist, Pennsylvania State University

The next decade will find beverages sold in edible cans, candy bars dispensed in edible wrappers and many other products marketed in containers which will not add to waste and pollution.

University Park, Pa./ The Dallas Times Herald, 4-2:(A)22.

Ralph E. Lapp
Nobel Prize-winning physicist

(On possible energy shortages due to environmental considerations): I believe there is severe danger of environmental backlash . . . If a worker in Illinois comes home from the factory and finds his can of beer warm and the television off, he's going to have different feelings about environmentalists. His attitude will be, "What do I care about the reproductive habits of certain fish in the Mississippi? Turn the (power) plant on."

April 12/The Washington Post, 4-13:(A)2.

Charles A. Lindbergh
Former aviator

I don't want to be a member of a generation that allows the loss of fauna and flora that has been developed through epochs. It is in our generation that the world has become vulnerable to disruption. Therefore we face the need for action unparalleled in the past.

Interview, Canberra, Australia/ Los Angeles Times, 8-21:(1)2.

Patrick L. Lucey
Governor of Wisconsin

Because our earth obviously does not contain unlimited supplies of coal and other fossilized forms of energy, and because we are already depleting our resources at a rapid rate, an alternative to the continued use of these forms of energy generating must be used. Nuclear energy appears to be the answer to meeting the demands of a growing population for necessary electrical power far into the future.

The Christian Science Monitor, 5-24:7.

Michael McCloskey
Executive director, Sierra Club

. . . 1971 was not a good year for the environment. The opposition has stiffened, and politicians are no longer afraid to vote against us. We don't have the public involvement we had a year ago. The Earth Day euphoria has worn off. The problems are no longer dramatic and simple. It's no longer enough to be against pollution, for example. We have had to get down to the morass of endless regulations, hearings and technical details. This can't be avoided, but it's hard to keep everybody aboard and plugged in. The basic public support is still there; but people who were expecting miracles have dropped out, and the hard work has begun. You might say 1971 was the year the environmental movement had to face reality.

Interview, San Francisco/ San Francisco Examiner & Chronicle, 1-2:(This World)28.

Charles B. McCoy
Chairman and president, E. I. Du Pont de Nemours and Company

(On the theory that further economic and industrial growth is impermissible in order to preserve the environment): You couldn't take our civilization the way it has developed and with the system of values and the incentives that people respond to and now—or even a couple of decades from now—put it on a no-growth basis. Damn, I don't know how. You would have to muzzle an awful lot of people. You would get a hell of a strong dictatorship. The strongest guys would take over. You would have to go to a much more rigid society, a Chinese situation. I don't know how in the world you would do it. Any organization, as soon as it stops growing—depending on how you define growth—begins to die . . . If you consider that way down the line somewhere there has to be a levelling out of population just because there is not enough air, water or space to support an infinite number of people, I can agree with that. There is a finite amount of all resources available on the globe. We've skimmed the cream off in most cases, taking the easiest coal, the easiest copper, the easiest iron ore. In time, you either go to lower grades of these materials or you recycle the materials you have already taken from the earth. I think market forces will bring that around in an orderly way. The most conspicuous candidates for recycling are the piles of junked autos you see around the country. Roughly speaking, a pile of junked autos will produce a pile of new autos. Or a new bridge some place.

Interview, Wilmington, Del./ Los Angeles Times, 2-25:(2)7.

George S. McGovern
United States Senator, D–S.D.; Democratic Presidential nominee

. . . to make progress in cleaning up our environment, we must be willing to face down industrial polluters. And that is a cost—a political cost—that (President) Nixon, the natural friend of big business, is not willing to incur.

Washington, Aug. 12/ The Dallas Times Herald, 8-13:(A)30.

Margaret Mead
Anthropologist

This (concern for the environment) is a revolution in thought fully comparable to the Copernican revolution by which, four centuries ago, men were compelled to revise their whole sense of the earth's place in the cosmos. Today we are challenged to recognize as great a change in our concept of man's place in the biosphere. Our survival in a world that continues to be worth inhabiting depends upon translating this new perception into relevant principles and concrete action.

At United Nations Conference on the Human Environment, Stockholm/ The New York Times, 6-18:(4)7.

Every baby born in the United States is more costly to the world because it will use up more resources and cause more pollution (than babies in undeveloped nations). Countries with highest standards of living endanger the world more . . .

News conference, San Francisco/ Los Angeles Times, 8-1:(4)4.

Arjay Miller
Dean, School of Business Administration, Stanford University; Former president, Ford Motor Company

People have demanded a small, low-pollutant automobile; and we are now fast ap-

(ARJAY MILLER)

proaching that goal. We can do more to clean up our environment through the recycling of cans, bottles and waste paper. We can clean up our lakes and other waterways . . . We (can) relieve congestion in our cities and make better housing available for more people. These are not beyond our grasp; and we must spend more time and effort in finding ways to get them done, either acting alone or in conjunction with government, rather than in explaining why they can't be done.

At White House Conference on the Industrial World Ahead, Washington, Feb. 7/ The Dallas Times Herald, 2-8:(A)5.

Rogers C. B. Morton
Secretary of the Interior of the United States

The environmentalists tell us that we cannot go on using our natural resources as we are . . . they are right. Those responsible for meeting our nation's needs for goods and services tell us we cannot go back where we came from . . . and they are right, too. And I say, we cannot stay where we presently are, either; and I think I am right!

Quote, 6-11:562.

Edmund S. Muskie
United States Senator, D–Maine

Again and again, President Nixon has sacrificed environmental protection in the wake of pressure from corporate lobbyists. Again and again, he has allowed those who make a profit from pollution to dictate his policy on pollution control . . . It is all part of a pattern—a pattern of influence-peddling and closed-door deals that have led millions of Americans to believe that this Administration is willing to trade their future for a campaign contribution. What we face is not just a failure to fund the fight against pollution; the President has also failed to enforce conservation bills he himself signed into law.

Before Wisconsin Resource Conservation Council, Madison, March 25/ San Francisco Examiner & Chronicle, 3-26:(A)13.

Richard M. Nixon
President of the United States

The starting point of environmental quality is in the hearts and minds of the people. Unless the people have a deep commitment to new values and a clear understanding of the new problems, all our laws and programs and spending will avail little.

Quote, 10-1:314.

Gunnar A. Peterson
Executive director, Chicago-area Open Lands Project

We have to think in terms of becoming a lower energy-use society. Americans have to face the possibility of cutting back to a single car, riding more bicycles and having fewer air conditioners. Energy resources need to be shared on a worldwide basis, particularly with developing nations. Otherwise, there is no hope that these underdeveloped countries can ever improve their standard of living.

At environmental hearings held by U.S. Secretary of State's office, Chicago/The Christian Science Monitor, 3-20:4.

Peter G. Peterson
Secretary of Commerce of the United States

There is a kind of dream-world quality in the public's perception of what it will take to clean up the environment. For example, over 40 per cent in a recent public-opinion survey said they would not be willing to pay *anything* for cleaning up the environment. Yet everyone wants a clean environment. They want all the benefits but none of the costs . . . Up to now, as a nation, we have not begun to reconcile the conflicts between environmental and economic concerns. It is a dialogue of the deaf. The ecologist and the economist are talking right past each other . . . The present national debate on the environment is one that has produced an unfortunate polarization. If you are *for* the environment, then you have to be *against* economic growth; and conversely, if you are for economic growth, then you are automatically assumed to be against the environment. That kind of thinking must stop. A partnership must be formed, a kind of team spirit developed, that will allow an objective search for answers to begin in earnest.

At National Environmental Information Symposium of U.S. Environmental Protection Agency/ The National Observer, 12-2:13.

John B. M. Place
President, Anaconda Company

Our ability to meet foreign competition is now being further hampered by our efforts to meet new environmental standards. Costs for building and operating environmental-quality systems have become an important factor in raising the costs of American metal producers. Unfortunately, many decisions in this area are being made for the wrong reasons, often out of ill-considered and unnecessary emotionalism . . . The over-all adverse effect on the American economy, and on our efforts to ensure a supply of minerals and energy, will continue to grow under pressure from developing nations. They are afraid that expensive pollution controls may be out of their reach, but they are anxious to industrialize as a means of eliminating poverty. I am not advocating degradation of the environment. My company is continuing its commitment to solving the problems of pollution control and to developing and installing workable environmental-quality systems. But I am saying that we must look clearly at all the implications of programs that can affect the competitive position of American industry.

Before Rocky Mountain Mineral Law Foundation, Missoula, Mont./ The New York Times, 8-6:(3)12.

Ronald Reagan
Governor of California

We must consider the adverse environmental impact of every major activity in our society and find reasonable, workable ways to minimize that impact, but without at the same time bringing economic development to a standstill . . . Too often, some in the communications media searching for the sensational will accept without challenge any figure, any horror story that will add to the drama until some of us find ourselves reading letters from frightened children who believe they will smother in poisoned air before they finish school or live in a desert of stumps with all the forests gone the way of the dinosaurs.

Before Joint Service Club, Long Beach, Calif., April 7/ San Francisco Examiner, 4-7:9.

Dwight F. Rettie
Executive director, National Recreation and Park Association

(Recreation, parks and leisure activities) can no longer be regarded as a frill and a luxury. They are a vital human necessity that touches a root cause of much personal and civic discontent. (They) must be considered in dealing with such symptoms of the identity crisis as drug abuse, student unrest, delinquency and crime, the resentments of our production workers and the broad distrust of public and private institutions.

Washington/ The Washington Post, 7-17:(A)2.

R. S. Reynolds, Jr.
Chairman and president, Reynolds Metals Company

The best-kept secret in America today is that we are moving forward on a legislated

(R. S. REYNOLDS, JR.)

rapid timetable to prevent the ecological doom the pessimists keep predicting. Actually, it's too rapid a timetable, one conjured up and legislated in a false crisis atmosphere. Air and water quality standards have been set on both a national and local basis that are far more stringent than needed, in most localities, for public health and safety. Arbitrary deadlines are forcing industry into pell-mell installations of costly, improvised solutions based on today's technology. What we need is more time to develop better technology . . . Probably the second-best-kept secret is the tremendous price of the environmental overkill we are asked to achieve by the deadlines of the mid-1970s and early 1980s. I fear it may prove too heavy a price, reducing the living standards of our people and pre-empting a good deal of national income that might be better spent on other social needs . . . If we restore a sense of balance and proportion to the ecological crusade, we can achieve a total environment that delivers everything our people want—cleanliness, recreation and culture, efficiency, prosperity and equality of opportunity for all.

Before Tennessee River Valley Association, Huntsville, Ala., Oct. 24/ Vital Speeches, 12-15:154,156.

Hyman G. Rickover
Vice Admiral, United States Navy; Director, Division of Naval Reactors, Atomic Energy Commission of the United States

(Saying natural fuels are being exhausted at a dangerously swift rate): In 1850 . . . fossil fuels supplied 5 per cent of the world's energy; men and animals, 94 per cent. By 1950, the percentages had reversed themselves—93 per cent coming from coal, oil and natural gas, 1 per cent from water power and only 6 per cent from the labor of men and animals. The fossil-fuel age may well prove to have been one of the briefest major epochs in man's long history on earth.

Before House Interior Committee, Washington/ The Dallas Times Herald, 4-20:(A)24.

Paul G. Rogers
United States Representative, D–Fla.

Noise from transportation has created acoustical slums in almost every major city in our nation.

San Francisco Examiner, 3-1:2.

William D. Ruckelshaus
Administrator, Environmental Protection Agency of the United States

Since everybody is for clean air, pure water and unspoiled land, the environment is a tempting bauble for any aspiring politician. It is tempting to propose simple solutions.

Human Events, 1-29:4.

Thomas Jefferson should be re-read today as we take stock of what we have done and left undone in the almost 200 year-old American experiment. Speculating once upon the role of man and his relation to the earth, he said: "The earth belongs always to the living generation. They may manage it then, and what proceeds from it, as they please during their usufruct." The concept of "doing as we please" has always appealed to us Americans. We expect to live where we please, think as we please, drive where we please. But now we see consequences of mindless license which Jefferson's generation could not even imagine, except on a small scale. We know that man's works can threaten the air, the oceans and even the land itself. But note that term "usufruct." Under an agreement of usufruct, a tenant may use the fruit or the orchard and the land, but he is bound to preserve the basic resources as they were received. He has the use of the land in his own time, but must pass it on without damage. So Jefferson saw all generations merely as tenants for a time. Behind this concept of freedom to do as you please was an implicit call for conserving resources and handing them on to the next generation in perpetual husbandry.

Before General Assembly of Virginia, Williamsburg/The Wall Street Journal, 3-6:8.

Only once in a century do you come across an issue which unites men of all races, all social classes, all political beliefs. In the brief span of a year or two, the condition of our physical environment has become such an issue. There is also the potential in this issue to rip hell out of society.

Newsweek, 6-12:46.

If we viewed success in the past as a constant increase in the Gross National Product, that may in fact be a net decrease rather than increase in the quality of life in the country. If a power plant is constructed and pours out sulfur oxide, the sale of the power from that company to the consumer is part of the GNP. And yet sulfur oxides . . . may cause health problems, chronic or acute. The doctor bills that are paid, and hospital bills, are also part of the GNP. So I think they ought to be subtracted from the GNP, to give us a Net National Product, or a quality-of-life measurement.

Interview/ Los Angeles Times, 6-29:(2)7.

Of course we're (the EPA) political. Most governmental activities are accommodations of conflicting interests. What you get when you have all the facts on the table is a political judgment of what is workable. But that doesn't mean we're not enforcing the laws. It has nothing to do with partisan politics or caving in to special-interest groups. The criterion is what is in the public interest. A policeman, if he's any good, doesn't deal with a truant the same way he does with a bank robber. A program that will arouse a storm of public resentment defeats the objective. Those are the kind of "political" decisions we have to make.

Interview, Washington/ The New York Times, 8-6:(3)5.

Arthur Schulert
Former biochemist, Vanderbilt University; Founder, Environmental Science and Engineering Corporation

Environmental pollution is a matter of great concern, but not for panic. Pollution is the inevitable consequence of people and even some of their most desirable activities. We must better understand and control pollution, but we can never completely eliminate it.

Mt. Juliet, Tenn./ The New York Times, 5-9:59.

Hugh Scott
United States Senator, R–Pa.

If you were in my position, you would hear many complaints nowadays from industrialists as to whether they can find the money with which to finance anti-emission and anti-pollution legislation. I think we have got to be within the bounds of realism, within the bounds of what can be achieved in a given year and over a given period. Some of the ecological statements will not hold water, if I may use the phrase.

TV-radio interview, Washington/ "Meet the Press," National Broadcasting Company, 1-23.

Glenn T. Seaborg
Professor of Chemistry, University of California, Berkeley; Former Chairman, Atomic Energy Commission of the United States

Up to now, the physical sciences and their related technologies have been employed primarily to increase greatly man's consumption of natural resources with little consideration of their replacement and still less of the impact of their use and the resulting waste. I believe that all this is beginning to change now and that our economic advances at the cost of environmental degradation will soon stop. But what will halt and eventually reverse it should not be a "stop everything" approach. Trying to turn off technology as a solution to improving the condition of man and nature could, at this point, be even more disastrous than letting that technology continue at its current course.

At International Science and Engineering Fair, New Orleans/ The Dallas Times Herald, 5-7:(AA)10.

There will come a day . . . when, instead of 100-car coal trains crossing a section of the country or huge coal barges crossing the ocean, our coal-burning power plants mainly will be plants at the mouths of mines, the power from which will be shipped as clean electricity via high-voltage underground cables to distant load centers. This may also be a time when, instead of nuclear power stations being built one by one in locations opposed by one or another local citizens' groups, we will see clusters of such nuclear plants and their fuel reprocessing facilities in "power parks"—areas set aside for their use which do not impinge on lands needed for other purposes. And such power parks themselves might be created so that they are attractive preserves in an otherwise undisturbed natural setting.

Before Power Engineering Society, San Francisco, July 11/ Los Angeles Times, 7-12:(2)2.

Maurice H. Stans
Secretary of Commerce of the United States

Industry has been indiscriminately accused by some of ignoring the pollution problems of our times and being responsible for most of them. The charge is dead wrong and it is unfair. Industry, of course, must bear a share of the blame. But the fact recognized by too few people is that many of the worst polluters are outside of industry—municipalities, other governments, agriculture and the public itself. Witness the fact that hundreds, perhaps thousands, of American communities pour millions of tons of untreated sewage into waters every day. By contrast, almost across the board, industries have launched vastly complex and expensive efforts to help clean up the air, water and landscape of the country . . . Unfortunately, business has failed to make these achievements credibly known to the American people. The idea still persists in many quarters that industry is doing almost nothing to fight pollution and what it does do is only because it is being dragged across the line. Neither is true. There are deliberate polluters, of course, but most business has been working at pollution-control for a long time—and it can be proud of its conservation record.

Houston/The National Observer, 2-26:10.

Maurice F. Strong
Secretary General, United Nations Conference on the Human Environment

Could there, one wonders, be any undertaking better designed to meet (the world's) needs, to relieve the great convulsions of anxiety and ingrained hostility that now rack international efforts to restore the hope, the beauty and the salubriousness of the natural environment in which man has his being (than the forthcoming Conference in Stockholm)? If the problems of the human environment are to be resolved . . . it is necessary to add a new dimension to man's thinking . . . This is for man to see himself not as a separate, antagonistic, exclusive exploiter of the earth, but as the steward and wise manager of earth's precious and limited resources. The Stockholm Conference can be a turning point.

San Francisco Examiner & Chronicle, 5-28:(This World)27.

I do not believe we can cease to grow. No growth is not a viable policy for any society today. Indeed, people must have more, not fewer, opportunities to express their creative drives. But these can only be provided within a total system in which man's activities are in dynamic harmony with the natural order. To achieve this, we must control and redirect our processes of growth. We must see it in terms of enriching the lives and enlarging the opportunities of all mankind.

At United Nations Conference on the Human Environment, Stockholm, June 5/The New York Times, 6-6:4.

There is much difference of opinion in the scientific community over the severity of the environmental problem and whether doom is imminent, or indeed, inevitable. But one does not have to accept the inevitability of catastrophe. We need subscribe to no doomsday threat to be convinced that we cannot—we dare not—wait for all the evidence to be in. Time is no ally here unless we make it one.

At United Nations Conference on the Human Environment, Stockholm, June 5/The New York Times, 6-11:(4)7.

The dominant image of the age in which we live is that of the earth rising above the horizon of the moon—a beautiful, solitary, fragile sphere which provides the home and sustains the life of the entire human species. From this perspective, it is impossible to see the boundaries of nations and the other artificial barriers that divide men. What it brings home to us with dramatic force is the reality that our common dependence on the health of our only-one earth and our common interest in caring for it transcends all man-made divisions.

Los Angeles Times, 11-1:(1-A)7.

Russell E. Train
Chairman, President's Council on Environmental Quality

Most of us march to the tune "Produce or Perish," and this has helped make of Americans a nation of high achievers. But with all the benefits from continued economic growth, as a people we are beginning to question whether more is really better. Communities from coast to coast are more and more willing to forgo new industries to prevent pollution and impairment of the local environment. The President's population commission concluded after two years of research that "no substantial benefits would result from continued growth of the nation's population."

Before World Affairs Council, Los Angeles, March 29/ The New York Times, 3-30:19.

We are learning that it is far less costly and more effective to build the necessary environmental quality into new plants and new communities from the outset than it is to rebuild or modify old facilities. The time to do the job of environmental protection is at the outset, not later. This holds true for every country at every state of development.

At United Nations Conference on the Human Environment, Stockholm, June 6/The New York Times, 6-7:3.

Environment quality cannot be allowed to become the slogan of the privileged. Our environmental visions must be broad enough and compassionate enough to embrace the full range of conditions that affect the quality of life for all people. How can a man be said to live in harmony with his environment when that man is desperately poor and his environment is a played-out farm. Or when the man is a slum-dweller and his environment is a garbage-strewn street. I reject any understanding of environmental improvement that does not take into account the circumstances of the hungry and the homeless, the jobless and the illiterate, the sick and the poor.

Quote, 9-17:272.

Morris K. Udall
United States Representative, D–Ariz.

(On possible energy shortages due to environmental considerations): I think there is a very great danger that the public is going to say during an energy brownout, "To hell with the environment, my food is spoiling in my refrigerator and my job is gone. Power at any cost!"

April 12/The Washington Post, 4-13:(A)2.

Stewart L. Udall
Former Secretary of the Interior of the United States

If there was one decision I made in all my tenure as Secretary of the Interior that I regret and, if I had the chance, that I would retract, it would be the (granting of) off-shore oil leases in the Pacific.

The New York Times, 3-19:(4)9.

E. B. Walker
Executive vice president, Gulf Oil Corporation

There's no way we can avoid a dramatic increase in our dependence on imported oil in the next 15 years. We don't have enough domestic oil and gas to meet our growing needs; and it's going to take a lot of money and a lot of time to develop synthetic fuels.

The Dallas Times Herald, 7-25:(B)2.

Pinkney Walker
Commissioner, Federal Power Commission

The most alarming aspect of the energy problem is that the vast majority of Americans do not realize that there is a problem. Moreover, most of those who recognize that some problem exists fail to understand (the) severity of its possible ramifications. Or stated another way, most Americans do not realize the importance of energy in their everyday lives, and therefore are unaware that these lives and living styles are in imminent danger of change because of inadequate supplies of reliable and economical power.

The Dallas Times Herald, 6-14:(B)4.

Barbara Ward
Economist

(Advocating sensible use of the earth's finite resources): To act without rapacity, to use knowledge with wisdom, to respect interdependence, to operate without hubris and greed are not simply moral imperatives. They are an accurate scientific description of the means of survival.

Stockholm/ The New York Times, 6-19:33.

Harrison A. Williams, Jr.
United States Senator, D–N.J.

As we consider imposing pollution controls to protect this planet's environment, one of my greatest fears is the threat of trade dislocations unless there are uniform approaches to the problem . . . It is obvious that high pollution-abatement costs can result in serious trade disadvantages. Further, the possibility of a trade disadvantage can retard the trend toward environmental protection in many nations . . . What this means . . . is that countries whose environmental policies, or lack of them, permit industries to operate under less restraint than others, could conceivably become "pollution havens" in much the same way that the tax structure of some states or countries attract investment.

Before Senate Foreign Relations subcommittee, Washington/ The Dallas Times Herald, 5-7:(A)8.

M. A. Wright
Chairman, Humble Oil & Refining Company

Helping give impetus to the "no-growth" concept is increasingly widespread recognition of the interdependence of man and his natural environment. Some conclude that economic growth and environmental conservation are irretrievably inconsistent. Somehow, the need for economic progress as a source of the means to repair past environmental damage and prevent future harm is all too often overlooked. The even broader social significance of continued economic progress also is too frequently ignored.

At Harvard Business School Southwest Regional Conference, Houston, March 25/ The Dallas Times Herald, 3-26:(A)30.

Foreign Affairs

Spiro T. Agnew
Vice President of the United States

The President's sole responsibility for developing and initiating foreign policy comes directly from our Constitution. The brevity of the Constitution in treating with this grave responsibility is in startling contrast with the complicated language we find in important documents today. Actually, the Constitution's simplicity on this subject reflects the realities of the time when it was drafted. The United States then was separated from possible enemies by a long ship voyage, and the Founding Fathers reasonably could view international problems in a fairly relaxed way. Today, on the other hand, the frightening presence of the nuclear age hangs over the world, and nations face destruction within minutes after a decision to attack may be made. Because of the time limitations, foreign policy cannot be conducted by consensus. The complexity of the issues, coupled with the frequent need for secrecy, inhibits the formulation of an informed consensus in time to make vital policy judgments. Therefore, we are fortunate that these critical determinations are vested clearly in our President, rather than in the Congress, or the members of the professional bureaucracy, or an outside panel of experts.

At Republican fund-raising dinner, Chicago/
San Francisco Examiner, 9-27:4.

William Blackie
Former chairman,
Caterpillar Tractor Company

In 1964 I was a member of the Presidential committee appointed to examine East-West trade, the so-called Miller Committee, and it was our recommendation that, through trade and any other available means, we try to break down the barriers that were dividing the world into hostile camps. Whether it be sports or cultural exchange or trade, the more we can deal with each other, meet each other on a people-to-people basis, the more we will whittle away at world misunderstandings.

Interview/
Nation's Business, August:43.

Eugene Carson Blake
Former general secretary,
World Council of Churches

Powerful nations use their power to protect their own interests—this country (the U.S.) as do others. Because we have so much power, we are considered the most dangerous country in the world. We are not seen by people overseas as the white-hatted cowboys we consider ourselves to be, but as the simple purveyor of power.

Pasadena, Calif., Dec. 10/
Los Angeles Times, 12-11:(2)8.

Zbigniew Brzezinski
Director, Institute on Communist Affairs, Columbia University

We no longer live in an age in which peace and war can be sharply differentiated. We live in a "neither-neither" land, and we have peace and competition at the same time. The need of the moment in my judgment is to create a stable framework of international cooperation, and this means not only accommodation between the United States and the Soviet Union, but simultaneously a consistent effort by the United States to improve its relationships with Western Europe, with Japan, so that the framework of international cooperation is created to which the American/Soviet relationship can be adjusted.

TV-radio interview, Washington/ "Meet the Press," National Broadcasting Company, 5-21.

John Buchanan
United States Representative, R–Ala.

Man's inhumanity to man makes countless thousands mourn, as Robert Burns once said. But the humanity of the United States to its fellow man through the work of the Peace Corps has helped dry some of the tears in distant lands and should be permitted to continue doing so.

Quote, 4-2:322.

James L. Buckley
United States Senator, C–N.Y.

. . . if we are to maintain effective alliances, we must decide as a people that ours is a long-term commitment, and we must restore confidence in our capacity as a nation to sustain our role of leadership. If we should appear to falter, to grow weary of the role–if we appear unable to match the tenacity of the Communists–then the framework for regional security, which we have constructed at so great a cost, will surely fall apart. And we must also be able to demonstrate that we will not fall victim to our own good nature. Because we have no aggressive designs on others, we find it hard to understand that others have a driving compulsion to dominate. Because we seek peace, we assume that others seek it with an equal intensity. Because we negotiate in good faith, we are too often tempted to place a dangerous reliance on the good faith of others. It is this beguiling streak of innocence embedded in our nature which may raise the greatest question as to our ultimate capacity to meet the responsibilities which have been thrust upon us. I believe that we may now be entering a point in history . . . which will test whether or not Leo Durocher stated a rule of universal application when he said, "Nice guys finish last."

Before National Press Club, Washington, Feb. 11/ Vital Speeches, 5-15:455.

Clifford P. Case
United States Senator, R–N.J.

. . . the establishment of an American (military) base in a foreign country is a very serious matter, which should require the advice and consent of the Senate. The stationing of American troops overseas can lead to war. Explicitly or implicitly, it may involve the United States in a commitment toward the host country.

Washington, Jan. 6/ The New York Times, 1-7:2.

Shirley Chisholm
United States Representative, D–N.Y.

Our country pours millions of dollars in financial and economic aid to countries abroad. Our nation espouses egalitarian principles. And yet, in spite of that espousal and what the United States Constitution and the Declaration of Independence say, we have been pouring the taxpayers' dollars into countries that are propping up military dictatorships at the expense of the liberties of the citizens who reside in those countries. We have not been really carrying forth the democratic principles as such. Therefore, I would say that (if elected President) I would cut off financial assistance and/or aid to those countries that do not respect human freedom and human life. I'm talking about Portugal. I'm talking about Cambodia. I'm talking about Greece.

Interview/ The Washington Post, 2-13:(B)4.

Winston S. Churchill II
Member of British Parliament

There was a time, not so very long ago, when the people of America were in love with the world. Today, you seem to eye her with less enchantment, even with some diffidence. One senses that you are tempted to find more congenial the rarified atmosphere of the planets—where the problems are not human, only technological—and more easily overcome. But as history has shown . . . there can be no shorter cut to disaster for us all than if America turns her back on the world. Only with the firm commitment and resolve of the people of the United States—looked to today, as ever before, as the inspiration of free men everywhere and indeed of those who yearn to be free—is there hope that those "gaunt marauders" that so afflict humanity—war, tyranny, poverty, disease and famine—can be overcome.

At Westminster College commencement, Fulton, Mo., May 21/ Vital Speeches, 7-15:580.

Clark M. Clifford
Former Secretary of Defense of the United States

(President) Nixon still perceives each problem of international relations as part of a global chess game between the United States and the Soviet Union; at times it is a three-sided game in which (Communist) China is also a contestant. In this game, one player's gain is automatically the other player's loss. This is an obsolete view, because it fails to acknowledge the reality that many countries, and indeed large areas of the world, have long since demonstrated a progressive independence and neutrality in the great power struggle.

Before House Foreign Affairs Committee, Washington, May 18/ The Washington Post, 5-21:(B)5.

John B. Connally, Jr.
Secretary of the Treasury of the United States

The conduct of foreign economic policy today is characterized by traits of ponderousness, division of responsibility, rivalry and, in some sectors, innocence.

New York/ The Washington Post, 3-23:(G)6.

John B. Connally, Jr.
Former Secretary of the Treasury of the United States

America was the lone survivor of World War II. We stood alone. Men could and did reason that the strength of the U.S. was a strength that others could cling to . . . If we do not exercise (the) role of leadership, no other nation can or will. If we do not, there will be cheering long and loud in the capitals of nations that do not hold freedom dearly.

Before Dallas and Forth Worth Chambers of Commerce, Fort Worth, Tex., Oct. 26/The Dallas Times Herald, 10-27:(B)1.

Robert Conquest
Former British diplomat; Authority on the Soviet Union

. . . the trouble is, in a democratic country like yours (the U.S.), a trip (by the President) to Peking leads to the most unlikely expectations. People say: "This is marvelous. It's a real move toward peace. So why not have another peace session in Moscow? And then everything will be wonderful; we will settle all of the world's problems; there will no longer be ideological or self-serving confrontations." One has to deal with public opinion in the West, and that is the difficulty. Shrewd American leadership can handle the problems of over-all diplomacy. But if you have a sudden wave of ostrich-like politics in this country—a sort of burying one's head in the sands—you could suddenly reach a situation in which an American government, pushed by public opinion, might feel compelled to sign something—almost anything. I'm sure (President) Nixon wouldn't do that, but it's a danger you have to watch for. The United States might end up signing meaningless treaties with both Peking and Moscow, and everyone would think that the world had been saved from catastrophe.

Interview/ U.S. News & World Report, 5-22:33.

John Sherman Cooper
United States Senator, R–Ky.

More and more I believe that our greatest influence in the world would be an example of justice and morality in our own country.

Quote, 11-5:434.

Archie K. Davis
President, Chamber of Commerce of the United States

. . . we in America must wake up . . . to the realization that we are not necessarily invincible. Burdened down with frustration, war-weary, disillusioned and fed up with taxes, acutely sensitive to the thanklessness of our friends and allies whom we have supported over the years, and somewhat embarrassed by many aspects of our own mismanagement, we stand in imminent danger of committing the cardinal error of withdrawal, and saying to hell with it. That is human nature; but we had better think twice. We must cut the cloth of our strategy to fit the pattern of a clearly-defined national purpose; and that purpose must embrace the long-range goals and aspirations of a nation that stands for peace but must always be strong enough to keep the peace. In that sense, we can yield leadership to no other.

At world trade dinner, Atlanta Chamber of Commerce/ The Wall Street Journal, 1-6:8.

Milovan Djilas
Author; Former Vice President of Yugoslavia

The United States won the cold war because of the internal disintegration of Communism. Because you (the U.S.) remained strong, you were able to accelerate this inevitable process . . . you have emerged stronger on the world scene because the Communist world divided into factions while, at the same time, the United States succeeded in enlarging some of the basic democratic ideas–like individual human rights–thus helping to erode the Communist system. And economically you succeeded in pressing the Marxist world into collaboration with you. You proved the truth of your theory that no economic system can develop isolated from others. And you stayed strong enough.

Interview, Belgrade/ The New York Times, 8-18:29.

Thomas F. Eagleton
United States Senator, D–Mo.

The powerful forces of international economics and technology–forces that were in their infancy in the '20s and '30s–have revolutionized the previously predictable business of diplomacy. Power relationships have broken down to a complicated ferment of overlapping special interests. A multiplicity of variables has been added to the bilateral affairs of nations. Long-standing alignments have grown flexible by necessity. Military allies may be economic competitors–political foes trading partners. So in our fatigue and disillusionment after Vietnam, we have to act. We must devise a policy–uncluttered with cliches about "isolationism"–that will make the turbulent reality of international relations serve us.

The New York Times, 10-23:31.

Luis Echeverria (Alvarez)
President of Mexico

It is impossible to understand why the United States does not apply the same boldness and imagination that it applies to solving complex problems with its enemies to the solution of simple problems with its friends.

Before joint session of Congress, Washington, June 15/ The New York Times, 6-16:11.

J. William Fulbright
United States Senator, D–Ark.

(Criticizing the USIA, *Radio Free Europe* and *Radio Liberty*): These programs keep alive the cold war. These programs are not presented to promote understanding or compassion.

Before Fulbright-Hays scholars, Washington, March 20/ The Washington Post, 3-21:(B)3.

(On the USIA and its Director, Frank Shakespeare): They have their own survival in mind. They are only incidentally . . . knowledgeable in how to approach our relations with the Communist world. What they are interested in is perpetuation of their own bureaucracy . . . I think Mr. Shakespeare is a very inadequate man for that position, but there's nothing I can do about that.

Radio interview/ "Capitol Cloakroom," Columbia Broadcasting System, 3-29.

As a member of the Senate Foreign Relations Committee, I object to the shift of responsibility from the Secretary of State to the National Security Council (and adviser Henry Kissinger). This insulates the makers of foreign policy from consultation with and information to the Committee. It is important that policies should be exposed to discussion and not just made by one or two fellows without any adversary discussion. You get the impression that what we have now is a kind of intuitive policy-making system. Consultation on basic policy is desirable. But the President is able to insulate policy from Congressional interference. All Chief Executives regard Congress as a damned nuisance.

Interview, Washington/ The New York Times, 4-28:37.

Our posture has been to preserve the status quo around the world by arms . . . We've overspent—and continue to overspend—and are overcommitted. We have too many bases abroad, and we continue to neglect priorities at home. In the old days, when we had all the money and all the gold, that was all right; but this is no longer so. A lot of people in my state can't understand why they can't get assistance for sewer and water projects—and I can't explain it.

Interview/ U.S. News & World Report, 5-15:65.

Indira Gandhi
Prime Minister of India

For many of us who were in the freedom struggle in India, the U.S. was a source of inspiration. The speeches and sayings of Thomas Jefferson and Abraham Lincoln—we looked to these with great admiration. But look what happened: The U.S. has taken to supporting regimes that are alienated from their own people—in Pakistan, in Vietnam, throughout the world. In fact, if we look at this recent history, we must ask whether America, with all its talk of democracy, is really supporting democracy anywhere.

Interview, New Delhi/ Parade, 8-13:9.

Barry M. Goldwater
United States Senator, R–Ariz.

The majority of the members of the Foreign Relations Committee of the United States Senate want to isolate America. And yet if you accuse them of being isolationists, they act as though you have questioned their paternity, their loyalty, their Americanism. Nevertheless, every action they take links them with the forces that would set America apart from the rest of the world by unilateral disarmament and isolationism.

At Los Angeles Philanthropic Foundation dinner, Beverly Hills, Calif./ Los Angeles Herald-Examiner, 6-26:(A)12.

Vance Hartke
United States Senator, D–Ind.

(Americans) demand and insist on a rational foreign policy to prevent future international tragedies. We can begin by halting all shipments of military weapons to dictators.

Announcing his candidacy for the Democratic Presidential nomination, Manchester, N.H., Jan. 3/ The Washington Post, 1-4:(A)1.

Bruce Herschensohn
Former Director, Motion Picture and Television Service, United States Information Agency

(On Senator J. William Fulbright's efforts to cancel Federal spending for *Radio Free Europe* and the *Voice of America):* What is disturbing to me, and I should think to most Americans, is that Senator Fulbright is not simply espousing the end of some information programs. It is that by doing so, he is bringing about the beginning of a monopoly of ideas.

News conference announcing his resignation, Washington, April 3/ Los Angeles Times, 4-4:(1)22.

Donald K. Hess
Director of the Peace Corps

There's a sweep of neo-isolationism in this country. *The Washington Post*, for instance, and all the other media are looking inward. There is less attention paid to what's happening overseas and fewer people to write about what's going on. We seem to have so many profound problems at home. And we think that any (foreign) involvement may entangle us in another Vietnam . . . What are we going to do—just leave those people out there? Our problems pale when compared with the Third-World problems. It's going to catch us one of these days.

The Washington Post, 12-24:(A)2.

Paul G. Hoffman
Administrator, United Nations Development Program

Our whole thinking has always been clouded and obscured by the term "foreign aid," as such. If you try deliberately to use aid to win friends and influence people, you won't win any friends and you won't influence any people. On the contrary, you will make bad friends.

Interview/Time, 1-17:31.

Townsend Hoopes
Former Deputy Assistant Secretary of Defense of the United States

(On Pentagon advocates of foreign military aid): (They assume that) there is a clearly-defined entity called the Free World, and that every part of this entity is threatened militarily by an expanding Communism and that the United States should be prepared to defend militarily against every such threat. Such a conception, of course, makes life easier for the military planners, but does not accurately reflect the more complicated relationships in the present-day, real world.

The Washington Post, 5-7:(A)18.

Hubert H. Humphrey
United States Senator, D–Minn.

. . . I happen to think that (President) Nixon has done well in foreign policy in some areas . . . Nixon going to (Communist) China—that was right. That fruit on the tree was ready for picking. He did it. The fact that he did it—a man who built his whole political career on hunting down anybody who could even spell China—is rather unusual; and that in itself gives it extra meaning. Second, his visit to the Soviet Union, his effort to improve relations—I don't think we ought to talk about normalizing; it is a matter for improving relations. Thirdly, he has spent a lot of time on other aspects of foreign policy, on monetary problems, on trade problems. We are going through a difficult period. I think that the Nixon Administration is a plus on foreign policy—not without limitations, but a plus.

Interview, Washington/ Los Angeles Herald-Examiner, 7-2:(A)13.

John N. Irwin II
Under Secretary of State of the United States

(On international affairs by the year 1980): The relatively simple bipolar days of the cold war will have given way to a less predictable situation in which there will be different constituencies and groupings for different issues. To take hypothetical examples, while the United States and the Europeans have been united, and I hope will remain united, to oppose Soviet designs on Europe, it is not too difficult to imagine a situation in which the Europeans and the Soviets might find a common interest in opposing some United States-backed trade or investment policy, or conversely, in which the United States and the Soviets might join in questioning trade policies of the European community. Traditional alignments, in other words, may become more flexible and subject to change on specific, ad hoc, issues . . . The power and dominance of the two superpowers (the U.S. and the Soviet Union) should decline in relative importance. Nuclear parity should tend to diminish the political significance of our nuclear weapons. Both powers will not only have to continue to get along with each other, but also pay even more attention to getting along with the new emerging power centers in Western Europe, Japan and China.

The New York Times, 6-19:12.

Jacob K. Javits
United States Senator, R–N.Y.

I would like to see the American role in the world along the following lines: We should be—give and take the usual 10 per cent for the frailties of any nation in respect to nationalism, commercialism, self-interest and all the things that go with it—we should be the world's moral power because we are big. There are lots of small powers that could be the moral power easier than we could, but it wouldn't mean enough. If we were the moral power—and that doesn't mean we have to be mawkish or pacifists, but it means that, where there is a choice between morality and immorality in national terms, that we would make the moral choice. I think that is a great role for us . . . I don't think we can go any further than is prudent. The moral choice would have dictated going after the Russians when they beat up Czechoslovakia—or Hungary or Poland—but that would have been highly imprudent, even more imprudent than Vietnam, which was imprudent enough. Yet I was for the action we took in Korea because it was under UN auspices. It was a situation that, strategically because of its bearing on Japan, we could not allow to occur. That had good reasons. But I think that, having accepted the morality, you still can't become the world's policeman.

Interview, Rome/ San Francisco Examiner, 1-7:52.

We have plenty of carrots to induce co-operation (from foreign countries). The recent (world monetary) crisis again proved America's importance to Europe. We are still the biggest economic factor in the world.

News conference, London, Jan. 11/ The New York Times, 1-12:59.

U. Alexis Johnson
Under Secretary for Political Affairs, Department of State of the United States

It is now fashionable to question our (the U.S.'s) motives and accomplishments in the post-war era. I find such questions extraordinary. As to our motives, I will simply note that (the late British Prime Minister) Winston Churchill—an observer with some experience in these matters—characterized our effort in the early post-war years as the "most unsordid act in history." To my mind, our accomplishments speak for themselves: Our bitterest enemies of three decades ago are now among our closest friends; and surely it is better to have strong friends than strong enemies. The dreadful prospect of another world war, this time between the Communist and non-Communist powers, seems now more remote than at any time since the mid-1940s. The American people have prospered to an unprecedented degree during this period. More than 60 free nations came into being in the remarkable and largely peaceful liquidation of some 400 years of

(U. ALEXIS JOHNSON)

colonial history; not a single one of these nations has chosen the Communist system. A new sense of the interdependence of nations has grown in only a few decades from being a bitterly-disputed premise to a commonplace statement of the obvious. We have kept the atomic genie in his bottle and have made significant progress in establishing international limits which lessen the atomic threat to mankind—and enhance the potential of the atom's beneficial use. We have made a singular contribution to the economic recovery of the world from World War II and have witnessed record levels of prosperity in large parts of the world. We have helped create an international economic system which has resulted in an explosion in trade between nations on a scale unprecedented in history with immeasurable benefits to the people of the world, notably including our own. These are not negligible accomplishments. They are, in fact, historic accomplishments. I do not think that we need be apologetic or defensive about them.

The Washington Post, 8-15:(A)18.

Edward M. Kennedy
United States Senator, D–Mass.

(Advocating limitation of the President's war-making authority): From Korea to the invasion of the Dominican Republic and finally to Vietnam, we have seen mounting evidence of the President unilaterally assuming the power to commit the nation to war.

Washington, April 13/
The Dallas Times Herald, 4-14:(A)13.

Henry A. Kissinger
Assistant to the President of the United States for National Security Affairs

The great advantage of secret negotiations is that you can leapfrog public positions without the turmoil that any change in public positions brings about internationally and domestically in some of the countries involved.

Jan. 26/The Washington Post, 10-1:(A)1.

Everyone assumes I am determined to go on and on (at his job), but that is not my goal . . . It's a fact that at some point I have to disassociate myself before the centrality of my role becomes an issue in foreign policy. I haven't decided (when that will be). Quite honestly. I'm not playing games on that. It depends on many things. First of all, it depends on how much has been accomplished; how much remains to be done; whether I think I can make a peculiar difference by staying on. But I have to get out before this becomes too personal a job. I would like to leave ideally when there is no foreign crisis, when I am not embroiled in a bureaucratic fight and when there can be no question in anybody's mind of my relations with the President.

Newsweek, 2-7:17.

My job is to make available to the President the maximum number of choices. It is the secret dream of the bureaucracy to give him yes-and-no alternatives. I've got to see that that doesn't happen . . . When all opinions are in, I sum up. I also give the President my judgment. But I'm fair. This system doesn't deprive the State Department of its rightful powers. The State Department's input is very important. In fact, under this system, the State Department has a say over matters like the Defense Department budget. That was never the case before. But we help the President forge national-security policy, which includes foreign affairs and defense. In national-security policy, the input comes from many sources . . . 99 per cent of the diplomatic business of the American government is still conducted by the Department of State. My office has done very little about Latin America and Africa. We have concerned ourselves only slightly with the Middle East and, until the recent crisis, with South Asia. We are only involved with that part of foreign policy that overlaps security. The State Department is still the government's principal arm in dealing with the other nations of the world.

Interview, Washington/ The New York Times Magazine, 2-27:35.

The factors which perpetuated that rivalry (between the U.S. and the Soviet Union) remain real and deep. We are ideological adversaries, and we will in all likelihood remain so for the foreseeable future. We are political and military competitors, and neither can be indifferent to advances by the other in either of these fields. We each have allies whose association we value and whose interests and activities impinge at numerous points. We each possess an awesome nuclear force created and designed to meet the threat implicit in the other's strength and aims. Each of us has just come into possession of power singlehandedly capable of exterminating the human race. Paradoxically, this very fact, and the global interests of both sides, creates a certain commonality of outlook, a sort of interdependence for survival between the two of us. Although we compete, the conflict will not admit of resolution by victory in the classical sense. We are compelled to coexist. We have an inescapable obligation to build jointly a structure for peace. Recognition of this reality is the beginning of wisdom for a sane and effective foreign policy today.

At Congressional briefing, Washington, June 15/The Washington Post, 6-16:(A)18.

Melvin R. Laird
Secretary of Defense of the United States

The Nixon Doctrine provides for a realistic approach to the problems of foreign policy. I think that doctrine will have to be applied during the 1970s and beyond. It calls for building strong partnerships with our friends and allies that we are committed to in our treaty arrangements that have been approved by the United States Senate under our Constitutional process. We must build strong partnerships, strong military strength during this period of time in co-operation with our partners. In some cases, this will require military assistance to our partners and to our friends throughout the world. But as we build for strong military strength and partnership, then and only then can we move into meaningful negotiations with our adversaries throughout the world. We should show at all times a willingness to negotiate, whether it be with the (Communist) Chinese, the Russians or any other nations in the world. We can have meaningful and successful negotiations, however, only if our partnerships are strong and we maintain our military strength.

Washington/ San Francisco Examiner, 2-10:56.

I believe that great nations today can be peaceful adversaries without being belligerent antagonists. But to continue to move in this direction we must have confidence on both sides that any agreements we do enter into are, in fact, being honored. To put it bluntly, this President (Nixon) and this Secretary of Defense are not going to place the destiny of the United States, or of our friends and allies, at the mercy of the hoped-for good will of any other power. That's why verification (of mutual arms-limitation) agreements is so important as we seek to resolve what can be resolved in our relationships with the Soviet Union and to control what cannot be immediately resolved.

Interview, Washington/ U.S. News & World Report, 3-27:42.

Those who fashioned our foreign policy in the past decade perceived the role of the United States as the ultimate guarantor of peace in the world—in effect, the problem-solver for all of the world's security ills . . . (Now, under the Nixon Administration) the unifying thrust in both domestic and foreign policy is an underlying trust in the ability and willingness of others to do a needed job—local officials and local citizens

(MELVIN R. LAIRD)

of America, governments and their citizens in their nations.

Before Associated Press Managing Editors, Kansas City, Nov. 16/ The Dallas Times Herald, 11-16:(A)6.

Alfred M. Landon
Former Governor of Kansas

(President Nixon's world peace plan is working because) it is based on the mutual recognition among governments of the legitimate needs and interests of other nations—a principle that historically, and tragically, has seldom been recognized. This means the most significant issue facing the American voter (in the Presidential election) next November is the overreaching value of the acquaintanceships and understandings existing between Mr. Nixon and the heads of other governments . . . (Democratic Presidential nominee Senator George McGovern's) only specific reference to foreign policy is his pledge to take America completely out of Vietnam by April, 1973. President Nixon, however, is treating the Vietnam settlement as part of the overall, intricate pattern of international relations that it is.

Before business and labor officials, Kansas City, Mo., Aug. 29/ Los Angeles Herald-Examiner, 8-30:(D)8.

Lee Kuan Yew
Prime Minister of Singapore

There has been a decline in the U.S.' willingness to meet its obligations and see problems through, as in Cambodia. There has been a decline in the U.S. economic position and a deterioration of U.S. social conditions at home. These events have an accumulative effect on U.S. prestige . . . It is also the American Congress niggling at money for Cambodia which, by accident and not of its own choice, has now become the major battleground in Indochina. The total impression is that the U.S. wants to lessen its defense load considerably and quickly. This leads to a diminution of influence.

Interview, Singapore/ San Francisco Examiner, 2-9:36.

Mike Mansfield
United States Senator, D–Mont.

(On foreign aid): In my judgment, the Senate will be well advised to stand fast in its insistence on at least a drastic cut and complete overhaul of what has become largely an irrelevant exercise in government spending. The majority policy committee is actively considering suggestions which range from reduction to elimination of foreign aid. Certainly, at the very least there is strong sentiment for a drastic cut in these expenditures for the 1970s.

Washington/ The New York Times, 1-26:7.

I think what has been happening is a decline in the influence of the State Department and an increase in the influence of the foreign affairs adviser of the President (Henry Kissinger). The person closest to the President's elbow will always have great influence. Secretary (of State William) Rogers has developed ideas of his own, for example, on the Middle East. Nevertheless, the base of operations has shifted from the State Department to the White House. Presidents are the chief foreign-policy makers of the United States, but they seem to depend more on their advisers and staff than on the State Department. A metamorphosis has taken place, and it goes back probably to the time of Jack Kennedy. The close friendship of Nixon and Rogers makes it more possible for Rogers to ride along with criticism and to continue to function in his job. Nixon is extremely fortunate to have a man at his side with the brilliance of Kissinger. If Nixon has made any marks in his Administration it is in the field of foreign policy.

Interview, Washington/ The New York Times, 4-28:37.

The pursuit of ideological struggle has not led us to any victories. Rather, it has projected us into a hodgepodge of foreign aid, military alliances and into overseas propaganda and other dubious manipulative operations. The warm human concern of Americans for other people has been distorted by ideological warfare; and we have plunged, without warrant, into the internal political and social affairs of other nations everywhere in the world. (History) may well record that we pursued the correct foreign policies into the early 1960s; that we bought time, through containment and counterforce, to permit the gradual moderation of Marxist power. However that may be, it has been apparent for some time that we persisted in these policies too long. We were blind to change elsewhere and to the possibility of adjusting to mutual interest. In the end, we came to the disaster of Vietnam. It is part of the price which has been exacted for the obstinate pursuit of the obsolete in foreign policy.

At Montana State University commencement, June 10/ The New York Times, 6-11:(1)19.

(Criticizing the Executive Branch for increasingly making Executive agreements with foreign nations, thereby by-passing the need for Senate approval): The Executive Branch has made it clear that it will ignore the Senate pleas for observance of the Constitutional requirement that important agreements with foreign governments be submitted to the Senate as long as the pleas are not backed up by action. Are we lackeys of the Executive Branch or are we members of the Senate with separate Constitutional responsibilities, and are we members of a co-equal branch of the government? The Constitution says so. What does the Senate say?

Before the Senate, Washington, June 19/ The New York Times, 6-20:15.

Gale W. McGee
United States Senator, D–Wyo.

We in the U.S. must not harbor the delusion that (our) recent summit diplomacy with (Communist) China and the Soviet Union suddenly relegates the balance-of-power concept to the dim, dark past. The direct opposite is true. While the recent SALT agreements have put a limitation on the nuclear capabilities of the U.S. and the U.S.S.R., and may be evidence that both super powers are committed to preventing a nuclear confrontation, we are still faced with the real world in which policies thought by some critics to be outmoded are not only still pursued but are also still effective. Witness the new presence of the Soviet Union in the eastern Mediterranean, the Red Sea, the Indian Ocean and the China Seas—all ushered in with old-fashioned naval power.

At national security policy meeting sponsored by American Enterprise Institute/The Wall Street Journal, 11-27:12.

George S. McGovern
United States Senator, D–S.D.

I'm not a pacifist. If we confront another Hitler or a clear threat to our national interests, I'd respond with power. It's a dangerous world, and some people only understand force.

Time, 6-26:17.

I don't like Communism, but I don't think we have any great obligation to save the world from it. That's a choice other countries have to make.

Time, 6-26:18.

American foreign policy since the early 1950s has been based on an obsession with an international Communist conspiracy that existed more in our minds than in reality. For example, we built Communist China into a threat, when it can barely feed its people and defend its own shores. Even the Soviet threat has been vastly overestimated. As a consequence, we've invested an in-

(GEORGE S. McGOVERN)

credible amount of money on foreign bases. We've overextended ourselves encircling the Soviet Union and China. We have mutual-security pacts with more than 40 countries, but we're really incapable of defending them; Vietnam has proved that. A new foreign policy has to move away from paranoiac anti-Communistic negativism to a recognition of the world's diversity. It is neither desirable nor possible for us to play a unilateral role in the world. We must acknowledge the limitations of American power.

*Interview/
The Washington Post, 7-5:(A)11.*

I think this country is a great and marvelous land that has wandered away from what the American people really want it to be. They want it to stand for peace in the world . . . I think the American people are at the present time unhappy about the condition of the country and about our standing in the world, and they want once again to be proud of this country. So you're going to hear a lot of this theme (during the upcoming Presidential election campaign): "Come home, America"—but not in any isolationist sense. I'm the former director of the Food for Peace program. I have traveled the world around. I'm a strong believer in the United Nations. I'm a great believer in the Good Neighbor policy with our friends in Latin America. My mother was a Canadian citizen; I have always thought friendship with Canada was essential to us. I believe in our important and close relationship with Western Europe and Japan, improving relations with the Soviet Union and China. But first and foremost, I intend to call the country to a new affirmation of the great historic ideals that America began with 200 years ago.

*Interview/
U.S. News & World Report, 8-7:18.*

I think the American people are getting tired of us trying to play a world-policeman role and that the old notion that we used to cling to—that the force of the American example was a great tool of foreign policy—needs to be revived; because the best thing America has ever had going for us in world affairs was the power of our own example as a decent and free society. Other peoples around the world have thought we were a good people and that we were fair-minded and that we weren't bullies and that we wouldn't abuse our great power. I would like to see that vision of the country restored around the world.

*Interview, Los Angeles, Oct. 15/
The Washington Post, 10-20:(A)16.*

(This country) must avoid the kind of reflexive interventionism that has foolishly involved us in the internal political affairs of other countries. While we are deeply involved and have vast influence in the world, forces beyond our control will have the most to do with shaping the political arrangements of the future . . . This is also the time to turn away from excessive preoccupation overseas to rebuilding our own nation.

U.S. News & World Report, 11-6:29.

Klaus Mehnert
*Professor of Political Science,
Technical University,
Aachen, West Germany*

(On U.S. President Nixon's recent meetings in Peking and Moscow): I would say that the two summits have decreased the revolutionary prestige of both Peking and the Soviet Union in the eyes of revolutionary-minded people everywhere. When Nixon was in Peking, I happened to be in Moscow; and Soviet TV showed on the one hand Nixon and (Communist Chinese Premier) Chou En-lai clinking champagne glasses and, on the other hand, American bombs falling on Vietnam. I don't know what the Chinese did on TV (when Nixon was in Moscow), but they could equally well show champagne glasses clinking in the Kremlin and bombs still falling on North Vietnam—and probably mines floating around Haiphong without the Russians doing anything about it. A possible effect is that radicals throughout the world will be increasingly disillusioned about both Peking and Moscow. There might be either an increase in nonaligned radicalism, not tied to either Peking or Moscow, or there could be general disillusion—a getting tired of revolutionary causes because the two great Communist powers have been so reticent in supporting that cause for which the radicals throughout the world have been marching these last years; namely, the cause of Vietnam.

Interview/
U.S. News & World Report, 6-12:69.

Richard M. Nixon
President of the United States

(On his forthcoming trips to Communist China and the Soviet Union): Summits which are held for the sake of having summits are a very bad idea. But when you are dealing with governments which have basically one-man rule . . . then, for the major decisions, summitry sometimes becomes a necessity. I became convinced that, with regard to China and with regard to the Soviet Union, that it would serve our interests and their interests in avoiding those confrontations that might lead to war . . . This will be tough, hard bargaining between people who have very great differences, but people who have one thing in common, and that is that we had better talk about differences or we may end up fighting about them.

Television interview, Washington/
Columbia Broadcasting System, 1-2.

In our foreign policy, we have entered a new era. The world has changed greatly in the 11 years since President John Kennedy said in his inaugural address: "We shall pay any price, bear any burden, meet any hardship, support any friend, oppose any foe, to assure the survival and the success of liberty." Our policy has been carefully and deliberately adjusted to meet the new realities of the new world we live in. We make today only those commitments we are able and prepared to meet. Our commitment to freedom remains strong and unshakable. But others must bear their share of the burden of defending freedom around the world. And so this, then, is our policy: We will maintain a nuclear deterrent adequate to meet any threat to the security of the United States or of our allies. We will help other nations develop the capability of defending themselves. We will faithfully honor all of our treaty commitments. We will act to defend our interests, whenever and wherever they are threatened any place in the world. But where our interests or our treaty commitments are not involved, our role will be limited; we will not intervene militarily, but we will use our influence to prevent war. If war comes, we will use our influence to stop it; and once it is over, we will do our share in helping to bind up the wounds of those who have participated in it.

State of the Union address,
Washington, Jan. 20/
The New York Times, 1-21:18.

Not so long ago, our alliances were addressed exclusively to the containment of the Soviet Union and the People's Republic of (Communist) China. But now there has to be more to our alliances. It is fairly simple to unite about what you are against. It is a lot more complicated to hold together an alliance on the basis of what you are for. We do not shy away from this complexity because now, in this time of breakthroughs, there has never been a greater need for a sense of common purpose among the non-Communist nations. There is no requirement that we all march in lockstep, but there is a need to move forward in the same direction. That is why we encourage initiative and self-reliance on the part of our allies. That is why our alliance is becoming what we need in the real world of the '70s—a dynamic coalition of self-assured and independent nations. Our former dependents

(RICHARD M. NIXON)

have become our competitors; that is good for us and good for them.

Radio address, Washington, Feb. 9/ The Washington Post, 2-10:(A)13.

Let us imagine for a moment what the world would be like if the United States were not respected in the world. What would the world be like if friends of the United States throughout the non-Communist world lost confidence in the United States? It would be a world that would be much less safe. It would be a world that would be much more dangerous, not only in terms of war but in terms of the denial of freedom; because when we talk about the United States of America and all of our faults, let us remember that in this country we have never used our power to break the peace, only to restore it or keep it–and we have never used our power to destroy freedom, only to defend it.

Floresville, Tex., April 30/ U.S. News & World Report, 5-15:100.

Great powers have learned this fact of life: Agreements based on exploiting the presumed weakness of one party only cause it to redouble its efforts to catch up; but agreements based on mutual respect and reciprocity have a far greater chance of enduring . . .

During U.S.-Soviet summit meeting, Moscow/ San Francisco Examiner, 5-25:37.

Speaking for the United States, I can say this: We covet no one else's territory; we seek no dominion over any other people. We seek the right to live in peace, not only for ourselves but for all the peoples of this earth. Our power will only be used to keep the peace, never to break it; only to defend freedom, never to destroy it. No nation that does not threaten its neighbors has anything to fear from the United States.

Broadcast address, Moscow, May 28/ The New York Times, 5-29:3.

Strength and resolution command respect. They are an incentive for negotiation leading to peace. But weakness and naive sentimentality breed contempt. They are an open invitation to pressure tactics and aggression leading to war.

Radio broadcast campaigning for the forthcoming Presidential election, Washington, Oct. 29/ The New York Times, 10-30:22.

The problem of the relationship between the President's international affairs adviser (currently Henry Kissinger) and the State Department has always been a difficult one. It is particularly at this time because we have had so many initiatives that had to be undertaken at the Presidential level. But I think (Secretary of State) Bill Rogers put it very well. He said, "When the team is winning, you don't have to complain because the second-baseman may be getting more publicity than the shortstop . . ."

Interview, Nov. 5/ The Washington Post, 11-10:(A)6.

Mohammad Reza Pahlavi
Shah of Iran

I think the United States realizes it can't be an international gendarme and that world stability should be assured by countries that can assume this responsibility in different regions. How many times can you repeat the Vietnam experience?

Interview, Teheran, Jan. 15/ The New York Times, 1-17:3.

Otto E. Passman
United States Representative, D–La.

If I had to meet my Maker in three minutes, and the last decision the Good Lord would let me make . . . it would be to abolish the Peace Corps. Then I could die in peace.

The Washington Post, 2-13:(B)7.

William Proxmire
United States Senator, D–Wis.

(Saying U.S. military aid missions abroad have too many Generals and Admirals): The big salaries and perquisites of office for military flag officers in this program make a mockery of U.S. economic aid designed to help the weak and poor of the world help themselves. In most cases, a warrant officer could run the program. In some cases, a private first class should be in charge.

Washington, June 16/
The New York Times, 6-17:3.

William P. Rogers
Secretary of State
of the United States

My objective is to help make the foreign policy of this country successful. It doesn't matter at all whether people think I'm the historical equal of some other Secretary of State. The truth is that the President (Nixon) and I think a lot alike. Our instincts are alike, and the decisions I favor are apt to be the decisions he makes. I normally don't have to fight for the positions I favor, since those are the positions toward which the President already tends. I can count on my fingers the times when a major Presidential decision on foreign policy was not foreshadowed by discussion between the President and me. Occasionally, there have been decisions with which I did not agree. Occasionally, I've had to go to the President and try to get a decision changed. But remember that the people don't elect a Secretary of State. They elect a President, and he's responsible for foreign policy.

Interview, Washington/
The New York Times Magazine,
2-27:12.

I don't accept the chessboard theory, that we lose countries or gain them. In the Eisenhower Administration, I remember my colleagues wringing their hands and crying, "Indonesia is lost" or, "Ghana is lost." Well, they weren't lost; and we see more clearly now that foreign affairs is always in flux. There is no final chapter. And unless we are ready to risk war or intrude recklessly in others' affairs, we must recognize that some problems are beyond our capacity to solve.

Interview, Washington/
The New York Times Magazine,
2-27:38.

Anyone that suggests, for political or any other reason, that it would serve our national interest to become isolationists, anyone that feels it would serve the cause of peace to have us withdraw from the world, just doesn't know about where we stand in the world. The progress that has been made under President Nixon's leadership is because we have taken a responsible position in world affairs. We have 60 per cent of the direct foreign investment in the world. We're involved all over the world. It's natural for Americans to be involved; and we have to be, whether we like it or not. So any tendency toward isolationism, I think, is a dangerous one.

Before Commonwealth Club,
San Francisco, July 18/
Los Angeles Times, 7-19:(1)4.

(The Nixon Administration believes a democratic system offers) the best hope for achieving the spiritual and material aspirations of people everywhere. But the choice, except as it applies to our own country, is not ours to make. It would be the ultimate arrogance of power to think that we can, or should, impose our will on others—to threaten or coerce others even in the name of conscience. The kind of government other countries have must, in the final analysis, be what their people want or will permit.

Before Order of the Hellenic Educational
and Progressive Association, Atlanta,
Aug. 24/The New York Times, 8-25:3.

Eugene V. Rostow
Professor of Law and Public Affairs,
Yale University

Many of the critics of our foreign policy recognize our vital national interest in preserving our alliances with Western Europe and with Japan—great centers of power

(EUGENE V. ROSTOW)

whose loss would be a catastrophe to us. But why, they ask, do we have to worry about the small, weak countries in the Third World? The answer is that we haven't tried to protect every small, weak country in the Third World against takeover. But some of them are vital to the preservation of our decisive national interests in Europe and in Japan. South Korea and Taiwan, for example, are indispensable to the security of Japan; and Soviet predominance in the Middle East would outflank Europe and could threaten NATO itself and our presence in the Mediterranean. We have not opposed the Soviet presence in Syria or in Egypt or in Algeria or in Iraq. We do not oppose internal revolutions. But we must oppose and do oppose the use of international force behind the mask of revolution, to engulf the whole region, which would make it possible for the Soviet Union to neutralize Europe and to dominate it. We could not long remain a democracy at home if we were beleaguered in a hostile world and threatened by nuclear weapons and nuclear blackmail. The national interest of the United States and of its key allies—Western Europe and Japan—is to achieve a system of peace; an accepted equilibrium of power in a world of wide horizons, based on reciprocal respect for the rules of public order which are codified in the United Nations Charter. But the Charter doesn't enforce itself. The only way to achieve that end is to continue the patient, difficult course we have pursued, difficult as it has been, and difficult, I'm afraid, as it almost surely will be again.

Television broadcast/ "Comment!" National Broadcasting Company, 5-7.

Arthur M. Schlesinger, Jr.
Historian;
Former Special Assistant to the President of the United States

I would suggest that the postwar (World War II) American imperial impulse, which came to its terrible culmination in Indochina, arose from a number of pressures and temptations—pressures and temptations exerted by the vacuums of power created by the Second World War; by the misapplication of the valid belief in the necessity of creating an international structure in which the United States would accept her full global responsibilities; by the grandiose overextension of America's mission to uplift suffering mankind; by the reformist faith in the American capacity to instruct and rebuild other nations; by the quite real menace of Stalinist Communism; by the counter-ideology of anti-Communism, persisting in rigid and absolutist form long after the circumstances that had produced it had begun to change; and by the institutionalization of the cold war, especially in the increasingly influential military establishment.

Before Senate Foreign Relations Committee, Washington/ The National Observer, 5-27:17.

Hugh Scott
United States Senator, R–Pa.

I have known all the Presidents since F.D.R. Every one of them has been enchanted with having their hand on the rudder of the ship of state. They love foreign policy. Domestic policy tends to be regarded as more drudgery, and it is more difficult to get any President down into the nitty-gritty of domestic policy . . .

TV-radio interview, Washington/ "Meet the Press," National Broadcasting Company, 1-23.

I believe today that—I hope I'm not too old to change my mind—containment of Communism is not the answer. What is the answer is to recognize that the world has many systems—socialism as in Yugoslavia, national socialism, Communism, small country systems, big country systems, democracy—and all of these systems have got to get together if people aren't going to destroy themselves on the battlefield or in a nuclear holocaust.

Television broadcast, May 20/ San Francisco Examiner & Chronicle, 5-21:(A)1.

Eric Sevareid
News commentator, Columbia Broadcasting System

A lot of stray thoughts cross a lot of minds at the spectacle of (U.S. President) Richard Nixon, who built a career on rigid anti-Communism, wining and dining in the Kremlin (during the current U.S.-Soviet summit meeting in Moscow). He has changed; so has the Russian leadership, so have the world's circumstances. The Soviets used to be 10-feet tall in many imaginations—a mammoth juggernaut ready to strike. But with an occasional exception, like their military investment in Egypt, they have proved cautious and predictable. The United States has proved more unpredictable.

News commentary, May 23/ The Christian Science Monitor, 6-1:16.

Frank Shakespeare
Director, United States Information Agency

(Advocating continuing support for *Radio Free Europe* and *Radio Liberty*): For us who live in this country, it is difficult to conceive of the hunger for truth among people who have no access to truth—whose television, radio, newspapers, magazines and theatre are total instruments of the state; whose educational institutions are not places in which to search for the truth but in which to indoctrinate the young; who cannot travel abroad, who fear to be seen talking with foreign visitors lest they arouse the suspicions of the security police; whose very thoughts of God must be in private, to avoid the frowns of their authorities. For such people, to be able to hear, through the miracle of radio, free voices talking to them from afar, is a ray of light. To argue that the existence of such radios is a cold-war anachronism is to tragically misunderstand the needs of the human spirit. For us as a people to extinguish or to dim the light would not only be political folly, but would be an act of shame.

Television broadcast/ "Comment!" National Broadcasting Company, 4-9.

In the last decade, there has been an increasing questioning in much of the Western world about our (the U.S.') root premises, about the philosophy that we stand for, about our traditions and about the rightness of our approach to human freedom, to the organization of society. In part, that's because we're in a constant stage of evolution, and Americans are a questioning people. The other side—led essentially by the Soviet Union—adopts a very simplistic, iterative, hard-line, nondeviating approach in saying that its system is the best and that it is the wave of the future, the way the world is going. The other side tells nothing about itself which is bad. The outside world rarely hears about the bad except when it involves an external action of a major sort, such as the Soviet invasion of Czechoslovakia in 1968. It is very, very difficult to get a continuing flow of news stories out of the Soviet Union because of the restrictive nature of their society. In the West, on the other hand, there is a constant flow of news—both bad and good. We have been in ferment; and many of the problems we are wrestling with are widely reported abroad—often in a disturbing way. So what gets through to many parts of the world is a picture of turmoil and uncertainty in the West, as against an appearance of a sort of solidity within the Communist regimes. This impression of Communist solidity is, in fact, just a cover—but it's what they present to the world. Now, in

(FRANK SHAKESPEARE)

that context, I think ideas are formed in the minds of many people that are not in accord with reality. And to the extent that that's true, the Soviet Union has done a better job in the promulgation of its concepts than the West has done.

Interview, Washington/
U.S. News & World Report, 5-1:50.

Maxwell D. Taylor
General, United States Army (Ret.); Former U.S. Ambassador to South Vietnam

President (Dwight D.) Eisenhower was elected—to some extent, at least—on his promise to end the war in Korea. And he did, while all over the United States Americans shouted: "No more Koreas! No more Koreas!" Maybe I shouted it, too. That was in 1953. But the next year, in 1954, the first step into our involvement in Vietnam was taken . . . I heard no dissenting voices at the time. Congress voted the necessary appropriations. Everybody was happy, since we were making the world safe for democracy in the good old American way . . . I mention this just to make the point that we are a volatile people; we change awfully fast. And some of these same Americans who have been saying, "Get out of South Vietnam," have also been saying, "Let's go over and help Israel." So don't ever bet on a stable bias on the part of the American public for or against forceful action. Having said that, I certainly hope that our leaders in the future will realize that they had better go very, very slow before getting committed to any course of action which may require military force, particularly if there is not a national interest so obvious it stands out and strikes you right in the eyes.

Interview, Washington/
U.S. News & World Report, 11-27:23.

Nobuhiko Ushiba
Japanese Ambassador to the United States

The basic fact is that, in the long run, the hopes for peace and prosperity of Western Europe, the United States and Japan depend even more on their own inter-relationship than on detente with the Communist powers. Moreover, this inter-relationship turns so much on trade and financial matters that these economic factors have come to dominate and largely determine even our political relationships. In its most dramatic context, the challenge and question ahead of us is whether the United States, Europe and Japan will form a cohesive, cooperative partnership or whether they will split into rival economic blocs. Needless to say, rival economic blocs will have a high potential for becoming rival political blocs as well.

The New York Times, 7-19:47.

Leonard Woodcock
President, United Automobile Workers of America

In the foreign field, this (Nixon) Administration has some pluses going for it. Nixon's (Communist) China trip and his trip to Russia made sense. The record of the Administration in the Near (Middle) East, too, is on the credit side. But when you look at Indochina, you get a big negative that wipes out all the pluses.

Dallas, Aug. 12/
The Dallas Times Herald, 8-13:(A)1.

Bella S. Abzug
United States Representative, D–N.Y.

I think there should be and must be more people coming to Congress who are prepared to fight for the people they represent and the ideas and the views that are really merited of a democracy, and not just coming here as though this is a career in which you occasionally pass a piece of legislation and make sure you'll be re-elected the next time around.

Washington/ The Washington Post, 9-5:(C)3.

Spiro T. Agnew
Vice President of the United States

Our Federal system . . . is under stress because of a lessening of the ability of state and local governments to cope with the problems facing their constituencies—a stress compounded, if not actually generated, in recent decades by the gradual passing of power into the hands of centralized, bureaucratic government. This inability of grass-roots governments to handle problems has led many people to believe that the system is growing ineffective. President Nixon's New Federalism, including the enactment of a workable revenue-sharing bill and government-reorganization proposals, is specifically aimed at this problem. We must reverse the flow of power from the grass roots to Washington. By reversing this flow, we can restore public confidence in the ability of our system to handle the problems facing us.

Interview/ U.S. News & World Report, 3-13:39.

(On the Vice Presidency): No office has been concurrently so ridiculed and dignified, so disdained and coveted, so examined and ignored. A President lives in the spotlight; but a Vice President lives in the flickering strobe lights that alternately illuminate or shadow his unwritten duties. It is sometimes uncomfortable. It is sometimes ego-diminishing. But it is also quietly rewarding—this office of the Vice Presidency—particularly rewarding if you serve with a great President, as has been my good fortune.

Accepting the Vice-Presidential nomination of the Republican Party, Miami Beach, Aug. 23/The Washington Post, 8-24:(A)18.

Myles J. Ambrose
Commissioner of Customs of the United States

Never ask . . . a Congressman, "What have you done for me lately?" You'd be surprised at the results you get from asking, "What are you going to do for me today?"

The New York Times, 1-29:8.

Jack Anderson
Political columnist

Yes, I like my job. I don't mind raking the muck. I have a sense of outrage, and I'm glad. I think public office is a public trust. I think sunlight is the best disinfectant. I don't believe that our government should work in the dark. The big question is, does the government have the right to lie? (Presidential National Security Affairs Adviser Henry) Kissinger orchestrates our foreign affairs, and he operates in total darkness. Foreign policy is being made in the dark recesses of Henry Kissinger's basement office or offices. These days, every time some kid blows his nose, it's a state secret.

Interview, Bethesda, Md./ The Washington Post, 1-16:(G)8.

(JACK ANDERSON)

In the Communist countries, the government hides its errors and shortcomings and prints in its papers all the good things it has done. Here in the U.S., the (Nixon) Administration has seen fit to "classify" all their blunders and poor moves, and says it is because of security precautions. Now, what is the difference between Nixon's classification system and the Kremlin's censoring? I am sure the President believes he knows what is best for the country and knows it better than anyone else; and that is why he does not give the public access to all information. But is that not what the Kremlin does, and probably for the same reasons?

Before Sigma Delta Chi, Dallas, Nov. 17/ The Dallas Times Herald, 11-18:(B)1.

(The President is) elected to serve the people (but is) fawned upon by admirers, has helicopters that swoop from the sky to lift him over those traffic jams the lesser of us in Washington must cope with, and has instant communications with anyone in the world any time he wishes. After four years of this, the man we have elected to be our servant doesn't feel like a servant. He begins to feel like a master. He begins to think we should serve him.

Cranston, R.I., Dec. 17/ The Sacramento (Calif.) Bee, 12-19:(A)4.

John M. Ashbrook
United States Representative, R–Ohio

(On President Nixon's State of the Union address): On the domestic front, there does not appear to be a single area in which the President sees no role for the Federal government. In no field does he advocate ending or even cutting back an existing government program, no matter how ineffective. The march of the new bureaucracy, new deficits and new controls continues without a pause. This, apparently, is what the President's New American Revolution is all about. It seems to me more like the New American Regimentation.

Human Events, 1-29:1.

Charles E. Bennett
United States Representative, D–Fla.

Lobbying is a much misunderstood process, sometimes abused and often carrying bad connotations. Lobbying is nonetheless a vital part of the daily interchange between the people and their government.

Los Angeles Times, 3-17:(1-A)6.

Edward W. Brooke
United States Senator, R–Mass.

It is the privilege of every American to differ with his President; but it is the obligation of every American to be fair in judging a President's performance.

At Republican National Convention, Miami Beach, Aug. 21/ The New York Times, 8-22:34.

Dean Burch
Chairman, Federal Communications Commission

The end product of the government regulatory craft is inherently unglamourous. It is all but incomprehensible to the layman. And because it generally molds a mixed bag of conflicting options, a set of rules is at best a pale copy of the good, the true and the beautiful.

Daily Variety, 2-22:4.

Arthur F. Burns
Chairman, Federal Reserve Board

The propensity to spend more than we are prepared to finance through taxes is becoming deep-seated and ominous.

The Dallas Times Herald, 7-30:(B)2.

John W. Byrnes
United States Representative, R–Wis.

(Criticizing the passage of Federal revenue-sharing with state and local governments which can use the money as they see fit): Nothing that has been done here in my 28 years (in Congress) gives me more concern about its impact on the fabric of our government. It launches us on the road to financing with Federal revenues general activities of local governments, giving them a blank check. It says we think the states have problems. So we throw some money at them and say, "Okay, children, be satisfied." But it will just whet their appetites. It will grow and grow, and the categorical grants will still be there with this on top of them. Really, we ought to have our heads examined as we embark on this historic mistake.

Before the House, Washington, Oct. 12/ The Washington Post, 10-13:(A)2.

Lawton M. Chiles, Jr.
United States Senator, D–Fla.

. . . democratic self-government and an informed citizenry just naturally go hand in hand, making essential the conduct of public business in the open, "in the sunshine." Only with such openness can the public judge and express, through its vote or voice, whether governmental decisions are just and fair. Since I came to the Senate last year, I have become very disturbed by the great amount of public business I have found being conducted behind closed doors and by the attitude of secrecy I have seen in our Federal government agencies. I am not surprised that people are suspicious of our motives and are losing confidence in their government when they are shut out of the decision-making process.

Before the Senate, Washington, Aug. 4/ The Washington Post, 10-4:(A)22.

Frank Church
United States Senator, D–Idaho

It is nothing less than folly to pass this huge revenue-sharing bill without raising a dime to pay for it. The Federal government has no revenue to share, only mounting debts. It is foolhardy to go further into debt, borrowing the billions this bill would give away to state and local governments.

Washington/ The Dallas Times Herald, 9-11:(A)12.

John B. Connally, Jr.
Former Secretary of the Treasury of the United States

In any free society there has to be an Establishment. There is an Establishment that runs our road system and our school system and our health system and our governmental system. Everything has to be part of a system, and you can't just tear it asunder. You can't tear it apart without doing violent damage to this country and what it stands for. I suppose I am very much like Hamlet. I would rather bear those ills I have than flee to others I know not of.

TV-radio interview, Washington/ "Meet the Press," National Broadcasting Company, 7-23.

Clifton Daniel
Associate editor, "The New York Times"

I don't mean to disparage our own leaders; they're quite adequate. But, you see, we don't require great men at the moment. We require *good* men, men who'll do their jobs well, get on with business and not go around creating crises and antagonizing people. Great times turn up great leaders, and we're just not at a "great and challenging" period of history right now. And that may not be such a bad thing.

Interview, New York/ "W": A Fairchild Publication, 4-21:19.

Thomas F. Eagleton
United States Senator, D–Mo.

. . . I think a Vice President very much has to be philosophically, politically and personally compatible with the President. We have only one President. It's not a shared Executive. If he had a disagreement with the President on a very serious issue of conscience and of national importance, then of course he might have to disagree with his President. But otherwise, he should be at the call of the President to do that which the President wants done—serve on a commission, travel to a foreign country, give a speech, head up a research project, or what have you. He's got to be truly the President's assistant and helper, and at the beck and call of the President.

Interview, Washington, June 30/ The Washington Post, 7-14:(A)13.

Thomas F. Eagleton
United States Senator, D–Mo.; Democratic Vice Presidential nominee

Trust (in government) can only be founded on the people's confidence that the men and women they elected will be sensitive to their needs and act in their interests.

Before National Audio-Visual Association, Kansas City, July 15/ The Dallas Times Herald, 7-17:(A)10.

John D. Ehrlichman
Assistant to the President of the United States for Domestic Affairs

There is a certain chemistry involved in dealing with this President (Nixon) . . . I would describe it as a willingness and a sensitivity (on the part of his assistants and advisers) to devote yourself to solving the problems of the Presidency. The associate who brings Mr. Nixon his own problems to solve instead just isn't encouraged.

The Christian Science Monitor, 5-19:14.

There shouldn't be a lot of leeway (for government department officials and Cabinet officers) in following the President's policies. It should be like a corporation, where the executive vice presidents (the Cabinet officers) are tied closely to the chief executive. Or, to put it in extreme terms, when he says jump, they only ask how high.

Interview, Miami Beach/ Los Angeles Times, 8-23:(1)26.

Sam J. Ervin, Jr.
United States Senator, D–N.C.

I want to have faith that the Executive Branch is fully responsive to the Congress and the American people, and that it is willing to tell the Congress and the people what they have a right to know about its actions and policies . . . How can a government be responsive to the people if it will not answer the people's questions, explain its actions and describe its policies to the only national body directly responsible to the people—(the Congress)?

The Christian Science Monitor, 2-4:5.

Gerald R. Ford
United States Representative, R–Mich.

(Advocating a limit on Federal spending to be administered by the President rather than by Congress): We are in a crisis. When a government is in a crisis, drastic action has to be taken. When a person is faced with a financial crisis, that individual, if he wants to straighten out his financial affairs, goes into bankruptcy. He does not like to do it. He does not like to turn over to other authorities the management of his financial affairs; but the pressure of crisis itself forces him to take that drastic action. When a business, whether it is a corporation or otherwise, gets into a financial crisis, what does it do? It goes into chapter 10 or chapter 11 in order to get some breathing space to straighten out its circumstances and get back on a profit basis. I do not say these are totally-accurate analogies, but I think they do point out that, when either a person or a family or a corporation gets into financial trouble, they have to do something they do not want to do and it is drastic in its implications. Here we are today, after going along blithefully forcing more spending, either by authorizations or increased obligation authority—and now we know that we are going to have a bigger deficit of $7 billion or more, which means increased inflation or more taxes. It seems to me that, when we look at the hard realities, we have to step up and take a point of view that is different and unusual, but it is necessary.

Before the House, Washington, Oct. 10/Congressional Digest, December:312.

Bill Frenzel
United States Representative, R–Minn.

Perhaps the strongest reason for the six-year single term (for the Presidency) is to reduce partisan attacks on the President and Presidential partisanship itself. Now the President's greatest critics are his competitors in the Congress who are struggling to be elected to his job. It is to their advantage to destroy or weaken the credibility of his program whether it serves the national interest or not. An unfriendly Congress can force vetoes by overburdening good bills or by not allowing the President to achieve any of his programs, particularly in the two years before a campaign. Perhaps worse than causing legislative mischief, such action cannot help but undermine public confidence in any President. On the other side of the coin, the President is always thought to be acting in a very political way prior to the re-election year. Whether he is doing so or not, he is accused of so doing. Rightly, sometimes, or wrongly, sometimes, a President standing for re-election is accused of developing short-run programs which are principally calculated to return him to office. In addition, every President standing for re-election makes some use of his office for campaign purposes; this is unavoidable even with the best of motivations. Even a totally unselfish President is supported by a large executive staff which feels a great need to re-elect its boss. Even if the President is not taking advantage of his office, frequently his staff may be.

Before the House, Washington, Jan. 31/Congressional Digest, March:84.

J. William Fulbright
United States Senator, D–Ark.

(On the growing power of the Presidency): A strong President has been regarded as not one who strengthens and upholds our constitutional system as a whole but as one who accumulates and retains as much power as possible in the Presidential office itself.

Time, 5-22:18.

John W. Gardner
National chairman, Common Cause

(State legislatures are) among the most scandalously-operated instrumentalities in this country. It's going to be a long time before we have full-time state legislatures, but it would be cheaper at the price, believe me . . . Most of them are riddled with conflict of interest, riddled with corruption and wholly inadequate instruments of self government. The conflict of interest in the state legislatures is the worst evil that they have. There are men making laws who most of the time are in the employ of the interests they are making laws about.

Interview, Washington, Jan. 3/ San Francisco Examiner, 1-3:2.

Arthur J. Goldberg
Lawyer; Former Associate Justice, Supreme Court of the United States

Without adequate information from the Executive Branch of the government, Congress cannot appropriately perform functions entrusted to it under the Constitution. Moreover, nothing can contribute more to the weakening of Congress and to an undue concentration of power in the Executive than the Executive's recalcitrance in ap-

(ARTHUR J. GOLDBERG)

propriate sharing of information with Congress . . . It is an understatement to say that we are witnessing an increasing confrontation between the Executive and the Legislative Branches in this information area. We must promptly take all necessary steps to prevent this confrontation from becoming a Constitutional crisis.

Before House Government Information Subcommittee, Washington/ The Dallas Times Herald, 3-26:(G)2.

Barry M. Goldwater
United States Senator, R–Ariz.

If you don't stay in shape, you just don't stay in the (Senate) business very long. I've been in the military—and that's pretty rough—but I've never experienced anything that required the physical stamina of this job.

The Washington Post, 10-1:(F)2.

Julian Goodman
President,
National Broadcasting Company

Government processes start with one purpose and then go on forever, careening in various directions, often ending up with results directly contrary to the original purpose. Theory is in conflict with reality, and reality is losing out.

Before International Radio and Television Society, New York, March 9/ The Hollywood Reporter, 3-10:6.

Mike Gravel
United States Senator, D–Alaska

(Secrecy in government) is the most important problem facing our democracy today. It permitted us to go into Vietnam. It leads to autocracy and dictatorship. How can the people agree or disagree with policy if they don't know what is going on?

The Washington Post, 5-4:(A)22.

Durward G. Hall
United States Representative, R–Mo.

(Advocating limiting Senators to two terms of office and Representatives to six): . . . a term limitation should be imposed on both houses of Congress, just as we have on the Executive, which would prevent election to office from becoming a way of life, and contribute significantly to the demise of the seniority system . . . I have developed the strong conviction that none of us here-assembled are so wise and indispensable, or so highly qualified that an unfillable void would be created if our longevity was curtailed. I have never held that repeated election to public office is qualification enough for committee chairmanship; on the contrary, it could very well serve as a reason for not providing an individual with the power that comes from ascendency to the chair. I have sat in these chambers for 12 years—on many occasions listening to our younger members orate at length about the evils of the seniority system. Now I am giving them an opportunity to help end it once and for all. I think we owe it to the representative system of government in a republic, and to the American people.

Before the House, Washington, March 14/ The Washington Post, 3-22:(A)22.

Vance Hartke
United States Senator, D–Ind.

People today have an uneasy feeling that the government has slipped away from them and they are on the outside looking in.

Quote, 4-23:385.

James D. Hodgson
Secretary of Labor
of the United States

The recent phenomenal growth in government was not imposed on us. We voted—or our elected representatives did—for all those public services supplied by all those governmental jurisdictions . . . Still, we do pay an awful lot for those services. And many of us apparently are beginning to think we're paying too much . . . The message is clear. A lot of people don't think they're getting their money's worth out of government, and they're not very happy about it.

U.S. News & World Report, 6-19:80.

Hubert H. Humphrey
United States Senator, D–Minn.

I don't want a government that does everything for me; because if it does everything *for* me, it can do anything *to* me.

At Junior Chamber of Commerce convention, Daytona Beach, Fla., Jan. 30/The Washington Post, 1-31:(A)9.

This country needs a President who not only reads what people say but looks into the eyes of the American people and reads there what they cannot say. The President is the lobbyist for the people. Everyone else is organized–the bankers, the lawyers, the businessmen, labor. But there are millions and millions of people who have no spokesman but their President.

The Washington Post, 5-7:(B)4.

(On whether he would accept the Vice-Presidential nomination this year): I have been Vice President. It is an interesting job, and someone who has not had the experience should get it. It builds character.

Miami Beach, July 10/ The Washington Post, 7-11:(A)10.

Lyndon B. Johnson
Former President of the United States

(Advocating a one-term, six-year Presidency): I believe that, if a man knew that he just had one term and he had to get everything through in six years, that he didn't have to play to any political group and he didn't have to satisfy any segment of our society, and this was the only chance he was going to have and he couldn't put it off, I think it would probably–and I say probably–be in the best interests of the nation.

Television interview, Austin, Tex./ Columbia Broadcasting System, 1-27.

Edward M. Kennedy
United States Senator, D–Mass.

Our present difficulties do not flow, I think, so much from the fact that people mistrust their government, as from the fact that the government so obviously mistrusts the people.

Before Washington Press Club, Jan. 17/The New York Times, 1-18:17.

Henry A. Kissinger
Assistant to the President of the United States for National Security Affairs

. . . between what you must do *as* President, and what you must do to be *elected* President, the disparity is staggering. Getting to be President takes so much energy that you stumble exhausted into the White House. What you do *as* President is make decisions. The Presidency is a constant series of choices–choices in which the pros and cons are fairly evenly balanced; otherwise, a subordinate will already have made them. Furthermore, the people who present these choices to the President are all strong and plausible men. So the man in the White House has a high incentive to give each advocate *something.* If the choice were absolute good over absolute evil, it would be a cinch to be President.

Washington/Newsweek, 8-21:19.

Richard G. Kleindienst
Deputy Attorney General of the United States

I believe that not only is the First Amendment right of free speech the most important right we have, but I also believe it important that the government, to the extent that it can, should create and maintain an atmosphere where people feel free to exercise that right.

Interview/Newsweek, 1-3:12.

Russell B. Long
United States Senator, D–La.

As sure as there are governments, there are going to be some men who make mistakes on this side of heaven.

Before the Senate, Washington, Sept. 7/ The Washington Post, 9-8:(A)16.

Richard G. Lugar
Mayor of Indianapolis

There are very few Governors in this country who ever do anything. They mostly smile a lot.

Campaigning for the re-election of Illinois Governor Richard B. Ogilvie, Mount Vernon, Ill., Oct. 12/ The New York Times, 10-15:(1)46.

Mike Mansfield
United States Senator, D–Mont.

(Criticizing the Senate for absenteeism, immaturity and unwillingness to work): I don't intend to get down on my knees to this body. If you won't face up to your responsibilities, there's nothing, not a thing, that the leadership can do to force you to. I don't intend to lose any more sleep, as I have over the past month, over the conduct of this body . . . these people who are supposed to be mature . . . Sometimes I wonder just how much conscience this body has . . . Sometimes I wonder how much longer Senators can think of themselves primarily and the Senate secondarily . . . There are thousands of people back in our respective states who are smarter than we are, have more ability than we do and who could do a better job than we're doing. But they haven't had the breaks we've had, and so we are here and they are not.

Before the Senate, Washington, Feb. 9/ Los Angeles Times, 2-10:(1)23.

Charles McC. Mathias, Jr.
United States Senator, R–Md.

(Criticizing a proposal for imposing a Federal spending limit to be administered by the President rather than by Congress): I have the highest confidence in the wisdom and capabilities of President Nixon, but each of us must realize that most of the spending decisions would be made—not by the President—but by some nameless, faceless bureaucrat not answerable to the people of America. Perhaps these decisions would be made wisely; I hope so; but we have no way of knowing. And we would be setting a very dangerous precedent for the future. I contend that our duty to the people and the Constitution demands that we (Congress) make these fundamental decisions ourselves. The Constitution gives Congress the power of the purse, the power to raise revenues and to direct how those revenues are to be spent. The power of the purse was the great victory won by the barons at Runnymede and guaranteed in the Magna Carta in the year 1215. Thousands of Englishmen have given their lives and fortunes to protect that fundamental principle in the centuries that have followed. Millions of people in other countries have died trying to gain a similar check on their rulers. Our Founding Fathers considered this power so vital that they spelled out in the Constitution that only the House of Representatives could initiate revenue legislation. The purpose of that provision was made clear by Hamilton and Madison: The Representatives are more accessible to and more responsible to the people of the United States; and the power to make these critical decisions should be shared by a large number of elected officials close to the general populace . . . In the final analysis, each of us must admit that we have been derelict in our duties, that we have neglected our responsibility to reform programs to meet the challenges of the modern Federal budget. But we should not now take the easy way out—by not only passing the buck, but also passing the power of the purse—with no commitment to reform our procedures in the future beyond a new committee to study the problem. I cannot support such action. If cuts be necessary—and I think they are—let us make them ourselves. If time be required, let us take it. If wisdom and responsibility be demanded, let us rise to the occasion and find it in ourselves. Only thereby shall we meet our full obligations to the people and the nation we serve.

Before the Senate, Washington, Oct.16/Congressional Digest, December:297.

(On the loss of Congressional authority to the Presidency): Congress today has become a third- or fourth-class power, a separate and thoroughly unequal branch of our national government.

The Christian Science Monitor, 12-7:1.

George S. McGovern
United States Senator, D–S.D.

Tens of millions of Americans have lost faith in government. We need leadership in Washington that will convince the average citizen of our cities that his government is being run for his benefit and is working to make his life better.

At U.S. Conference of Mayors, New Orleans, June 20/ The Dallas Times Herald, 6-20:(A)9.

(On how, if he were elected President, he would use his Vice President): I think that, depending on who it is, you ought to figure out his areas of greatest talent and then really give him major responsibility in supervising those areas, so that there might even be some division of responsibility for everyday operations for supervising, energizing, accelerating and serving in the role of a kind of second President in areas where the Vice President had the greatest competence.

Interview, Washington/ Los Angeles Times, 6-24:(1)13.

Abner J. Mikva
United States Representative, D–Ill.

(Advocating higher pay for members of Congress): There's always a sacrifice in politics, and I don't say that's unreasonable. But it shouldn't be so great that it becomes a deterrent. It's an expensive hobby —and that's too bad. The more we underpay public servants, the less we're going to get the kind of government we want. A lot of people are just frozen out of government.

The Washington Post, 12-25:(A)39.

Wilbur D. Mills
United States Representative, D–Ark.

We (in government) have failed to maintain a responsible fiscal policy. We have exhorbitantly outspent our revenue resources. We have unnecessarily opened the public coffers to wasteful programs which have caught the public fancy and which have produced few tangible results.

Campaigning for the Democratic Presidential nomination, Gardner, Mass., April 14/ The Washington Post, 4-15:(A)2.

(On government spending): The root of most all problems we have today is the uncontrollable appetite of politicians in Washington to dish it out.

Before Commonwealth Club, San Francisco, June 2/ San Francisco Examiner, 6-3:7.

William S. Moorhead
United States Representative, D–Pa.

(By classifying government documents and papers as "secret" and thus unavailable for public scrutiny, a) President could safely stay in office for his full two Constitutional terms, totaling eight years, and at the same time make it possible for his Vice President, or another of his supporters, to succeed him without the public knowing the full details of major defense or foreign-policy errors his Administration had committed. In other words, the same political party could control the Presidency for 12 years, when, perhaps, the public would

(WILLIAM S. MOORHEAD)

throw it out of office (sooner) if only the facts were known.

Before House Subcommittee on Government Information, Washington, March 10/ The New York Times, 3-11:14.

(On secrecy in government): Secrecy is the blood enemy of democracy. Secrecy subverts any representative system, just as it is essential to maintain a totalitarian dictatorship.

Before Federal Editors Association, Washington, May 11/ San Francisco Examiner, 5-11:2.

Rogers C. B. Morton
Secretary of the Interior of the United States

. . . kids are idealists . . . and I don't think government will ever perform to the satisfaction of people between 17 and 28.

Claremont, N.H., Feb. 4/ The Washington Post, 2-5:(A)4.

Edmund S. Muskie
United States Senator, D–Maine

What has changed is the faith which many Americans have (toward government) and the responsiveness of their leaders and the honesty of their responses to questions from the people. The anger of the American voter in these (Presidential) primaries—and I have been exposed to it—is not just the anger of those with whom others do not agree. It is the anger of those who are frustrated and who have begun to believe that there is no way in which they can improve their own lives or the lives of their children. They are part of the frustration which has contributed to the helpless feeling which seems to underlie the brutal desperation of the assassin, and which may be in the lives of others who feel themselves without hope in this nation today.

At La Salle Academy, Providence, R.I., May 19/The New York Times, 5-20:14.

Pat (Mrs. Richard M.) Nixon
Wife of the President of the United States

Being First Lady is the hardest unpaid job in the world.

Monrovia, Liberia/ San Francisco Examiner, 3-16:25.

Richard M. Nixon
President of the United States

As President, an individual is expected to maintain a quality of dignity; a quality of aloofness. Yes, of course, to be friendly too; but people don't want the President of the United States to be a little sloppy or lewd or vulgar. They want to think he is one of them but not too much so. If they see the President kicking up his heels, eating too much or drinking too much, the confidence factor is weakened. People want to think that, if there is a crisis, he will be cool and sober. They also want to think that he's a human guy who likes his wife and kids and a good time.

Interview, Washington/ Time, 1-3:19.

(Criticizing excessive spending by Congress): The Congress operates the way a family would if all the individual family members went out on their own, spent what they wanted, or signed up for long-term payments for things they desire, without regard to what other members of the family were spending, and without regard to the total income of the family and the total of the bills all of the members of the family were running up on their own.

Broadcast address, Camp David, Md., Oct. 7/ San Francisco Examiner & Chronicle, 10-8:(A)12.

The central question which goes to the heart of American government and is sure to affect every person in this land is this: Do we want to turn more power over to bureaucrats in Washington in the hope that they will do what is best for all the people? Or do we want to return more power to the people and to their state and local governments, so that people can decide what is best for themselves? Now, people of good conscience differ on this issue. Certainly, in the past generation there were cases in which power concentrated in Washington did much to help our people live in greater fairness and security and to enable our nation to speak and act strongly in world affairs. When the will of the people is best expressed by the nation acting as one people, I strongly support the use of effective Federal action. But the concentration of power can get to be a dangerous habit. Government officials who get power over others tend to want to keep it. And the more power they get, the more they want.

Radio address, Oct. 21/
U.S. News & World Report, 12-4:32.

It is very easy for politicians to call for fresh millions to be allocated for every new . . . spending proposal that spins out of any ivory towers. But the President must carefully weigh the cost of new proposals against their merits. And there are times when he must have the strength to say "No" for the sake of the American taxpayer.

Radio address campaigning for the forthcoming Presidential election, Washington, Oct.25/
The New York Times, 10-26:33.

(Saying there should be less government influence and more individual public initiative in domestic programs and affairs): Now, I realize what I have just said—in many quarters in Washington in which we live, and the Georgetown cocktail set—that (it) will be tut-tutted by those who are living in another era. They honestly believe that the answer to the problem is always some new massive government program. I totally disagree with that. Sometimes a new program is needed. But what we need now, rather than more government, is better government. I realize that is a cliche; but rather than more it is better, and many times the better is not the fatter but the leaner.

Interview, Nov. 5/
The New York Times, 11-10:20.

. . . generally speaking, whether they are Democratic Administrations or Republican Administrations, the tendency is for an Administration to run out of steam after the first four years, and then to coast, and usually coast downhill. That is particularly true when there is what you call a landslide (Presidential re-election) victory. As I have put it to some of my closest colleagues, generally when you think of a landslide (such as he just won), you are submerged by it and you also think in terms of a landslide pushing you downhill. What I am trying to do is to change that historical pattern. The only way that historical pattern can be changed is to change not only some of the players but also some of the plays, if I may use the analogy to sports. What I am suggesting here is that, when a new Administration comes in, it comes in with new ideas, new people, new programs. That is why it has vitality and excitement. A second Administration usually lacks that vitality. It lacks it not because the men and women in the Administration are any less dedicated, but because it is inevitable, when an individual has been in a Cabinet position or, for that matter, holds any position in government, after a certain length of time he becomes an advocate of the status quo; rather than running the bureaucracy, the bureaucracy runs him. It has been my conviction for years that elected officials in this country too often become prisoners of what we would call the bureaucracy which they are supposed to run. This is no reflection on the bureaucracy. There are millions of dedicated people working for government throughout this country who are not elected officials or people who are appointed by the elected officials. It is, however, simply a statement of fact that it is the responsi-

(RICHARD M. NIXON)

bility of those who are elected to the highest office in this land to see to it that what they consider to be the directions that the people want them to follow are followed out and not that they simply come in and continue to go along doing things as they have been done in the past.

News conference, Camp David, Md., Nov. 27/ The New York Times, 11-28:40.

Robert Packwood
United States Senator, R–Ore.

(Arguing against Congress relinquishing to the President the right to determine government spending): We went from the time of our Constitutional Convention all through the 1800s with Congress perfectly able to draw budgets, determine priorities and raise money . . . We can do it again if we want to. When people say, "It is beyond us; that was 1921; we were talking about a budget of $3 or $4 billion; we cannot do it now with a budget of $250 billion; nobody in Congress can fathom that"—I say that is baloney . . . I look at us and say, "Why the dickens do we do it? Why are we willing to give away this power?" I can only come up with two reasons. One is that we really do not want it . . . It is easy to give the power to the President. Let him make the tough decisions; we will not have to do it. Let him decide where to spend $2 or $3 billion. We will sit back, and if it is unpopular, we will criticize him . . . If he happens to make a popular decision and cuts something nobody likes, we applaud him, and we all get re-elected together . . . In addition to not wanting it, I think we have gotten in the habit in Congress of saying, "Can't—can't be done." We cannot run the Post Office. We cannot determine wage and price policies. We cannot determine where military bases ought to be placed overseas. We cannot set the Executive salaries. We cannot fathom the Federal budget. So we delegate it to the President. I think this Congress is fiscally corrupt. I do not think we have the discipline or courage to raise taxes or lower the expenditures . . . So we are faced with a Hobson's choice: either we delegate these powers to the President in order to save the country from Congress, or we keep the powers in Congress and perhaps run the country into bankruptcy. What it amounts to is a choice between a *fiscally* irresponsible Congress and a *totally* irresponsible Congress. If I have to make a choice between the two, I will choose the fiscally irresponsible Congress, because anything we do that is wrong, if we keep the power, we can right.

Before the Senate, Washington, Oct. 13/ The Washington Post, 10-22:(B)6.

Claiborne Pell
United States Senator, D–R.I.

. . . I think the true judge of effectiveness of a Senator or a Congressman is not the headlines he gets in *The Washington Post* or any other paper . . . but the true judge of effectiveness is the amount of new ideas that would not have been put into legislation and into law if it wasn't for that man.

Interview/ The Washington Post, 11-1:(A)8.

Charles H. Percy
United States Senator, R–Ill.

To lower the age of eligibility for service in the House and Senate would further participation of young people in making changes in our government. The youth of this country have too often been overlooked by our democratic system. Far too many have lost faith in being able to influence change which is necessary for a representative democracy to function properly in such a highly-skilled and technocratic society as we have. We must provide the opportunity for younger people to serve in our legislative bodies . . . Our young people are subject to the taxes Congress levies on them and the military draft we ask them to accept. It is time to give young people the opportunity to help decide the future of our nation. They are the ones who will have to live in this country, and they must be given the opportunity to take an active interest in helping to solve our problems. We cannot afford to isolate ourselves from the innovations, idealism and creativity these young citizens can bring to our councils.

Before the Senate, Washington/ Human Events, 10-28:18.

William Proxmire
United States Senator, D–Wis.

(On his having the best voting attendance record of any Senator): There are other measures of Senatorial influence, but the vote is the cutting edge, the basis of decision on the big issues that come before the Senate. This is the job I was elected to do.

The New York Times, 3-24:41.

Ronald Reagan
Governor of California

In those states where they have (government-run) lotteries and where they have turned to gambling of one kind or another in an effort to raise revenues for the state, they haven't proven all that successful. As a matter of fact, they have made very little impact on the state's financial picture. I just think that, in a state like California, with the size and wealth and power of California, we should appeal to the people's strengths rather than their weaknesses in order to get the funds we need to run state government.

News conference, March 21/ Los Angeles Times, 3-23:(2)6.

With the average citizen spending almost a third of his work week just earning the money to pay his taxes, there is still an urgent need to reduce the size and cost of government. Those working men and women who—if I can paraphrase—never have asked what government can do for them, but have constantly been told what they can do for their government, are the social and economic backbone of our state. They deserve more consideration than they have had from all the governments they pay for with the fruit of their toil.

State of the State address, Sacramento/ Los Angeles Herald-Examiner, 4-20:(A)10.

In some dim beginning, man created the institution of government as a convenience for himself. And ever since that time, government has been doing its best to become an *in*convenience. Government bureaus and agencies take on a life and a purpose of their own. But I wonder if it happens because so many of us—all of us probably—read and hear and just repeat what we think is a truism—that when a public problem develops, government is *forced* to step in. That is utter nonsense. Government can hardly wait to step in. As a matter of fact, government is in the position of the fellow who will make a speech at the drop of a hat.

Before Chamber of Commerce of the United States/ The Wall Street Journal, 9-25:8.

George E. Reedy
Former Press Secretary to the President of the United States

If you were ever to establish as a principle that information were to be coordinated from the White House, I think you could forget freedom of information and access to information and everything else. The way the public really does get a break is that the government is so huge that frequently the left hand does not know what the right hand is doing—that's the way the public learns something from time to time.

Before House Government Information Subcommittee hearing on government secrecy policies, Washington, March 6/ San Francisco Examiner, 5-7:2.

(GEORGE E. REEDY)

We talk of the "great powers of the Presidency." The reality is that there are few powers in the office itself. A more precise way of saying it is that the Presidency is an office through which great powers can be exercised, providing the occupant has those powers and knows how to use them. We speak of a newly-elected President as carrying a "mandate from the people." All that has really happened is that he has been selected from a narrow field of candidates to manage our affairs for a four-year term. Maybe he has a mandate, maybe he doesn't; but it cannot be measured by the size of his vote. He may have been elected because he was the lesser of two evils, because he looked a little bit better to the public than his opponent, or possibly just because he was popular personally. It may have had nothing to do with his policies and his programs, and the vote for him did not necessarily mean support for what he wants to do. Unfortunately, once he is elected, we wrap him in a mystical mantle, and isolate him so thoroughly from the world of people, where real power lies, that he is incapable of taking the actions that are necessary for dynamic leadership in a democratic society.

Television broadcast/"Comment!" National Broadcasting Company, 7-9.

Edwin O. Reischauer
Professor, Harvard University; Former United States Ambassador to Japan

The world needs leadership more than ever simply because of the speed at which things change. You can come to a catastrophe much more rapidly in the sort of society in which we now live. But, while we need leadership, it's much less likely to be the type of leadership we've seen in the past, of a great man like Roosevelt or Churchill. Then, what do we do? Well, we've just got to get better at the techniques of group leadership. We need a synthesis of the various forms of leadership that already exist—from intellectual leadership, through business leadership, to the various kinds of political leadership. We need some sort of committee kind of rule. That isn't far-fetched or radical. The U.S. Constitution was set up for group leadership. The "strong President" is only a fairly recent development . . . We already have intellectual leaders who think of new concepts, new ideas, new ways to go. They play a very large educational role. The mass media will become even more important, bringing across to the public all these different perceptions, often conflicting ones, but out of which will come a synthesis leading us in the right direction. And the role of the so-called political leader will become a fairly small one. The techniques of education are being done by others. The politician can be the catalytic agent, perhaps, but he's not the man who can do the whole thing. Life is just too complicated to be left to a single great man.

Interview, Belmont, Mass./ "W": A Fairchild publication, 4-21:5.

Elliot L. Richardson
Secretary of Health, Education and Welfare of the United States

Nothing is more damaging to public confidence in the ability of government to function than its propensity for subdividing a person's problems, parceling them off for solution to a veritable host of different agencies—most of which maintain little if any contact within—while the whole person is himself lost sight of . . . This (Nixon) Administration is determined to build bridges between service agencies at all levels of government, to rid them of their petty jealousies and predilection for bureaucratic infighting, and to make them begin treating people with problems as just that—people.

At Kansas State University, Jan. 24/ Vital Speeches, 3-1:297, 298.

The President has the most complex and broadest choices to make. He must, within the constraints imposed on him, select from among efforts to improve the environment, to improve transportation, to make the nation more secure at home and abroad, to bring sense and humanity to our welfare system, and from among a host of other worthy and pressing objectives. The Secretary of HEW must choose among efforts to bring health services into poor neighborhoods, to increase the educational opportunities of children living in those same neighborhoods, to reduce the isolation of the aged, to offer alternatives to delinquency and drugs, and among many other objectives, all of which again are worthy and compelling. And down through the tiers of government it goes, the inescapable necessity of choosing. Choice is the basic reality; and for us it is doubly difficult and saddening, because whatever we have to give up is not something bad or trivial, but something that is only somewhat less-important, if that, than what we have selected to do . . . The hard choices, in the end, are bound to depend on some combination of values and instincts—and, indeed, it is precisely because the content of choice cannot be reduced to a mathematical equation that we need the political forum to reach the final, most-difficult decisions. To recognize this, however, reinforces the importance of being as honest and explicit as possible in articulating the nonmeasurable considerations that transcend the limits of objective analysis. Only if these considerations are exposed to full view can we bring those whose expectations have to be deferred—or overruled—to accept the legitimacy of the process by which this was done. Only thus can we hope to reconcile the loser to losing and encourage the impatient to wait.

Before HEW employees/ Los Angeles Times, 2-20:(G)6.

Hyman G. Rickover
Vice Admiral, United States Navy

As a realist, I must say that about the only real power Congress has left is the negative power of denying funds . . . When Congress does not exercise the power vested exclusively in it to make the laws that govern the United States, its power to do so atrophies. Indeed, I submit that Congress has already lost much of its power by not using it. Congress may change the Administration's budget by 1 or 2 per cent; but to all intents and purposes, Congress no longer has control over the budget. Like any other parliamentary body in a free society, it does, however, have the power of legislative oversight as well as the right to refuse to vote appropriations if it judges that in the past they have not been used in accordance with the laws it has enacted . . . Since Congress itself can no longer control in detail how appropriated moneys are spent, its Constitutional control of the purse strings now depends more than ever on the judicious exercise of its investigatory function and on the negative power to refuse funds.

Before Senate Armed Services Committee, Washington/The New York Times, 4-27:43.

Dean Rusk
Former Secretary of State of the United States

(On leaks of secret government documents to the press): It is the duty of the government official to keep his mouth shut.

The Dallas Times Herald, 1-9:(A)42.

Robert L. Saloschin
Chairman, Freedom of Information Committee, Department of Justice of the United States

(On leaks to the press of classified government material): With all due respect to the public's right to know—and the public does have a right to know—the people have elected a President and a Congress to protect the national security; and (court) judges should, in my opinion, exercise great restraint in ruling on questions of defense and foreign policy.

Interview/ Los Angeles Times, 1-30:(A)5.

Arthur M. Schlesinger, Jr.
Historian; Former Special Assistant to the President of the United States

The discipline of consent—i.e., the need to persuade Congress and the electorate of the soundness of a proposed policy—is the heart of democracy. More than that, the debate generated by this need to persuade is vital to the education in public affairs that alone produces an informed citizenry.

San Francisco Examiner & Chronicle, 1-9:(This World)2.

John G. Schmitz
United States Representative, I–Calif.; American Party Presidential nominee

Any government that's big enough to give you everything you want is big enough to take away everything you've got.

San Francisco Examiner & Chronicle, 10-29:(A)15.

Neil Sheehan
News correspondent, "The New York Times"

Governments in general will try to hide what they think they can hide from the public.

News conference, Norfolk, Va., May 25/ The Washington Post, 5-27:(A)22.

R. Sargent Shriver
Democratic Vice-Presidential nominee

Politics is being aware of the deep needs that people have, such as shelter, quiet and an orderly environment for their families. What people want from the government is an atmosphere where they can achieve those things themselves. They don't want the government to hand it to them. Government, that is all of us working together, should concentrate on trying to make it easier for people.

Interview, Rockville, Md./ Newsweek, 8-21:13.

George P. Shultz
Secretary of the Treasury of the United States

Until now, mood and attitude have been, "The more you (in government) spend, the greater a guy you are." We have to get that turned around into an attitude that says, "The more careful you are with the taxpayer's dollar, the better a guy you are." Because what we're talking about in reality is not so much spending as it is taxing. If we're going to spend and spend, then taxes will have to go up. That's really the issue; and the President (Nixon) is determined to do everything in his power to keep taxes from going up. The people who want to do the spending must also sooner or later realize that taxes must go up. The people who are trying to keep spending under control are also trying to keep taxes under control. That, I might say, should be the number one plank on the tax-reform program—keep spending under control so that taxes are under control.

Interview, Washington/ U.S. News & World Report, 8-28:26.

Margaret Chase Smith
United States Senator, R–Maine

(On Senators traveling at taxpayers' expense): There are two kinds of junkets: one to become informed, and one to have fun. Too many Senators have taken the latter.

Quote, 4-2:313.

David T. Stanley
Senior fellow in governmental studies, Brookings Institution

Government agencies can and should be put through an organizational wringer to squeeze out unproductive layers of supervision and proliferated staff units . . . It takes an outside strike force, armed with hatchets.

U.S. News & World Report, 6-19:78.

Herbert Stein
Chairman, Council of Economic Advisers to the President of the United States

Too often, the Federal budget is less an instrument of economic management than a live grenade tossed back and forth between the Administration and Congress.

Before World Affairs Council, Los Angeles, Sept. 22/ Los Angeles Herald-Examiner, 9-23:(A)3.

Leonor K. Sullivan
United States Representative, D–Mo.

I think the main reason the President's (Nixon) programs are in trouble is that he sends us one message after another and then waits until it is almost time to quit before we get the exact recommendations in legislative terms. We get more beautiful generalities than anything else. Revenue-sharing is an example of a proposal the deeper you get into the less you see how it can be done. For one thing, there is so much confusion from the Administration. One witness comes up and says one thing. Next week, another witness will tell us something else. This sounds terribly partisan, and I'm not that partisan a person. But I think Congress has been getting 3½ years of a whirl of confusion from the Administration. Their people don't know who is doing what.

Interview/ U.S. News & World Report, 5-15:66.

Stuart Symington
United States Senator, D–Mo.

I don't get enough information (from the Executive Branch) on which to make my decisions, and I resent that. If we could just get this passion for secrecy out of the way . . . Having run quite a few businesses, I have a difficult time voting other people's money in the blind. There's just no true accountability.

Interview/ The Christian Science Monitor, 3-22:13.

I don't think there's any substitute for the wisdom that comes from experience, particularly in government. I knew (former West German Chancellor Konrad) Adenauer when he was in his 80s, and I knew (former British Prime Minister Winston) Churchill when he was in his 80s. They were both still very able men. You take (U.S. Senator) Allen Ellender. He's 81. I work out in the Senate gym with him every night. He's in tremendous shape, strong as a bull. And he's probably the hardest-working man in the Senate.

Interview/ The New York Times Magazine, 6-11:39.

Morris K. Udall
United States Representative, D–Ariz.

It must be apparent to anyone studying the present situation that the Nixon Cabinet has been downgraded to a dangerous degree. The plain fact today is that on most matters Cabinet members tend to deal with underlings who have far more influence on the President than the Cabinet member himself. Most major policy formulation is now made by a kind of medieval court where the king's favorites struggle for power, owing no allegiance except to their master, and the public good is consistently subordinated to private gain. The real point . . . is that everyone should be made aware of a very subtle change in our system of government.

Washington/ San Francisco Examiner, 4-25:2.

Charls E. Walker
Deputy Secretary of the Treasury of the United States

Spending is not easy to control in our system of government. Spending is popular, and Congressmen naturally attempt to respond to the wishes of their constituents, as they are doing now in exceeding President Nixon's requests in almost every major area. But there is one effective way of getting spending under control, and that is

(CHARLS E. WALKER)

for Congress to enact a tough, iron-clad, no-exceptions ceiling for Federal outlays for the current fiscal year and for each fiscal year in the future. With such a firm ceiling, the President would be required to hold spending to that figure regardless of increases in uncontrollable items such as interest on the debt.

Dallas, July 25/
The Dallas Times Herald, 7-25:(D)8.

Caspar W. Weinberger
Director, Federal Office of Management and Budget

We ought to have learned by now that throwing the taxpayers' money at social problems is not the automatic way to solve them, as so many seem to think. We ought to become much more modest about our estimate of government's ability—particularly by the Federal government's ability—to correct these problems by starting a spate of big, expensive, untested programs under the misguided assumptions that we know the solutions.

Before Congressional Joint Economic Subcommittee, Washington, June 27/
The New York Times, 6-28:22.

I don't hold any particular brief for a (government budget) surplus. If you're in a situation where you have a surplus, you're collecting too much in taxes, and you should then redress this by reducing taxes, unless this would produce inflation in that particular year. A government should not be in business to make money. It should do the necessary things, perform the necessary services, create the kind of atmosphere in which problems can be solved, and give the private sector and the free market as much rein as possible. I don't feel there's any particular justification for a tax system that produces a surplus each year. On the other hand, I certainly wouldn't favor spending enough to wipe out any potential surplus. A lot of people approach it that way.

Interview, Washington/
U.S. News & World Report, 7-17:24.

Caspar W. Weinberger
Director, Federal Office of Management and Budget; Secretary-designate of Health, Education and Welfare of the United States

I was pretty young when the New Deal came in. I did not like it. It seemed to me at that time that it involved an enormous increase in government power over the lives and rights of individuals. It also came on very rapidly, it seemed to me. It came without necessary preparation and with a very glib assumption that, because there was a problem, we needed a Federal solution. This is not to say I am opposed to all government action or exercise of power; frequently, it is necessary, obviously. Only the Federal government can be responsible for the security of the country and the conduct of foreign policy . . . But government power should be used very sparingly and with full knowledge that it is not always the solution and sometimes it is the wrong approach. I am suspicious of automatic, across-the-board approaches—the kind of thinking that says we have got a serious problem and, therefore, we should bring the Federal government into it.

Interview, Washington/
Los Angeles Times, 11-29:(2)7.

Spiro T. Agnew
Vice President of the United States

It's just another of these radical ideas that everything will be all right if everybody is allowed to have an equal share of the income. Well, that's ridiculous. If we have that, we're dead. You could give everybody in the country today the same amount of money, and by the end of the year there would be rich people and poor people all over again. There has got to be an incentive system. People have to be able to gain from hard work and discipline. A system that didn't have a competitive edge for some who are industrious wouldn't be worth living in. If we are going to live in a sea of nonachievers, we might just as well quit. If that ever happens to this country—where the wealth is redistributed every year—then the competitive spirit and individual initiative that have made America great will have died.

Interview/ U.S. News & World Report, 3-13:40.

Tax reform is easier to demand than to design—especially in an election year when ambitious candidates are prone to invoking visions of fiscal fantasylands where the "rich" pay but everybody enjoys a heaven on earth.

Before National Association of Counties, Washington, June 27/ The Washington Post, 6-28:(A)27.

Frank E. Barnett
Chairman,
Union Pacific Corporation

We have no expectations of getting eight hours of work a day from our labor force . . . If we get up to four or five hours a day, we'll feel this is a substantial improvement.

Plainview (Tex.) Daily Herald, 7-11:6.

P. T. Bauer
Professor of Economics,
University of London

The market system delivers the goods people want, but its supporters cannot explain why. The socialist system does not deliver the goods, but its supporters readily explain why it does not, cannot or should not do so. The one system is long on desired goods and short on effective arguments. The other system is short on desired goods but long on successful arguments.

The Sacramento (Calif.) Bee, 10-19:(A)18.

Joseph A. Beirne
President,
Communications Workers of America

The young worker never experienced the big Depression. He is well-educated and has been taught to be independent. He doesn't feel the work ethic that is so important to his parents. Young workers don't have a clear idea of what they want, any more than young people ever did. So the labor movement must be flexible and keep up with change. A lot of us aren't flexible enough. That's why organized labor is not keeping up with the growth of the labor force.

U.S. News & World Report, 2-21:25.

(On labor union jurisdictional disputes): This is something that is going on in hundreds and hundreds of communities every single day of the week and every single

(JOSEPH A. BEIRNE)

day of the year. I don't think there's any statistic anybody could compile that would give an actual picture of the time and energy and everything else that's wasted and lost in these jurisdictional fights between unions. Hundreds and hundreds and hundreds of man-hours, with all the countless thousands of dollars behind every one of those man-hours, are involved where two unions are battling for one plant or five unions are trying to organize the same group of workers.

The Washington Post, 4-9:(A)21.

(On mergers of labor unions, such as that possible between his union and two postal unions): If you look at life in terms of how sweet everything is, then this merger doesn't present any advantages. But if you look at things as they are in this country, you see that numbers count. American culture is enthralled by bigness. So, okay; if this is the way things are, let's get big. It will make the Postal Service and AT&T sit up and take notice when they are dealing with a union with 1.25 million members.

Interview/
The New York Times, 12-20:18.

Lloyd M. Bentsen
United States Senator, D–Tex.

Age discrimination practices, whether they relate to the age of hiring, restrictions on promotion, or direct and indirect encouragements to retire, are not to be condoned. Many of our citizens are (as) productive at 60 as they were at 25; and measures taken to remove them from the work force are both callous and unrealistic.

Before the Senate,
Washington/Quote, 4-9:338.

Hale Boggs
United States Representative, D–La.

The (Nixon) Administration has been so undecided between the policies that would allegedly cure inflation and those which would expand employment that we have had inactivity, indecision, unemployment and inflation all at the same time.

Before National Rural Electric
Cooperative Association,
Las Vegas, Nev., Feb. 28/
San Francisco Examiner, 2-29:2.

George H. Boldt
Chairman, Pay Board,
Federal Cost of Living Council

(On the resignation from the Pay Board of three labor representatives): The AFL-CIO has alleged that the public members have been part of "an unholy alliance" with the business members and have acted to thwart the development of an equitable program (to control inflation). This allegation has been part of a steady drumfire of accusations and abuse that has been directed at the public members from the first day that the Pay Board convened. We unequivocally reject the assertion that the public members have been concerned with any objective or consideration other than the goals of the stabilization program and the economic welfare of all Americans. Moreover, each of the public members states categorically that there has been no attempt by (Nixon) Administration officials to influence any votes by the public members. We think we have reached the right decisions, but we know that we reached them independently.

News conference,
Washington, March 22/
The New York Times, 3-23:34.

Arch N. Booth
Executive vice president,
Chamber of Commerce
of the United States

If monopolistic unions are to continue to get preferential treatment by using the strike weapon and arrogant threats of coercion, it is difficult to conceive how the vast majority of the American people can be expected to show the restraint necessary to make the anti-inflation program work.

Plainview (Tex.) Daily Herald, 1-19:6.

James L. Buckley
United States Senator, C–N.Y.

Although our economic system is one of enormous complexity, essentially it is based on a quite simple principle which the American Economic Foundation has reduced to the following formula: Man's material welfare equals his natural resources, plus the muscular and mental human energy he applies to them, multiplied by the efficiency of his tools. Better living depends upon better tools. Tools come from savings. Savings come from self-denial. Self-denial is inspired by reward. This is the fundamental formula which explains and justifies capitalism. But to fully understand the American system of capitalism, it is necessary to add an additional ingredient to our equation, and that is freedom–economic freedom. By this I mean the preservation of the widest feasible range of options for every participant in our economy–the entrepreneur, the manager, the worker, the investor, the consumer; freedom from arbitrary or artificial restraints, whether they be imposed by private monopoly or governmental edict. It is this system of capitalism, operating within the disciplines imposed by the marketplace, which has served us so well. For it has combined the fullest incentive to investment with the free marketplace's weeding out of the inefficient.

Before Queens County (N.Y.) Chamber of Commerce, Dec. 5/ Human Events, 12-30:8.

Arthur F. Burns
Chairman,
Federal Reserve Board

We have experienced in recent years many strikes against government–Federal, state and local. These strikes have had an encouraging effect on other unions elsewhere in the economy. That is because: 1) The strikes against government are conspicuous strikes; 2) they have by and large been successful strikes; and 3) even though they are successful, they are still illegal strikes. This encourages lawlessness, extravagant demands. It even serves to limit the power of influence of responsible union leaders. The rank-and-file say, "Look what illegal strikes have won! Ours is legal, so we will demand still more."

Interview, Washington/ Los Angeles Times, 1-21:(2)9.

It is important to distinguish between money income and real income. The first is the number of dollars in your paycheck; the second is what those dollars will buy after taxes. In recent years, while their money incomes were going up, many millions of American families have actually lost ground economically. That we have to stop. This is not to say that we have to give up the hope of pay raises except when a person is promoted into a higher job. Productivity in the American economy–the output per man-hour–has tended to go up at a rate of three per cent a year, and with good economic management we can hold it at that rate or even increase it. In any event, that is all we have to distribute, and wage increases of 10 per cent a year are simply an illusion. The average of incomes cannot increase faster than the increase in the nation's productivity . . . There's no sleight-of-hand. We must all strive to be more efficient, more innovative and work harder.

The Reader's Digest, February:72.

(Advocating sweeping reforms to fight inflation rather than assuming it is inevitable): If a nation with our traditions attempted to make it easy to live with inflation, rather than resist its corrosive influence, we would slowly but steadily lose the sense of discipline needed to pursue governmental policies with an eye to the permanent welfare of our people.

Before American Economic Association and American Finance Association, Toronto, Dec. 29/ The Washington Post, 12-29:(D)5.

Earl L. Butz
Secretary of Agriculture of the United States

Don't ask me to apologize for beef prices. I say, isn't it about time that beef prices got up to the levels of 20 years ago?

At livestock association meeting, St. Paul, Minn., Feb. 10/ San Francisco Examiner, 2-11:2.

As a consumer, I know price controls won't work. I vividly remember the OPA days of World War II and what happened—black markets, rationing priorities and a host of government officials checking prices, weighing packages and hauling people into court. And empty meat counters! Some consumers, either too young or too forgetful to remember, may think they want controls. They should read history. It would be easier to learn what's wrong with price control for meat by reading history than to learn it again while standing in line at a half-empty meat counter.

Before Texas and Southwest Cattle Raisers Association, Houston, March 14/ The New York Times, 3-15:28.

(The) main cause of the present inflation is the concentrated economic power exercised by special-interest groups—by some labor-union leaders, for instance. Wages throughout manufacturing and service industries keep going up—and never come down.

Before Texas and Southwest Cattle Raisers Association, Houston, March 14/ The Washington Post, 3-15:(A)2.

The American consumer this year is going to buy his food with 15.6 per cent of his take-home pay. Last year it was over 16 per cent, and two years ago it was 23 per cent. Never has the consumer bought food so cheaply as he does now . . . Farm prices are only 7 per cent higher than they were 20 years ago. You can't blame the farmer (for inflation). Farm prices are now just getting back to where they were 20 years ago, and farmers are beginning to get a little black ink on their books for a change. (The price of steak) is just right. If it was any higher we could not afford it, and if it was any lower there wouldn't be enough to get around . . . The farmers are not the ones who are striking for higher wages; they're not the ones walking off the wage-price board; they're not the ones demanding a 24 per cent wage increase like the dock workers.

At Southern Regional Republican Women's Conference, Atlanta, March 24/ The Washington Post, 3-25:(A)6.

I stood behind a housewife the other evening in a supermarket check-out line. I watched what she put on the counter. She had a quart of milk, a pound of bacon, a package of dry breakfast cereal, a 10-pound package of detergent for the automatic washer, a 25-pound sack of dog food. She had a whole mess of kitchen towels and kitchen soap. And she had two pairs of panty hose she had gotten off the impulse counter down at the end of the store. She had eight decorated tumblers at $1.28. She had two skillets at $12.98. And the whole bill came to $27.28. She turned around to me and she said, "Golly, food is expensive, isn't it!" And that girl thought she was buying food in this modern department store we call the supermarket, and came home thinking that she was being gouged on food prices. Now, the plain truth is that in 1972 the American housewife will spend only 15.6 per cent of disposable income for food. Last year, this figure was better than 16 per cent. Twenty years ago, it was 23 per cent of disposable income for food. Compared with 20 years ago, she gets an entirely different market basket. She now gets much more built-in maid service. One-fourth of the potatoes we market in this country are now processed—frozen french fries or chips—because many housewives won't peel potatoes any more. This costs money and you pay for it. Twenty years ago, our mothers stirred up a cake in the kitchen—made it from scratch. Now they rip the top off a box, break an egg in it and there's a cake. All this costs money.

Interview, Washington/ U.S. News & World Report, 4-10:53.

William W. Carlson
President,
University of Toledo

The unemployment situation has come as a shock to many college students who, up to this time, had considered stories of the Great Depression as part of American folklore. The idea that the opportunity to have a job is something to be cherished is a new concept for some of them.

San Francisco Examiner, 3-6:30.

Edwin S. Cohen
Under Secretary of the Treasury
of the United States

(Saying most rich people pay huge taxes and do not escape through loopholes): We should be slow to condemn a Federal income tax system that produces by voluntary assessment these huge amounts of tax on high adjusted gross income groups merely because a fraction of one per cent of the cases report no tax due.

Before Joint Congressional Economic Committee, Washington, July 21/ The Washington Post, 7-22:(A)2.

John B. Connally, Jr.
Secretary of the Treasury
of the United States

The philosophy of this Administration basically is against wage and price controls. Conditions were reached in this nation that made it imperative that we have them. You do have them. Now you are asking: "How long are we going to have them?" I can answer that one, too. You are going to have them so long as it is necessary to bring inflation down to the goal we have set—of 2-to-3 per cent. That is how long you are going to have them. Now, when does that time come? That time comes largely when you want it to come. That time is going to depend upon how cooperative you are, and how forceful you are, and how ambitious you are to end these controls . . . We conceive the government, and what we can do, as an instrumentality to work cooperatively with you in trying to solve some of our common problems. But I will say to you, in all candor—without any embarrassment whatsoever—that you cannot look to the government for the complete answer to your problems. When we end wage and price controls is going to depend on you. It is going to depend on you and labor relations across the bargaining table. It depends upon labor. When each of you makes up your mind that you can no longer negotiate and expect anybody to support unconscionable and unreasonable wage demands in this country; when you make up your mind that you have to increase your productivity; that you cannot continue to expect to raise your prices in unconscionable fashions, then we are going to stop inflation.

Before Chamber of Commerce of the United States, Washington, Jan. 20/ The New York Times, 1-22:44.

. . . the rest of the world is at work while we are worrying. That is the truth of the matter. They are outworking us; they are outplanning us, day after day. Those of you who are dealing in the international markets, those of you who compete in the international field, know full well what I am talking about. Now, somehow, you have got to lead a resurgence of the American spirit of work. We have to return to our puritanical system of work if we are going to survive; if we are going to build, if we are going to grow; if we are going to expand.

Before Chamber of Commerce of the United States, Washington, Jan. 20/ The New York Times, 1-22:44.

(JOHN B. CONNALLY, JR.)

Our main problem in this country is to bring down interest rates. There is more to think about than what the international bankers and the bankers in Europe are concerned about. The thing we need in this country is continued pressure to bring down interest rates, not particularly the short-term rates, but intermediate rates and long-term rates which are still too high. The only way (to bring down rates) is to keep fighting the idea that we are inevitably linked with inflation. If we can ever get this idea across, we will squeeze inflation out of interest rates and they will come down.

Before Joint Congressional Economic Committee, Washington, Feb. 16/ Los Angeles Times, 2-17:(3)12.

(On the criticism by Democrats of the Federal budget deficit): I am reminded of remarks the President (Nixon) and I had when I was invited to take this position. I said I would feel out of place as a Democrat in a Republican Cabinet. "No, John," he said. "We're going to make you feel at home." He has. He's given me the biggest budget deficit in history and the biggest balance-of-payments deficit in history.

At Washington Press Club/ The Dallas Times Herald, 2-20:(A)20.

Labor is out to get what it can. It is out to represent the interests of its members just as you (businessmen) are out to represent stockholders. You are both out to do the best job possible. But there comes a time when we all have to give for the public interest.

Plainview (Tex.) Daily Herald, 3-6:2.

(On criticism of tax "loopholes"): Loopholes? Loopholes? What loopholes? One man's loophole is another man's bread and butter, another man's livelihood. Let's take capital gains. Anybody want to knock that out? You want to destroy real estate values in the U.S.? You want to destroy the value of insurance companies in the U.S.? You want to destroy the stock market?

U.S. News & World Report, 5-22:58.

John T. Connor
Chairman,
Allied Chemical Corporation

Those who criticize corporate profits conveniently overlook the fact that a substantial part of corporate profits goes to pay taxes, which help support the countless programs of Federal and state governments. The rest of the profit dollar is what keeps our economy regenerating itself. Part of it is paid out as dividends to the millions of Americans who have invested their savings in our private-enterprise system in the expectation of getting a return on that investment. And a large part of the balance is spent directly to build the new plants and buy the new equipment needed to provide more jobs, and better jobs, for American working men and women. It is this function of profits—providing the funds for the continual modernization and expansion of the means of production—that is so vital to the future of our economy and is so little appreciated.

Before Democratic Party Platform Committee/ Vital Speeches, 10-15:20.

Stewart S. Cort
Chairman,
Bethlehem Steel Corporation

It seems to me that the power labor unions have today has become a serious liability to the unions themselves. This power tends to lock union officials into a set behavior pattern at the bargaining table. It carries over into administering the labor agreement. And it's a pattern that's sure to hurt the interests of their general memberships in the long run. It's hard to think of anything worse than being pushed into a position that will lead to pricing one's own people out of jobs. Union officials are now in that position. The very survival of labor unions may depend on changes in the structure of collective bargaining that will remove this kind of pressure and ensure settlements of disputes that are really beneficial to employees, to employers and to the general public.

Before Economic Club, New York, Jan. 19/ The Wall Street Journal, 5-2:14.

Everybody's talking about tax reform; but watch out for rhetoric about "closing the loopholes" that only benefit the "rich and powerful." As *The Wall Street Journal* commented the other day, one of the biggest so-called "loopholes" is the provision enabling homeowners to deduct mortgage interest and property taxes from Federal taxable income. Well, there are many millions of homeowners in this country and they aren't all "rich and powerful." Most of them are just ordinary citizens. And as a matter of fact, I always thought there was a sound public policy behind those deductions—to encourage people to own their own homes. Take the deductions away and I doubt you'd prevent wealthy people from owning homes, but you'd surely make it tough on everybody else.

Before Rotary Club, Jacksonville, Fla., June 12/ Vital Speeches, 7-15:588.

As for business taxation, one of the (Presidential) candidates said this: "The time has come for a tax system that says to big business—you must pay your fair share." That's a reasonable demand; but it implies that we aren't already paying our "fair share." My own company has been tagged with that sort of accusation despite the fact that over the past 10 years our taxes have averaged $37 million a year more than our net income. Our total tax bill added up to nearly $200 million last year, $155 million in 1970 and more than $1.7 billion for the 10 years from 1962 through 1971. So please think twice before swallowing all this baloney about large corporations not carrying their fair share of the tax burden.

Before Rotary Club, Jacksonville, Fla./ The Wall Street Journal, 8-1:8.

Walter Dance
Senior vice president, General Electric Company

We see a potential problem of vast significance to all industrial companies. This involves the slowly-rising feeling of frustration, irritation and alienation of the blue-collar worker, the "hard hats" if you will, but not just the activists in big cities. It involves a gut feeling on their part that industrial society has left them with the dull, hard, dirty jobs—and doesn't care.

At stockholders' meeting/ The Washington Post, 4-18:(A)12.

John H. Dent
United States Representative, D–Pa.

In the 40 years I've been a legislator, I've yet to see any labor organization without well-prepared testimony. It is usually very factual—based on their viewpoint—but always logical and designed to achieve their aims. Industry does the same kind of job. It's up to us lawmakers to draw the line and not allow either labor or industry to bowl us over in the legislative process.

U.S. News & World Report, 2-21:24.

Otto Eckstein
Professor of Economics, Harvard University

The interesting part of (Senator George) McGovern's tax-reform agenda is the part that deals with wealth—that is, his plan to tax gifts and inheritances much more heavily. McGovern people perceive that the real disparity of economic status in the U.S. is not based on current income but on accumulated and inherited wealth. Where this approach will lead intellectually remains to be seen, but the attack on wealth is a relatively new issue and an issue that has a future. It just won't go away.

Time, 6-19:75.

Paul J. Fannin
United States Senator, R–Ariz.

If we are to survive as a leading manufacturing nation, we must have a return of what once was known as the work ethic. American workmen must once again take pride in being the best—rather than just the best paid—in the world. Our (labor) union leaders must start acknowledging the realities of economics. Workers must be allowed to produce; they must be encouraged to produce.

Quote, 4-30:418.

Edgar R. Fiedler
Assistant Secretary for Economic Policy, Department of the Treasury of the United States

The wage and price freeze was a resounding success. (But) the jury is still out on Phase II. We don't know how to judge Phase II. The Price Commission and Pay Board have a lot of work to do. We should not judge success by a handful of statistics, but we must wait for more statistics. No one is sure whether the policies of the Price Commission and the Pay Board will prove to be compatible with each other and whether they will be compatible with an expanding economy. My own view is that the stabilization program has a good chance to achieve its goal of slowing the inflation to an annual rate of 2 to 3 per cent by the end of 1972. Some uncertainties remain also about the impact of the major changes that have been made in the international monetary system. How freely consumers will spend is always a matter of some doubt. We will no doubt experience a number of economic surprises this year. However, the best bet is a healthy rise in business activity—not a rampant boom—but an advance that is vigorous enough to put a significant dent in the unemployment rate in 1972.

Before Dallas Federal Business Association, Feb. 23/ The Dallas Times Herald, 2-24:(C)9.

Robert H. Finch
Counsellor to the President of the United States

Everybody (during the upcoming election campaigns) is going to play the numbers game on the economy. We'll say that there's more employment; they'll cite all the people who are unemployed. It's a question of whether the glass is half-empty or half-full.

The Washington Post, 5-21:(A)18.

Charles T. Fisher III
President, National Bank of Detroit

Profits generate economic growth and create jobs. Profits require investment and investment requires profits. Our rising standard of living has occurred because of continued increases in productivity. These, in turn, have been made possible by additions to our stock of capital goods which in turn are financed by retained earnings and new equity and debt issues. The willingness of investors to invest their savings in such securities is directly related to the past and prospective earnings of those companies seeking new capital. The incentive to improve technology, to develop new products and to find better ways of making goods and providing services comes from the hope of higher profits. The profits debate is much more than a wrangle between capital and labor on the division of economic wealth; it deals with the material well-being of all our people and it reaches into the social system that guarantees our freedom. Profits create jobs, whether these jobs are in business or in government, because corporations and their employees pay the bulk of all taxes collected and spent by government. The record clearly shows that there is a close relationship between profits and employment. If profits are a problem, then sooner or later unemployment becomes a problem too.

Before Citizens Research Council of Michigan, Bloomfield Hills, Sept. 12/ Vital Speeches, 10-15:19.

Gilbert W. Fitzhugh
Chairman, Metropolitan Life Insurance Company

The obvious cause of inflation is fiscal irresponsibility—terrific Federal deficits, over a long period of years, and undue monetary expansion. You can't have inflation without too much money. But too many people talk about a trade-off between inflation and unemployment. They say you have to have a little inflation or you have to have unemployment. That is for the birds. Those mulitbillion-dollar deficits, in themselves, don't produce one more loaf of bread, one more automobile, one more square mile of clean air, one more unpolluted river. And the Federal Reserve issuing another billion dollars doesn't, by itself, produce one more of any one of those things, either. All it does is raise the price of available goods. The only way you can produce those things is to produce them. The real answer is productivity. People's wants will never be satisfied. They always want more—and that is good; that is what makes the country grow. But you have to provide for those wants by work and investment. You always come back to hard work and thrift. I am an old-fashioned duck and I don't think there is anything wrong with that.

Interview, New York/
Nation's Business, July:43.

Frank E. Fitzsimmons
President, International Brotherhood of Teamsters

(Affirming his intention of remaining on the Federal Pay Board despite other labor members' resignations): I have maintained from the beginning that inflation must be checked, that the Teamsters will participate in any effort to achieve that . . . goal as long as the basic rights of workers are protected, and that we can best speak for the two million Teamster members by participating in Pay Board activities.

March 22/
The Washington Post, 3-23:(A)1.

Milton Friedman
Professor of Economics, University of Chicago

It is inconceivable to me how big business can be so happy and excited with the advent of government economic controls. In the end, it can mean only more government control over productivity and our personal freedom. I think we are getting closer to the day when Big Brother will always be there looking over our shoulder.

Before Merchants and Manufacturers Association, Los Angeles, Jan. 4/
Los Angeles Times, 1-5:(3)12.

I would set (1972 economic) policy the same as I would have for 1970 and 1971: steady and moderate monetary growth; lower government spending and lower taxes, with a roughly balanced full-employment budget; elimination of price and wage controls—both the new ones established by President Nixon and such older ones as farm price supports and regulated air fares. The key need in policy-setting is to reverse the growth of government; to leave more of our incomes for us to spend in accordance with our own values; to reduce the extent to which our Big Brother in Washington runs our lives for us.

Panel discussion/
Newsweek, 1-31:75.

John Kenneth Galbraith
Professor of Economics, Harvard University

Our tax system is by way of being a scandal. And we need to get back to the principle that a buck is a buck is a buck; and however one is enriched by a dollar, he pays the same general tax on it, the same progressive tax on it. We should get the graft out of the tax system.

TV-radio interview, Washington/
"Meet the Press,"
National Broadcasting Company, 1-2.

Richard C. Gerstenberg
Chairman,
General Motors Corporation

The subject of our nation's economic productivity should concern every American. The effect of productivity on the daily lives of everyone is nothing less than enormous. Yet few people appreciate it or even understand it—and even fewer are trying to do anything to increase it. Productivity is not a matter of making employees work longer or harder. Increased productivity results mostly from sound planning, from wise investment, from new technology, from better techniques, from greater efficiency—in short, from the better exercise of the functions of management. Productivity also depends upon the conscientious effort of every employee, a willingness to do a fair day's work for a fair day's wages. If America is to improve its productivity—and we must—then productivity must be everybody's job.

The Dallas Times Herald, 6-4:(A)41.

The managers of American business must remember what Woodrow Wilson said—that labor is not a commodity but a form of cooperation. We in management and the leadership of our unions must stretch ourselves above our experience. We must reach for better ways of constructive cooperation with our work force. There is no way that we can turn back the clock of history; nor would we want to return the worker to the unrewarded drudgery of another day. Instead, we must move constructively with the times. To do this, we must take a common-sense perspective on the status and the aspirations of the American worker. We must look deeper than the headlines and gain a better understanding of the real life-style and aspirations of the men and women who produce the goods that make our economy flourish. I speak from my own experience at General Motors—and I echo the experience of all who work most closely with our employees—that at least 95 per cent of them are conscientious and hard-working men and women. To the imagination, the ingenuity, the energy and the dedication of American workers such as these, our country owes its present eminence in the world. The American work force is still the best-educated, still the most inventive, still the nation's greatest resource—and we must never forget it. All of us, therefore—all of us who care about the future of our country—must regard the resource of labor not as a commodity but as a form of cooperation. All of us in management must resolve to make every effort to work in close cooperation with our employees and with the union leadership to meet the legitimate needs of the changing American work force, remembering always that we have more in common than in conflict. By our work together we can maintain and enlarge the strength of the free American economy which has so enriched our nation and all its people.

Before Tax Foundation, New York, Dec. 6/ U.S. News & World Report, 12-25:57.

Nat Goldfinger
Research director, American Federation of Labor-Congress of Industrial Organizations

We (labor unions) are the only group in American society—the only organized group—that works day in and day out on a broad range of progressive social and economic issues. There is no other such group in the country. We are the solid-core base of progressive social and economic change in America. Without us, there's nothing.

The Washington Post, 4-9:(A)1.

I think the public attitude toward the worker has declined substantially; and the American worker is now looked down upon on the radio and television and news media generally. You make fun of the plumber and the carpenter and the working man . . . Who in American society in the past 15 or 20 years pays any attention to the importance of skilled manual work? The emphasis in society has been on the Ph.D. degree, upon the mathematician, the scientist, the engineer and so forth. I use words which sound kind of phony—the dignity and honor of manual work—but I think all of this has been very sharply downgraded in the society. And most recently you find it in all the fun that's poked at the hard hats: The hard hat is the bigot, the racist, the sexist, the male chauvinist pig. He's viewed almost as the enemy within.

Washington/
The Washington Post, 4-9:(A)21.

Victor Gotbaum
New York City director,
American Federation of State,
County and Municipal Employees

If an individual who is able-bodied and willing to work can't find a job and he has to face an undignified life, our society stinks! The government must be the employer of last resort and guarantee full production. If the government has the will to do it, it can do it.

Newsweek, 1-24:54.

Edwin H. Gott
Chairman,
United States Steel Corporation

The quickest way to destroy a society like ours is to shut down its economic engine.

Before American Society of
Civil Engineers, Cleveland/
Los Angeles Times, 4-26:(1)2.

C. Jackson Grayson, Jr.
Chairman, Price Commission,
Federal Cost of Living Council

(Agriculture Secretary Earl Butz' call for higher farm prices—is damaging to the stabilization program. I realize the Secretary is speaking in behalf of his constituency; but if the leader of every sector of the economy did that, the efforts to achieve price stability would be wrecked . . . (Butz) is no different than a labor leader claiming that a particular set of workers needs more than the wage guidelines permit them to "catch up," or a business leader saying that his firm needs more than the price rules permit them to "catch up." The name of the "catch up" game is inflation.

News conference, Washington,
March 17/The Washington Post,
3-18:(A)1,4.

. . . to my surprise, I am finding more and more businessmen who want (wage-price) controls continued. Many are among the best-known in their trade in the East. At one meeting alone, 20 top people said they favored keeping some type of controls. There are a number of reasons. The most common one is they don't think they can control labor any more.

Interview,
San Francisco, April 6/
San Francisco Examiner, 4-7:13.

We (the Price Commission) have been accused of being ineffective, of failing our job, of being pro-business, of being a pass-through agency, of being a phony cover to permit controls to be placed on wages . . . We are not pro-business. Nor are we anti-business, either. We're simply and implacably anti-inflation.

Before Associated Press leaders,
New York, April 24/
San Francisco Examiner & Chronicle,
4-30:(This World)9.

There has been the illusion that the United States is so far ahead in the world productivity and economic leadership that we can coast. Not true. The reality is that we are lagging and others are gaining. Our country in recent years has ranked eleventh in productivity gains among the eleven most industrialized nations in the world. That's last place. And whether we are nice guys or bad guys, nobody is going to wait for us to catch up.

Before Business Equipment
Manufacturer's Association,
Washington, Oct. 25/
Vital Speeches, 12-15:135.

(C. JACKSON GRAYSON, JR.)

(On government wage and price controls): There is an illusion–nurtured and fostered by the technique of constant repitition–that prices are not actually being controlled, but that wages are being held down. The known facts absolutely refute this. And the reality is that "real spendable earnings" have risen, which means that wages have gone up faster than prices.

Before Business Equipment Manufacturer's Association, Washington, Oct. 25/ Vital Speeches, 12-15:135.

Fred R. Harris
United States Senator, D–Okla.

The economic problems of America will not be solved by more government intervention, but by more economic liberty. As someone wisely said, the Nixon Administration may not be soft on Communism, but it's damn sure hard on capitalism.

Quote, 9-3:219.

Philip A. Hart
United States Senator, D–Mich.

Once we start with limited (wage-price) controls, and they don't work, it's a little too tempting to add some more controls, and eventually to end up with an economy based on big business, planned and controlled by the Federal government . . . The trade-off–less power in the hands of a few citizens for more power in the hands of government–to me is a bad bargain.

Before the Senate, Washington, July 24/ The Washington Post, 7-23:(A)8.

Gabriel Hauge
Chairman, Manufacturers Hanover Trust Company, New York

The economy is not fundamentally inflationary. We have plenty of capacity, good management, the best financial system in the world and a generally tolerant attitude of government. We get into trouble because of bad economic habits and we need some preventive medicine. This time, we got into trouble because of the calamitous decisions that weren't taken in 1965 and 1966 when we piled a war on top of an economy already at full employment. How do you avoid that? I suppose you avoid war. You avoid overloading the economy. You pursue a credit policy that's reasonably stable.

New York/ The Washington Post, 4-30:(F)1.

Walter W. Heller
Professor of Economics, University of Minnesota; Former Chairman, Council of Economic Advisers to the President of the United States

I think that with the Pay Board and Price Commission, as with a child or a dog, you can have a few accidents and still housebreak them.

Time, 1-10:25.

Now that the United States economy is at long last on the move, and inflation is at long last on the wane, the voice of over-cautious conservatism is raised again at the other end of Pennsylvania Avenue: "Reach for the brakes; slash the budget; seek an end to the wage-price restraints."

San Francisco Examiner & Chronicle, 8-6:(This World)2.

(President) Nixon has been pre-empting one economic issue after another from the Democrats. He has taken the Democratic game plan, so about all the Democratic (Presidential) candidate can say to the voters will be: "Since you've got the Democratic economic plan, you might as well have a Democrat as President."

San Francisco Examiner & Chronicle, 8-27:(This World)2.

Walter E. Hoadley
Executive vice president and chief economist, Bank of America

. . . there is now and will continue to

be less inflation in the United States than in any other major nation. In no small part, this is due to the persistent will of our country to resist—not to succumb to—inflation. The average citizen in our country still fights inflation by more saving, in contrast to more spending elsewhere. In addition, there is strong voter pressure for anti-inflation measures by government, business and labor. All this means that a turn has come for the better. Our economic intelligence from around the world as well as at home indicates that the dollar is on a firming base, and will continue so despite some temporary waves of pressure in the international currency markets. Prospects are excellent that ample funds will be available to meet the needs of our growing economy with continued moderate upward pressures on interest rates as near-full to full employment is achieved.

At American Life Convention, San Francisco, Oct. 18/ U.S. News & World Report, 11-6:38.

James D. Hodgson
Secretary of Labor of the United States

The old arguments about the sacred right to strike are no longer relevant in today's economically-intermeshed world. Major strike-induced economic setbacks caused by transportation emergencies are intolerable to the public . . . The East Coast (dock) strike story is much the same (as on the West Coast)—a drop in exports, the loss of foreign markets, damage to our balance of trade, a decline in farm prices, as wheat and corn overflowed grain elevators and backed up on barges in the Mississippi. Couple all this with increased government expenditures on agricultural programs, the shutdown of sugar-refining companies, huge layoffs among importers and exporters, losses among truckers, U.S.-flagship operators and railroads, and the ripple effects go on and on without end.

Los Angeles Herald Examiner, 1-30:(B)7.

We (the Nixon Administration) feel that we've been building a record of accomplishment that shows that we have intense concern for the American worker, and we have been attempting to establish a record of fairness to organized labor . . . If one were to go back and examine much of the labor press before the election in 1968, there were horror stories about the kind of anti-labor legislation that could be expected. That has not occurred. We have not proposed anti-labor legislation. We have chosen to work with, rather than around or against, organized labor.

Interview, Washington/ San Francisco Examiner, 3-13:18.

Productivity is a bloodless, abstract concept that most Americans have trouble with . . . We've got to put more sex and soul into the concept . . . and show (the worker) how more productivity will indeed translate into more purchasing power in his own pocket . . . To build productivity, we must build people—people who regard their work as challenging, respected, rewarding and worthwhile. In the final analysis, productivity . . . depends on the success of managers in providing conditions for high motivation.

At Conference Board Productivity Conference, New York/ San Francisco Examiner, 5-24:69.

Today our nation is undergoing severe transitional pains, and the going for many is rough. I find a number of sincere people seizing on organized labor as a handy villain. They point to labor's mistakes, to labor's excesses, and take comfort that they have identified the source of our troubles. So doing, they retreat to some high and dry ground of satisfied moral superiority. I am convinced such a conclusion is inaccurate and such an attitude is unhelpful. When labor makes a mistake, we should remedy the mistake. When labor's excesses create a problem, we should solve the problem. But this nation needs strong, responsible institutions working together to attack its many

(JAMES D. HODGSON)

difficulties. Working together requires mutual trust. Carping criticism destroys trust. Joint efforts build it. The next decade will require joint effort and good will—both with labor and on the part of labor. I believe a changing labor movement is preparing to do its part.

At 1972 Spring Business Conference, University of Colorado, Boulder, June 8/ Vital Speeches, 7-15:583.

Hubert H. Humphrey
United States Senator, D–Minn.

(The Treasury Department) has become the blocking back for big business Republicanism, seeking to wedge out bigger loopholes in the tax structure for big special interests to run through. The little guy, meanwhile, has no one running interference for him in Washington. He's asked to shoulder heavier and heavier tax loads, while the wealthy and the special interests avoid paying their fair share through a variety of gaping tax loopholes.

Fond Du Lac, Wis./ The Dallas Times Herald, 2-27:(A)31.

The American tax system is unfair and unjust. It is rigged against work, against wages, against salaries. It is rigged against the elderly. It is rigged against the middle-income workers. It is rigged against the poor. It is rigged in favor of unearned income.

Quote, 2-27:193.

. . . I consider (President) Nixon's economic policies a colossal failure. I think that those policies have worked an undue hardship upon this country; and today, I might add, that the price-control program of the Nixon Administration is a hoax, a sham, a public-relations gimmick that is not protecting the average wage earner and the working family of this country and is causing great hardship to people on fixed incomes. On that basis the Administration is a failure.

TV-radio interview, Washington/ "Meet the Press," National Broadcasting Company, 3-12.

(Criticizing Senator George McGovern's tax program as being anti-business): We need jobs in the private sector, and we won't have jobs if we scare the living daylights out of everybody that provides them, with a tax program that doesn't make any sense at all. You cannot provide jobs without factories, without shops, without investment. When you start to have confiscatory taxation, even against some of the big ones, you're not going to provide any jobs. That doesn't make you a liberal; it makes you a fool. And there's a lot of difference.

Campaigning for the Democratic Presidential nomination, Fresno, Calif., May 29/ Los Angeles Times, 5-30:(1)25.

Henry M. Jackson
United States Senator, D–Wash.

It is hard to believe that . . . more than 100 Americans with 1970 incomes in excess of $200,000 . . . didn't pay any Federal income tax . . . We cannot justify a (tax) system that lets millionaires off tax-free while wage earners in the $5,000 to $15,000 brackets pay 45 per cent of all Federal income taxes.

The National Observer, 5-6:16.

Vivien Kellems
Former industrialist

The Supreme Court has held that taxpayers may be classified for purposes of taxation; but the classification must be reasonable. It must be based upon some sound ground. Since there are in this country six million more single women than single men, is it a reasonable classification to penalize these women because there aren't husbands enough to go around? What do you do if you can't get a husband? Should you be taxed for that? Is it a reasonable classification when a woman loses her husband and her taxes immediately go up? Isn't it penalty enough that she loses her husband without having to pay increased taxes? Where is the reason in this?

Before House Ways and Means Committee, Washington, April 10/ Human Events, 6-3:10.

Edward M. Kennedy
United States Senator, D–Mass.

To me, the (proposed Federal) value-added tax would be the wrong tax in the wrong country at the wrong time. It would be nothing more than a national sales tax piled on top of countless state and local taxes that now exist, another regressive gimmick to divert the nation from the job of real (tax) reform.

Washington, March 21/ The New York Times, 3-22:25.

Theodore W. Kheel
Lawyer; Labor mediator

The right to strike and the right of an employer to take a strike is indigenous to the process of collective bargaining . . . Any over-all system of compulsory arbitration must ultimately break down. Compulsory arbitration, labor courts, the Taylor Law, fact-finding, won't work. The only way to achieve true collective bargaining–there is no other way–is to include provisions for the right to strike and the right to take a strike.

Before Commission of Inquiry Into the Use of Injunctions and Jail Sentences Against Public Employees, New York/ The New York Times, 3-12:(1)32.

John V. Lindsay
Mayor of New York

(America's) first priority program (must be) a full-scale employment program to create one million jobs by the end of 1972. But jobs come last on the Nixon economic agenda–bail out business, push up profits, reward the stockholders and take care of the banks, then worry about jobs. And the people most in need are last in line, as usual.

Minneapolis, Feb. 19/ The New York Times, 2-20:(1)37.

Russell B. Long
United States Senator, D–La.

(On proposed value-added or national sales tax): It's the kind of tax the rich corporations would like to stick on the poor. These big companies would just pass the tax on in higher prices, and the Administration could get more revenue without raising corporate taxes. First of all, I don't think the House will pass such a plan if (President) Nixon proposes it. If the House does, the Senate will kill it–I can promise you that.

San Francisco Examiner, 1-21:2.

. . . I would like to see some additional taxes on people who are paying nothing, such as those who pay all that money into foundations where, theoretically, they are giving to charity and it turns out that the charity they are giving it to is themselves. Some of these groups manage to get by with paying nothing. It was my suggestion, long before it was suggested by someone else, that we ought to have a minimum income tax law, so if we missed you with everything else, we could catch you with that.

Broadcast interview, April 1/ The Washington Post, 4-2:(A)22.

George H. Mahon
United States Representative, D–Tex.

We have been trying to buy ourselves out of inflation and huge deficits; but these efforts have failed . . . No one should believe that with whopping deficits in the $20-to-$30-to-$40-billion range that we can really win the fight against inflation. This government will have to borrow about $44 billion in the current fiscal year 1972–from the highway fund, the Social Security fund and other funds, and from the private

(GEORGE H. MAHON)

sector—mostly from the private sector. When the government goes to the money market and borrows in the magnitude of $38 billion to $40 billion from the private sector, this inevitably will have a marked effect upon the economy of our country. Among other things, such borrowing will put pressure on interest rates. Such a course is . . . highly inflationary and will tend to create further economic dislocations . . . No candidate for President is probably going to go before the voters and advocate new taxes. I doubt that will happen. But as certainly as I stand on the floor of this House today, when the (1972) election is over and when an Administration takes over in January of 1973, we will be standing at fiscal crossroads. Whoever is elected President, whether he be Democrat or Republican or Independent, will be faced with a critical situation which can no longer be side-stepped.

Before the House, Washington/ Human Events, 2-5:3.

Mike Mansfield
United States Senator, D–Mont.

(Food processors) are the culprits responsible for the high prices of meat and bread, and they go unscathed. The consumer gets it in the neck and the farmer gets it in the neck. The consumer continues to pay, pay, pay, and the farmer is blamed, blamed, blamed.

News conference, Washington, March 21/The Los Angeles Times, 3-22:(1)9.

George S. McGovern
United States Senator, D–S.D.

Men who work for a living in the factories of Manchester (N.H.), or the mills of Berlin (N.H.), or who own a small business here in Concord (N.H.) . . . and who earn ten or twelve thousand dollars a year, are paying more in taxes than men in Boston and New York who earn more than $200,000 a year from buying and selling commodities they never see. Americans don't mind paying taxes; they only want to know the system is fair—and today they know it is not.

Formally announcing his candidacy for the Democratic Presidential nomination, Concord, N.H., Jan. 4/ The Washington Post, 1-11:(A)15.

George S. McGovern
United States Senator, D–S.D.; Democratic Presidential nominee

. . . honest work must be rewarded by a fair and just tax system. The tax system today does not reward hard work—it penalizes it. Inherited or invested wealth frequently multiplies itself while paying no taxes at all; but wages on the assembly line or in farming the land—these hard-earned dollars—are taxed to the very last penny. There is a depletion allowance for oil wells, but no depletion for the farmer who feeds us or the worker who serves us all. The (Nixon) Administration tells us that we should not discuss tax reform in an election year. They would prefer to keep all discussion of the tax laws in closed rooms where the Administration, its powerful friends and their paid lobbyists can turn every effort at reform into a new loophole for the rich and powerful. But an election year is the people's year to speak; and this year the people are going to insure that the tax system is changed so that work is rewarded and so that those who derive the highest benefits will pay their fair share rather than slipping through the loopholes at the expense of the rest of us.

Accepting the Democratic Presidential nomination, Miami Beach, July 14/ The New York Times, 7-15:11.

The Nixon (economic) record is one of giveaways to the big corporations and takeaways from the average taxpayer. By the end of (President) Nixon's term, the average family of four will have lost about $3,000 in potential income, thanks to the stagnant Nixon economy. Nixon has thrown almost

5 million Americans out of work and increased the tax burden on the average taxpaying family. Nixonomics has raised food prices by 4 per cent a year and has added a total of well over $450 to the average family's grocery bill.

*Washington, Aug. 5/
San Francisco Examiner & Chronicle, 8-6:(A)14.*

Deliberately throwing people out of work—that is "Nixonomics" . . . And that's not accidental; it's by design. The plan was to stem inflation by slowing down the economy . . . A tax structure which rewards those at the top and gouges those in the middle—that is "Nixonomics." It's the same old Republican approach—business gets a stern look once in a while, and workers get clobbered.

*Before Amalgamated Meat Cutters, Miami Beach, Aug. 8/
The Dallas Times Herald, 8-8:(A)1.*

When the (Vietnam) war is ended and waste is stopped, we can end wage and price controls; and I think that can be done within 90 days of the (McGovern Presidential) inauguration. And I'm committed to that goal.

*Before Illinois labor leaders, Springfield, Aug. 15/
San Francisco Examiner, 8-16:9.*

Jobs are the cornerstone of my policy. I will take whatever steps are necessary to guarantee a job opportunity to every man and woman in America who is able to work, including idle youth able and willing to work. I have previously urged a $10 billion Federal investment in new jobs through government contracts with industry. Our highest economic priority is the lowest possible unemployment—to be achieved by vigorous action in both the public and the private sectors.

*Before New York Society of Security Analysts, Aug. 29/
The Washington Post, 8-30:(A)12.*

. . . the Republicans say I want to soak the rich. I don't want to soak the rich, but I want them to pay their fair share of the cost of government in this country. What I'm really interested in is that we develop the kind of a tax system that stops soaking the ordinary taxpayer of this country. That's what I'm concerned about. And every tax loophole in the law in this Internal Revenue code is on the backs of the people in this audience today. When (former Treasury Secretary John) Connally and his oil-billionaire friends get by with paying little or no taxes, that means that every man and woman in this audience has his tax bill lifted as a consequence. You pay for every martini lunch that a businessman deducts, while you can't deduct the price of a baloney sandwich. And when you stand at that lathe or at that factory bench, or work in that mine or in that mill or in that home from morning to night, just remember that out of every dollar you earn, part of that goes to sustain a loophole that makes the rich richer, the powerful more powerful, the concentration of wealth all the greater.

*Campaigning for the forthcoming Presidential election, Barberton, Ohio, Sept. 4/
U.S. News & World Report, 9-18:81.*

The President (Nixon) says inflation is under control. I say let him try to feed his family for a week on an average paycheck. Whenever you shop at the local grocery store, you find out that Richard Nixon cost(s) more. The Nixon inflation is ground into every pound of hamburger you buy.

*Campaigning for the forthcoming Presidential election, Ohio, Sept. 4/
San Francisco Examiner, 9-4:1.*

(President) Nixon and his men do not subscribe to the principles of organized labor because they have fought those principles throughout their political careers. They will not preserve what you have won, because they would have preferred it if you

(GEORGE S. McGOVERN)

had lost. The heart of this Administration does not burn for working people. Their romance is with the special interests, the powerful men who have filled their campaign coffers; and these men don't work in factories and they don't work on construction sites.

Before building trades leaders, Los Angeles, Oct. 27/ Los Angeles Herald-Examiner, 10-27:(A)2.

George Meany
President, American Federation of Labor-Congress of Industrial Organizations

(Labor unions) have never had a large proportion of the work force in this country—nothing like Britain, nothing like the Scandinavian countries, nothing like the Germans . . . We've done quite well without it. And we are not tied to any political party; and we feel that we've got along without that, too. We've delivered more to the American worker than any labor movement that ever existed—today, yesterday or in the past—and we inherited a good deal of our labor movement: its principles from the Germans and, to a lesser extent, from the British. With all of our complaints, we have the highest standard of living in the world. Why should we worry about organizing groups of people who do not appear to want to be organized? If they prefer to have others speak for them and make the decisions which affect their lives, without effective participation on their part, that is their right . . . Frankly, I used to worry about the membership, about the size of the membership. But quite a few years ago I just stopped worrying about it, because to me it doesn't make any difference. It's the organized voice that counts—and it's not just in legislation, it's anyplace. The organized fellow is the fellow that counts. This is just human nature.

Interview, Washington/ U.S. News & World Report, 2-21:27.

. . . the trouble with a lot of collective-bargaining relationships is that, once a contract is signed, the two sides sort of get divorced. They don't see one another, they don't even talk to one another, until three years later when they meet again, and they again have an adversary situation. I think that that is one of the things we have got to overcome. If they are going to have this relationship, they should really know one another better, not just meet one another when there is a fight on.

Interview, Washington/ U.S. News & World Report, 2-21:28.

In politics, your mathematics are a little different than if you are not in politics. Now, 2.5 per cent (unemployed) was always considered by the theoreticians and the people from the academic world—the eggheads—as full employment. In other words, it was always 2.5 per cent of (the) people who were either between jobs or who were not looking for jobs or for reasons of their own decided to take a six-month layoff. Now we are getting to the point where this (Nixon) Administration has said that 4 per cent looks better, and now they are going to talk about 5 per cent as full employment. Five per cent is a little over 4 million people unemployed. Right now, we are at about 6 per cent. So I suppose the attitude is: "We can't bring this unemployment rate down, so let's change the method of looking at it and the arithmetic for measuring it." And if they decide that 6 per cent unemployed represents basically full employment, well, then we will have them making speeches saying, "Isn't it wonderful now—we have full employment."

Interview, Washington/ U.S. News & World Report, 2-21:33.

In the guise of an anti-inflation policy, the American people are being gouged at the supermarket and squeezed in the paycheck . . . It is our duty to report, now, to the membership of the trade-union movement and the American public, that we have no hope for fairness, equity or justice in the (Federal) Pay Board . . . In a supposedly free country, in time of peace, with no national emergency defined, or like sacrifices required of the affluent elements of society, it is not tolerable to subject free American workers to control at such hands.

News conference announcing his resignation from the Federal Pay Board, Washington, March 22/ Los Angeles Times, 3-23:(1)15.

Reports indicate that the nation's 100 largest corporations scored a sensational 76 per cent rise in profits last year. While prices are going up and profits are soaring, workers' wages have been held down. The (Nixon) Adminsitration's so-called new economic policy is heavily loaded against the worker and consumer in favor of the profits of big business and the banks, and is dominated by the view that economic progress begins and ends in the stock market and corporation financial report. There is no fairness, no equity, no justice in the Administration's economic program.

March 22/ San Francisco Examiner, 3-23:9.

(Arguing that Federal Price Commission policies do not work in favor of consumers): Mrs. Adler's matzoh ball soup was famous for years and years with four matzoh balls in a can. Now, same can, same price, but only three matzoh balls. This is the sort of thing I mean.

Before Federal Price Commission/ San Francisco Examiner & Chronicle, 4-9:(This World)9.

There's such a thing as a worker's pride in his work, which I know quite a bit about. To me, as a young fellow, this was all-important. This was *really*—well, you almost worshipped the skilled craftsman. I mean, you'd look at an older man as if he were almost God because of his tremendous skill. And there was one thing I recall in my younger days: You never wanted to be disgraced. If you were fired for doing shoddy work, you were disgraced. If you got fired for being unable to produce the proper type of installation or do it properly, boy, that was a disgrace! Around the trade, a fellow who got into that situation was dubbed a "boot." Nobody ever wanted to be called a boot.

Interview/ The Washington Post, 4-11:(A)8.

I have never been enchanted with (labor) strikes. They are not funny—they are grim. There are casualties in every strike—economic, human, social casualties. And I'd like to avoid any of these consequences. Any responsible labor leader considers, as I do, that a strike is never more than the lesser of two evils, adopted by workers as last resort to protest some grievance that, to them, is worse than not working at all

At forum sponsored by Institute of Collective Bargaining and Group Relations, New York, May 19/ The New York Times, 5-21:(1)62.

The flood of imports is drowning whole communities . . . The labor movement never has and never will espouse isolationism, but it is not isolationism and it is not protectionism to have the United States open its eyes and see that the rest of the world is stealing jobs, capital and technology from this country.

San Francisco Examiner & Chronicle, 6-11:(This World)2.

The (wage-price) control mechanism has not worked equitably as far as prices are concerned. It has controlled wages; it has held wages down to this 5.5 per cent, mostly. But it has not controlled prices; and unless they come up with machinery that will really control prices, they should drop controls.

Chicago/Newsweek, 9-11:54.

Wilbur D. Mills

United States Representative, D–Ark.

The only way to get taxes at the Federal level, or revenues at the Federal level, in

(WILBUR D. MILLS)

my opinion, the safest and best way to do it, is through the income tax. I would not want to incorporate into our structure the value-added tax, a sales tax—they are both the same; the value-added tax to me is worse than a sales tax because of the discriminatory nature of it, the fact that it compounds, rather than the sales tax just being paid at the manufacturing level or at the retail level. I would assume, if taxes had to be increased in the future, that these would be additional burdens on the great masses of the people in the middle brackets because there are so many of them. That is where you get your money.

TV-radio interview, Washington/ "Meet the Press," National Broadcasting Company, 6-11.

John G. Mohay
Executive vice president, National Meat Packers Association

We in the meat-packing industry are puzzled and concerned by the recent furor regarding meat prices (that they are too high). Our profits structure is a disgrace. If our net profit reaches 1 per cent of sales, we are elated . . . I sometimes wonder whether instead of being called meat packers we wouldn't more rightly be called philanthropists. We give away every profit potential we develop or invent. Competition is so keen we are constantly cutting the price to get the business . . . In spite of our efforts, some sources have accused meat packers of being the fat cats in the meat distribution chain. That, if I may mix metaphors, is hogwash.

Before House Livestock Subcommittee, Washington, April 10/ San Francisco Examiner, 4-11:51.

Edmund S. Muskie
United States Senator, D–Maine

. . . with respect to this (Nixon) Administration, I would say that its basic economic problem is the lack of confidence, (1) in its management, (2) in its economic convictions, (3) in its implementation of those convictions. On all of these counts, the perception of the American consumer—whose welfare is at the heart of our economic problems—is one of uncertainty, confusion and doubt. And when you have that with respect to any Administration's economic policy, you have an uncertain economic future.

Interview/ The Washington Post, 2-27:(C)4.

Unless we win sweeping tax reform, we will propose our programs and speak about our solutions and enact laws, and we will still find social and economic justice beyond our grasp. We must change our tax system so we can change this country without telling poor and middle-class Americans to sacrifice beyond their means.

Campaigning for the Democratic Presidential nomination, Miami, March 9/ The New York Times, 3-10:20.

Progress is always expensive; and almost always we have financed it on the backs of average-income Americans . . . Our people will no longer accept the injustice of paying more taxes while . . . a Federal tax system . . . protects special . . . privilege to such an extent that we now read ads for tax shelters addressed to "Mr. and Mrs. Fortunate Taxpayer."

The National Observer, 5-6:16.

Delfim Netto
Minister of Finance of Brazil

A little inflation is like a little pregnancy. It gets bigger.

San Francisco Examiner, 12-4:38.

E. L. Nicholson
Chairman and president, CNA Financial Corporation

I am a strong believer in the free-enterprise system—not because it is equated with motherhood and the flag, but because it is the most effective and efficient system of getting products and services to the most people, thereby improving their standard of living. Believing this, as I do, and at the same time observing a deterioration of the system, leads me to believe that there is a breakdown in performance, to suspect that we are not working hard enough to support this system. And to the extent it fails, the public loses.

Before Pennsylvania Chamber of Commerce, Philadelphia, Oct. 18/ Vital Speeches, 12-15:143.

Richard M. Nixon
President of the United States

If we were ever to permit this nation to turn isolationist in its foreign policy, we would be inviting another war or the destruction of our freedom. If we were to let this nation turn protectionist in its economic policy, we would be inviting a trade war—and like the other kind of war, every nation on this planet would lose. We are not going to let either of these things happen. After years of lagging productivity . . . we made a comeback last year—back to a 3.6 per cent rise. Now we have momentum. And we must never again forget the secret of American success. For too long, I think . . . too many of us in this country—too many businessmen, too many workingmen—thought of the American economy as a kind of giant turtle. It may have been fat and lazy, but it had a protective shell that seemed impregnable. But let me point out to you that nature played a trick on the turtle. The only way he can move forward is to stick his neck out. Well, the time has come for that turtle, this great giant American economy . . . to stick its neck out and get moving. As it does, it will show that America's competitive spirit is alive and healthy, ready to lead the world into a new prosperity.

At White House Conference on the Industrial World Ahead, Washington, Feb. 7/ The National Observer, 2-19:2.

We have cut inflation in half, but we must cut it further so that we can continue to expand on the greatest achievement of our new economic policy—for the first time in five years, wage increases are not being eaten up by price increases. As a result of the millions of new jobs created by our new economic policies, unemployment today is less than the average for the peacetime years of the 1960s. But we must continue the unparalleled increase in new jobs so that we can achieve a goal of our new prosperity—a job for every American who wants to work, without war and without inflation.

Accepting the Republican Presidential nomination, Miami Beach, Aug. 23/ Los Angeles Times, 8-24:(1)21.

Because of our American economic policies, we have built a great building of economic wealth and might. It is by far the tallest building in the world, and we are still adding to it. Because some of the windows are broken, they (his opponents) say tear it down and start again. We say, replace the windows and keep building.

Accepting the Republican Presidential nomination, Miami Beach, Aug. 23/ Los Angeles Times, 8-24:(1)22.

The United States recognizes the importance of a strong, non-inflationary domestic economy, both in meeting the needs of our own citizens and in contributing to a healthy world economy. We are firmly committed to reaching our goals of strong growth, full employment and price stability. We are encouraged by the record of our current economic performance. We are now experiencing one of the lowest rates of inflation, and highest rates of real economic growth, of any industrial nation. Recent gains in the productivity and real income of American workers have been heartening. We intend to continue the policies that have produced these gains.

Before International Monetary Fund, Washington, Sept. 25/ The New York Times, 9-26:70.

(RICHARD M. NIXON)

There is no country in the world today in which there is a dictator and in which there is also a free trade-union movement. And there is no country in the world today which has a free trade-union movement in which there is a dictator . . . a free trade-union movement is essential if we are going to have free governments.

Before African and Latin American labor representatives, Washington, Oct. 17/ The Washington Post, 10-18:(A)2.

I am convinced that the total tax burden of the American people—Federal, state and local—has reached the breaking point. It cannot go higher. If it does go higher, I believe that we will do much to destroy the incentives which produce the progress we want.

Interview, Nov. 5/ The New York Times, 11-10:20.

Arthur M. Okun
Former Chairman, Council of Economic Advisers to the President of the United States

No previous incumbent Administration has created as much uncertainty about what its policies would be like in a second term of office (as the Nixon Administration). We have had diametrically opposed Nixon economic policies in every area. On wage-price controls, where would a second Nixon Administration stand between total non-intervention and complete freeze? On the job front, would we get the Nixon Administration that promised to hold unemployment down when it was 3.5 per cent or the one that dismissed 6 per cent as the hole in the doughnut? On taxes, where would the 1973 Nixon stand on the value-added tax? How would he honor his promise of property-tax relief? What did the President have in mind in his Texas speech when he pointed to new unspecified tax preferences?

The New York Times, 9-1:27.

Leif H. Olsen
Senior vice president and chief economist, First National City Bank, New York

(On wage-price controls): A program which achieves some arbitrary standard of equity in allocating labor income, corporate income and investment income is not necessarily a program that enhances the growth and performance of the economy, nor one that assures the maximum reduction in the rate of inflation. If monetary and fiscal policies are kept on a noninflationary path, the controls will appear to work and probably will get the credit—and hopefully (be) retired early. The widespread opinion that controls represent an efficient means of forcing prices to behave runs contrary to theory and also to a long and unhappy chain of experience.

The New York Times, 1-9:(NES)2.

Harold C. Passer
Assistant Secretary for Economic Affairs, Department of Commerce of the United States

We're close to the target in terms of the over-all economy. One area that has fallen a little short is consumer spending because of the extra tax withholding and the mild weather in the Northeast. But in residential construction and capital spending, we are ahead of the target, and that should help us to achieve the $100 billion gain in the gross national product we still expect for the year. The economy is really going along pretty well, and we are encouraged by the general tone of what we see.

Interview/ The New York Times, 4-2:(3)12.

Enoch Powell
Member of British Parliament

If you really want to attack (inflation) . . . then you tell the government to stop it . . . Remember, nobody but government causes inflation, because nobody but government manufactures or destroys money—apart from forgers. Inflation is caused by government because it is growth of money in a certain relationship to the growth of goods and services offered. The government controls money. Indeed, government is the creator of money. Government says to the people, "Look, see this; this is money."

Interview, London/
Nation's Business, April:74.

The net effect of labor unions has been to make workers slightly worse off than they otherwise would have been . . . And to the extent that labor unions, by a legalized duress, are able to prevent people from freely seeking their own advantage, they make themselves—as well as nearly everybody else—worse off. They probably don't make the leaders worse off.

Interview, London/
Nation's Business, April:76.

William Proxmire
United States Senator, D–Wis.

It is time the President recognized that the only way to cope with the inflation problem is to concentrate on those huge corporate conglomerations and those massive unions, each of which have supra-bargaining power, and forget about the small union and firm that must hold wages and prices down to meet competition.

Washington, March 10/
The New York Times, 3-11:32.

Seven and one-half months after the price freeze, prices continue to go up and up and up. The Price Commission functions entirely in secret. Its rulings and procedures are so complicated that the ordinary citizen is lost in a bureaucratic maze if he tries to lodge a complaint. Now there is talk of extending peacetime controls into the areas of highly-competitive markets and industries. Having prescribed the wrong medicine, we now may get a double dose.

Washington, March 31/
The Dallas Times Herald, 3-31:(A)4.

If we can't find less-damaging ways of controlling inflation than either creating unemployment or imposing complex and unfair controls, we should give serious consideration to learning to live with inflation as the lesser of two evils . . . The wage-price regulations are so prolific, so complicated and so secretive that they have become totally ineffective.

Interview/
The New York Times, 5-1:39.

(Criticizing the U.S. Chamber of Commerce's favoring extension of wage and price controls past the April 30, 1973, expiration date): Business wants to rely on the government to set prices for them, and more important, to protect them from the demands of labor unions . . . Your (the Chamber's) support of these price and wage controls makes me wonder if the controls aren't really becoming a shield for business which protects them from having to rely on competition and from having to rely on their own initiative in negotiating with labor.

At Congressional Joint Economic Committee hearing, Washington, Nov. 14/Los Angeles Times, 11-15:(1)8.

Ronald Reagan
Governor of California

Unless we are prepared to accept second-place status as a world trading nation, we must end needless conflict between business and labor and start an era of cooperation. I have every confidence in the American working man; but some of our national labor leaders had better acquire some statesmanship and stop thinking the calendar still reads 1933 . . . The kind of national strikes we have—which cripple whole industries—are virtually unknown in Japan and other major nations which compete against us in the world marketplace. We have got to change the curious and untrue attitude that business and labor, and business and government, are adversaries playing a game of economic touch football. We are going to have to work together—business, labor and government—to increase

(RONALD REAGAN)

our productivity, wind down the inflationary spiral and revitalize the competitive spirit that changed America from a small backward agricultural nation to the world's foremost economic and industrial power.

Before Sacramento (Calif.) Metropolitan Chamber of Commerce, Jan. 24/ San Francisco Examiner, 1-25:15.

(Arguing against the welfare eligibility of labor strikers): The first day of a strike finds an immediate surge in applications for both public assistance and food stamps at the adjacent welfare offices. This substantially bolsters the financial ability of the union and its ability to prolong a strike. The effect is to place (government) on one side of a management-labor dispute.

Before Senate Finance Committee, Washington, Feb. 1/ Los Angeles Herald-Examiner, 2-1:(A)3.

(Advocating Federal legislation to prevent massive labor strikes): It doesn't come easy for me to suggest government interference with labor and management. I was in labor too long, and I know when I was doing it I didn't want government sticking its nose in. But I think we have to recognize that there are certain areas of our economy now in which too many other people are penalized by a labor dispute that drags on this way (like the West Coast dock strike) —people who don't have a voice at the bargaining table.

News conference, Sacramento, Feb. 8/ Los Angeles Herald-Examiner, 2-9:(A)11.

Ogden R. Reid
United States Representative, R–N.Y.

There is a growing suspicion in this country that there is not one wage and price policy, but two—a policy of strict restraint for the wage earner and small businessman and a separate, more generous one for the more powerful economic interests . . . Unless we compel Federal officials to return to the original policy and apply it with even-handed fairness, we will soon slip back into the spiral of inflation.

Before United Auto Workers locals from N.Y., N.J. and Pa., Kiamesha Lake, N.Y., March 13/ Los Angeles Herald-Examiner, 3-13:(A)4.

Henry S. Reuss
United States Representative, D–Wis.

The Republicans have been referring to the economic performance out of Washington in 1971 as "historic." If this characterization merely means that 1971 is now over, one cannot fault it much. But if it means the Republicans—or for that matter the Democrats—think they deserve the Nobel Prize in economics based on performance, it seems presumptuous.

Before American Economic Association, New Orleans/ The Wall Street Journal, 1-5:10.

With one minor exception, the percentage of people who escaped all taxes rose steadily (in 1970) in every income bracket from $15,000 up to $1 million. Only 0.12 per cent of those in the $15,000-$20,000 bracket paid no tax; but the percentage was almost four times as high—0.45 per cent—in the $100,000-$200,000 bracket, and nine times as high—1.07 per cent—among people reporting incomes of $500,000 to $1 million . . . Income from the interest on state and local bonds is not included, nor is one-half of all long-term capital gains. If income from these sources was included in the Treasury statistics, the number of wealthy non-taxpayers would skyrocket . . . for every wealthy person who pays no taxes at all, there are many, many more who pay only a small pittance.

The Washington Post, 3-20:(D)7.

Pierre A. Rinfret
Economist

(The election of Senator George McGovern as President would be) an economic disaster for the U.S. . . . It can stand no other label. McGovern represents the socialist economic trends of thought in the U.S.

Before New York Society of Securities Analysts, July 17/ The Washington Post, 7-18:(D)7.

The greatest disaster to free enterprise is sustained inflation. It ultimately results in more government controls and more government intervention, and breaks down the confidence of the people, and destroys the morality of the system.

News conference, Los Angeles, Oct. 30/ Los Angeles Herald-Examiner, 10-30:(B)3.

George W. Romney
Secretary of Housing and Urban Development of the United States

The skepticism with which Wall Street continues to greet Senator (and Democratic Presidential nominee George) McGovern's economic proposals . . . is based on the clear fact that he does not understand how the American economy . . . works. His demagogic "soak the rich and share the wealth" concepts have been demonstrated by economic history . . . to be a certain road to economic destitution. In the name of helping the poor, he would set loose forces that would beggar the entire population.

Before Channel Club, Santa Barbara, Calif., Sept. 11/ Los Angeles Times, 9-12:(1)18.

Donald Rumsfeld
Director, Federal Cost of Living Council

Some people don't understand that profits aren't inflationary—prices are. My only concern about growing profits is that some people might think the money all flows to rich Wall Streeters with fat money belts. Increasing profits are what business uses to expand, to increase productivity, to provide jobs. What's inflationary about that?

Interview/ Los Angeles Times, 8-13:(1)1.

(On the results of the Nixon Administration's wage-price controls): Well, I would have to ask in answer to the question: "How are we doing compared with what?" Compared with where we were a year ago? Pretty good. Compared with what the President's goals were? Quite good. Compared with where we would have been if we had not had an economic-stabilization program? Clearly, I think we're doing considerably better than where we would have been had the President not instituted the new economic policy.

Interview/ U.S. News & World Report, 8-21:14.

Paul A. Samuelson
Professor of Economics, Massachusetts Institute of Technology

If permanent price controls could solve the problem of "stagflation," they would be a necessary evil. But there is little in the experiences of other countries to suggest to anybody but (Harvard economist) John Kenneth Galbraith that permanent controls can be made to work and produce the desired results in our mixed economy. I suspect that, before or after the (1972 Presidential) election, the American people will turn against controls. The next phase will be saying, "What's so bad about a little inflation?" We will be introducing escalation devices, such as cost-of-living adjustments in Social Security, to make creeping inflation more tolerable. The phase after that, I fear, will be stop-go driving of the economy with occasional flings at wage-price controls. I hope I am wrong,

(PAUL A. SAMUELSON)

but that is what experience suggests. And the world can survive it.

Panel discussion/ Newsweek, 1-31:75.

Congress has responsibly insisted upon budget deficits that by historical standards would have been considered large, but which have been shown to be vitally necessary to turn an anemic expansion into a vigorous one.

Plainview (Tex.) Daily Herald, 10-18:8.

Hugh Scott
United States Senator, R–Pa.

(Saying farmers should not be held responsible for high food prices, such as in restaurants): There have been the mark-ups of numerous middlemen, and as a result eggs, if you add a little bread and coffee to them at New York's Pierre Hotel, are about $30 a dozen. The farmer gets about 30¢ for the same eggs, so I don't think the farmer should bear the brunt.

San Francisco Examiner, 5-24:38.

R. Sargent Shriver
Democratic Vice-Presidential nominee

Once we looked on massive unemployment only as a problem of the ghetto. But now it appears in Youngstown, as well as Watts; in the steel mills of Buffalo and the aerospace industry of California and the textile mills of Lowell. Tragedy falls upon a man when his plant closes, or his job is taken by a machine in Japan or an exporter of shoes from Italy; when he suddenly loses his medical coverage and the seniority and pension rights built up over the years, and feels the clutching fear of not enough money to meet the mortgage or put dinner on the table.

Accepting the nomination, Washington, Aug. 8/ The New York Times, 8-9:18.

George P. Shultz
Secretary of the Treasury of the United States

When you think about almost any major economic problem these days, you can see that there are international foreign-policy ramifications to it, there are often defense ramifications to it, and there are interactions through all sorts of aspects of domestic policy that one can think of.

The Christian Science Monitor, 12-13:17.

Rocco A. Siciliano
Member, Pay Board, Federal Cost of Living Council

Capitalism is a dirty word in some parts of the world, and even in some quarters in this country; but generally we accept the private-enterprise system here. It really accounts for our great growth. And it succeeds because of its acceptance by the public. Nonetheless, in recent years there have been more and more questions about business corporations. I think there's going to be increasing administrative and legislative concern over how the system operates. (That attitude means) the danger of controls. It means giving the President authority, such as he now has, to continue to call into play certain kinds of strictures if the economy is not functioning properly. This may be merely an exhortation kind of control, or an incomes policy, or something like we now have—an in-between kind of program which is still basically voluntary. So I think that any Administration in the future is going to be given more tools than Administrations have had in the past.

Interview/ Nation's Business, July:25.

Harold R. Sims
Acting executive director,
National Urban League

Phase Two (of President Nixon's economic program of Aug., 1971) is not an economic program for America but an economic program for the rich. It is not for the working man but for the highly-organized union member. It is not for the businessman but for the big-business man. It is not for the consumer but for the upper-middle-class white consumer living in suburbia.

Interview, New York/
The New York Times, 1-9:(1)45.

Howard K. Smith
News commentator,
American Broadcasting Company

There isn't much good to say about the Wisconsin (Presidential) primary . . . but this: Never have so many active politicians voiced a sentiment long expressed in this space—that is, our tax is cockeyed. It penalizes those who work, as against those who live on capital. It bankrupts the small businessman or farmer and pays bounties to the big ones. Middle America pays the nation's bills; the rich and big pay little, and, in conspicuous cases, no tax at all. Well, scared by (Alabama Governor) George Wallace, every candidate has, in Wisconsin, come up with detailed plans for tax reform—from (Senator Edmund) Muskie's which promised to close $14 billion worth of tax loopholes, to (Senator George) McGovern's which neatly doubles the promise to $28 billion. Oh, for a Harry Truman now—someone to say to them: "Put your actions where your promises are. Come back to Washington where you are paid to be anyhow, prove you mean it by enacting those tax reforms now before (the Presidential election in) November. Yours is the majority party. So do it."

News broadcast, American
Broadcasting System, April 4/
The Christian Science Monitor,
4-15:14.

If the nation is going to finish this century in viable shape, our leaders are going to have to think some unthinkable thoughts about things we now take for granted—like (labor) strikes. Originally, the strike was the poor workers' only way to force a management to share its income with them. But unions have grown so mighty, they can demand more than their share. Moreover, many managements are so nearly monopolistic, strikes are no longer against them; they can simply pass on raises in higher prices to the public—the real victim. The sum result is inflation and inability to compete with other nations. The eventual answer is going to have to involve labor and management becoming mere advocates before a court of public representatives, whose rulings will have to be binding in wage disputes as in those price rises not subject to supply and demand. It is one more subject about which all those men asking us to vote for them for President ought to do some solid thinking—out loud.

Reader's Digest, June:16.

Maurice H. Stans
Secretary of Commerce
of the United States

I think there is a real question which the President (Nixon) himself has expressed a number of times about the attitude of the American people toward the work ethic. There isn't the stimulus, there isn't the desire of people to work, to succeed, as there once was. That is a bit pathetic, because when you travel in other countries you find that that still prevails. In Greece and Spain and the Soviet Union and in many other countries that I have been in, there is still the belief that it is worthwhile and valuable to work hard and thereby to find a means of success individually.

TV-radio interview, Washington/
"Meet the Press,"
National Broadcasting Company, 1-30.

Herbert Stein
Chairman, Council of Economic Advisers to the President of the United States

(Only three serious efforts have been made in the past 40 years) to bring the (Federal) budget into balance while the economy was significantly below full employment. One was President Hoover's effort in 1931-32, which was followed by disastrous economic and political developments. A second was President Roosevelt's 1936-7, followed soon thereafter by one of the sharpest recessions in American history. The third was President Eisenhower's in 1959-60, followed by the recession of 1960 and the election of John F. Kennedy. I don't think any government will ever again try to balance the budget while the economy is well below full employment.

Before House Appropriations Committee, Washington, Jan. 27/ The Dallas Times Herald, 1-30:(A)19.

The arithmetic is just not consistent with the notion that we can get a lot of revenue from (tax) loophole-closing simply by closing those loopholes which are of maximum benefit to the rich. The fact is that the tax preferences enjoyed by the upper-income brackets are not large enough to be a potential source of revenue to alter our budget position seriously.

Before Virginia Bankers Association, Hot Springs, June 17/ The New York Times, 6-18:(1)1.

We are now in the course of a vigorous economic expansion. Production and employment are rising strongly. Unemployment is declining. The rate of inflation has been reduced. Our international economic position is improving.

Before Joint Congressional Economic Committee, Washington, July 24/The New York Times, 7-25:17.

We must not make a fetish of annual Federal budget balance, but we must not make deficits a way of life. We must work with the (wage-price) controls, but not become infatuated with them. We must press for our interests in the international economy, but we must not relapse into isolationism.

Before Republican National Convention Platform Committee, Miami Beach/ San Francisco Examiner, 8-16:58.

John G. Tower
United States Senator, R–Tex.

(Criticizing the resignation from the Federal Pay Board of three AFL-CIO members): Big labor management is so used to having its own way, so used to being the beneficiaries of labor legislation passed in the 1930s, that it can only act like a spoiled child when asked to cooperate with the rest of the nation in the public interest.

Washington/ The Dallas Times Herald 3-23:(A)2.

Charles A. Vanik
United States Representative, D–Ohio

Corporate taxation is rapidly vanishing as they become freeloaders on the American scene. I feel very sorry for the average taxpayer of America who earns $10,000 per year, has three dependents and pays a heavy share of the tax load of this country.

Before the House, Washington, March 21/ Los Angeles Times, 3-22:(1)17.

George C. Wallace
Governor of Alabama

We're sick and tired of the average citizen being taxed to death while these multibillionaires like the Rockefellers and the Fords and the Mellons and Carnegies go without paying taxes. They got billions of dollars in tax-shelter foundations, and they don't pay as much tax as you do on a percentage basis. And the church commercial property—the churches own businesses, shopping centers, hotels, skyscrapers, all competing with private enterprise. A fair tax on this $200 billion in untaxed wealth would bring in $12 billion to the Treasury. We've got to close up these loopholes on those who've escaped paying their fair share so we can lower taxes for the average citizen—the little businessman, the farmer, the elderly, the middle class.

Campaigning for the Democratic Presidential nomination/ Newsweek, 3-27:23.

The candidates (for the Democratic Presidential nomination) are stealing all my stuff after (the primary in) Florida. Didn't they all come up here and start talking about tax reform? And all those years when the only words you ever heard from them were tax, tax, tax and spend, spend, spend.

Campaigning in Wisconsin for the Democratic Presidential nomination/ The New York Times, 4-1:8.

Henry C. Wallich
Professor of Economics, Yale University

Trying to substitute wage and price controls for sound monetary and fiscal policies may be tempting to some, but it is a prescription for disaster. A market-oriented form of restraint on wages and prices would be something else. For instance, a tax on corporations granting excessive wage increases would stiffen the backbones of employers who now find it easier to put pressure on the consumer than on the union.

Panel discussion/ Newsweek, 1-31:75.

Theodore H. White
Author, Journalist

We now have a Republican President (Nixon) who has a controlled economy. If anyone thinks we are going back to free prices and wages, he is crazy. We'll have a semi-controlled economy the rest of our lives.

Interview, New York/ Los Angeles Times, 10-6:(2)7.

Elmer L. Winter
President, Manpower, Inc.

One of the best-kept secrets in industry today is the cost of absenteeism, low productivity, boredom on the job and frequent turnovers among employees. We may be paying a heavy price for lack of interest and motivation on the part of employees. I sometimes think that many companies have a four-day week without knowing it . . . We know now, I think, that we have to change the mode of work. People can't get the satisfaction out of some specialized jobs—broken down as they are so often into components for improved efficiency. We need to put in a job-enrichment factor. We've got to do a whole new job of human engineering to find ways to keep interest and motivation high . . . I think people want to work, but they want satisfaction out of their work experience. And I'm afraid we've kept a lot of people trapped who had great potential.

Interview/ The New York Times, 5-14:(3)3.

Leonard Woodcock
President, United Automobile Workers of America

The groups of workers we traditionally have represented are growing smaller. There has been a union breakthrough among white-collar employees, but mainly in government. As for office workers in the auto

(LEONARD WOODCOCK)

industry, managements give them the same raises the union wins for production workers, and frequently add something extra for the office group. Office workers have told us frankly that they are content to stay out of the union because they don't have to pay dues or go on strike but get the same raises. They admit it's the union that wins them their raises.

U.S. News & World Report, 2-21:23.

(On his leaving the Federal Pay Board): We leave because the whole Nixon (wage-price) control program is an abomination; and the UAW cannot in good conscience maintain any connection whatsoever with that system.

The Dallas Times Herald, 3-24:(A)1.

Spiro T. Agnew
Vice President of the United States

(Criticizing some poverty-program attorneys): What we may be on the way to creating is a Federally-funded system manned by ideological vigilantes who owe their allegiance not to a client, but only to a concept of social reform. Program attorneys have been heavily involved in every social issue of the day. In Evanston, Ill., it's draft counseling; in Texas, California, Colorado, Florida and other places, it's underground newspapers; in Boston, it's women's rights; in California, it's the rights of penitentiary inmates; in numerous other places, it's students' rights, antiwar protests, free-speech movements. The list of causes is seemingly endless. Is this right? Is that what the legal services were meant to do? Did Congress in its enactment or the bar in its support contemplate a program where a destitute mother of five can't get help with an eviction notice, but a middle-class drop-out can get legal counseling in setting up his underground newspaper?

Before Texas Bar Association, Houston, July 7/ Los Angeles Herald-Examiner, 7-9:(A)2.

Joseph L. Alioto
Mayor of San Francisco

Justice in America is fast becoming a luxury commodity reserved for a select few —the very rich and the very poor. The blunt fact is that the legal procedures in this country are archaic, the costs outrageously high, and the people are turning elsewhere for justice.

Before young lawyers section, American Bar Association, San Francisco, Aug. 11/ Los Angeles Times, 8-12:(1)21.

F. Lee Bailey
Lawyer

I get paid for seeing that my clients have every break the law allows. I have knowingly defended a number of guilty men. But the guilty never escape unscathed. My fees are sufficient punishment for anyone.

Interview/Los Angeles Times, 1-9:(Calendar)43.

The public regards lawyers with great distrust. They think lawyers are smarter than the average guy but use their intelligence deviously. Well, they're wrong: Usually they're not smarter.

Interview/Los Angeles Times, 1-9:(Calendar)43.

. . . I think there are two ways to look at the definition of (a) great legal writer. One is a good legal mind who's a great writer; and the other is a great legal mind who's a good writer. I think the two greatest legal writers, as far as putting the words together in a spellbinding order, are Benjamin Cardozo and Oliver Wendell Holmes. Brandeis was good, and Frankfurter had flashes of brilliance; but as far as people whose opinions are solid, lucid and just damn good workable law regardless of the degree of the flight of rhetoric used to express it—because that sometimes creates as many problems as it creates delights—I can't think of anyone particularly. But I do think of a number of judges who repeatedly, but not consistently, will come out with that kind of opinion. Learned Hand was one of them; and I'll never forget Cardozo's great line—really a gorgeous line—in a case called McPherson against Buick, where an owner was trying to sue the manufacturer and skip the dealer on a breach of warranty. The defense was that there was no "privity of contract" between the owner and the manufacturer. Cardozo opened up by saying, "The assault upon the citadel of privity continues these days apace."

Interview/
The Washington Post, 4-2:(Book World)2.

The American people are very suspicious of lawyers. Juries think we are there to con them. And the public believes the mark of success for a lawyer is just getting people off.

Life, 11-17:97.

Melvin Belli
Lawyer

Justice is a means; justice is a system; justice is a *modus operandi* whereby you achieve the right to be heard and the right to be brought before impartial triers who judge you according to the mores of the time. Two men, X and Y, commit the same crime. Yet, perhaps X may be found guilty and Y found innocent. And the only reason would be that X lives in a different state than Y. You have different mores in different communities, so you have different justice depending on the geography.

Interview, San Francisco/
Los Angeles Times, 4-9:(West)39.

I'm pretty disgusted with the law now, with what (U.S. Chief Justice Warren) Burger and (President) Nixon have done to it. Burger has said, "Don't go into the law if you want social change." He said that up at Harvard and they booed him. He tried to clarify what he really meant but it didn't go over. Law for him is on the side of the establishment; it's a staid, fixed thing. But I say you don't have a Constitution unless you read it in context, and the only way to do that is to relate it to social activity . . . a hell of a lot of (young prospective lawyers) were going to law school because they figured that they could change the system within the law. By learning the law, they could file writ upon writ in consumer cases, ecology cases, all the rest of those. But Burger says, in effect, like hell you will.

Interview, San Francisco/
Los Angeles Herald-Examiner, 9-3:(California Living)7.

Kingman Brewster, Jr.
President,
Yale University

It's a terrible American weakness to believe that if you've got a problem all you have to do is pass a law. It may be important to pass the law and observe it; but even more important in the long run is the active concern of the private citizen for the values involved.

Interview, Yale University/
The Dallas Times Herald, 6-15:(B)16.

Warren E. Burger
Chief Justice of the United States

Our basic system of justice, of course, lies within state power and it should remain that way, with Federal courts functioning, as the Constitution intended they should, as courts of special and limited jurisdiction.

Before American Law Institute, Washington, May 16/
San Francisco Examiner, 5-16:2.

A graph of the docketed cases in the Supreme Court over the past 20 years looks like a one-sided profile of the Eiffel Tower. I put it to you whether there is any basis to assume that the Supreme Court, which was hard-pressed to deal with 1,100 cases in 1942, and 1,400 in 1952, can deal adequately with 4,500 cases in 1972 or the 7,000 we can anticipate by 1980.

State of the Judiciary address before American Bar Association, San Francisco, Aug. 14/
Los Angeles Times, 8-15:(1)3.

Ideas, ideals and great conceptions are vital to a system of justice, but it must have more than that—there must be delivery and execution. Concepts of justice must have hands and feet or they remain sterile abstractions. The hands and feet we need are efficient means and methods to carry out justice in every case in the shortest possible time and at the lowest possible cost. This is the challenge to every lawyer and judge in America.

Before American Bar Association, San Francisco, Aug. 14/ Vital Speeches, 10-1:743.

(On a compulsory retirement age for Federal judges): Laying aside the question how this could be done, I see no valid basis for applying to judges rules that are fundamentally different from those you apply to most people in private business, in the professions, in corporate life or the military, where 65 and 68 are prevailing retirement ages. Of course, there is no limit to age in Congress; but there is the balancing factor that at least the voters have a choice every two and every six years for members of Congress. Frankly, I see no basic objection to reasonable age limits, but on the whole we have managed pretty well without them in government. If you analyze the periodic complaints, you will see that the critics want age limits for people they don't agree with.

Interview, Washington/ U.S. News & World Report, 8-21:39.

My concern for the problems of state courts derives from a conviction based on a lifetime of experience as a lawyer and a judge—that the problems of justice are indivisible and that the basic system of justice in this country is and always must be the state courts. If they are not strong and effective and provided with adequate support, all the appropriations, all the plans and all the work of 500 or 600 Federal judges will not give us a meaningful system of justice.

Before National Institute of Justice/ The New York Times, 12-13:35.

Harry F. Byrd, Jr.
United States Senator, I–Va.

(Advocating periodic reconfirmation of Federal judges and Supreme Court Justices): Why should any official in a democracy have a lifetime tenure? In the modern world, only kings, queens, emperors, maharajahs and United States Federal judges hold office for life.

Before Senate Judiciary Subcommittee on Constitutional Amendments, Washington, May 19/ The Washington Post, 5-20:(C)13.

Fred J. Cassibry
Judge, United States District Court for the Eastern District of Louisiana

In the United States, no man is so small as to be disregarded by the law; neither is any man so great as to be above it.

New Orleans, Jan. 5/ San Francisco Examiner, 1-6:15.

Angela Davis
Political activist

(On her recent murder-conspiracy trial in which she was acquitted): If you're implying that my acquittal changes my mind about the American judicial system, then you're wrong . . . the only fair trial would have been no trial.

Los Angeles Herald-Examiner, 6-25:(B)2.

William O. Douglas
Associate Justice, Supreme Court of the United States

We're actually hearing and deciding fewer cases (on the Supreme Court) now than when we were when I went on the Court . . . The judges have changed; the idea of what is important has changed in the minds of the judges—a highly selective considera-

(WILLIAM O. DOUGLAS)

tion. Is this case fit to take? Should we take it? And so on. And we take fewer and fewer. When I went on the Court, we sat six days a week. Under (former Chief Justice Earl) Warren, we sat five days a week, a conference on Friday. And now it looks as if our trend will be to three days a week, with a conference on Saturday. The job takes about four days a week.

Television interview, Sept. 6/ The Dallas Times Herald, 9-7:(A)18.

Percy Foreman
Lawyer

I don't charge by the hour or the day. I'm not a mechanic. I'm an artist. If you are going to use the time to be a book-keeper, you can't be a trial lawyer.

At District Court hearing, Houston, May 11/ The Dallas Times Herald, 5-12:(A)22.

Arthur J. Goldberg
Former Associate Justice, Supreme Court of the United States

The Supreme Court recently spoke of courts in general as "palladiums of liberty" and as "citadels of justice" . . . to some elements of our population, the judicial system is viewed as anything but a "citadel of justice." And there are some who profoundly believe that justice is not only delayed but that it is denied. I am not referring to the view taken by those who style themselves revolutionary and who are blind to our Constitutional commitment to the rule of law. I am describing the perceptions of some of the residents of our racial ghettos, of our urban and rural poor, of the economic and socially deprived . . . They are people for whom in criminal cases a plea or verdict of guilty is almost an inevitable conclusion; for whom the concept of due process may appear, in such cases, to mean no more than completing the paperwork necessary to carry out judgment and sentence.

At Hastings-American Trial Lawyers Association banquet, San Francisco, Aug. 26/ San Francisco Examiner & Chronicle, 8-27:(A)29.

L. Patrick Gray III
Acting Director, Federal Bureau of Investigation

The out-of-court conduct of most of these attorneys (who disrupt courtroom proceedings during trials) has been no less than scandalous. They exploit misunderstandings; they encourage confrontation; they appeal to those who place rule by mob above rule by law. One of the legally-trained agitators to whom I refer has been quoted as telling a street audience in our nation's capital last September, "I have come out of a prison yard . . . where I was privileged to meet, yes, convicted murderers, child molesters, holdup artists, second-story men—and they were the finest and most decent men I ever met." Is it any wonder that disrespect for law, contempt for authority and distorted values prevail among those to whom this activist directs his strongest appeal?

At crime-control conference, Biloxi, Miss., May 25/ Los Angeles Herald-Examiner, 5-27:(A)2.

Lord Hailsham
Lord High Chancellor of the United Kingdom

It seems to me that the only law which there is any merit in obeying is the one you do not agree with either because you think it is mistaken or because you think it operates against your interest; and the only law which there is any merit in enforcing is the law which at least somebody would not obey if it were not enforced.

Before magistrates, Exeter, England/ Los Angeles Times, 4-23:(G)6.

R. J. Henle
President,
Georgetown University

Too often, practitioners of the law are simply sort of journeymen of legal practice and are not creators of legal justice and do not in fact understand the philosophical bases of law, its ultimate goals or its importance in any society, and above all in a democratic society. I find one of the weaknesses of American general education to lie in the fact that practically nobody, except a graduate student in law or political science, or a very bright law student, really gets any kind of a full understanding of the meaning of the law and of the legal system in a democracy. This great cultural creation of civilized man is hardly appreciated by the millions of people whom it protects and whose institutions it perpetuates. It should be the role of universities to communicate this understanding, not only to law students but to all educated people. It should be the role of universities to constantly explore the possibilities of improving the rule of law, of constantly studying the extension of the rule of law, of constantly working for the universalization of the basic principles which lead to an international conformity of basic law. It should be the role of universities to study the extension of law to other areas of human disputes and arguments and violence, so as to substitute basic principles and rational procedures for prejudice and violence and force.

On 10th anniversary of Georgetown University Center for Strategic and International Studies, Sept. 7/Vital Speeches, 10-15:12.

Frank S. Hogan
District Attorney,
New York County, N.Y.

There is no finality in the law any more. To move a case to trial, we first have to run an obstacle course of motions. More of our time is consumed in this preliminary skirmishing than in the actual litigation. Many motions are made merely to gain delay. They are frivolous. They are not intended to obtain a legitimate remedy but as a weapon in a war of attrition to exhaust the prosecution in hope that the case will fade away or, at worst, that the prosecution will finally settle for a lesser plea . . . If the defendant is found guilty, our task has just begun. Years of litigation follow as the case threads its way through complicated review. Every imaginable aspect—even things that were never thought of at the trial—will be argued and reargued . . . English criminal proceedings are concluded with much more dispatch and finality than ours. Since appeals there are not allowed as a matter of right, there is likely to be no appeal at all. If there is, it is a once-only affair. There are no rehearings and no further proceedings by way of collateral attack. I hope the day will soon come when we can reach a fair compromise between the bare English minimum of appellate practice and our maximum indulgence of remedies after conviction.

Interview, New York/ Los Angeles Times, 8-14:(2)7.

J. Edgar Hoover
Director,
Federal Bureau of Investigation

The courts are now experiencing some of what law enforcement for years has suffered in full measure—violent disrespect for the law and diabolical schemes to prove that the system of justice does not work in America.

Quote, 2-27:193.

. . . the law is the principle which holds society together. Take away the law—through disrespect or actual disobedience—and the whole keystone of society crumbles, and with it the dignity of man as a child of God.

Interview, Washington, May 1/ San Francisco Examiner & Chronicle, 5-7:(B)7.

Henry M. Jackson
United States Senator, D–Wash.

If I were President of the United States, I would see that court reform received the priority it deserves. I would see that the states received the money they need to make our criminal courts function effectively, with more judges and more prosecutors and more public defense counsel. But I would impose a condition that the states guarantee that any person accused of a crime of violence be brought to trial within 60 to 90 days after arrest.

News conference, Columbus, Ohio, April 18/ The New York Times, 4-19:47.

Leon Jaworski
President, American Bar Association

When entering the profession, a lawyer does not engage in a popularity contest; but he does assume a special creed . . . "to safeguard every man's right to a fair trial." It is disquieting to observe in these days a growing tendency of some of the most capable members of the bar to shun the acceptance of representation of those in public disfavor.

At Law Day ceremonies, St. Mary's University School of Law, San Antonio/ The Dallas Times Herald, 4-16:(A)29.

Thomas F. Kavanaugh
Chief Justice, Supreme Court of Michigan

Today, as perhaps never before in the history of the judicial system—with the courts under attack from various sources—it is more imperative than ever before that all members of the judiciary conduct themselves in a manner to reflect only honor on the system.

The New York Times, 9-8:33.

Richard G. Kleindienst
Attorney General of the United States

One of the chief factors that has slowed and frustrated the justice process has been the interminable collateral attacks made possible by the post-trial use of the Federal writ of habeas corpus. While I recognize the place of collateral attack in the justice process, I do deplore the abuse of it that has mushroomed in the last 20 years.

Before National Association of Attorneys General, Stateline, Nev., June 27/ San Francisco Examiner, 6-28:14.

William M. Kunstler
Lawyer

I know the law. It is used to oppress those who threaten the ruling class. The judicial decree has replaced the assassin . . . I remain a lawyer, I stay with the law, only because the law is maneuverable, it can be manipulated. But in the future?

Pittsburgh/ Human Events, 2-12:6.

George S. McGovern
United States Senator, D–S.D.

I believe in the rule of law when it works against me, and I believe in it when it works for me.

At Texas caucus of Democratic National Convention, Miami Beach, July 9/ The Washington Post, 7-11:(A)12.

John N. Mitchell
Attorney General of the United States

Any lawyer prefers the legislative approach to a Constitutional amendment if it can accomplish the same purpose.

The Dallas Times Herald, 3-3:(A)32.

Stanley Mosk
Associate Justice, Supreme Court of California

It has been our lot, as lawyers, to be in the forefront of every effort to preserve liberty through and under law during

America's history. It is our responsibility to continue these efforts, regardless of the obstacles placed before us by unthinking zealots and thinking fanatics, situated on every political extreme and in the dead center of apathy.

San Francisco Examiner & Chronicle, 5-21:(This World)2.

Edmund S. Muskie
United States Senator, D–Maine

If justice delayed is justice denied, there is far too little justice in American courts.

The National Observer, 5-6:16.

Richard M. Nixon
President of the United States

. . . I promised in the election campaign (in 1968) that I would appoint judges to the Federal courts–and particularly to the Supreme Court–who would recognize that the first civil right of every American is to be free from domestic violence. I have kept that promise. I am proud of the appointments I have made to the courts and particularly to the Supreme Court. I pledge again tonight, as I did four years ago, that, whenever I have the opportunity to make more appointments to the courts, I shall continue to appoint judges who share my philosophy that we must strengthen the peace forces against the criminal forces in America.

Accepting the Republican Presidential nomination, Miami Beach, Aug. 23/ Los Angeles Times, 8-24:(1)22.

I said several times that I intend to continue to appoint conservative judges to the (U.S. Supreme) Court. I do. The courts need them, and they need men like (Justices William) Rehnquist and (Warren) Burger and (Harry) Blackmun and (Lewis) Powell on their Court–not reactionary judges but men who are Constitutional conservatives, because the trend has gone too far in the other direction. I don't mean that there weren't well-intentioned judges calling them as they see them. But I don't believe that that was the right trend for this country, and I think we have got to continue to reverse that trend in the whole field of law enforcement.

Interview, Nov. 5/ The New York Times, 11-10:20.

Henry E. Petersen
Assistant Attorney General, Criminal Division, Department of Justice of the United States

(Criticizing the rule which excludes illegally-obtained evidence from a trial): It has failed to discourage police officers from conducting unreasonable searches and seizures. It is difficult to perceive how suppression of reliable and probative evidence can discourage unreasonable police conduct. Unlike coerced confessions, probative evidence is reliable regardless of the manner in which it is seized. Moreover, the rule provides no flexibility. It imposes suppression without regard to the nature of the misconduct–whether honest mistake or outrageous behavior.

At American Bar Association annual meeting, San Francisco, Aug. 13/Los Angeles Times, 8-14:(1)17.

Lewis F. Powell, Jr.
Associate Justice, Supreme Court of the United States

(On whether he enjoys being on the Supreme Court): The answer is "no." (But) if one asked not whether I enjoy my new status, but whether I would make the same decision to go on the Court that I made when the lightning struck last fall, the answer is plainly "yes." I do not enjoy being away from Richmond (Va.), my friends of a lifetime and my home. At this point I do not enjoy learning what in many respects is a new profession. I do not enjoy working 6½ days a week and almost every night at a time when I had planned to be tapering off. (Nor) do I enjoy the limitations which the ethics of our profession impose upon a judge in

(LEWIS F. POWELL, JR.)

terms of nonparticipation in so many interesting phases of life—social, political and business. The truth is that I'd rather be a lawyer than a judge. I was never in any doubt as a lawyer as to which side I was on. I really prefer to be competitive rather than neutral, detached and disinterested.

Before Virginia Bar Association, White Sulphur Springs, W. Va., July 15/ The Washington Post, 7-17:(A)2.

The Supreme Court is an awesome place. It's responsibility and power under our form of government are greater than that of any other court in the world. Whether wisely or not, the Court is regarded at times, perhaps even more than the Legislative Branch, as the most direct means of achieving social progress and reform. It always has been the guardian of the most sacred rights and liberties of our people.

Before Virginia Bar Association, White Sulphur Springs, W. Va., July 15/ The Washington Post, 7-17:(A)2.

Ronald Reagan
Governor of California

(On the not-guilty verdict in the Angela Davis murder-conspiracy trial): Many of those who have been demonstrating and protesting, and who have, incidentally, found the United States and our system of justice guilty without a trial, might have second thoughts now and be willing to accept that our system does work. If they're really fair-minded and really interested in justice, then they ought to sit down and think a little bit about whether they want to run around staging any more demonstrations again. I think they've had pretty good proof that this society of ours leans over backward to give the accused every opportunity.

News conference, Sacramento, June 5/Los Angeles Times, 6-6:(1)23.

Long delays between arrest and conviction, endless appeals of questionable merit, the resort to legal gimmicks involving technical rules . . . all of these things contribute to the lack of confidence in the legal system. To many of our people, it seems the prime goal of defense attorneys is not an early hearing on the merits of the case to win acquittal or a resolution of the case on the facts. Instead, delay becomes a tactic in itself; a way not to assure justice, but to thwart it. The legal system itself must lead the effort for reforms, provide the effective means of dealing with disrespectful and contemptuous conduct toward the court (and support) regulations to prohibit the antics of defendants who see their day in court only as an opportunity to publicize and dramatize a social or political cause. For more than 180 years, the advocacy system in our courts has been one of the legal system's major strengths in assuring justice. Today, it seems, the advocacy system has become a means of exploiting the weaknesses of our system . . . using the legitimate safeguards built into our legal system to prevent it from functioning effectively.

Before State Bar of California, Monterey, Sept. 27/ Vital Speeches, 11-15:68.

Arthur M. Schlesinger, Jr.
Historian

The (U.S.) Supreme Court is becoming a wholly-owned subsidiary of the rich and powerful, instead of the impartial and compassionate tribunal it has been.

At University of North Carolina, Chapel Hill/ The New York Times, 10-24:30.

Eric Sevareid
News commentator, Columbia Broadcasting System

Years ago, despairing citizens . . . used to say, "There oughta be a law." There is a law. There are lots of laws. What there oughta be is severe—and equal—enforcement of the laws . . . In one area after another of our public life we are seeing a reversion to that frontier phenomenon—citizens taking the law into their own hands, not to enforce it themselves, but to force the official enforcers to enforce it.

Television broadcast/"Evening News," Columbia Broadcasting System, 4-3.

R. Sargent Shriver
Democratic
Vice-Presidential nominee

Our people deserve a new and genuine Department of Justice—one which sees as its responsibility the expansion of justice for all of our citizenry and which perceives its task to confront injustice wherever it is found; one which opposes private lawlessness by a slum landlord and official lawlessness by a General (John D.) Lavelle bombing (North Vietnamese) cities against orders; one which chooses civil rights and liberties over regressive tactics and suppression of dissent. As I conceive the role of the Department, it should have two Deputy Attorneys General; one would be in charge of the traditional law-enforcement activities, the other would head a new office charged with the duty of expanding justice . . . Some time ago, I proposed the creation of a national institute of justice devoted to improving our entire legal system, coordinating legal research and long-range planning, revising legal education, reforming criminal and correctional systems, developing techniques for resolving disputes and exploring other methods of bringing justice closer to the people. This branch of the Department of Justice also should deal with official injustice. We know of such injustices—agencies arrogant with power that fail to protect the public interest, neglect to carry out the law, and callously submerge citizens in delay and mind-boggling red tape. We have all seen such injustices—agencies that summarily evict families from housing, cut off Medicare, deny claims, bar citizens from voting, refuse children free lunches, remove students from schools, and many more.

Campaigning for the forthcoming Presidential election, Drake University/ The New York Times, 10-11:39.

John R. Silber
President, Boston University

The lawyers' contribution to the civilizing of humanity is evidenced in the capacity of lawyers to argue furiously in the courtroom, then sit down as friends over a drink or dinner. This habit is often interpreted by the layman as a mark of their ultimate corruption. In my opinion, it is their greatest moral achievement; it is a characteristic of humane tolerance that is most desperately needed at the present time.

At dinner celebrating the centennial of Boston University School of Law, Westport, Mass./ The Wall Street Journal, 3-16:10.

Harold H. Titus, Jr.
United States Attorney-designate for the District of Columbia

I'm tired of the social-worker aspect of people thinking my job is to put the rights of the victim behind the rights of the defendant . . . I'm mad; I'm a damn mad prosecutor. I'm mad at the emphasis being given to the defendant and his rights.

Interview/ The Washington Post, 4-10:(A)10.

Civil rights, Constitutional rights I'm not complaining about. But extensions of them to the point of absurdity I vomit at, I vomit at.

Interview/ The Washington Post, 4-10:(A)10.

John G. Tower
United States Senator, R–Tex.

(On Congressional legislation vs. Constitutional amendment): The fatal weakness of a statute is that a statute can be overturned by the Supreme Court. The Supreme Court has no inhibition about telling those of us in Congress that we don't know what the Constitution says.

The Dallas Times Herald, 2-23:(A)28.

George C. Wallace
Governor of Alabama

Some of my lawyer friends say I ought to be cool and dignified and not talk about the judges that have just about ruined this country. Why not? They talk about me, don't they? They don't hang their britches on the wall and go jump in them; they pull them on one leg at a time just like regular folks. And the people didn't elect them, either, like they did me.

Before Tiger Bay Club, Miami/ The National Observer, 2-19:4.

Earl Warren
Former Chief Justice of the United States

A man might be a very great liberal in political life, and he might be equally as conservative in judicial process (as a Supreme Court Justice), because they're entirely different. You see, in the political process, the legislative bodies have the oversight, within Constitutional limits, of everything in their jurisdiction. And if they see something they don't like, something that needs to be remedied, they can single that out and bring it in and try to legislate on it. And they can; they're in what you might call free-wheeling to advocate anything they want to accomplish that accomplishes that purpose. And if they can't get a whole loaf, why, they settle for a half-loaf; and if they can't get a half-loaf, they may settle for a quarter; and if they can't get that, maybe they'll bypass the whole thing and let it go to another time. But the Court is not a self-starter in that respect. It can never reach out and grab any issue and bring it into Court and decide it, no matter how strongly it may feel about the condition it's confronted with. It is a creature of the litigation that is brought to it. So when they come to the Supreme Court, the members of the Court have no way of determining what they want to hear . . . And so many people can't understand that, because they believe that a lot of the people (Justices) come there committed to a definite course of conduct and action depending upon their views, their political views. And they think if they see something they don't like, they just pull it into the Court and decide it. But that is not true; the Court is very limited in its jurisdiction.

Broadcast interview, Boston/ The New York Times, 12-20:43.

Edward Bennett Williams
Lawyer

If someone robbed you tonight . . . I, a trial lawyer, would be able to keep him at liberty for from 18 months to two years before he faced the day of reckoning, by various maneuvers that I would be able to employ in order to postpone the day of reckoning for him.

Television interview/ "Thirty Minutes With . . . ," WETA-TV, Washington, 6-8.

Samuel W. Yorty
Mayor of Los Angeles

Everybody knows our criminal court system has fallen down. It's got to be overhauled . . . Justice must be swift and sure . . . A way must be found to cut through this useless procedure and get down to the basic question: Is the defendant guilty or innocent?

News conference, Los Angeles, Jan. 26/ Los Angeles Times, 1-27:(2)2.

Evelle J. Younger
Attorney General of California

Our citizens will wait just so long for the judiciary and bar to take practical and long-overdue action to drag the criminal justice system into the space age . . . If the criticism must be given a catchy title, let's call it "the courts are handcuffing the courts." That statement reflects my firm conviction that appellate courts in the last 15 years have seriously reduced the effectiveness of criminal courts. Their obsession with procedural matters has turned a criminal trial into a game which is only remotely and incidentally concerned with guilt or innocence.

At California Conference on the Judiciary, Los Angeles, Jan. 13/ Los Angeles Times, 1-14:(2)3.

National Defense • The Military

Spiro T. Agnew
Vice President of the United States

(On the arms-control agreement concluded by President Nixon during his recent summit meeting with the Soviet Union): Had we entered the talks in a position of weakness caused by unilateral abandonment of our military capability, a favorable agreement would not have been possible. Had the Congress voted down the ABM program in 1969, there would have been no incentive for the Soviets to agree on limiting defensive systems in 1972. We would be well advised to remember that fact as pressures begin to mount for irresponsible cuts in our defense budget.

At National Governors Conference, Houston, June 5/ The Washington Post, 6-6:(A)8.

(On Democratic Presidential nominee Senator George McGovern's proposals to cut back on defense spending): The McGovern defense proposal must be based on the assumption that we will never face the challenge of a limited non-nuclear war. It guarantees that we can't fight such a war, because it restricts the size of our traditional forces and leaves us with weapons systems rapidly becoming obsolete in the face of continuous modernization of conventional armed forces by other world powers. It leaves us with only one course of action—nuclear retaliation if attacked—and it restricts that capability to the point that in a few short years we might have to back down in a confrontation with a major power.

Before members of Rotary Clubs, St. Louis, Sept. 20/ Los Angeles Herald-Examiner, 9-21:(A)8.

We don't need to glorify our military men; but neither should we denigrate them. They neither seek nor should be accorded special status; but they do need and deserve our strong support.

Veterans Day address, College of Southern Idaho, Oct. 23/ Los Angeles Times, 10-24:(1)18.

James B. Allen
United States Senator, D–Ala.

My vote against the nuclear weapons limitation treaty with Russia (concluded during President Nixon's summit meeting in Moscow earlier in the year) was one of only two cast in opposition to leaving the American people virtually defenseless from nuclear attack. Mine will probably be one of only a relative handful of votes against the interim agreement which will give the Russians a 3-to-2 advantage over us in offensive nuclear weapons . . . My position . . . is that the Russians can be trusted to live up to an agreement only so long as it serves their purposes, and we should not freeze ourselves into a position of inferiority in nuclear strength in comparison with Russia. My sympathies are with efforts to end the scourge of war as a means of settling disputes, and it is my hope that mankind can look forward to the day when all nations will forever renounce war as an instrument to effect international policies. But the dream for peace must not keep us from promoting the strength and honor of our country in our dealings with foreign nations. We must keep America the strongest nation in the world, and the treaty and agreement do just the opposite.

Human Events, 10-14:23.

John M. Ashbrook
United States Representative, R–Ohio

(On arms-control agreements concluded

by President Nixon recently during the U.S.-Soviet summit meeting in Moscow): There is no question in my mind that the President has signed agreements dooming the United States to nuclear inferiority and to a decade of danger.

San Francisco Examiner & Chronicle, 6-11:(This World)2.

Frank R. Barnett
President, National Strategy Information Center, Inc.

It seems to me that it is more practical to deduce a nation's intentions and strategies by looking at the profile of its defense budgets than by listening to the words of its diplomats. If one looks at the Soviet defense budget, one sees first of all that they are spending more than we are on strategic weaponry and research and development of advanced weapons. Our defense budget, totally, has been greater than the Soviet Union's only because we have been spending so much on conventional war.

At Navy League Seminar on Soviet Seapower, New York/ The National Observer, 3-11:13.

James L. Buckley
United States Senator, C–N.Y.

I find no cause for rejoicing over the announced terms of the SALT agreement (signed by the U.S. and the Soviet Union during President Nixon's summit meeting in Moscow); nor will our friends in Europe, Asia and the Middle East who depend for their security on our continuing ability to hold our ground in any future confrontations with the Soviet Union. It is quite clear that the United States is being asked to pay a very high price in order to buy five years' time within which to achieve major qualitative improvements in its strategic arsenal. Aside from grave misgivings over the proposed ABM treaty, I fear that the announcements of the SALT agreements will have the effect of lulling the nation into a totally unwarranted sense of security.

The Dallas Times Herald, 5-28:(B)33.

A nation's military establishment is not a luxury but a necessity. No nation with peaceful intentions requires or can justify a defense establishment which is larger than that which is necessary to meet the needs of her own security. But the adequacy or inadequacy of a nation's defense is determined not by considerations of domestic priorities, but by the power relationships within which that nation must operate. And we must keep in mind that in the real world no country can conduct an effective foreign policy without a military capability which is appropriate to its responsibilities.

Human Events, 8-19:15.

Bernard A. Clarey
Admiral, United States Navy; Commander-in-Chief, Pacific Fleet

I think the Russians are expanding (their Navy). They understand the use of sea power. Their understanding was highlighted, in my view, at the time of the Cuban crisis, when we forced them to take those missiles back. The big push in the build-up of the Russian Navy has been since 1962. They are building about 15 nuclear submarines a year now. Very soon they will have the same number of the *Yankee*-class submarines that we have of *Polaris*-type and *Poseidon* submarines. Their Navy is spread out, showing the flag. Their merchant marine is operating all over the world. They are expanding the operations of their oceanographic-research vessels and their fishing fleet. For these very reasons, we (the U.S.) must keep our Navy modern and strong.

Interview, Washington/ U.S. News & World Report, 4-17:77.

Jack Donohew
Major General, United States Air Force; Commandant, Air War College

We study wars (at the Air War College), yes, and how to fight wars and win wars.

(JACK DONOHEW)

But we sure the hell study how to stop wars, too, and what makes wars, and how they escalate, and how to stop the escalation, and how to get out of war.

Los Angeles Times, 1-9:A.

Thomas F. Eagleton
United States Senator, D–Mo.

The ultimate objective of our foreign policy is a simple and pragmatic one—the safety and improvement of our people's lives. That means, first of all, survival—a plausible military deterrent. Today we have a fat, slack deterrent—plausible enough because of its cost. In the annual Pentagon struggle to save its line items in the budget, the initiative for innovation and streamlining somehow gets lost.

The New York Times, 10-23:31.

Richard G. Eaves
Assistant Professor of History, Auburn University

The "military-industrial complex" is (a) term about which we hear much exaggeration. Some people seem almost to see a "military-industrial complex" under every bed, so to speak. Of course, it would not be appropriate for our military leaders, or any other leaders, to be unchallenged on everything they propose. The fact is, however, that they are almost constantly challenged—probably much more than in the past, and rightly so. Even those most dedicated to a strong defense have a right to expect the most and best for the defense dollars; and defense appropriations *are* getting intense scrutiny today—another example of "the system" working. There are those, however, who speak of the "military-industrial complex" as if they are filled with hate for the military and big business. We should know most definitely that our country would be a pitifully weak fourth-rate nation if it were not for our "military-industrial complex." It has provided protection for the weak and the strong during the cold war era, and it has brought us to be the strongest nation in all the world. This is quite a record indeed! While we work to improve it, and to correct any abuses, we need to remember how much we owe to our "military-industrial complex" and that it is the *main* barrier against totalitarian expansion by military force in the world today.

Before Daughters of the American Revolution, Auburn, Ala., March 7/ Vital Speeches, 4-15:394.

Sam J. Ervin, Jr.
United States Senator, D–N.C.

The *defensive* power of the U.S. is vested in the President. Congress should declare *offensive* wars.

Quote, 5-7:433.

John S. Foster, Jr.
Director of Research and Engineering, Department of Defense of the United States

We must buy insurance to protect against nuclear war because the consequence of being wrong could be the very loss of our country. In preparing against conventional war, we do cut prudence a bit fine because we know that the consequences of a mistake could be offset. In nuclear war, however, we must have an extra margin of safety. We must make it clear by our actions that we are determined to maintain an adequate retaliatory force. It is not enough for us to believe it. Our potential adversaries will have to be convinced beyond doubt that we will be able to strike back effectively. I do believe that we are maintaining, and can continue to maintain, enough weapons of the right kinds to preserve an effective deterrent. I believe also that in the long run, through appropriate modernization and through negotiations, we can prudently reduce throw weight and total numbers of weapons on both sides, and even find workable and verifiable constraints to certain types of technological advance. National security is best served by hard, objective thinking, by a careful balance in numbers and quality of weapons and by firm negotiation for bilateral, eventually multilateral, but not solely unilateral, arms control.

Before Air Force Association/ The New York Times, 10-21:31.

Robert F. Froehlke
Secretary of the Army of the United States

We have had a reordering of national priorities in recent years, and in many ways this was necessary; but now the time has come to get back and make sure that the armed forces have sufficient funds. In 1960, the United States had military superiority over the Soviet Union. Now we have parity. In our opinion, parity is sufficient; but if the trend lines continue as they are, our deterrent may not be enough.

News conference, Beverly Hills, Calif., Feb. 15/ Los Angeles Times, 2-16:(2)5.

(Commenting on the Army's military intelligence branch): I know every embassy in this town has people attached to it who are looking at what I might be doing. I don't take it personally at all. I don't see the "moral issue" in intelligence-gathering. I think the nation has the right to defend itself. And that is what intelligence is all about. The only way for the United States to defend itself is to be prepared. And one of the facets of being prepared is: "What are they doing?"

Interview, Washington/ The Washington Post, 2-27:(C)3.

J. William Fulbright
United States Senator, D–Ark.

(On the arms race between the U.S. and the Soviet Union): More force, greater spending and additional weapons will not make either side more secure. More can only lead to a deepening of the balance of terror which has enslaved this world for more than a decade. A further drive for more to achieve a shifting parity can only heighten the possibilities of a holocaust, which neither side would consider thinkable.

At Senate Foreign Relations Committee hearing, Washington, June 19/ The New York Times, 6-20:3.

Barry M. Goldwater
United States Senator, R–Ariz.

(Criticizing a proposed bill to limit the President's war-making authority): The bill set(s) out four narrow situations in which it authorizes military action to commence. If a situation does not fit one of the imminent emergencies which the draftsmen of the bill have foreseen, the President is prohibited from acting until Congress authorizes him, no matter how fixed and untenable the situation may eventually become as a result of our failure to act. Even when the President is allowed to move, the bill states that his activity shall not continue beyond 30 days unless Congress grants an extension of his authority. Another provision of the bill enables Congress to stop whatever action the President has started before 30 days are up, so that he cannot even count on having 30 days for action even in those cases where it said he has the power to act. What the bill gives with one hand it takes away with the other . . . this legislation is unrealistic, unwise and unconstitutional. It makes no sense from the standpoint of safe or intelligent military planning. It is disruptive of our entire mutual-security system which now safeguards world order. It is totally without any statutory precedent in American history. And it invalidly prohibits the President in the exercise of his Constitutional powers of national defense.

Before the Senate, Washington/ The National Observer, 4-22:6.

I think the civilian Pentagon has grown out of all proportion to their need. We've got thousands of people over in the Pentagon that don't know what the hell

(BARRY M. GOLDWATER)

they're doing. I'm not talking about the man in uniform—I'm talking about civilians.

At Senate Armed Services Committee hearing, Washington, May 12/ The New York Times, 5-13:33.

As a conscientious American and a United States Senator and a Republican, I am most anxious to find myself in a position to support the SALT agreements recently arrived at in Moscow. However—and I say this reluctantly—the more hearings I attend on the subject, the more confused I become, because it is obvious to me by now that no one person either knows the extent of our commitments or is willing to talk about them or is allowed to do so. I have received two different answers on one important question, and I have sat through hearings where the chief negotiator did not feel that he should discuss certain commitments made to the Russians. Because of this obvious muddle and the seeming desire to keep some of the facts from the American people, I cannot at this particular moment in history tell my constituents or myself that I will unhesitatingly support our SALT agreements. I hope that somehow in the very near future all the facts and figures of the negotiations and discussions can be brought to light so that we can act intelligently upon them and not be pressured into an agreement merely because they have a good sound to them which the facts at this point do not support.

Human Events, 7-8:3.

Michael J. Harrington
United States Representative, D–Mass.

The . . . requisite equipment that should come with service on the (House Armed Services) Committee is a bucket of whitewash and a brush. I say it because we (of the Committee) are regularly too responsive . . . to what the Department of Defense wants done. They know it; and they use it that way.

At House Armed Services Committee hearing, Washington, April 18/ The Washington Post, 4-30:(A)2.

F. Edward Hebert
United States Representative, D–La.

Since our potential enemies know of the gaping holes in our air defenses, I think it is high time that the American people were let in on this open secret. They should know, for example, that there is a 1,500-mile open stretch from Florida to California devoid of military surveillance and air defense command control. For the past 10 years, I have been fighting against the emasculation of our continental air defenses in the name of the economy. We are now reaching a point where our weakness in this area constitutes a threat to our very survival.

Human Events, 1-22:4.

In war, they don't pay off for second place. There's one bet, and you've got to have the winner. (As Chairman of the House Armed Services Committee) I intend to build the strongest military we can get. Money's no question.

The Washington Post, 3-26:(E)4.

John Q. Henion
Major General and head of Recruiting Command, United States Army

(Regarding a new program of taking young men on four-to-five-day tours of an Army post as a means of increasing full-time volunteers): The young men will be able to sample Army life and determine in their own minds if the Army wants to join them. If the young man likes the Army, and the Army wants him, we'll offer him a written guarantee assuring him of the training for which he enlists. If, on the other hand, he is not interested in us, or we're not interested in him, we'll shake hands and wish him the best of luck; he'll be under no obligation to the Army . . . All too often, the young man's only contact is with the recruiter; that's his only experience with the Army until he enlists. At the Selection Center, however, he'll be living on an Army post, coming into daily contact with career enlisted and officer personnel, eating Army food and sleeping in Army quarters. By the time his four days are up, he should have a pretty good idea of what Army life is all about.

Los Angeles Times, 3-3:(1)14.

Harold E. Hughes
United States Senator, D–Iowa

(On Senate-hearing testimony by two top military officers that they could not guarantee that further unauthorized bombings in Vietnam, such as that ordered by Air Force Gen. John D. Lavelle, wouldn't take place): These admissions stun the imagination. They strongly suggest that the sense of security we derive from our powerful military machine is a false sense of security–that subordinate military commanders in the ranks of Generals and Admirals have sufficient leeway in their command functions to permit them to involve us in hostilities that could engulf this nation in war.

Before the Senate, Washington/ The New York Times, 10-15:(4)2.

Hubert H. Humphrey
United States Senator, D–Minn.

I am opposed to unilateral disarmament and unilateral troop reductions. I know it makes good copy. I know it appeals to a lot of people who are weary of our long period of defense expenditures. But we are in a tough world. I want to negotiate these reductions. I want the Soviet Union to reduce their manpower and the Warsaw Pact countries to reduce theirs . . . If you stick with it and you negotiate and you don't capitulate, you can get reductions. And that's what I'm for.

Before Commonwealth Club, San Francisco, May 26/ The Washington Post, 5-27:(A)2.

Senator (George) McGovern is proposing a 40 per cent cut in our defense forces, cutting the Navy in half and the Air Force by more than half, without any similar disarmament agreement from the Russians. It shocks me. No responsible President would think of cutting our defenses back (to) the level of a second-class power in the face of the expanding Russian Navy and Air Force.

Campaigning for the Democratic Presidential nomination/ The New York Times, 6-1:36.

Henry M. Jackson
United States Senator, D–Wash.

I'm very proud that I stood up and supported the men in uniform when they were being kicked around . . . I say the first priority is survival, make no mistake about it. I say thank God for the military-industrial complex, thank God for the military, and thank God for a free industry that can provide the weapons systems we need to remain strong.

Campaigning for Democratic Presidential nomination, Fort Walton Beach, Fla., Jan. 5/ Los Angeles Times, 1-6:(1)16.

A fundamental question facing Americans in 1972 is this: How safe a world will our children live in; what kind of America will we pass on to future generations? Thus far, the primary (election) campaigns have been hiding this crucial issue, not illuminating it. There has been so much pandering to the popular passions of the moment that a major problem facing the nation has been obscured. Just as 35 years ago, when many chose to ignore the greatest foreign danger we have ever faced (Nazi Germany), so the American people are once again being kept from the truth about a growing foreign danger (Soviet military expansion) and what it means for the future of America and of individual liberty.

Before American Society of Newspaper Editors, Washington, April 20/ Los Angeles Herald-Examiner, 4-23:(A)17.

(HENRY M. JACKSON)

(On the arms agreements recently concluded between the U.S. and the Soviet Union): The stark facts are these: The United States—a country with 2-to-1 economic *superiority* over the U.S.S.R., a country with innovative and technological superiority over the U.S.S.R.—has accepted agreements which guarantee the United States 3-to-2 *inferiority* in crucial categories of strategic offensive systems. All Americans hope for progress toward a lessening of international tensions and the instabilities that cause wars. All Americans want to see the strategic-arms balance become more stable. We all desire the increased security that flows from a potential aggressor's knowledge that he simply can't execute a disarming first strike against our deterrent forces. Unfortunately, I see nothing in the present agreements that lessens the threat to the security of these deterrent forces. On the contrary, far from placing us in a condition of stable deterrence, the agreement permits the Soviet Union to continue its offensive build-up in a way and on a scale that could prove highly dangerous. Simply put, the agreement gives the Soviets more of everything: more light ICBMs, more heavy ICBMs, more submarine-launched missiles, more submarines, more payload, even more ABM radars. In no area covered by the agreement is the United States permitted to maintain parity with the Soviet Union.

June 16/
U.S. News & World Report, 7-3:60.

Roger T. Kelley
Assistant Secretary for Manpower and Reserve Affairs, Department of Defense of the United States

I regard the typical man and woman in the armed forces, active and reserve, to be the personification of the American ideal.

Quote, 6-25:601.

Edward M. Kennedy
United States Senator, D–Mass.

Let us recognize the advances that have been made in the science of detection (of underground nuclear tests), and in gathering intelligence through satellites. Let us offer to negotiate a total test-ban treaty (with the Soviet Union), without demanding the right number of on-site inspections that have blocked such a treaty for a decade. Unless we do all we possibly can to end the arms race now, we shall be violating the trust we hold for future generations, and we shall be false to the goal the President (Nixon) has so eloquently set—a generation of peace for America and the world.

Jan. 15/
The Washington Post, 1-16:(A)2.

Glenn A. Kent
Lieutenant General, United States Air Force; Director, Weapons System Evaluation Group

(Citing advantages of bombers over missiles): In the first place, bombers are recallable. Once you've launched a missile, there's no calling it back. Secondly, bombers can be used short of going to war. When we sent the B-52s into the air during the 1962 Cuban missile crisis, the Soviets knew we meant business.

The Christian Science Monitor, 4-4:11.

Henry A. Kissinger
Assistant to the President of the United States for National Security Affairs

The Soviet Union has more intercontinental ballistic missiles than the United States. The Soviet Union has been building intercontinental ballistic missiles; the United States has not and has no such program at the moment. The Soviet Union has been building submarine-launched ballistic missiles at the rate of eight submarines a year. The United States has at this moment no submarines under construction. Therefore, the question to ask in assessing the freeze (on arms reached with the Soviet Union during the just-completed U.S.-Soviet summit meeting in Moscow) is not what situation it perpetuates, but what situation it prevents. The question is where would we be without the freeze. And if you project the existing building programs of the Soviet Union into the future, as against the absence of building programs over the period of the freeze in either of the categories that are being frozen, you will get a more direct clue to why we believe that there is a good agreement and why we believe that it has made a significant contribution to arresting the arms race . . . The reason it was possible to achieve such an agreement is because we are confident it will be seen to be in the common interest of both countries and in the common interest of humanity.

Moscow/
The Christian Science Monitor, 5-31:3.

(On the arms-control agreements concluded between the U.S. and the Soviet Union during President Nixon's summit meeting in Moscow): The agreements on the limitation of strategic arms (are) . . . not merely a technical accomplishment, although it is that in part, but it must be seen as a political event of some magnitude. This is relative to the question of whether the agreements will be easily reached or circumvented. Given the past, no one can answer that question with certainty; but it can be said with some assurance that any country which contemplates a rupture of the agreement or a circumvention of its letter and spirit must now face the fact that it will be placing in jeopardy not only a limited arms-control agreement, but a broad political relationship.

At Congressional briefing,
Washington, June 15/
The Washington Post, 6-16:(A)18.

Alexei N. Kosygin
Premier of the Soviet Union

(On the arms-control agreement made by the U.S. and Soviet Union during U.S. President Nixon's summit meeting in Moscow): The agreement will go down in history as a major achievement on the road toward curbing the arms race . . . a great victory for the Soviet and American people for bringing about international detente.

The Dallas Times Herald, 5-28:(A)9.

Melvin R. Laird
Secretary of Defense
of the United States

I believe we have adequate defense forces today, but I am concerned about the period from 1975 on. I don't want any future President of the United States to be in a position where he has to crawl to any negotiating table anywhere in the world. That's what we are talking about as far as the real issues of the defense budgets are concerned—the maintenance of the future strength of the United States. Since I became Secretary of Defense, I have tried to inform Congress and the American people about the program that the Soviet Union embarked on in 1965 to modernize both their conventional and strategic forces. Based on the evidence I see, it is my belief that the Soviet Union is trying for military superiority over the United States by the latter part of the 1970s and during the 1980s. And we are not matching this effort at the present time.

Interview, Washington/
U.S. News & World Report, 3-27:41.

In my view, a vast majority of the American people may perhaps be willing to accept parity in the area of strategic nuclear weapons, but under no circumstances would they or should they accept inferiority. Certainly, as Secretary of Defense, I would never recommend or accept inferiority. The sufficiency of our armed forces is a matter that cannot be judged strictly from the standpoint of military realities. Global political realities are also very much involved. I am concerned about what the political effect would be on our allies—or, for that matter, on the people of the

(MELVIN R. LAIRD)

United States—if the Soviet Union acquired a vastly superior nuclear force, whether on land, at sea or in the air. In other words, it is crucial to the achievement of lasting peace that neither our own citizens nor our friends and allies ever have reason to question the adequacy of our strength or our resolve.

Interview, Washington/
U.S. News & World Report, 3-27:43.

(On the arms agreements recently concluded between the U.S. and the Soviet Union): I believe the ABM Treaty and the Interim Agreement on Offensive Weapons now before the Congress are good for America. They enhance our security. They permit us to maintain needed strength. They help us to maintain confidence in the effectiveness and realism of our strategic deterrent. But by themselves they do not automatically guarantee these national-security gains . . . Peace cannot be bought cheaply. The opportunities for peace embodied in the SALT agreements would be nullified and our national security jeopardized unless there is continued strong support for an adequate defense budget. The success of SALT and prospects for ultimate peace depend on sustained strength.

Before Senate Armed Services
Committee, Washington, June 20/
U.S. News & World Report, 7-3:62.

I have always thought that the American people would not, on a long-term basis, be willing to devote more than 7 per cent of the gross national product to national-security requirements. As a rule of thumb, I have always used a figure along that line. I believe that when it gets above that figure, the people would seriously question devoting more of our effort. We're down to 6.4 per cent now, the lowest period of any time in the last 23 years.

News conference,
Los Angeles, Aug. 24/
Los Angeles Times, 8-25:(2)5.

Gene R. La Rocque
Rear Admiral, United States Navy (Ret.); Director, Center for Defense Information

Frequently, (military) information is classified so that only portions of it can be released selectively to the press to influence the public or the Congress. The ritual begins each spring with the Pentagon implying that a potential enemy is developing a very threatening weapon, "but unfortunately the exact details are classified." These incomplete statements are the stock-in-trade at appropriations time to persuade the Congress to authorize military appropriations. Last year, it was big holes in the ground in the Soviet Union. This year, it is evidence of a Soviet ship under construction which might be a carrier or a merchant ship.

Before House Government Information
Subcommittee, Washington, May 24/
Los Angeles Times, 5-25:(1)6.

John V. Lindsay
Mayor of New York

We must have a President who will control the awesome power of the Pentagon in this democratic society. There is no institution in this country that influences our leaders more or distorts our relations with other nations as much. The growth of this vast, unchecked, unexamined power since the end of World War II is perhaps the single most important phenomenon of government in our day.

At University of California,
Los Angeles, Feb. 23/
Los Angeles Times, 2-24:(1)33.

George S. McGovern
United States Senator, D–S.D.

(Disputing charges that he is too far from the political "center" to win the

Presidency): . . . the establishment "center" has constructed a vast military colossus based on the paychecks of the American worker. That military monster, now capable of blowing up the entire world a hundred times over, is devouring two out of three of our tax dollars. It inflates our economy, picks our pockets and starves other areas of our national life.

At Jefferson-Jackson Day dinner, Detroit/The New York Times, 4-25:41.

I am proposing (if elected President) a $55 billion (defense) budget, and that's not beans. It is five times the spending at the time of Pearl Harbor . . . I would include a nuclear deterrent more devastating than in any country or combination of countries on the face of the earth. I would maintain the strength of the Sixth Fleet in the Mediterranean and the Seventh Fleet in the Pacific. I would increase our submarine capability . . . I would not close a single air base in California. I recognize the need to maintain a mobile force . . . As a former bomber pilot, I would never advocate a defense budget that would weaken the defense muscle of this country.

Before Sacramento (Calif.) Press Club, May 27/ Los Angeles Herald-Examiner, 5-28:(A)12.

By exercising restraint, I believe we could have prevented both Soviet and American MIRVs. But because we were so determined to play them, we have lost those bargaining chips. And now the (Nixon) Administration is back before the Congress demanding more. Certainly, our ability to build these systems should be just as effective for (arms-control) bargaining purposes as actual construction. My approach would be similar to that followed by Presidents Eisenhower and Kennedy in achieving the nuclear test ban treaty—to buy and build weapons according to military necessity, rather than on negotiating cheekiness, and to hold fast against actions which can only push up the terms of ultimate arms-control agreements. That means that, instead of accelerating the ULMS (submarine) and B-1 (bomber) programs now, we should be back at SALT immediately seeking a mutual freeze on further deployment.

Before Joint Congressional Economic Committee, Washington, June 16/ The Washington Post, 6-17:(A)10.

We need a new definition of national defense, which goes beyond the size of our weapons that are stockpiled. We need a definition which understands that the defense of a city, the defense of a country, is as closely tied to the quality of its goals, the health of its people, the housing in which they live, the services that are provided.

At U.S. Conference of Mayors, New Orleans, June 20/ Los Angeles Times, 6-21:(1)4.

The guys who are supposed to be the toughest of all—the Pentagon brass—they're going to find out I'm tough if I get to be President. I think that is going to be the chief test of the next President—whether he can stand up to the military—and I don't mean the Russians or the Chinese—I mean our own.

Interview/Life, 7-7:41.

George S. McGovern
United States Senator, D–S.D.; Democratic Presidential nominee

It is necessary in an age of nuclear power and hostile ideologies that we be militarily strong. America must never become a second-rate nation. As one who tasted the bitter fruits of our weakness before Pearl Harbor, 1941, I give you my sacred pledge that, if I become President of the United States, America will keep its defenses alert and sufficient to meet any danger. We will do that not only for ourselves, but for those who deserve and need the shield of our strength—our old allies in Europe and elsewhere, including the people of Israel who will always have our help to hold their promised land.

Accepting the Democratic Presidential nomination, Miami Beach, July 14/ Los Angeles Herald-Examiner, 7-14:(A)3.

I fully understand the dangers of war and the needs of security. But the desire for money and new weapons has no limit. We reduce our involvement in Vietnam, but military spending goes up. We sign arms-control agreements with Russia, but military spending goes up. We open new relationships with (Communist) China, but military spending goes up. My proposed defense budget is larger than that of President (Dwight) Eisenhower at the height of the cold war. It is designed, like his, to satisfy the needs of security rather than the appetites of a military-industrial complex. It will produce only one white flag—when a handful of professionals and industries surrender their claim on money which has wiser and more urgent uses.

Broadcast address, Washington, Aug. 5/ The New York Times, 8-6:(1)36.

Everyone who ever served in the armed forces knows that our military spending is riddled with waste and inefficiency. We need an invincible and invulnerable defense. But we also need to rein in the high-flying military spenders who think the sky is the limit.

At American Legion convention, Chicago, Aug. 23/ The Dallas Times Herald, 8-23:(A)8.

I will never (if elected President) permit America to become a second-rate power in the world. Neither can we permit America to become a second-rate society. And if we choose a reasonable military budget, we will not have to choose between the decline of our security and the deterioration of our standard of life. A nation does not live by weapons alone. And the waste of scarce wealth on excess firepower will finally make us, not a stronger nation, but a beleaguered fortress nation groaning under the dead weight of excessive arms and a demoralized military bureaucracy.

Before New York Society of Security Analysts, Aug. 29/ The Washington Post, 8-30:(A)12.

Thomas H. Moorer
Admiral, United States Navy; Chairman, Joint Chiefs of Staff

The strategic nuclear balance, at least in quantitative terms, is turning against us . . . the Soviets have already overtaken us in strategic offensive megatons, and this year they will overtake us in strategic offensive delivery vehicles. If they move vigorously into MIRVs, they could narrow the gap in strategic offensive warheads and bombs as well.

News conference, Dallas, March 24/ The Dallas Times Herald, 3-25:(B)1.

Edmund S. Muskie
United States Senator, D–Maine

(On the U.S.-Soviet arms-control agreements reached during President Nixon's recent summit meeting in Moscow): No sooner were the accords signed than the Secretary of Defense (Melvin Laird) told Congress that, as a result of the SALT agreements, we must increase defense spending—not reduce it. We are told that the Secretary of Defense and the Joint Chiefs of Staff, who presumably speak for the same President who negotiated the agreements in Moscow, cannot support the SALT agreements unless Congress votes more money for nuclear weapons not covered by the accords—advanced bombers, new-generation submarines, a new strategic cruise missile and a variety of other technological improvements. The American people will not accept that. If we have stunted the Soviet offensive weapons development—as the President has assured us—how can we justify to the world, to ourselves, new efforts to breed new giant species of nuclear weapons?

Before Town Hall, Los Angeles, June 16/ Los Angeles Times, 6-17:(2)10.

Richard M. Nixon
President of the United States

. . . we've got to take this awesome power in nuclear weapons and see if there is a way that we can stop this escalating arms race and also slow down the prohibitive rise in arms cost. A perpetual rise in those costs, in terms of diverting resources that could be used to raise the standard of living of the Russian people and the American people, is simply not defensible. Therefore, it's in the interest of peace to have arms limitation, and it's also in the interests of domestic progress. The Soviets want it for that purpose. We want it for that purpose.

Interview/ The Reader's Digest, February:64.

. . . I have studied the strategic balance in great detail with my senior advisers for more than three years. And I can assure you, the members of the Congress and the American people tonight, that the present and planned strategic forces of the United States are without question sufficient for the maintenance of our security and the protection of our vital interests. No power on earth is stronger than the United States of America today. And none will be stronger than the United States of America in the future. This is the only national-defense posture which can ever be acceptable to the United States.

Before joint session of Congress, Washington, June 1/ The New York Times, 6-3:30.

(On the arms-control agreements concluded between the U.S. and the Soviet Union during his recent summit meeting in Moscow): I know there is a disagreement among various members of Congress with regard to what our defense levels ought to be. I think, however, I owe it . . . to the nation to say that (Soviet Communist Party Secretary Leonid) Brezhnev and his colleagues made it absolutely clear that they are going forward with defense programs in the offensive area which are not limited by these agreements. Under those circumstances, since they will be going forward with their programs, for the United States not to go forward . . . with its offensive programs—or worse, for the United States unilaterally to reduce its offensive programs—would mean that any incentive that the Soviets had to negotiate the follow-on agreement would be removed. It is for that reason, without getting into the specifics as to what the level of defense spending should be, as to what the offensive programs should be, I am simply saying that if we want the follow-on agreement, we have to take two steps: First, to approve these (present) agreements; and second, we need a credible defensive position so that the Soviet Union will have an incentive to negotiate a permanent offensive freeze. That is what we all want.

At Congressional briefing, Washington, June 15/ The Washington Post, 6-16:(A)18.

(Asking for Congressional approval of the arms-control agreements he concluded with the Soviet Union during his summit meeting in Moscow): This is an election year, and I realize that in an election year it is difficult to move as objectively as we ordinarily would move on any issue; but I would respectfully request the members of the House and Senate, Republican and Democratic, to approach this in the spirit (the former President Woodrow) Wilson explained in that period when they were debating whether they should go forward with the League of Nations, remembering that our clients are the next generation, that approval of these agreements—the treaty limiting defensive weapons, the agreement limiting offensive weapons in certain categories, and also the continuation of a credible defense

(RICHARD M. NIXON)

posture—will mean that we will have done our duty by our clients, which are the next generation.

At Congressional briefing, Washington, June 15/ The Washington Post, 6-16:(A)18.

For the United States unilaterally to reduce its strength with the naive hope that other nations would do likewise would increase the danger of war in the world. This would completely remove any incentive for other nations to agree to a mutual limitation or reduction of armaments. The promising initiatives we have undertaken to limit arms would be destroyed. The security of the United States and of the nations in the world that rely upon us would be dangerously threatened. We have cut defense spending in our Administration so that it now takes the lowest percentage of our national product in 20 years. We should not spend more on defense than we need. But we should never spend less than we need. Spending what we need will cost us money. Spending less than we need could cost us our lives.

Accepting the Republican Presidential nomination, Miami Beach, Aug. 23/ Los Angeles Times, 8-24:(1)23.

(Criticizing Democratic Presidential nominee Senator George McGovern for his promises to cut back on military spending): I have never gambled—and I will never gamble—with the safety of the American people under a false banner of economy. Lasting peace is built only on strength. Economy, always. Weakness, never.

At American Legion convention, Chicago, Aug. 24/ Los Angeles Herald-Examiner, 8-24:(A)1.

There are those who ridicule military expenditures as wasteful and immoral. Our opponents in this (Presidential election) campaign have even described the great bipartisan tradition of negotiating from strength as one of the most damaging and costly cliches in the American vocabulary. If the day ever comes when the President of the United States has to negotiate from weakness, that will be a dangerous day, not only for America, but for the whole world. Those who scoff at balance-of-power diplomacy should recognize that the only alternative to a balance of power is an imbalance of power; and history shows that nothing so drastically escalates the danger of war as such an imbalance.

Radio broadcast campaigning for the forthcoming Presidential election, Washington, Nov. 4/ San Francisco Examiner & Chronicle, 11-5:(A)8.

David Packard
Former Deputy Secretary of Defense of the United States

The Defense Department's first and foremost commitment is to the security, the strength and the world leadership of the United States. This commitment comes before any well-intentioned individual loyalty to the Army, the Navy, the Air Force or the Marines . . . But, while some progress has been made, there are still those . . . who have not accepted the larger commitment. Within the Defense Department, for example, there continues to be a degree of competition between the services—and frequently between parts of a service—that is unacceptable because it is inconsistent with the common commitment. Some competition is healthy, but not when it begins to affect such major matters as funding, missions and roles. Jealousies and in-fighting will only serve to draft our nation's energies.

At Forrestal Award Dinner, March 9/The Washington Post, 4-26:(A)16.

Otis G. Pike
United States Representative, D–N.Y.

(Arguing against further U.S. offensive weapons spending): Obviously we've got the power to blow the Soviets to smithereens.

And all we're talking about here is how fine a powder to grind the other peoples of the earth into.

Washington/
Los Angeles Times, 6-28:(1)10.

William Proxmire
United States Senator, D–Wis.

The GAO report (criticizing the performance of the C-5A cargo plane) demonstrates that the Air Force is the biggest satisfied customer of lemons in the history of military procurement.

Washington, April 6/
The New York Times, 4-7:1.

If the Pentagon steps up the bombing in Vietnam and proposes huge increases in funds for manned bombers, submarines, (aircraft) carriers, bomber defense and other weapons, let them pay for it by cutting back on military spending in other areas. The "All this and heaven, too" policy toward military spending must end.

The New York Times, 6-30:4.

(Criticizing a Senate bill which would do away with kitchen-police duty in the armed forces): Every housewife does KP three times a day. Most husbands do KP. Most Senators do KP, including this one . . . What kind of namby-pamby military are we going to have when you don't have to get your hands dirty?

Quote, 11-12:458.

Jeannette Rankin
Former United States Representative, R–Mont.

We (the U.S.) must have absolutely unilateral disarmament. If we disarmed, we would be the safest country in the world. After all, you have to have a worthy adversary to fight. Would Cassius Clay fight a Boy Scout?

San Francisco Examiner & Chronicle, 1-30:(This World)2.

Hyman G. Rickover
Vice Admiral, United States Navy

In my opinion, we are at a very critical moment. Either the Soviets slow down (their military expansion) or we must speed up. If we do not own up to these realities, the United States will soon find that American foreign policy objectives have become irrelevant because we will be without the means of supporting them. Complacency is the accomplice of catastrophe. When you've stopped changing and meeting challenges–you're through. The Russians surely realize this, even if we don't; and to suppose they will refrain from using their new strength in political power plays is simply an act of faith.

Before House Appropriations Committee, Washington/
Los Angeles Herald-Examiner, 8-30:(A)12.

As the war in Vietnam begins to close out for us and we strive for a zero draft, I can see where it is going to become more and more difficult for the military service to acquire the talents it will need. Depending on the economic situation in the country, it is difficult for me to see how the military can attract the smart high-school graduate. He can easily attend college now that they are so accessible, and he can find a reasonable-paying job without a great deal of difficulty. What incentive does he have to join the military, especially if the mood of the nation is anti-military? What could easily happen is that the military will attract those who either cannot make the grade in a civilian environment or do not want to exert the effort. In a sense, the military could become a large government-sponsored social correction agency.

Before House Appropriations Committee, Washington/
The New York Times, 10-9:31.

Leon Salzman
Clinical Professor of Psychiatry, Albert Einstein School of Medicine, New York

(On the performance of women if they were subject to the military draft): Women don't take to killing comfortably; but then,

(LEON SALZMAN)

no one really does. I think women would make very effective killers if they got the same kind of training our Vietnam soldiers do. I have never believed that women, by their nature, are softer or more sentimental. It really is a matter of cultural training. Women could be trained just like men to despise and kill the enemy.

Los Angeles Times, 4-9:A.

William B. Saxbe
United States Senator, R–Ohio

(On the Senate vote for a fourth $1 billion atomic-powered aircraft carrier): What we're talking about here is the dodo of modern warfare. We're whistling in the dark on vulnerability, and this is not going to be solved by putting $1 billion into one target.

Plainview (Tex.) Daily Herald, 8-20:(A)4.

James R. Schlesinger
Chairman, Atomic Energy Commission of the United States

The recently-concluded SALT agreements (between the U.S. and the Soviet Union) reflect the inherently dualistic nature of the task of maintaining the arms balance. Undoubtedly, they represent a great historic milestone. On the one hand, it may be hoped that these agreements prove to be a watershed event which will substantially alter the character of international politics for future generations. On the other hand, were the agreements to lull this country into a sense of false security and into stagnation, they might very well tempt the Soviet in ways that would upset the stability for which we strive. Which way the agreements lead will depend in great measure on the decisions and actions taken by the Soviet Union in the years ahead. But it will also be critically dependent upon the response here in the United States. The agreements are not an end but a beginning, and it is essential that they be so recognized. If they generate euphoria and lethargy, they will ultimately prove to be self-defeating. It is of paramount importance that the nation temper hope with prudence, and continue to take steps that will maintain the underlying balance of forces that have made these agreements and these brighter prospects possible.

Before Commonwealth Club, San Francisco, Sept. 22/ Vital Speeches, 10-15:29.

Margaret Chase Smith
United States Senator, R–Maine

. . . the people's emotions are appealed to by those who are calling for greater cuts in our defense. There should be an increase in defense spending rather than a decrease. The $30-to-$32 billion cuts that some Democrats have talked about is perfectly ridiculous. Our Navy has deteriorated and we have to keep our Army up-to-date. There is talk about cutting defense spending and spending more on welfare. We need welfare, and we need it badly. But we must not sacrifice defense. Public opinion is not being correctly read. I think public opinion supports defense–but it is easier to get headlines for welfare.

Interview/ U.S. News & World Report, 5-15:65.

Curtis W. Tarr
Director, Selective Service System of the United States

(Voicing his opposition to drafting women for the armed forces): You can't put women in tough combat jobs. There are so many things they can't do physically. Tell one to take a mortar casing over the hill and, by thunder, she can't even get it over a log.

The Dallas Times Herald, 4-14:(A)28.

Edward Teller
Physicist

The Russians are ahead of us in every military field today with the exception of the Navy, where they are getting ahead of us now and will be ahead of us within a few years. In missile defense, the Russians are many years ahead of us. There is no question about that.

Before aerospace engineers and scientists, San Diego, Calif./ San Francisco Examiner, 2-18:3.

Emmett H. Tidd
Rear Admiral and Chief of Recruiting, United States Navy

Achievement of the all-volunteer (armed) force will be historic. I for one, as a commanding officer, would prefer to have volunteers serve with me. For more than 30 years the military has required drafted men in the armed services. The all-volunteer force will not only improve our national security, but will offer young Americans a choice in ordering their careers.

Portland, Ore./ San Francisco Examiner, 7-25:2.

George C. Wallace
Governor of Alabama

I think you must deal from a position of strength with the Soviets and (Communist) Chinese, and that's all they understand at this stage of history. And I think that if we reach a parity or inferiority, that it bodes evil for this country. They're not going to unilaterally disarm, and so I think we ought to have—since we've announced that we would never be a first-strike country—we must have an overwhelming nuclear capability to retaliate, which would be our deterrent. But if we get down on a parity or inferior, where a first strike could put you out of commission, nobody knows what would happen. I don't think we should gamble with it. While the SALT talks have gone on, they've (the Soviets) increased their ICBMs to what—1,200 and some odd?—and we've remained static.

Interview, Washington, Feb. 23/ The Washington Post, 3-5:(D)4.

I believe in equal opportunity (for women). But I don't go for this idea that women ought to serve in the armed forces under the draft. That's folderol and silly stuff.

News conference, Salisbury, Md., May 12/ The Washington Post, 5-13:(A)6.

Caspar W. Weinberger
Director, Federal Office of Management and Budget

(On Senator George McGovern's proposal to reduce the defense budget by $32 billion): I think this is totally and completely unrealistic. I think it's a proposal that could only be made by a person who has no real idea of the facts or of the composition of the defense budget. About 56 per cent of the defense budget goes into pay and allowances. That's a very high figure, and it has moved up dramatically in recent years, because we've started to pay market wages for people in the armed forces. When you have that high a proportion of your total budget in payroll, and then talk about saving as much as 32 billions, it means you're either going to have a great many empty bases and rusting airplanes and tanks with nobody to man or maintain them, or you're going to have people standing around with no equipment to use. But worst of all, such a proposal would completely destroy our ability to negotiate with—or, indeed, even be listened to by a potential opponent, because it would destroy the strength which they respect and which enabled us to have the talks (with Communist China and the Soviet Union) the President has just completed . . . There's another factor in defense spending that's unique. In education, in health, in welfare and in almost any other field, what the Federal government doesn't do, other levels of government or the private sector will attempt to do. But the only unit of government that pays for defense is the Federal government. What we don't do in defense at the national level doesn't get done. So you have an added responsibility in looking over the defense budget to insure that it is adequate. And anyone who talks about cutting 30 to 35 billions, depending upon what state he's speaking in or which day of the week it is, not only is totally unrealistic but displays an ignorance of the situation that I find frightening.

Interview, Washington/ U.S. News & World Report, 7-17:23.

(Criticizing Democratic Presidential nominee Senator George McGovern's plan to cut $30 billion from defense spending): It has been estimated that a cut of $30 billion in the defense budget would mean a reduction in direct employment of approximately 1.8 million jobs nationally, not to mention the indirect effects. We do not maintain an adequate defense or lead the world in space exploration as a means of keeping people employed, but neither can we ignore the employment aspects of these programs, nor the unemployment that would rise from crippling or terminating these vital activities.

At "Skylab" space project "roll-out" ceremony, Huntington Beach, Calif., Sept. 7/The New York Times, 9-8:20.

William C. Westmoreland
General and Chief of Staff, United States Army

(Today) soldiers understand only one system of rank. It is the rank of dedication to duty, of care and concern for the mission and your men—of integrity of character, of willingness to learn, of readiness to admit one's error and seek a better way, of devotion to principle.

At United States Military Academy commencement, West Point, N.Y., June 7/The New York Times, 6-8:32.

(At ceremony on his retirement): This last parade is at once a moment of recollection, gratitude, renewed faith and pride: pride in an Army that has defended our country and met our commitments with dedication and selflessness; pride in an Army that has played a significant role in building our country and in meeting the needs of our society; pride in an Army that has given total loyalty to the leadership of our country and to the people it supports. As I bid farewell, I say to the American soldier who stands tall today around the world: The country you serve today is the greatest on earth—whatever its present problems and whatever its present torments. As I look back on my life, I thank God for the opportunity that was given to me to be a soldier. If given that opportunity again, I would—with the same pride and with even greater humility—raise my hand and take once again the soldier's oath.

Fort Myer, Va., June 30/ The Washington Post, 7-1:(A)12.

Elmo R. Zumwalt, Jr.
Admiral, United States Navy; Chief of Naval Operations

(On whether women should be sent into combat if they so desired): I believe any man or woman should be able to serve his country in any capacity he wishes . . . When you look at the level to which our society has developed, there is no reason in theory, in sociology or in equity why women should not have the same opportunities the men have.

News conference, Washington, Aug. 8/ The Washington Post, 8-9:(A)4.

I. W. Abel
President, United Steelworkers of America

Can you give me just one reason why I should support (Senator) George McGovern (for President of the U.S.)? There are no reasons. I will not support him.

Miami Beach, July 13/ Los Angeles Herald-Examiner, 7-14:(A)5.

I don't buy this bull that you (the leadership of a labor union) have to support somebody (in a Presidential election). The lesser of two evils is still evil. In fact, the evil foisted on you may be preferable to the evil you choose. It's a case of rape or rape with consent.

Human Events, 7-22:6.

Spiro T. Agnew
Vice President of the United States

. . . I think it probable that the idea there is a bloc "youth vote" will be dispelled next November (in the national election). The view that youth is a monolithic entity and that all or most young Americans think or act alike is largely a media myth. Who, for example, can say that a young construction worker or young policeman doesn't have more in common, at least in terms of electoral interests, with his fellow workers or policemen of all ages than he has, say, with a young person attending a university or of a different economic stratum?

Interview/ U.S. News & World Report, 3-13:39.

What most Americans are fed up with is the doctrinaire and, yes, the cavalier treatment given their interest by liberal elitist spokesmen, both in and out of government. From the confines of Georgetown and insulated editorial offices, the "infallibles" claim some mystic mandate to speak for "the people."

Before California Republican Assembly, Palo Alto, April 8/ The New York Times, 4-10:59.

Countless numbers of Democrats are unable to stomach the bleeding-heart tactics of (Presidential candidate-Senators) McGovern, Humphrey and Muskie, who express more sympathy for our enemies than for our allies. Their efforts to court the young, black and poor as a monolithic mass will not be successful, because the young, black and poor are individuals who can think, smell, read and walk, yes, and vote their own convictions, not those dictated to them by the arrogant pontificators who would usurp their individuality.

Shreveport, La., April 24/ The Washington Post, 4-26:(A)9.

. . . if you have your heart set on becoming President of the United States, you have to have an issue. And unfortunately for these would-be Presidents (the Democratic Party candidates), (President) Richard Nixon has eliminated their best issues one by one. He is getting us out of the Vietnam war. He is improving our relations with Russia and mainland (Communist) China. He is cleaning up the environment. He is curbing inflation. And he is shifting the economy into high gear.

Before Los Angeles Chamber of Commerce, June 9/ Los Angeles Times, 6-10:(2)1.

Sooner or later, the people of this country are going to find out what

(Senator and Presidential candidate) George McGovern is really like. They are going to discover his far-out, left-wing voting record. They are going to learn of his former ties with Henry Agard Wallace and his recently reaffirmed support of the policies of Henry Agard Wallace. And they are going to see how he feels about marijuana and school busing (for racial balance), and abortions and amnesty for draft dodgers, and they are going to drop George McGovern like a hot potato.

At Republican fund-raising dinner, Omaha, June 10/ The New York Times, 6-12:36.

(On election-year politics): It is a season when demagogues busily pack old pork into new barrels, and try to obscure its rancidness with catchy slogans and outlandish promises.

Before National Association of Counties, Washington, June 27/ The Washington Post, 6-28:(A)27.

The Democratic Party was once thought of by many as the party of the immigrant, the worker, the producer. Today, under its new leadership, it is becoming the party of the radicals, the welfarists, the elitists. The old liberal Democratic establishment has lost the power which once made it the dominant force in American politics.

Before Heritage Group, New York, June 30/ The Washington Post, 7-1:(A)8.

There is nothing new about crusades against progress. My own research convinces me that there has never been a significant improvement in all of history that didn't have its Senator (George) McGoverns and Senator (Edward) Kennedys and Senator (Edmund) Muskies to ridicule it and fight it every step of the way. If ours were an alien society, these opponents of progress would be the "no-no birds." As you know, the "no-no-bird" is a strange little creature that spends most of its time with its head in the sand. And when it does fly, it flies backward because it doesn't want to know where it's going; it just wants to know where it's been.

At Printing Industries of America convention, New York, July 12/ The Washington Post, 7-13:(A)15.

(On Democratic Presidential nominee Senator George McGovern's campaign tactics): It really doesn't do any service to our country when a man who seeks his nation's highest office spends his total time running down all of the establishment of the country without any facts to back him up—stirring the basic hates and suspicions of people around the land and relying solely on a campaign of smear and innuendo to attempt to discredit the national leadership of this country, which, after all, was put in by the people to lead for four years. I urge that Senator McGovern return to the real issues of this campaign, return to an examination of the programs that he advocates to improve the conditions of Americans—and that's sometimes pretty hard to do because he's changed those positions so often in this campaign, we don't know what they are. I guess we've got to just accept the fact that he does not have a plan for America, that about all that the fractional and truncated plans that he offers seem to do is make him very popular in some sections of North Vietnam society. It's just not sensible for us to sit and listen to the wild imprecations which are founded on an incandescent hunger for personal popularity on the part of this candidate. The people of the United States are getting pretty tired of listening to what bad people they are, because they know the record doesn't bear that out. If this is the way that you create unity in a country, if this is the way you bring people together, by telling them that they're basically running down a trail that leads to national dishonor, then I just have to frankly tell you, my South Dakota friends, I just don't understand the United States.

But I think I do understand the United States. I think you are the United States, and I think you will repudiate the policies of George McGovern emphatically in November.

Campaigning for the forthcoming Presidential election, Rapid City, S.D./ The New York Times, 10-11:39.

(On hecklers who try to disrupt his speeches): Our democracy is not enhanced by this small, unrepresentative group, ladies and gentlemen. We pity them; for in the mindless expression of their visceral hatred, they demonstrate that they have no notion of how lucky they are to live in this great country. These demonstrators are offensive to you because they are violating one of the central concepts of our society, the concept of civility. The structure of a democratic society, unlike a totalitarian structure, is a fragile one. Democracy works only if reasonable people listen to one another carefully, accepting or rejecting, but always listening courteously. If a majority of people in a democracy suddenly decided to disrupt all communication they disagreed with–to stop being civil–then a democracy could no longer function . . . Let us hope that their destructive emotionalism will soon give way to constructive maturity. And I'm sure it will, once they get to work and find themselves making tangible contributions to this society which has so patiently nurtured them.

Campaigning for the forthcoming Presidential election, Wilmington, Del., Oct. 26/ The New York Times, 10-27:24.

(On Democratic charges of Republican espionage against them): A calculated attempt to prove corruption on the part of the Administration . . . has fallen flat as a pancake in the eyes of the American people. The American people are tired of having all these insinuations made about the Nixon Administration. We've seen it tried from every angle, and yet there is nothing but smoke. We haven't seen a bit of fire yet, and I'm not sure there's going to be any fire . . . I still don't see a connection between the President of the United States and the Watergate (Democratic headquarters bugging and break-in) case . . . What disturbs me greatly is the moral outrage of the same people who have in the past condoned this kind of conduct . . . I didn't see any of these cries of moral indignation against the person accused of stealing the "Pentagon Papers."

TV-radio interview/ "Issues and Answers," American Broadcasting Company, 10-29.

George D. Aiken
United States Senator, R–Vt.

(On the just-concluded series of Presidential primaries): Frankly, it seems to me that we are still at the point where we started on March 7 when the New Hampshire voters started this new season of political confusion, bewilderment, unsubstantiated charges and downgrading of candidates. After 23 primaries, numerous state conventions, each with its own set of rules and customs, millions of voters are now convinced that none of the candidates are qualified for the job.

Before Senate Subcommittee on Constitutional Amendments, June 21/ Los Angeles Herald-Examiner, 6-22:(A)7.

Herbert E. Alexander
Director, Citizens' Research Foundation

I like to make the point that there are pretty complex reasons for people making political contributions . . . A lot of people give money without respect to policy or jobs or favors or anything like that. A lot of people can't get into the Social Register; but there's a kind of "political register," and you get into it if you contribute political money. For the person of wealth, for *nouveau riche*, for a minority person–and I think this often explains some of the Jewish money–contributing money is easier

(HERBERT E. ALEXANDER)

than contributing time, and contributing money gives a kind of social status. You get invited to the White House or to the Governor's mansion. A contributor once told me that he gave because he liked to be able to call the Senator by his first name, or even better, have the Senator call *him* by his first name. In other words, there are ego gratifications involved.

Interview, Princeton, N.J./ The National Observer, 9-9:5.

Anne Armstrong
Co-Chairman, Republican National Committee; Counsellor-designate to the President of the United States

I've been amazed at the industry, the long working-hours and the decency of people in politics. The pleasantest surprise is that people in government, people of both parties, are hard-working and good and that politics is not at all a dirty business.

Interview/ The Dallas Times Herald, 12-27:(G)1.

John M. Ashbrook
United States Representative, R–Ohio

What is the future of conservative politics in America if the national leaders of both major parties become irrevocably committed to liberalism?

May 3/ San Francisco Examiner, 5-3:16.

I have listened to my friend (Vice President) Spiro Agnew . . . pointing out to the American people the danger that comes from "effete, intellectual, sophisticated snobs" . . . This (Nixon) Administration has its share of effete, arrogant, intellectual snobs . . . and if you're wondering who I am talking about, I am talking about people like (Presidential National Security Affairs Adviser) Henry Kissinger.

Before United Republicans of California, San Jose, May 6/ San Francisco Examiner, 5-8:16.

Yes, semantics is a wonderful thing. When you say you are for peace, that has a pretty well-defined meaning to us. To the Communists, it literally means the state of the world when capitalism is crushed and Communism is supreme. When the Communists stage an invasion, we call it armed aggression and they call it liberation. Semantics has perverted the word "liberal," also. The (current) liberals robbed a good name. In the historic sense, they have little connection with liberals of the past who fought against government encroachment and decentralized power in the hands of parliaments and peoples' representatives. The modern liberals are totalitarians, bent on placing power into fewer and fewer hands . . . We are gradually being brainwashed through semantics, and little by little we are coming to believe that government action and control are good and individual action is bad. One of these days we will wake up and believe that individual freedom is tyranny and government control is really liberty. It will largely have been accomplished by the polished art of political semantics.

Human Events, 9-16:23.

Reubin Askew
Governor of Florida

I was told over and over again—you can't be honest with the people. I was sure you could. After my election, I got telephone calls from politicians all over the country. They wanted to know how we did it. I told them: Make an inventory of all the sacred cows in your state and take them on all at once. Don't take on one at a time; if you do that, you look like Don Quixote. Take them all on and make sure you go after each one.

The New York Times Magazine, 3-5:55.

Russell Baker
Newspaper columnist

Sitting here in Washington talking to ourselves, we (in the news media) begin to look down on the electorate . . . We think of them as bigoted, reactionary, mean-spirited. And almost every election, it seems to me, they surprise us in a delightful way . . . They usually go for decency. They very rarely can be sold a bill of goods when the chips are really down.

Interview/ The Washington Post, 8-27:(Potomac)21.

Joseph A. Beirne
President, Communications Workers of America

I think it impossible for any labor leader to sit out an election. There can be no real neutrality in the political processes of America.

U.S. News & World Report, 8-21:23.

Julian Bond
Georgia State Legislator

The root of all social evils rests in politics—so in politics will answers to these evils be found.

At Utah State University, April 4/ San Francisco Examiner, 4-5:9.

Those blacks who urge us to vote for the man (President Nixon) who gave us (former U.S. Supreme Court nominees) Carswell and Haynsworth and "benign neglect" are members of a new American political party, neither Democratic nor Republican nor independent. These new political prostitutes belong to the Small Business Administration party, the Housing and Urban Development party, the Health, Education and Welfare party, the Washington Rent party. They praise the President as "the greatest savior since Jesus Christ"; they applaud the wizard of the wiretap, the architect of law and order: the former Attorney General (John Mitchell); and wonder of wonders, they attend a formal dinner honoring the old Dixiecrat himself, (Senator) Strom Thurmond. It is imperative that we (black people) come together now to drive Richard Nixon from the White House. He says he will get 20 per cent of the black vote in November. That's 100 per cent more than he deserves.

At National Urban League convention, St. Louis, Aug. 2/ The New York Times, 8-3:18.

Daniel J. Boorstin
Director, National Museum of History and Technology

(Referring to the attempted assassination shooting of Alabama Governor George Wallace): When an unbalanced young man slips into a crowd and shoots, there is a chorus of dismay (from politicians). But these very same politicians are very cautious when the violence is not done by one unbalanced person—who probably will be put away and not be able to vote for many years, if ever—but instead is done by crowds of young people who have the vote, or by Negroes, "Jewish defense" organizations, "Women's Lib" groups—you name it . . . It seems that when groups of voters appear receptive to disorderly instincts, the politician says: "Wait a minute—maybe this is a great thing. Maybe women are great, or 'black power' is great, or maybe it's marvelous that students should burn a professor's manuscript or seize a government office." That is the serious symptom of disorder I see.

Interview/ U.S. News & World Report, 5-29:18.

Tom Braden
Political columnist

One would have to go back to (Warren) Harding, at least, to find an Administration so devoid of intellectuals as that of (President) Nixon. Except for (National Security Affairs Adviser) Henry Kissinger, there is hardly a man on the appointment list whom one would suspect of reading, let alone reading seriously. As for intellectual content, this is the Administration which has used electronic spying devices more widely than any in history; which con-

(TOM BRADEN)

ducted a systematic campaign against the press; which saw nothing disgraceful in trying to put Judge (G. Harrold) Carswell on the Supreme Court. It is headed by a man whose taste in music runs to country-Western and Lawrence Welk; who put comic-opera uniforms on the White House police; and who could think of nothing more discerning to say to a student war protester from the University of Syracuse than to ask him about the "Orangemen."

On CBS-TV's "Spectrum"/ The National Observer, 11-4:13.

David Broder
Political columnist

Rather than being able to say that the (big) issue for the voter this year is the economy, or the war (in Vietnam), or busing (of school children for racial balance), or law and order, the real question is: Which side are you on? Are you one of us, or are you one of them—the ones who have been running things? . . . It's very basic, gut-level politics, where what has to be determined is: Whose government is it?

Interview/ The Washington Post, 8-27:(Potomac)21.

Edward W. Brooke
United States Senator, R–Mass.

Many people think participation in politics merely means registering and voting and perhaps even ringing doorbells for their favorite candidates every few years. But those who wait for bienniel or quadrenniel elections are participating in politics only in a limited sense. They are like diners in a restaurant who must select from a very limited menu; it is the people who prepare the menu who have the greatest influence on the meal that is finally served . . .

The Washington Post, 7-11:(A)18.

Edmund G. Brown
Former Governor of California

You know what I miss about not being Governor? The power and authority to do things. I still take the *Sacramento Bee*, you know; have to keep up with things in Sacramento. But, God, it's frustrating. I read about all (Governor Ronald) Reagan's doing, all those horrible things, hurting the schools and vetoing bills to help crippled children and all, destroying the things that make California great—no compassion, no feeling, no humanity—and I can't do anything, not a damn thing.

Interview, Beverly Hills, Calif./ Los Angeles Times, 3-19:(West)9.

Edmund G. Brown, Jr.
Secretary of State of California

(On the controversy surrounding an alleged favoritism shown to Sheraton-ITT by the Federal government in return for a large contribution to the Republican convention upcoming in San Diego): I don't think it takes any insight to see that big business is getting big write-offs and benefits, and at the time they are making massive contributions. For many years, many of us have suspected that giant companies can virtually buy and sell politicians. The Sheraton-ITT contribution is the latest example of big business dominating our government.

News conference, Los Angeles, March 20/ Los Angeles Times, 3-21:(1)3.

James MacGregor Burns
Professor of Government, Williams College, Williamstown, Mass.

People can't make Ted (Senator Edward) Kennedy disappear; and even he (Kennedy) can't make Ted Kennedy disappear. He is a brooding presence way down in the psyches of practicing politicians all over the country.

Washington, Feb. 9/ The Washington Post, 2-10:(A)4.

Earl L. Butz
Secretary of Agriculture of the United States

(On the attack on his appointment by the Democratic Party): The Democrats will regret their attack on a new Secretary of Agriculture which made him a national figure. He is a chap who is rather articulate; he is a chap who doesn't straddle issues; he is a chap who is not afraid to speak out. He has now become a political asset sought after by the Republican National Committee. As a matter of fact, I was the only Cabinet member to address the entire meeting of the Republican National Committee Workshop recently in Washington; the only Cabinet member to do that. The Republicans who wondered whether (President) Nixon made a mistake when he named the new Secretary of Agriculture now recognize that here's a man who'd be an asset for anything.

The New York Times Magazine, 4-16:93.

John H. Chafee
Former Governor of Rhode Island

(On his current campaign for the U.S. Senate): I have two rules when I work a shopping center: never go into a beauty shop; never enter a bar. In beauty shops, you only embarrass the women when they are having their hair done. In bars, if you buy drinks for the house, you're a spendthrift; if you don't, you're a cheapskate.

Providence, R.I./ Los Angeles Times, 12-21:(1)14.

Shirley Chisholm
United States Representative, D–N.Y.

(On her candidacy for President): My gut commitment is the Presidency with a black man as Vice President, a woman as head of Health, Education and Welfare, an Indian as Secretary of the Interior and other Cabinet posts reflecting all the people.

At Mills College, Oakland, Calif., Jan. 11/ San Francisco Examiner, 1-12:19.

Watch now what the other candidates (for President) say to you, watch what they have done. I can't put on a show like they can. I can only speak from the heart . . . I'm the only un-bought and un-bossed candidate now running for President. I'm a shaker-upper. Your humble servant is a catalyst for change.

At Whittier (Calif.) College, Jan. 13/ Los Angeles Times, 1-14:(2)2.

I am not the candidate of black America (for President), although I am black and proud. I am not the candidate of the women's movement of this country, although I am a woman and I am equally proud of that. I stand here now without endorsements from any big-name politicians or celebrities or any other kind of prop. I do not intend to offer you the tired and glib cliches which have for too long been an accepted part of our political life. I am the candidate of the people, and my presence before you now symbolizes a new era in American political history . . . I stand before you today to repudiate the ridiculous notion that the American people will not vote for a qualified candidate simply because he is not white or because she is not a male. I do not believe that, in 1972, the great majority of Americans will continue to harbor such narrow and petty prejudices.

New York, Jan. 25/ The Washington Post, 1-26:(A)5.

The black people can't do it (influence the forthcoming national political conventions) alone. The women can't do it alone. The Chicanos can't do it alone, and the Indians can't do it alone. But together, the have-nots and the disillusioned can come together as convention delegates to tell those people who have been dominating these conventions for years: "Not this time, fellows."

Boston, April 6/ The Washington Post, 4-8:(A)10.

(SHIRLEY CHISHOLM)

(On her campaign for the Democratic Presidential nomination): I'm tired. But it's a good kind of tired. When I first started my campaign, the big boys said, "Oh, Shirley's on an ego trip. Look at that little 90-pound thing; she's going to collapse." But now the staff members of other candidates are asking me what I'm thinking. And they've got to think you're important to do that.

At fund-raising dinner, Washington, June 21/ The Washington Post, 6-23:(B)3.

The Democratic Party must shake off the old custodial type of liberalism with its litany of welfare projects, its stress on numerical quantitative aspects of problems and politics, and its self-styled pragmatists, contemptuous of those who challenge the familiar routine of power politics and Main Street wisdom.

Before Democratic Platform Committee, Washington, June 24/ The New York Times, 6-25:(1)34.

(On her seeking the Democratic Presidential nomination): Never before in this country, ever since the inception of the Republic, have you had a woman seriously running for the Presidency. I am not talking about someone nominating someone at the convention as a mere gesture of symbolism and tokenism; I am talking about someone going out in the highways and byways in the past seven and a half months and saying to the American people that, indeed, this is a multi-faceted society, that Mrs. Chisholm can also be considered as a person who can run for the Presidency of this country. I was breaking a tradition, in which only white males have been the gentlemen in this country that have guided the ship of state; so you don't expect people—black, white, men or women—to suddenly overcome a tradition that has been steeped ever since the inception of this Republic. I understand that I have broken the ice.

TV-radio interview, Washington/ "Meet the Press," National Broadcasting Company, 7-9.

William Clay
United States Representative, D–Mo.

(On black entertainers who support President Nixon for re-election): It is both sickening and disgraceful for any blacks—especially entertainers, who are where they are because of black support—to be duped by shrewd political con men and then to have the gall to try to con black people into believing that one of their greatest oppressors, Richard Milhous Nixon, is their friend and should be supported for re-election. This is nothing but pure bull.

Oct. 16/The Washington Post, 10-18:(A)15.

John B. Connally, Jr.
Secretary of the Treasury of the United States

(On his being a Democrat in a Republican Administration): My party loyalty is not as strong as my adherence to my own conscience and convictions. Nor can I ever put my party above my country.

Washington/ San Francisco Examiner & Chronicle, 2-6:(Sunday Scene)2.

(On why he has not made any political talks): I don't like to engage in forensic futility.

The Dallas Times Herald, 5-12:(A)32.

John B. Connally, Jr.
Former Secretary of the Treasury of the United States; Chairman, Democrats for Nixon

According to a national poll just completed, 20 million Democrats have already decided that their choice this year will be

President Nixon over Senator (George) McGovern (in the November Presidential election). We (who support President Nixon) open our doors to all those millions of Democrats who realize that in this Presidential election, President Nixon is simply the better choice . . . (I am) disturbed about the trend that my own (Democratic) Party has taken under the leadership of Senator George S. McGovern. Far from becoming a more open party, the Democratic Party under Senator McGovern's leadership is becoming an ideological machine closed to millions of Americans who have been the Party's most loyal and steadfast members.

News conference, Washington, Aug. 9/ Los Angeles Times, 8-10:(1)23.

Frankly, I hope I never seek public office again . . . I've been in politics since 1935. It's a tough, hard grind. No man can do it without being pilloried. It takes the skin of a rhinoceros and the stubbornness of a Cape buffalo.

News conference, Los Angeles, Oct. 10/ San Francisco Examiner, 10-11:4.

(Democratic Presidential nominee Senator George McGovern) may have captured the machinery and nomination of the great Democratic Party—but he does not stand in its traditions and he has not captured its heart.

Television broadcast, Oct. 20/ Los Angeles Herald-Examiner, 10-21:(A)2.

(On the just-concluded Presidential election in which President Nixon defeated Democratic Presidential nominee Senator George McGovern): McGovern misread the American people. He talked about revolution and radical change and that's not what they wanted. In the 1960s they witnessed massive social and political change. They've been overwhelmed by it; they couldn't be assimilated by it. The people were not looking for massive change, but for stability . . . Given a little time, the Democrats will trim their sails and move with it. Now that they know where the winds are blowing, you can expect them to tack to the right.

The Washington Post, 11-9:(A)6.

Harry S. Dent
Special Counsel to the President of the United States

There is a common misconception, that the Democrats foster, that "Republican" means wealth, that Republicans care more about themselves than people. We have to refute this myth. If we can't do something about that problem soon, I would be a strong advocate of a committee sitting down and coming up with a new name. This is our biggest problem.

Interview/ The Christian Science Monitor, 12-9:11.

Thomas F. Eagleton
United States Senator, D–Mo.

. . . I think that some of the more bombastic and caustic divisiveness has been executed by the Vice President of the United States, Mr. (Spiro) Agnew, on behalf of the President (Nixon). Someone said that Agnew is Nixon's Nixon, meaning that Agnew's performing the role as Vice President that Richard Nixon performed as Vice President under President (Dwight) Eisenhower. And I think there's some truth to that statement. That is, where the President on occasion is projecting the role of statesman and taking the high, noble road, he has his Vice President running around the country in a fashion that is divisive, that is contentious.

Interview, Washington, June 30/ The Washington Post, 7-14:(A)13.

Has President Nixon been truly a national leader trying to bring this country together? That was the slogan, you know, he used in his inaugural address, when he reminisced about the young girl who waved a sign saying, "Bring Us Together." I, for one, don't think that the President and the

Vice President have brought this country together. I think the country's more divided. There's more internal friction within the American populace than existed in early 1969 when he took office as President; and I think that that is a national issue that can and will be raised.

Interview, Washington, June 30/
The Washington Post, 7-14:(A)13.

Thomas F. Eagleton
United States Senator, D–Mo.;
Democratic Vice-Presidential nominee

When (Senator and Presidential nominee) George McGovern asked me to be the nominee of the Democratic Party for Vice President, he told me what he perceived the office of Vice President to be. We know it's the second-highest office in the land; and he wanted it to be filled by a person whose objectives are compatible with those of the President himself, but who will not hesitate to make his views known to the President. And, most important, it's an office whose occupant must understand and appeal to the highest—to the highest, not the basest—motives of our fellow Americans . . . If there's one thing which the present occupant of the White House (President Nixon) has made perfectly clear . . . it is that he does not share that view of the role of his Vice President. And so, tonight I pledge to you that we will restore the dignity of the office of the Vice Presidency. It will not be a platform for cheap rhetorical attacks that divide our nation.

Accepting the Democratic
Vice-Presidential nomination,
Miami Beach, July 14/
The New York Times, 7-15:12.

(Referring to the Nixon Administration): From the people who promised to bring us together, we've gotten deception and more distrust; from the people who promised a lift of a driving dream, we have a sodden mound of trampled hopes. And so, we have an electorate so jaded by gimmickry that their healthy skepticism about politics, indeed their healthy skepticism about politicians, has escalated into a total lack of confidence in this Administration.

Accepting the Democratic
Vice-Presidential nomination,
Miami Beach, July 14/
The New York Times, 7-15:12.

(On AFL-CIO president George Meany's opposition to the Democratic Presidential nominee Senator George McGovern): I would like to talk with Mr. Meany and try to point out to him that, whatever reluctance he may have about the McGovern-Eagleton ticket, I wish he would just write down McGovern-Eagleton on a piece of paper, then write down Nixon and Agnew or Nixon and Connally on another piece of paper and look at the two pieces of paper. Which one of those tickets . . . comports the most with the basic philosophy of the AFL-CIO? If you look at those two and just go back and forth, there's no question that the McGovern-Eagleton ticket comports more closely with the philosophy and the legislative policies of the AFL-CIO.

TV-radio interview/
"Face the Nation,"
Columbia Broadcasting System, 7-16.

On three occasions of my life I have voluntarily gone into hospitals as a result of nervous exhaustion and fatigue. A few in this room know me well . . . and they know me to be an intense and hard-fighting person. I sometimes push myself too far . . . I still am an intense person; I still push very hard. But I pace myself a great deal better than I did in earlier years. The past six years, from 1966 to date, I've experienced good, solid, sound health . . . So I believe, and I have every confidence, that at age 42 I've learned how to pace myself and learned how to measure my own energies and know the limits of my own endurance. Insofar as this campaign is concerned, I intend to give it all I have, but on a measured basis, and not to repeat the experiences that I have experienced as heretofore mentioned.

News conference, Custer, S.D., July 25/ The New York Times, 7-26:20.

(On his recent revelation of past hospitalizations for nervous exhaustion): I did tell Senator (and Democratic Presidential nominee George) McGovern that, if my candidacy at any time became an embarrassment to him or in any way a hindrance to his campaign and his chances of achieving the Presidency, I would withdraw as a candidate for the Vice-Presidency. He very promptly and very magnificently said that he didn't even consider that within the reach of possibility.

July 26/ San Francisco Examiner, 7-26:4.

(On columnist Jack Anderson's charges that he has a history of drunken and reckless driving): I have never been more determined in my life about any issue than I am today about remaining on this (Democratic) ticket. I am not going to bow to Mr. Anderson. I'm not going to let a lie drive me from this ticket. I will label it for what it is—a lie. And we'll see what develops therefrom.

News conference, Honolulu, July 27/ Los Angeles Times, 7-28:(1)20.

(Announcing his withdrawal as Democratic Vice-Presidential nominee because of the disclosure of past health problems): I will not divide the Democratic Party, which already has too many divisions. Therefore, I am writing to the Chairman of the Democratic Party withdrawing my candidacy. My personal feelings are secondary to the necessity to unify the Democratic Party and elect (Senator) George McGovern President of the United States. My conscience is clear. My spirits are high. This is definitely not my last press conference, and Tom Eagleton is going to be around for a long, long, time. I'm for George McGovern, and I'm going to continue working to see him elected President of the United States.

Washington, July 31/ San Francisco Examiner, 8-1:4.

Thomas F. Eagleton
United States Senator, D–Mo.

(On whether, despite his withdrawal as Democratic Vice-Presidential nominee because of the disclosure of past health problems, he would again accept the nomination if he had it to do over again): I definitely would. If I passed up the Vice-Presidential offer, I guess time and again I would have said to myself, "I had a chance to be really somebody, and I passed it up. I'm one of a hundred (Senators); I am somebody, but I could have been one of two" . . . A hundred years from now, in some primer on American history, there might be a footnote that says some person named Eagleton, for 15 days, was a Vice-Presidential nominee.

Interview, Washington, Aug. 1/ The New York Times, 8-2:20.

Sam J. Ervin, Jr.
United States Senator, D–N.C.

(Criticizing the Subversive Activities Control Board): The sole function of this board is to intimidate people. If I could see ghosts of Communists in all the corners I could support it. There is nothing in the Constitution against a man being politically or intellectually obnoxious . . . to those of us who belong to the established order.

Washington, June 15/ San Francisco Examiner, 6-16:4.

M. Stanton Evans
Editor, "Indianapolis News"

What has happened to our politics is that, for almost 40 years, from 1932 to 1972, we have lived under a political technique, a political style, that I designate for shorthand purposes as welfare politics, the welfare coalition—a congeries of interest groups, each of whom believes that it has

(M. STANTON EVANS)

something to gain from the big-government, big-spending, big-taxing formula. The arithmetic of this is relatively simple. You articulate American society into a number of blocs—farmers, labor-union members, black, ethnic groups of some other type, consumers, whatever the case may be—and go to each of these groups, saying to them in convention assembled, "What is it you want from the Federal government? I will provide it for you. Do you want a subsidy? Do you want some kind of Federal aid or assistance? I will make sure you get it." And if each of them thinks that is the most important thing in life, in political life at least, and believes that you are the man who can deliver this, and enough of them come to that conclusion, eventually you will assemble a majority, and you will be elected. That is the way most elections—not only at the national level but at the state level—in America are conducted.

Interview, Washington, Sept. 18/ Human Events, 10-7:9.

Robert H. Finch
Counsellor to the President of the United States

. . . I am totally opposed to the idea of a national Presidential primary. And I do not think that the way to reform the problems posed by 25 primaries in 1972 is to add 27 more for 1976. In effect, a national primary would create a second and equally expensive and cumbersome national election just three months before the real one in November. Indeed, if the results of the national primary required a run-off, that would mean a third national election; and that is just too much to ask or expect. At the same time, a national primary would serve to eliminate the positive aspects of the visibility function of primaries. I think that there is an important role played by primaries in getting the politicians and the issues out among the people, in different settings, and under different pressures.

Lecture, Westminster College, Fulton, Mo., April 4/Vital Speeches, 6-1:492.

Frank E. Fitzsimmons
President, International Brotherhood of Teamsters

(Democratic Presidential nominee Senator) George McGovern is no friend of American labor. And moreover, the Teamsters have consistently stood firmly by the President (Nixon) in his effort to bring this (Vietnam) war to an honorable conclusion and to secure the release of our prisoners of war. We do not want the U.S. to surrender or to beg to Hanoi or to any other enemy power. We (Teamsters Union leaders) have voted today to endorse the re-election of President Nixon. We will urge our members to work and vote to keep Mr. Nixon in office for another four years. We believe America needs in these perilous times a man of President Nixon's courage, vision and experience. Our members work hard for their wages. They are entitled to what they earn, and they figure that the government ought to get off of our back and out of our pockets. The policies of Mr. McGovern only promise more of the "big brother," not less. Our members are, for the most part, hard-working family men and women who are not in favor of legalizing pot, encouraging abortion or granting amnesty to those who deserted their country in time of need.

La Costa, Calif., July 17/ Los Angeles Times, 7-18:(1)21.

Betty Friedan
Founder, National Organization for Women

All the (political) candidates are suddenly making noises like feminists. But they had better know that rhetoric isn't enough. Women are emerging as a real political force, and we intend to pin down all the candidates on their talk and promises.

Los Angeles Times, 3-31:(1-A)2.

George Gallup
Political analyst

(On vigorous campaigning by political candidates): This is the biggest myth in American public life. Running up and down a state and shaking hands loses more votes than it wins. All these people succeed in doing is wearing themselves out and making fools of themselves. As a matter of fact, you can make a hell of a good case that TV does not change things, or very little, except perhaps for an unknown candidate. The public makes up its mind on the basis of a candidate's personality and his ideas—the issues.

Interview, Princeton, N.J./ San Francisco Examiner & Chronicle, 5-14:(This World)20.

John W. Gardner
National chairman, Common Cause

I think it would be the biggest bargain the American people ever got if they just took over the cost of (political) campaigning themselves. Because when they hand the cost of campaigning over to these big interests, what comes back to those big interests in political favors is 10, 20, 30, 100 times as much money out of our taxpayers' pockets.

Interview, Washington, Jan. 3/ San Francisco Examiner, 1-3:2.

In the 1972 election campaign, the citizen will be the victim of the most sophisticated sales blizzard ever inflicted on any voting population anywhere. It will combine all the wizardry of Madison Avenue, computer technology and the electronic media. The aim of the new approach will not be to make the voter think, not to clarify the issues, not to give him a greater grasp of his role as a citizen or a deeper understanding of the candidate. The aim will be to sell him an illusion, to move him to act without thinking, to con him psychologically. The essence of the new approach is to remove from public view as completely as possible the real flesh-and-blood candidate—that anachronistic soul who dashed around meeting honest-to-God people, answering unrehearsed questions, debating real issues, letting himself be seen and heard and judged as a human being. Not until he is safely removed can the political manager proceed with the carefully contrived image that he will project over the electronic media. As one cynical operator put it: "Given today's techniques, the best way to handle the candidate is to lock him in a broom closet. Let him out occasionally, apply the makeup, rehearse him in some easy dialog and run him through a TV spot. Then—back to the closet."

At meeting of New Hampshire Common Cause, Concord/ The National Observer, 3-25:15.

John J. Gilligan
Governor of Ohio

(On the campaigning for the Democratic Presidential nomination): (Alabama Governor) George Wallace is out there raising questions of excruciating relevance, and what does (Senator Edmund) Muskie offer? Typical programmatic Senate answers, with long, involved discussions of details you get in committee. Who gives a damn about Title 8, Subsection 6, applicable only to gooney birds in Wyoming? Not the voters. They want straight talk—maybe oversimplified talk—and they have had enough of programs. They're fed up to here. Muskie is not getting to the guts of the voter.

Interview, Columbus, April 10/ The New York Times, 4-12:22.

Barry M. Goldwater
United States Senator, R–Ariz.

(On charges that U.S. Attorney General-designate Richard Kleindienst was involved in a favorable legal ruling toward ITT in return for political contributions): We are being treated to theatre of the absurd for the personal profit and pleasure of a gossip monger (columnist Jack Anderson who made the charges) and the personal satisfaction of a few politicians who would like

(BARRY M. GOLDWATER)

a nice scandal to direct attention away from the considerable problems of their own (Democratic) party.

March 10/ Los Angeles Times, 3-11:(1)6.

Politically, I'm somewhat to the right of President Nixon, and somewhat to the left of Vice President Nixon.

Before Gridiron Club, Washington, April 8/ The Washington Post, 4-10:(B)1.

(On Democratic Presidential nominee Senator George McGovern's supporters at the recent Democratic National Convention): What I listened to and saw on my television set made me question whether I was sitting in the United States or someplace else. I was reminded, when I listened to their constant complaints, of the coyotes who live on my hill with me in the desert of Arizona. These coyotes, particularly on a moonlight night, just sit and bay and moan and cry at the moon. That's what this little handful of angry people who live with us in America and who were in Miami last month do. They remind me of coyotes.

At Republican National Convention, Miami Beach, Aug. 21/ Los Angeles Times, 8-22:(1)1.

It's a strange thing about conservatives. They are the most anti-Communist group in America, and yet they practice the same thing for which they criticize the Communists—namely, if you don't agree with them 100 per cent, then you're wrong.

Parade, 9-24:26.

Albert Gore
Former United States Senator, D–Tenn.

No one who has ever served in high elective office can deny the personal importance to him of a handful of large contributors. With economic power goes political power; and the escalation of campaign costs . . . has vastly concentrated this political power. I am not at all sure our system as we know it can long withstand the corruption of money in politics.

Before Senate Antitrust Subcommittee, Washington, Jan. 18/ The Washington Post, 1-19:(A)10.

Gus Hall
General Secretary, Communist Party of the United States

. . . fundamentally, the Democratic Party remains the party of big business and monopoly capital. Let's say (Democratic Presidential nominee Senator George) McGovern was not nominated. Because McGovern represents some of the mass movements, I think there would have been a split in the Party. Possibly, a new party might have emerged. That would have been a positive step. At some point in American politics, that's going to happen. I'm convinced pressures will grow and, when they can't be resolved in the Democratic Party, a new party will emerge that will bring into its ranks an anti-monopoly, socialist party.

Interview/ San Francisco Examiner, 10-3:30.

Leonard Hall
Former Chairman, Republican National Committee

(Chicago) Mayor (Richard) Daley is really the last big political boss in the country. As long as he is around you have to expect that he will be a factor (at the upcoming Democratic National Convention). He is the last of the Mohicans. There is no one else around like him. With the exception of Daley, the old political bosses are as dead as a dodo bird.

Interview, New York/ Los Angeles Herald-Examiner, 6-25:(A)15.

W. Averell Harriman
Former United States Ambassador-at-Large

The reason I am for (Senator and Presidential candidate Edmund) Muskie and shall continue to work for Muskie is because it is impossible for Muskie not to tell the truth. That's what I've got against (President Richard) Nixon—it's impossible for him to tell the truth.

Washington, May 11/ The Washington Post, 5-13:(B)3.

Louis Harris
Public opinion analyst

. . . if all we (opinion analysts) did (in conducting political polls) was say who is ahead or who is behind, I would have been out of this business long ago. It is my firm conviction that our real contribution is to try to explain how the voters in this democracy make the most important decision we can make, which is the selection of the Chief Executive for the country every four years. If we can tell what are those elements working on the voters, what are the things in the minds of the voters, I think, one, it can keep a man who is elected President honest in terms of what the mandate really was; I think politicians are bad about reading mandates as they will. Number two, I think it ought to be documented how the American people made their decision. This is our job.

TV-radio interview, Washington/ "Meet the Press," National Broadcasting Company, 10-22.

We will probably have more ticket-splitting this November 7 (general election) than we have ever had before. In fact, I think the suspicion is so high in the country that we now get, by a 2-to-1 margin, voters saying to us they think it is the right thing to have the Congress of one party—the Democrats—and the Republicans controlling the White House. People want the system of checks and balances with a vengeance, if you will.

TV-radio interview/ "Meet the Press," National Broadcasting Company, 10-22.

Vance Hartke
United States Senator, D–Ind.

The American people, and the world, cannot afford four more years of Richard Nixon's failures. (But) if the Democratic Party expects to receive the mantle of leadership, it had better start leading. This (Presidential) campaign is all about a country which is fighting for its life. The Democratic Party is entitled to have a candidate ready to lead the fight. I am ready.

Announcing his candidacy for the Democratic Presidential nomination, Manchester, N.H., Jan. 3/ San Francisco Examiner, 1-3:2.

Richard G. Hatcher
Mayor of Gary, Ind.

. . . in the eyes of all decent people, (Democratic Presidential nominee Senator) George McGovern is concerned about the poor and the black. His positions show he has more courage than any others. He says frankly to the people with great wealth: "You must share." If he could accomplish one-half of what he has promised, he would be the greatest President we have ever had. And I could be a proud American again.

Interview, Gary, Ind./ The Christian Science Monitor, 8-15:13.

Hugh M. Hefner
Publisher, "Playboy" magazine

The major difference between a conservative-Ayn Rand individualism or conservative-Republican individualism and the kind of individualism I believe in is simple: *I* think people are important, and *they* think that property is important. The kind of freedom that (William F.) Buckley is concerned with says: Let me do whatever I want to do with my property. It's *people* that this country's supposed to be all about. It's protecting people that the Constitution is all about. And you'll find that's where it really splits politically. Over and over again,

(HUGH M. HEFNER)

you'll find property rights and personal rights bumping into one another.

Interview, Los Angeles/ Los Angeles Times, 2-27:(West)23.

James D. Hodgson
Secretary of Labor of the United States

The average American working man can be characterized as one who works hard, pays his taxes, loves his country and likes to lead an orderly, responsible existence. This kind of an individual is not, in our judgment, particularly attracted to things that are characterized as being "liberal" these days. Such things as unlimited busing (of school children for racial balance), unlimited amnesty (for draft-dodgers), unlimited pot smoking. The worker is concerned about his home and his family, and for this reason, these things hold no particular attraction for him. So from our standpoint, we believe that workers in greater numbers than ever before will be attracted to the record and principles of President Nixon, (as contrasted) with the record of what appears to be the opposition.

Interview/ The Washington Post, 7-3:(A)2.

Sidney Hook
Professor of Philosophy, New York University

No one can expect to have his professions of liberalism taken seriously who is not outspokenly *both* anti-Communist and anti-Fascist.

Plainview (Tex.) Daily Herald, 7-14:8.

Thomas L. Hughes
Director, Carnegie Endowment for International Peace; Former diplomat

Democratic Administrations have a soft spot for unused intellectuals. But that doesn't really indicate anything at all about the use of ideas. The intensity and clash of ideas is greater, but they may be mutually cancellable.

The Washington Post, 2-27:(A)12.

Hubert H. Humphrey
United States Senator, D–Minn.

Persistence and tenacity are old American virtues. I was defeated for Mayor (of Minneapolis) the first time I ran for office –but I was elected the second time. I was defeated for the Vice-Presidential nomination the first time–but I was later nominated and elected. I was defeated for the Presidential nomination in 1960–but I was nominated in 1968. I was defeated in the Presidential election of 1968–but I return to the battle determined to do my best to achieve victory in 1972.

Announcing his candidacy for the Democratic Presidential nomination, Philadelphia, Jan. 10/ U.S. News & World Report, 1-24:50.

It's not the silent majority, it's a deaf Administration that afflicts this country today. It's not because there are not able men in the (Nixon) Administration who know how the government works, because they do. It is because they are insensitive to the needs of hundreds of thousands of people throughout the country. (As a result, there is) a government in Washington that stands there as stupified and as stupid as a stunned ox.

Campaigning for the Democratic Presidential nomination, St. Petersburg, Fla., Jan. 12/ The New York Times, 1-15:14.

. . . I consider this (Nixon) Administration anti-people. I just don't think they like people. I think this Administration is primarily interested in what we call the polemics of politics, rather than the programs and the policies and the issues of politics that affect people's lives . . . This is the most closed, highly-disciplined, non-published Administration that we've had in this country in my lifetime. It communicates with the people when it wants to. It has waged a relentless battle with the media on what should be known and, may I say, (it has) done rather well at it.

Interview/
The Washington Post, 1-16:(B)1.

Why let (Alabama Governor) George Wallace pick up the biscuits out here (in Florida, for the Democratic Presidential primary)? Why let him be for law and order? *I* was for law and order before he could spell it. Why let him run around here and wrap himself in the Flag? *I'm* a patriot. *I* love my country every bit as much as he does.

While campaigning in Florida/
Los Angeles Times, 3-2:(1-A)1.

(On his campaign for the Democratic Presidential nomination): Look at the way I'm working. Tired? Hell, yes, I'm tired. But I've got to go, got to go, go, because I want to win. This is it for me. It's now or never. I don't want to be some rerun on the late show.

Interview,
St. Petersburg, Fla., March 10/
The New York Times, 3-12:(1)53.

I am not going to be diverted from the main effort by spending all of my time in some kind of argument, a running battle with the Governor of Alabama (George Wallace), when all he is is the Governor of Alabama. I'm not running for Governor—I'm running for President. Where was he when I was fighting for 100 per cent (farm) parity? Where was this Governor of Alabama? I'll tell you what he was doing. He was down there keeping people poor.

Campaigning for the Democratic
Presidential nomination, Arnott, Wis./
The New York Times, 3-17:16.

(On charges that Deputy Attorney General and Attorney General-designate Richard Kleindienst and other Nixon Administration officials gave favorable legal decisions to friends and political contributors such as International Telephone and Telegraph Co.): There is a cloud hanging over the government today and over the Justice Department . . . Mr. Kleindienst has been involved in it, and unless that cloud can be removed, unless this pallor of uncertainty and suspicion and doubt about the ITT case can be removed, then Mr. Kleindienst ought not to be Attorney General and, frankly, he ought to step aside.

TV-radio interview/"Issues and Answers,"
American Broadcasting Company, 3-26.

(On political campaigning): In each state, there are certain little issues and you try to get your material around so it hits those issues, and you end up looking like a pretzel once in a while.

The Washington Post, 5-28:(B)1.

(Arguing against the Democratic Party nominating Senator George McGovern for President): If the Democratic Party falls into the hands of any narrow, ideological elite, if it focuses its concern on matters of interest to only a handful of the privileged, or if it neglects the day-to-day concerns of the many, then the long and scrupulously planned "emerging Republican majority" may well be upon us.

Before Democratic platform subcommittee,
Washington, June 24/
San Francisco Examiner & Chronicle,
6-25:(A)16.

If the Democratic Party gets into the position of representing only the college campus, the militant youth movement, racial minorities, then it will face the same problems the Republicans face—namely, it will look like it is a special-interest party. The only way I know that you can win elections is to recognize that the majority of the American people are not poor, that there is what we call Middle America, and that it is made up mostly of working peo-

(HUBERT H. HUMPHREY)

ple; and that great middle section represents victory or defeat for a political party.

Interview/
U.S. News & World Report, 10-2:26.

(Asking the nation to unite around President Nixon's second inaugural, even though he and others may disagree with Administration policies): I ask you to unite in the 1973 inaugural. As (the late U.S. President) John F. Kennedy said, (an inauguration is) not a victory of party but a celebration of freedom . . . I did all I could to have another man for President and Vice President . . . (But) after all, I live in a free society. I respect the will of the majority, and will seek to change it on the next occasion. I don't have much time for people who, once the (election) is over, spend their life in anger.

Interview, Minneapolis/
The Washington Post, 12-28:(D)1,4.

Henry M. Jackson
United States Senator, D–Wash.

This newspaper *(The New York Times)* and its national news service has downgraded my campaign (for the Democratic Presidential nomination) since its beginning. They have virtually dismissed my candidacy, despite a strong third-place finish in Florida ahead of the candidates they appear to find more palatable, Senator Edmund S. Muskie, Senator George McGovern and (New York) Mayor Lindsay. They have downgraded the issues that I have been articulating, and they are downgrading the people of America who understand far better than *The New York Times* what is troubling the nation. *The New York Times* is not going to run this country. The people, not *The New York Times*, are going to choose the issues. And I am going to take my case to the people, with or without the cooperation of *The New York Times.*

News conference,
Milwaukee, April 2/
The New York Times, 4-3:22.

(Arguing against nomination for President by the Democrats of Senator George McGovern): I don't want the Democratic Party to make the mistake the Republicans made in 1964. Senator McGovern could be the Democrats' Goldwater. Nominating him may make some people feel good for the moment, but it could spell disaster at the polls in November. Extremism on the left is gaining "respectability" (and) the main vehicle of this suicidal drift is the candidacy of Senator McGovern.

San Francisco Examiner & Chronicle,
4-30:(This World)8.

Jesse L. Jackson
Civil rights leader;
Former director, Operation Breadbasket,
Southern Christian Leadership Conference

This country today needs jobs or income. That's what it needs. It needs health care. It needs medicine. It needs peace and nonracism . . . The issue ain't no more to save the Democrats; the issue is not to save the Republicans; but the democracy and the Republic are at stake, and unless someone rises with the power to reconcile black and white, young and old, he is not qualified to save the nation. The issue in (the Presidential election of) 1972 is not to save your party, not even your pride, but to save the Union.

March 18/
The New York Times, 3-23:43.

Jacob K. Javits
United States Senator, R–N.Y.

In a number of states . . . the Governor and Lieutenant Governor run separately and are elected separately. Since the present method of nominating Vice Presidents is definitely unsatisfactory, we could go to separate elections for national office. Why not? Running separately would greatly upgrade the Vice President. In the states, a number of candidates usually contest for the nomination of Lieutenant Governor, and if Vice Presidents ran separately, once they were nominated by the conventions, it would have the effect of stimulating competition for the Vice-Presidential nomination. The Vice President would have to run on his own just as the President does. It is possible, of course, that you might end up with a President of one party and a Vice President of another. What's wrong with that? . . . What would be wrong with a President and Vice President of different parties, if that is the way it came out? I am not convinced that anything would be. You have now a President of one party and a Congress of another. That is a hell of a lot more important than the Vice President.

Interview/
Los Angeles Times, 7-31:(2)7.

I always found that the best political principle is to do what you are doing in the best possible way.

News conference,
New York, Oct. 17/
The New York Times, 10-18:26.

Lyndon B. Johnson
Former President of the United States

I think every candidate for public office is beholden to groups and people with means.

Television interview/
Columbia Broadcasting System, 1-27.

Edward M. Kennedy
United States Senator, D-Mass.

(On the attempted assassination shooting of Alabama Governor and Presidential candidate George Wallace): Once again, democracy in America has been scarred by senseless and unforgivable violence. I am saddened beyond measure that tragedy has again stained and darkened the process we use to select our political leaders.

May 15/
Los Angeles Times, 5-16:(1)11.

The tragedy of our election apathy is compounded by the fact that the highest proportion of America's non-voters are in the under 30 age group. They never have voted in proportion to their number. They are the worst drop-outs in America today—drop-outs from the political process, drop-outs from our democracy.

Quote, 5-28:521.

(The Republicans) had their chance and they failed, and the failure of leadership will be rewarded with failure at the polls in November. For there is a new wind rising over the land. Starting faintly amid the plains and rocky hills of South Dakota, it spread its gathering momentum to New Hampshire and Wisconsin and Massachusetts, sweeping across the nation to California and back to New York, and now to Miami. In it can be heard many things—promises, anguish, hopes for the future, echoes of the past, and our most cherished prayer: America, America, God shed his grace on thee, and crown thy good with brotherhood, from sea to shining sea.

Introducing Democratic Presidential nominee Senator George McGovern at Democratic National Convention, Miami Beach, July 14/
The Washington Post, 7-15:(A)10.

(On President Nixon's campaign for the forthcoming Presidential election): The President has been resting at Camp David, but he has had (White House Communications Director) Herb Klein in New York City, (Presidential Counsellor) Bob Finch in Philadelphia, (Transportation Secretary) John Volpe in Atlanta, (Housing and Urban Development Secretary) George Romney in Portland, Oregon, (Agriculture Secretary) Earl Butz in Minneapolis, (Interior Secretary) Rogers Morton in St. Louis and (Presidential National Security Adviser) Henry Kissinger in Moscow. They say they are surrogate candidates, but you know

(EDWARD M. KENNEDY)

what they are—elephants walking around a ring, each one holding the tail of the one in front of him.

At Democratic rally, Waterbury, Conn., Sept. 14/ San Francisco Examiner, 9-15:8.

The Four Horsemen of ancient days bore the names of war and pestilence, famine and death. Now, in the Nixon Administration, the Four Horsemen are riding again. They bear the names of incompetence, favoritism, secrecy and corruption. It isn't easy to be found with your hand in the till, your foot in your mouth, your tongue in your cheek and your eye on the polls all at the same time; but that's what this Nixon Administration is doing.

Campaigning for Democratic Presidential nominee Senator George McGovern, Hackensack, N.J., Oct. 20/ The Washington Post, 12-13:(A)29.

If I read the future correctly, then I see the range of foreign and domestic issues before us as a field that presents a very great opportunity for effective cooperation between Congress and the (Nixon) Administration, especially in vital areas such as national security and the economy and health and education. And I say that because there is more good-will in Congress now toward Mr. Nixon than perhaps at any time in his career in public life. We have differences in policies, to be sure, and some of those differences are profound; but they are no longer necessarily colored by the difficult partisan passions that so often obscured the issues before. Without abandoning any of the basic principles we have fought for, we in Congress, and I for one, will extend the olive branch to the Administration in the coming Congress. I am confident that we can close ranks and join together in launching a new and effective era of progress on every issue that matters deeply to our people.

At fund-raising dinner for Jerusalem's Hebrew University, Beverly Hills, Calif., Dec. 11/ The Washington Post, 12-13:(A)29.

Richard G. Kleindienst
Deputy Attorney General, and Attorney General-designate, of the United States

(On charges that he took favorable legal action toward Nixon Administration friends and political contributors): I'm no penny-ante two-bit little crook . . . I came to Washington with my honor and a little money. I still have my honor and less money. If anyone can produce just one iota of evidence that I've done anything dishonest in this job, or that I have tampered with justice for political reasons, I'll resign this job.

Broadcast interview, March 19/ The New York Times, 3-20:22.

Earl F. Landgrebe
United States Representative, R–Ind.

Like it or not, what the new Democratic Party has become, in the words of one newspaperman, is "a huge meeting of clients and their social workers . . . a vast coming together of . . . (so-called) teachers, students, researchers, nebulous paper-shufflers, staff people, members of all the bureaucracies." Just who is left out of this party?—the union membership, who have to work and can't afford, in the words of (Steelworkers union president) I.W. Abel, to "stay up to all hours and talk politics"; the middle class, whose values are derided by the McGovernites; professional people, farmers, young working people; the Southerners, who have been all but read out of the Party; and many minority members who cannot accept the extreme and slick slogans handed them by their self-proclaimed representatives. No, there is nothing new in the politics of (Democratic Presidential nominee Senator) George McGovern.

It is the "something for everybody" philosophy which has crippled the Democratic Party since the days of the New Deal. Now, however, we see added to it the fuzzy righteousness of a candidate whose future performance will be as it was in Miami (at the Party convention)—shabby, opportunistic and shallow. Yes, America does need to come home, but not to the fantasyland of George McGovern.

Human Events, 8-5:23.

Alfred M. Landon
Former Governor of Kansas

I liked him (Democratic Presidential nominee Senator George McGovern) better a few months ago. But this (Senator Thomas) Eagleton affair and some other incidents have shown that he just doesn't know how to handle himself in an embarrassing situation. It doesn't seem that he does his homework. McGovern reminds me of a minor leaguer who is just getting to the major leagues. He's finding it very difficult to adjust.

Interview, Topeka, Kan./ Los Angeles Times, 8-21:(1)22.

Giovanni Leone
President of Italy

The best politicians are in fact lawyers, capable of insulting each other in court and then going out to dinner together.

Quote, 1-23:73.

John V. Lindsay
Mayor of New York

Every time there is a decisive problem, whether it is race, poverty or the environment, you'll find that crowd in Washington —the Nixon Administration—doing something to appeal to the worst in people instead of the best in people.

San Jose, Calif., Feb. 24/ The New York Times, 2-25:22.

(On charges that U.S. Attorney General-designate Richard Kleindienst was involved in a favorable legal ruling toward ITT in return for political contributions): I'm deeply disturbed by recent revelations about Mr. Kleindienst's role in the ITT settlement. I had strong reservations when he was first proposed for Attorney General because of his record in civil rights, civil liberties and crime fighting. Now I think there is just too big a cloud over the Kleindienst appointment.

Jacksonville, Fla./ The Christian Science Monitor, 3-6:14.

(Alabama Governor) George Wallace is talking about keeping black and poor people down. He is not talking about law and order. He is talking about perpetuating injustice. That is what Wallace and Wallacism is all about. Regardless of the issue—whether it is busing (for racial balance in schools) or poor people, race or law and order, war abroad or peace at home, the answer is always the same: Suspend the Bill of Rights; put aside the Constitution; pull the trigger or drop the bombs; lock them up, lock them out, beat them down and keep them in their place. It is always the same.

Campaigning in Florida for the Democratic Presidential nomination/ Los Angeles Times, 3-11:(1)12.

(On his dropping out of the race for the Democratic Presidential nomination): I have no regrets on making such an effort; I'd always be prepared to do it again, given the same circumstances. It was impossible to assemble the resources and the money to carry on . . . I was not able to push through my message as effectively as I had hoped. Maybe it was too maverick a situation for a Mayor, which is unusual, to run for President.

News conference en route to New York, April 5/ The New York Times, 4-6:31.

. . . it's unlikely I'll run for Mayor again. I'm not closing doors, though, because things change so fast. In this busi-

(JOHN V. LINDSAY)

ness, six months is a lifetime, a year is forever.

Interview, New York/ Los Angeles Times, 6-22:(1)16.

Russell B. Long
United States Senator, D–La.

(On the attempted assassination of Alabama Governor and Presidential candidate George Wallace): Governor Wallace is another victim of those who do not understand that human beings must learn to live together peacefully. It is the ballot rather than the bullet which should determine America's destiny.

May 15/ The Washington Post, 5-16:(A)13.

Clark MacGregor
Director, Committee for the Re-election of the President (Nixon)

. . . frustrated, 26 points behind in the polls, with three weeks to go (before the election), (Democratic Presidential nominee Senator) George McGovern–and his confederates–are now engaging in the "politics of desperation." We are witnessing some of the dirtiest tactics and hearing some of the most offensive language ever to appear in an American Presidential campaign. Lashing out wildly, George McGovern has compared the President of the United States to Adolf Hitler, the Republican Party to the Ku Klux Klan, and the United States government to the Third Reich of Nazi Germany. His personal assaults on the President have been characterized by such terms as "most corrupt," "murderous" and "barbaric," and his running mate (Vice-Presidential nominee R. Sargent Shriver) has served as an echo chamber . . . It is said that this (1972 campaign) is a dirty campaign; but all the dirt is being thrown by only one side. The mud-slinging, the name-calling, the unsubstantiated charges, the innuendoes, the guilt by association, the character assassination, the second-hand hearsay are all tactics exclusively employed by the McGovernites and their apologists. President Nixon will remain on the high road, discussing issues of real concern to the American people in a fair, forthright and hard-hitting manner.

News conference, Oct. 16/ The Washington Post, 10-18:(A)16.

Frank Mankiewicz
National political director for Democratic Presidential nominee Senator George McGovern

(On Republican Presidential campaign tactics): This fight reminds me of those British spy stories, Bulldog Drummond vintage, I used to read at school. By chapter five, at the latest, there always came a moment when an English colonel would turn to one of our fellows and say: "These are desperate men and they will stop at nothing." That is exactly how we must think of our Republican opponents in the 1972 election, where billions of dollars and immense power are at stake.

Washington/ San Francisco Examiner, 10-14:4.

Mike Mansfield
United States Senator, D–Mont.

(Advocating a single national Presidential primary, rather than individual state primaries): I've been fed up for years with these circuses taking place in various states. It's expensive and hard on the candidates . . . For the underfinanced and understaffed candidate, the effect is always fatal. For the American voter, the effect is one of bewilderment, confusion and at times revulsion.

The Dallas Times Herald, 3-13:(A)22.

(Referring to the "circus" atmosphere of state Presidential primaries such as in Florida): What is happening in Florida today gives one cause to suggest that the winter quarters of Ringling Brothers-Barnum and Bailey have failed to close on schedule this year . . .

Before the Senate, Washington, March 13/ The Washington Post, 3-14:(A)2.

I think elections (political campaigns) are entirely too long. They become too boring from constant repetition. They cost too much and they wear out the candidates and the people.

Helena, Mont., Oct. 29/
The Washington Post, 10-30:(A)11.

Eugene J. McCarthy
Former United States Senator, D–Minn.

We haven't had a good platform in the Democratic Party, that was projected into the future and dealt with current problems, since 1948. That was a real platform. There were real commitments in it–things like civil rights, public housing, the Marshall Plan, the United Nations and a number of other issues. From that time on, the Democratic platforms have been largely kind of second-guessing Republicans; and they get longer and longer, and they write more and more of the history of the (Franklin) Roosevelt Administration.

TV-radio interview, Washington/
"Meet the Press,"
National Broadcasting Company, 2-6.

(On the decreasing influence of national political-party chairmanships): Being national chairman is like an Irish inheritance. The smaller it is, the more they fight over it.

Washington/
Los Angeles Times, 12-14:(8)4.

Paul N. McCloskey, Jr.
United States Representative, R–Calif.

I run for the Presidency because I got fed up with people lying to us in Washington. They have made deception a habit.

Durham, N.H./
The New York Times, 1-6:23.

(On his being a candidate for the Presidency): The Presidency doesn't hold any terror for me, but the fact that I might not know everything I should in order to make judgments does.

Interview/
The Washington Post,
1-30:(Book World)2.

(Announcing his withdrawal as a candidate for the Republican Presidential nomination): The harsh reality of the situation is that you cannot run a credible Presidential campaign without large sums of money. I obviously don't have that money.

News conference,
Menlo Park, Calif., March 10/
Los Angeles Times, 3-11:(1)18.

Politics is a grueling business. You get so involved in causes, you lose your sensitivity to other people. And there's such an artificial environment in this field. It's all those goddamn cocktail parties where you do half your business. It's the demeaning bit of begging for money to sell yourself. It's the tendency to try and absorb more and more information so that you can do a better and bigger job. You know, a friend once said about me, "Pete's a great guy. He'll do anything for his country, his friends and his family–in that order–which is not very good for his family." He was right.

Interview/"W":
a Fairchild publication, 7-14:4.

George S. McGovern
United States Senator, D–S.D.

(Advocating disclosures of political campaign contributors): For too long, Presidential candidates have catered to special interests, to the rich, to the corporations and others who use secret conduits to mask their real influence. (With full disclosure) power brokers will no longer have any place to hide.

Washington, Feb. 28/
The New York Times, 2-29:1.

I love the United States, but I love it enough so that I want to see some changes made. The American people want to believe in their government, they want to believe in their country; and I'd like to be one of those that provides the kind of leadership that would restore that kind of faith. I don't say I can do it alone; of course, I can't. But the President can help set a new tone in this country. He can help raise the vision and the faith and the hope of the American people. And that's what I'd like to try to do.

Campaigning for the Democratic Presidential nomination/ The New York Times, 5-2:30.

(On whether he thinks he will be the next President of the United States): Yes, I think I will be. I think the conditions of the times almost demand it, if that doesn't sound too arrogant. I think my time has come, maybe that's the way to put it. Candidates are usually elected by historical forces more than by what the candidate does. I think the historical situation today is going to propel me into the White House. I think the country is ready for a change. The country is way ahead of its political leadership. People want new standards, new directions. I think 1972 could be a watershed, the beginning of a new era. I tremble for the future of this country if we don't undertake fundamental change after 1972.

Interview, Washington/ The New York Times Magazine, 5-14:13.

(On the attempted assassination shooting of Alabama Governor and Presidential candidate George Wallace): . . . I must say I am terribly shocked by this savage act. If we have gotten to the point in this country where a public figure can't express his views on the issues of the day, can't seek the Presidency of this country, without being shot, then I tremble for the future of our nation.

Kalamazoo, Mich., May 15/ Los Angeles Herald-Examiner, 5-16:(A)2.

I don't accept the notion that I'm a left winger. I don't think it's left-wing to say that corporations ought to pay their fair share of taxes. I don't think it's left-wing to say we ought to end the (Vietnam) war. I don't think it's left-wing to say people who are hungry ought to be fed, people who are jobless ought to have jobs.

Interview, Detroit/ The New York Times, 5-19:42.

(On the controversy concerning alleged ITT contributions to the Republican Party in return for favorable government legal rulings): In the case of ITT, we saw how a timely political contribution, plus a good paper-shredding machine, can erase the antitrust laws from the statute books of this nation.

Before California Federation of Teachers, Coronado, Calif., May 29/ Los Angeles Times, 5-30:(1)3.

I don't want to be President if I have to make deals that compromise my essential convictions. This country can always get a new President, but I can't get a new conscience.

Interview, San Francisco, June 2/ Los Angeles Herald-Examiner, 6-4:(A)9.

What is this "Southern strategy" (of President Nixon's)? It is not very complicated. When you ask about education for your children, it replies: Fear the black man. When you seek peace abroad and reasoned discourse at home, it replies: Fear the young. When you demand jobs and expanding opportunity, it replies: Fear the poor.

Columbia, S.C., June 28/ Los Angeles Times, 6-29:(1)6.

(On his candidacy for the Democratic Presidential nomination): In every campaign I've ever had since '56, that's been the standard line against me—that I'm too radical. Stooge of Walter Reuther; stooge of the left-wingers; stooge for John Kennedy; always an ADA apologist. I do consider myself a radical in the sense that I am willing to go beyond the conventional view. I think fundamental change is what's needed; so in that sense I don't mind people calling me a radical.

Interview/Life, 7-7:41.

I'm not where I am as a serious candidate for the Presidency because I have a narrow base . . . I believe I have the best and broadest grass-roots organization ever built in American politics. That organization is going to be at the service of every Democrat running for office in 1972, from the courthouse right on up to the Congress and the White House. I believe that many people who are now fearful of my candidacy are going to hail it as one of the great steps forward for our Party when they feel its impact.

TV-radio interview, Miami Beach/ "Meet the Press," National Broadcasting Company, 7-9.

George S. McGovern
United States Senator, D–S.D.; Democratic Presidential nominee

To anyone in this hall or beyond who doubts the ability of Democrats to join together in common cause, I say never underestimate the power of (President) Richard Nixon to bring harmony to Democratic ranks. He is our unwitting unifier and the fundamental issue of this campaign. And all of us together are going to help him redeem the pledge he made 10 years ago: "Next year you won't have Richard Nixon to kick around any more."

Accepting the Democratic Presidential nomination, Miami Beach, July 14/ Los Angeles Herald-Examiner, 7-14:(A)3.

(On his nomination for President): This is a people's nomination; and next January we will restore the government to the people of this country. And I believe that American politics will never be quite the same again. We are entering a new period of important and hopeful change in America—a period comparable to those eras that unleashed such remarkable ferment in the periods of Jefferson and Jackson and Roosevelt. I treasure this nomination especially because it comes after vigorous competition with the ablest men and women our Party has to offer: my old and trusted friend and neighbor, (Senator) Hubert Humphrey; a gracious and good man from the state of Maine, (Senator) Ed Muskie; a tough fighter for his own convictions, (Senator) Scoop Jackson of Washington; and a brave and spirited woman, (Representative) Shirley Chisholm; a wise and effective lawmaker from Arkansas, (Representative) Wilbur Mills; a man from North Carolina who over the years has opened new vistas in education and public excellence, Terry Sanford; the leader who in 1968 combined both the travail and the hope of the American spirit, Senator Eugene McCarthy. And I was moved, as were all of you, by the appearance in this convention hall of the Governor of Alabama, George Wallace. His votes in the primaries showed clearly the depth of discontent in this country; and his courage in the face of pain and adversity is the mark of a man of boundless will.

Accepting the Democratic Presidential nomination, Miami Beach, July 14/ The New York Times, 7-15:11.

(On the AFL-CIO executive council's opposition to his Presidential nomination): Now, either that's a calamity or it's a signal that a new day is here in which we're going to test now over the next few months whether the union power brokers are alive or dead. And I don't know the answer to that. But I must tell you that I won the nomination over their active opposition, so that it may be a signal of things to come . . . The question is whether Governors any longer can deliver their states. Can a Mayor deliver his city? Can a union leader deliver his union? Can a priest deliver his parish? Those are the kinds of questions that I think we are now waiting for answers on.

Interview, Custer, S.D., July 19/ The Washington Post, 7-20:(A)1,6.

The Republicans are afraid to tell us where that $10 million has come from that is bank-rolling their campaign. We're proud of the fact that the McGovern-Eagleton

(GEORGE S. McGOVERN)

campaign is financed by contributions of thousands of people all over the country. We published every name.

News conference, Custer, S.D., July 24/ The Washington Post, 7-25:(A)2.

(On Vice-Presidential nominee Senator Thomas Eagleton's revealing that he had been hospitalized three times for nervous exhaustion): . . . I think Tom Eagleton is fully qualified in mind, body and spirit to be the Vice President of the United States and, if necessary, to take on the Presidency at a moment's notice . . . I know fully the whole history of his illness. I know what his performance has been in the Senate over the last four years and I don't have the slightest doubt about the wisdom of my judgment in selecting him as my running mate, nor would I have any hesitance at all trusting the U.S. government to his hands. I wouldn't have hesitated one moment if I had known everything Senator Eagleton said (about his health) here today.

News conference, Custer, S.D., July 25/ The New York Times, 7-26:20.

(On Vice-Presidential nominee Senator Thomas Eagleton's revealing that he had been hospitalized three times for nervous exhaustion): I don't believe in polls in terms of an issue like this. I don't think they're very helpful. It's really trying to make a judgment of what the implications are of this on substantive grounds. Does it any way impair his capacity for leadership? Does it arouse anxiety in a public that's already nervous and uptight about its national leadership? Does it damage our chances of winning the election? Those are all the things that I frankly cannot answer at this point . . . If the campaign were to turn into a debate on the Vice President's medical history, it would be a catastrophe . . . I said I was backing him 1,000 per cent and I stay with that. There won't be any change made that is not a mutual decision. I will not ask Senator Eagleton to leave the ticket unless he and I jointly reach a decision that that is a proper thing to do.

News conference, July 30/ Los Angeles Times, 7-31:(1)14.

(Announcing the withdrawal of Senator Thomas Eagleton as Vice-Presidential nominee because of the disclosure of past health problems): . . . the public debate over Senator Eagleton's past medical history continues to divert attention from the great national issues that need to be discussed. I have referred to the growing pressures to ask for Senator Eagleton's withdrawal. We have also seen growing vocal support for his candidacy. Senator Eagleton and I agree that the paramount needs of the Democratic Party and the nation in 1972 are unity and a full discussion of the real issues before the country. Continued debate between those who oppose his candidacy and those who favor it will serve to further divide the Party and the nation. Therefore, we have jointly agreed that the best course is for Senator Eagleton to step aside.

News conference, July 31/ The New York Times, 8-2:21.

Now we move toward what President Nixon has called the clearest political choice of a century. I agree with the President. For it is not just a choice of men, but between competing principles and traditions and purpose. It is a decision between the belief that political power exists to serve private power, and the conviction that political leadership must take up the people's cause against those who seek advantage at their expense. It is a decision between the desire to preserve things as they are, against the confidence that this nation can do better, that life in this nation can be more rewarding—for every citizen. It is a choice—this choice of the century—between your hopes and your fears, between today's America and the one you want for your children; between those who believe we must abandon our ideals to present realities, and those who wish to shape reality to our American ideals.

Broadcast address,
Washington, Aug. 5/
The New York Times, 8-6:(1)36.

I would have been surprised if (Democrat and former Treasury Secretary John) Connally had been for me. I don't think it's just an accident that all these big fat-cat tycoons are lining up behind (President) Richard Nixon. Does it really surprise anyone that the big oil millionaires in Texas are supporting Richard Nixon? He's not for us. He's not for the ordinary people, and neither are those oil millionaires. These are Mr. Connally's friends. They're for Connally, they're for Nixon, they're for the people that are milking the ordinary citizen of this country. I never expected their support, and I don't regard it as a handicap that these selfish interests of privilege and greed are lined up behind Richard Nixon.

Campaigning for the Presidential
election, Manchester, N.H., Aug. 10/
Los Angeles Times, 8-11:(1)10.

(Accusing the Nixon Administration of being at least indirectly responsible for a break-in at Democratic National Committee headquarters in Washington June 17): What is to prevent an Administration that co-operates with that kind of thing from wire-tapping your house, or your union hall, or something else they want to get? Now, this is the kind of thing that you expect from a person like Hitler. You would not expect it from a country like this that is supposed to be a free society.

Campaigning for the Presidential
election, Lordstown, Ohio, Aug. 15/
Los Angeles Times, 8-16:(1)7.

. . . if I'm going to be elected President, we have to reach out beyond the groups that got us the nomination. That doesn't mean that I have to betray my principles; but it does mean that in dealing with people I've got to make a deliberate effort to ask for support from Party regulars. I did call (Chicago) Mayor (Richard) Daley . . . Some people with tender skin are going to be offended by that. But the fact remains that Mayor Daley is a power in Illinois. If we want to carry that state, it's helpful to have his support. Anybody with a little common sense who wants to see me elected will see that as a wise move, not as a betrayal of principle.

Interview/Time, 8-21:10.

The only way the President (Nixon) can achieve a new majority in this (forthcoming Presidential) election is to trick the vast majority of the voters. So just as he tried to do when John Kennedy was the Democratic nominee, Richard Nixon is now trying to make the nation fear the Democrats. He is trying to make people afraid that Democrats are extremists who want to tax too much and spend more than we have. But that is the oldest lie in the reactionary Republican book of partisan smears. And just because the election comes a week after Halloween is no excuse to use the campaign as a time to scare the country.

At AFL-CIO picnic,
Oakland, Calif., Sept. 4/
Los Angeles Times, 9-5:(1)28.

I know this fight (for the Presidency) is uphill. I know that I'm behind in the polls. I know we're short of money. I know we've made some mistakes. But I've had to fight uphill every single step of the way in 16 years in public life, so this is nothing new to me. I'm ready for this uphill fight against (President) Richard Nixon, and I think we're going to win. I think we're going to win primarily for one reason, and that's because we have some sense of the greatness and the decency and the goodness of America that the people of this country want restored to the very highest councils of government.

Campaigning for the forthcoming
Presidential election, Seattle, Sept. 4/
The New York Times, 9-6:32.

(GEORGE S. McGOVERN)

I'm involved in this campaign for the Presidency because I believe that no political party can serve two masters. You cannot serve the people and the enemies of the people at the same time. And, by heritage and by choice, I believe that to be the fundamental difference between the philosophy of the Democratic Party and the Republican Party in this country. As Democrats, we are not beyond making mistakes; but for 175 years we have, year in and year out, been the party that spoke for the people of this country. And all too often, the Republican Party—and especially under this (Nixon) Administration—is a party whose heart breathes for the special interests and the forces of privilege in this land.

Campaigning for the forthcoming Presidential election, Barberton, Ohio, Sept. 4/ U.S. News & World Report, 9-18:79.

(On alleged Republican Party connection with the bugging and break-in at Democratic Party headquarters at Washington's Watergate apartments earlier this year): The American people have begun to realize how serious the spreading scandal of the Watergate is . . . what has been called a caper is, in fact, a serious crime with connections reaching deep into the Republican apparatus. It now appears that the headquarters of one of the two major political parties in the United States was treated, for a prolonged period, as if it were the headquarters of a foreign government.

News conference, Albuquerque, N.M., Sept. 9/ San Francisco Examiner & Chronicle, 9-10:(A)4.

(On the government investigation of the alleged break-in and bugging of the Watergate apartments headquarters of the Democratic Party earlier in the year): The Nixon Administration asks us to believe that the Watergate Five, plus two lowly White House operatives, dreamed up and carried out this shabby scheme to spy on the Democratic Party all on their own, with no authority from above. (The indictments are a) blatant miscarriage of justice . . . ordered to spare the White House embarrassment in an election year. Through their evasiveness and delaying tactics, (the Nixon Administration has) made this case of political espionage a major issue in this Presidential campaign. What is involved here is not only the political life of this nation, but the very morality of our leaders at a time when the United States desperately needs to revitalize its moral standards. And that is why I shall pursue this case the length and breadth of this land.

News conference, Washington, Sept. 16/ The Washington Post, 9-17:(A)16.

(On the government's investigation of the alleged break-in and bugging of the Watergate apartments headquarters of the Democratic Party in Washington earlier in the year): I charge that the Nixon Administration commanded that the Democratic bugging case be whitewashed by the Justice Department and the grand jury under its control. I charge that the failure of the grand jury to determine who ordered and paid for this act of political espionage—and who received the stolen information—was engineered by the White House through its Attorney General, Mr. (Richard) Kleindienst. I charge that at all stages of this investigation it remained a political case under the total direction and control of Mr. Nixon's political operatives, working through Mr. Kleindienst.

News conference, Washington, Sept. 16/ The Dallas Times Herald, 9-17:(A)16.

I don't think you're going to see (President) Richard Nixon in Logan County (W. Va.). He sneaks out once in a while in a helicopter and drops in someplace for a few minutes. But he's sitting there in the White House, smugly on top of his Gallup

Poll, thinking that everything is safe and sound and that all he has to do is print those slogans around the country—"Re-elect the President." He doesn't even tell us what his name is. He just says, "Re-elect the President." But if my name was Nixon, I'd keep it a secret, too.

Campaigning for the forthcoming Presidential election, Logan, W. Va., Sept. 18/ The New York Times, 9-19:38.

I make no apology for changing my mind in light of additional insight and reflection. Indeed, a leader who is afraid to change his mind for fear of losing face is no leader at all.

Before United Press International editors and publishers, Washington, Oct. 2/ The Washington Post, 10-3:(A)9.

The Nixon Administration is the most morally bankrupt Administration in the entire history of our country. At no time in the history of our land has corruption been so deep, so pervasive as it is today . . . The influence of big money is corrupting the integrity of government on a scale never seen before.

At Democratic fund-raising dinner, New York, Oct. 2/ San Francisco Examiner, 10-3:4.

(On his dropping, earlier in the year, of Vice Presidential nominee Senator Thomas Eagleton because of Eagleton's reported health problems): To those who are troubled that a Presidential candidate could back his chosen running mate "1,000 per cent" and then ask him to step down a week later, I can only say that, in politics as in real life, compassion must sometimes yield to more reflective and painful judgment . . . I took the course that I believe was in the national interest—a course that was only possible with Tom's respect and full cooperation. We wanted this campaign to center not on the issue of one man's history, but on the great issue of war and peace, the American economy, the quality of our society and the condition of our constitutional government.

Campaigning for the forthcoming Presidential election, St. Louis, Oct. 7/ The Washington Post, 10-8:(A)2.

(On alleged Republican espionage activities against the Democrats): During 18 years in politics, I have never seen such efforts to poison the political dialogue. These Republican politicians have fouled the political atmosphere for all of us who see public service as a high calling. They do not seek to defeat the Democratic Party—they seek to destroy it.

Television campaign address, Oct. 25/ Los Angeles Times, 10-26:(1)16.

George S. McGovern
United States Senator, D–S.D.

(On the just-concluded Presidential election in which he was defeated by President Nixon): The first Presidential concession that I remember hearing was that of Adlai Stevenson in 1952. He recalled the old Lincoln story of the boy who had stubbed his toe in the dark, and when he was asked how it felt, he replied, "Well, it hurts too much to laugh, but I'm too old to cry." It does hurt all of us in this auditorium and many others across the country to lose; but we're not going to shed any tears tonight about the great joy that this campaign has brought to us over the past two years. All of the satisfaction and joy that we have found in these past 22 months are not going to be washed away with the tears and regrets on one night. We have found the greatest outpouring of energy and love that any political effort has ever inspired, at least in my lifetime . . . The Presidency belongs to someone else; but the glory of those devoted working friends and their dedication to the noble ideals of this country sustains us now and it will sustain our country. We will shed no tears because all of this effort,

(GEORGE S. McGOVERN)

I am positive, will bear fruit for years to come.

Concession speech, Sioux Falls, S.D., Nov. 7/ The New York Times, 11-9:22.

(On the just-concluded Presidential election in which he was defeated by President Nixon): I know there's going to be a lot of talk about how humiliating my defeat was. It won't bother me. I feel quite secure in my own person. I've taken quite a pounding along that line for quite a while. During the campaign it was widely predicted that I'd be overwhelmingly rejected. I resisted the thought, but it's certainly nothing new to be told that I am unacceptable . . . I don't regard my loss so much as a personal rejection, as a rejection of the things I stood for. Many people who are far greater than I am have been rejected in history and then turned out in the long run to be right. There's no doubt at all in my mind that, if history follows its likely course, those things I advocated will come to be embraced by the majority four to eight years from now. You have to remember that at various times in history the forces of irrationalism and fear have temporarily triumphed. Then the other side has its day.

Interview, Nov. 8/ Life, 11-17:12.

(On the recently-concluded Presidential election in which he was defeated by President Nixon): As I look back on the campaign, we (Democrats) made mistakes. (But) the other (Republican) side made deliberate deceptions. There's a vast difference, which I think the public did not comprehend. I think they equated mistakes of the heart as being serious—in fact, more serious—than massive crimes, like the bombing of innocent civilians in Indochina or sinister plots like the espionage and sabotage (against the Democrats) carried out by the Committee to Re-elect the President, or secret campaign funds running to tens of millions of dollars. Those were not mistakes. Those were conniving, deceitful, underhanded deals. Any one of them should have been enough to have defeated this (Nixon) Administration—but they weren't.

Interview, St. Thomas, Virgin Islands, Nov. 12/ The New York Times, 11-14:36.

(On the just-concluded Presidential election in which he was defeated by President Nixon): The only way a Democrat could have won in 1972 would be if (Alabama Governor George) Wallace had run as an independent and siphoned off the 15 or 20 million votes I'm convinced he would have gotten away from Nixon had he run . . . I think that, of the 45 million votes Nixon got, I think Wallace would have gotten 20 million. He was much stronger in '72 than in '68. He had become a fairly acceptable figure to many rank-and-file Democrats by the time the primaries were over.

Interview, St. Thomas, Virgin Islands, Nov. 13/ Los Angeles Times, 11-14:(1)7.

John J. McKeithen
Former Governor of Louisiana

(On his leaving the Democratic Party): If (Senator George) McGovern is elected President, God save America. I have no hesitancy about leaving the Democratic Party. The Democratic Party left me.

The New York Times, 8-13:(1)36.

George Meany
President, American Federation of Labor-Congress of Industrial Organizations

(On New York Mayor John Lindsay's running for the Democratic Presidential nomination): . . . my antipathy toward him is based on a lot of reasons. For one, I'm a New Yorker, and I see what a mess he made of my city, and I don't want him here in Washington. Another thing: He stood up in Central Park and advised kids to resist the (military) draft. I can't buy that kind of a guy. Maybe I'm old-fashioned. I'm *that* old-fashioned, anyway.

Interview, Washington/
U.S. News & World Report, 2-21:31.

I'm not predicting, but it's my belief that he (President Nixon) is not nearly in as good shape as some of his people think. They think he's a shoe-in (for 1972 re-election), and a lot of newspaper political experts think that. I don't think so. I think this business of making these great television addresses can be overdone. Every television appearance he makes is good. I mean, he's a real pro. But the whole trouble is that, 36 hours after he makes that TV appearance, everybody has second thoughts. They wonder . . . More and more people whom I meet say that it's not that they don't like Nixon or something. They say, "We don't know what he's going to do next." I tell them, "It's not so bad that I don't know what he's going to do next. What worries me is I am not sure *he* knows what he's going to do next."

Interview, Washington/
U.S. News & World Report, 2-21:34.

If I were to make a bet now, hell, I'd bet that (President) Nixon's going to win (the upcoming Presidential election). I haven't the slightest doubt about that, in spite of all the nasty things I've been saying about him.

San Francisco Examiner, 4-17:30.

I will not endorse, I will not support and I will not vote for Richard Nixon for President of the United States. I will not endorse, I will not support and I will not vote for George McGovern for President of the United States.

News conference,
Washington, July 19/
Los Angeles Herald-Examiner, 7-19:(A)2.

There is a misconception that I am an organization Democrat. There is a misconception that Meany will come home to the Democratic Party (in the November Presidential election). Neither the Democratic nor the Republican Party has been my home. My home is the labor movement.

The Dallas Times Herald, 8-31:(B)2.

Arthur Miller
Playwright

When I said, "I hate politics," that doesn't mean I turn my back on politics. You can't. Politics is something like tying your shoes or making a living. And, God help us, I know our fate is political. Yet I also think politics now is becoming less and less connected to what's really going on. It's never been so true as it is now that it hardly matters which party is in.

Interview, Roxbury, Conn./
The New York Times Magazine,
2-13:38.

Wilbur D. Mills
United States Representative, D–Ark.

(On why he would not accept the Democratic nomination as Vice President): As Chairman of the Ways and Means Committee, I can contact the President, whoever he may be, quite readily on the telephone. As a Vice President, I don't know whether he'd listen to me or not.

TV-radio interview/
"Face the Nation,"
Columbia Broadcasting System, 6-4.

John N. Mitchell
Former Attorney General of the United States; Former re-election campaign director for President Nixon

(Denying any prior knowledge of the alleged Republican bugging and break-in at the Watergate apartments headquarters of the Democratic Party in Washington earlier in the year): Anyone in a campaign who has ordered something like that should have his head examined. That whole disgusting episode was counter-productive. I still don't know how it happened.

Interview, Washington/ Los Angeles Times, 10-19:(1)20.

Edmund S. Muskie
United States Senator, D–Maine

. . . the President must lead. A President must find and touch the common chords of our experience, challenge us to respond to our best instincts, to realize America's ancient dream that somewhere on this planet there can be full justice for every member of a society. It would be foolish to blame all the nation's ills on the present (Nixon) Administration; some are part of the stresses of modern society; others are rooted in the injustices of history. But government can lead; it can be truthful. And if our present leadership had been candid with the country –if they had been straightforward–we could have done far more than we have . . . I am seeking the Presidency not merely to change Presidents but to change the country. I intend to lead, to ask you to make America what it was to Abraham Lincoln–"the last best hope of mankind." I intend to ask you to try, and to be willing to try again if we fail. And I intend to ask everyone of you to pay a fair share of the costs of a decent society . . . Ultimately, of course, what is at stake is your future. I am not telling you that I can guarantee the best of all possible worlds. All I am asking is that we pledge a new beginning.

Broadcast address announcing his candidacy for President/ Columbia Broadcasting System TV and radio, 1-4.

(Concerning his statement last year that the Democrats could not win the 1972 Presidential election with a black Vice-Presidential nominee): My statement was not an expression of preference; it was a statement of judgment as to what I thought were the political realities . . . I happen to resent the fact that those are the realities, and I commit myself to eliminate, insofar as I can and insofar as it is in my power, the discrimination which results in that kind of reality.

Miami, Jan. 8/ The Dallas Times Herald, 1-9:(A)12.

The recent charges about Nixon Admininstration favoritism for ITT (in exchange for ITT political contributions) have again shaken the confidence of Americans in the integrity of the political process and the even-handedness of government.

Campaigning for the Democratic Presidential nomination, Tampa, Fla., March 12/ The Washington Post, 3-13:(A)1.

(Referring to his emotional attack on a newspaper editorial which was critical of his wife): For three years now I've been told I have no emotions. So on one occasion I show emotion about an attack on my wife; and if I can't show emotion in that instance, I guess the conclusion is that I've got to be an iceberg as President.

Interview/Time, 3-13:20.

(On the victory by Alabama Governor George Wallace in the Florida Democratic Presidential primary): Of course we know that I have lost. But what disturbs me most is not that I have suffered a personal defeat . . . The results reveal to a greater extent than I had imagined that some of the worst instincts human beings are capable of are too strong an influence in our elections. George Wallace's victory here is a threat to the unity of this country . . . to the underlying values of humanism and decency and progress . . . George Wallace believes that the way to advance himself is to exploit the fears of the people he appeals to. He is a demagogue of the worst possible kind. I pledge to you that, as long as his kind of politics and his kind of values threaten the nobility of our country,

I will fight him with everything that I've got.

Miami, March 14/ Los Angeles Times, 3-15:(1)15.

(On his finishing fourth in the Wisconsin Democratic Presidential primary): I've always said that winning isn't everything. And now I want to say that losing isn't *anything.*

Milwaukee/Life, 4-14:(A)48.

I have made the decision to withdraw . . . to withdraw from active participation in the remaining Presidential primaries. I do so with regret, but I have no choice. I do not have the money to continue . . . I will continue to speak out on the issues around the country and from the Senate floor. I will be more actively involved in legislative work, pressing for the changes in public policy I have been urging in the course of the campaign. The American people, in the course of the primaries to date, have clearly indicated their determination to achieve at least four basic goals: 1) an end to the war in Vietnam; 2) an anti-inflation policy which controls prices as well as wages and which produces jobs instead of unemployment; 3) a more equitable distribution of the burdens and the benefits of our society; and 4) an open government which confides in them, responds to their needs and opinions and which is free from the corrupting influence of special interests. Those goals are my goals as well, and I will continue to fight for them. To achieve them requires the defeat of (President) Richard Nixon in November. I am committed to that objective.

Broadcast address, Washington, April 27/ The New York Times, 4-28:22.

(On the recent attempted assassination of Alabama Governor and Presidential candidate George Wallace): We must relearn the fundamental truth that there is no short cut to change in a free society. The assassin seeks a short cut to change. The burning of buildings, the shouting down of those with whom we disagree, the bombing of churches—these are attempts to find a short cut to change.

At La Salle Academy, Providence, R.I., May 19/ The Washington Post, 5-20:(A)2.

(On his losing bid for the Democratic Presidential nomination): (Senator Hubert) Humphrey has his constituency. It is the blacks, the Jews and the elderly. They love him. (Senator George) McGovern has his. It is the young, the anti-war groups and the blue-collar workers and the suburbanites. (Alabama Governor George) Wallace has his in the working man. But Muskie? He had no constituency. He was squeezed out.

Interview, New York/ "W": a Fairchild publication, 6-30:6.

Richard E. Neustadt
Professor of Government, Harvard University; Chairman, Democratic Party Platform Committee

I think one misunderstands the purpose and character of a (political party's) platform either now or as it has been in the past, if one takes it to be a detailed prescription which a candidate must follow in detail during his campaign or which a President and Congress will follow in specific detail thereafter. I think you will find that, in general, platforms do forecast the policy attitudes of Administrations when they come in. And if you look back over a period of, say, a decade, you will find that the pledges in particular platforms are pretty thoroughly carried out by parties; but if you try to apply this year-by-year or month-by-month, it won't work. The main significance of a platform is its use before it is completed, not afterwards. What is critical are the terms under which the platform is adopted, under which agreement is sought and reached on a range of goals upon which the party delegates can agree. The terms and conditions under

(RICHARD E. NEUSTADT)

which goals are set forth in a platform very much represent, though in rough (form), the voter coalition to which a majority of that party convened in convention hopes to appeal and the aspirations it hopes to serve; and those terms and conditions set by the final adoption of the platform are of very considerable importance. Thus, what goes into making the platform is more important in the nominating process than the specific terms that come out.

TV-radio interview, Washington/ "Meet the Press," National Broadcasting Company, 7-2.

Richard M. Nixon
President of the United States

(On keeping Vice President Spiro Agnew as his running mate in the 1972 Presidential election): My view is that one should not break up a winning combination. I believe that the Vice President has handled his difficult assignments with dignity, with courage. He has at times been a man of controversy; but when a man has done a good job in a position, when he has been part of a winning team, I believe that he should stay on the team. That is my thinking at this time.

Television interview, Washington/ Columbia Broadcasting System, 1-2.

. . . my strong point is not rhetoric; it isn't chop and chip; it isn't big promises—those things that breed the glamor and the excitement that people call charisma and warmth. My strong point—if I have a strong point—is performance. I always do more than I say, and I always produce more than I promise . . .

Television interview, Washington/ Columbia Broadcasting System, 1-2.

There are more candidates for the Presidency in this chamber today than there probably have been at any one time in the whole history of the Republic. And there is an honest difference of opinion, not only between the (political) parties, but within each party, on some foreign-policy issues and on some domestic-policy issues. However, there are great national problems that are so vital that they transcend partisanship. And so let us have our debates. Let us have our honest differences. But let us join in keeping the national interest first. Let us join in making sure that legislation the nation needs does not become hostage to the political interests of any party or any person.

State of the Union address, Washington, Jan. 20/ The New York Times, 1-21:18.

(On the current controversy surrounding charges of favorable legal action toward ITT by the Justice Dept. in return for political contributions): . . . It is significant to note that ITT became the great conglomerate that it was in the two previous Administrations primarily, the (John) Kennedy Administration and the (Lyndon) Johnson Administration. It grew and grew and grew, and nothing was done to stop it. In this Administration, we moved on ITT. We are proud of that record. We moved on it effectively. We required the greatest divestiture in the history of the antitrust law. We also, as a result of the consent decree, required that ITT not have additional acquisitions so that it became larger. Now . . . that not only was a good settlement, it was a very good settlement. I think, under the circumstances, that gives the lie to the suggestion that this Administration, in the handling of the ITT case, just using one example, was doing a favor for ITT. If we wanted to do a favor for ITT, we could just continue to do what the two previous Administrations had done, and that is nothing; let ITT continue to grow. But we moved on it and moved effectively.

News conference, March 24/ The Washington Post, 4-21:(A)24.

(Saying that he will not make a political issue out of Democratic Vice-Presidential nominee Senator Thomas Eagleton's revealing that he had been hospitalized three times for nervous exhaustion): The issues that divide the opposite side and this Administration are so wide—in fact, the clearest choice in this century—that we must campaign on issues. There is an honest difference of opinion on foreign policy, an honest difference of opinion on domestic policy and an honest difference of opinion on most major defense issues.

News conference, Washington, July 27/ The New York Times, 7-28:27.

When it gets down to the final tough decision, he (Vice President Agnew) is, from my evaluation, always cool and poised, and is one who therefore could be expected to make decisions in the future in a calm, cool, judicial way. Now, that does not mean that all of his decisions will be good, because calm, cool, judicial men make bad decisions just as emotional men sometimes make good decisions. But my point is that, in all of the so-called mini-crises and major crises we have had in the Administration, he has been strong, courageous and loyal.

News conference, Washington/ The Washington Post, 8-8:(A)19.

I don't think the youth vote is in anyone's pocket. I think they will be independent. They are casting their first vote. We (Republicans) have just as good a shot at it as the other (Democratic) side, and we're going to get it.

At young Nixon voters rally, Miami Beach, Aug. 22/ Los Angeles Times, 8-23:(1)1.

Six weeks ago, our opponents (Democratic Presidential nominee Senator George McGovern and his supporters) in their convention rejected many of the great principles of the Democratic Party. To those millions who have been driven out of your home in the Democratic Party, we say come home—not to another party but to the great principles we Americans believe in together. I ask you to join us, not in a coalition held together only by a desire to gain power. I ask you to join us as members of a new American majority bound together by our common ideals. I ask everyone listening to me tonight—Democrats, Republicans and independents—to join our new majority; not on the basis of the party label you wear on your lapel, but what you believe in your hearts.

Accepting the Republican Presidential nomination, Miami Beach, Aug. 23/ Los Angeles Times, 8-24:(1)21.

(On the alleged Republican Party connection with the break-in at Democratic headquarters at the Watergate apartments in Washington earlier in the year): With regard to who is investigating it now, I think it would be well to notice that the FBI is conducting a full field investigation. The Department of Justice, of course, is in charge of the prosecution and presenting the matter to the grand jury. The Senate Banking and Currency Committee is conducting an investigation. The Government Accounting Office, an independent agency, is conducting an investigation of those aspects which involve the campaign spending law. Now, with all of these investigations that are being conducted, I don't believe that adding another special prosecutor would serve any useful purpose . . . Within our own staff, under my direction, Counsel to the President Mr. (John) Dean has conducted a complete investigation of all leads which might involve any present members of the White House staff, or anybody in the government. I can say categorically that his investigation indicates that no one in the White House staff, no one in this Administration, presently employed, was involved in this very bizarre incident.

News conference, San Clemente, Calif., Aug. 29/ The Washington Post, 8-30:(A)16.

(RICHARD M. NIXON)

We are seeking in this (forthcoming Presidential) election something that no President has had since 1956, with the exception of President (Lyndon) Johnson in '64 after his landslide, and that is a majority, because there was none in 1960 and there was none in 1968 because of third-party candidates. I think what we need now is a clear majority of the American people. That means a clear mandate, mandate for what I have described as change that works, for progress . . . One thing I should mention when I speak of the new majority, I reject the idea of a new coalition. A coalition is not a healthy thing in a free society. Coalition automatically adds up the young against the old, the black(s) against the whites, the Catholics against the Protestants, the city people against the country people, et cetera, et cetera. What we are doing is to make our appeal across the board and try to build a new majority on the basis of people from all the groups supporting us on the basis of what we believe.

News conference, San Clemente, Calif., Aug. 29/ The Washington Post, 8-30:(A)16.

(On why he has not done much campaigning for the forthcoming Presidential election): . . . I believe my first obligation is to do my job as President of the United States of America. That is the reason why, whenever it is necessary, when I feel it is necessary to stay in Washington to do the job that the people elected me to do, I will be there. When I can, I will be campaigning.

At Republican fund-raising dinner, San Francisco/ Los Angeles Herald-Examiner, 10-1:(A)14.

(On Democratic Presidential nominee Senator George McGovern's election campaigning): I am not going to characterize the Senator's campaign. As a matter of fact, I don't question his motives. I think he deeply believes in a number of actions that he believes that this government should take, that I think would be disastrous for this nation . . . Consequently, as far as I am concerned, I will discuss those issues; but I am not going to raise any doubts about his motives. Incidentally, I have no complaint with his doubts about mine. That is his choice.

News conference, Washington, Oct. 5/ The New York Times, 10-6:28.

(On alleged Republican espionage activities against Democratic headquarters at the Watergate apartments in Washington earlier in the year): One thing that has always puzzled me about it is why anybody would have tried to get anything out of the Watergate. Be that as it may, that decision having been made at a lower level, with which I had no knowledge . . . I certainly feel that, under the circumstances, that we have to look at what has happened and to put the matter into perspective . . . (In the FBI investigation of the case) I wanted every lead carried out to the end, because I wanted to be sure that no member of the White House staff and no man or woman in a position of major responsibility in the Committee for the Re-election (of the President) had anything to do with this kind of reprehensible activity.

News conference, Washington, Oct. 5/ Los Angeles Times, 10-30:(1)18.

. . . with the advent of television, we have to realize that (political) campaigns now bore the people to death, because they are simply too long and they see them on the tube a lot. Then you can read about it in the newspaper or put it aside. But when the evening news comes on, month after month—it isn't just two of the regular campaigns: you hear of the convention; you hear it between the conventions; but then the campaign begins two years before when they start speculating about who is going to run in the primaries and then the polls are taken; then you have the primary campaigns. By the time you get to the election, the people say, "Oh no; not more politics."

Interview, Nov. 5/
The New York Times, 11-10:20.

. . . the liberal establishment, during the four years I have been in office, thought that I was out of touch with the country. That is not true. What this (forthcoming Presidential) election will demonstrate is that out across the country—and including up in the Northeast, which is considered to be the playground of the limousine liberal set—you find that a solid majority of the American people do not want to go to the Far Left. What this election will demonstrate is that, when a candidate (Democratic Presidential nominee Senator George McGovern) takes basically an extreme position on issues, he inevitably splits his party and assures his defeat, even when it is a majority party; always when it is a minority party, but even when it is a majority party, as is the Democratic Party.

Interview, Nov. 5/
San Francisco Examiner & Chronicle, 11-12:(A)15.

(On the just-concluded Presidential election in which he defeated Democratic Presidential nominee Senator George McGovern): I tried to conduct myself in this campaign in a way that would not divide our country—not divide it regionally or by parties or in any other way, because I firmly believe that what unites America today is infinitely more important than those things which divide us . . . I had noted in listening to the returns a few minutes ago that several commentators have reflected on the fact that this may be one of the great political victories of all time. In terms of votes, that may be true. But in terms of what a victory really is, a huge landslide margin means nothing at all, unless it is a victory for America. It will be a victory for America only if in these next four years we, all of us, can work together to achieve our common great goals of peace at home and peace for all nations in the world; and for that new progress and prosperity which all Americans deserve.

Victory speech to the nation,
Washington, Nov. 7/
The New York Times, 11-9:21.

Robert Novak
Political columnist

Every (political) campaign has a character of its own. Most politicians don't understand that. They always used to say that the French general staff made the tragic error of always fighting the last war. Politicians make the mistake of always fighting the last campaign. They extrapolate information from the past that doesn't apply to the present.

Interview/
The Washington Post, 8-20:(Potomac)46.

Dallin H. Oaks
President,
Brigham Young University

I hope we can achieve a moratorium on the use of the words "liberal" and "conservative" on this campus. I am persuaded by observation and experience that the damage caused by the use of these words far exceeds the value of the communication they foster. Among intimate friends, thoroughly familiar with one another's connotations and intent, these words may convey a clear meaning. But when these labels go out into the world to be repeated by others less knowledgeable and intimate, they become the enemies of understanding. So many different meanings proceed under these labels —political, religious and otherwise. Under the category of "otherwise" are the characterizations of my children, who say I am liberal with love and praise but conservative with allowance and the family car. When we are tempted to employ these labels, I suggest that we substitute more precise descriptions. The possibilities include "loyal

(DALLIN H. OAKS)

or disloyal," "dynamic or immovable," "wise or unwise" and scores of others.

At his inauguration/ The National Observer, 2-19:11.

Lawrence F. O'Brien
Chairman,
Democratic National Committee

I want the Democratic Party to regain the Presidency. (But the candidate must be able to offer leadership) that unites rather than divides, that does not seek to startle the people with sudden, ill-planned shiftings of course. Those in power today have defaulted; and now it is up to us, as the party that claims to represent the American people, to provide the answers and lead the way.

At (John and Robert) Kennedy Memorial Dinner, Los Angeles, April 14/ Los Angeles Herald-Examiner, 4-15:(A)3.

If any institution is to remain alive in a self-governing society, it must respond truthfully to the voices of those being squeezed by the problems—to the voices of those who see their lives destroyed, their sons dead, their hopes blighted, their freedoms restricted—while their institutions sit in fat and splendid isolation, and their cries of distress become minor statistics in bureaucratic reports. Those cries come from every section of American life . . . As the Democratic National Chairman, it is tempting for me to capitalize on these feelings with the standard old political remedy: "Send a Democrat to the White House. Throw out Mr. Nixon and his Republican friends, and your problems will be over." Such a message would have two weaknesses: It wouldn't be true; and nobody would believe it. Now, make no mistake—I am proud to be a Democrat, and I am proud of our Party's record. In good men, good women, good ideas and good works, the party of the people is unmatched. But an excessive pride in the past, coupled with future promises that few people believe, have brought our Party—along with other institutions—to the present crisis of truth. Both political parties and their leaders are on trial this year.

At Democratic National Convention, Miami Beach, July 10/ The Washington Post, 7-12:(A)26.

James G. O'Hara
United States Representative, D–Mich.

The Democrats are trying to make the Party bigger than its candidates. Now it is so oriented to the Presidential election that when we lose, the Party becomes bankrupt and when we win, it becomes moribund.

San Francisco Examiner, 6-28:38.

Robert Packwood
United States Senator, R–Ore.

(On political primary elections): These extravaganzas take the form of citrus circuses in Florida and winter carnivals in Wisconsin. They leave the candidates tired and broke. They leave the public bored or bewildered and—far too often—disgusted. In the process, the candidates (lose) their credibility and the office loses its dignity.

Quote, 5-21:494.

Wright Patman
United States Representative, D–Tex.

(On the refusal of Nixon Administration officials to appear before his House Banking and Currency Committee to answer questions on alleged Republican espionage activities against the Democratic Party): This is a sad spectacle, a massive cover-up and concealment of the greatest political espionage ever carried out in the history of this nation. We have now reached the point where the major political operatives for the President are shrinking out of sight. They now speak to the Congress and the public only through faceless attorneys. They do not reply over their own signatures and they do not appear before either the

Congress or the press to answer even the most basic inquiries. It is the first time that a Presidential campaign has been carried on as if it were being operated as a "secret society."

Washington, Oct. 11/
The New York Times, 10-12:40.

Endicott Peabody
Former Governor of Massachusetts

(Advocating public election of the Vice President): I think the method by which we pick our Vice Presidents . . . is an absolutely corroding process. It demeans the office and it demeans the man. Now, a man who's in there because he earns his vote, because he has run for the office, because he was put there by the people or the people's delegates will have a dignity and status of his own. A Vice President shouldn't be waiting the crumbs the President throws him.

Miami Beach, Fla./
The Washington Post, 7-11:(A)14.

Charles H. Percy
United States Senator, R–Ill.

We (Republicans) depend too much on the popularity of an individual, such as (Dwight) Eisenhower, who can win despite his Party. And now (President) Nixon, who will win (re-election) despite the lack of strength in his own Party. He will run much bigger than his Party. In 1948, (Harry) Truman won because of his (Democratic) Party strength. That's a luxury we never can afford. We always have to have someone who is stronger than the Party.

Interview/
The National Observer, 8-26:5.

Henry C. Petersen
Assistant Attorney General, Criminal Division, Department of Justice of the United States

(On the government investigation of the alleged break-in and bugging of the Watergate apartments headquarters of the Democratic Party earlier in the year): All aspects of the alleged break-in and bugging were studied in detail, including questions about the sources and distribution of any funds. The FBI investigation was carried out by 333 agents operating from 51 field offices and in four foreign capitals. They developed 1,897 leads, conducted 1,551 interviews and expended 14,098 man hours. As the trial goes forward, the thoroughness and objectivity of the grand jury investigation will become apparent.

Sept. 16/
The Washington Post, 9-17:(A)16.

Kevin Phillips
Political columnist

The (Democratic Presidential) nomination of George McGovern isn't the wave of the future. It's like the last big wave washing up on a beach, after the tide has turned and is going out. There are plenty of signs that the tide has turned. Social tension is fading. The campuses are quiet again. The urban riots that filled our August TV screens (some years ago) are fortunately only a memory. No more *Oh! Calcutta's* are opening on Broadway. Rather than see George McGovern stir it all up again, rekindling the turmoil of the '60s, with his counter-culture morality and social experiments, millions and millions of traditional Democrats appear to be switching to (President) Richard Nixon. If so, this is the key to the new Nixon coalition. Appalled by the McGovernite takeover of the Democratic Party, many conservative and moderate elements of the old New Deal coalition are looking for a new political faith. Chief among them are Southerners, Catholics, Jews, ethnics and blue-collar workers. In the past, this is the sort of realignment that has led to a new political era, and I think a new political era is coming again. Even if McGovern loses badly (in the Presidential election) in November, his New Left forces will maintain a powerful role in the Democratic Party—too powerful, I think, for conservative Southerners and ethnics to

(KEVIN PHILLIPS)

come back into the fold. Thus, if Richard Nixon plays his cards right—and I think he will—he has a tremendous opportunity to secure the new majority, and the place in history that he cherishes so much.

Television broadcast/ "Comment!" National Broadcasting Company, 8-20.

Ronald Reagan
Governor of California

(The 1972 Presidential election) is not just another election; it is an election that will match a solid and consistent performer (President Nixon) . . . against a group of politicians who have been on every side of almost every issue in the last few years. This will match the man who has wound down the war (in Vietnam), who reformed the draft, balanced the Supreme Court and came to grips with the hard, knotty problems of inflation and unemployment against those who are known not for their constructive criticism but more for their nonconstructive criticisms rather than for any worthwhile accomplishments.

News conference, Los Angeles, Feb. 4/ Los Angeles Times, 2-5:(2)1.

(On the attempted assassination shooting of Alabama Governor and Presidential candidate George Wallace): We all must recognize that we can disagree, we can debate and we can continue to disagree; but there is no place for the kind of disagreement which kindles personal vilification and hatred. Isn't this an outgrowth of the hatred that has been injected into what has been peaceful competition? As God is in heaven, do we have to hate ourselves to the point where people with less balance are stimulated to deeds of this kind?

May 15/ Los Angeles Herald-Examiner, 5-16:(A)2.

I think, regardless of who the (Presidential) candidate is on the Democratic side, we (Republicans) have to take them very seriously, because we are a minority party, we're outnumbered. Having been a Democrat for a great part of my life—until I progressed and learned more—I know how difficult it is to get someone to leave his party and vote the other ticket. So I always run a little scared.

News conference, Rome, July 14/ Los Angeles Times, 7-15:(1)18.

Ogden R. Reid
United States Representative, R–N.Y.

(Announcing his plans to switch to the Democratic Party): I believe that I cannot in good conscience remain with the (Republican) Party. The Democratic majority has shown greater responsiveness to the needs of all the people. It has displayed the ability to tolerate dissent, the strength to undertake reform, concern with justice and equality and the courage to hammer out its positions on the issues in open debate, responsive to the people, not ideology.

New York, March 22/ Los Angeles Herald-Examiner, 3-22:(A)8.

James Reston
Vice president and political columnist, "The New York Times"

Never since before the last world war, not even in Lyndon Johnson's time, have I seen a trickier Administration than this (Nixon) one. There is a crisis of confidence in all government in this country because government is not working as it should. The (Vietnam) war is a disgrace, the economy is a mess and the financing of our politics is a scandal . . . (This Administration) evades the Congress whenever they can and have turned the press conference from an honest accounting of Executive stewardship into an instrument of political propaganda. Overwhelmed by their problems, they have sought to deal with the consequences of their failures by adopting all the techniques of commercial advertising and by trying to manipulate, or intimidate, or discredit their critics.

Before American Society of Newspaper Editors, Washington, April 21/ The New York Times, 4-22:15.

Frank L. Rizzo
Mayor of Philadelphia

(Senator and Democratic Presidential nominee George) McGovern represents the radical left. The American people will not be fooled by his double-talk. The worst thing that could happen to the country would be if McGovern were ever elected. I'm absolutely certain he won't be; but I have a standing order to buy a ticket to Australia if he is.

News conference, Philadelphia, July 18/ The Washington Post, 7-19:(A)2.

Felix G. Rohatyn
Member, board of directors, International Telephone and Telegraph Corporation

(On the controversy surrounding possible ITT contributions to the 1972 Republican National Convention in exchange for favorable antitrust action by the government): In view of everything that's happened, it seems to be inevitable that there are going to be questions asked as to what happened and how it happened and whether in the future we should be doing things differently . . . In view of all this flak . . . there certainly is a question to be raised as to whether any involvement with anything that looks political is a reasonable business proposition for a company. By that I would include (the forthcoming convention in) San Diego, even though it's completely innocent and even though it has nothing to do with anything.

Interview, New York, March 18/ The Washington Post, 3-19:(A)14.

George W. Romney
Secretary of Housing and Urban Development of the United States

(Referring to President Nixon): No recent figure in American political life has attracted a more savage and continuing attack upon his character, motives and accomplishments. For more than two decades, President Nixon has been the object of an unrelenting criticism by newspaper columnists, magazine writers, television and radio commentators and the intellectual elite in the universities, foundations and churches . . . There is no question in my mind, and I believe all fair-minded people will agree, that the nation is in better shape today than seemed possible in 1968 (before President Nixon entered office). We may not find him eulogized by the contemporary press and television. But I feel confident that he will go down in history as one of our great Presidents. I feel confident that his period in office will be recorded as the time when America found herself again and resumed the path to greatness.

Before Booster Club, San Francisco, June 15/ San Francisco Examiner, 6-16:55.

James Roosevelt
Former United States Representative, D–Calif.

(On why he is supporting re-election of President Nixon rather than Democratic Presidential nominee Senator George McGovern): Father (the late Democratic President, Franklin D. Roosevelt) always said, "Look, I've supported Republicans when I thought they were the better man," and that's what I'm doing. Father said the Democratic Party had an obligation to put up the best man available. And if not, the Party not only would lose the election but would also betray and fail to advance at all the aspirations of the millions who believe in it . . . the Democratic Party has not put up a man good enough for me to

(JAMES ROOSEVELT)

believe that he will push for the basic things for which our Party stands, or always has stood—not when the heat comes on. I knew George McGovern in Congress; and when the heat comes on, he simply isn't there. He sidesteps, seizes opportunities, is unpredictable, is not reliable. If McGovern were elected—and I don't think there's much chance of that—people would swing so far the other way in disgust with the Democratic Party that the next time, in 1976, we never would get a good man in the Presidency. So, yes, you could say that the Party should trade a defeat now for a chance of victory the next time. I don't see any harm to the country or the Party as long as we continue to elect the Congress, and the Democrats control the Congress, and I am working for that.

Interview/ The New York Times Magazine, 10-1:74.

Francis Sargent
Governor of Massachusetts

To me, a (political) party that seeks leadership will only survive if the leadership meets the needs of the people it seeks to serve. If its policies are not relevant or workable, then ultimately the party will indeed wither and die. In my opinion, the way to get the right solution is to know the problem. That means listening to people, all kinds of people. A party must try to have all groups represented within it—the young, the senior citizens, ethnic groups, as well as minorities, women as well as men . . . The purpose of a political party is to lead, but it can't do it if its programs reflect only the views of a very narrow segment of the population. It must represent the people as a whole. That party will serve this nation best which most accurately reflects the desires and needs of the American people.

Television broadcast/ "Comment!" National Broadcasting Company, 8-20.

William B. Saxbe
United States Senator, R–Ohio

It's just typical of the politics of today when both parties are trying to fool the people . . . The country's full of con men, and a lot of them are in politics.

San Francisco Examiner & Chronicle, 11-5:(This World)2.

Richard M. Scammon
Political analyst

Any politician, to be successful in America, cannot lose his sense of empathy for Middle America . . . If he represents only the very poor or only the very rich, he is going to lose . . . At the present time, any candidate who comes out and says, "I represent the left wing" or another who comes out and says, "I represent the right wing" and makes no effort to reach into the center, into Middle America, is simply going to lose. The polls I have seen . . . all indicate that the moderate is the dominant element; and those who call themselves liberal are actually in a smaller number than those who call themselves conservative, and the center is the place where you win or lose elections.

TV-radio interview, Washington/ "Meet the Press," National Broadcasting Company, 5-14.

Not to have a (political) convention would be like making the intentional walk in baseball automatic. It would ruin the game, because you never know when the catcher is going to drop the ball and the guy on third can score.

San Francisco Examiner & Chronicle, 8-27:(This World)2.

Arthur M. Schlesinger, Jr.
Historian; Former Special Assistant to the President of the United States

What television has done is to render obsolete the structure of American politics. It (politics) used to be tripartite: There were the candidates, the political leaders and the voters. The political leaders and intermediate agencies, like chambers of commerce, labor leaders and ethnic groups, interpreted the candidates to the voters and told the candidates about the voters. Through television, the voters are presented to the candidates directly, and public opinion polls give candidates information about the voters. The voter no longer depends, say, on a union leader. He makes his own decision.

Interview, New York/ "W": A Fairchild publication, 4-21:5.

The beauty of American politics is its continuing unpredictability. The electorate insists on outwitting forecasters and pundits.

Interview, New York/ "W": A Fairchild publication, 4-21:5.

By inauguration day in 1973, it will have been nearly a decade since the country was accustomed to believing its President.

Quote, 7-2:1.

John G. Schmitz
United States Representative, I–Calif.; American Party Presidential nominee

Socialism has never moved so fast in this country as in the four years under (President) Richard Nixon.

News conference, Los Angeles, Aug. 25/ Los Angeles Herald-Examiner, 8-26:(A)5.

The choice between (Republican President) Nixon and (Democratic Presidential nominee Senator George) McGovern is the choice between two professional wrestlers. Four years ago, (Alabama Governor) George Wallace said there wasn't a dime's worth of difference between the two parties. Today, well, you could get 8 or 9 cents in change. The two parties have given you a choice between a man you can't stand and a man you're afraid of—a choice between a man who broke every campaign promise he made and a man who you'd pray would break every campaign promise he's making now. One man is endorsed by Peking and Moscow, and the other man is endorsed by Hanoi and the Manson family.

Campaigning for the forthcoming Presidential election, Memphis/ The National Observer, 9-30:4.

Eric Sevareid
News commentator, Columbia Broadcasting System

(On news coverage of political events): It's not the business of reporters to be prophets . . . What I don't like is this constant race to see who can guess first how something is going to happen. The reason that you have primaries and a convention is that the people decide. This passion to know how elections will come out has always struck me as rather silly. It's a weakness of a lot of journalists.

Interview/The Washington Post, 8-20:(Potomac)14.

Anybody who pretends to be absolutely sure how things are going to turn out in an election is either a knave or a fool . . . I've felt reasonably sure in the past . . . But this year just baffles me . . . You don't know how people are going to jump (in the forthcoming Presidential election). This is a real transitional period (in politics), and it may go on for a long time, with the (political) parties reshaping themselves completely.

Interview/The Washington Post, 8-27:(Potomac)21.

R. Sargent Shriver
Former United States Ambassador to France

(On being designated by Democratic Presidential nominee Senator George McGovern as his new choice for the Vice-Presidential nomination): I've been blessed with incredibly good health; I haven't been sick for 30 years, thank God. I've got a wonderful wife and family. Look where we are—this beautiful setting here (at his home). How many guys in the world have this magnificent situation I've got? It's really one of the reasons I want to run. Because I'm so grateful to this country and to God for the things I've been given.

News conference, Rockville, Md., Aug. 6/ Los Angeles Times, 8-7:(1)13.

R. Sargent Shriver
Democratic Vice-Presidential nominee

Three months from today (in the Presidential election), Americans will choose between jobs and unemployment, between peace and four more years of war, between special treatment for corporate interests and general neglect of the public interest, between equal justice for all versus special justice for some. We choose not merely between two men or two parties . . . but between national greatness and national decline. In 1960, Richard Nixon represented national decline—the people rejected him. In 1972, Richard Nixon has created national decline—the people will reject him again.

Accepting the nomination, Washington, Aug. 8/ The New York Times, 8-9:18.

I am not embarrassed to be (Presidential nominee) George McGovern's seventh choice for Vice President. We Democrats may be short of money. We're not short of talent. Pity (President) Nixon—his first and only choice was Spiro Agnew.

Accepting the nomination, Washington, Aug. 8/ The New York Times, 8-9:18.

In 1972 the polls and the millionaires say (Democratic Presidential nominee Senator) George McGovern can't win. But I believe that lightning will strike again, just as it did in 1948. We will make it clear that, while (former Treasury Secretary) John Connally and his so-called Democrats for Nixon have the millionaires, we have the people. They've got the money, but we've got the heart; and I predict the party with the heart is going to beat the party with the dollar.

Campaigning for the forthcoming Presidential election, Houston, Aug. 18/ San Francisco Examiner, 8-18:5.

He's (President Nixon) like those professional football teams. They've got what they call the big front four. Those are those guys that are built wide like this—heavy here and rather thick sometimes, too. And who's he got? Up there he's got Big John Mitchell (former Attorney General). And next to Big John Mitchell is Big John Connally (former Treasury Secretary). And next to Big John Connally is Big Spiro Agnew (Vice President). And next to Mr. Agnew is Big Melvin Laird (Defense Secretary). Behind that front four they've got Tricky Dicky (Nixon) at quarterback dancing around out there.

Campaigning for the forthcoming Presidential election, Galveston, Tex., Sept. 26/ Los Angeles Times, 9-27:(1)27.

(Criticizing alleged Nixon Administration campaign tactics): When John F. Kennedy ran for President, he said politics was a noble profession. He encouraged young men and women to go into politics to serve their fellow man. And now, under Nixon, it looks as if you can't succeed in politics unless you have a spy, an electronic bug to put on your opponent's telephone, unless you forge, unless you steal, unless you go burglaring in the night. That's the degradation of politics.

Campaigning for the forthcoming Presidential election, Parma, Ohio, Oct. 12/ The Dallas Times Herald, 10-13:(A)12.

(On alleged Republican espionage activities against the Democrats during the current Presidential campaign): This is not ordinary finagling around among politicians. This is the introduction into the life of the people of America of covert, subversive acts of the type that have only been permitted outside the United States (by the CIA, etc.). That devil is coming back home to corrupt us here and I say the American people will not tolerate that. (President Nixon is) still the same old Nixon he always was. He may dress like a President, look like a President, talk like a President, act like a President, walk like a President—but it's still Nixon, and that's the big issue in this campaign.

Campaigning for the forthcoming Presidential election, Buffalo, N.Y., Oct. 16/ Los Angeles Times, 10-17:(1)18.

Every Italian-American in Congress except one is a Democrat; every Polish-American member of Congress except two are Democrats; every Greek-American member of Congress is a Democrat; every Spanish-speaking Congressman except one is a Democrat; every black Congressman is a Democrat; and every Irishman is a Democrat, who's any good.

Campaigning for the forthcoming Presidential election/The Washington Post, 10-23:(A)1.

(Running for the Vice-Presidency) has challenged all the intelligence, energy, emotion, experience—every quality I've got. There's nothing in your life that goes wasted in an experience like this. It's a test of everything you've ever done, everything you've ever thought. It's like a great big comprehensive exam at the end of four years in college. The nation examines you.

Interview/ The New York Times, 11-5:(1)53.

John J. Sparkman
United States Senator, D–Ala.

The trouble with politics is that usually you either have to brag about yourself or say something adverse about one of your opponents, or, worse yet, all of your opponents.

Television interview/ The Washington Post, 3-23:(G)3.

Benjamin Spock
Physician, Author

. . . we're not going to make this country what it can be as long as the two (political) parties are so tied up with industry. It's the industrialists who pay for the election of public officials. We can't do what has to be done as long as the old parties dominate the system . . . Of course, history shows no instance of a voluntary surrender of power. But the gradual process of radicalization—of policemen and soldiers and workers, as well as of students—will undermine the confidence of industry in its ability to hold on. And once confidence begins to recede, there may be no way to stop the system from crumbling.

At University of Vermont/ The New York Times Magazine, 6-4:58.

(On his being a candidate for the People's Party Presidential nomination): America is a lot more radicalized than what the newspapers think and miles beyond what the Congress of the United States thinks. Give me a platform and I'll radicalize the whole middle class of humanity.

At People's Party convention, St. Louis, July 27/ San Francisco Examiner, 7-28:6.

Maurice H. Stans
Republican Presidential campaign finance chairman

(On his suit against former Democratic Party chairman Lawrence O'Brien who accused him of financing the alleged bugging of Democratic headquarters earlier in the year): I have brought this action not only to defend my reputation against a vicious and wholly unfounded attack, but to serve notice on Mr. O'Brien and his agents that, so long as they persist on the low road of smear and character assassination, they will be held strictly accountable not only to the American people but before the law. This is a personal action by one who treasures his reputation and who believes in fighting back when falsely attacked. In a broader sense, it is a class action on behalf of all Americans who believe in fair play and in a man's right to protect his good name even in the political season.

Washington, Sept. 14/ Los Angeles Times, 9-15:(1)22.

Herbert Stein
Chairman, Council of Economic Advisers to the President of the United States

What the "new politician" seeks is not the consensus issue but the divisive issue. He seeks the issue on which he can divide black against white, young against middle-aged, poor against rich and women against men. Of course, for the professional politician who wants to win an election and not merely lead a demonstration, this selection of issues creates a certain difficulty. Having done his best to polarize the society, he then finds himself wanting the support of both poles. This has created an identity crisis for certain members of the (Democratic) opposition.

Before Virginia Bankers Association, Hot Springs, June 17/ The New York Times, 6-18:(1)36.

Charles P. Taft
Chairman, Fair Campaign Practices Committee

Historically, dirty politics always peaks during the last two weeks of the campaign. If the present trend continues, we will have a new high in political low blows during 1972. First, this appears to be the year for the great stamp robbery. Already, half way through the 1972 (political) campaign, the Committee has received more complaints about members of Congress abusing their free mailing privilege than we received throughout the entire campaign period in previous years. Second, this seems to be a negative year, with many candidates attacking their opponents' positions instead of taking a positive stand on the issues. A negative attack in a close race most often results in dirty politics.

Washington, Oct. 9/ San Francisco Examiner, 10-9:6.

Kakuei Tanaka
Prime Minister of Japan

A politician is like a machine designed to meet as many people as possible.

Time, 7-17:25.

John G. Tower
United States Senator, R–Tex.

You can generally count on people who are low on the socio-economic spectrum to vote Democratic and people who are high in it to vote Republican. Then there is that vast majority of America in the middle that really determines the outcome of an election and is (for) the most part a table element which rejects extremes.

Interview, Miami Beach/ The Dallas Times Herald, 8-24:(A)12.

(Urging Democrats to vote for President Nixon this year instead of Democratic Presidential nominee Senator George McGovern): This is a year when we have to put partisan politics aside. The late (President) John F. Kennedy once said sometimes party loyalty demands too much. I have great respect for the fine tradition of the Democratic Party, steeped as it once was in the tradition of Thomas Jefferson. But I think if Thomas Jefferson were alive today, the founder of the Democratic Party, he would be voting for Richard Nixon and John Tower.

Campaigning for the forthcoming election, Galveston, Tex., Sept. 16/ The Dallas Times Herald, 9-17:(A)29.

I believe (Democratic Presidential nominee Senator) George McGovern is intellectually honest and, because he believes in what he says, he is eminently more dangerous than if he was a mindless demagogue. Thus, his defeat must be made certain, or we may see the sun set on the great democratic experiment.

Campaigning for the forthcoming national election, El Paso, Tex., Oct. 25/ The Dallas Times Herald, 10-26:(A)26.

George C. Wallace
Governor of Alabama

I speak the majority viewpoint of the people of America, and I intend to make a serious effort to win the Democratic (Presidential) nomination. I want to show the Democratic Party that they are not representing the people. I'm an Alabama Democrat of the old school . . . It's time to return the Party to the people, away from the outer liberals. These intellectual snobs have looked down their noses too long at the average citizen. The people want to be left alone.

Announcing his candidacy for President, Tallahassee, Fla., Jan. 13/ Los Angeles Times, 1-14:(1)1.

If I broke a leg right now and had to get out (of the race for the Democratic Presidential nomination), I could feel that I had done a lot. Who would have thought that a little country boy like me could make those fellows (other Democratic candidates) adopt my platform? That's what they're doing. Now they're talking about law and order and welfare loafers, and they're waffling on all over the place on busing (of school children for racial balance). And they're all promising the people they will cut their taxes even though all they've been doing as Senators all these years is to raise these same taxes. But they changed their positions—and they've all broken their backs while they were doing it. I've always known that the important issue in this country is the remoteness and aloofness of government for the average man. Now the others are beginning to see it. So I've already accomplished much of what I set out to do. You know, they called me evil when I talked about law and order in 1968. Now they are all talking about it. It's a good feeling. Yep, the chickens sure have come home to roost.

Interview, Eau Claire, Wis./ The Christian Science Monitor, 4-4:1.

Senator (George) McGovern has been in Congress 14 years; but he's managed—by picking up what I said in Florida and saying it in Wisconsin first—to establish himself as an anti-establishment (Presidential) candidate; but he is part of the establishment. He voted for the establishment's Tonkin Gulf (Vietnam) resolution; he voted for the establishment's (racial-balance school) busing bills; he voted for the establishment's foreign aid giveaways.

News conference, Boston, April 24/ San Francisco Examiner & Chronicle, 4-30:(This World)8.

Mike Wallace
News correspondent,
Columbia Broadcasting System

(President) Nixon got elected and he thought the press (had) kicked him around. Roosevelt got elected way back in the '30s and (he also) felt the press had done it to him. Harry Truman was regarded by the press as a sure loser. Need I say more? The American people have a remarkable genius for reading, listening, watching and then making up their own minds in some strange and independent way.

Interview/ The Washington Post, 8-20:(Potomac)15.

Jean Westwood
Chairman,
Democratic National Committee

(Criticizing black supporters of President Nixon): Blacks who blow their horns and run to Washington to raise money for that kind of Administration are back-stabbers. They are working for the increasing unemployment of their brothers and should be repudiated. They help bleed our poor

(JEAN WESTWOOD)

while pretending to work for community uplift.

Before Southern Christian Leadership Conference, Dallas, Aug. 16/ The New York Times, 8-18:52.

Leonard Woodcock
President, United Automobile Workers of America

The day has passed when the (labor union) leadership declaring for this candidate or that meant anything. We found that out last May in Michigan when tens of thousands of auto workers voted for (Alabama Governor) George Wallace (in the Democratic Presidential primary) after we had urged them and pleaded with them not to.

The New York Times, 7-17:18.

Samuel W. Yorty
Mayor of Los Angeles

Our Democratic Party is threatened with suicidal radicalization by Senator George McGovern's lavishly-financed (California Presidential primary) campaign of deception and demagoguery . . . I have some differences with Senator (Hubert) Humphrey, particularly in foreign policy, but I regard him as a realistic, loyal American, unwilling to resort to demagogic deception to win the election. He plays politics, as do most politicians, but he stops far short of appealing to extremists and confused idealistic dreamers to garner votes. This has put him at a disadvantage in competing with the computer-programmed McGovern propaganda machine.

News conference, Los Angeles, June 5/ Los Angeles Times, 6-6:(1)1,21.

(On the Democratic Party's nomination of Senator George McGovern for President): The Party is now generally dominated by the left. That great old coalition of farmers and labor and small businessmen has been broken up. Unless it's put back together, this could become a minority party for quite a while.

Miami Beach, July 13/ Los Angeles Times, 7-14:(1)22.

Spiro T. Agnew
Vice President of the United States

The welfare situation certainly requires some reform; and it requires a recognition by the people who are administering these programs that there is a need to tighten up procedures and investigatory methods to make certain that welfare fraud is eliminated and that the work requirement, where it is feasible, is strictly enforced. This is a point of philosophical difference among many of our citizens—this business about what kind of work a man has to take if he's able to work. But I believe that the idea of going ahead with a welfare reform on a pilot basis and making changes based on what comes out of the experiment is a pretty wise one. One thing we have got to stop thinking is that the mere provision of money, without providing the means to constructively utilize the money, is the answer to a problem. The "liberal" point of view in the country is that the mere providing of dollars answers the problem automatically. I have found in some cases it's just the opposite.

Interview/
U.S. News & World Report, 3-13:39.

John B. Anderson
United States Representative, R–Ill.

. . . I am afraid that many of our current enthusiasts for reordering national priorities have a rather simplistic and naive view of what will be necessary to find solutions to the great problems that confront us as we move into a new decade. Put simply, this view is based on the assumption that the amount of new Federal money that we throw at a problem symptom, such as the decay of our central cities or inadequate housing, is a direct measure of the progress we are making in arriving at a solution to these problems, and is an indicator of our national commitment or lack thereof to deal with them. Nothing could be more mistaken. National priorities cannot be measured by means of simple budgetary classifications and arithmetic. The great domestic problems that we face today are far too complex and stubborn to yield readily to new Federal spending panaceas; if we have learned anything from the vast disappointment of the Great Society period it should be that. Solutions to the problems of poverty, of the environment, of urban decay, of full participation in American society by our long-deprived minorities cannot be obtained by means of mere budget shifting alone. At bottom, they are related to the health and productivity of the entire American socio-economy, of both the public and private sector; and until we begin making progress on those larger problems, the battle will not even have yet been joined.

Before the House,
Washington, April 20/
Congressional Digest, 6-7:183.

William E. Brock III
United States Senator, R–Tenn.

(Opposing government intervention in support of child day-care centers): This . . . would motivate the dissolution of family care, family sharing, family concern. To me, there is no possible way to calculate the cost of that to the child . . . For the life of me, I cannot see how the government could create an incentive program to encourage a woman to choose the work market over her responsibility of trying to provide her child with every ounce of love available to it, so that it can

(WILLIAM E. BROCK III)

grow up with dignity and love for other people. I do not think that can be found in a child-development center.

Human Events, 7-1:4.

Shirley Chisholm
United States Representative, D–N.Y.

The FHA, marked by a legacy of racism and profiteering in the administration of previous housing programs, has knowingly tolerated the development of Federal-financed slums, the perpetuation and acceleration of segregated housing patterns and the gouging of the poor by speculators, builders and bankers who all pocket Federal dollars for violating Federal laws.

At Phillips Academy, Andover, Mass., April 21/ The New York Times, 4-25:47.

Frank Church
United States Senator, D–Idaho

We could abolish poverty among the elderly for what it costs to run the war in Southeast Asia for just three months. We could broaden Medicare coverage to include out-of-hospital prescription drugs for what we now spend for an aircraft carrier. We could establish a comprehensive manpower program for older workers for the cost of one submarine.

Before the Senate, Washington, Feb. 7/ Quote, 4-30:416.

No Administration to date—whether it be Democratic or Republican—has really come to grips with the predicament of the elderly . . . The retirement-income crisis which now affects millions of older Americans . . . deserves no less than a national commitment to eliminate poverty for the elderly and to allow them to share in the economic abundance which they have worked most of their lives to create.

U.S. News & World Report, 3-27:40.

John B. Connally, Jr.
Former Secretary of the Treasury of the United States

We know that countries around the world think the United States is a rich and powerful nation and say, "Why don't you give us more?" Well, rich and powerful are relative terms. We have a great deal of poverty in the United States, and it's pretty difficult to tell millions of our own people why we give anybody any money. They say, "Help us." You (in Afghanistan, for example) wouldn't classify them as below the poverty level; I understand that. Poor people in many nations would call our poor rich.

News conference, Kabul, Afghanistan, July 7/ The New York Times, 7-10:7.

John B. Connally, Jr.
Former Secretary of the Treasury of the United States; Chairman, Democrats for Nixon

(On Democratic Presidential nominee Senator George McGovern's economic views): You and I are seeing today the most bitter attack on the free-enterprise system ever launched in the history of the United States. We are witnessing the full flowering of a philosophy that men who work must be taxed to the limit to support those who don't or won't—a philosophy that the welfare state is the only answer to poverty and suffering—a philosophy that America should be ashamed of its wealth, growth and strength.

Before Veterans of Foreign Wars, Minneapolis, Aug. 21/ Los Angeles Herald-Examiner, 8-22:(A)6.

Roger A, Freeman
Senior fellow, Hoover Institution, Stanford University; Former Special Assistant to the President of the United States

Maybe we should consider whether a child is always best off with his mother, or whether growing up in a well-run institution may not give it a better chance in life than living under inferior parental care or in a detrimental environment.

San Francisco Examiner, 2-1:30.

Mitchell I. Ginsberg
Dean, Columbia University School of Social Work

There is no way of significantly improving the welfare program if we don't put it under Federal administration and financing . . . Welfare is the only subsidizing program in the United States which is not Federally administered. The states and cities can't handle it any more. And any Federal program is better for the poor.

Before Golden Gate Chapter, National Association of Social Workers, San Francisco, Jan. 31/ San Francisco Examiner, 2-1:22.

Martha W. Griffiths
United States Representative, D–Mich.

We purport to build into the welfare system work incentives, but truth is stranger than fiction. The welfare system is inequitable alike to the recipient and to the taxpayer. It does not have work incentives; it has work disincentives.

Quote, 8-6:122.

Edward M. Kennedy
United States Senator, D–Mass.

(The) central issue (on domestic policy is) are we going to have a government that is responsive to the people, or only the special interests? Do we want welfare only for Lockheed and the giant farmers? . . . And for those who live in poverty–shall we spend our dollars on a space shuttle and on (an) SST for a few to fly to the heavens, when the many here on earth have simple unmet needs like homes and schools and health?

At Washington Press Club, Jan. 17/ San Francisco Examiner, 1-18:2.

Elizabeth Duncan Koontz
Deputy Assistant Secretary and Director, Women's Bureau, Department of Labor of the United States

The fact is that women with small children *do* work, and the children often have no place to go. Day care *is* a necessity, but I don't know how quickly we'll have it. What some people forget is that the wealthy have always had child care. The flak comes when we try to provide it for the poor. In order to please women, politicians pay lip service to child-care services; but one can't be sure what they'll do in the clinch.

Parade, 6-25:17.

Russell B. Long
United States Senator, D–La.

Fraud and misrepresentation and simply bad management of the welfare system have led to the inclusion on the welfare rolls of literally thousands of people all around the country who should not, under reasonable interpretation, be eligible for benefits, or whose benefits should be substantially less than they are receiving. It has been said that a few bad apples should not discredit the whole barrel and that welfare recipients, in general, should not be tarred with the same brush that paints horrible pictures of welfare cheating and malingering. I agree completely with the thesis that millions of people on welfare rolls are there through no fault of their own . . . But I am concerned–gravely concerned–that the welfare system as we know it today is being manipulated and abused by malingerers, cheats and outright frauds to the detriment not only of the American taxpayers whose dollars support the program, but also to the detriment of the truly needy on whose behalf the Federal-state system of cash assistance was founded.

Before the Senate, Washington, March 14/ U.S. News & World Report, 4-3:54.

(On his plans for a welfare work-requirement program): I think that we will

(RUSSELL B. LONG)

have about six good ways that we can increase the income of people who ought to be working to help improve their own conditions. We will provide job opportunities for them; we will provide tax advantages for them if they will take the job; we will provide tax incentives for people who will hire them; we will provide training opportunities. We are going to do about everything any reasonable man can think of to make work more attractive so that people who have never worked before might be tempted to take the job.

Broadcast interview, March 20/ The Dallas Times Herald, 3-20:(A)8.

William S. Lowe
President, Chamber of Commerce of the United States

. . . subsidizing people for not working is not a good thing. There are a few who will claim it is. Its defenders say it is a necessity—maybe not a good thing, but a necessity. I agree completely that, in a society as opulent as ours, the lame and the blind must have adequate help. But when you get into the area of those who see fit not to support themselves, then there is the question of how many we who work can support. It must be kept in mind that, when you subsidize indolence and complacency, you continue to breed these same characteristics; you don't cure them.

Interview, Mexico, Mo./ Nation's Business, May:45.

Mike Mansfield
United States Senator, D–Mont.

As an oil well is used up, we give the owner a depletion allowance to compensate him for his lost asset. We do the same for gravel and the other minerals—it is an accepted practice. But there is no depletion allowance for the people—the greatest asset—as they wear out. Our Social Security System, although providing only a bare subsistence, was an enormous breakthrough. But what of the man and woman who are made old before their time . . . ? Their bodies and spirits can be exhausted long before the age of general retirement. Every job has its cost. The manual laborer may be physically depleted before the office worker; white-collar workers may be psychologically depleted . . . ; the assembly-line employee may be dehumanized long before his statutory retirement age.

Before the Senate, Washington, Sept. 29/ The Washington Post, 10-8:(D)6.

George S. McGovern
United States Senator, D–S.D.

I propose that every man, woman, and child receive from the Federal government an annual payment. This payment would not vary in accordance with the wealth of the recipient. For those on public assistance, this income grant would replace the welfare system.

At Iowa State University, Jan. 13/ The New York Times, 7-8:10.

I think the individual and our whole society are both losers when we act as if age 65 were a mystical milestone that somehow deprives people of their physical and mental resources. The truth is that about 80 per cent of all American citizens over age 65 are capable of discharging all normal responsibilities. Some live in financial poverty. But all 16 million of the healthy aged have been forced to make their own way out of the prison of enforced idleness.

Before the Senate, Washington, Feb. 15/ Quote, 3-19:281.

George S. McGovern
United States Senator, D–S.D.; Democratic Presidential nominee

Most of us can . . . agree that our present welfare system must be abolished.

Those who can work should have jobs, even if the government must provide them. And all our citizens—those who work and those who cannot—should be assured an adequate income which will let them feed and clothe and house their families. President Nixon himself has proposed a guaranteed annual income. We do not disagree on that principle. But poverty cannot be ended by providing less than people need for the barest necessities of a decent life; and every worker and every merchant will do better when poverty gives way to new purchasing power.

Broadcast address, Washington, Aug. 5/ The New York Times, 8-6:(1)36.

When I read this Republican propaganda, this rubbish, about what I stand for, I scarcely recognized the person they're talking about. I'm not for increasing the welfare rolls—I'm for increasing the employment opportunities. I came out of a background where, at the age of 14, from that day on, I earned every penny that has supported my existence. I'm not here to boast about myself other than to say that I know something about the work ethic. I came out of a poor family; I worked my way through school; I fought for this country as a bomber pilot in World War II. I've worked every day of my life—harder than (President) Richard Nixon worked.

Campaigning for the forthcoming Presidential election, Cleveland/ The Washington Post, 9-10:(A)4.

When 6 million senior citizens live in poverty—in hovels instead of homes, without enough food, gouged by the high cost of drugs and health care, without decent clothing and shelter—when a society as wealthy as ours provides such treatment for those who worked to build it—then there is something wrong in America.

At senior citizens luncheon, North Bergen, N.J., Sept. 20/ Los Angeles Herald-Examiner, 9-20:(A)8.

Federal insurance already covers bank deposits, home mortgages, securities losses resulting from the failure of brokerage houses, and the Lockheed loan. Why should it not be extended to cover retirement income earned by working people and set aside for them in pension plans . . . More than 35 million American workers are enrolled in private pension plans, yet more than half of them will receive absolutely no pension benefits when they retire and many others will receive only minimal returns. The Nixon Administration has largely ignored this injustice. For two years it had made no serious proposal for pension reform. Last year it finally made a proposal which fits neatly into the traditional Republican mold—discriminating heavily in favor of the rich and doing nothing for many of those in greatest need.

Campaigning for the forthcoming Presidential election, Philadelphia, Oct. 19/ The Fresno (Calif.) Bee, 10-19:(A)12.

It is true that, in my search for a way out of the welfare mess, I once discussed a plan, a plan by some of the nation's leading economists, for a $1,000 grant to every citizen that would be taxed back from those who do not need it. But it is also true that I have rejected this idea, just as (President) Nixon advocated and then rejected a similar guaranteed income plan. Attacking me for it now makes no more sense than attacking Mr. Nixon for it.

Television campaign address, Oct. 20/ The Washington Post, 10-21:(A)1.

The best job incentive is a job opening. The best answer to welfare is work . . . By guaranteeing jobs, we can reach the point where 3½ million Americans are living on the earnings of breadwinners rather than relief.

U.S. News & World Report, 11-6:30.

Robert Moses
Government planner and builder; Former New York City Parks Commissioner

My definition of a slum is an area

(ROBERT MOSES)

where a large number of people are living in buildings which are unfit for human habitation but which can't be repaired. Can we get rid of slums? If you accept that as a definition, yes. There is no reason why you shouldn't have a city free from that kind of slum. But you take the kind of places the blacks are living in in New York. Some of them are in absolutely inhuman condition. Eight people in a room. Disease. Crime. Degeneracy. There are 1.2 million people living in such slums in New York. People won't tolerate them any more. They'll smash them up or burn them down. They are going to get mad enough so that they will sabotage those communities. When they do, there will be no fire engines, no water, no lights. They will kick the daylights out of the whole community.

Interview, New York/ Los Angeles Times, 6-27:(2)7.

Richard Nathan
Deputy Under Secretary for Welfare Reform Planning, Department of Health, Education and Welfare of the United States

. . . if you go into your own cities and look at the welfare administration offices, you will see that many of them are absolutely inundated with paper. There is a paperwork flood in many welfare systems in the nation today. In one of the offices that I was recently in, all of the records are kept on top of filing cabinets, in corners, dusty corners, wherever space can be found; in beer cartons, because in this particular state the state forms that they are required to keep fit very conveniently into beer cartons. But this is not unusual. I have been into welfare offices in other parts of the country where the workers, the eligibility workers, are unable to find a place to sit to interview recipients, because all around their desks and on chairs and on tables are cartons, boxes, file folders, records in large amounts.

News conference/ The Washington Post, 1-11:(A)14.

Richard M. Nixon
President of the United States

. . . looking at the welfare program, I believe that the position that we (his Administration) have taken, a position that has been overwhelmingly approved by the House, is the right position. It provides for welfare for those people who need it. It provides also for incentives that will move people from welfare rolls to jobs, and it does so at a cost we can afford . . . I want welfare reform and the country wants welfare reform; but we cannot have welfare reform that moves in the direction of increasing the cost and putting more people on, rather than getting them off.

News conference, Washington, June 22/ The Washington Post, 6-23:(A)9.

(On a proposed 20 per cent increase in Social Security benefits): The problem with the 20 per cent increase which the Senate will consider is what it does to the Social Security System, and also what it does to the cost of living and to future taxes in this country. We must realize that, if a 20 per cent Social Security (increase) is passed by the Senate and by the Congress, that the increased payroll tax to pay for it will completely wipe out the tax reduction that was given to middle-income and lower-income wage earners in 1969. And that's a question that the Congress has got to address itself to. If, on the other hand, the Congress passes the 20 per cent increase in Social Security and does not finance it adequately, it will seriously jeopardize the integrity of the Social Security trust fund and it could be highly inflationary, which would, of course, hurt most of the Social Security people, the retired people. And so these are some considerations that have motivated me in expressions of concern. It isn't that we do not want an increase in

Social Security; it isn't that we don't want as high an increase as possible. But the increase must be a responsible one. It should be funded; and the Congress, if it does not fund it, would be doing something that would not be in the interest of retired people, who would be faced with (an) increase in the cost of living.

News conference, Washington, June 29/ The New York Times, 7-1:8.

The incomparable productivity of our farmers has made it possible for us to launch a winning war against hunger in the United States and makes us the best-fed people in the world with the lowest percentage of the family budget going to food of any country in the world. People on welfare in the United States would be rich in most of the nations of the world today.

Accepting the Republican Presidential nomination, Miami Beach, Aug. 23/ Los Angeles Times, 8-24:(1)21.

I say that, instead of providing incentives for more millions to go on welfare, we need a program which will provide incentives for people to get off welfare and go to work. It is wrong for anyone on welfare to receive more than someone who works. Let us be generous to those who can't work without increasing the taxes of those who do work . . . Let us never destroy the principle that has made America the world's most prosperous nation—that a person should get what he works for and work for what he gets.

Accepting the Republican Presidential nomination, Miami Beach, Aug. 23/ Los Angeles Times, 8-24:(1)21,22.

The people who advocate the welfare ethic spend their time discussing how to cut up the pie we have—but those who believe in the work ethic want to bake a bigger pie, and I am for baking a bigger pie . . . The work ethic tells us there is really no such thing as something for nothing and that everything valuable in life requires some striving and some sacrifice. The work ethic holds that it is wrong to expect instant gratification of all our desires and it is right to expect hard work to earn a just reward . . . The welfare ethic, on the other hand, suggests that there is an easier way. It says that the good life can be made available to everyone right now, and that this can be done by the government . . . it sees the government, not the person, as the best judge of what people should do, where they should go to school, what kind of jobs they should have and how much income they should be allowed to keep.

Labor Day message, San Clemente, Calif., Sept. 3/ Los Angeles Times, 9-4:(1)1.

Richard B. Ogilvie
Governor of Illinois

In the bluntest possible terms, I believe the present disaster in the administration of public welfare presents a serious challenge to the viability of our Federal system. The imposition of a detailed and increasingly-rigid structure of administrative regulations has given the Federal welfare bureaucracy, quite literally, a life-or-death grip over the ability of state governments to act in the best interests of their citizens in this important activity. But of even more immediate concern, the present system is threatening the states—especially the major industrial states like my own—with financial chaos.

Before Senate Finance Committee, Washington, Jan. 25/ U.S. News & World Report, 2-14:22.

Wright Patman
United States Representative, D–Tex.

Many of these (Federal housing) programs start out with high-sounding purposes and what appear to be really outstanding concepts. Then someone comes along and insists that we add in the profit margin for

(WRIGHT PATMAN)

each real-estate interest as the program moves forward. There's a little bit for the land speculator, the builder, the lender, the closing attorney, the title company, the insurance company and on down the line. By the time the project reaches the end of the line, it is so top-heavy that you can't be sure just who did get the subsidy . . . After all these years, we really don't seem to have what can be honestly regarded as a coherent national policy on housing. It's still little more than a patchwork of overlapping, inadequate programs glued together with high-sounding preambles and pronouncements. I don't think anyone, in or out of Congress, has been giving enough thought to these rambling housing bills that seem to roll forward every year.

At National Housing Conference/ The New York Times, 3-13:25.

Ronald Reagan
Governor of California

(Criticizing the "guaranteed income" portion of President Nixon's welfare-reform plan): It is commonly understood that a government guaranteed income, not based upon individual productivity, is a giant step toward a welfare state with its inherent loss of individual identity and pride . . . It doesn't seem right to reduce a man's take-home pay with taxes and then send him a government dole which robs him of the feeling of accomplishment and dignity which comes from providing for his family by his own efforts.

Before Senate Finance Committee, Washington, Feb. 1/ Los Angeles Herald-Examiner, 2-1:(A)3.

The welfare problem is the gravest domestic issue our nation faces. I believe the individual states have both the power and responsibility for its solution, if only the Federal government will give us the elbow room to do it. In spite of the seemingly endless maze of Federal bureaucratic regulations which hamstring and frustrate effective state reforms, we in California nonetheless have brought our welfare program back in check. Fifteen months ago, California's welfare system was spawning 40,000 new welfare recipients a month. It was literally out of control; and without drastic action it threatened to bankrupt the state. We began implementing a series of strong actions designed to curb ludicrous abuses of the system, in which people earning as high as $16,000 a year were still drawing welfare checks. By tightening eligibility requirements, we were able to get many of these freeloaders off the rolls, while increasing by 30 per cent the grants to the truly needy, including the aged, disabled and blind. We adopted plans to crack down much harder on welfare cheaters, and to track down absent fathers who, because of non-support, pushed their families onto the rolls. We enacted a law which set up a project to require able-bodied, employable welfare recipients to either seek work, accept a job if offered, take part in job training or work in selected jobs for their community in return for their welfare grants. If they do not comply, they'll be cut from the welfare rolls. Today, there are 182,000 fewer Californians on welfare than there were 10 months ago. Without our reforms there would now be more than half a million more Californians drawing welfare than there actually are, at an increased cost to our taxpayers of $1.1 billion this year and next. We've turned the welfare monster around in California, and we're convinced our approach to reform is the right answer to the problem. The states can and must do the job. The welfare problem will not be solved, but will only be made much worse if turned over to the Federal welfare bureaucracy.

Television broadcast/ "Comment!" National Broadcasting Company, 3-26.

George W. Romney
Secretary of Housing and Urban Development of the United States

The forces that cause abandonment and

the decline of large neighborhoods are not primarily physical, but are primarily human, social and governmental. We will not solve this crisis if we pretend that it is just a housing crisis. Housing didn't take the jobs away. Housing didn't reduce the population. Housing didn't reduce the public services. Housing didn't destroy the quality of education in the schools. Housing didn't bring the drug addiction in. Deep social changes are at work that have little if anything to do with housing. Yet too often the *result* is accused of being the *cause* . . . I acknowledge with deep regret the things that have gone wrong with our housing subsidy programs. I am angered and determined to eliminate incompetence, conflict of interest, favoritism, graft, bribes, fraud, shoddy workmanship and forms of "legal" profiteering that take advantage of technicalities to defraud the home buyer and the tax-paying public . . . Our Department has made mistakes, but we have not made the mistake of abandonment.

Detroit/
The National Observer, 4-8:5.

I think we need to put an end to this concentration of people with problems in public housing. I don't think you can have a viable public-housing program when you build up concentrations of low-income families with problems and you don't have a suitable mix of stable families with problem families . . . England is very wise in not excluding any family, regardless of income. If higher-income families want to live in public housing, they are free to do so. It provides a better mix and greater stability.

News conference,
Washington, Dec. 22/
Los Angeles Times, 12-23:(1)6.

R. Sargent Shriver
Democratic Vice-Presidential nominee

(If Democratic Presidential nominee Senator George McGovern becomes President), the regular people of America will be coming to dinner in the White House. At least occasionally, we'll invite people who are hungry. The first McGovern dinner at the White House will be for poor people.

Campaigning for the forthcoming Presidential election, Wheeling, W. Va., Aug. 14/The New York Times, 8-15:24.

Stuart Symington
United States Senator, D–Mo.

(Advocating more domestic and less military spending by the government): There are those in this body who can hear the farthest drum before they can hear the cry of a single hungry child.

Before the Senate, Washington/
Plainview (Tex.) Daily Herald, 1-7:6.

Robert Taft, Jr.
United States Senator, R–Ohio

Our welfare laws have been generally structured simply to feed people and keep them alive, rather than renewing their lives and regenerating their productive abilities. We must focus on the rehabilitation of people, enabling them to renew their lives and to give them hope for a better tomorrow.

Before the Senate,
Washington, March 17/
Quote, 4-9:352.

James Tobin
Professor of Economics, Yale University; Former member, Council of Economic Advisers to the President of the United States

(Advocating financial aid to the poor financed by more taxation of the wealthy): Think of the alternatives. One of them would be to socialize industry. It would really change the basic nature of property ownership of the country. That would be the more radical way, less efficient. Or another alternative would be a rather detailed series of controls on prices, wages, dividends and so forth that would also

(JAMES TOBIN)

create much more bureaucratic, more extensive interference with the mechanisms than by doing it with taxation. When you do it with taxation, you let the system operate in the best way it can. You do not interfere with the basic structures of industry and management. You are simply taking the results of a market economy and saying, "Let us redistribute them a little differently." All this is nothing new in the United States or in other Western countries. We have been doing it for a long time with the progressive income tax, at least in theory. But over the years it was shot full of so many holes by various ways of having income escape taxation that it really doesn't work the way it is supposed to.

Interview, New Haven, Conn./ Los Angeles Times, 6-19:(2)7.

John V. Tunney
United States Senator, D–Calif.

There is a fundamental hypocrisy in the way a society with such great resources as ours classifies people as poor, declares that they must be helped when they need help, and yet ultimately issues a check which simply insures that they will have to live below a poverty line which is itself drawn in very frugal terms indeed.

Quote, 4-9:350.

George C. Wallace
Governor of Alabama

Too long this (Democratic) Party has been controlled by the so-called intellectual snobs who feel that big government should control the lives of American citizens from the cradle to the grave.

News conference, Tallahassee, Fla., Jan. 13/ San Francisco Examiner, 1-13:2.

. . . (Senator Hubert) Humphrey, four years ago, when I said get the loafers and chiselers off the welfare rolls, he said I was a demagogue. And you know what he said this time? "Get the loafers and chiselers off the welfare rolls."

Campaigning for the Democratic Presidential nomination, Dallas/ The Dallas Times Herald, 4-16:(A)36.

Henry C. Wallich
Professor of Economics, Yale University

(Advocating corporate aid for social activities): The use of money . . . will be in the hands of corporate executives, who are trained to get the most value for a dollar, whether in production, or marketing, or in social activities. Consider the alternative. If corporations do not do what needs to be done, using stockholders' or customers' money, it will be done by government, using taxpayers' money. There are many reasons to think that a political body, working through a centralized system, will often get less value per dollar than the decentralized and results-oriented business system. In terms of how and at what prices to get a job done, there is much to be said for handling social responsibilities through corporate channels.

At American Marketing Association's Industrial Marketing Conference, Cleveland/ The Wall Street Journal, 5-31:16.

Earl Warren
Former Chief Justice of the United States

When hundreds of millions of dollars are given to bankrupt railroads, failing defense manufacturers, shipping interests and the like, the words "welfare" or "relief" are not used. Instead, such things are done to "strengthen the economy." Perhaps welfare to needy individuals can some day be discussed with the same particularity and with the same equanimity.

Plainview (Tex.) Daily Herald, 7-20:8.

Transportation

James M. Beggs
Under Secretary of Transportation of the United States

(Referring to AMTRAK): They are trying to reverse a 22-year-old trend that has led most Americans to do their traveling by automobile; and trends do not reverse easily.

Plainview, (Tex.) Daily Herald, 1-16:(A)8.

We know that buses can be attractive, comfortable, efficient and fast. We know that subways can be clean, safe, reliable and efficient. And perhaps most importantly, we know that American engineering and design genius can produce almost any technological miracle that society can define. The space program taught us that. The problems lie in artificial obstacles—the multitude of institutions and governmental jurisdictions that must be included in technological growth and development. I recall Dr. Wernher Von Braun once saying that transportation systems are much more complex than space systems. What he was really saying, I think, is that you don't have to go through Kansas City on the way to the moon: There are no toll-takers, councils of government, counties, states or communities that have to agree on the best space route to take.

At Metropolitan Growth Conference sponsored by Mid-America Regional Council, Kansas City/ The Wall Street Journal, 6-2:8.

B. F. Biaggini
President, Southern Pacific (Railway) Company

If you believe in nationalization (of railroads), you can rationalize the nationalization of any industry. I think a privately owned transportation system is more efficient and cheaper than any other transportation system in the world . . . Every state-owned railway system in the world loses tremendous amounts of money; it ranges from $300-to-$600 million a year for the British, the Italians and the Japanese. I think the French win the prize—they are up around 900 million a year in losses. And you're talking about countries that aren't as big as the state of Pennsylvania. It would be just a matter of time and the same thing would happen here.

Interview/ U.S. News & World Report, 1-3:46.

. . . when the decline in rail patronage resumed right after the war (World War II), railroad management mistakenly assumed it could win customers back by new equipment, service and promotion. Management proceeded to take its best shots—with the most beautiful, best-riding, most streamlined trains, equipped with barber shops, valet service, maids, couriers, nurses and dining cars where you got the thickest steaks, and with high-speed trains at 90 and 100 miles an hour, clockwork on-time performance and, above all, low fares like the $7.50 price in 1950 on Southern Pacific's fine Coast Daylight between San Francisco and Los Angeles or the $49.37 rate between Chicago and San Francisco. But the postwar public simply wasn't buying. It had two new darlings—comfortable automobiles and fast airplanes, with the government generously providing excellent facilities on which to operate both. The finest trains on earth no longer could hold the patronage of the socialites, the political leaders, the movie stars, the wealthy and, most importantly of all, the businessman, who found he could no longer afford the time it took to go by train. Business travel is both the bread and the butter of passenger service; and when the railroads lost this, they lost everything. So when someone complains that we don't showcase trains like some other countries, tell them we did, once. And remind him that we had many more of them than any state-owned railroad has today—and that's a tribute to the competitive capitalistic, free-enterprise system. Anyone who wants a nationalized system should just stop and recall his own experiences with the present government bureaucracies here and abroad.

Before Executives Club, Chicago, Jan. 28/ Vital Speeches, 3-1:310.

Claude S. Brinegar
Vice president, Union Oil Company; Secretary of Transportation-designate of the United States

(On his nomination as new Transportation Secretary): I've flown a million miles in the last seven years and I've sat on the Harbor Freeway (in Los Angeles) for hours in traffic jams. I've experienced all the obvious open issues that you and I see. I now plan to dig very hard into the issues that all the country sees.

News conference/ San Francisco Examiner & Chronicle, 12-17:(This World)8.

Secor D. Browne
Chairman, Civil Aeronautics Board of the United States

We recognize there is pressure on the airlines to raise capacity again. There are some 60 or more wide-body jets set for delivery in 1972. The Board urges the carriers not to put them into service on a one-to-one basis, replacing a narrow body with a wide body. This would be disastrous . . . If an airplane has 35 per cent of the seats and 25 per cent of the market, they are out of their minds. This inefficiency has to be translated into higher fares.

Interview/ U.S. News & World Report, 3-6:31.

(On airliner hijacking): To me, it is economic nonsense to suggest that the carriers or the airport operators are capable of policing the system. My thesis is that this is a national responsibility, and the Federal government must act before the sands run out and we have a real catastrophe . . .

June 9/ U.S. News & World Report, 7-3:13.

(On airliner hijacking): As it stands now, virtually every criminal skyjacker knows there is some place in the world where he can be safe. Cuba is not the only such haven—there are others, like Algeria and Libya—but it is the closest, handiest and easiest to get to. So an agreement to end (Cuba's) use as a safe haven would go far in putting a stop to the increasingly violent hijacking of United States airliners.

U.S. News & World Report, 12-4:44.

Roy D. Chapin, Jr.
Chairman, American Motors Corporation

Product development will emphasize smaller cars, because this is where need and demand will continue to accelerate. The market for larger or luxury cars will not disappear in this decade, but it is difficult to foresee any real growth. Styling will have to be highly functional and highly appealing. A square box on wheels, however useful and economical, will not sell any better in the 1970s than it would have sold in the 1960s.

Before Rubber Manufacturers Association, Washington, Nov. 16/ Los Angeles Times, 11-17:(3)19.

James M. Collins
United States Representative, R–Tex.

We should commend those who worked so hard in AMTRAK to try to make the system a success; but the plain facts are that the public is no longer riding trains for the long haul and there is no need to keep them running.

San Francisco Examiner, 3-24:36.

Benjamin O. Davis, Jr.
Assistant Secretary for Safety and Consumer Affairs, Department of Transportation of the United States

(On airliner hijackings): We must instill in all parties . . . an increasing determination to resist hijack and extortionist demands to the fullest extent possible consistent with the safety of human life. Too often, hijackers have been afforded service and responsiveness that is not provided even the first-class traveler. Too often, funds have been raised and provided extortionists in amounts and with a speed that approach the fantastic.

News conference, Washington, June 7/ The New York Times, 6-8:82.

(On airliner hijackings): The solution to this problem remains on the ground. The airlines must, in addition to obeying the Federal Aviation Administration's rules regarding passenger screening, use a lot of common sense with respect to limiting carry-on baggage, the examination of certain types of carry-on baggage, the permitting of people to board aircraft with certain things that can be used as weapons. There's going to have to be a lot of effort by local jurisdictions to provide law-enforcement personnel to give an atmosphere of security at airports. Airport operators are going to have to take stringent measures to prevent unauthorized people and vehicles from getting to the operational side of airports. All these efforts are going to have to be intensified. They are being intensified; and I think that we'll come to a point where it will be much more difficult for a potential hijacker to board an airplane. That is what we really want: We want to avoid the necessity for the violent actions that take place aboard an airplane filled with passengers. When it comes to that, it represents a failure on the part of our system, because the first effort must always be to prevent the hijackers from ever getting aboard in the first place.

Interview/ U.S. News & World Report, 7-17:28.

Alejandro DeTomaso
Italian automobile designer

My criteria for a city car are quite rigid. The car must be large enough to transport at least one adult and two children, perhaps along with a load of baggage or groceries. It must be very cheap, $1,000, and weigh less than 1,000 pounds. The maximum speed does not have to be higher than 50 miles an hour . . . For my city car, the power choice is a very basic two-stroke motorcycle engine. It will have a displacement of 500 to 600 cubic centimeters, be air-cooled and coupled to a simple three or four-speed transmission. The time is fast approaching when a car like our city car will no longer be an oddity; it will be a necessity.

Turin, Italy/ San Francisco Examiner & Chronicle, 3-12:(B)6.

Henry Ford II
Chairman, Ford Motor Company

Today, except for the most densely populated central cities, the car continues to be the means of transportation with the highest level of comfort and convenience. There is movement to large metropolitan areas; but there is also great movement within these urban-suburban complexes. Where formerly we had one central business area surrounded by residential districts, we now have multi-activity centers—clusters of business, shopping and cultural facilities—scattered throughout a metropolitan area.

(HENRY FORD II)

We expect this trend to continue, and we expect that the private automobile will continue to be the most convenient means of transportation between home and activity center.

The New York Times, 4-2:(1A)8.

Ola Forsberg
President, International Federation of Air Line Pilots Associations

(On the forthcoming pilots strike to protest airliner hijackings): This drastic action is the result of the lack of effective international measures to stem the tide of unlawful interference with civil aviation and constitutes a strong expression of deep concern and solidarity on the part of the world's aviation community. The UN must clearly go on record to the effect that unlawful interference with civil aviation is a threat to international peace and security and must be dealt with as such, including the application of enforcement procedures.

June 16/
The Dallas Times Herald, 6-17:(A)1.

Richard C. Gerstenberg
Chairman,
General Motors Corporation

Most Americans who ride in cars don't use safety belts, unfortunately. The studies show that 30 per cent use the lap belts and only 4 per cent use the shoulder belts. Yet everyone who buys a car must pay for these—whether he wants them or not. Society can understandably require good brakes or good steering mechanisms, because these affect the safety of people outside the car—pedestrians and other motorists. But when people are required to buy equipment whose only purpose is to protect the buyer, then government has invaded the principle of consumer sovereignty.

Before Industrial Executives Club,
Flint, Mich., March 29/
Vital Speeches, 5-1:430.

(On the recall of automobiles by manufacturers because of mechanical defects): . . . there is nothing, absolutely nothing, that happens in our business that we dislike as much as a recall. We spend terrific sums of money trying to prevent this. We employ right now about 35,000 people who devote their full time to inspection and quality control. Last year, those people worked a total of 70 million man-hours. This is just to discover any defects that occur during the production process. We inspect all principal components as the parts are built. We inspect the complete vehicle once it has been assembled. We test it before it leaves our plants. We have the dealer again test that vehicle upon receipt. We give these cars and these components a terrific amount of testing at our proving grounds. Outside of Detroit we have a proving ground of about 8,000 acres. We drive 50 million miles a year on those proving grounds, and about 20 million of those miles is spent in just durability testing of our cars. We drive our cars for 30,000 to 36,000 miles on a durability test; and incidentally, we drive our competitors' cars the same way. And when that is finished, we tear them all apart to see where the wear and tear has been. We go every length we possibly can to discover these things before they leave the plant. But we are all human. We do make mistakes. I make them as well as others. We do our very, very best, though, to see that these things do not happen.

TV-radio interview, Washington/
"Meet the Press,"
National Broadcasting Company, 9-3.

L. Patrick Gray III
Acting Director,
Federal Bureau of Investigation

(On airliner hijacking): While hijackings are troublesome to authorities, they have proved to be much more distressing to a great majority of their perpetrators. Well over 90 per cent of all hijackers during the period January 1, 1968, to August 26,

1972, have been identified. In all but one hijacking in which money was obtained, either the hijacker has been apprehended or his ransom denied him. Five hijackers have been killed in the commission of their crime, six more have been wounded and three others chose suicide. Considering that a few more than 200 persons have been involved in the crime, the statistics prove that hijacking ranks with the most futile of criminal enterprises.

Quote, 11-26:515.

Knut Hammarskjold
Director general, International Transport Association

(On the recent terrorist attack at Tel Aviv's Lod Airport): The airlines are doing everything in their power to protect their passengers without bringing air transport to a stop. They cannot, however, succeed without equally energetic action by governments through legislation and severe punishment of those perpetrating acts of armed aggression against civil aviation.

Geneva, June 1/
The New York Times, 6-2:4.

J. Herbert Hollomon
Provost, Massachusetts Institute of Technology

What is the social cost of urban transportation? The total cost, whether it is borne by you and me or the society in general, is on the order of $100 billion. Recently, I attempted to make a "guesstimate" of how much it cost the society for you and me to drive a car in the central city of the United States. It is a difficult thing to calculate, for one must include the displacement of land, the change of property values, the traffic-safety costs, the street costs, the pollution costs, the health costs, the cost of welfare that is attributable to the lack of mobility. The cost to society of inadequate mobility within the large city is also difficult to calculate: How much does it cost in unemployment compensation? How much does it cost in racial strife? How much does it cost in crime? How much does it cost in decreased property values? It is difficult to calculate, but congestion costs alone in London have been estimated to be of the order of $1 a mile. I suspect that in the central core of many cities the total cost of driving a private car is at least $1 per mile. We do not know what various people will do if given different options for urban transportation. It is very clear that, with a system that costs about 10 per cent of the total gross national product—a cost that affects the whole fabric of American life—we need to look again at the nature of the problem.

At International Conference on
Urban Transportation, Pittsburgh/
The National Observer, 4-15:13.

Lee A. Iacocca
President, Ford Motor Company

I think the days when we produced all-new (automobile) models every year or two are gone forever. The need to hold down costs and, equally important, the need to meet current and proposed legislation prompted our decision to make fewer model changeovers. However, I think styling will always be an important factor to many customers. Beauty sells better than ugliness; it's as simple as that. And we don't have to look far for an example. We at Ford had only four all-new models this year; and while total sales in the model year have gone up across the board, sales of those four all-new cars jumped spectacularly.

The New York Times, 4-2:(1A)8.

John W. Ingram
Administrator,
Federal Railroad Administration

The short-haul trains are the real money-losers. The Kansas City-St. Louis run, for example, has so few passengers (that) it would be cheaper for us to buy each one a Cadillac convertible and drive the route. But I don't think that's exactly what the government had in mind when it set up AMTRAK.

San Francisco Examiner & Chronicle, 10-1:(This World)2.

James L. Kerrigan
President, Greyhound Bus Lines

Today, the greatest single obstacle to improving the quality of bus transportation is the 96-inch Federal width limitation. So long as this limitation exists, the width of passenger seats on intercity buses cannot be increased. That is because Greyhound and other large intercity bus companies operate approximately 80 per cent of their total miles on the interstate system.

Before Senate Subcommittee, Washington/ The Christian Science Monitor, 1-10:9.

William P. Lear
Industrialist

As far as I can see, the internal-combustion engine is as dead as a dodo bird. It and its accompanying diesel engine have already become extinct and are going to be oddities in the future, because there are so many better ways to produce power.

Plainview (Tex.) Daily Herald, 1-31:2.

R. Dan Mahaney
Manager, Dulles International Airport, Washington, D.C.

When we get around to executing them (airliner hijackers), we'll be much more ahead. I loved the way the Israelis handled that last one (when they killed one plane's hijackers). We have to stop this. If you let one go, it encourages the next one. Each one refines a little more on the last one.

Interview/ The Washington Post, 6-4:(D)1.

Lee Metcalf
United States Senator, D–Mont.

(On letters he has been receiving complaining about AMTRAK service): . . . there is a similar refrain describing hours of waiting in dirty depots, delayed arrivals and departures, cold, dirty cars, unfriendly personnel, oversold reservations and locked bathrooms.

San Francisco Examiner, 4-6:10.

John J. O'Donnell
President, Air Line Pilots Association (United States)

(Announcing a 24-hour pilots strike protesting air piracy): It is truly unfortunate that hundreds of thousands of airline passengers will have their travel plans interrupted for this period. But it is inevitable that, unless hijack sanctuaries are eliminated, many thousands of future passengers will continue to face the horrors of air crimes.

News conference, Washington, June 6/ San Francisco Examiner, 6-16:1.

Theodore W. Parker
New York State Commissioner of Transportation

Transportation is becoming more and more a government responsibility. The government must take over because we cannot leave people without transportation, even if it has to be a deficit operation.

Interview, Albany, N.Y./ The New York Times, 8-20:(3)24.

John J. Riccardo
President, Chrysler Corporation

In spite of the size and diversity of the American automobile industry today, our products have outstanding quality. If each company were producing a single car model, similar in all respects to the one next to it on the line, the quality would be even higher. But the driving public, which is expected to purchase more than eight million American-built cars this year, does not want uniformity and in fact insists on choice. And with the addition of each option or accessory, the quality problems and chances for human error increase.

The New York Times, 4-2:(1A)8.

William P. Rogers
Secretary of State of the United States

We need to remember that threats and acts against international air travel are an aspect, a very important aspect, of the international terrorism that threatens the lives of innocent people, regardless of nationality. The international community must take firm and prompt action to effectively prevent air piracy. If we can do this, we will have denied to terrorists and would-be terrorists one of their most effective weapons and will have taken a major step to subdue international lawlessness and terrorism.

Before International Civil Aviation Organization, Washington, Sept. 6/ Los Angeles Times, 9-7:(1)24.

William J. Ronan
Chairman, New York State Metropolitan Transportation Authority

The technological challenge of mass transportation on earth is ever so much more complex than moon junkets, because out there (in space), all we must do is adapt man and machine to a given set of natural phenomena–and down here we must attempt to persuade man and adapt machine to an unpredictable and irrational set of variables which are in a constant state of flux.

At Engineering Foundation Conference, New England College, Hennicker, N.H./ The Wall Street Journal, 7-25:14.

William D. Ruckelshaus
Administrator, Environmental Protection Agency of the United States

There is going to be some limitation, I think, or some change, in the way we transport ourselves in this nation. I don't believe we can go on producing automobiles at the rate we are and utilizing them at the rate we have and have cities that aren't constantly clogged, that are not going to have air that's . . . in some difficulty.

Interview/ Los Angeles Times, 6-29:(2)7.

Americans all want cars, and one of the problems is that 75 per cent of us get them. The very popularity of the automobile now seriously threatens its usefulness. In many of our cities we are confronted by pollution, congestion, noise, delay, ugliness and urban breakdown on a scale that has not been seen since the last days of imperial Rome . . . We need more flexibility of choice; we need means of transportation that bring people into contact with each other and not just with machines. If necessary, fares (for public transportation) should be subsidized or abolished. No one expects the police or the schools to make a profit, yet transit has been so-obligated in most metropolitan areas. The automobile is here to stay. It will continue to have a dominant role in the exurbs, on the farm, between cities over short distances and as an alternate mode of transportation everywhere. But we must supplement it if we are to get the most efficient service out of it.

Before American Automobile Association/ The New York Times, 10-14:31.

John H. Shaffer
Administrator, Federal Aviation Administration

The future of America rests with a strong and growing aviation industry. Without air transport, this country cannot survive. New York City is an excellent example. Three years ago, New York had 11 per cent of all the passenger business. Today it has dropped to 6 per cent, and the decline is continuing. In recent years, 29 major corporations left New York City because they have no good air transport . . . One day soon, New Yorkers will awaken to find they have what they want. They will have a quiet airport, that is, a dead airport. And the city soon will die with it.

Before American Institute of Aeronautics and Astronautics, Los Angeles/ Los Angeles Herald-Examiner, 1-21:(C)12.

Hijacking an aircraft for profit is the world's greatest exercise in futility. I realize the typical hijacker-extortionist is neither a stable nor rational personality. But I would think that even the most disturbed individual would have gotten the message by now. That message is that, when a person buys a ticket on an airliner with the idea of hijacking it for profit, he has really bought himself a ticket to prison or the morgue.

Los Angeles Times, 7-25:(1)1.

Robert L. F. Sikes
United States Representative, D–Fla.

It should be obvious that nothing really has been accomplished toward putting an end to the practice of (airplane) hijacking . . . Hijackings are a heinous thing, not a lark. They have made the airlines and the law-enforcement officials appear ridiculous, and it is time to put a stop to it. The airline companies seem to have no difficulty in paying whatever amount of money the hijackers demand for blackmail. This could lead to the deduction that they are making too much money to care what happens to it; and it may be well to look into the matter of raising their taxes to reduce the supply of cash available for hijackers.

Before the House, Washington/ The National Observer, 6-10:17.

Donald G. Stokes
Managing director, British Leyland Motors

I see a risk of the automobile being so safe for its occupants that, with their being un-hurtable whatever the car hits, the pedestrian is going to be exposed to greater risk.

San Francisco Examiner, 1-13:32.

Stuart G. Tipton
President, Air Transport Association of America

(On airliner hijacking): The efforts that we (U.S. commercial airlines) have followed have taken two forms. One is the attempt to stop hijackers on the ground and to make sure that our government gives us the law-enforcement aid that we need. In the international field, we have backed the efforts strongly taken by the United States to establish an international law that says that the nation that holds a skyjacker and neither prosecutes nor extradites is an outlaw nation. That, we think, is the proper way to drive at this problem.

June 18/ U.S. News & World Report, 7-3:13.

Lionel Van Deerlin
United States Representative, D–Calif.

AMTRAK must be denied all of the $170 million (Federal subsidy) . . . until they prove they're running the ship . . . (Relating an experience he had using AMTRAK): It seemed that a friendly barge pilot took out a key railroad bridge. We had to be bused 165 miles to meet up with the train; and when we got there, it turned out that all the passengers were on time, but the railroad had forgotten to bring our luggage on the same bus. That made us two hours late getting started. (At another point, waiting for a broken-down freight train to be cleared from the track), we sat there on that darn siding an hour longer than it takes me to fly home from Washington. What they are doing is destroying confidence in AMTRAK instead of building it up as they should be. There is no evidence at all that things are any better under AMTRAK than they were under the old system. And that must change if they are to see any of the $170 million.

News conference, Los Angeles/ The Dallas Times Herald, 1-9:(A)4.

John A. Volpe
Secretary of Transportation of the United States

(On airliner hijacking): The fact is that, prior to this time, we were depending upon voluntary cooperation on the part of airlines and airport operators to get this job (protecting against hijacking) done within our own continental limits. The fact is that some airlines responded and responded extremely well; other airlines did not . . . We believe the airlines themselves have got to take a very great role in this total picture, and get a good part of this job done themselves . . .

June 14/ U.S. News & World Report, 7-3:13.

(On airliner hijackings): Piracy on the high seas came to an end when the ports of call were closed to the plunderers of ships. Piracy in the skies will die the same death when the doors of welcome are universally slammed on hijackers around the world.

At anti-hijacking conference, Washington, Sept. 4/ Los Angeles Times, 9-5:(1)7.

Edgar D. Whitcomb
Governor of Indiana

It is frightening to contemplate just how much worse our urban traffic congestion would be today without these multi-lane high-volume expressways. But we are still being told that highways are "strangling and mutilating" our cities.

San Francisco Examiner & Chronicle, 10-1:(This World)2.

Leonard Woodcock
President, United Automobile Workers of America

Needless to say, I am not opposed to the automobile, nor to the construction of highways to facilitate its use. This attitude does not rest solely on the fact that the UAW represents about 850,000 auto workers. It rests also on the fact that the automobile is the only efficient mode of transportation in many areas and for many purposes. (But) in our large population centers, the automobile is fast becoming a threat to our health, our safety, our comfort and our efficiency . . . Clearly we must develop, construct and operate more efficient modes of transportation . . .

Before Senate Commerce Committee, Washington, March 16/ Los Angeles Herald-Examiner, 3-16:(A)7.

Urban Affairs

Joseph L. Alioto
Mayor of San Francisco

A city is a place where people who are oppressed and who have lost hope can come. The heartland of America is not some wheatfield. That's nonsense. The heartland of America is its vibrant cities, where the personality can be developed to its fullest.

At inauguration for his second term in office, San Francisco, Jan. 8/ San Francisco Examiner & Chronicle, 1-9:(A)3.

Earl L. Butz
Secretary of Agriculture of the United States

. . . one of the problems that has been created in inner cities has been the exodus of rural people to downtown Baltimore, Philadelphia, Detroit, St. Louis and New York, without the skills to be a productive citizen, without the cultural background to live there. They constitute a breeding ground for crime and delinquency, and cause welfare rolls to skyrocket. We should have kept them in the country. We could keep them much cheaper out there, much more productive out there than we have them in the ghettos of the inner cities.

The New York Times Magazine, 4-16:90.

William T. Cahill
Governor of New Jersey

I don't really think (President) Nixon understands or knows what the people are really thinking about in New Jersey. We have no one really close to the Administration. I have no communication with the White House. Nixon never talks to me. He'll see me and he'll say, "How are things in New Jersey?" and I'll say, "Pretty good." And he'll say, "How am I going to do in New Jersey next year?" and I'll say, "You could win here today." But what about our problems? I'd like to see Nixon come to New Jersey and leave all the fanfare in Washington and see the Newarks as I see them. If he ever saw Newark through my eyes, he'd change: He'd build Newark; he'd spend some money on it. It doesn't do any good for a man to come to Newark and have a press conference and make a speech . . . If he'd only forget the prepared scripts and stop saying what his media advertisers tell him to say; if he wasn't so intent on making sure that he does nothing to hurt his chances for re-election . . . he ought to sneak into Newark on a Sunday night and walk up and down the streets and see what I've seen there in the streets of Paterson and Camden and Elizabeth. Then he'd know why there is so much unrest in the country.

Interview, Trenton, N.J./ The New York Times, 2-21:22.

Constantinos A. Doxiadis
Architect; City planner

Man has not abandoned the city. He has enlarged it. One problem today is that too many people are still planning for the small cell city instead of the larger area. All cities everywhere are spreading out. You have more abandonment in the central sections of the U.S. because there is more room to spread out, and higher mobility because there are more autos.

U.S. News & World Report, 4-10:44.

Philip Houser
Director, population research center, University of Chicago

The major problem of the cities in 1972 is the complete inability of the cities to deal with their problems. Complete inability, because there isn't a city in the United States that has the sources of revenue to deal with its problems. The reason is that we in the United States are still dealing with the 18th century form of governments we inherited from England; England has long since got rid of it. We're still struggling with it because we don't have the good sense to deal with these problems the way other countries do . . . You ask the Mayor what does he think about going in the direction of metropolitan government. He says, "Hell, no." The same is true of the suburbs. And the answer is simple: The Mayor in control of the Democratic machine in the city and the Republicans in control of the Republican machine in suburbia would much rather preserve their own realms of dominance. This frontier orientation of "how do I get mine and the hell with everybody else" threatens the very viability of our society . . . We in the localities are proving year after year that we're too adolescent, too bigoted and too stupid to govern ourselves, so Washington is going to have to do it for us.

Interview/ San Francisco Examiner & Chronicle, 1-2:(B)9.

Hubert H. Humphrey
United States Senator, D–Minn.

There are no answers to the problems of urban America if there are no answers to the problems of rural America—none.

Before Oklahoma Legislature, Oklahoma City, March 23/ The Washington Post, 3-24:(A)6.

I long for the day when we look upon even a great metropolis as but a center, and around it like spokes on (a) wheel, going on out, are autonomous villages and communities that are viable, that can live by themselves.

Before New Jersey Mayors, Princeton, May 17/ The New York Times, 5-18:36.

We've spent it ($160 billion trying to revitalize the cities) like a kid who goes to the circus—no plan, no concept of what it is all about, except that there's a need and somebody rushes in with a package of Band-Aids, aspirin tablets and a bottle of iodine to touch things up.

Campaigning for the Democratic Presidential nomination, San Francisco/ The Dallas Times Herald, 5-27:(A)8.

I don't think either of the major political parties has faced up to the realities of the urban crisis. I suggest we quit talking about the urban crisis and put it as the American crisis, because America is essentially urbanized. What some people once thought to be a comfortable existence in the suburbs is becoming a mish-mash of problems of zoning, sanitation, transportation, and the tax rates are going up and the schools are having problems.

At U.S. Conference of Mayors, New Orleans, June 20/ Los Angeles Times, 6-21:(1)4.

Moon Landrieu
Mayor of New Orleans

. . . in the last five years the Federal government will have reduced taxes by some $75 billion, while cities and states and local units of government will have increased taxes by $7 billion. Let me tell you . . . what that does to my city. We have placed in the last six years a one-cent sales tax for school purposes, a half-cent sales tax for general government, another one-half cent sales tax for general government, supported a one-cent sales tax at the state level in order to get some state revenues here, plus garbage service charges, water rate increases, transit rate increases,

(MOON LANDRIEU)

to a point that you simply began to drive people out of the cities and only maintain your head above water.

TV-radio interview, New Orleans/ "Meet the Press," National Broadcasting Company, 6-18.

John V. Lindsay
Mayor of New York

(Responding to criticism of his frequent trips around the country campaigning for the Democratic Presidential nomination): I know what it takes to run a city. Unless I take the battle to the steps of Congress and the state house and whoever will listen, I am not doing my job . . . I don't think the Mayors should be excluded from the political process. If they keep us strapped to our chairs and off the streets, we can't do our job. There's no statute that prohibits me from walking the streets of any part of the country if it will help my city.

News conference, New York, Jan. 12/ Los Angeles Herald-Examiner, 1-13:(A)13.

The cities are not the problem. They are the solution . . . The city is not the creator of social problems, and it doesn't spread them. It solves them; for the city is the machine of social change.

Plainview (Tex.) Herald, 10-16:6.

Tom Luken
Mayor of Cincinnati

. . . financing touches all the problems. If we had enough money, we could buy the bus system, install more pollution-control monitors and solve the other problems. But Cincinnati . . . has a small central city. We're a city of 450,000 in a metropolitan area of a million and a half. And those most in need are those in the central city who are least able to pay. So more and more we shall have to look elsewhere for money.

Cincinnati/ The Christian Science Monitor, 1-10:5.

Henry W. Maier
Mayor of Milwaukee

Basically, the . . . central cities of the country have to handle the young and the attendant costs and the aged and the attendant costs and the poor and the attendant costs. These three classes in our society—services to the poor, education for the young, recreation for the young and aid to the aged—are the most expensive business we (in the cities) have.

TV-radio interview, New Orleans/ "Meet the Press," National Broadcasting Company, 6-18.

Sam Massell
Mayor of Atlanta

As a person earns more money and is able to better himself, he starts looking for a little better home—a larger yard and more space. If he starts looking in the core city, chances are he's not going to find what he wants. It's just not there. So if he wants a new home, he goes out farther—not because it's beyond the city limits, but because it's a nice new place.

U.S. News & World Report, 4-10:44.

As of 1970, 73.5 per cent of the total U.S. population resided in urban areas, which is a 19.1 per cent increase over the 1960 figure. In 1985, the urban population is projected at 85 per cent; so we can expect more pollution, more traffic congestion, more crime and more of every other condition of density that goes unchecked.

At annual Congress of Cities, Indianapolis, Nov. 27/ San Francisco Examiner, 11-28:2.

Paul Moore, Jr.
Episcopal Bishop of New York

I do not believe it is the will of God that New York shall die, nor that Yonkers dies, nor Newburgh, Poughkeepsie nor any other place. Yet they are all doomed. Someone has to say it. Our cities will die within the next 20 years—as surely as Sodom and Gomorrah. Our sin is not as colorful as Sodom's but deeper. It is the sin of Cain, the murder of our brothers. New York murders her children in the tenements, on the streets, in the schools; while those who can escape understandably seek an illusory Eden in the suburbs.

At his installation as Bishop, New York, Sept. 23/ The New York Times, 9-24:(1).

Edmund S. Muskie
United States Senator, D–Maine

We are told (by President Nixon) that more studies will be conducted to find an alternative to the property tax—as if high-level words about the problem could point us toward a solution. We know now, as we have known for years, what the real solution is—not only to the property tax, but to the total crisis in urban finance and urban services. The only solution is a real commitment of Federal resources instead of more official rhetoric.

Philadelphia, Jan. 20/ U.S. News & World Report, 1-31:16.

In a nation where three-quarters of the people live in urban areas, the state of the Union is determined by the state of the cities.

Before City Council, Philadelphia, Jan. 20/ The New York Times, 1-21:20.

The urban problem is the nation's problem. The urban problem is the concentration of all the pressure and problems and unmet needs of our society. We cannot abandon the cities without destroying the nation.

At U.S. Conference of Mayors, New Orleans, June 20/ Los Angeles Times, 6-21:(1)4.

Lawrence F. O'Brien
Chairman, Democratic National Committee

I fervently hope and I deeply believe that the party I represent will once again recognize in 1972 that the city is its bedrock; that it cannot claim to represent and to lead the American people until it has sought them out and helped them where they hurt the most, fear the worst, breathe the dirtiest, enjoy the least and live the most briefly.

At U.S. Conference of Mayors, New Orleans, June 19/ The Dallas Times Herald, 6-19:(A)9.

Ralph J. Perk
Mayor of Cleveland

(Protecting the environment) is not a new problem. It is a problem that cities have struggled with for time immemorial. I feel that it is one of our greatest challenges; and how we meet this challenge will determine whether our cities will survive or perish.

At conference of Mayors of the world's major cities, Milan, Italy, April 20/The Washington Post, 4-20:(E)8.

Desmond Plummer
Chairman, Greater London Council (England)

Cities are indeed national assets, but they are not permanent assets. Like all assets, they need to be preserved and developed. And it is time that central governments recognized more clearly that investment in the future of their cities is as vital to national prosperity as it is to the well-being of the cities themselves.

At Conference of the World's Great Cities, Tokyo, Nov. 28/ The New York Times, 11-29:16.

Nelson A. Rockefeller
Governor of New York

While New York (City) is still the cultural and financial capital in this coun-

(NELSON A. ROCKEFELLER)

try—and we've got to keep it that way—for the people who live there it is presently a place where housing can't be found, streets are unsafe, corruption undermines public trust, traffic is unbearable, garbage isn't picked up often enough and, worst of all, no one can ever seem to get anything changed for the better because, as things now stand, there is not actual control over the functioning of city government despite the almost total centralization of power in City Hall.

State of the State address, Albany/The New York Times, 1-23:(4)3.

George W. Romney
Secretary of Housing and Urban Development of the United States

It has been estimated that 50 per cent of the jobs in the metropolitan areas are now outside the central city, and the movement of jobs from the central city to the suburb is accelerating very rapidly. The flight of the middle- and upper-income groups to the suburbs, the concentration of problem populations in the central city with higher welfare costs, higher crime-control costs, higher educational costs and a decreasing tax base—both in terms of residential property and in terms of manufacturing and commercial property—results in a growing fiscal crisis for the central city. At the very same time, municipal workers are becoming more organized and more able to pressure annual wage increases. The economic resources of the city administrations to meet these increased demands and to maintain services is deteriorating sharply. The more city services decline, and the more the general environment appears to be deteriorating, the more is accelerated the flight to the suburbs by both business and the individual . . . We would do a disservice to ourselves and to the nation if we continue to approach this problem with any sense of easy optimism. There are those who say that a frank statement of the problem is so demoralizing that it contributes to making the problem worse. It is my belief that it is essential that we face the problem in all its stark reality and full dimensions, particularly because of its contagious character. For the problems of the central cities are beginning to penetrate the suburbs. As the Vice President (Agnew) has pointed out: A city is like an apple—if it rots at the core, soon the whole apple will be rotten . . . We have been throwing billions of dollars into these problem areas without making a dent upon them. It is now foolish to say that if we will only spend a little more money we will resolve these difficult issues . . . The truth is, none of us are now sure what are the right things to do.

March 6/ U.S. News & World Report, 4-10:46.

Look at the growing parade of Mayors and Council leaders from city after city—once the unchallenged base of the Democratic Party—who are singing the praises of the Nixon Administration and endorsing the President for re-election. That didn't just happen. It happened because this Administration proved it understood urban problems, understood the problems of local leadership and responded creatively to local needs.

Before Republican National Convention Resolutions Committee, Miami Beach, Aug. 15/ The New York Times, 8-16:20.

George Sternlieb
Director, Center for Urban Policy Research, Rutgers University

The size of the constituency which lives outside the cities but still wants to preserve them at any cost grows smaller day by day. It is not exploitation that the core areas must fear. It is indifference and abandonment. The crisis of the cities is a crisis of function. The major problem of the core areas of our cities is simply their lack of economic value. Except for insurance companies, banks and other institutions that find it difficult to leave because of legal rules, business institutions are virtually deserting the central city. All major department-store chains now do the bulk of their business in the suburbs. Smaller retailers in secondary urban shopping areas on the "trolley-car streets" are also leaving or going out of business. The old "Mom and Pop stores," grocery and candy stores on every block, the fish stores and neighborhood bakeries are things of the past. There has also been a flight of the professionals. In the last 10 years, Newark (N.J.) has lost half its physicians, and many of those who remain have one foot in the suburbs and are just waiting for their practices to take hold there before they move out.

U.S. News & World Report, 4-10:43.

Herman E. Talmadge
United States Senator, D–Ga.

Fun City isn't fun any more. Since the conclusion of World War II, we have been on a national joy ride that has produced the greatest migration of human beings in history. We have shoved untold millions of people into cities, because we failed to commit ourselves to the need for balanced growth. Rural people couldn't find jobs, so they left. They lacked clean water to drink, could not get sewer systems, telephone service or natural gas, so they left. Small farms could no longer support families, so they left. Rural decay set in; institutions that hold communities together fell apart. Not only were no new jobs created, existing jobs began to disappear. Now, I do not propose a national policy of "back to the farm." I do advocate a sensible policy of balanced growth to strengthen rural America, a program that will also relieve cities of some of their problems. The migration of rural people to major cities has created an urban crisis, in fact a national crisis. The economic renewal of rural America will not only benefit country people, but by turning off the mass migration, we will be helping hard-pressed Mayors of every big city throughout the land. Rural development is an idea whose time is long overdue. Never before has a nation had such an opportunity to raise the quality of life for all Americans, whether they live on the farm, in the small town, or in the big city. In the final analysis, we want to assure every citizen of his right to live and work, in comfort and economic security, wherever he pleases.

Television broadcast/ "Comment!" National Broadcasting Company, 6-25.

Hans-Jochen Vogel
Mayor of Munich, West Germany

A few years ago, I said Munich was not New York. But today, I'm no longer so sure . . . Cities can also die, or at least alter their character so that they are no longer places of peace, well-being and fulfilled living, but concrete jungles dominated by hatreds, violence, decadence and decline.

Los Angeles Times, 3-24:(2)7.

Albert Walsh
Commissioner of Housing and Development of New York City

Our new society is based on automobile wheels and airplanes–not trains and rivers. Our old cities are built around trains and rivers. We have to recognize the change and adjust. There is no question that some cities will decay indefinitely. Some cities are obsolete. They should be torn down. I am not sure we can or should try to stop decay where there is no reason for a city to exist.

U.S. News & World Report, 4-10:43.

Evelle J. Younger
Attorney General of California

A city is like an apartment house. If it is filled, there should be no effort to bring in any more people. The concept that "there's room for one more" just doesn't apply.

At environmental conference/ San Francisco Examiner, 10-21:5.

Women's Liberation

Bella S. Abzug
United States Representative, D–N.Y.

(There is a) duality of American life . . . the myths. Women are beautiful and silent, but they talk too much. They can't balance the checkbook, but they control the wealth. Women are fragile, but it's perfectly all right for them to carry children and move furniture. Women can't pilot planes, but they can pretend to be a plane and invite men to "fly them" (as in airline advertising). Women are no longer imprisoned by man-made myths. We are coming down from our pedestal and up from the laundry room. We want an equal share in government and we mean to get it . . . although we seek not only equality for ourselves but also diversity. What is good for women will turn out to be good for our country.

Interview,
Beverly Hills, Calif./
Los Angeles Times, 11-20:(4)10.

Birch Bayh
United States Senator, D–Ind.

The magnitude of the evil of sex discrimination is plain. It cannot be denied. Nor can it be denied that the best way to remedy this blight on the American dream is by a Constitutional amendment. It is time to resolve that the women of this country shall no longer be subject to second-class citizenship. It is time to resolve that they, like their fathers, husbands and sons, and every American, are first-class citizens of this great nation.

Before the Senate,
Washington, March 17/
San Francisco Examiner, 3-17:2.

William H. Brown III
Chairman, Federal Equal Employment Opportunity Commission

Many people consider sex discrimination rather comical. Their minds see visions of women steelworkers or lady bricklayers, or bra-burnings in Atlantic City. Or, conversely, male Playboy Bunnies! But sex discrimination is not funny . . . Sex discrimination denies employment to people who need jobs . . . Clearly, women's lib is going to keep waging war on sex discrimination until business, labor and government clean their own houses.

U.S. News & World Report, 12-11:92.

James L. Buckley
United States Senator, C–N.Y.

I not only believe that the great majority of American women find fulfillment in their roles as wives and mothers, but I suspect that the great majority of American women are inclined to resent the demeaning, derogatory and cynical posture taken against marriage and motherhood by some of the outspoken advocates of the women's liberation movement, as if marriage and motherhood were the hallmarks of inferiority and servitude. To be sure, not all feminists share this jaundiced view, a fact for which we can all be thankful. There are many articulate and engaging activists in the movement, and they have made a compelling case for altering many of our laws which unjustly discriminate against women, especially in the area of job opportunities. With many of their grievances I am in great sympathy; but . . . I am satisfied that present Constitutional and statutory law provide ample opportunities for redress. I am not at all convinced that the "liberation" of some women requires the removal of legal protections from others or the imposition of greater legal burdens upon those who do not share the goals of the liberationists.

Before the Senate,
Washington, March 22/
Vital Speeches, 6-1:496.

Barbara Castle
Member of British Parliament

The challenges facing our society today are so big and exciting that this is the moment for women to be widening their horizons, not narrowing them as the American Women's Lib movement is doing on trivialities. Let us get ourselves obsessed with something bigger than sexual politics.

San Francisco Examiner, 2-24:30.

Carl N. Degler
Professor of History,
Stanford University

The women's movement is the most significant radical social phenomenon in all history. It makes the impact of Marxism seem old hat. Because, if we intend to carry it out to its logical extremes, if we really want an egalitarian society, then we naturally must revise the entire concept of the traditional, patriarchal family as we have always known it. And it will be the first time in the tradition of the Western world that the family has been altered so drastically, that men and women mutually agree to share the child-rearing and domestic roles so that both can pursue careers.

Interview/
Los Angeles Times, 11-21:(4)9.

Nicole de Hauteclocque
Mayor of Paris

I have no interest in (women's liberation) whatsoever. I'm very happy to be a woman. I like men. I think a woman should be able to take the role of a man. But to set men aside, to get rid of them, what an idea!

Interview, Paris/
The Christian Science Monitor,
7-24:8.

Sam J. Ervin, Jr.
United States Senator, D–N.C.

(Opposing an equal-rights amendment for women): I have had a number of conversations with militants of the extreme wing of women's lib. They have been unable to convince me that God made a mistake when He created two sexes instead of one, and that the most effective way to repair this mistake of God is to adopt a Constitutional amendment under which the daughters of America could be drafted for compulsory military service or enlisted for combat service and sent into battle to have their fair forms blasted into fragments by the bombs and shells of the enemy. That is precisely what this amendment . . . would do . . . This amendment is intended to rob Congress and all of the states of their powers to protect women . . .

Before the Senate, Washington/
The National Observer, 4-1:5.

Betty Friedan
Founder,
National Organization for Women

Female chauvinism, and those who preach or practice it, seems to me to be corrupting our movement for equality (for women) and inviting a backlash that endangers the very real gains we have won these past few years . . . Men can and must be with us if we are to change society. If we make men the enemy, they will surely lash back at us.

News conference, New York, July 18/
Los Angeles Times, 7-19:(1)1,7.

Wilma Scott Heide
President,
National Organization for Women

No significant change in the future is possible without women's human rights and

(WILMA SCOTT HEIDE)

liberation from centuries of blatant and subtle bondage. Only those women and men free enough from stereotyped notions of "femininity" and "masculinity" to be secure about our common humanity are as yet liberated enough to move with the level of self confidence to create an androgynous society and world. Women will demand it. Men will eventually welcome it. Our children deserve it. No woman should ever have to stand alone or (be) criticized for advocating and creating our own—our mother's, our sister's, our daughter's—personhood. It's a matter of human justice.

At University of Nebraska, Lincoln, March 6/ Vital Speeches, 4-15:409.

Jeanne M. Holm
Brigadier General, United States Air Force; Director, Women in the Air Force

. . . in the '50s we went through a unique period in our country. There was a tendency for the woman to go back to the home and for our culture to say, "That's where you belong." But that was not typical of what women have done historically in this country. Women have worked, historically. I think that notion of "women's place" has affected everyone's attitude. Any time women have gone into a profession that was essentially dominated by men, we've had problems of acceptance. The first women who went into Civil Service had a terrible time. The first women who were nurses had a miserable time. In World War II, women in the service had a difficult time in terms of acceptance. But I think those attitudes are disappearing, particularly as the new generation of male comes into the Air Force. They don't have those hang-ups; neither do the women. The women are learning to walk that professional line and still be women. It's important for a woman herself to recognize that there's nothing unfeminine about being a professional—it's bad only if she acts like a man and gets confused in her role.

Interview/ U.S. News & World Report, 1-17:65.

Matina S. Horner
President, Radcliffe College

Young men and women of today still tend to evaluate themselves and behave in ways consistent with age-old stereotypes and expectations. These stereotypes argue that independence, competence, intellectual achievement and leadership are all positive attributes of maturity and mental health. These very characteristics are at the same time viewed as synonymous with what is "male" and as basically inconsistent with what is "female." The implication is that a feminine woman cannot be a healthy, mature adult; and Margaret Mead's statement that "each step forward as a successful American is a step back as a woman" is very much to the point. Thus, one of the challenges to our generation will be to help women resist and dissolve the persistent myth that the fulfillment of any of their non-traditional aspirations is a denial of their femininity and proof of their inadequacy as potential wives and mothers. This myth prevents educated women from walking through doors now open to them, from taking advantage of opportunities now available to them. What a tremendous waste of both human and economic resources this represents! The price is too high. It is paid for by our students and by women in general in an easily-recognizable loss of confidence and self-esteem, in an attrition of aspirations, in a persistence of low expectations for the future, and in the presence of a pervasive, often self-defeating sense that they are second-class citizens. These are impossible conditions for personal and intellectual growth and development.

At her installation as president of Radcliffe College/ The National Observer, 12-30:11.

Sophia Loren
Actress

When a woman gives up her apparent inferiority, she doesn't realize how much pleasure she loses. In Italy, the woman has always been the real head of the house, while letting the man think he was.

San Francisco Examiner & Chronicle, 8-27:(Datebook)12.

Clare Boothe Luce
Former American diplomat and playwright

. . . (women's liberationists) Gloria Steinem and Germaine Greer are sort of the White Panthers of Women's Liberation. I'm not saying they are more militant than necessary, because any movement or crusade will inescapably set the mark in order to have other people toe it. And every movement in history has produced its exaggerated fringers . . . I stand with the more traditional women's liberationists who have simply plunked for equal pay for equal work and for the opening of opportunities on an equal basis with men. I agree with those who are not trying to get into the personal sexual relationships with male and female.

Interview, Hawaii/ Los Angeles Times, 5-14:(West)26.

I disagree with (author and women's rights advocate) Gloria Steinem in that I believe women should be quite free to choose privileges instead of rights. The great majority of women in every country in the world would rather be married than unmarried. Most of them (are) fairly well pleased by domestic life. I simply say if that's what a woman wants, why shouldn't she have it?

San Francisco Examiner & Chronicle, 7-9:(This World)2.

David J. Mahoney
Chairman and president, Norton Simon, Inc.

We are determined to continue our efforts to eliminate all barriers to advancement (by women) which are unrelated to merit. We are determined to be responsive to the changing wants and needs of women, as well as men. Above all, we are determined to continue to listen to the voices of women, both inside and outside our company. The law demands it. Self-interest compels it. The future requires it.

Nation's Business, August:15.

Norman Mailer
Author

(Women's Liberation is) a terrorist movement. It is precisely those women who have been dominating men for the last 20 years who are leading the movement. The men are terrified.

San Francisco Examiner & Chronicle, 10-29:(This World)2.

Marya Mannes
Author, Journalist

It's ridiculous to think that women can evolve alone. Men are their greatest potential allies. Women, of course, should be freed from the role of "Little Woman," a frustrated housewife whose only outlet is exercising power over her children and her husband. The ultimate by-product of women's liberation is the liberation of men from the incubus of having to seal themselves up in an office for 40 years to support a totally dependent wife.

Interview, New York/ "W": a Fairchild publication, 9-22:16.

George S. McGovern
United States Senator, D–S.D.; Democratic Presidential nominee

(President) Nixon's Administration has treated the women's movement as a joke. Out of 12,000 top policy positions in the Administration, 105 have gone to women. That's eight-tenths of a percentage point—not a very likely record to take to an electorate in which 51 per cent are women.

(GEORGE S. McGOVERN)

It is not only unjust, but it is stupid politics.

Washington, Aug. 26/ Los Angeles Herald-Examiner, 8-27:(A)10.

Golda Meir
Prime Minister of Israel

Women's Lib is just a lot of foolishness. It's the men who are discriminated against. They can't bear children, and no one's likely to do anything about that.

Newsweek, 10-23:52.

Walter F. Mondale
United States Senator, D–Minn.

Although in some quarters the women's rights movement prompts only humor and cynicism, the concerns the movement addresses are neither funny nor trivial. Discrimination against women is a documented, proven fact in many aspects of American life, and a cruel reality that mars the ambitions of untold numbers of American women.

Quote, 4-9:353.

Richard M. Nixon
President of the United States

I would say that, as we consider the role of women in American political life, that a woman could serve in the office (the Presidency). I am not suggesting that that is going to happen soon. I am suggesting, however, that looking to the future, as the place of women as executives in our society is recognized, as women develop respect for themselves as executives rather than as women, that their place in political life is going to be recognized more and more. Now . . . as far as I am concerned, I have the greatest respect for women in both capacities–those who are home-makers and those who decide to go into business–but let us have freedom of choice for women.

Television interview, Washington/ Columbia Broadcasting System, 1-2.

Paul VI
Pope

True feminine emancipation does not lie in formal or material equality with the other sex, but in the recognition of that thing which is specific to the feminine personality–the vocation of a woman to be a mother.

Before Italian Catholic jurists, Vatican City, Dec. 9/ San Francisco Examiner, 12-9:2.

Jeannette Rankin
Former United States Representative, R–Mont.

I tell these young women (of women's liberation) that they must get to the people who *don't* come to the meetings. It never did any good for all the suffragettes to come together and talk to each other. There will be no revolution unless we go out into the precincts. You have to be stubborn–stubborn and ornery. And when the men make fun of you, that's when you *know* you're getting on well.

Life, 3-3:65.

Francoise Sagan
Author

I think men in general are fragile. They are human beings. It is stupid to say men are bad. That's why I don't think the women's movement is a good way. I see it as a false solution.

San Francisco Examiner & Chronicle, 12-17:(This World)2.

Jacqueline St. John
Assistant Professor of History, University of Nebraska

American women represent 53 per cent of the nation's population. That in itself does not make us a majority; it makes us a minority. We are a minority because we do not effectively mobilize our strength—politically, economically or socially. We are invisible in government, whether in the White House, the State House or the House of Representatives. We are absent from the Supreme Court, from the Cabinet, from the highest levels of our national government—those levels significantly concerned with policy decisions that affect our daily life. We have our tokens: female generals, but no astronauts; Presidential assistants, but no Presidents! We are invisible in the stock exchanges, invisible in the banking directorates, invisible on the board of directors of most major business corporations. Let us face the harsh truth—we are the "silenced majority"! Any woman who is so foolish as to believe that "we have come a long way, baby" is living in a child's temporary paradise—the chocolate factory, also inhabited by the tooth fairy, Tinkerbell and the Easter Bunny. It is this situation, the deteriorating condition of women in America, together with the increasing spread of egalitarian ideas, that has led to the resurgence of feminism in the '70s. What is now demanded is an end to the domination and exploitation of 53 per cent of the citizens of this nation. What immediately lies ahead, however, is conflict, turmoil, hostile reactions and possibly even violence, as the new feminist movement surges ahead to boldly challenge tradition-mired sexist practices. Women's liberation consequently has the potential of becoming the most broadly-based and politically-potent social movement of America in the '70s and '80s. At the same time, the majority of women believe that this new feminism, women's liberation, is erratic and eccentric. This stereotyped image has been fostered by the mass media which first ignored us, then misrepresented us all as bra-burners, and finally ridiculed us. We are burning, certainly—with indignation that American women are not only considered inferior to men in today's society, but, more tragically, that American women believe that they are in fact inferior.

At Institute for Business Women, April 26/ Vital Speeches, 6-15:529.

Alexandra Symonds
Assistant Clinical Professor of Psychiatry, New York University School of Medicine

What Women's Lib has done is provide a framework, or a language, if you will, for those women unable to articulate their frustrations. The leaders of the movement are articulate, educated women who are able to conceptualize the case for women who are not very verbal. But they do these women great disservice when they go overboard. Different kinds of women need different kinds of help. Highly-educated women who are trying to get into the professions need one kind of help. The working woman stuck with no money needs another kind. Women's Lib lumps all of them together as if they were all the same.

Family Weekly, 7-2:4.

Barbara Walters
Television commentator, "Today Show," National Broadcasting Company

I've always felt one of the major problems with Women's Lib is they try to make women who don't want to work sound hopeless and the ones who do sound glamorous. Well, there are many jobs that are much more stultifying than staying at home.

Interview, New York/ Los Angeles Times, 4-20:(4)21.

Barbara M. Watson
Administrator, Bureau of Security and Consular Affairs, Department of State of the United States

Very often you have the situation where men have not been accustomed to having women as bosses. The important thing is to know how to deal with that so that you lead but you don't lead, if you know what I mean. This takes skill and is great fun

(BARBARA M. WATSON)

once you know how to do it. It is just like the man who thinks he is the head of the household, but it turns out that he is doing everything that his charming, very smart wife has determined she wants to do—only it comes out, in his estimation, as his idea.

Interview/
U.S. News & World Report, 1-17:68.

Wade Wilson
President, Cheyney (Pa.) State College; Member, executive committee, National Education Association

The National Education Association calls upon parents and all groups involved in public education to join in a nationwide effort to reduce the negative effects of sex-role stereotypes, the standardized mental pictures of male and female that permeate all areas of our lives . . . Women's potential contributions to this nation and to their communities has gone largely unrecognized and undeveloped. The National Education Association seeks to move ahead in developing that potential. We seek ways to free women from illogical social expectations that deny self-fulfillment . . . Men also pay the price of sex-role stereotypes. They have been forced, through admonition and example, into "masculine" roles and behaviors which rob them of the full range of human emotion and experience . . .

News conference,
Washington, Nov. 22/
Los Angeles Herald-Examiner, 11-23:(A)18.

PART TWO

International Affairs

Africa

Ignatius K. Acheampong
Chief of State of Ghana

Total emancipation of Africa from colonial domination will continue to be a cardinal principle of Ghana's foreign policy. Accordingly, we will give support, both moral and material, to independence movements in Africa.

Before foreign diplomats, Accra, Jan. 17/ The Washington Post, 1-18:(A)16.

Ghana is basically an agricultural country; but over the years we have been relying on foreign aid as far as food is concerned. And not only that; we rely more on foreign assistance as far as raw materials. So we have decided that we must be self-reliant in this respect. We must produce the food we eat; we must produce the raw materials we need for the factories.

The Washington Post, 7-26:(A)21.

Justin Ahomadegbe
President of Dahomey

I am an authoritarian, but I'm not a mean man and I pardon easily.

Interview, Cotonou, Dahomey/ The New York Times, 5-28:(1)3.

John J. Akar
Former Ambassador to the United States from Sierra Leone

I am happy to say that, when I was confronted with the choice in April of last year to continue as Ambassador under a dictatorship or to stand up and be counted, I chose democracy. I have no regrets at all, in spite of the enormous sacrifices and great hardships which I have since encountered. Life is meaningless without high principles. I think we must remind ourselves that the sea recedes and returns eternally. I have great faith in God that democracy will return to Sierra Leone after President Siaka Stevens has exhausted all other alternatives. The genius of man has not invented any institution better than democracy, regardless of the screeching, strident propaganda of leftist ideologies.

At Boy Scout banquet, San Francisco/ San Francisco Examiner, 2-10:42.

Idi Amin
President of Uganda

(Saying the first stage of Uganda's "economic war" is the current expelling of more than 50,000 Asians): The second phase will be for black Ugandans to buy all shops, factories, cotton gins and businesses owned by Europeans and Asians whether they like it or not . . . My top priority is to Ugandans. Even if you go to Russia, Britain, the United States of America and other developed countries, they give top priority to their own citizens. If you go to America and your pass expires, they will tell you to go away. All I want is to see Uganda enjoying its true independence.

At police training college, Kampala, Aug. 26/ The Washington Post, 8-27:(A)30.

(On the economic problems in his country caused by his expulsion of non-Ugandan Asians): I know the people of Uganda will suffer. But this doesn't matter. We can eat what we grow and live without importing. Any suffering will be temporary.

The Washington Post, 12-25:(A)28.

Habib Bourguiba
President of Tunisia

(Libyan Premier Muammar el) Qaddafi came to me and proposed union (between Libya and Tunisia), and even that I become President of the two states. Unity on paper is worth nothing. Mentalities must change. It takes years and even centuries. We saw the unity that (the late Egyptian) President Nasser tried to form with Syria and even with you, Qaddafi. Where is it now? In Libya, people in the Fezzan district are still in the stone age. Before unity, we must have economic progress, exchanges. While we waste our time in meetings, the advanced countries move forward daily.

During public debate between the two leaders, Tunis/ The Christian Science Monitor, 12-19:7.

Kofia A. Busia
Former Prime Minister of Ghana

The military coup (ousting him as Prime Minister) has no justification whatsoever. It can bring nothing but disaster. It violates the first principle of democracy, namely, that governments should be changed not by the use of the gun but by the people exercising their choice through their votes at an election.

News conference, London, Jan. 21/ The New York Times, 1-22:7.

Robert K. Gardiner
Ghanian economist; Executive Secretary, United Nations Economic Commission for Africa

(Advocating more international aid for the poorest world areas, such as Africa): The specter of poverty, stagnation, paralyzing inflation and balance-of-payments nightmares stalks our land . . . One of the declared aims of international development policy is to reduce growing international inequalities. This principle so far has been applied only to the income gap between the developed and the developing countries as a group. What African countries are asking for . . . is that the development policies of the 1970s should in much greater proportion be directed to those with lowest incomes and lowest development prospects.

At United Nations Conference of Trade and Development, Santiago, Chile/ Los Angeles Times, 5-15:(3)10,12.

Omar Arteh Ghalib
Foreign Minister of the Somali Republic

(On Britain's veto of a UN Security Council resolution calling on Britain to stop its agreement to resume normal relations with Rhodesia): Africa is awake; and veto or no veto, nothing will deter or diminish the pace of our march to freedom and economic development.

Addis Ababa, Ethiopia, Feb. 5/ Los Angeles Times, 2-5:(1)18.

Haile Selassie
Emperor of Ethiopia

In Ethiopia, as in other countries, there are regions and provinces known by different names; but the nomenclature of these regions do not constitute any handicaps in the way of national integration. Ethiopians always stood firm, always shared the feeling of oneness and belonging together to keep our country united. All within the nation have equal opportunities. In the private sector there might be differences because everyone works according to his own abilities. But in the government every Ethiopian stands equal.

Interview, Addis Ababa/ Los Angeles Times, 7-23:(H)6.

Hassan II
King of Morocco

In contemplating the Mediterranean pact, or even a conference to discuss one, it is necessary to consider evident contradictions.

The Mediterranean has become both too big and too little. It is too little because the smallest tempest there involves us all; and it is too big because political and economic distances between different Mediterranean lands are too wide. In any thought of such a grouping, one could not exclude NATO allies like Italy or Turkey, or non-NATO lands like Spain, or a country like Egypt that has been closely linked to the Soviet Union. All of them border the same area . . . Just suppose the Mediterranean nations wanted this (non-alignment of the area) and asked the Russians and Americans to pull out their ships. Do you suppose they would agree? And how would anyone be able to push them?

Interview/
The New York Times, 7-23:(4)11.

(On the recent assassination attempt on him by some members of the armed forces): This Army which I created, for which I sacrificed everything, this Army which I love, I am now seeing stray, to the detriment of the great family that is Morocco.

San Francisco Examiner & Chronicle, 8-27:(This World)14.

Felix Houphouet-Boigny
President of the Ivory Coast

(The Ivory Coast's economy) remains vulnerable because it is essentially agricultural and, therefore, at the mercy of any vicissitude. It is dependent on foreign countries where everything is decided without—and often against—us.

The Washington Post, 8-31:(G)2.

Jack Howman
Foreign Minister of Rhodesia

(On the agreement reached between Britain and Rhodesia providing for a return to normal relations and eventual rule in Rhodesia by the black majority): In spite of the uncharitable remarks made by certain of our critics and opponents reflecting upon our integrity and honesty of purposes, it is our firm intention to honor the agreement reached, both in the letter and in the spirit.

Salisbury, Jan. 6/
The Washington Post, 1-7:(C)3.

Huang Hua
Communist Chinese Ambassador to the United Nations

The white racist regimes of South Africa and Rhodesia and the Portuguese colonial authorities dare to defy world condemnation and stubbornly push their brutal colonial rule and barbarous policy of racial discrimination mainly because they have the political, economic and military support of a handful of countries, such as the United States and Britain.

At UN Security Council meeting, Addis Ababa, Ethiopia, Jan. 31/
San Francisco Examiner, 1-31:6.

Yakov A. Malik
Soviet Ambassador/ Permanent Representative to the United Nations

. . . at the present time, it is precisely the continent of Africa which has become the target of aggression and colonial wars, which are carried out from three sides by the forces of international imperialism, the shock detachments of which are the Portuguese colonialists, the South African and Southern Rhodesian racists and the Israeli racist Zionists. These are the contemporary propagators of the racist-fascist ideology of the "chosen people."

At United Nations, N.Y./
The New York Times, 10-22:(1)14.

J. B. Mills
South African Ambassador to Australia

We (in South Africa) have admittedly been playing God to the black man for three centuries. We now realize that we have been riding a tiger, and it is plain to us that we must dismount . . . more agonized thinking on racial realities is going

(J. B. MILLS)

on in South Africa than in any other part of the world.

Sydney/
Los Angeles Times, 2-22:(1)2.

Joseph Mobutu
President of Zaire
(formerly the Congo)

(On his changing the name of his country): What does it mean? I no longer have a borrowed soul. I no longer have borrowed thoughts or ideas. I no longer speak in a borrowed language. My manner of speaking is authentically Zaireois. A Zaireois soul inhabits my body. I am first of all Zaireois before anything else.

San Francisco Examiner & Chronicle, 6-25:(This World)26.

Julius K. Nyerere
President of Tanzania

(Explaining the problems his country is having in implementing socialism): A man who has inherited a tumbledown cottage has to live in even worse conditions while he is rebuilding it.

The Washington Post, 4-2:(A)1.

(On Uganda President Idi Amin's decision to expel Uganda citizens who are Asians): This is clearly racialism and representative of the same thing that Africans are deploring . . . Either they are citizens or they are not; and once they are, you are enjoined to accord them the same treatment that you accord all the others.

At opening of educational institute, Dar es Salaam, Tanzania, Aug. 21/
Los Angeles Times, 8-22:(1)22.

Muammar el Qaddafi
Premier of Libya

The single impediment in our relations is your (the U.S.'s) unlimited support of Israeli aggression (in the Middle East). In fact, after the evacuation of the (former American) Wheelus air base, I summoned Ambassador (Joseph) Palmer to my office and asked the United States for artillery, especially 175mm guns, transport planes and F-5 jet fighters, all for purely *defensive* purposes—please underline "defensive." We have still received no answer from Washington.

Interview/
The New York Times Magazine, 2-6:70.

Gabriel Ramanantsoa
Chief of State of Madagascar

To preserve national unity there must be mutual confidence. This is especially important because several tendencies—French, Chinese, American—seek a place on Madagascar and would swallow up the Malagasy people. I am taking over the direction of Madagascar myself.

Address to the people after being given full power by the President to lead the country/
The New York Times, 5-21:(4)4.

In our Army, tradition is that we take care of the private first and then the officers. We'll take care of the masses first, the poorest above all.

After being given complete control of the country by the President, Tananarive/
San Francisco Examiner & Chronicle, 5-28:(This World)16.

Ian Smith
Prime Minister of Rhodesia

(Referring to the terms of the tentative agreement between Rhodesia and Britain to normalize relations): If the present generation of Africans are so stupid as to reject this offer of advancement for their people, they will bear the curses of their children forever.

Broadcast address, Salisbury, Jan. 21/
The New York Times, 1-22:3.

William R. Tolbert, Jr.
President of Liberia

Our task is to eradicate whatever we identify as unwholesome in our society, while preserving those things that are worthy. Waste cannot escape removal, attitudes cannot remain unpurposeful.

Inaugural address, Monrovia, Jan. 3/ The New York Times, 1-4:3.

We reaffirm our friendship with the United States of America, with whom we share the pursuit of liberty, dignity, order and justice.

Inaugural address, Monrovia, Jan. 3/ The New York Times, 1-4:3.

John Vorster
Prime Minister of South Africa

The philosophic basis of separate development (of the races in his country) is not—and I repeat not—that we are better or more learned or richer because we are white. But it is a simple fact—and you can't explain away a fact—that we are different. We whites feel we have every right to maintain our identity. Just as we are proud of our identity, so the black nations are proud of theirs.

U.S. News & World Report, 2-7:36.

(Referring to UN Secretary General Kurt Waldheim's forthcoming trip to South Africa to discuss the rights of non-whites in that country): . . . if he wants to come to South Africa to act as the mouthpiece of the extremists of the Organization of African Unity and others, and to put across resolutions taken in that connection, he will still be very courteously received by us—but I can tell him in advance that he will be wasting his time.

The Washington Post, 3-6:(A)12.

Roy Wilkins
Executive director, National Association for the Advancement of Colored People (United States)

In South Africa you have people who carry the banner for individual and human freedom—no matter what the color of the individual is. Indeed, this is one of the compensations of this trip; to discover that, in spite of the monolithic front of this nation, there are people—white, black and Coloured—who are interested in freedom for the individual and do not hesitate to criticize their country and its policy which denies that freedom.

At University of Cape Town, South Africa/ The Christian Science Monitor, 4-4:2.

Essiah Zhuwrara
Leader in the Front for the Liberation of Zimbawe (South Africa)

The proposition in South Africa is whether Africans can conquer whites or whether whites will continue to rule throughout the world. The time has come for Africans to move from peace and diplomacy. It is unfortunate if Africans still think a smile is what wins battles.

At conference of black organizations on Africa, Washington/ The New York Times, 5-27:3.

Alpheus H. Zulu
Bishop of Zululand

Very few whites in this country (South Africa) are committed to non-violence, and there is no reason why blacks should be. After the disillusionment which followed the quelling of the black passive resistance movement in the middle '50s, it has become unreasonable to gain support for the hope of a non-violent solution (to the South African civil rights problem). The harshness with which discrimination is enforced by law and custom makes a black man look simple and naive if he continues to believe and talk of non-violence ever becoming effective. This is a fact, although nobody speaks of violence.

Before students at University of Cape Town, South Africa, May 17/ The Christian Science Monitor, 5-22:10.

(ALPHEUS H. ZULU)

I say South Africa has a great future and that future is within reach, if you will increasingly acknowledge the humanity of the black people whose land you have taken; if you will accord them the respect and rights which are due to them as human beings; if you will accept them as partners in the development of the country, investing at least as much money in their development and training as in armaments; if you will boldly test the honesty of the nations of Africa and outside, which threaten to fight you on account of your inhuman white-black relations, by granting that freedom now. This you can do by making new laws and by providing opportunities for the educational, economic and social advancement of black people.

Before students at University of Cape Town, South Africa, May 17/ The Washington Post, 5-19:(A)27.

Salvador Allende (Gossens)
President of Chile

We export copper, not revolution. We don't export and we don't import political panaceas. Besides, we are realists; and we know that, in order for a Popular Unity government like our own to come into power through democratic elections, a country must have a parliament, unions, elections, parties. Many Latin American countries have none of these. Where political democracy does not work, we don't expect social democracy to succeed. We are content to try to lead Chile toward socialism without bloodshed, without violence, but within the rules set up by capitalist democracy and in accordance with our traditions, our history and particular circumstances.

Interview, Santiago/ The Christian Science Monitor, 2-11:7.

Chile's foreign policy is based fundamentally on our desire to have good relations with all countries, irrespective of their regimes. Nonintervention and self-determination are the two principles that we hold as superseding all others in carrying out our diplomacy. That is to say, we abide by no doctrines such as the Monroe Doctrine or the so-called Brezhnev Doctrine or any other of that sort. Furthermore, we belong to two groups of nations: the Latin American group and the group of the 77—the developing nations. We take both these "belongings" very seriously. Of course, we also enjoy warm relations with the socialist countries while regretting that some important difficulties exist between some of them. We hope to stay clear of these differences and pursue a positive, constructive foreign policy—one that makes no difference between white, yellow or black skins . . . As for foreign bases (in Chile), Chile will never allow any to be built that can be used against the United States. Chile will never allow her territory to be used for a military base against the United States and will never contribute to injure U.S. sovereignty.

Interview, Santiago/ The Christian Science Monitor, 2-11:7.

They said if I was elected there would be no more elections. They said that I was going to destroy the family. They said that I was going to persecute religions. They said that I would fill the jails with political prisoners. What has happened? There are no political prisoners in Chile. I (the government) have lost three elections. There are no journalists in prison—although there are some who deserve to be.

Interview, Santiago/ San Francisco Examiner, 3-31:16.

Chile is not self-supporting. This country must buy machines, motors, petroleum, foodstuffs and raw materials. Some would say: "Buy in the socialist world." *No se puede*—It is not possible. They do not produce materials for the machinery we use; they don't produce for the installations which we have. The economy of those countries is planned. They have their five-year plans of production, and they export in accordance with the necessities of the nations with whom they maintain relations; and they cannot tomorrow night satisfy the demands of a republic like ours in all of its aspects.

News conference, Talcahuano, Chile, February/ The New York Times Magazine, 5-7:75.

I am horrified to hear people talking irresponsibly about a possible civil war. I

(SALVADOR ALLENDE [GOSSENS])

will fight with all my strength to maintain normalcy in the country; for if there were to be a civil war, even if we (his government) were to win—and we would have to win—it would mean the destruction of the Chilean economy and brotherly coexistence for several generations.

Before State Technical University students, Santiago/ The New York Times, 9-3:(4)5.

We are going to establish an economic politics of wartime. This will be a tough policy but not an unfair one. This political policy will mean that the people who have a lot will have to hand over more and more.

Broadcast address, Valdiva, Chile, Oct. 7/ San Francisco Examiner & Chronicle, 10-8:(A)19.

(Criticizing the U.S. and U.S. interests for interference with Chile's government and economy): From the very day of our election triumph on September 4, 1970, we have felt the effects of large-scale external pressure against us, which tried to prevent the inauguration of a government freely elected by the people, and which has tried to bring it down ever since. It is action that has tried to cut us off from the world, to strangle our economy and to paralyze trade in our principal export, copper, and to deprive us of access to sources of international financing . . . Each and every Chilean is suffering from the consequences of these measures, because they affect the daily life of each citizen and naturally his internal political life . . . Such misuse represents the exertion of pressure on an economically weak country, the infliction of punishment on a whole nation for its decision to recover its own basic resources, and a form of intervention in the internal affairs of a sovereign state. In a word, it is what we call imperialism.

At United Nations, N.Y., Dec. 4/ The New York Times, 12-5:1.

Joaquin Balaguer
President of the Dominican Republic

This is the opportune time to reject, with all sincerity and all the energies of my spirit, the frequently-made charge against us of being a regime that remains in power to serve as an instrument of the interests of the oligarchy and to represent our traditional conservative forces. The truth is to the contrary. We are as revolutionary as or more revolutionary than those who claim to be in the forefront of social revolution in our country and the world.

Before National Congress, Santo Domingo, Feb. 27/ The New York Times, 4-26:6.

Pedro G. Beltran
Former Prime Minister of Peru; Publisher, "La Prensa," Lima

It is a wonder to our people how the Communist threat moves you (the U.S.) to such an extent so far away, at the opposite end of the world, when you appear indifferent to the problems of the restless peoples right near you. (Latin Americans) feel that you hardly show any interest in them as compared to what you are doing in other parts of the world.

Accepting the Americas Award, New York/ The New York Times, 10-14:30.

Ruben Berrios
President, Puerto Rican Independence Party

By 1976, we will declare the Republic. The United States will have to negotiate with us. We will become the Socialist Republic of Puerto Rico . . . Socialism and democracy. But neither the socialism of

Russia nor the democracy of the U.S. They have defamed the concepts; we want to rescue them. By socialism, I mean a multiparty system ruled by the dictates of the constitution we will write. By democracy, I mean individual rights fully guaranteed—not the kind of democracy one of our poets, Luis Llorens Torres, described: "The poor have the freedom of expression to tell each other their misery in the slums at night." There may be a civil war, but that will depend on the empire. We think it will be a massive confrontation, not civil war. We can paralyze the American empire through mass strikes, mass boycotts, noncooperation, civil disobedience, refusal to pay taxes. We won't fall into the trap of the imperialists who want us to use violence so they can arrest us.

The New York Times Magazine, 5-21:31,32.

R. J. Bilodeau
President,
Honeywell, Ltd., of Canada

The key to a successful and amicable future in our dealings with the U.S., I contend, depends upon Canada establishing clearly, and soon, just what it wants from the U.S. Obviously, we want relatively free entry to its markets; we also want access to American sources of capital, for borrowing purposes at least; we want the U.S. to take certain steps on the pollution-control front in border areas, for example cleaning up the Great Lakes; and we have many other demands involving widely-diverse subjects from nuclear testing to immigration quotas. At the same time, the U.S. wants certain things from us—access to our markets, energy, water, natural resources and so on. Only when our respective wants are diligently thought out and precisely expressed can we engage in any sensible negotiations.

Before Data Processing Management Association, Quebec City/ The Wall Street Journal, 6-7:12.

Forbes Burnham
Prime Minister of Guyana

The independent English-speaking Caribbean states, exercising their sovereign right to enter into relations with any other state and pursuing their determination to seek regional solidarity, will seek the early establishment of relations with Cuba, whether economic or political or both. To this end, the independent English-speaking Caribbean states will act together on the basis of agreed approaches.

At West Indies summit conference, Port of Spain, Trinidad, Oct. 14/ The Washington Post, 10-15:(A)20.

Luckner Cambronne
Minister of Defense and the
Interior of Haiti

(Promising amnesty to Haitian political exiles): I know there are some Haitians who do not want to return. Some have been condemned to death. But I give my word that we will issue a decree of amnesty for all. Haiti does not belong only to those who run the government. It belongs to all Haitians, including those in New York and elsewhere.

News conference, Washington, March 15/ The Washington Post, 3-16:(A)29.

Fidel Castro (Ruz)
Premier of Cuba

We have never thought about talking to (U.S. President) Nixon about anything. What have we got to tell him? That he stops being an imperialist? That he raises the blockade of Cuba? That he stops being an aggressor?

News conference, Sofia, Bulgaria, May 26/ Los Angeles Herald-Examiner, 5-26:(A)2.

Today, the revolutionary ideas are spreading on the whole (American) continent. They are also spreading among the citizens of Latin America. But what is even more—the revolutionary ideas have also begun spreading in the United States proper. We have no doubt what the historic result will be. We are certain that these revolutionary ideas will some day triumph in all of Latin America, and that some day these revolutionary ideas will also be victorious in the United States. The historic realities are in favor of these ideas and they are paving the way toward their victory.

Dresden, East Germany, June 16/ Los Angeles Herald-Examiner, 6-17:(A)4.

Maybe what hurts the imperialists most is that this small country in the middle of the Yankee patio, the Caribbean, has been able to defend and maintain itself. They will never forgive the Cuban revolution for this. We did not make any concessions when we were weak. We will not want anything now, precisely at a moment when we are advancing, when prospects seem brighter. We are ready to survive five, 10, 15 or 30 years without relations with the United States.

At "26th of July" celebration, Havana/ Seattle Post-Intelligencer, 7-28:(A)11.

(On talks with the U.S. on curbing U.S. airliner hijackers from landing in Cuba): We are discussing a solution to the problem of the airplanes . . . a problem that worries the entire international community, and we will try sincerely to find a solution for this problem. But no one should think for a moment that we want reconciliation with Yankee imperialism. (U.S. President) Nixon has said he will not change his position on Cuba. What do we care what Mr. Nixon thinks in that ultra-reactionary and Fascist brain of his? . . . There can be no talks between the blockaders and the blockaded.

At rally honoring Chilean President Salvador Allende, Havana, Dec. 13/ Los Angeles Herald-Examiner, 12-14:(A)18.

Jacques Chonchol
Minister of Agriculture of Chile

In many countries trying to implement socialism, the opposition has tried to use the church as a center of reaction. But the Chilean church has not taken the traditional Latin American position that a Catholic cannot vote for a Marxist.

The Washington Post, 1-30:(A)27.

Norris R. Crump
Chairman, Canadian Pacific, Ltd.

The United States is running out of clean water, energy resources and a lot of things. So they're talking about "continentalism" (sharing Canada's natural resources). I'm all for it, providing they pay—exactly the same as if we were exporting wheat or auto parts.

Montreal/ San Francisco Examiner, 5-5:17.

Miguel Angel Flor de la Valle
Foreign Minister of Peru

The prolonged isolation (by the OAS) of the Republic of Cuba constitutes a disturbing factor which interferes with the necessary, normal relations among our countries . . .

At Organization of American States General Assembly, Washington, April 12/ Los Angeles Times, 4-13:(1)23.

Carlos Sanz de Santamaria
Chairman, Inter-American Committee for the Alliance for Progress, Organization of American States

(U.S.) President Nixon still stresses the special relationship with Latin America. But the Latin Americans are skeptical. The U.S.

withdrawal of interest has left a vacuum for a democratic ideology in Latin America. But if the United States is still willing to take Latin America as a priority area, then everything will be okay. I should believe it to be a great error if the U.S. does not realize that the most important continent for the U.S. is Latin America. The world will not stop with the balance of powers as they are today. It will continue to change and change.

Interview, Washington/ Los Angeles Times, 2-27:(G)6.

Luis Echeverria (Alvarez)
President of Mexico

Our people are aware that their poverty produces wealth for others. The resentments that have accumulated against political colonialism have now changed to resentment of economic colonialism.

Before joint session of Congress, Washington, June 15/ The Washington Post, 6-16:(A)4.

(Advocating lifting of OAS sanctions against Cuba): If the most powerful country of the hemisphere (the U.S.) endeavors to overcome differences with other overseas powers, we should all bring to an end inter-American policy that implicitly denies the right of member states to adopt the system best-suited to their interests.

Before Organization of American States, Washington, June 16/ The New York Times, 6-17:8.

Let Washington listen to this carefully: We do not want to be a colony, a satellite country, nor a sphere of influence of the United States of America.

The Washington Post, 11-2:(A)19.

Luis A. Ferre
Governor of Puerto Rico

The people of Puerto Rico desire permanent union with the United States and the full enjoyment of their American citizenship. Until (our) people determine otherwise, we will continue to reaffirm and strengthen these principles in our relationship with the United States . . .

San Francisco Examiner & Chronicle, 4-9:(This World)20.

Richard Fulton
United States Representative, D–Tenn.

If the world's prospects for survival have increased with (U.S. President Nixon's) China visit and again should brighten with the summit in Moscow, isn't it a fair assumption that having our President in Havana (Cuba) would prove our positive effort in search of positive effects?

San Francisco Examiner, 2-25:2.

Herb Gray
Revenue Minister of Canada

Foreign investment (in Canada) plays an important role in Canadian development; but it brings with it costs as well as benefits. While there are a variety of opinions among Canadians about the balance of benefits and costs of foreign direct investment, there is certainly no disagreement that foreign investment should work in the interests of this country.

Before House of Commons, Ottawa, May 2/ The New York Times, 5-3:74.

Robert P. Kaplan
Member of Canadian Parliament; Chairman, House of Commons Standing Committee on Finance, Trade and Economic Affairs

. . . we are sometimes warned in Canada that future prosperity lies in trading blocs. There is some convincing evidence of this. If there is to be free trade within blocs and relative protectionism among them, Canada, as the industrial country most dependent in the world on foreign trade, would have to adapt. One solution would be for us to join a trading community. And the logical one would be North American. I believe that every good argument that can be made for

(ROBERT P. KAPLAN)

Britain joining the European Common Market can be made for Canada joining the United States. Except this: that Britain joined over 200 million Europeans who were divided into six countries of which Britain is one of the largest. Britain can easily retain its identity, especially with a different language and a deep cultural sense which reinforces its difference. Canada, on the other hand, would be 22 million persons joining only one other country of over 200 million and that is an English-speaking one. What would happen to our identity?

Before National Association of Manufacturers, New York, Aug. 8/ Vital Speeches, 10-1:756.

Edward M. Kennedy
United States Senator, D–Mass.

Just as the goal of world peace justified bridging the 9,000 miles to the People's Republic of (Communist) China, so is the goal of hemispheric peace and stability worthy of spanning the 90 miles to Havana.

Washington, April 17/ San Francisco Examiner, 4-17:1.

Alejandro Agustin Lanusse
President of Argentina

(Challenging Brazil's position of leadership in Latin America): Today no state is so powerful as to forego the others, because all know the limits of their power. We Argentines, we Latin Americans, will not accept under any conditions a second-rate destiny.

At state banquet, Brasilia, Brazil, March 13/ The New York Times, 3-15:25.

I have force. I can exercise force in a moral way for my country, and I will exercise it. Argentina is a country that must be managed like one manages a horse in the cavalry. You must hold the reins firmly. It must be strong, but not too strong. Firm.

Interview/ The New York Times Magazine, 8-20:83.

Gale W. McGee
United States Senator, D–Wyo.

(On Cuba's accusation that Puerto Rico is part of the United States colonialism and should be granted independence): If the people of Puerto Rico vote for a commonwealth, so be it. If they vote for statehood, so shall it be. If they vote for independence, so shall it be. And that is not a determination subject to the decision of Cuba . . . not subject to the decision even of this body (the UN). This decision alone belongs to the people of Puerto Rico.

At United Nations, N.Y., Oct. 19/ Los Angeles Times, 10-20:(1)12.

George S. McGovern
United States Senator, D–S.D.

I would hope that we could open up relations with Cuba with some of the same kinds of things the President's (Nixon) now doing with Peking. I really can't believe that it's more important to isolate Cuba than it is Peking. You could begin either by inviting (Cuban Premier Fidel) Castro or some designated person to Washington, or vice versa. Whether they would permit an American Embassy there I have no idea. But at least we ought to keep that door open. I've never understood the theory that you're safer by not maintaining relations with a country than you are when you maintain diplomatic contact.

Interview, Washington/ Los Angeles Herald-Examiner, 7-9:(A)11.

Richard M. Nixon
President of the United States

I would have to say quite candidly that we have had very little success to date in our negotiations with our Canadian friends (on such matters as trade, the environment, etc.); which shows, incidentally, that sometimes you have more problems negotiating with your friends than you do with your adversaries. But that is as it should be. They have a right to their position and we have a right to ours.

News conference,
Washington, March 24/
The New York Times, 3-25:12.

(On U.S.-Canadian relations): Through the years, our speeches . . . have often centered on the decades of unbroken friendship we have enjoyed and our 4,000 miles of unfortified frontier. In focusing on our peaceful borders and our peaceful history, they have tended to gloss over the fact that there are real problems between us. They have tended to create the false impression that our countries are essentially alike. It is time for Canadians and Americans to move beyond the sentimental rhetoric of the past. It is time for us to recognize that we have very separate identities; that we have significant differences; and that nobody's interests are furthered when these realities are obscured. Our peaceful borders and our peaceful history are important symbols, to be sure. What they symbolize, however, is the spirit of respect and restraint which allows us to cooperate despite our differences—in ways which help us both. American policy toward Canada is rooted in that spirit.

Before Parliament,
Ottawa, April 14/
The National Observer, 4-22:2.

(Referring to Canada): No self-respecting nation can or should accept the proposition that it should always be economically dependent upon another nation (such as the U.S.). Let us recognize once and for all that the only basis for a sound and healthy relationship between our two proud peoples is to find a pattern of economic interaction which is beneficial to both our countries—and which respects Canada's right to chart its own economic course.

Before Parliament,
Ottawa, April 14/
Los Angeles Herald-Examiner,
4-14:(A)2.

We recognize that diversity has resulted in different kinds of governments, with varying national goals and methods, in Latin America. We realize that all of this presents problems. But the United States is no stranger to policy differences and to the efforts needed to forge strengths from the fires of discord. Consequently, we stand prepared to work as a mature and equal partner on the inevitable differences that have arisen, and will continue to arise, because of the developing new realities in the American hemisphere.

At dinner honoring
OAS members' foreign ministers,
Washington, April 15/
The Washington Post, 10-20:(A)18.

(U.S. policy is) a new practical acknowledgement that the general term "Latin America" connotes a plurality of views rather than a uniform voice . . . Let us all recognize that some things will not change as far as United States policy is concerned: We will continue to give special priority to our unique relationship with Latin America. We will deal realistically with governments as they are—never seeking to impose our political structure on other nations.

At dinner honoring
OAS members' foreign ministers,
Washington, April 15/
San Francisco Examiner & Chronicle,
4-16:(A)13.

Juan D. Peron
Former President of Argentina

I am certain that the Argentine economy can be immediately re-established. Our country is rich. It can produce 10 to 20 times more than it now produces. This

(JUAN D. PERON)

amounts to a question of good internal administration and resistance to imperialism. But all the governments since my fall (in 1955) have only handed over the economy to the clutches of imperialism. The banks, our most important industries, our agricultural and pastoral riches have fallen into these hands, and the Army has let it happen! And one wonders why she has lost prestige! In view of this general "decapitalization" of the country, our fight must be one of liberation. We must liberate Argentina from the stranglehold of the old democratic-liberal capitalist system which has ruined us.

Interview, Madrid/
The New York Times, 11-17:45.

(On his impressions of the country upon returning after 17 years in exile): Gentlemen, when I see what is happening today (in Argentina), I lack words to describe my astonishment. The social situation of the people is miserable and painful.

News conference,
Buenos Aires, Nov. 25/
The New York Times, 11-26:(1)2.

I am not a dictator, as some say. But if the Peronist movement—that is, the Argentine people—ask me to be a candidate for President, I will agree. I am a slave of the people.

News conference, Rome/
Time, 11-27:33.

Nikolai V. Podgorny
President of the Soviet Union

(Addressing Chilean President Salvador Allende): You are not alone in your struggle (for liberation). On your side are the sympathy and support of the Soviet Union, your brother socialist countries and the solidarity of all contemporary progressive forces. The Soviet people associate themselves with the peoples of Latin America who rose up in struggle against the domination of foreign monopolies and local oligarchy, for elimination of economic backwardness, for taking up a wide road of really free and progressive development.

At banquet, Moscow, Dec. 6/
Los Angeles Times, 12-7:(1)29.

Guillermo Rodriguez (Lara)
President of Ecuador

(On his recent assumption of power by military coup): There is no political tendency in our revolution and no ideology. There is nationalism; there is the fatherland at the beginning, the middle and the end; and there is a desire to serve the Ecuadorian people.

The New York Times, 3-9:11.

William P. Rogers
Secretary of State of the United States

Cuba's continuing interventionist behavior and its support for revolution—even though on a different scale than in the past—still constitute a threat to the peace and security of the Hemisphere within the meaning of the 1964 OAS decision which established diplomatic and economic sanctions. Moreover, Cuba continues its close and active military ties with the Soviet Union, a matter of obvious concern to this Hemisphere.

Before Organization of American
States General Assembly,
Washington, April 12/
The Washington Post, 4-13:(A)11.

Mitchell Sharp
Secretary of State for External Affairs of Canada

Every Canadian should pray morning and evening that the United States will continue to prosper. So closely are we tied together that we will thrive together or suffer together.

U.S. News & World Report, 3-27:30.

Robert L. Stanfield
Leader, Conservative Party of Canada; Conservative candidate for Prime Minister

I don't want to become Prime Minister badly enough to go after it with the single-minded intensity of a (late U.S. President John) Kennedy or a (U.S. President Richard) Nixon. I'm not going to die an unhappy man if I don't become Prime Minister of this country. Okay, I have no lust for power.

San Francisco Examiner & Chronicle, 10-8:(This World)27.

Omar Torrijos (Herrera)
Head of Government of Panama

(On conditions which are necessary to a realistic defense arrangement for the Panama Canal): The first is a good neutrality treaty with every country in the world. Second is the emergence of conditions that would enable the people of Panama to look upon the Canal with tenderness rather than wanting to throw rocks at it. Third is the need for a new defense treaty with the United States, a treaty that would not presuppose the physical presence of the Army of the United States. You don't really need the American Army, and many U.S. Army Generals have stated that.

Interview, Rio Hato, Panama, Oct. 6/ The Washington Post, 10-8:(A)14.

In our foreign relations, we want to maintain Panama as unmarried. We no longer want to be hitched to one country (the U.S.). The Panamanian people and this government are reluctant to have any foreign power give it a list of enemies and friends that they should have. We want to choose our own friends and enemies.

Interview, Rio Hato, Panama, Oct. 6/ The Washington Post, 10-8:(A)14.

The (U.S.-controlled Canal) Zone is a social cancer in the heart of my country. It is a socialist economy populated by a privileged class of people who are neither Americans nor Panamanians—the Zonians. I cannot sleep at night knowing that I will see that (U.S.) flag over the Zone every morning.

Los Angeles Times, 11-1:(1-B)10.

Pierre Elliott Trudeau
Prime Minister of Canada

The U.S. and Canada love each other as neighbors, as good neighbors. It doesn't prevent them from being nationalist in the patriotic sense of the word. They each prefer to keep their country developing along an independent course rather than be absorbed or absorb the other.

U.S. News & World Report, 4-17:67.

(On whether anti-Americanism in Canada is a serious problem): I don't think so. I think even the most outspoken supporters of Canadian nationalism would say that they are not anti-American. They say they want more Canadian control of our domestic economic environment, but they wouldn't say that this is anti-American or anti-British or anti-Japanese or anti anything else. In my opinion, it would be politically very unpopular to be anti-American; and if it's unpopular politically, I suppose that means the overwhelming majority of Canadians don't want to be associated with any party which could be defined as anti-American. Often in my political peregrinations, I am picketed by Canadians carrying signs saying: "Trudeau is the Lackey of American Imperialism" or "Please Take Our People Out of Vietnam." This is obviously a way of using American issues to protest against the government in Canada. But this type of anti-Americanism is extremely marginal.

Interview, Ottawa/ U.S. News & World Report, 7-3:34.

There are nationalists in Quebec who think the French-speaking people of that part of Canada would be better off going

(PIERRE ELLIOTT TRUDEAU)

it alone. As a movement, it has had its ups and downs. It began to have an up in the early '60s when there was an awakening in Quebec of political consciousness. Since then, a legitimate political party has come into existence—the *Parti Quebecois*—which is dedicated to the independence of Quebec from the rest of Canada, but, curiously enough, still linked with it in a sort of association. It's not full independence; it's independence in a kind of a common market with a common currency and other common features. The movement exists; it is there; and it is motivating a lot of young people in Quebec, just like socialism or Fabianism may be motivating a lot of young people in other countries . . . This government is dedicated to combatting separatism. Obviously, I believe it is not a good idea. And I also believe it will disappear if the right things are done in Quebec and in the rest of Canada. One of those right things is promulgation and application of a policy of bilingualism. We've done a great deal along this line.

Interview, Ottawa/ U.S. News & World Report, 7-3:35.

Erico Verissimo
Brazilian writer

Censorship (in Brazil) is highly prejudicial to the cultural life of the country. Everything is suffering—the theatre, the novel, the cinema and teaching—whether it is political or not. The man in the street has reached a stage where he is afraid to have opinions or even to think. People tell me that Brazilians don't need liberty, but food, housing, medical assistance and a chance to work. I agree that all these are of major importance. But I don't understand the rationality of those who think these things can be achieved only under an authoritarian regime.

Interview, Porto Alegre, Brazil/ Los Angeles Times, 3-16:(1-A):2.

Asia and the Pacific

Spiro T. Agnew
Vice President of the United States

(On President Nixon's forthcoming trip to Communist China): The Chinese are not our friends. We are going to see them at their house and see if we can make them less hostile; that is all.

Television interview/ "Today Show," National Broadcasting Company, 2-14.

(On the return by the U.S. to Japan of Okinawa and other Ryukyu Islands): This is my first visit to Japan, and I am especially honored to be here for this unique occasion—unique because the ceremony which we are here to celebrate is unprecedented in history and has special significance for Americans and Japanese and for all mankind. The decision to end the American administration and restore Japanese dominion over these islands was mutual and amicable. As such, it is an example for all nations and for men of goodwill everywhere, demonstrating the efficacy of our common democratic institutions and our high regard for man.

Tokyo, May 12/ Los Angeles Herald-Examiner, 5-12:(A)4.

We place the highest value on our relations with Japan. A balanced relationship between our two countries, based upon inter-dependence, equality and reciprocity, is essential not only to our mutual well-being, but also to the continued political and economic development of the rest of Asia.

At ceremonies marking the return of Okinawa to Japan, Tokyo, May 15/ The Dallas Times Herald, 5-15:(A)1.

Zulfikar Ali Bhutto
President of Pakistan

(On restoration of democracy in his country): I will be the last to see the curse of the generals' dictatorship further ruin my country. Before the day is done, if I'm still here, I will ensure that the night of terror will never return to this country. I can only set the pace and direction; better men than I may complete the job. You will see that I'm not an enemy of private enterprise. Foreign investment will be encouraged and welcomed and never touched.

Interview/Time, 1-10:29.

We do not want eternal enmity with India; we have never wanted it. We want a *modus vivendi* built on justice and equity. Vindication of national honor does not mean chauvinism but acceptance of the 1947 arrangement agreed upon by India and Pakistan and acknowledged by the world. All we seek is for that rationale of live and let live to come to fruition in the interests of the people of both countries.

Interview/Time, 1-10:29.

Please do not take (Bangladesh Prime Minister) Sheik Mujibur Rahman literally (when he said all links between their two countries are permanently severed). How is it possible to snap all ties? I cannot imagine the ties between Muslim Bengal and this part of Pakistan can be broken forever.

News conference, Lahore, Pakistan, Jan. 13/ Los Angeles Times, 1-14:(1)14.

(On Pakistan's withdrawal from the British Commonwealth because of Britain and two other members' decision to recog-

(ZULFIKAR ALI BHUTTO)

nize Bangladesh): Our decision to quit the Commonwealth is not an antagonistic one. We have taken this decision reluctantly. We have excellent bilateral relations with Britain and other Commonwealth countries. We hope to expand these relations. The decision to quit the Commonwealth is in vindication of our national honor and self-respect. This is how Pakistan will survive. I am certain the nation will endorse this decision.

News conference, Rawalpindi, Jan. 30/ Los Angeles Times, 1-31:(1)13.

India will lose from its aggression (against Pakistan) in the long run. It has sown the seeds and will reap a bitter harvest in India itself. By sponsoring Bangladesh, you will see that India will lose West Bengal and Assam. And it is preposterous to think that, in an association with a great power like Russia, the great power's own interests will not prevail. It is absurd of India to think that with its ancient wisdom and the rope trick it can lasso the Soviet Union. The Soviet Union will demand its full pound of flesh. There will not be anything immediate and sensational like Soviet bases. There will just be an undercurrent of subtle gains . . . And if our links with East Pakistan (Bangladesh) remain permanently broken, that part of the world too will come under Communist influence, either Soviet or Chinese. In either case, it will be red.

Interview, Rawalpindi, Feb. 8/ The New York Times, 2-13:(1)16.

I have no ideology that can be described in a simple phrase. I have always been sickened by poverty and economic injustice. I have always had a fire in my heart and a desire to revolutionize our society, to throw away dead weights and build a beautiful new face. And we are building. We are reducing tyranny and cruelty. I can't define my doctrine. Doctrines everywhere are becoming flexible. You can't define things. How can you define Communism? In Russia? In China? In Yugoslavia? In Albania?

Interview, Rawalpindi, Feb. 8/ The New York Times, 2-13:(1)16.

(On U.S. President Nixon's forthcoming trip to Communist China): This Nixon trip is a welcome development. The dialogue will be welcome. Nothing sensational will come of the talks, but that is good; nobody wants an earthquake. Let the stream flow gently and build relations gradually on the basis of mutual confidence. Nixon showed admirable statesmanship in moving for this meeting.

Interview, Rawalpindi, Feb. 8/ The New York Times, 2-13:(1)16.

We recognize the realities of the (India-Pakistan) postwar situation. But it's hard to figure out what (the Indians) really want. Already, hostile propaganda has resumed on their radio. Border incidents, too. Isn't half our country enough? The 93,000 Pakistani prisoners of war (in Indian hands) have to come back sooner or later. They are a wasting asset for India . . . First I released Mujib (Bangladesh Prime Minister Mujibur Rahman) unconditionally. I thought this would be a happy augury for a new era. I was wrong. Well, now I have less birds in the cage. My nightingale has gone. You can't expect me to follow up one unilateral concession with another. If India releases our prisoners, then I could take the next step. I am quite prepared to recognize Bangladesh—but there must be a quid for my quo.

Interview/Newsweek, 4-3:42.

(On new military equipment needed by Pakistan): You can look at these things in two ways: one, that we want toys to play around with and, on the other hand, we want to safeguard our security. Well, we do not want toys to play around with. We want to safeguard our security. We are a state that has suffered greatly to military conquest and military aggression, so we will never disarm. The extent to which we arm will depend on the attitudes and the ambitions of others.

News conference, May 7/ The New York Times, 6-3:1.

We have no intention of curbing the freedom of the individual to pursue his vocation. We accept that private enterprise has a role to play in the economic progress of Pakistan; but we must rid the economy of concentrations of economic power in the hands of the few to end the exploitation of the many.

Before businessmen, Karachi, May 23/ The Washington Post, 6-5:6.

(On his forthcoming conference with Indian Prime Minister Indira Gandhi): I believe we should give peace a chance . . . The past 25 years has been an era of confrontation and war in the sub-continent, with what result to the peoples of the region? They remain among the poorest, most underfed, illiterate, ill-housed and disease-ridden—the worst conditions in the world. It has been a heavy price.

Address to the nation/ The New York Times, 7-2:(4)3.

(Referring to Indian Prime Minister Indira Gandhi): I have always seen her like this: a diligent and hard-working student, a woman devoid of intelligence and imagination. With all her saris, her red mark in the middle of her forehead, her little smile, she will never succeed in impressing me . . . She irritates me. God! Don't make me think about it!

Interview/Newsweek, 7-3:23.

Hale Boggs
United States Representative, D–La.

(On his just-completed trip to Communist China): We were advised by high officials that the policy of the Peking government is that disarmament will not be unilateral disarmament, and there was specific concern expressed rather emphatically with regard to the possibility of continued Soviet armament and American disarmament . . . As they put it, there are two superpowers—the United States and Russia—and if Russia becomes the greater superpower, then much of the world is in difficulty.

News conference, Washington, July 8/ San Francisco Examiner & Chronicle, 7-9:(A)1.

Houari Boumedienne
President of Algeria

(On the India-Pakistan war of 1971): We saw Pakistan taken apart by force—and, I might say, without any help from its U.S. ally. Even if our political relations with India are in some ways closer than with Pakistan, we were frightened to see a country militarily torn apart. This was a serious precedent for us to watch.

Interview, Algiers/ The New York Times, 7-30:(4)13.

Leonid I. Brezhnev
General Secretary, Communist Party of the Soviet Union

Facts—that is, the subsequent deeds of the United States and (Communist) China—will say the decisive word about the significance of the Peking talks (between U.S. President Nixon and Chinese officials). However, it is impossible to overlook some statements of the participants in the Peking talks that make one think the dialogue goes beyond the framework of the bilateral relations between the United States and China. How else can one assess the statement made at a banquet in Shanghai that today our peoples—that is, the American and the Chinese—hold in their hands the future of the whole world?

At Soviet Trade Unions Congress, Moscow, March 20/ San Francisco Examiner, 3-20:10.

(LEONID I. BREZHNEV)

Speaking bluntly, what does Peking's (Communist China's) foreign policy amount to today? It amounts to absurd claims to Soviet territory; to malicious slander of the Soviet social and political system, of our peace-loving foreign policy. It amounts to undisguised sabotage of the efforts to limit the arms race and of the struggle for disarmament and for a relaxation of international tension. It amounts to continuous attempts to split the socialist camp and the Communist movement, to foment discord among the fighters for national liberation, to range the developing countries against the Soviet Union and the other socialist states. Lastly, it amounts to undisciplined alignments on anti-Soviet grounds with any, even the most reactionary, forces—the most rabid haters of the Soviet Union from among the English Tories or the revenge-seeking elements in West Germany, the Portuguese colonialists or the racists of South Africa. What can one say about this policy? We hold that it is unnatural for relations between socialist countries, that it acts against the interests not only of the Soviet, but also of the Chinese people, against the interests of world socialism, of the liberation and anti-imperialist struggle, against peace and international security.

At celebration of 50th anniversary of the formation of the Soviet Union, Moscow, Dec. 21/ The New York Times, 12-22:10.

James L. Buckley
United States Senator, C–N.Y.

(Referring to Nationalist China): It is my conviction that the United States will continue to make available the military means required to preserve and protect this outpost of Chinese freedom. I say this not just because my President (Nixon) has stated time and again that we will not turn our backs on our alliances, but because of my deep belief that the American people will not abandon you.

At World Freedom Day rally, Taipei, Jan. 23/ The New York Times, 1-24:3.

We are a Pacific power just as we are an Atlantic power. The control of Asia and its vast manpower and mineral resources by a power hostile to the United States would be as intolerable a threat to our security as would be the control by a hostile power of the human and industrial resources of Western Europe. If the rimland of eastern Asia were to fall in hostile hands, the threat against the island republics extending from Indonesia around through Japan would be palpable, and our own continued access to vital waterways and resources would be placed in jeopardy. Moreover, the geographic and political isolation which would follow would dangerously reduce the alternatives which would be available to us in planning for our own defense. This is why every American President for over 100 years has understood the need to maintain an American military presence in the western Pacific.

Feb. 11/ The New York Times, 2-29:33.

(On the results of President Nixon's recent trip to Communist China): . . . a disastrous venture in American diplomacy which has done enormous damage to American credibility. If this is an example of Richard Nixon's summitry . . . I do not know if I will be campaigning for him.

Washington, Feb. 29/ National Review, 3-17:273.

George Bush
United States Ambassador/Permanent Representative to the United Nations

(On the U.S.' stand favoring Pakistan in the India-Pakastani conflict): . . . we were on the same side of the issue with them (Communist China), but so were 102 other countries, too. There was a very small handful on the other side. Most people seem to think we were on the wrong side. Only India and Russia and a handful of Soviet satellites were against what we were trying to do. We were on the overwhelming side of world opinion as the United Nations tried to take action that would enforce the fundamental character principle that one country should not be taken over by another by force.

Interview, Washington/ The Dallas Times Herald, 1-28:(A)4.

Y. B. Chavan
Minister of Finance of India

All-round economic progress since independence has radically altered the character of our economy and brought about a significant increase in real incomes generally. But the absolute number of those living in abject poverty has scarcely diminished; economic disparities appear to have widened; unemployment has become a seemingly intractable problem.

The Washington Post, 8-15:(A)16.

Chiang Kai-shek
President of Nationalist China

The purpose of our bitter struggle still lies in the complete recovery of the mainland (Communist China), in the final rescue of our hundreds of millions of compatriots there.

Upon his re-election by the National Assembly, Taipei/ The Washington Post, 5-21:(A)26.

Chiao Kuan-hua
Deputy Foreign Minister of, and chief United Nations General Assembly delegate from, the People's Republic of (Communist) China

Dear Mr. Soviet Representative, why can't you just withdraw your troops and dismantle your bases from the People's Republic of Mongolia instead of unabashedly uttering empty words about the renunciation of the use of all force? . . . The stark facts have shown that the Soviet leaders have neither laid down their butcher's knives nor will they become Buddhas.

At United Nations, N.Y., Nov. 13/ The Washington Post, 11-14:(A)20.

Chou En-lai
Premier of the People's Republic of (Communist) China

(On U.S. President Nixon's forthcoming trip to Communist China): The inevitable in history often comes about through the accidental. The fact that the people of the United States and China wanted contacts became ripe, and (Chinese Communist Party) Chairman Mao happened to take an interest . . . China places high hopes on the American people. It is our belief that the future will be decided by an awakening among them. Their potential and prospects are boundless.

Interview, Jan. 31/ The New York Times, 2-6:(4)2.

When we stated at the United Nations that we are not a superpower and would never attempt to be one, one superpower (the Soviet Union) laughed and said China could not exist without a nuclear umbrella. As our Chinese proverb has it, that fellow "does not know how high the sky is or how deep the earth."

Peking/Time, 2-14:30.

(Addressing U.S. President Nixon): The social systems of China and of the United States are fundamentally different, and there are great differences between the Chinese government and the U.S. government. However, these differences should not hinder China and the United States from establishing normal state relations on the basis of mutual respect for sovereignty and territorial integrity, mutual nonaggression, noninterference in each other's internal affairs, equality and mutual benefits and peaceful coexistence. Still less they should lead to war.

At banquet for President Nixon, Peking, Feb. 21/ The Washington Post, 2-22:(A)6.

(CHOU EN-LAI)

(Toasting U.S. President Nixon): There exists great difference of principle between our two sides. Through earnest and frank discussions, a clearer knowledge of each other's positions and stands has been gained. This has been beneficial to both sides. The times are advancing and the world changing. We are deeply convinced that the strength of the peoples is powerful and that whatever zigzags and reverses there will be in the development of history, the general trend of the world is definitely toward light and not darkness. It is the common desire of the Chinese and American peoples to enhance their mutual understanding and friendship and promote the normalization of relations between China and the United States. The Chinese government and people will work unswervingly toward this goal.

Peking, Feb. 25/
The Washington Post, 2-26:(A)7.

(On his country's relations with Japan): We are going to end the abnormal state of affairs which has existed between the two countries up to now. The termination of the state of war and the normalization of relations between China and Japan—the realization of these long-cherished wishes of the Chinese and Japanese people—will open a new chapter in the relations between our two countries and make a positive contribution to the relaxation of tension in Asia and the safeguarding of world peace.

At farewell banquet in honor of visiting Japanese Prime Minister Kakuei Tanaka, Peking, Sept. 28/
Los Angeles Herald-Examiner, 9-28:(A)1.

Chow Shu-kai
Foreign Minister of Nationalist China

(On possible contacts between his country and Communist nations): . . . if our contact with these foreign countries will not affect our national policy, and if these nations are not the puppets of Communist China, we can still find ways to develop trade and economic and other relations which will be good for both sides. Whether to establish diplomatic relations with any other country should be decided on the basis of whether it would be good for us.

Before Central Committee of Kuomintang Party, Taipei, March 7/
The New York Times, 3-8:6.

(On U.S. President Nixon's recent trip to Communist China): The reception of the President by Communist China was very calculated. In Taiwan, we have plenty of bananas; but in Japan a banana is so precious they don't usually give you one banana—they give you one-third, one-half, or, on very special occasions, they give you a whole banana. I call the reception of the President by the Chinese leaders the banana tactics. They give you one-third to start with and then hang onto the rest.

Interview, Taipei, March 9/
Los Angeles Herald-Examiner, 3-9:(A)3.

Frank Church
United States Senator, D–Idaho

(Humorously endorsing President Nixon's forthcoming trip to Communist China): I do think this trip is necessary. I admit we've always had somebody mad at us, but this is the first time I can recall when we've had everybody mad at us. So I say, if the Chinese are willing to talk, let's talk. We've got to make a friend somewhere!

At "Salute to Congress" dinner, Washington, Jan. 26/
The Washington Post, 1-28:(D)1.

Bernard A. Clarey
Admiral, United States Navy; Commander-in-chief, Pacific Fleet

I think it's unlikely in the foreseeable future that we're going to have to get out of Japan . . . or the Philippines. They are two principal bases. And when I say Japan, I include Okinawa. If circumstance required us to leave those bases, that would, in my view, represent a major political change out there, which would affect more than just the Fleet. It would affect the whole American posture in the area. So I think it would have a big impact on U.S. foreign policy and U.S. actions if we were forced out of all our bases out there for some reason.

Interview, Washington/
U.S. News & World Report, 4-17:79.

Harlan Cleveland
President, University of Hawaii;
Former Undersecretary of State
of the United States

I was myself for many years a practitioner of secret diplomacy. But on the basis of that experience, I must say that my government's tactics in the arrangements for President Nixon's visit to Peking were both unwise and unnecessary. Some months of advance consultation on the general problem of building a new relationship with Peking could have preceded the dramatic shift in American strategy. Political consultation, like other key human relationships, is subject to a golden rule of its own: Don't surprise your friends if you don't want them to surprise you.

Seoul, South Korea, Feb. 9/
The Washington Post, 2-10:(A)4.

James C. Corman
United States Representative, D–Calif.

It seems to me there is a substantial amount of pro-American feeling among people in government and the general populace we've been exposed to so far (in Bangladesh). It would be very unfortunate for Bangladesh and the United States if this were allowed to dissipate because of our refusal to recognize the country.

Interview, Dacca, Jan. 26/
Los Angeles Times, 1-27:(1)26.

Gerald R. Ford
United States Representative, R–Mich.

(On his just-completed trip to Communist China): Among high Chinese officials there was a great deal ot interest shown and many questions asked about the sufficiency of our military capability, and what our direction might be in the future with respect to Defense Department funding and its program . . . They don't want the United States to withdraw from the Pacific or other points . . . They believe our presence is important for the stability of the world now and in the future.

News conference,
Washington, July 8/
San Francisco Examiner & Chronicle,
7-9:(A)1.

Takeo Fukuda
Foreign Minister of Japan

The question of American relations with (Communist) China and the problem of our relations with (Communist) China are not at all the same; and Japan will not necessarily follow the same course as that of the U.S. in pursuing its China policy. In the event that the two countries find their paths diverging on the China issue, both sides should seek to understand what the other is doing. This is very, very important.

News conference, Tokyo, Jan. 4/
The Washington Post, 1-5:(A)8.

With development of nuclear weapons, it became evident that, if they are used, mankind will be annihilated. I can't foresee a third world war. Consequently, economic strength becomes much more important than military strength. Japan could make nuclear weapons but has no intention of doing so. Instead, we wish to employ our economic strength to gain an increasing voice in the international community. The tradition once was that a nation used its economic power to become a military power; but that is not the case with us today. I think this is unprecedented in history, at least in modern history.

Interview, Tokyo/
The New York Times, 3-10:37.

Largely due to the cooperation of the United States, Japan is among the major

(TAKEO FUKUDA)

nations today. When you look at history, economically powerful nations have become powerful militarily as well. But Japan will not take that path. Because we experienced defeat for the first time in our history (in World War II), most of our people are pledged never to fight again. This consensus is established among the Japanese. Particularly strong is our feeling on nuclear weapons. We have a nuclear allergy. We should not have nuclear arms or any substantial military means. Being an economic power, but declining to be a military power, we have a certain reserve of power. We can use it for the development of the less-advanced parts of the world and by that means contribute to the development and prosperity of the world. That is Japan's new role as I envision it, and it is also the vision of the Japanese people, as I see it.

Interview/Newsweek, 5-15:44.

As far as (U.S.) President Nixon's visit to (Communist) China is concerned, I certainly welcome it. But the way it was done—in that sudden, abrupt manner—is not something I really appreciate. That particular method gave rise to uncertainties in various countries in the world and also could undermine the relation of trust between the U.S. and Asia. It should never be repeated.

Interview/Newsweek, 5-15:44.

I am sure that Japanese-American relations will remain stable in the future . . . We believe the relations with the United States are more important to us—more important than our relations with any other country.

Interview, Tokyo, June 16/
Los Angeles Times, 6-18:(B)1.

Indira Gandhi
Prime Minister of India

(On India's involvement in the war with Pakistan over the independence of East Pakistan, now Bangladesh): If India had allowed a nation (East Pakistan) to be stifled and a people to be suppressed, it would have been a disgrace for us. If a country does not raise its voice against injustice elsewhere, it can't fight injustice at home. We are proud that we helped put down the genocide next door.

At Congress Party rally,
New Delhi, Jan. 2/
Los Angeles Times, 1-3:(1)9.

There have been suggestions that we were pressured into the cease-fire (during the India-Pakistan conflict) by the Russians, who in turn were being pressured by the Americans. Hah! The decision was made right here, at the moment of the surrender in Dacca. We were able to inform the Soviet Union right away only because (Soviet Deputy Foreign Minister) Mr. Kaznetsov happened to be here. I am not a person to be pressured—by anybody or any nation.

Interview, New Delhi/
Time, 1-3:34.

The leaders of the Asian countries should realize that the big powers do not want Asian nations to become stronger and are trying to weaken them instead. Asian countries could build themselves into stronger and prosperous ones by getting united and working with cooperation among themselves. The time has now come for Asian countries to consider seriously whether they want to continue to be suppressed under the domination of rich and big nations or whether they want to work for prosperity and peace for their people.

Kutch, India, Jan. 3/
San Francisco Examiner, 1-3:4.

I think the United States always has had difficulty understanding India. Western nations have a habit of regarding the West as the center of the world. But obviously, we can't see always through the same eyes.

And even when the United States spoke of supporting India (in the India-Pakistan war), it was arming Pakistan. I think the United States made many wrong assessments from the start. It tended to look at things in terms of being Communist or non-Communist, and not in terms of what people were actually doing. I don't want Communism for my country. But if someone calls himself a Communist and at the same time really behaves like a democrat, I don't have anything against him.

Interview/The New York Times, 2-17:15.

The Soviet Union is a friend of India, and we value this friendship. However, anyone who imagines that we shall allow ourselves to be dictated to by third parties in our negotiations with Pakistan or in any other matter, foreign or domestic, is quite off the mark.

Before Parliament, New Delhi, April 4/ The Washington Post, 4-5:(A)17.

We are quite willing to forget what has happened and to make a new start with the United States. We want your friendship. But the Nixon Administration has shown no real desire to improve its relations with India. The American people—that's another story. They have consistently been sympathetic. I, personally, get such a vast number of letters from Americans—in every state, and every age—all expressing their friendship for India. We are grateful for this support. And we sincerely hope that the U.S. Administration, too, will try to understand our point of view and our problems. It is never too late or too early to be friends.

Interview, New Delhi/ Parade, 8-13:6.

Although the old empires have receded, Asia remains an arena for the contest of world powers. Most of the conflicts since World War II have erupted on our continent. Many have been the outcome of the interference of outsiders, and not one has helped the people of Asia in any way.

At opening of Asian International Trade Fair, New Delhi, Nov. 3/ Los Angeles Times, 11-4:(1)6.

There is a constant feeling—or so we are told—that we are pro-Russian. We are certainly friends. They helped us in difficult times. But we pay for whatever we get from them. The Soviet Union does not influence policy decisions in Delhi and does not try. Geography alone dictates some of our actions, of course.

Interview/ San Francisco Examiner & Chronicle, 12-10:(This World)2.

Marshall Green
Assistant Secretary for East Asia and Pacific Affairs, Department of State of the United States

I believe that I helped in reassuring Asian leaders (on his recent trip) that our (the U.S.'s) seeking a closer relationship with the People's Republic of (Communist) China will not be at the expense of their nations. On the contrary, it will be in accordance with their—and our—long-range interests. I was able to explain to them that what we seek through improved contacts with Peking is a lessening of tensions and dangers; that we did not negotiate behind the backs of our friends and that we will continue to stand by them.

Before House Foreign Affairs Committee, Washington, March 23/ The New York Times, 3-24:3.

Andrei A. Gromyko
Foreign Minister of the Soviet Union

The Soviet Union desires that other countries have friendly relations with (Communist) China . . . However, the relations between China and the Soviet Union have deteriorated not on the responsibility of my country but on the responsibility of China. The Soviet Union has no objection to Japanese policy toward the

(ANDREI A. GROMYKO)

improvement in its relations with China. However, any nation that hopes to have friendly relations with the Soviet Union must carry out such a policy on the premise that it would not affect adversely the safety and interests of the Soviet Union.

News conference, Tokyo, Jan. 28/ The New York Times, 1-29:7.

William Randolph Hearst, Jr.
Editor-in-chief, The Hearst Newspapers

The Russians are in the Pacific around the Indian Ocean. They are moving in to fill any vacuum, and the (Communist) Chinese take a dim view of it. That's dandy. If anybody's going to get in a scrap, I can't think of two better countries . . . as long as we (the U.S.) don't think we have to choose sides.

Before International Salon Forum, Los Angeles, May 2/ Los Angeles Herald-Examiner, 5-4:(A)16.

Kenneth B. Keating
United States Ambassador to India

India is working out its own brand of socialism. But because they're socialist-oriented, they feel more comfortable with the Russians. They've been closer to the Soviet Union than to the United States since the time of Nehru.

Interview, New Delhi, July 22/ The Washington Post, 7-24:(A)15.

Edward M. Kennedy
United States Senator, D–Mass.

The India-Pakistan war has become the Achilles heel of the Nixon foreign policy. It (U.S. support for Pakistan) demonstrates how warped our policy really is, how prostrate toward Peking our policy has really become.

At Washington Press Club, Jan. 17/ San Francisco Examiner, 1-18:2.

Although our government has not recognized you (Bangladesh), the people of the world do recognize you and recognize all you have accomplished in the name of freedom. The people of America were with you in recent months, although our government was not. We are brothers in liberty, and no man, no policy, no government can change that fact.

At Dacca (Bangladesh) University, Feb. 14/ San Francisco Examiner, 2-14:6.

Kim Il Sung
Premier of North Korea

It is my assertion that we should attempt direct North-South talks right away. To raise the question of the right of American troops to remain in South Korea is to miss the point. The withdrawal of American troops is not a precondition for political talks. (If) North and South met and talked in a single room, they ought to be able to find many points in common. We have no intention of pushing South Korea into socialism. On the other hand, we have no intention of having capitalism thrust upon us from the South. Even with the South Korean system as different as it is, it is possible to build a unified country.

Interview, April 28/ Los Angeles Times, 4-29:(1)19.

Nearly 20 years have passed since the signing of the armistice agreement (in Korea), and what kind of necessity do you (the U.S.) have for stationing forces in South Korea under the signboard of the United Nations forces? Some people say you are staying in South Korea to protect the South Koreans because we want to invade South Korea. But we have declared time and again we have no intention at all of invading South Korea. Therefore, I think it is high time for you to put an end to your role of police. If you withdraw, we Koreans can do things in common for peaceful unification . . . Our policy toward the United States is as follows: If the

United States government stops its unfriendly attitude toward us and stops obstructing the unification of our country, then there is no reason why we should have hostile attitudes toward the United States. So I should say relations between ourselves and the United States entirely depend on the United States and not on us.

Interview, Pyongyang, North Korea/ The New York Times, 5-31:14.

The most important thing in war preparation, in my opinion, is that we educate our people in the spirit of hating the enemy. Without educating our people in this spirit we cannot defeat the U.S., which is superior in technology. Therefore, we frankly tell you (the U.S.) we are always making preparations for war. We do not conceal this matter. We are making preparations openly. Nobody can tell, neither you nor I can tell, what time you'll pounce upon us. Therefore, I think it is quite natural and quite all right to educate people with the spirit of hating the target of our struggle.

Interview, Pyongyang, North Korea/ The New York Times, 5-31:14.

We propose that a confederation of North and South Korea would be all right if we can't reunify the country right away. This means forming a Supreme National Committee to consult and discuss matters of common concern for the nation while retaining different social systems intact in North and South Korea. Even now we want economic cooperation. So we think if we give South Korea what they have not and if they give us what we have not, we can develop our economy faster in exchanging in that way. So we think we must proceed from the interests of the nation. We propose an exchange of trade, economics, culture and scientists. We propose political negotiations on a broad basis and meetings between parliamentary members on a broad basis. They (the South Koreans) have closed their doors, not we. We are not afraid of capitalist influence coming in. We are not afraid of it because there is no reason why we should fear it. Everything will be solved if South Korea opens its doors.

Interview, Pyongyang, North Korea/ The New York Times, 5-31:14.

The peaceful reunification of the country can be attained by way of establishing a unified government through the elections to be held throughout the whole of Korea or by setting up a confederation system as a transitional step. The elections we demand should be free elections without the interference of any outside forces. It is desirable to set up the unified government through democratic elections based on universal direct principles and principles of equality. But if the unified government cannot be set up right away, it may be good, as well, to achieve the reunification through a confederation system slowly, leaving the present systems in the North and the South intact. In this way, the reunification of the country may be realized gradually. We think to settle all the problems for the peaceful reunification of the country, it is necessary first of all to achieve a great unity of the nation, transcending the differences of systems, belief and political views; and for this purpose it is essential to remove misunderstanding and distrust between the North and the South and create an atmosphere of mutual understanding, respect and trust. This is our contention.

Interview, Pyongyang, North Korea, June 21/ The Washington Post, 6-26:(A)18.

When the American people joined the common front against Fascism and fought against Hitlerite Fascism and Japanese imperialism during the Second World War, they won high praise and support from the Korean people. Subsequent aggravation of relations between Korea and the United States is attributable to the United States intervention in the internal affairs of Korea (during the Korean War) and its hostile and

(KIM IL SUNG)

aggressive policy toward the Democratic People's Republic of (North) Korea. If the United States gives up its hostile and aggressive policy toward us even now and does not encourage the division of Korea or obstruct the reunification of Korea, we are also ready to change our policy toward the United States. We Korean people distinguish the American people from the U.S. imperialists. The Korean people wish to promote friendship with the U.S. people not only now but also in the future.

Interview, Pyongyang, North Korea, June 21/ The Washington Post, 6-26:(A)18.

Kim Jong Pil
Premier of South Korea

(On recent discussions between North and South Korea toward easing relations between them): This is just like a soccer game, and the South and the North have just agreed to play a game. Before we even start to play, the spectators in the stand try to meddle in the game. But such an attempt would only hurt our sincere effort to pursue a peaceful solution to the problems of the Korean peninsula . . . It is not time for the United Nations to take up the Korean issue. In terms of their authority and competence, they should first ascertain that there is no possibility of renewed armed aggression from the North. In terms of helping us to expedite our dialogue or our reunification, they should leave us alone, because we have just begun and we are trying to have our own dialogue.

Interview, Seoul/ The New York Times, 8-11:6.

We know we cannot insist on having our own way . . . but a hasty withdrawal of U.S. forces from Korea will put us in a more difficult situation rather than helping us in what we are trying to attain. I am one who wants U.S. forces to remain. It is an iron rule that, when you deal with Communists, you must negotiate from a position of strength . . . The North Koreans have only *indicated* they will seek a peaceful solution to reunification . . . No matter how outsiders may look at it, the cold fact is that a threat from the North does exist.

Interview, Seoul, Aug. 19/ Los Angeles Times, 8-20:(A)17.

Norman E. Kirk
Prime Minister-elect of New Zealand

A Prime Minister should be able to hear what the bloke living next door says and not just what the head of a (foreign) government says. What the public wants is important. You can't give them everything they want, but it's their government and they are the ultimate power.

The New York Times, 11-27:3.

Henry A. Kissinger
Assistant to the President of the United States for National Security Affairs

We have said on many occasions, and I will say it again here, that as far as the United States is concerned, our relationship with the People's Republic of (Communist) China is not directed against the Soviet Union; and while the People's Republic is well able to speak for itself, and my megalomania has not reached the point where I believe that I can speak for it, I believe that it is clear to us that neither is the policy of the People's Republic of China in its relations with us directed against the Soviet Union. We are pursuing our policy with the People's Republic of China on the ground that a stable peace in the world is difficult to envisage if 800 million people are excluded from a dialogue with the most powerful nation in the world, and we are conducting our discussions with the People's Republic entirely on the merits of that relationship.

News conference, Shanghai, Feb. 27/ The New York Times, 2-28:16.

(On U.S. President Nixon's recently-concluded trip to Communist China): The basic objective of this trip was to set in motion a train of events and an evolution in the policy of our two countries which both sides recognized would be slow at first and present many difficulties and in which a great deal depended on the assessment by each side of the understanding by the other of what was involved in this process and of the assessment by each side of the reliability of the other in being able to pursue this for the amount of time necessary to see it prevail.

Feb. 27/
Los Angeles Times, 2-29:(2)6.

Melvin R. Laird
Secretary of Defense of the United States

The Soviet Union, in my opinion, is a major contributor to the continuing conflict that exists in Southeast Asia. The prospects for peace in that area of the world or in other areas like Southeast Asia rests, it seems to me, to a major degree with the Soviet Union.

News conference, Washington, April 7/
Los Angeles Times, 4-8:(1)12.

Tran Van Lam
Foreign Minister of South Vietnam

(On a communique issued by the U.S. and Communist China at the end of U.S. President Nixon's visit to Peking): No peace-loving person can criticize it, because its ultimate goal is to reduce tension in relations between the two big powers, thus avoiding an armed conflict detrimental to both sides. It proves the United States' great efforts and hopes in normalizing relations with a hostile country after nearly a quarter of a century.

Interview, Saigon, March 2/
Los Angeles Times, 3-2:(1)9.

Lee Kuan Yew
Prime Minister of Singapore

A net loss for the Americans in this area is not necessarily a net gain for (Communist) China. China will need time to develop the military and economic sinews of a great power. Japan has the economic sinews and Russia has the military sinews; they and others will be preempting as much as they can.

Interview, Singapore/
San Francisco Examiner, 2-9:36.

Liu Chieh
Former Nationalist Chinese Ambassador to the United Nations

One thing is certain (about U.S. President Nixon's forthcoming trip to Communist China): The hostility of the Maoist regime toward the United States will remain unchanged. It is rooted in Maoist ideology. The United States is the principal nation that stands in the way of the Communist grand design of world domination.

News conference, Los Angeles, Jan. 6/
Los Angeles Herald-Examiner, 1-6:(A)6.

Kafiludden Mahmood
Chief Secretary of Planning of Bangladesh

As for foreign aid, we hope we can turn all that goodwill for Bangladesh into a little food.

Interview, Dacca, Jan. 5/
The New York Times, 1-6:4.

Andre Malraux
Author; Former Minister of State for Culture of France

Five years ago, the hatred of the United States in (Communist) China was total. At that time, the Chinese position was still what I would term a highly or very revolutionary position versus a capitalist position. That, of course, was before the "Cultural Revolution" . . . At this time, what (Party Chairman) Mao is interested in is not the revolutionary problem, because you don't start waging every morning a battle that you have already won; what interests him most vitally—and that which

(ANDRE MALRAUX)

was the goal of the revolution—was how to raise the standard of living of the Chinese. Because you must understand that, if the United States represents for him a means to improve the standard of living of the Chinese, the fact that the United States is capitalist does not matter . . .

News conference,
Washington, Feb. 15/
U.S. News & World Report, 2-28:20,21.

I do not think that (U.S. President) Nixon gave up anything on Taiwan (during his recent trip to Communist China) because there has been, between Peking and Taipei, an agreement for at least five years (that Taiwan would come under Communist China's control) linked to the death of Chiang Kai-shek. But they did not think Chiang Kai-shek would live so long.

Interview, Paris, March 2/
Los Angeles Times, 3-3:(1)4.

. . . Russia today wants to encircle (Communist) China—Siberia, Bangladesh, Vietnam. On this, Russia is playing for keeps. It is the Russians who have been rebuilding the Indian Army for three years. They are driving hard now, and China, in my opinion, will not fight; because what China wants now is not at all a new conflict with Russia—it's the development of China. They dazzle us with a sort of Chinese revolution that is supposed to be conquering Asia. They're doing nothing. It's the Russians who are fighting.

Interview/
The New York Times Magazine,
8-6:58.

In four years, Japan will be the second-greatest economic power in the world, behind the United States but ahead of the Soviet Union. And at that moment, America . . . will be forced to adopt a Japanese policy—that means, giving them atomic bombs. If the Americans do not, then the Russians will. We have four years. Then, we're in a serious situation; the Americans and the Russians wooing this ravishing maid—which one will go to bed with her?

Interview/
The New York Times Magazine,
8-6:56.

Mike Mansfield
United States Senator, D–Mont.

(Reporting on his trip to Communist China): The cities are clean, orderly and safe; the shops well stocked with food, clothing and other consumer items; policemen are evident only for controlling traffic and very few carry weapons; soldiers are rarely seen. The housing is of a subsistence type but is now sufficient to end the spectacle of millions of the homeless and dispossessed who in the past walked the tracks and roads or anchored their sampans in the rivers of China and lived out their lives in a space little larger than a rowboat. Crime, begging, drug addiction, alcoholism, delinquency are conspicuous in their absence. Personal integrity is scrupulous. In Canton, for example, a display-case for lost-and-found articles in the lobby of the People's Hotel contained, among other items, a half-empty package of cigarettes and a pencil.

Before the Senate,
Washington, May 11/
The Dallas Times Herald, 5-12:(A)3.

Ferdinand E. Marcos
President of the Philippines

The Nationalist Chinese can, I believe, withstand any attempt by the Red Chinese to take over Taiwan militarily in the next five to 10 years, provided no other power intervenes and provided the United States stands by Nationalist China. Even if the United States were to stay away from fighting, I don't believe the Red Chinese would be able to take Nationalist China—short of the use of atomic weapons. But I don't believe the Red Chinese would use atomic weapons merely for the purpose of solving the Taiwan question.

Interview, Manila, March 15/
San Francisco Examiner, 3-15:12.

Most certainly, Russia has always maintained that it was an Asian power . . . Asia has now become like all the rest of the world. Russia has now become more flexible. Flexibility seems to be the line now for everyone in Asia. Everyone is housebroken.

Interview/
Los Angeles Herald-Examiner, 3-19:(B)11.

(On his declaration of martial law to combat Communist subversion): This is not a military take-over. I have proclaimed martial law in accordance with the powers vested in the President by the Constitution of the Philippines. I, as your duly-elected President, use this power which may be implemented by military authorities to protect the Republic of the Philippines and our democracy which is endangered by the peril of violent overthrow of the duly-constituted government, insurrection or rebellion. Such a danger confronts the Republic of the Philippines today. We will eliminate the threat of violent overthrow of government, and we must now reform our political, economic and social institutions. We are falling back and have fallen back to our last line of defense. The limit has been reached because we have been placed against the wall.

Broadcast address,
Manila, Sept. 23/
The Dallas Times Herald, 9-24:(A)1.

(On his declaring martial law): We do not want any Vietnams in the Philippines. We do not want the repetition of the bloodshed that occurred in Indonesia. We want to fight Communism now. If we do not fight it now, we may not be able to overcome it. (The American people should be proud of this action because) here we show that the Filipino people have been able to succeed where perhaps in Vietnam you (the U.S.) failed. In Vietnam you wanted the Vietnamese people to stand alone, proud, and defend themselves—self-reliant. And here you have the Philippines, proud, dignified, self-reliant—a country where the people would like to fight their own problems internally against the threat of rebellion, against a Communist threat, if you will. It is what the United States wanted with respect to the program of Vietnamization. (The U.S. had to send) half a million soldiers to Vietnam. Here, we don't ask you to send any American soldiers. All we ask is that we be allowed to strike the Communist threat with all the weapons at our command under the Constitution—and martial law is one of them.

TV-radio interview,
Manila/"Meet the Press,"
National Broadcasting Company, 10-8.

I have always maintained there is a security gap in Asia, and there is no nation that can counterbalance the (Communist) Chinese nuclear capacity except the United States. There has been talk among some regional leaders of neutralizing Southeast Asia, which is laudable but impractical. Of course, the Red Chinese will demonstrate that they are "housebroken" and respectable, but the threat remains; and I personally feel that the only acceptable deterrent right now is the American defense umbrella.

Interview, Manila/
U.S. News & World Report, 10-16:38.

(On the goals of the current martial law in his country): Peace and order above everything else. Land reform, of course, with tenants taking over the ownership of land they now work. (For martial law to be considered a success by next year), judicial reform must have worked and (so must) the restructuring of the government to eliminate the corrupt and inefficient. We will also have to have educational reforms under way, changing general high schools to technological colleges and generally relating the educational system to our economic

(FERDINAND E. MARCOS)

development. We will also have to have our manpower-training scheme under way to cut unemployment and diversify and increase our exports and overseas markets . . . Of course, (democracy) can work. But it must demonstrate its ability for self-rejuvenation, its ability to correct itself. But it need not be an American type of democracy. It could just as well be the British or French variety . . . Remember that when (the late French President Charles) de Gaulle sought to save France, he asked for practically dictatorial powers . . . I hope the situation is so well in hand (next year) that we can have a (Constitutional) plebiscite.

Interview, Manila/ Newsweek, 10-30:56.

(On how he finally decided to declare martial law): I wanted a period in which I would commune with myself and commune with God and ask him whether it was correct for me to proclaim martial law. I asked for a sign and He gave me several signs. I told myself if this occurs I will immediately order martial law . . . and it did occur. It seems as if I was being led and guided by some strange mind above me.

Before Philippine Historical Association, Manila, Nov. 28/ Los Angeles Times, 11-29:(1)5.

Paul N. McCloskey, Jr.
United States Representative, R–Calif.

(On U.S. President Nixon's trip to Communist China): I don't think much will happen. I welcome breaking down barriers between our two countries. The trip is primarily for home consumption. The Chinese are great negotiators. They may gently drop his pants around his ankles and he'll never know it.

Feb. 5/ San Francisco Examiner & Chronicle, 2-6:(A)8.

George S. McGovern
United States Senator, D–S.D.

I would give (U.S. President) Nixon a complete zero, an F-minus, on the way he handled that whole India-Pakistan war matter, because—just to oversimplify the issue—I would have come out on the side of the Indians instead of the West Pakistanis. Now, that's an oversimplification, but it makes the point that the moral position of the Indians and the political, military, diplomatic position was on much sounder grounds than this savage onslaught that the West Pakistani government launched against Bangladesh. I think that for a country that started with the way we did—with a Declaration of Independence and so on—our sympathy should have been with East Pakistan (now Bangladesh); that on humanitarian grounds, we should have reacted much more strenuously than we did to the slaughter that was going on; that on political grounds, we should have identified with the people who won the election in Pakistan instead of with the government that immediately turned on the winners and tried to suppress them, put their leaders in jail and started attacking the Awami League.

Interview/ The Washington Post, 1-9:(C)4.

There's no place for the white man in Asia any more.

News conference, Los Angeles, April 6/ Los Angeles Herald-Examiner, 4-6:(A)2.

Our withdrawal (from Southeast Asia) is not going to mean automatic stability in that part of the world. But it does mean that the political, revolutionary forces that are moving will work themselves out without the kind of massive introduction of modern weapons and killing that we've brought in.

Interview, Milwaukee, Aug. 18/ The New York Times, 8-20:(1)44.

Mujibur Rahman
President of Bangladesh

(On the recent conflict between West Pakistan and East Pakistan, now Bangladesh): . . . we (Bengalis) were the majority in the whole of Pakistan. And I was the majority leader of the whole of Pakistan. And my party was the absolute majority party. That they (West Pakistanis) can't tolerate—that Bengalis should rule Pakistan, because I have got a majority, absolute majority. They played with me. And they played dirty games to perpetuate their rule and to exploit Bengal as a colonial power. They don't know Bengal. But my people know them, and I hope now that West Pakistan will understand what Bengal means.

News conference, London, Jan. 8/ The New York Times, 1-9:(1)2.

. . . I appeal to the world that millions of my people may not die. My roads have been destroyed (in the conflict with West Pakistan). My railroads have been destroyed. Thousands of buildings have been burned. My economy has been destroyed. You know Bengal is a wonderful country. It has very big resources, very fertile lands, but unfortunately exploited for hundreds of years by foreign powers. I appeal to you, for the sake of humanity, all over the world to come to our aid to save the hungry millions of my people, because they are dying.

News conference, London, Jan. 8/ The New York Times, 1-9:(1)2.

I am at last going back to my Bangla, the land of my dreams, after a period of nine months. In these nine months, my people have suffered. When I was in captivity, they fought; and now, when I go back to them, they are victorious. Now I go back to sunshine and to the victorious smiles of millions of my people. I go back now to the free, independent and sovereign Bangladesh. I go back not with hatred in the heart toward anyone, but in the realization that truth at last triumphs over falsehood, sanity over insanity, courage over cowardice, justice over injustice.

New Delhi, India, Jan. 10/ Los Angeles Times, 1-10:(1)11.

Let me tell (Pakistani President Zulfikar Ali) Bhutto that all links with Pakistan are snapped for good. I have no animus against the people of West Pakistan. I wish them well; I wish them happiness. Let them be free in their own country; and let us be free in our country. You (Pakistanis) have killed millions of my countrymen, dishonored our mothers and sisters, burned innumerable houses and driven one crore (10 million) of my people into neighboring India. Even then, I do not harbor any hatred against you. You have your independence and let us have our independence.

Dacca, Jan. 10/ The Washington Post, 1-11:(A)12.

Mujibur Rahman
Prime Minister of Bagladesh

. . . I understood what had been happening in my country even during my months in solitary confinement (in Pakistan). You see, I know my people; I know my forces; I know my organizational leadership; I know my student front; I know my labor front; and I knew they would fight every inch of the way. I sensed what was happening all those months (during his imprisonment), though I was alone with nothing to do but to think. I always knew my people were behind me. I knew that God would help me. I knew, too, that in a war between falsehood and truth, falsehood wins the first battle and truth the last. That's what kept me going. I never wept during all those months in solitary confinement. I never wept when they put me on trial. But I wept when I arrived back here and saw my wonderful *sonar Bangla* (golden Bengal).

Interview, Dacca/Newsweek, 1-24:29.

Why was the U.S. government giving arms to Pakistan (during the recent Pakistan war from which Bangladesh was created) when the massacre of my innocent country-

(MUJIBUR RAHMAN)

men was going on in towns and villages? Did not the U.S. government know of it while it had machinery functioning there at the time? I request the U.S. government to see that democracy, about which they talk so much, functions everywhere . . . And because India helped us, the United States cut off aid to India. While today I express my gratitude to the many countries who have recognized us, I cannot express gratitude to the United States.

Calcutta, Feb. 6/
The Washington Post, 2-7:(A)1.

(Peace) can be achieved only when our part of the world ceases to be a cockpit of contending powers from outside this region. We are opposed to efforts of some big countries to chalk out their spheres of influence in the region by encouraging divisive elements and reviving old bodies.

Toasting Indian Prime Minister Indira Gandhi, Dacca, March 17/
Los Angeles Times, 3-18:(1)3.

I am glad to learn that the United States has accorded formal recognition to Bangladesh as a sovereign, independent state. I hope this will open a new chapter in the development of friendly cooperation and understanding between the United States and Bangladesh for the mutual benefit of our two peoples.

Dacca, April 5/
The New York Times, 4-6:3.

Yashuhiro Nakasone
Minister of Trade of Japan

The imbalance in payments between the United States and Japan has as its cause the disparity between the two countries in competitiveness resulting from different rates of increase in price(s), standards and productivity. To go back further to the very source, the imbalance can be traced to the underlying differences in patterns of investment by the two countries. Japan has consistently channeled a large part of her resources to the modernization, improvement and expansion of her domestic industrial plant and equipment. Unlike the United States, Japan has not emphasized overseas investment nor the growth of multinational corporations.

The Washington Post, 8-31:(A)9.

Richard M. Nixon
President of the United States

(On U.S. diplomatic recognition of Communist China): Recognition in the conventional sense will not be one of the results (of his forthcoming trip to Peking). They do not expect that. We do not expect that. The reason it cannot be one of the results is that, as long as we continue to recognize Taiwan, which we do, as long as we continue to have our defense treaty with Taiwan, which we will, the People's Republic will not have diplomatic relations in the conventional sense in that country.

Television interview/
Columbia Broadcasting System, 1-2.

There is what I would term a natural interdependence between Japan and the United States. We both are nations of the Pacific; we are nations that have a responsibility for peace in the Pacific. Peace in the Pacific is indispensable for peace in the world.

San Clemente, Calif., Jan. 7/
The Washington Post, 1-8:(A)12.

It causes concern among our other friends in Asia when the United States moves to have a more normal relationship with mainland (Communist) China, in view of that country's record in Korea, in Indonesia and, for that matter, in supporting the North Vietnamese. Under those circumstances, our friends begin to wonder whether the United States, in making a move toward China—with a quarter of the earth's population—will do so at the expense of the 300 million people who live on the rimland of Asia in non-Communist countries. The answer is, we're not going to do that—just as the Communist Chinese are not going to change their attitudes with regard to the commitments to North Korea, for example . . . We have to weigh the short-term dangers of acting against the danger, long-term, of *not* acting. Long-term, we have to realize that China, now with 750 million people and, in 20 years, perhaps a billion people, will be a very significant economic power. It will be a major nuclear superpower if it wants to be. If China, there in the heart of Asia, with those very able people and with all that power, is isolated from the rest of the world, it creates an unacceptable danger not only to its neighbors but to the rest of the world. It is ironic that it is the United States rather than the Soviet Union that can make this move. But as I looked at history down the road—not just for the next election or even the next five or ten years, but for 15 and 20 years—it seemed to me that anyone sitting in this position, with all the power the United States represents, has an obligation to try to mitigate the danger of an isolated China.

Interview/
The Reader's Digest, February:62.

When it came to dealing with the People's Republic of (Communist) China, 25 years of hostility stood in the way. Accordingly, I began what is now three years of the most painstaking and necessarily discreet preparation for an opening to the world's most populous nation. In two weeks, I shall begin my journey for peace to Peking. The agreement to meet, and the mutual trust needed to make the arrangements for the first American state visit to the People's Republic of China is a breakthrough of great importance. We do not expect instant solutions to deep-seated differences; but the visit is a beginning. Now, in the relations between our countries, the old exchange of denunciations can be replaced with a constructive exchange of views.

Radio address, Washington, Feb. 9/
The Washington Post, 2-10:(A)13.

(Addressing Communist Chinese Premier Chou En-lai): As we discuss our differences, neither of us will compromise our principles. But while we cannot close the gulf between us, we can try to bridge it so that we may be able to talk across it. And so let us, in these next five days, start a long march together, not in lock step but on different roads leading to the same goal—the goal of building a world structure of peace and justice in which all may stand together with equal dignity; in which each nation, large or small, has a right to determine its own form of government free of outside interference or domination. The world watches, the world listens, the world waits to see what we will do . . . What legacy shall we leave our children? Are they destined to die for the hatreds which have plagued the old world? Or are they destined to live because we had the vision to build a new world? There is no reason for us to be enemies. Neither of us seeks the territory of the other. Neither of us seeks domination over the other. Neither of us seeks to stretch out our hands and rule the world. Chairman Mao has written: "So many deeds cry out to be done and always urgently. The world rolls on. Time passes. Ten thousand years are too long. Seize the day. Seize the hour." This is the hour. This is the day for our two peoples to rise to the heights of greatness which can build a new and better world.

At banquet, Peking, Feb. 21/
The Washington Post, 2-22:(A)1,6.

(On his just-concluded trip to Communist China): The primary goal of this trip was to establish communication with the People's Republic of China. We have achieved that goal . . . we hope too that the seeds planted on this journey for peace will grow and prosper into a more enduring structure for peace and security in the Western

Pacific. But peace is too urgent to wait for centuries. We must seize the moment to move toward that goal now; and that is what we have done on this journey.

On his arrival in Washington, Feb. 28/ Los Angeles Times, 2-29:(1)6.

. . . there is now an unfavorable balance of trade between Japan and the United States of three and four-tenths billion dollars a year. Naturally, that is not healthy for the United States; but responsible Japanese leaders do not believe it is healthy for Japan—because what will happen if that kind of imbalance continues? It will inevitably feed the fire of those in this country who would want to set up quotas and other restrictions, and that interest of Japan and the United States will better be served by freer trade rather than more restrictive trade.

News conference, San Clemente, Calif., Aug. 29/ The Washington Post, 8-30:(A)16.

Masayoshi Ohira
Former Foreign Minister of Japan

We are, of course, very much interested in peace and detente in Asia. But I think it would be too optimistic to predict peace and order in Asia in the foreseeable future. Asia remains always under a gray sky; it has been, is and will remain unstable. We do not have any illusions about Asia. We will build a foundation with care and patience. Even if this rose tree does not produce any flowers, we will keep watering it. We will keep this attitude toward Asia. As for a revival of Japanese militarism, I say absolutely no. Japan must be aligned with pacifism. Japan's existence and prosperity depend on global peace. We should be positive in nipping the buds of militarism and making that a state policy.

Interview/Newsweek, 5-15:44.

Park Chung Hee
President of South Korea

(On U.S. President Nixon's forthcoming trip to Communist China): Our government is watching the forthcoming talks in Peking with deep concern . . . I want to make clear our basic position that we will not accept any decision on the Korean question made without consultations with our government and our participation in it.

News conference, Seoul, Jan. 11/ The New York Times, 1-12:3.

The time for depending totally on the United States and other allies is gone. We must now make greater efforts to establish a self-reliant national defense posture.

News conference, Seoul, Jan. 11/ The New York Times, 1-12:3.

(On recently-improved relations with North Korea): Now we are on the threshold of a hopeful new era. This is one of the most important moments in the annals of our national history . . . because I believe that now we can achieve peaceful unification of our fatherland with our own strength. Now is the time when we can inscribe a brilliant new chapter of our national history before all of the nations of the world.

On 27th anniversary of Korea's liberation from Japanese rule, Seoul, Aug. 14/ Los Angeles Times, 8-15:(1)4.

(On proposed amendments to South Korea's Constitution): We can no longer sit idle while wasting our precious national power in imitating the systems of others. Just as we make our clothes to fit our own measurements, I believe that we will have to (creatively) develop a democratic political system of our own, commensurate with our historic and cultural tradition and present reality.

Seoul, Oct. 27/ Los Angeles Herald-Examiner, 10-28:(A)4.

Ronald Reagan
Governor of California

(Regarding U.S. President Nixon's trip to Communist China): If you look back at the record of international affairs under Democratic Presidents, you would have to believe that a Democratic President was going there appeasement-minded and willing to trade away things of value to this country. If this were a Democratic President going to China, I'd be standing on the walls screaming "no" as loud as I could.

News conference, Des Moines, Iowa, Feb. 22/ Los Angeles Times, 2-23:(1)6.

Edwin O. Reischauer
Professor, Harvard University; Former United States Ambassador to Japan

(Regarding the effects on Japan of U.S. President Nixon's current trip to Communist China): I am very much concerned about that. The whole trip of the President to a country that we don't recognize, spending a longer time there than any President has ever spent in any country, is just plain quixotic. It is a strange thing to do. It is an unpredictable thing to do. The rest of the world wonders what this can mean, and they are rather worried about it. The Japanese are in the process of going through a great change in their relationship with us. As they see themselves, the third-largest country in the world economically, they have got to establish a relationship of real equality with us. This is a very difficult thing to do, (with) deep psychological changes on both sides—and just at this time we seem to them extremely unpredictable, unreliable. They begin to wonder if they can go on counting on us as a real defense partner when we seem to forget all about them, when we get excited about China, and so on. So I think we have done very serious damage there, and I think there is some damage done in lots of other countries, too.

TV-radio interview, Washington/ "Meet the Press," National Broadcasting Company, 2-20.

William P. Rogers
Secretary of State of the United States

(Announcing U.S. diplomatic recognition of Bangladesh): We now enter into an official relationship with the government and the people of Bangladesh. I want to express on behalf of all the American people our good wishes for the future. I also want to reaffirm our intention to develop friendly bilateral relations and be helpful as Bangladesh faces its immense task of relief and reconstruction.

Washington, April 4/ Los Angeles Times, 4-5:(1)4.

Carlos P. Romulo
Foreign Secretary of the Philippines

(SEATO) needs to redefine its purposes in the light of rapidly-evolving times . . . It needs to change its orientation to meet the new requirements of Southeast Asia. It needs to take full account of the popular aspiration to be free from all kinds of interference in internal affairs. It may be (that), in refashioning SEATO in accordance with that prescription, the old SEATO will cease to be.

Before SEATO Ministerial Council, Canberra, Australia, June 27/ Los Angeles Herald-Examiner, 6-27:(A)3.

Abdus Samad
Foreign Minister of Bangladesh

We are aware of the machinations of some powers who are trying to strangle our infant state at birth. But our determination and the justice of our cause shall frustrate all their attempts. No power on earth can bring us back within the fold of Pakistan.

New Delhi, India, Jan. 7/ The New York Times, 1-8:4.

(ABDUS SAMAD)

We are not beggars. We will choose wherefrom we'll have our friends and get our help or assistance . . . If a friend offers me a glass of water, I will accept without hesitation. But if any enemy of yesterday, or friend of my enemy, offers me a glass of water, I will hesitate to take this water directly. Rather, I may apprehend there might be some poison in that water. There might not be any poison, but it is a natural apprehension.

News conference, New Delhi, India, Jan. 9/ The New York Times, 1-10:1.

Eisaku Sato
Prime Minister of Japan

I had not been able to fully trust the United States since the sudden announcement of the President's (Nixon) plan to visit (Communist) China and its dollar-defense measures that included the 10 per cent import surcharge, in spite of its promises to keep commitments with its old friends. Indeed, I sometimes felt contradictions in some of Nixon's remarks. But I can say that the United States is a trustworthy country now that it has showed us all sincerity in the course of the negotiations on Okinawa reversion (to Japan).

Before youth and women's division of Liberal Democratic Party, Tokyo, Jan. 13/ The New York Times, 6-16:(1)8.

For Japan, our relations with the United States are more important than those we have with any other country. Today, no matter how multi-polarized international relations have become, this fact has not changed in the slightest degree.

Before the Diet (Parliament), Tokyo, Jan. 29/ The Dallas Times Herald, 1-30:(A)3.

In view of the admission of the People's Republic of (Communist) China to the (UN) Security Council last year, and on the recognition that there is only one China, the Japanese government considers that there is an urgent need to begin discussions on a governmental basis with a view to normalizing our relations with the government of the People's Republic of China. If there should be misunderstanding or distrust on the Chinese side with respect to our true intentions, our government will do its utmost to eliminate such fears. If relations between Japan and China become stable over the long term, that will have a far-reaching significance in the maintenance of peace not only in Asia but also in the world.

Before the Diet (Parliament), Tokyo, Jan. 29/ The Washington Post, 1-30:(A)21.

According to my understanding, Taiwan is a part of China; and since the (Communist) People's Republic is now the government representing China in the United Nations, when we say China we mean Peking . . . The government representing China is definitely the People's Republic; and it is natural to say, therefore, that the representative of China, with authority over Taiwan, is the People's Republic.

Before the Diet (Parliament), Tokyo, Feb. 28/ The Washington Post, 2-29:(A)1,14.

(On U.S. President Nixon's recent trip to Communist China): I don't think the visit of the President will have any effect on Japanese-American relations. We attach great importance to our relations with the United States . . . I believe the President's visit to China should be highly appreciated. I don't think there will be an immediate outcome of the visit, but I think it represents a change in American policy—from the policy of containment to the policy of dialogue. That change is highly appreciated.

Interview, Tokyo/ Los Angeles Herald-Examiner, 3-15:(A)6.

We don't even have conscription. There are still people in Japan who say we shouldn't have any self-defense forces at all. It is odd that a country like this should be accused of militarism by countries that are nuclear powers. The American nuclear umbrella is a guarantee that Japan will not become a nuclear power.

Interview/Time, 3-27:60.

Hugh Scott
United States Senator, R–Pa.

(Reporting on his trip to Communist China): China as a totality adds up to something radically different from our knowledge, experience and concepts. In the case of China, we have a strong culture determined to go its way, to assimilate what it wants of the West with retention of its own identity and direction . . . Most definitely, the Chinese are not backward in energy. There is no apathy, no toleration of any tendency toward deterioration. In the factories, on the communes and in the street, one senses vigor, vitality and dedication—a desperate struggle to move ahead.

Before the Senate, Washington, May 11/The New York Times, 5-12:19.

Eric Sevareid
News commentator, Columbia Broadcasting System (United States)

(Communist) China is the only big nation we can think of that has actually reduced its central bureaucracy—drastically—because (Party Chairman) Mao Tse-tung thinks the way he does and remains a kind of diety . . . (But) the moment any society begins to industrialize, it says good-bye to true egalitarianism, because the tasks become extremely complex; advanced education is required; elites grow up; pay scales begin to vary; economic, then social classes, appear. "To each according to his ability" becomes the rule; "to each according to his needs" becomes the vanishing dream of true Communism. If the state is to preside over it all, an immense bureaucracy becomes inevitable. It is the road China wants to avoid; it is the road it will take the more it industrializes.

News commentary, May 23/The Christian Science Monitor, 6-1:16.

Mohammed Musa Shafiq
Prime Minister of Afghanistan

Our experience is that there is a need for marriage between traditional values in Afghan culture and the need to live in the 20th century. This marriage has had difficulties in the last 10 years and we felt we would give it a new start to prevent a divorce. Isolation imposed by geography has made it easy for Afghans not to worry much about things. Modern life, fortunately or unfortunately, is based on worry. We want our people to worry now about things.

Interview, Kabul/The Dallas Times Herald, 12-14:(A)16.

James C. H. Shen
Nationalist Chinese Ambassador to the United States

Naturally, we were terribly disappointed by our expulsion from the United Nations last year (and the admission of Communist China). But we will not try to get back into the UN. This is because we would have to declare our independence from the mainland, and this we are not inclined to do. We may be confined to the island of Taiwan, but we are the government of China. It's a question of moral responsibility. Because we have tasted the fruits of freedom, we want the people of the mainland to have an opportunity to enjoy them.

Interview, Los Angeles, April 19/Los Angeles Herald-Examiner, 4-20:(A)5.

Norodom Sihanouk
Exiled former Chief of State of Cambodia

I think the Russians consider themselves white, and they do not want yellow people to become too strong. It would be difficult for the U.S.S.R. not to help North Vietnam, which belongs to the socialist family of nations. But I have seen what the Russians give the North Vietnamese. I have seen the jet planes, the radars, the missiles. None of this equipment is up-to-date. In terms of both quantity and quality, the Russians have not given Hanoi a quarter of what they have given the Egyptians. Why? Because the Russians don't want Hanoi to win. They will give the Vietnamese just enough to keep them from losing the war, but not enough to enable them to win it. Speaking as an Asian, I feel that the Russians want to keep Asians in a state of subserviency. There is, in the Russian mind, a neurotic fear of an imaginery "yellow peril" embodied by China. By hindering the Indochinese, the Russians are aiming at China.

Interview, Peking/
The New York Times Magazine,
1-23:28.

I can tell you the (Communist) Chinese are not aggressive. Except for Korea, when United States troops reached their borders, they have sent no soldiers abroad. They are friendly . . . What China wants is not to colonize, not to replace an American imperialism in Southeast Asia with a Chinese imperialism. Not true. Not true. China simply doesn't want American forces so close, any more than you (the U.S.) would want foreign troops in Mexico. She wants a neutral Indochina as a buffer.

Interview,
Peking, Jan. 25/
The New York Times, 1-26:11.

The shaking of hands by (Communist Chinese Premier) Chou En-lai, (Communist Chinese Party Chairman) Mao Tse-tung and (U.S. President Richard) Nixon is a result of Chinese-Russian antagonism. China is trying to isolate its number one enemy, Russia. The U.S. is the number two enemy. For Russia, China is the number one enemy, and the U.S. is number two.

Interview, Shanghai/Time, 3-20:23.

Adlai E. Stevenson III
United States Senator, D–Ill.

(Regarding the 1971 India-Pakistan war over East Pakistan which resulted in the formation of Bangladesh): What happened in Bengal and the decision of (U.S. President) Nixon to support (Pakistani President) Yahya Khan in his repression must go down in history as a despicable act. Now that I have been in Bangladesh, I have seen evidence of these atrocities (by the Pakistan Army). We don't know how many thousands of people were massacred there, but we know the figure could be as high as three million, with many others raped and tortured. In spite of the brutality which is here—it surely is one of the most terrible atrocities in the history of the world—Mr. Nixon sides with Yahya Khan, the oppressor, against the people of Bangladesh and their liberators, the Indians.

News conference, New Delhi/
San Francisco Examiner, 1-31:4.

Kakuei Tanaka
Minister of International Trade
and Industry of Japan

(On U.S. President Nixon's announcement last year, without prior notification to or consultation with Japan, of his plans to visit Communist China): The Japanese are a very cautious people. The kind of move Mr. Nixon made to Red China without reference to Japan—this is not the way we would have done it. We would have given you advance notice. Courtesy is something Orientals respect. As for our relations with China, I know there are obstacles. The Chinese have still not forgotten the actions of Japanese armed forces during World War II. And we have widely-different political systems. Still, we have had 2,000 years of interchange. We are of an almost identical ethnic group, aren't we? So, between Japan and China I don't think there is any fundamental obstacle preventing normalization.

Interview/Newsweek, 5-15:45.

Kakuei Tanaka
Prime Minister of Japan

The basic stance of our foreign policy is to deepen U.S.-Japanese relations. It goes without saying that this is the most important and vital thing. It's a relationship that has developed over the past quarter-century, and our people have come to take it for granted, like water and air. But there is a necessity for people to reflect on the necessity of air and water.

Interview/Time, 7-17:24.

There is an identity of interests between Japan and the U.S. The two nations are like inseparable brothers.

U.S. News & World Report, 9-4:35.

It is regrettable that, for several decades in the past, the relations between Japan and (Communist) China had unfortunate experiences. During that time, our country gave great troubles to the Chinese people, for which I once again make profound self-examination. After World War II, the relations between Japan and China remained in an abnormal and unnatural state. We cannot but frankly admit this historical fact. But we should not forever linger in the dim blind alley of the past. In my opinion, it is important now for the leaders of Japan and China to confer in the interest of tomorrow. That is to say, to conduct frank and sincere talks for the common goal of peace and prosperity in Asia and in the world as a whole. It is precisely for that goal that I have come here. We hope that we can establish friendly and good-neighborly relations with Great China and its people and that the two countries will, on the one hand, respect each other's relations with its friendly countries and, on the other, make contributions to peace and prosperity in Asia and in the world at large.

At banquet, Peking, Sept. 25/ The New York Times, 9-26:3.

The normalization of our relations with (Communist) China has an aspect of orienting Japan's foreign policy toward the continent of Asia. This new relationship with China and the maintenance and development of the close ties Japan already has with her friends, such as the United States, can be and should be made compatible.

Before Japan-American Society, Tokyo, Oct. 18/ Los Angeles Times, 10-19:(1)21.

Nguyen Van Thieu
President of South Vietnam

Southeast Asia includes 10 states–North Vietnam, South Vietnam, Thailand, Cambodia, Laos, Burma, Malaysia, Singapore, Indonesia and the Philippines. These 10 nations–and I include North Vietnam–should discuss among themselves their common attitude, and we are perfectly willing to include Hanoi in such meetings. I do not think neutralization is the correct word to describe our goal. The three superpowers (the U.S., Communist China and the Soviet Union) should be neutralized while the weak states in Southeast Asia should be turned into a buffer zone which is not violated by anyone. We do not want to be violated by anyone or to attack anyone. We do not want any foreign bases here or any alliances in this area.

Interview, Saigon, Feb. 23/ The New York Times, 2-25:2.

Nobuhiko Ushiba
Japanese Ambassador to the United States

Certainly, the most important and dramatic new element in the Far East is (U.S.) President Nixon's planned trip to (Communist) China. This can and should be a very significant contribution to peace and stability in Asia. But it might–however unintentionally and contrary to American desires–be the beginning of a process of unraveling our mutual security in the Far East. Which of these two positions becomes a reality, in my opinion, will depend in

(NOBUHIKO USHIBA)

very large measure on the real nature of U.S.-Japanese relations in the critical period to come. If our consultation and collaboration are intimate and substantial, and they repose on mutual confidence, then I believe we can view the future with optimism. But if they should become largely *pro forma* and cosmetic, then I would worry about what the future holds in store. Both of us have far too much at stake to risk getting out of tandem on the important subject of China . . . The Japanese government thoroughly approves of the policy of bringing China into the mainstream of world affairs. In my opinion, this has been long overdue. But we Japanese feel that it is of greatest importance that U.S. rapprochement with China take place in a manner which will also improve Japan's relations with China, while reinforcing U.S. ties with Japan. Indeed, anything which would have a contrary effect would sow the seeds for a very serious problem in the future, including the danger of ultimate deterioration of the security of both our countries in the Far East.

Before Commonwealth Club, San Francisco, Jan. 10/ The Washington Post, 1-16:(B)6.

(On U.S. President Nixon's forthcoming trip to Communist China): The President's trip to Peking is already having enormous impact in Asia. I hardly need tell you of the effect it has had in Taiwan, which is suddenly left to fend for itself. At the same time, (South) Korea has also been considerably shaken by these events, wondering if at some future date it might also go the way of Taiwan—with the credibility of U.S. protection suddenly cast in doubt, even if that doubt is unfounded. And in Southeast Asia, where ethnic Chinese have great influence on economic life in many countries, the President's trip to Peking was interpreted as an immediate signal that these countries should trim their sails in the direction of Peking.

Before Commonwealth Club, San Francisco, Jan. 10/ Vital Speeches, 2-15:281.

Albert C. Wedemeyer
Major General, United States Army (Ret.); Commander, United States forces in China in 1944

(On U.S. President Nixon's trip to Communist China): I knew them all in Chunking, and I don't see how the President can avoid making concessions to them. The Communist leaders are dishonest bargainers and, while Mr. Nixon will follow Christian ethics, they will unscrupulously pursue their own aims.

Interview/Newsweek, 2-21:12.

Gough Whitlam
Prime Minister of Australia

(On his country's opening negotiations with East Germany aimed at establishing diplomatic relations): (The move will make European countries) more aware that there is a new government in Australia which is not concentrating on Southeast Asia and the Pacific to the exclusion of our highly important relations in Europe . . . Following the recent moves between West and East Germany to normalize their relations, I consider it important, both for political and commercial reasons, to normalize Australia's relations with East Germany.

News conference, Canberra, Dec. 19/ The New York Times, 12-20:5.

(On his government's decision to grant recognition to Communist China): While it has long been recognized that Australia's geographical position gives it special interests in the Asian region, up until now Australia has not come to terms with one of the central facts of that region: the People's Republic of China.

Dec. 22/The New York Times, 12-23:8.

Masao Yagi
Japanese Ambassador to Indonesia

A common headache for all Japanese Ambassadors, particularly in Southeast Asia, is how to dispel and dissipate the hatred, fear and suspicion created by our business ventures.

Quote, 5-14:457.

C. K. Yen
Vice President and Premier of Nationalist China

(Referring to U.S. President Nixon's discussions with Communist Chinese leaders in Peking): Some non-Communist countries, lacking foresight and oblivious of the difference between right and wrong or advantage and disadvantage, have given up their principles and come to consider foes as friends. As a result, they have played into the hands of the enemy. People are searching for peace but have forgotten some of the cherished and eternal values of civilization and are neglecting the necessity of upholding principles of righteousness and justice.

Before National Assembly, Taipei, Feb. 29/ San Francisco Examiner, 2-29:4.

. . . the Communists have never published any accurate figures, but many experts of China have more or less estimated that the Communists constitute about two per cent of the population of the Mainland; that even in the Communist Party, many people are forced into it, but more than 90 per cent (of the) people are opposed to the regime. If they were given an opportunity of free choice, they would choose freedom. That was very clearly indicated more than 10 years ago, after the so-called Korean War. Many Chinese war prisoners were given the option of where do you want to go; do you want to go back to your homeland or do you want to remain in Korea or go somewhere else? Fourteen thousand of them, which constituted a majority, came here. Actually, they were young boys, and they were brought up entirely under Communist indoctrination. The little freedom that they first saw was in the prison camps. It means that even this little freedom they experienced in the prison camps was more desirable than the way of life on the Mainland.

Interview, Taipei, March 8/ Los Angeles Herald-Examiner, 3-8:(A)10.

. . . we are not going to have any kind of negotiations with the Communists because we think that Communism is entirely foreign to China and Communism cannot be tolerated in my country. While we say Taiwan is a part of China, Taiwan is not a part of Communist China. We think that Taiwan belongs to China; that any part of China belongs to China. We think that the Chinese nation should be entitled to have all of China. But China must be under a non-Communist democratic regime.

Interview, Taipei, March 8/ Los Angeles Herald-Examiner, 3-8:(A)10.

Paul Cardinal Yupin
Member of the Presidium, National Assembly of Nationalist China; Former Roman Catholic Archbishop of Nanking

(U.S.) President Nixon's visit to (Communist) China has doomed Mao Tse-tung politically. In that respect, it was a blessing from heaven for the Republic of (Nationalist) China. The American President's visit has ruined the credibility of Mao's claim to be the true leader of the Communist world revolutionary movement. It has destroyed what little confidence the militant Chinese Communists had left in Mao's leadership. It will probably lead to the ousting of him from power, if he lives much longer. I have told my people the President's visit was a blessing in disguise. He made a mockery of Mao's claim to be the leader of the anti-imperialist forces of the world. He has placed Mao in the position of endorsing the

(PAUL CARDINAL YUPIN)

policy of peaceful coexistence with the United States—the Khrushchev policy for which the Chinese Communists so bitterly denounced the Soviets and which was one of the main reasons for the Sino-Soviet split. Mao can never recover from that. He is now finished as inspirational leader of the world Communist movement. His prestige has been ruined. His popularity among the militant, true believers in the Communist world is finished. He has lost his struggle to challenge Russia for leadership of world Communism.

Interview, Taipei/
Los Angeles Herald-Examiner,
3-12:(A)7.

THE WAR IN INDOCHINA

Creighton W. Abrams
General, United States Army;
Commander, U.S. forces in Vietnam

There's no question in my mind that they (South Vietnamese troops) can defend their country. It's whether they believe they can do it. The big thing about Vietnam is what the Vietnamese people believe they can do. The rate at which you take out our forces cannot be faster than what the Vietnamese people believe they can handle. Hanoi is counting on them to not believe thay can handle (it), but I believe they can.

Interview, Saigon, March 17/
San Francisco Examiner, 3-17:12.

(On the training being received from the U.S. by South Vietnamese soldiers): The French never let these people have an army of their own; never gave them an automatic weapon, let's say. Sure, the French had their pets–Vietnamese who had been educated in French, spoke French, had learned to drink red wine and liked brie, who ate French bread instead of rice, and who could no longer bear nuoc-mam, the traditional Vietnamese fish sauce. The French offered these people citizenship, forgetting the peasants. People forgot that the basic people of Vietnam, the peasants, are tough as hell; they threw the Chinese out of here twice . . . But the French didn't understand. They occasionally integrated their units with South Vietnamese, true. But the only Vietnamese who was a commander at Dienbienphu had only the rank of company commander. He's now Commanding General of the first ARVN division.

Interview, Saigon/
San Francisco Examiner, 3-21:31.

Bella S. Abzug
United States Representative, D–N.Y.

(President) Nixon says American honor is at stake in Indochina, and respect for his office as President is at stake. Well, honor and respect have long been buried under the bodies of Asians in Indochina.

At antiwar rally,
Washington, May 21/
The Washington Post, 5-22:(A)14.

Spiro T. Agnew
Vice President of the United States

(U.S. involvement in Vietnam) has been one of the most unselfish acts in the history of the United States foreign policy. We answered the cry for assistance of people who sought for themselves only the right to determine how they would live, and we refused to abandon them to the invader and demonstrated oppressor from the North despite pressure in this country as well as on the battlefield . . . I believe history will record (our involvement) as a very worthwhile and moral accomplishment, perhaps the most moral act that the United States ever performed as a citizen of the world community. That is my answer to those who say this is an "immoral war."

At ceremony welcoming home the 101st
Airborne Division from Vietnam,
Ft. Campbell, Ky., April 6/
The Washington Post, 4-7:(A)2.

(SPIRO T. AGNEW)

Men who played a central role in pushing America into an ever-deepening involvement in Vietnam are now charging that the President (Nixon) desires a military victory more than he desires peace. This is a transparent lie . . . Some of these people now expressing outrage at the allied response to the enemy invasion have flatly predicted the failure of the President's Vietnam policies. They have staked their credibility—and some of them their political future—on the outcome of this struggle. If there is a collapse in Saigon, if there is a Communist take-over—then they will have been proven right. They can then denounce the President for having foolishly resisted the inevitable; they can then congratulate themselves for having bailed out at the right moment; they can then make the President pay the political price for trying to see the war through. And . . . there is *The New York Times*, an early and ardent advocate of getting America into Vietnam, doing public penance regularly by scourging the President who is getting us out.

Before American Society of Newspaper Editors, Washington, April 21/ The New York Times, 4-21:15.

In the society of nations, North Vietnam is a criminal—an international bandit that preys on its neighbors, that savagely bullies its way across borders established by treaty, that has already swallowed up pieces of Laos and Cambodia and South Vietnam and seems intent on conquering all three.

Accepting Father of the Year Award, New York, May 25/ The New York Times, 5-26:8.

Much of the coverage of this war (by the press) has been overwhelmingly lopsided (because it has discredited) the courageous South Vietnamese and the United States assistance of their defense effort, while seldom subjecting the North Vietnamese aggressors—our enemy, as I see it—to the same harsh criticism.

At Jaycees national convention, Atlanta/ Los Angeles Times, 6-20:(1)2.

(On Democratic Presidential candidate Senator George McGovern's statement that he would go to Hanoi and beg if necessary to obtain the release of American prisoners of war): Ladies and gentlemen, I find this an incredible admission by a man who would lead the American people. It expresses a philosophy so callow and short-sighted as to be repugnant to the tradition of a free people. Neville Chamberlain, an apostle of appeasement 35 years ago, had an umbrella as his symbol. But even Neville Chamberlain did not carry a beggar's cup to Munich—as George McGovern proposes to carry to Hanoi.

Before Heritage Group, New York, June 30/ The Washington Post, 7-1:(A)8.

(On amnesty for U.S. Vietnam-war draft-dodgers): On every ground I can think of—historical, legal, moral and practical—the idea of general amnesty without penalty or alternative service is totally without merit. The laws of this nation—statutes passed by duly-elected representatives of all the people—have been violated. To me, such violations should not be rewarded with a collective pardon and a rueful admission that it was the United States that was wrong.

Before Veterans of Foreign Wars, Aug. 25/The Dallas Times Herald, 10-29:(B)3.

. . . I am frankly amazed at the emphasis by . . . those who are responsible for bringing opinion to the American people, the thrust and emphasis on the (U.S.) bombing of the North (Vietnam), and a total obliteration of any query concerning rocketing of the cities in the South (by North Vietnam), the callow attitudes of the leadership of the North, the callousness as they have shot down fleeing refugees. When you consider that rockets have been thrown into marketplaces in Kontum and Saigon and An Loc, and large segments of the South Vietnamese populace have been destroyed by aggressive action from the North in a country that they (the North) don't belong in, to call attention to the retaliatory means that are employed to assist our allies in the South doesn't seem to make much sense. And I want to add one thing that I think is overridingly important. You talk about repression in the (South Vietnamese President) Thieu regime. Think of this: If there were really more repression in the South than the North, why is it that all the refugees run South when an area is under a heavy attack and when actual warfare is being conducted there, and the civilian population has the ability to go in either direction? If the South is so regressive, why don't they all run North? The plain fact is that, during the time this war has been going on, more than 800,000 people have fled South and only about 80,000 went North.

TV-radio interview, Burbank, Calif./ "Meet the Press," National Broadcasting Company, 8-27.

(On North Vietnam's recent release of several U.S. prisoners of war to an American anti-war group): Hanoi is using a handful of prisoners to raise the hopes of many American families . . . they are just exploiting these few people for their own propaganda gains. If they're really serious about the prisoners, they'd adhere to the Geneva Convention by allowing the International Red Cross to inspect prisons. They'd deal with the duly-elected government of the United States instead of dealing with every dissident anti-war group who is attempting to make the contact on behalf of . . . well, mainly of themselves . . . If we don't start dealing on a government-to-government basis, instead of all these informal conferences that are being held with people who really aren't in possession of the facts and haven't the ability to negotiate, it's going to impair all our efforts.

News conference, Fort Worth, Tex., Sept. 25/ The Dallas Times Herald, 9-26:(A)1.

(If the North Vietnamese) want to stop this war, they have only one thing to do: get those thousands and thousands of troops out of South Vietnam, sit down at the bargaining table under international supervision, have a cease-fire, allow the international community to witness a free election so that the South Vietnamese people can determine whom they want to govern them. Yes, it merely makes my heart bleed when I think of all of this focus on the bombing (of North Vietnam by the U.S.) when we are not even bombing civilian targets. Sure there has to be some hardship out of it. But what really makes my heart bleed is that these bleeding hearts don't have any sympathy for the people that stand in the South Vietnamese market place when (Communist) rockets were deliberately aimed at them.

Campaigning for the forthcoming Presidential election, Fort Wayne, Ind., Oct. 3/ The New York Times, 10-4:32.

Daniel Berrigan
Activist American Catholic priest

(Criticizing U.S. President Nixon's bombing of North Vietnam and other actions taken in response to the current North Vietnamese offensive): At some point we have passed beyond the politics of power to the pathology of power. I can't see any politics in the present moves at all, only a kind of personal vengefulness growing out of a long history of personal defeat. Any study of the history of bombing must tell you how untactical our moves are. They've only led us deeper into a desperate corner.

Interview, St. Jean-Cap Ferrat, France/ Los Angeles Times, 5-17:(4)15.

(DANIEL BERRIGAN)

I was in Hanoi during an American air raid. It was a turning point in my life. There I saw what we Americans bring about. The worst of all is that we're so big and mighty that, no matter what we do, we don't have to pay the price, we don't even notice the effect of our actions. That's what makes it so hard for people to make up their minds in our country. We ride roughshod over the weak and don't hear when they cry out in their death agony.

Interview, New York/
The New York Times, 5-23:39.

Mrs. Nguyen Thi Binh
Foreign Minister, National Liberation Front of South Vietnam-Viet Cong

(The sole purpose of Vietnamization in South Vietnam is to) use Vietnamese to kill Vietnamese. In this there is nothing new except the changing of the color of the dead.

Interview, Paris/
San Francisco Examiner, 4-10:4.

The United States eight-point (peace) proposal refers to the holding of "Presidential general elections" in South Vietnam and to the resignation of (President) Thieu-(Vice President) Huong one month before these elections, which means that these general elections would be held within the framework of the present regime in Saigon and under the control of its machine of coercion and repression, while those who wage the resistance war against United States aggression should give up their fight. By its very nature, to take this position is simply to demand that the South Vietnamese people accept the U.S.-set-up Administration and to deny the existence of the provisional revolutionary government (Viet Cong), the genuine and legal representatives of the South Vietnamese people. This is an absurd demand . . . (President) Nguyen Van Thieu should resign immediately, and the Saigon Administration should end its warlike policy, disband at once its machinery of oppression and constraint against the people, stop its "pacification" policy, dismantle the concentration camps, set free all persons arrested on political grounds and guarantee the democratic liberties as provided for by the 1954 Geneva agreements on Vietnam. The resignation of Thieu, the change of the Saigon Administration's policy and the dismantling of its machine of oppression and constraint are absolutely necessary if one wants the people to recover their democratic liberties and to proceed to really democratic and fair elections. After the above has been achieved, the provisional revolutionary government of the Republic of South Vietnam will immediately discuss with the Saigon Administration the formation of a three-segment government of national concord with a view to organizing general elections in South Vietnam, to elect a constituent assembly, work out a constitution and set up a definitive government of South Vietnam. The general elections will be held according to procedures agreed upon among the political forces in South Vietnam so as to insure effectively their free, democratic and fair character. The provisional revolutionary government does not demand monopoly of control on political life in South Vietnam. A "take-over," as the United States puts it, simply does not exist. On the contrary, we stand for the achievement of broad national concord.

At Paris peace talks, May 4/
The New York Times, 5-5:20.

Eugene Carson Blake
General secretary, World Council of Churches

. . . It appears to me that it is the task of the American churches to challenge, with whatsoever influence they have, not merely the policies of the United States in Southeast Asia, but also the basic moral assumptions used as the justification of these policies. (Present U.S. policy in Southeast

Asia is based on) a sophomoric view of the world that the U.S.A. is the number one nation in wealth and power and that our chief "game plan" is to defeat any effort to challenge our number one position.

At interfaith conference on the war in Southeast Asia, Kansas City/ The Dallas Times Herald, 1-17:(C)22.

The American explanation that the present weakness of the dikes (in North Vietnam) is due to neglect by the population is untrue . . . The American protests that no intentional bombing has occurred and that only accidental bombs have fallen on or near the dikes must also be untrue.

Geneva/ Los Angeles Times, 7-21:(1)2.

Leonid I. Brezhnev
General Secretary, Communist Party of the Soviet Union

The war in Indochina, which by admission of the U.S. President is the longest and hardest war in American history, has shown the utter untenability of the imperialist policy of aggression and oppression of nations. The U.S.A. now counts, above all, on local mercenaries in its attempt to strangle the national liberation struggle in Indochina in order to retain its political and strategic positions in this area. This is what Washington calls "Vietnamization" of the war. It wants to replace U.S. uniforms, tattered by the Indochinese patriots, by the uniforms of puppet soldiery; but the political lining remains the same—American. The patriots of Vietnam, Laos and Cambodia see through these maneuvers. With the assistance and support of the Soviet Union and the other socialist countries, the peoples of Indochina are carrying on their struggle against the aggressor on the military, diplomatic and political fronts. In this struggle, the Soviet people are entirely on the side of the peoples of Indochina. Helping them is our internationalist duty, and we shall fulfill it to the end. The Soviet Union wrathfully condemns the piratical bombings of the territory of the Democratic Republic of (North) Vietnam by the U.S. Air Force and demands that they be stopped . . . We demand that the invaders withdraw from Indochina. We demand independence for the peoples of this region and hold that they should be able to determine their destinies without any outside interference and pressure.

At Soviet Trade Unions Congress, Moscow, March 20/ Vital Speeches, 4-15:391.

In Washington, the Vietnam war is described as the longest in American history. That is true. It should be added, however, that it is also the dirtiest of all the wars known in American history. Now the world has become witness to new American imperialist crimes in Vietnam. Apart from the fact that, resorting to various unsavory maneuvers, the United States is artificially delaying the conclusion of an agreement on terminating the war, it some days ago resumed bombing towns and mining ports in the Democratic Republic of (North) Vietnam. Grave responsibility devolves on the United States government for these barbarian acts and for the bloodshed that it continues to inflict on the Vietnamese people. Like all peace-loving states, like all the peoples of the world, the Soviet Union angrily and resolutely condemns these acts of aggression. It is clear to everyone by now that the United States military adventure in Vietnam has failed. And now no new outrages can break the will of the heroic people of Vietnam or shake the determination of their friends to give them every possible support and aid in their just struggle of liberation.

At celebration of 50th anniversary of the formation of the Soviet Union, Moscow, Dec. 21/ The New York Times, 12-22:10.

James L. Buckley
United States Senator, C—N.Y.

Any cease-fire which would allow the North Vietnamese invaders to remain within

(JAMES L. BUCKLEY)

the territorial boundaries of South Vietnam, enabling them in effect to retain during the cease-fire period what they have conquered by force of arms, would not be acceptable. Only a cease-fire incorporating as an integral part of its structure the control of South Vietnamese territory by the legitimate government of South Vietnam would even begin to lead toward peace with justice.

Human Events, 5-27:2.

George Bush
United States Ambassador/ Permanent Representative to the United Nations

I think it is fair to observe, after talking to many UN Ambassadors, that (U.S.) President Nixon's most recent decisions regarding Vietnam (mining North Vietnamese ports and increasing bombing) are viewed by many as a reasonable response to an unreasonable enemy. The course of action which the President has taken was the only one permitted us by an enemy which apparently believes that its massive invasion (of South Vietnam) would go unchallenged.

Before Texas Jaycees, Corpus Christi, May 20/ The Dallas Times Herald, 5-21:(A)48.

(On charges that U.S. planes are bombing dikes in North Vietnam): I believe we are being set up by a massive propaganda campaign by the North Vietnamese in the event that there is the same kind of flooding this year—to attribute it to bombs—whereas last year it happened just out of lack of maintenance. There's been a study made that I hope will be released shortly that will clarify this whole question. (This study) would be very helpful, because I think it will show what the North Vietnamese are up to in where they place strategic targets . . . I think you would have to recognize that, if there was any intention (by the U.S. to attack the dikes), it would be very, very simple to do exactly what we are accused of—and that is what we are not doing.

Television interview, New York/ "Today Show," National Broadcasting Company, 7-26.

Chiao Kuan-hua
Deputy Foreign Minister of, and chief United Nations General Assembly delegate from, the People's Republic of (Communist) China

The three Indochinese countries are close neighbors of China, and the three Indochinese peoples are the Chinese people's brothers. We are duty-bound to support them in their just struggle against foreign aggression, and will never interfere in their internal affairs. On behalf of the Chinese government, I once again solemnly declare on this rostrum: As long as the war in Indochina goes on in whatever form, the Chinese government and people, not flinching from the greatest national sacrifice, will firmly support the three Indochinese peoples in fighting to the end.

At United Nations, N.Y., Oct. 3/ The New York Times, 10-4:4.

Chou En-lai
Premier of the People's Republic of China

U.S. imperialism has long violated the Geneva agreement and invaded Vietnam, Laos and Cambodia. So long as the United States does not cease its war of aggression in Indochina, no matter in what form the war is carried out, the three Indochinese peoples, we are convinced, will certainly fight to the end, and we will support them to the end until complete victory is achieved.

At banquet honoring North Vietnamese Politburo member Le Duc Tho, April 27/ San Francisco Examiner, 4-28:4.

Frank Church
United States Senator, D–Idaho

. . . I hope . . . that the South Vietnamese do hold out against this (North Vietnamese) offensive. My only disagreement is based upon a 30-year record that the North is going to continue to press this war, and by now either the South is able to defend itself or it looks to be very dubious that they will ever be able to defend themselves. If it takes this kind of American air power now, I can't see any time in the near future when it won't take this kind of American air power again. And I don't see Vietnamization ending our involvement, if that's the way Vietnamization is defined . . . I don't think you can negotiate a settlement with these people (North Vietnam), because you can't agree to their terms and they can't agree to yours. Now, it's just as plain as that. And they're not going to stop fighting. Now, either Vietnamization means that the South Vietnamese become self-sufficient and we give them the tools to defend themselves and we extricate ourselves from further involvement in the war, or . . . it means a continuous American involvement for the indefinite future, because the North isn't going to call this war off . . . When will an end come to our participation in this war?

Addressing Secretary of State William Rogers at Senate Foreign Relations Committee hearing, Washington, April 17/ U.S. News & World Report, 5-1:60.

(On his proposal for cutting off funds for the war by Dec. 31): It is not easy to plead for retention of an end-the-war amendment at a time when the enemy is pressing his attack on the battlefield. We are told this is not the right time, or this is not the right bill. Perhaps not. But we are now in the eighth year of the American ordeal in Vietnam. When will the "right time" ever come? When will we ever find the "right bill"? Too much blood has been lost, too much patience gone unrewarded while the war continues to poison our whole society . . . if we fail to erect a framework for completing our disengagement from this war, if we continue to acquiesce in a policy which leaves us partly in and partly out, we shall move inexorably closer, day by day, to that which the policy purports to avoid: a rendezvous with disaster and defeat.

Before the Senate, Washington, May 5/ The Washington Post, 5-6:(A)2.

Mark W. Clark
General,
United States Army (Ret.)

(On U.S. bombing in North Vietnam): When people yell "savagery" and "it isn't right, it isn't human," I say look at what the Vietnamese Communists have done to their own people—shooting into open cities, killing women and children. War isn't humane; but when you are in a war and you are trying to persuade the other side to stop fighting, you have got to bring the war home to their people. That's why Germany folded (in World War II). I would still be in Italy if we hadn't pounded away at the Ploesti oil fields in Romania and hit every possible target in Germany. North Vietnam is screaming that we have hit a dike. That's the thing they really fear. I think now is the time to turn the heat on. They're hurting.

Interview, Rome/ Los Angeles Herald-Examiner, 6-20(A)10.

Ramsey Clark
Former Attorney General of the United States

(Discussing his recent trip to North Vietnam): I think there is no question but that the (U.S.) prisoners (of war) will be released and will be released immediately when we stop this senseless, murderous bombing and end the war and get out, get home and get to the business of building

(RAMSEY CLARK)

the peace and giving happiness to little children around the world.

News conference, San Francisco, Aug. 13/ Los Angeles Times, 8-14:(1)1.

(Discussing his recent trip to North Vietnam): I've seen more apartments, villages, dikes and sluices destroyed (by U.S. bombing) than I ever want to see again. I do know that, in human terms, the bombing I've seen is without justification no matter what the cause and purpose.

Bangkok, Aug. 13/ Los Angeles Times, 8-14:(1)1.

(Discussing his recent trip to North Vietnam): Once I received Hanoi's invitation, I knew I had to go. Suppose I didn't go, and I could have made a difference? Suppose I could help one (U.S.) prisoner (of war)? Suppose I could see something that could be important? Suppose they had something they wanted to say? I felt the absolute compulsion and duty to go. Let me say that I do not believe in personal diplomacy. This world is too big and life too precious to entrust to a man on horseback . . . But I think I saw things and I think I brought things back that will help any open-minded person evaluate two questions on the prisoner issue: 1) are they humanely treated, and 2) will they be returned if there is a complete political and military settlement?

Interview/ Newsweek, 8-28:12.

Lucius D. Clay, Jr.
General and Commander-in-Chief/Pacific, United States Air Force

(On U.S. bombing of North Vietnam): I cannot categorically state that there have not been some people (civilians) injured from bombs. But there have certainly been no attacks against civilian centers per se. Every one of the attacks we have made has been designed to the best of our ability to minimize damage and injury to the civilian population. They have all been associated with what we call the "interdiction campaign" or war-making potential of the North Vietnamese—such things as power plants, motor vehicle repair yards, bridges, railroad yards and things of that nature. We are extremely conscious of the responsibility to hit only military targets and take every precaution.

Interview, Honolulu, June 18/ San Francisco Examiner, 6-18:(A)21.

Clark M. Clifford
Former Secretary of Defense of the United States

The national security of the United States is not threatened in Vietnam, regardless of the outcome of the fighting. The small, underdeveloped, nonindustrial nation of North Vietnam constitutes no threat to us, and it is equally clear that Russia and (Communist) China are not on the march in Southeast Asia. The war itself has been essentially an internal struggle among Vietnamese—a civil war—in which the Saigon government is being aided by the United States, and its opponents by Russia and China. One would hope that, by this late stage in the war, there would be no disagreement on this basic assessment. We are in Vietnam today only because we got into Vietnam yesterday.

Before House Foreign Affairs Committee, Washington, May 18/ The Washington Post, 5-21:(B)1.

What is so dangerous about the decision (by U.S. President Nixon) to mine Haiphong and establish an air and naval blockade of North Vietnam is that it constitutes a confrontation with the Soviet Union, and insists that the Russians terminate their assistance to North Vietnam. Whatever the misjudgments of past Administrations, the policy-makers of those years were careful never to widen the bitter local contest in Vietnam into a global confrontation of the superpowers, with all the imponderable risks of such a move. Thus the President is jeopardizing the basic American national interests involved in our relations with the Soviet Union for the sake of his policies in Indochina . . . The mining and blockading are not likely to be effective because Russian ships can unload at Chinese ports and their cargo can be transported overland to North Vietnam. Increased shipments can be sent by rail from the Soviet Union. There may be lulls, periods of reduced fighting, accompanied no doubt by spokesmen claiming that the other side is "fading away." The current (North Vietnamese) offensive may stall, particularly as the rainy season sets in, but the war will go on so long as Hanoi finds the situation in the South incompatible with its interest.

Before House Foreign Affairs Committee, Washington, May 18/ The Washington Post, 5-21:(B)5.

How can anyone possibly believe in the war in Vietnam any more? (American) men are sent off to support a corrupt government (in South Vietnam) and bomb other peoples. And we are told that the justification for their sacrifice is that it is necessary for "our national honor." Can we not see the sophistry in this position, when in fact our national honor is daily being soiled in the mud of Indochina? If the negotiations now in progress finally result in a settlement and an end to the bloodshed–and I pray to God that they will–the damage that this war has done to our national spirit will not disappear. Even on the day the war ends, we will be living with its dreadful legacy. Long ago, the war in Vietnam spewed forth a poison through the bloodstream of our nation, and the poison is still spreading. It has destroyed much of the confidence we had in our institutions, in our government and in ourselves. When we needed unity, we got divisiveness; when we needed honesty, we got duplicity; when we needed candor, we got deception.

Before Jewish Community Relations Council, Philadelphia/ The National Observer, 12-30:11.

John B. Connally, Jr.
Secretary of the Treasury of the United States

(On U.S. bombing of North Vietnam in response to the North's offensive in South Vietnam): We're there because the President of the United States has concern for the troops which remain. He deserves some plaudits for what he's trying to do. Instead, members of the Cabinet had to spend hours before that (Senate Foreign Relations) Committee defending our policy . . . In this political year, it is absolutely critical that those in the press and politics use some restraint in all-out criticism of our leadership.

Before American Society of Newspaper Editors, Washington, April 19/ Los Angeles Herald-Examiner, 4-20:(A)11.

(Referring to U.S. Democratic Presidential nominee George McGovern's pledge to bring home all U.S. troops and POWs from Southeast Asia within 90 days after his inauguration if elected): Obviously a President of the United States has no capacity, no power, to bring home prisoners of war in the hands of the North Vietnamese. It is an unfair statement, and it is a statement that, frankly, sabotages the efforts of this (Nixon) Administration and of the peace negotiators in Paris to try to bring the war to an end . . .

News conference, San Clemente, Calif., July 14/ San Francisco Examiner, 7-15:2.

Alan Cranston
United States Senator, D–Calif.

(Saying President Nixon's current bombing of North Vietnam is political and that he should not seek re-election): This could clear up the confusion that may be in the mind of the B-52 pilot on his bombing

(ALAN CRANSTON)

missions who may wonder whether he is acting as an arm of his Commander-in-Chief or as a precinct worker for Richard Nixon over Hanoi.

Before the Senate, Washington, April 19/ Los Angeles Times, 4-20:(1)20.

Richard J. Daley
Mayor of Chicago

Certainly, this is a hell of a war . . . I don't know a President in our history who wanted war; and I have known several Presidents very well. Who among us knows what the President knows about foreign relations? Let us stand behind our President (Nixon) and, with him, hope and pray he can end the war tomorrow.

At U.S. Conference of Mayors, New Orleans/ Los Angeles Herald-Examiner, 6-22:(A)8.

Ronald V. Dellums
United States Representative, D–Calif.

The United States is in the identical position of Germany during World War II. The Germans continued killing as many as possible, even when they knew they had lost. The U.S. has been beaten in Vietnam. It cannot win.

San Francisco, May 20/ San Francisco Examiner & Chronicle, 5-21:(A)11.

Robert J. Dole
United States Senator, R–Kan.

The American people have had enough rumors, enough leaks, enough "inside stories," enough lies. The American people want the truth. It is time the Congress showed them the respect they deserve and give them the truth . . . As American troop strength in Vietnam grew and grew through the mid-'60s, today's critics of the war were loyally supporting the policies of the war party . . . The fact that the Democratic Party—traditionally this nation's war party—is responsible for a conflict which has cost the lives of over 55,000 Americans is a source of some distress to the present crop of Democratic (Presidential) hopefuls.

Jan. 21/ San Francisco Examiner, 1-21:2.

Pham Van Dong
Premier of North Vietnam

In spite of the ever-heavier defeats on the battlefield in Vietnam, Laos and Cambodia, the chiefs in the White House and the Pentagon are still cherishing dark designs, and they continue to consider military and political adventures leading into a blind alley in an attempt to hang onto South Vietnam, Laos and Cambodia.

Hanoi, Feb. 5/ San Francisco Examiner, 2-5:1.

(U.S. President) Nixon seemed to consider that the war would end one day for lack of combatants. That's why until now he has always refused to negotiate seriously. But the war will not end until the day Nixon realizes that it will yield him nothing. He has everything to lose except the honorable exit that we are determined to give him.

Interview/ The New York Times, 5-18:14.

For the Vietnamese people, reunification of the country is a supreme demand. You (Americans) cannot understand all we feel about this. We can say that every Vietnamese lives in the belief that the country must be reunified . . . Generally speaking, we are not in a hurry. We have the utmost respect for the aspirations of our countrymen in the South. We will do nothing contrary to their aspirations. Reunification will be accomplished in a very democratic, peaceful and equal way.

Interview, Hanoi, Sept. 14/ The Dallas Times Herald, 9-22:(A)10.

(Saying reports that South Vietnam's Army is stronger today than before the current Communist offensive started are wrong): The fact that the U.S. was forced to impose a total blockade and massive bombing to save Saigon's hide was proof enough. If Vietnamization had been a success, then why bother? Unbelievable means have been brought to bear on us. And that's the most eloquent proof of failure.

Interview, Hanoi, Oct. 18/ Newsweek, 10-30:26.

(On speculation of reprisals by Communist forces if they gain power in South Vietnam): It is inconceivable that the (National Liberation) Front (Viet Cong) would allow reprisals after a settlement; that would be diametrically opposed to its policy of national reconciliation. It would jeopardize everything. These are errors that have to be avoided at all costs. Besides, reprisals could only be against their own families in many cases. If in America and Western countries one talks about a blood bath, it is simply a matter of bad faith.

Interview, Hanoi, Oct. 18/ Newsweek, 10-30:27.

Thomas F. Eagleton
United States Senator, D–Mo.

(On President Nixon's bombing of North Vietnam in response to the North's offensive in South Vietnam): A great man understands his fallibility and acknowledges error. A weak man admits no faults. What we are doing today in Vietnam is not a sign of greatness; it is a compensation for failure. The President's policy has been threatened and there is nothing more vengeful than the "wounded pride of a king."

Before the Senate, Washington, April 19/ Los Angeles Times, 4-20:(1)20.

(On U.S. bombing and mining in North Vietnam): From a military point of view, it's perhaps been more successful than I would have anticipated. It does appear that it's had the effect of dampening the aggressive potential of the North Vietnamese. I don't think in the long run, though, it's going to affect the ultimate outcome in Southeast Asia. I don't think that we're ever going to be in a position where we can say that we have won the war. But from a strictly narrow military point of view, it would appear that it has been at least partially successful.

Interview, Washington, June 30/ The Washington Post, 7-14:(A)13.

Cyrus S. Eaton
American industrialist

When are the American people going to realize that (U.S. President) Nixon and (National Security Adviser Henry) Kissinger are not sincere? Oh, certainly Kissinger had the meetings he said he had with the North Vietnamese, but they do not understand Hanoi's position. They (North Vietnam) will never accept the Thieu government (in South Vietnam). When my wife and I went to Hanoi in 1969, we talked to almost all the top Vietnamese leaders—Le Duan, Le Duc Tho, Pham Van Dong and others. When I told them the American leaders would listen to any peace plan I might bring back, one of them suggested to me that I might be "naive." When we came back, it was just as he said. What I was told in Washington by the highest officials was that these men in North Vietnam were "evil people" and they could not be negotiated with.

Interview, Northfield, Ohio/ New York Post, 2-2:36.

Milton S. Eisenhower
President, Johns Hopkins University

. . . if I were 19 years old, or any age subject to the draft, and I sincerely believed that the war was . . . either immoral or not in our national interests, or futile,

(MILTON S. EISENHOWER)

and yet I was subject to call, I think this would affect me deeply. Now, I was in the Army in World War I . . . and I did war work right at the fronts, first in Africa and then in Europe as a civilian in World War II; but I believed 100 per cent in the justice of those wars. But I can see it would affect me very deeply if I were a young man subject to the draft and I didn't believe in the justice of the war. This is a very traumatic experience that I think affects attitudes in many ways.

Interview, Baltimore/ The Washington Post, 1-2:(D)4.

Daniel Ellsberg
Former United States Government consultant, Rand Corporation

(On U.S. bombing of North Vietnam): . . . we are about to see, or are already seeing, a change in bomb targets from military to people. (As a result), the next million tons of bombs will kill more than the last 3 million tons that (U.S. President) Nixon has dropped. Any amount of killing and bombing will be allowed to prevent the loss of South Vietnam cities . . . By torturing the population of North Vietnam, President Nixon thinks he can coerce the country's leadership into accepting the demands they have been rejecting for 25 years.

Before Business Executives Move for Vietnam Peace, May 18/ The Christian Science Monitor, 5-23:4.

Richard Falk
Professor of Law, Princeton University

Even the most casual reading of "Pentagon Papers" (secret documents released to the press last year) reveals that the U.S. government has opposed a negotiated settlement of the conflict ever since we got involved in the French war in Indochina way back in 1950. Our leaders have insisted for more than 20 years that force was the only way to reach our objective in Indochina; and despite its claims to the contrary, the Nixon Administration has never wavered from this militarist policy. Why? While the military presence of the United States seems unsuccessful and immoral, it continues to provide the only leverage we have in Vietnam. Our one advantage there is superior military technology and our willingness to use it massively and cruelly to neutralize the political advantages of our adversary. Increasingly, our allies in Saigon have become the Benedict Arnolds of their country—traitors to the cause of their own national independence. When will this war end? It will not end so long as we persist in imposing this regime of villains and traitors on the Vietnamese people. It can only end when we accept the reality of negotiation, when we take our military forces out of the country, when we cease our support of the Thieu regime and when we agree in Paris on the establishment of a provisional coalition government that is composed of the main political tendencies in South Vietnam.

Television broadcast/"Comment!" National Broadcasting Company, 4-23.

Robert H. Finch
Counsellor to the President of the United States

(Arguing against immediate withdrawal of U.S. troops from the war): If we truly honor our dead, we cannot accept the shoddy compromise. The day we accept the back-room deal, that day we defile the race of mankind . . . Those who would have us dishonor (our pledged word) and forthwith withdraw from a tough, miserable, difficult struggle without regard to historical consequences fail to realize that the price is too high.

Veterans Day address, Los Angeles, Oct. 23/ Los Angeles Herald-Examiner, 10-23:(A)2.

Jane Fonda
American actress

(Addressing U.S. pilots on bombing missions over North Vietnam): (U.S. President) Nixon is continuing to risk your lives and the lives of the American prisoners of war under the bomb in a last desperate gamble to keep his office come November. How does it feel to be used as pawns? You may be shot down, you may perhaps even be killed; but for what and for whom? . . . The people back home are crying for you. We are afraid of what . . . must be happening to you as human beings. For it isn't possible to destroy, to receive salary for pushing buttons and pulling levers that are dropping illegal bombs on innocent people, without having that damage your own souls. Tonight when you are alone, ask yourselves: What are you doing? Accept no ready answers fed to you by rote from basic training on up; but as men, as human beings, can you justify what you are doing? Do you know why you are flying these missions, collecting extra combat pay on Sunday?

Broadcast on Radio Hanoi, July 21/Human Events, 8-19:12.

J. William Fulbright
United States Senator, D–Ark.

(On U.S. bombing of North Vietnam in response to the North's current offensive in South Vietnam): It is ironic and tragic that today, six years later (after massive U.S. involvement took place), after hundreds of thousands of lives have been lost, after much of North Vietnam, South Vietnam, Laos and Cambodia have been ravaged and destroyed, after the economic and social fabric of our nation has been seriously undermined, we're still discussing the war in Vietnam with members of the Cabinet even though we have a President (Nixon) who came into office in January of 1969 promising to end the war either through negotiations or through Vietnamization. Instead, three years after that President took office, we find the largest force of combat aircraft and naval vessels the United States has ever assembled in Southeast Asia, massive bombings of North Vietnam resumed and the port of Haiphong and the capital of Hanoi under attack at the risk of grave international complications. I, for one . . . cannot understand what possible national interest has dictated these military measures. Surely considerations of prestige would not warrant such drastic steps. Surely we are no longer under the illusion that a military victory can be achieved by bombing or that a renewal of bombing will improve the chances of negotiating a settlement or recovering our prisoners of war.

At Senate Foreign Relations Committee hearing, Washington, April 17/ The New York Times, 4-18:19.

(On the U.S. bombing of North Vietnam in response to the North's offensive in South Vietnam): The President (Nixon) has changed the character of the war insofar as American foot soldiers are concerned. He has reduced the loss of American lives, for which I am thankful. But at the same time, in changing the character of the war to unlimited air and naval bombardment, he has removed one of the normal human restraints upon the savage cruelty and inhumanity present in all wars.

Before the Senate, Washington, April 27/ The New York Times, 4-28:17.

Indira Gandhi
Prime Minister of India

(Criticizing U.S. involvement in the Vietnam war): A small nation has been able to withstand the world's mightiest power. Could there be a more glorious example of the immortality of the human spirit? I have no doubt that the people of Vietnam will triumph in the not so distant future.

At Asian trade union seminar, New Delhi, April 24/ The Washington Post, 4-25:(A)14.

John H. Geiger
National Commander, American Legion

The American Legion believes that most draft evaders and deserters consciously decided to refuse to accept their responsibilities as citizens under the law; that they evaded their responsibilities by flouting our laws and legal remedies rather than by going through the available legal channels of redress; that their actions in declining to obey certain laws distasteful to them is contrary to sound legal and moral standards; and that the obligations of citizenship cannot be applied to some and evaded by others . . . we of the American Legion firmly believe that giving any wholesale amnesty—whether conditional or unconditional—would make a mockery of the sacrifices of those men who did their duty, assumed their responsibilities in time of conflict and—in many cases—were killed, seriously wounded, or now lie in a prison camp somewhere in Indochina. Over 50,000 men have paid the supreme price of patriotism and citizenship. Another 302,602 have been wounded or injured. Over 1,600 are prisoners or missing in action in Vietnam, Laos or Cambodia. And the casualties have not ended. How can any general amnesty be explained to these men? How can amnesty be explained to parents, wives, children—all those who have lost a son, husband or a father in their country's service? How can we excuse ourselves to the prisoners of war, the missing in action, or to their suffering families for offering amnesty? Furthermore, what would be the effect on the morale of our armed forces if amnesty were granted to those who have violated the law and their oath of service by turning their backs and fleeing their country? In our opinion, it could only badly undermine that morale and cheapen the value of honorable service to one's country at the very moment these values are most in need of strengthening.

Before Senate Subcommittee on Administrative Practice and Procedure, Washington, March 1/ Vital Speeches, 4-15:402.

Vo Nguyen Giap
Minister of Defense of North Vietnam

(On the action taken in Vietnam by four U.S. Presidents): The Vietnamese people have defeated the neocolonialism invasion war of the Eisenhower Administration. We have defeated the special war of the Kennedy Administration. We have defeated the partial war and destructive war of escalation of the Johnson Administration. We are now defeating and definitely will defeat completely the war of Nixon—defeat completely all the adventurous and cruel escalations of the U.S. imperialists.

Radio Hanoi broadcast, May 7/ Los Angeles Times, 5-8:(1)14.

The United States hopes to bend the will of the Vietnamese people by mass-bombing North Vietnam. This will prove to be an illusory hope. Hanoi, Haiphong and other cities may be bombed and erased, but the Vietnamese peoples will never bend . . . In the course of our resistance, we have defeated the war of subversion by Eisenhower, the special war by Kennedy, the limited war by Johnson; we are defeating—we will defeat—the war of aggression conducted by the Nixon Administration.

At celebration of 28th anniversary of the North Vietnamese Army, Hanoi, Dec. 21/ The New York Times, 12-23:6.

Joseph Godber
Minister of State for Foreign Affairs of the United Kingdom

(On the U.S. mining of North Vietnamese ports and increased bombing in response to North Vietnam's offensive in the South): All war is hideous. All escalation of war carries dangers to others. But the American response on this occasion has been proportionate and directly related to the North Vietnamese invasion of the South.

Before House of Commons, London, May 15/ San Francisco Examiner, 5-16:4.

Barry M. Goldwater
United States Senator, R–Ariz.

No (Vietnam) peace proposal—no matter what it says and offers to do—will receive bipartisan support from Democrats so long as it bears the imprint of Richard M. Nixon. More and more it becomes apparent that the opposition is not so much to the plan but to the man who offered it.

Before the Senate, Washington, Feb. 9/ The Washington Post, 2-10:(A)14.

(On U.S. bombing of North Vietnam in response to the North's current offensive in South Vietnam): I, for one, am happy that the time of pussyfooting and kowtowing to every Soviet threat is over. We hear a lot about the risks run by the President (Nixon) in ordering the bombing of supply dumps and other targets in Hanoi and Haiphong. There is no denying this . . . But unless we are willing to back our foreign commitments with decisive action, the ultimate risk will be to freedom everywhere in the world. Sure, President Nixon took a risk, and I thank God he had the courage to take it before it was too late.

April 17/ The Washington Post, 4-18:(A)15.

(On the U.S. bombing of Haiphong in response to North Vietnam's offensive in South Vietnam): I say if a Russian ship is bombed at Haiphong, that's too damn bad. I hope we hit them all. They have no business being in Haiphong. They are our enemies when they supply our enemies with ammunition and weapons to kill our men . . . (I assail) the weak-kneed, jelly-backed attitude of members of this body and citizens of this country who think you can end a war overnight by snapping your fingers and starting to bring the troops home.

Before the Senate, Washington, April 19/ Los Angeles Times, 4-20:(1)20.

(On Democratic Presidential nominee Senator George McGovern's position on Vietnam): At this crucial point in our history, we face something shocking for the first time—a candidate of one of our (political) parties has already surrendered to the enemy before the election has even been held.

At Republican National Convention, Miami Beach, Aug. 21/ Los Angeles Times, 8-22:(1)1.

(On U.S. Air Force Gen. John D. Lavelle's disobeying orders by authorizing an air strike on a North Vietnamese radar site last spring): When the site was finally destroyed, it was on the orders of General (and Army Chief of Staff-designate Creighton W.) Abrams and General Lavelle, and they both caught hell from the Joint Chiefs of Staff—not because the JCS disagreed with the strike, but because the orders said you can't do it . . . I think it's time the American people know how we've been forced to fight a war that, in my humble opinion, could have been ended seven eight years ago. Would you ever believe that our country has come to the place that we would have orders of combat that prohibited us from shooting a known enemy?

Before American Fighter Aces Association, San Antonio, Tex., Sept. 16/ San Francisco Examiner, 9-18:9.

(On what he would have done if he had been elected President in 1964): If they'd handled (the war) the way I wanted to handle it, (Presidential National Security Affairs Adviser) Henry Kissinger wouldn't have to be traveling (and negotiating). I could have ended it in a month. I would have made North Vietnam look like a mud puddle.

The National Observer, 11-11:20.

Andrei A. Gromyko
Foreign Minister of the Soviet Union

The continuance and expansion of the American intervention in Vietnam and other

(ANDREI A. GROMYKO)

countries of Indochina provokes indignation and condemnation. Probably never before have so many declarations been made promising to leave Vietnam and to stop the war as have been made of late (by the U.S.). And never before has there been so striking a contrast between words and deeds.

At United Nations, N.Y., Sept. 26/ The New York Times, 9-27:4.

H. R. Haldeman
Assistant to the President of the United States

(Before President Nixon made his eight-point Vietnam peace plan known) you could say that his critics–people who were opposing what he was doing–were unconsciously echoing the line that the enemy wanted echoed. Now, after this explanation (of Nixon's plan)–after the whole activity is on the record and is known–the only conclusion you can draw is that the critics now are consciously aiding and abetting the enemy of the United States; and I think that kind of criticism is deeply disturbing to him, because it gets in the way of getting done what he so deeply believed must be done in trying to bring this war to an end through the negotiation route . . . (The President's peace plan) makes all the points that the critics of the President have sought–except one, which is turning over South Vietnam to the Communists, putting a Communist government in South Vietnam. The only conclusion you can draw now is that the President's critics are in favor of putting a Communist government in South Vietnam and insisting that this be done, too. That's something we aren't going to do.

Television interview/ "Today Show," National Broadcasting Company, 2-7.

F. Edward Hebert
United States Representative, D–La.

(Regarding amnesty for American draft dodgers in Canada who fled to avoid service in Vietnam): I am for amnesty for them in the most secure cells in the most secure jails in this nation for their lives . . . Those poor creatures in Canada . . . those cowards, those treacherous people, fled because they were not willing to defend that which these 50,000 people (Americans in Vietnam) died so uselessly for.

Columbus, Ga./ The Dallas Times Herald, 4-2:(A)32.

Lawrence J. Hogan
United States Representative, R–Md.

I am vehemently opposed to amnesty (for U.S. Vietnam war dodgers and deserters), not only because I feel that it would be a disservice to those who did answer their country's call, especially those who gave their lives or were wounded or imprisoned, but for an even more basic reason. I oppose amnesty because, if we allow some of our citizens to choose the laws they wish to obey and those they wish to disobey, the result will be anarchy.

Before Federal Bar Association, Washington, May 1/ Quote, 5-28:508.

Hubert H. Humphrey
United States Senator, D–Minn.

Our urgent, immediate need is to end the war–and to do it now. I served as the Vice President during the period of our heaviest involvement there (in Vietnam). Yet when I spoke to the American people during my campaign for the Presidency in 1968, I said that my experience had led me to the conviction that, however noble the intent of three Presidents who felt that our Vietnam involvement was essential to our national security, that position was no longer valid. I pledged in 1968 an end to the bombing, a cease-fire and an immediate troop-withdrawal program. I would have carried out that pledge. It is taking (President) Nixon longer to withdraw our troops than it took us to defeat Hitler. Had I been elected, we would now be out of that war. I repeat that pledge.

Announcing his candidacy for the Democratic Presidential nomination, Philadelphia, Jan. 10/ U.S. News & World Report, 1-24:50.

I . . . believe that we are leaving South Vietnam with a powerful military force: over a million men trained in the regular armed forces, the fifth largest navy; they have the best equipment that this country has been able to produce, and we have supplied it to them in vast quantities; they have billions of dollars of equipment in surplus; they have 500,000 troops in the militia. And I have a feeling that, if a government and a country with that amount of equipment and manpower can't take care of itself after 10 of the best years of our lives having been given to that country, there is no reason at all for us to stay a single extra day.

TV-radio interview, Washington/"Meet the Press," National Broadcasting Company, 3-12.

(On Senator George McGovern's saying he would be willing to go to North Vietnam and "beg" for release of U.S. prisoners of war): I wouldn't beg here, in Hanoi or anywhere. I do not believe the word beg represents sound morality. I think it's unfortunate that Senator McGovern used that term. There is a difference between tough negotiations and begging. I'm not a beggar.

TV-radio interview, Miami Beach/"Meet the Press," National Broadcasting Company, 7-9.

Jacob K. Javits
United States Senator, R–N.Y.

Once the Vietnam war is deprived of its "ideological" overcoat–as the alleged focal point of a global struggle between monolithic Communism and the free world–the residual international significance of the outcome of the struggle between Hanoi and Saigon is diminished to the relatively inconsequential framework of "balance of power" considerations within the Southeast Asia peninsula.

Quote, 4-9:351.

Edward M. Kennedy
United States Senator, D–Mass.

If ever a President was elected to end a war . . . Richard Nixon was elected for that purpose . . . Now, four years have passed since 1968. Twenty thousand more Americans have died, and still the war goes on. We know that the monstrous bombing will continue. And we know that thousands of soldiers of North and South Vietnam, and tens of thousands of innocent men and women and children, will die in Indochina in 1972, for the simple reason that President Nixon will not allow the Saigon government to falter until he is secure at home for another term of office . . . Let us end completely every aspect of our military involvement in Vietnam, once and for all. Let us abandon every one of the false dreams that led us into that swamp. Let us admit that as all men make mistakes, so do nations, and that we are large enough and courageous enough to disdain false pride, repair our errors and seek the path of decency once again.

Before National Press Club, Washington, Jan. 17/ U.S. News & World Report, 1-31:17.

I favor amnesty (for men who fled the country to avoid service in the Vietnam war), and I don't believe we ought to set conditions for people to receive amnesty. I think if you start right off and say that the war is wrong, as practically all political leaders would agree at this time . . . then you say that it was the government that was wrong, it was the leadership that was wrong at that time, and it was these young

(EDWARD M. KENNEDY)

people who left the country that were right about the war; and why they ought to be additionally penalized for their deep-seated feelings or beliefs is something that I don't understand.

Television broadcast, Washington, Feb. 12/ San Francisco Examiner & Chronicle, 2-13:(A)6.

(The Nguyen Van Thieu regime in South Vietnam) is nothing—(and it) will wash away in the stench of its own inconsequence . . . and corruption.

The National Observer, 5-6:1.

(Criticizing reported U.S. bombing of North Vietnamese dikes): If the dikes are in close proximity to a potential bombing target, the policy of the (Nixon) Administration is to bomb the target anyway, regardless of the consequences to the dikes. It doesn't take a Philadelphia lawyer to label this policy for what it is: a policy of deliberately bombing dikes.

Before the Senate, Washington, Aug. 4/ Los Angeles Times, 8-5:(1)9.

Henry A. Kissinger
Assistant to the President of the United States for National Security Affairs

On the political evolution, our basic principle has been a principle we have been prepared to sign together with them (the North Vietnamese), that we are not committed to any one political structure or government in South Vietnam. Our principle has been that we want a political evolution that gives the people of South Vietnam a genuine opportunity to express their preferences. The North Vietnamese position has been that they want us to agree with them, first, on replacing the existing government (in South Vietnam) and, secondly, on a structure in which the probability of their taking over is close to certainty. They want us, in other words, to do in the political field the same thing that they are asking us to do in the military field—to negotiate the terms of the turnover to them, regardless of what the people may think.

News conference, Washington, Jan. 26/ The New York Times, 1-27:14.

. . . there has been no issue of greater concern to this Administration than to end the war in Vietnam on a negotiated basis. We have done so because of what we felt the war was doing to us as a people and because we felt that it was essential that, whatever differences that may have existed about how we conducted the war, that we ended it in a way that showed that we had been fair, that we had been reasonable and that all concerned people could support. We have not approached these negotiations (with the Communist side) in order to score debating points. We have not conducted these negotiations in order to gain any domestic benefits. In the very first meeting that we conducted with the other side, we mentioned these principles: We said, one, we want a just settlement. Secondly, we recognize you will be there after we have left and, therefore, it is in our interest that we make a settlement that you will want to keep.

News conference, Washington, Jan. 26/ The Washington Post, 1-27:(A)4.

We have talked to you ladies and gentlemen (of the press) here very often about the negotiations with respect to the peace, and we have been very conscious of the division and the anguish that the war has caused in this country. One reason why the President (Nixon) has been so concerned with ending the war by negotiation, and ending it in a manner that is consistent with our principles, is because of the hope that the act of making peace could restore the unity that had sometimes been lost at certain periods during the war, and so that the agreement could be an act of healing rather than a source of new division. This remains our policy. We will not be stampeded into an agreement until its provisions are right. We will not be deflected from an agreement when its provisions are right. And with this attitude, and with some cooperation from the other side, we believe that we can restore both peace and unity to America very soon.

News conference, Washington, Oct. 26/ Los Angeles Times, 10-27:(1)16.

The war must be ended with principle, with judiciousness. And this is not the same thing as saying that it was right (for the U.S.) to enter the war.

Interview, Washington, Nov. 4/ San Francisco Examiner, 11-18:1.

(On his peace negotiations with North Vietnam): We (the U.S.) will not be blackmailed into an agreement. We will not be stampeded into an agreement. And, if I may say so, we will not be charmed into an agreement, until its conditions are right. For the President (Nixon), and for all of us who have been engaged in these negotiations, nothing that we have done has meant more than attempting to bring an end to the war in Vietnam. Nothing that I have done since I am in this position has made me feel more the trustee of so many hopes as the negotiations . . . in which I have recently participated. And it was painful at times to think of the hopes of millions . . . expecting momentous events to be occurring, while inside (at the talks) one frivolous issue after another was surfaced in the last three days. And so what we are saying to Hanoi is: We are prepared to continue in the spirit of the negotiations that were started in October. We are prepared to maintain an agreement that provides for the unconditional release of all American and allied prisoners, that imposes no political solution on either side, that brings about an internationally-supervised cease-fire and the withdrawal of all American forces within 60 days. It is a settlement that is just to both sides, and that requires only a decision to maintain provisions that had already been accepted, and an end to procedures that can only mock the hopes of humanity. And on that basis we can have a peace that justifies the hopes of mankind and the sense of justice of all participants.

News conference, Washington, Dec. 16/ The New York Times, 12-17:(1)34.

Herbert G. Klein
Director of Communications for the President of the United States

(On criticism of U.S. Vietnam policy by Democratic Presidential candidates): . . . these aspirants to the nation's highest office, perhaps unwittingly, become a funnel through which propaganda from Hanoi seeks to further divide us over the situation in Vietnam. If the candidates continue to align themselves with statements such as those being made by the North Vietnamese negotiators, we have to conclude that they believe the credibility of the Communists is greater than that of the United States.

Before South Carolina broadcasters/ The Dallas Times Herald, 2-10:(A)20.

Melvin R. Laird
Secretary of Defense of the United States

Strangely enough, some of those individuals who are going around the country today criticizing the program to withdraw Americans from Vietnam were silent in 1968 and before, when we were on the escalator going up and up and up as far as American troop involvement and military involvement in Vietnam. Now that we are going down, down, down, it seems that they have changed their position and are critical of the President (Nixon) and the program which he has approved to with-

(MELVIN R. LAIRD)

draw Americans from Southeast Asia and from Vietnam.

News conference, Washington, Jan. 13/ Los Angeles Times, 1-14:(1)19.

(On the current Communist offensive in South Vietnam): The enemy has scornfully rejected the American people's patience, restraint and desire for peace. Our patience has been met with propaganda and with provocation. Our restraint, in the form of troop withdrawals, has been answered by invasion. The enemy has escalated the actions and has committed new forces. He has dared us to abandon our allies, and we will not. He has challenged us to protect our men as they come home, and we will.

News conference, Washington, April 7/ The Washington Post, 4-8:(A)12.

. . . the President (Nixon) has presented the most forthright and generous peace offer at any time in history. If the enemy agrees to an internationally-supervised cease-fire and the return of our prisoners of war, we will withdraw our forces from Vietnam within four months. This will bring an end to the war and a return of our prisoners. It will allow us to continue the movement toward a generation of peace which is the goal of all Americans and is the goal of the Nixon Doctrine foreign policy, which is supported worldwide by our national security strategy of realistic deterrence . . . the American people always have supported our President when Americans are endangered and the cause of freedom has been threatened. This is no time for quitters or for a lot of talk about instant surrender. I don't think the American people want to clamber aboard some sort of a bugout shuttle.

News conference, Washington, May 10/ The New York Times, 5-11:18.

Pham Dang Lam
South Vietnamese Ambassador to Paris peace talks

(Addressing Vietnamese Communist delegations): Whether all the allied forces leave South Vietnam or there remain residual forces, and how long those forces will take to disengage, depends on whether or not you accept to negotiate seriously on the problem of troop withdrawal as part of an over-all settlement, as well as on the question of the release of prisoners of war . . . It (Vietnamization) is necessary because of the fact that you continue to have recourse to force and violence and continuously increase your military potential with massive aid from the Communist bloc, instead of seeking with us a peaceful settlement of the conflict.

At Paris peace talks, Jan. 13/ San Francisco Examiner, 1-13:1.

Tran Van Lam
Foreign Minister of South Vietnam

We all know that this Vietnam war is irreversibly drawing to a close because of the new trend in international relations, the winding up of the cold war between the great powers, which makes continuation of this bloody Indochina conflict look increasingly anachronistic and absurd.

Before Lions Club, Saigon, Nov. 13/ Los Angeles Times, 11-14:(1)14.

John V. Lindsay
Mayor of New York

If I were President, I would say I am hereby announcing a date of total withdrawal (of U.S. forces from Vietnam)—period. I would ask for an immediate cease-fire on the basis of the withdrawal announcement; but whether or not it is accepted, I would adhere to the withdrawal deadline.

Jan. 26/ Los Angeles Times, 1-27:(1)31.

(On Nixon Administration criticism of war critics): I've been arguing against the Vietnam war since 1964 when I spoke on the floor of the House of Representatives. If democracy can't survive that kind of difference of opinion, then there is something wrong with democracy.

Feb. 7/
The Washington Post, 2-8:(A)1.

Clare Boothe Luce
Former American diplomat

There isn't one of these Democratic (U.S. Presidential) candidates who has the guts to use the real word–surrender. They want the U.S. to surrender, and not one of them has the guts to say so. And surrender is just what we would have if we had to finish it (the war) tomorrow. The men in Hanoi just have to read the American press to see that if they hold on long enough they will probably get the next best thing to surrender, short of saying, "Sorry, we surrender; please give us back our prisoners, if you feel like it." That's surrender, isn't it?

Interview, Hawaii/
Los Angeles Times, 5-14:(West)29.

Mike Mansfield
United States Senator, D–Mont.

I'd say the whole country (Laos) is there for the grabbing, and I'd say that applied to Cambodia as well. If they (the Communists) want to take those two countries, they can. They are keeping up the pressure; they have gone farther than they have ever gone before. And they are very likely to go farther still . . . I think the Viet Cong, the Pathet Lao and their friends are increasing in strength and maintaining the pressure. They are showing that they're in good shape and going to keep on coming. The war is winding down but it isn't winding out. It will wind out only when there's a complete (U.S.) withdrawal from all of Indochina.

News conference,
Washington, Jan. 22/
The Washington Post, 1-23:(A)22.

What once was one war, winding down, has now become three wars sealed into one. That was the inevitable consequence of the (U.S.-South Vietnamese) invasion of Cambodia in 1970 and the military adventure into Laos in 1971. Since there is now a war distended to include all of Indochina, it is no longer enough to talk of a peace settlement for Vietnam. It is no longer enough to talk of peace only with North Vietnam. In that sense, what has transpired in Paris (at the peace talks) for many months has been a futile exercise. If negotiations are to have any chance of succeeding, an enlargement of the negotiation table is necessary. Places will have to be provided for Laos and Cambodia.

Before the Senate,
Washington, Jan. 24/
San Francisco Examiner, 1-24:4.

(The U.S. incursion into Cambodia in 1970 has brought not peace, but another costly extension of our involvement in Southeast Asia and one more expensive dependent government. Regrettably, the Cambodian situation is one in which we permitted our involvement–again as we did in Vietnam, as we did in Laos–to rise from the wetting of a toe up to the level of our necks.

Before the Senate,
Washington, Aug. 18/
The Washington Post, 8-19:(A)4.

(Criticizing the renewed and intensified U.S. bombing in North Vietnam): The bombing tactic is eight years old. It has not produced results in the past. It will not lead to a rational, peaceful settlement now. It is the "Stone Age" strategy being used in a war almost unanimously recognized in this nation as a mistaken one. It is a raw power play with human lives–American and others–and, as such, it is abhorrent.

News conference, Dec. 20/
The New York Times, 12-26:10.

John S. McCain, Jr.
Admiral and Commander-in-Chief/Pacific, United States Navy

The mining (by the U.S. of North Vietnam's port of Haiphong), we feel, has had a profound psychological effect on the North Vietnamese and a profound military effect . . . and, to the best of our knowledge, there has not been one ship to get in or out of that harbor since the mines were activated (in May) . . . Some of our countrymen are immune to the realities of the war in Indochina. Many are tired of strife and seek an easy way out. There is no easy way. And our nation must not be turned aside from its proper course in Southeast Asia.

Before Town Hall, Los Angeles, June 6/ Los Angeles Times, 6-7:(1)3.

Eugene J. McCarthy
Former United States Senator, D–Minn.

What they (the Vietnamese Communists) have been asking for all this time is our agreement to support a new government in South Vietnam to replace (President) Thieu and (Vice President) Ky . . . The agreement to replace the South Vietnamese government is the key. The promise of free elections is quite meaningless. The war wasn't fought over the issue of free elections . . . (U.S. President) Nixon has it twisted around to the point that it sounds as if the war were fought to free the prisoners; a consequence has become a case.

Jan. 26/ Los Angeles Times, 1-27:(1)31.

(On what he would do to end the war if he were President): Well, the easy one . . . is to negotiate an end to the war in Vietnam by . . . being willing to accept a new (South Vietnamese) government. And once you'd done that, you could begin to straighten out the prisoner-of-war question and most of the others in Southeastern Asia. I said what I'd do would be just to call the Pentagon and say, "Do you have a General who knows how to disengage and an Admiral who can load boats coming home . . . and an Air Force officer who can probably get bombs off a plane without dropping them?" And that would take care of that . . .

Television interview, March 16/ The Washington Post, 3-18:(A)14.

We've now had two Presidents (Lyndon Johnson and Richard Nixon) say they would not be the first President to preside over a U.S. military defeat. I think they should be more concerned about what history is going to say about this nation, rather than what history is going to say about them as individuals.

News conference, Los Angeles, May 9/ Los Angeles Times, 5-10:(1)3.

Paul N. McCloskey, Jr.
United States Senator, R–Calif.

I agree with the President (Nixon) that we should not overthrow the Thieu government (of South Vietnam); but we do not have to support that government, either. If it is overthrown by the natural political processes, our sole obligation is to provide political haven for those who wish to leave. Our goal should still be . . . to leave Vietnam if we get our prisoners (of war) back. The President, by insisting on the preservation of South Vietnam and its government, asks too much; and that is the sticking point in the negotiations.

Jan. 26/ The Washington Post, 1-27:(A)10.

We are bombing the North, killing God knows how many civilians, solely for the sake of pride, to prop up Saigon so that the United States does not suffer a diplomatic defeat, so our prestige is not hurt . . . What kind of country have we become? We have killed and maimed thousands of non-combatant old people and children . . . in a war we are no longer willing to fight ourselves, where our sole purpose is to prevent humiliation.

News conference, San Francisco, April 21/ San Francisco Examiner, 4-22:4.

William J. McGill
President, Columbia University

The object (for the U.S.), our policy-makers now tell us, is to get us out (of Vietnam) in some marginally respectable way. Regrettfully, that is no longer possible for us. Much of what America has always stood for before the rest of the world has become lost in Vietnam . . . Nearly everyone agrees that no purpose would be served now by seeking a military victory that nearly a decade of American anguish has been unable to achieve. The issue is when to get out and under what terms. It seems clear to me that the moral calamity into which we have fallen is so serious and so potentially destructive to the morale and outlook of nearly an entire generation of our young people that other considerations can no longer be seen as very important.

At Columbia University commencement, June 6/ The New York Times, 6-7:49.

George S. McGovern
United States Senator, D–S.D.

Two years ago, (U.S. President) Nixon chose to elevate (the prisoner-of-war issue) as a political weapon against the doves. How can we pull out when they have all these hundreds of American prisoners? Now that issue is going to blow up in his face. He's going to have to go around now and change those bumper stickers that say remember the POWs. He's going to have to say forget the POWs, because that's what he's doing. He's writing them off. And I would wager that there's a decision right now that's operative in this Administration that the prisoners of war are expendable; because they're more interested in preserving face and preserving General (South Vietnamese President) Thieu than they are in getting those prisoners out.

Interview/ The Washington Post, 1-9:(C)4.

(On the U.S. bombing of Haiphong and Hanoi in response to North Vietnam's offensive in the South): (The bombing is) a reckless act . . . that was not even tried at the height of the Vietnam war, when we had half a million citizens over there. It's a sad commentary that it was carried out by a man (President Nixon) who was elected on a platform that he had a secret plan to end the war.

April 16/ Los Angeles Times, 4-17:(1)18.

. . . sooner or later we've got to recognize that those (Vietnamese) people are going to settle their own future. Even if we stay there and bomb for the next five years, and Americans continue to die, and we spend another $100 billion, five years from now we're going to be right where we are now. So let's recognize that we made a mistake and these young men have given their lives, and let's quit killing other young men. Let's bring this war to an end.

Television spot for his Democratic Presidential nomination campaign/ The New York Times, 4-24:28.

(Disputing charges that he is too far from the political "center" to win the Presidency): It is the establishment "center" that has led us into the stupidest and cruelest war in all history. That war is a moral and political disaster–a terrible cancer eating away the soul of the nation. Yet those who charted its course brand its opponents as too far out to be electable. My answer to that is "Nuts!" My platform is to stop the bombing of the people of Southeast Asia immediately and then get every American out of Indochina, lock, stock and barrel, within 90 days.

At Jefferson-Jackson Day dinner, Detroit/ The New York Times, 4-25:41.

(GEORGE S. McGOVERN)

The President (Nixon) boasts of withdrawing 20,000 more troops by next July. But 20,000 Americans have died under the Nixon policy who could have been saved if he had ended the war three years ago. Instead, we have had three years of hypocrisy, three years of higher war taxes and higher wartime prices, and three more years of destruction and death. In the ancient words, Mr. Nixon has created a desert and called it peace.

April 26/
Los Angeles Herald-Examiner, 4-27:(A)3.

(On the U.S. bombing of North Vietnam in response to the North's offensive in South Vietnam): The President (Nixon) said we are bombing in response to the North Vietnamese invasion, but the bombing began much before the invasion. The President says we bomb to save our troops and to permit their withdrawal; but if we would state a total withdrawal date, both our troops and our prisoners could come home in safety. The President says we are bombing to save freedom in South Vietnam, but South Vietnam lives under a dictator—General Thieu; the President places the welfare of that dictator ahead of the release of our prisoners. The President says we bomb to prevent a bloodbath, but his immoral and outrageous bombing is the bloodbath. The President says we bomb to save South Vietnam from Communism; but each bomb creates more Communist sympathizers, more determined to hate and fight to the end.

April 27/
The New York Times, 4-28:1.

(On how, if elected President, he would end the war and get U.S. prisoners back): If it's necessary to go to Hanoi to accomplish that, I'll go to Hanoi to do it. If we can do it in Paris (at the peace talks), I'll go to Paris. I'll go anywhere in the world to meet with the leaders of the government of Hanoi to work out arrangements for an immediate end to the killing, the safe withdrawal of our forces and the release of our prisoners. I don't have any doubt at all that I can accomplish all of that—have the prisoners home, have our troops home and have it done within 90 days.

News conference,
Los Angeles, June 7/
The New York Times, 6-8:1.

The war is clearly immoral and unwise. Its pursuit is unrelated to any reality of (U.S.) national interest; and those who conduct it scarcely bother to assert any rational basis for its continuation. And now, the war clearly lost, we continue to fight and slaughter, to expend our resources and vitality, as if we were trying to prove how high a price we will pay for their victory. That is not realism or pragmatism or tough-mindedness. It is the ultimate and dangerous romanticism of the ostrich.

San Francisco Examiner & Chronicle,
6-18:(A)12.

(As President) I would go to Hanoi and beg if I thought that would release the boys (U.S. prisoners of war) one day earlier. Begging is better than bombing.

Before South Carolina Democratic
convention delegates,
Columbia, June 28/
Los Angeles Herald-Examiner, 7-1:(A)2.

. . . the Nixon bombing policy on Indochina is the most barbaric action that any country has committed since Hitler's effort to exterminate Jews in Germany in the 1930s.

Interview/
San Francisco Examiner, 7-1:2.

George S. McGovern
United States Senator, D–S.D.;
Democratic Presidential nominee

I have no secret plan for peace. I have a public plan. And as one whose heart has ached for the past 10 years over the agony of Vietnam, (if elected President) I will halt the senseless bombing of Indochina on Inaugural Day. There will be no more Asian children running ablaze from bombed-out schools; there will be no more talk of bombing the dikes or the cities of the North. And within 90 days of my inauguration, every American soldier and every American prisoner (of war) will be out of the jungle and out of their cells and back home in America where they belong. And then let us resolve that never again will we send the precious young blood of this country to die trying to prop up a corrupt military dictatorship abroad.

Accepting the Democratic Presidential nomination, Miami Beach, July 14/ The New York Times, 7-15:11.

A national-security memorandum prepared at the beginning of this (Nixon) Administration and published in the *Congressional Record* some time ago shows very clearly that the Administration was aware that North Vietnam had withdrawn a substantial number of its divisions from South Vietnam in 1968, that they were in fact giving us a sign that they were willing to ease off militarily, and they were expecting us to respond then with generous offers of negotiation. Instead of that, the bombing (by the U.S.) was accelerated, the military attack was increased and we blew the opportunity for a negotiated settlement several years ago.

Television interview, Aug. 13/ San Francisco Examiner, 8-14:4.

(Refusing White House briefings on the Vietnam situation which he, as a Presidential nominee, is being offered): They haven't been as accurate as some of the assessments of skilled journalists, in the main, who are on the scene and have no ax to grind, no policy to defend other than telling the truth. I frankly learn more about the realities of Vietnam from following the dispatches of good newspapermen.

Youngstown, Ohio/ San Francisco Examiner, 8-16:9.

The President (Nixon) has his chief foreign-policy specialist (Henry Kissinger) on a highly-publicized global junket on the eve of the Republican Convention. That is what is interfering with quiet, serious, professional peace negotiating far more than anyone else could possibly do. Mr. Nixon has manipulated Mr. Kissinger and American public opinion to appear to be negotiating when actually he has been stalling to prop up (South Vietnamese President) General Thieu and his corrupt military regime in Saigon.

News conference, Racine, Wis., Aug. 17/ The Washington Post, 8-18:(A)4.

I know they've (the Vietnamese Communists) done a lot of barbaric and cruel things, but I think they've probably been more careful in the way that they deal with the villagers and rank-and-file people than we have. We're the ones that have applied massive firepower and free-fire zones and this word, "pacification"—and cleared six million people out of their homes. And really, the massive suffering inflicted on the population, I believe, has come more from us than from the other side.

Interview, Milwaukee, Aug. 18/ The New York Times, 8-20:(1)44.

(If all U.S. military support is removed from South Vietnam), I think this Provisional Revolutionary group (the Viet Cong political arm) probably will move in during or immediately after that period—but with an effort to broaden the coalition. I think that they might even be willing to settle for a temporary leader like General (Duong Van) Minh or somebody of that kind. But what they're interested in is an administration that they can live with at least temporarily . . . I don't really think there is much sense of urgency about reunification with the North. I think you might see that some time over the next 10 years, but that will be preceded by a rather lengthy period of trade relations between the two areas and movements of people back and forth across the border in which the government in Saigon could have rather sizable non-Communist elements in it. It doesn't seem to me, however . . . that you are now going to see a quick all-Communist take-over in Saigon (if U.S. military support of the South is removed). I think it'll be more in the nature of an accommodation.

Interview, Milwaukee, Aug. 18/ The Washington Post, 8-20:(A)2.

. . . our soldiers and our sailors and our airmen and our Marines are fighting a confusing and unnecessary war. I think Americans will still fight and they will still die for a worthy cause that they understand. We always have. The Army that so fights will respect its officers—and it will be honored and admired and supported by the people back home. Our present problem, it seems to me, came about because the military was asked—and is still asked—to continue a war in which the nation no longer believes. War, under the best of conditions, is never fair. We shall always ask more of the men and women in service than we can ever give in return. But at least as a free society we can give them a mission in keeping with the honor and dignity of their service—a mission in keeping with their own self-respect as human beings—a mission they can proudly call American.

At American Legion convention, Chicago, Aug. 23/ Los Angeles Times, 8-24:(1)28.

. . . we used to say that we fought in Vietnam to stop Communist China or to stop Communist Russia. But these nations are now quarreling among themselves, and (President) Nixon's public-opinion ratings have gone up after he was wined and dined in the Communist capitals of Peking and Moscow. How can we really argue that it is good to accommodate ourselves to a billion Russian and Chinese Communists—but that we must somehow fight to the bitter end against a tiny band of peasant guerrillas in the jungles of little Vietnam? Incredible as it seems, when all is said and done, our purpose in Vietnam now comes down to this: Our policy-makers want to save face and they want to save the Saigon regime of (South Vietnamese President) General Thieu.

Television address, Washington, Oct. 10/ The Washington Post, 10-11:(A)18.

(President) Nixon says we must bomb and fight to free our prisoners (of war). But just the reverse is true. We must end the bombing—end the fighting—if we're ever to see these prisoners again. Prisoners of war come home when the war ends—not while the war continues.

Television address, Washington, Oct. 10/ The Washington Post, 10-11:(A)18.

(On what he would do if elected President): Immediately after taking my oath as President, if the war has not ended by then, I would issue a National Security Directive to the Secretary of Defense, to the Joint Chiefs of Staff and to our commands in the field, with the following orders: Immediately stop all bombing and acts of force in all parts of Indochina; immediately terminate any shipments of military supplies that continue the war; immediately begin the orderly withdrawal of all American forces from Vietnam, from Laos and Cambodia, along with all salvageable American military equipment—and we will assign whatever transportation is required to complete the process and to complete it within 90 days, a time period that I've been told by competent military authority is well within our capability. Secondly, I would issue the following instructions to our negotiators in Paris: notify the representatives of the other side that we have taken these steps to end the hostilities, and that we now expect that they will accept their obligation under their own Seven Point Proposal of 1971—to return all prisoners of war and to account for all missing in action—we will expect that process to be completed within 90 days to coincide with our complete withdrawal from the war; we would further notify all parties that the United States will no longer interfere in the internal politics of Vietnam, and that we will allow the Vietnamese people to work out their own settlement; the United States is prepared to cooperate to see that any settlement, including a coalition government, gains international recognition. Thirdly, I would send the Vice President to Hanoi to speed the arrangements for the return of our prisoners and an accounting of the missing. I would also instruct our diplomats to contact the opposing parties in Laos and Cambodia in order to secure release of prisoners held in those countries, and an accounting of missing in action, including American civilian newsmen now missing in Cambodia . . . Fourth, after all of our prisoners have been returned, and we have received a satisfactory accounting for any missing men, I would order the Secretary of Defense and the Joint Chiefs to close our bases in Thailand, to bring home any troops and equipment still there and to reassign eleswhere any ships still stationed in the waters adjoining Indochina. Fifth, as the political solution in Vietnam is worked out by the Vietnamese themselves, we should join with other countries in repairing the wreckage left by this war.

Television address, Washington, Oct. 10/ The Washington Post, 10-11:(A)18.

I want you to remember how they (the Nixon Administration) misled the American people in 1968, four years ago, when they said they had a secret plan to end the war in Southeast Asia. Now, with just two weeks before the election on November 7, they're telling us that they're going to end the war again. But why not four years ago? Why, Mr. Nixon, was it necessary to kill another 20,000 young Americans in this war before we end it? What did you gain by killing or wounding or driving out of their homes 6 million people, most of them in South Vietnam, by this incredible bombing that has gone on for the last four years? What did you get, Mr. Nixon, for the $60 billion you spent in the last four years on the destruction of Southeast Asia that we needed to build up our own cities, to combat crime, to combat drugs, to combat pollution, to build up our own country instead of destroying the land and the villages of another country 10,000 miles from our shores? I ask this question: What has changed that makes it any easier for us to get a peace settlement today than the one we could have had four years ago, if we had a President committed to peace four years ago? Did you make all these sacrifices, Mr. Nixon, to save your own political face from right-wing criticism?

Campaigning for the forthcoming Presidential election, Dayton, Ohio, Oct. 24/Los Angeles Times, 10-25:(1)18.

George Meany
President, American Federation of Labor-Congress of Industrial Organizations

I don't want to see him (President Nixon) defeated by somebody who is advocating surrender. I don't believe in surrender in Vietnam. There's one point, one deep end I will not go beyond. I will not go with a guy who advocates surrender, and this has nothing to do with the labor movement; it has nothing to do with Mr. Nixon. This is me. I will not go with a fellow running for President of the United States who advocates surrender in Southeast Asia.

Interview, Washington/ U.S. News and World Report, 2-21:31.

Duong Van Minh
General, South Vietnamese Army (Ret.); Former candidate for President of South Vietnam

It is amply demonstrated, now more than ever, that we cannot solve our problems by military means . . . It is quite clear that (South Vietnamese) President Thiệu cannot win the war militarily and does not have the support of the people to win the peace. This is why the other side refuses to negotiate with him . . . You (the U.S.) don't seem aware that a majority of Vietnamese do not accept the Communists and do not support Thieu. Perhaps 65 per cent of the people of South Vietnam are in that position . . . I don't ask your government to change its attitude. But the United States is here to help the nation of Vietnam and its people, not just one man. You have to solve the problems of Vietnam with the Vietnamese people, not just one man. You give American aid to the Vietnamese people, not just one man.

Interview, Saigon/ The Washington Post, 5-31:(A)10.

John N. Mitchell
Former Attorney General of the United States

(Commenting on former U.S. Attorney General Ramsey Clark's visit to North Vietnam, and his claim that U.S. prisoners are treated well there and that they would be released once the war is settled on Communist terms): Occasionally, a naive American has been duped into playing Hanoi's wretched game, into serving as an American megaphone for Communist propaganda. Such a naive American is Mr. Ramsey Clark.

The Dallas Times Herald, 8-16:(B)2.

Walter F. Mondale
United States Senator, D–Minn.

(On U.S. bombing of North Vietnam in response to the North's current offensive in South Vietnam): Coming into this chamber this morning to talk about the war in Indochina, I felt a deeply depressing sense of reliving all over again tragedies of the past which should be far behind us. We have been through so many springtimes of slaughter and folly and deception . . . Now, in the spring of 1972, it is happening again.

Before the Senate, Washington/ Time, 5-1:10.

Rogers C. B. Morton
Secretary of the Interior of the United States

From the beginning, the (U.S.) Democratic Presidential candidates have undermined our negotiating position at the conference table in Paris. Recently, one of their leading candidates–the junior Senator from Maine (Edmund Muskie)–rejected the President's peace proposals even before the enemy responded . . . What amazes me is that many of these critics were the architects of the policies we are trying to correct. They have repudiated their previous decisions without a blush of shame.

At Republican dinner, Concord, N.H., Feb. 4/ Los Angeles Times, 2-5:(1)5.

Edmund S. Muskie
United States Senator, D–Maine

. . . most Americans understand now–whatever their earlier view–that the war was wrong. It is not right. It is simply not right for a great country like ours, with its great capacity for applying firepower and destructive ability, to apply it to a backward country in a far corner of the world which is not able to retaliate out of its own resources. This is not the way to answer the political problems of Vietnam. It must be clear that at some point we are going to have to leave that tragic country; and that, when we do, the people involved are going to find their own way to settle their political problems; and that all that we would have done in the meantime–the 55,000 Americans who have lost their lives, the $130 billion of American treasure that we've spent, the more than five years of intensive American involvement to which we have been committed—all of this will have no effect upon the resolution of those political problems when that time comes, because it simply isn't possible for this country, powerful as it is, militarily, economically, politically—it is simply impossible no matter what our intentions, however good they may be—to settle the political problems of this country (Vietnam). It just will not work . . . The result, when it comes, may run counter to what we have been trying to do for the last five years. All I say to you is that we have little if any control over what that result will be, and the sooner we understand that the better off we will be, the better off the people of Vietnam will be.

Campaigning for the Democratic Presidential nomination, Manchester, N.H., Jan. 6/ The Washington Post, 1-13:(A)14.

We have no right to take for our own the awful majesty of God over life and death, destroying land and people in order to save them. We have no right to kill, wound or displace over 100,000 civilians a month by continuing to rain four million pounds of bombs a day on Indochina. We have no right to send young Americans to Vietnam as bargaining chips for the freedom of prisoners of war who would be free if those young Americans were not sent at all . . . Those of us who are out of power must welcome (Nixon) Administration proposals to move American troops out of Indochina. But we must question the wisdom of a course which attaches so many conditions to our leaving that it can only leave us where we are now, watching our sons fight and die, not for a cause but for a mistake, looking to a future where more human beings will suffer at our hands in a senseless and immoral conflict.

Before Church Women United, Washington, Feb. 2/ The New York Times, 2-3:20.

(On President Nixon's decision to mine North Vietnamese ports): The President is jeopardizing the major security interest of the United States. The planned Moscow visit and the SALT talks now have an uncertain future . . . This dangerous step is not the way to end the war, protect our troops or gain the return of prisoners. It is not the road to peace . . . The President is now trapped by his own failures and faced with a series of unpleasant options. He chose the worst option of all—escalation which is both dangerous and desperate.

May 9/The Washington Post, 5-10:(A)11.

Gunnar Myrdal
Swedish economist

I am chairman of the International Commission of Inquiry into U.S. War Crimes in Indochina. I don't say it's a pleasure; but for my conscience's sake I could not say no. We have sponsored five international conferences and we took much evidence. There was tremendous attention here in Europe, but not a word in the United States, except in underground or Communist papers. That is a defensive self-censorship. You (Americans) are sick and tired of it and don't want to hear anything about it. You are defending yourselves against knowing too well what the world thinks of you.

Interview, Stockholm/ The New York Times, 6-24:31.

Gaylord Nelson
United States Senator, D—Wis.

While under heavy pressure, the (U.S.) military finally stopped the chemical defoliation war and has substituted another massive war against the land itself by a program of patterns or carpet bombing and massive land clearing with a huge machine called a Rome Plow. The huge areas destroyed, pockmarked, scorched and bulldozed, resemble the moon and are no longer productive . . . This is impersonal, automated and mechanistic warfare brought to its logical conclusion—permanent, total

(GAYLORD NELSON)

destruction. The tragedy of it all is that no one knows or understands what is happening there, or why, or to what end. We have simply unleashed a gigantic machine which goes about its impersonal business destroying whatever is there without plan or purpose. The finger of responsibility points everywhere, but nowhere in particular. Who designed this policy of war against the land, and why? Nobody seems to know and nobody rationally can defend it . . . If Congress knew and understood, we would not appropriate the money. If the President (Nixon) knew and understood, he would stop it in 30 minutes. If the people of America knew and understood, they would remove from office those responsible for it–if they could ever find out who is responsible . . . when the members of Congress finally understand what we are doing there, neither they nor the people of this nation will sleep well that night.

Before the Senate, Washington/ The Christian Science Monitor, 5-10:16.

Pham Kim Ngoc
Minister of Economics of South Vietnam

(On U.S. bombing in Vietnam): Everything that has been written about the bombing makes it seem evil and senseless. But if this war had been prosecuted by any country but the United States . . . with its air resources . . . we would not have survived. I don't say that we are better off for having the war; but the war was fought on an agricultural country and that can't be damaged like an industrialized country. I am not being cynical. A dead tree is a dead tree; but there are still vast expanses of live trees. For the postwar period, I don't think, on balance, we have lost. When the peace comes, we will start with something, not with nothing . . . a network of roads, harbors and airfields.

The Washington Post, 12-10:(A)26.

Richard M. Nixon
President of the United States

(On amnesty for U.S. deserters and draft dodgers from Vietnam service): I, for one, would be very liberal with regard to amnesty, but not while there are Americans in Vietnam fighting to serve their country and defend their country, and not while POWs are held by North Vietnam. After that, we will consider it; but it would have to be on a basis of their paying the price, of course, that anyone should pay for violating the law.

Television interview, Washington/ Columbia Broadcasting System, 1-2.

Some Americans, who believed what the North Vietnamese led them to believe, have charged that the United States has not pursued negotiations intensively. As the record will show, just the opposite is true. Questions have been raised as to why we have not proposed a deadline for the withdrawal of all American forces in exchange for a cease-fire and the return of our prisoners of war; why we have not discussed the Seven-Point-Proposal made by the Viet Cong last July in Paris; why we have not submitted a new plan of our own to move the negotiations off dead center. As the private record will show, we have taken all these steps and more and have been flatly rejected or ignored by the other side . . . Here is the essence of our peace plan; public disclosure may gain it the attention it deserves in Hanoi. Within six months of an agreement: We shall withdraw all United States and allied forces from South Vietnam; we shall exchange all prisoners; there shall be a cease-fire throughout Indochina; there shall be a new Presidential election in South Vietnam. President Thieu will announce the elements of this election; these include international supervision and an independent body to organize and run the election, representing all political forces in South Vietnam, including the National Liberation Front (Viet Cong). Furthermore, President Thieu has informed me that, within the framework of the agreement outlined above, he makes the following offer: He and Vice President Huong would be ready to resign one month before the new election. The Chairman of the Senate, as caretaker-head of the government, would assume administrative responsibilities in South Vietnam, but the election would be the sole responsibility of the independent election body. There are several other proposals in our new peace plan; for example, as we offered privately on July 26 of last year, we remain prepared to undertake a major reconstruction program throughout Indochina, including North Vietnam, to help all these peoples to recover from the ravages of a generation of war. We will pursue any approach that will speed negotiations. We are ready to negotiate the plan I have outlined tonight and conclude a comprehensive agreement on all military and political issues . . . This has been the longest and most difficult war in our history. Honest and patriotic Americans have disagreed as to whether we should have been involved at all nine years ago, and there has been disagreement on the conduct of the war. The proposal I have made tonight is one on which we can all agree. Let us unite now in our search for peace—a peace that is fair to both sides—a peace that can last.

Broadcast address, Washington. Jan. 25/ The New York Times, 1-26:10.

. . . there is, in my view . . . a very great difference between criticizing policies that got us into war and criticizing the conduct of the war, and criticisms by a Presidential candidate of a policy to end the war and to bring peace. What we have here is a situation . . . where, within one week after a very forthcoming peace proposal has been made (by the U.S.), various Presidential candidates sought to propose another settlement which went beyond that. My own candid judgment is that that kind of action has the effect . . . of having the government in Hanoi consider at least that they might be well-advised to wait until after the (November U.S.) election rather than negotiate . . . I would strongly urge at this point that all candidates for the Presidency, Republican and Democrat, review their public statements and really consider whether they believe that they are going to help the cause of peace or hurt it; whether they are going to encourage the enemy to negotiate or encourage him to continue the war.

News conference, Washington, Feb. 10/ The New York Times, 2-11:20.

. . . under no circumstances are we going to make any further (peace) proposals without the consultation with and the agreement of the government of South Vietnam, particularly on political issues, because the political issues are primarily theirs to decide rather than ours . . . Under no circumstances are we going to negotiate with our enemy in a way that undercuts our ally.

News conference, Washington, Feb. 10/ The Washington Post, 2-11:(A)16.

(On the U.S. suspension of the Paris peace talks): There has been a three-and-a-half-year filibuster on the peace talks on the part of the North Vietnamese. They refuse to negotiate seriously, and they use the talks for the purpose of propaganda while we have been trying to seek peace. Whenever the enemy is ready to negotiate seriously, we are ready to negotiate—and I would emphasize we are ready to negotiate in public channels or in private channels. As far as the hopes for a negotiated peace are concerned, I would say that the way the talks were going, there was no hope whatever. I am not saying that this move is going to bring a negotiation. I do say, however, that it was necessary to do something to get the talks off dead center and to see whether the enemy continued to want to use the talks only for propaganda or whether they wanted to negotiate. When they are ready, we are ready; but we are not going to continue to allow them to use this forum for the purpose of bullying the United States in a propaganda forum rather than in seriously negotiating peace, as we tried to do . . .

News conference, Washington, March 24/ The New York Times, 3-25:12.

(RICHARD M. NIXON)

(On the current North Vietnamese offensive in South Vietnam): What we are witnessing here—what is being brutally inflicted upon the Republic of (South) Vietnam—is a clear case of naked and unprovoked aggression across an international border. The only word for it is invasion. This massive attack has been resisted on the ground entirely by South Vietnamese forces. No United States ground troops have been involved. None will be involved. To support this defensive effort by the South Vietnamese, I have ordered attacks on enemy military targets in both North and South Vietnam by the air and naval forces of the United States . . . I have ordered that our air and naval attacks on military installations in North Vietnam be continued until the North Vietnamese stop their offensive in South Vietnam . . . They (the attacks) will not stop until that invasion stops.

Broadcast address,
Washington, April 26/
The New York Times, 4-27:20.

I do not know who will be in this office in the years ahead. But I do know future Presidents will travel to nations abroad on journeys for peace as I have. If the United States betrays the millions of people who have relied on us in Vietnam, the President of the United States, whoever he is, will not deserve nor receive the respect which is essential if the United States is to play the great role we are destined to play of helping to build a new structure of peace in the world. It would amount to a renunciation of our morality, an abdication of our leadership among nations and an invitation for the mighty to prey upon the weak all around the world. It would be to deny peace the chance peace deserves to have. This we shall never do.

Broadcast address,
Washington, April 26/
The New York Times, 4-27:20.

In the event that one country, like North Vietnam, massively assisted with the most modern technical weapons by two Communist superpowers—in the event that that country is able to invade another country and conquer it, you can see how that pattern would be repeated in other countries throughout the world—in the Mideast, in Europe and in others as well. If, on the other hand, that kind of aggression is stopped in Vietnam and fails there, then it will be discouraged in other parts of the world. Putting it quite directly then, what is on the line in Vietnam is not just peace for Vietnam, but peace in the Mideast, peace in Europe and peace not just for the five or six or seven years immediately ahead of us, but possibly for a long time in the future.

Floresville, Tex., April 30/
The New York Times, 5-2:21.

I do not question the patriotism of any critics of this war. Reasonable and honest and decent Americans can disagree about whether we should have gotten into Vietnam. They can disagree about how the war should be conducted, disagree about who is at fault now and so forth. But let's look at the record as it is at the present time. Since I have come into office, we have withdrawn half a million men from Vietnam. We have offered everything that could be offered except impose a Communist government on the people of South Vietnam, and their (North Vietnam's) answer has been massive invasion of South Vietnam . . . Now, under these circumstances, instead of the critics criticizing brave Americans flying dangerous air missions, hitting military targets in North Vietnam, and military targets only—instead of criticizing them trying to prevent a Communist take-over, I think they should direct a little criticism to the Communists who are trying to keep this war going. That is what they ought to be doing.

Floresville, Tex., April 30/
U.S. News & World Report, 5-15:101.

I have . . . concluded that Hanoi must be denied the weapons and supplies it needs to continue its aggression. In full coordination with the Republic of (South) Vietnam, I have ordered the following measures which are being implemented as I am speaking to you: 1) All entrances to North Vietnamese ports will be mined to prevent access to these ports and North Vietnamese naval operations from these ports. 2) United States forces have been directed to take appropriate measures within the internal and claimed territorial waters of North Vietnam to interdict the delivery of supplies. 3) Rail and all other communications will be cut off to the maximum extent possible. 4) Air and naval strikes against military targets in North Vietnam will continue. These actions are not directed against any other nation. Countries with ships presently in North Vietnamese ports have been notified that their ships will have three daylight periods to leave in safety. After that time, the mines will become active and any ships attempting to leave or enter these ports will do so at their own risk. These actions will cease when the following conditions are met: First, all American prisoners of war must be returned. Second, there must be an internationally-supervised cease-fire throughout Indochina. Once prisoners of war are released, and once the internationally-supervised cease-fire has begun, we will stop all acts of force throughout Indochina. At that time, we will proceed with a complete withdrawal of all American forces from Vietnam within four months. These are terms which would not require surrender and humiliation on the part of anybody.

Broadcast address, Washington, May 8/
Los Angeles Times, 5-9:(1)8.

I know that many Americans favor (immediate withdrawal of all U.S. forces from Vietnam). They believe that the way to end the war is for the United States to get out, and to remove the threat to our remaining troops by simply withdrawing them. From a political standpoint, this would be an easy choice for me to accept. I did not send over one-half million Americans to Vietnam. I have brought 500,000 home from Vietnam since I took office. But abandoning our commitment in Vietnam here and now would mean turning 17 million South Vietnamese over to Communist terror and tyranny. It would mean leaving hundreds of American prisoners in Communist hands with no bargaining leverage to get them released. An American defeat in Vietnam would encourage this kind of aggression all over the world–aggression in which smaller nations, armed by their major allies, could be tempted to attack neighboring nations at will. World peace would be in grave jeopardy.

Broadcast address, Washington, May 8/
Los Angeles Times, 5-9:(1)8.

. . . I have had some experience–and a great deal of experience as a matter of fact–in this past year in dealing with Communist leaders. I find that making a bargain with them is not easy; and you get something from them only when you have something they want to get from you. The only way we're going to get our POWs back is to be doing something to them, and that means hitting military targets in North Vietnam, retaining a residual force in South Vietnam and continuing the mining of the harbors of North Vietnam. Only by having that kind of activity go forward will they have any incentive to return our POWs rather than not account for them, as was the case when the French got out of Vietnam in 1954 and 15,000 French were never accounted for after that. I shall never let that happen to the brave men who are POWs.

News conference, Washington, June 29/
The New York Times, 7-1:8.

As far as a coalition government (in South Vietnam) is concerned: No, we will not negotiate with the enemy for accomplishing what they cannot accomplish themselves, and that is to impose against their will on the people of South Vietnam a coalition government with the Communists.

News conference, Washington, June 29/
U.S. News & World Report, 7-10:52.

(RICHARD M. NIXON)

Looking back over the period of this very difficult war, we find that since 1965 there have been 600,000 civilian casualties in South Vietnam as a result of deliberate policies of the North Vietnamese Communists—not accidental, but deliberate. In North Vietnam, in the period from 1954 to 1956, in their so-called land-reform program, a minimum of 50,000 were murdered, assassinated; and according to the Catholic bishop of Danang whom I talked to when I was there in 1956, in South Vietnam, in addition to the 800,000 refugees who came south, there were at least a half-million who died in slave-labor camps in North Vietnam. Now, I did not relate this series of incidents for the purpose of saying, because they did something bad, we can do something bad. What I am simply saying is, let's not have a hypocritical double standard (of criticizing U.S. Vietnam policy while being silent about Communist Vietnam policy). The United States has been restrained, greater restraint than any great power has ever shown in handling this war. We will continue to be restrained.

News conference, Washington, July 27/ The Washington Post, 7-28:(A)10.

As far as our military commanders are concerned, while they do give me their judgment as to what will affect the military outcome in Vietnam, they have never recommended, for example, bombing Hanoi. You have seen some of these signs, "Bomb Hanoi"; in fact, they were around in '68 even, a few, as well as '64. Our military doesn't want to do that. They believe it would be counterproductive; and secondly, they believe it is not necessary. It might shorten the war, but it would leave a legacy of hatred throughout that part of the world from which we might never recover. So our military have not advocated bombing the dikes; they have not advocated bombing civilian centers. They are doing their best in carrying out the policy we want of hitting military targets only. When, as a result of what will often happen, a bomb is dropped, if it is in an area of injury to civilians, it is not by intent, and there is a very great difference.

News conference, Washington, July 27/ The Washington Post, 7-28:(A)10.

Standing in this convention hall four years ago, I pledged to seek an honorable end to the war in Vietnam. We have made great progress toward that goal. We have brought over half a million men home from Vietnam, and more will be coming home. We have ended America's ground combat role. No draftees are being sent to Vietnam. We have reduced our casualties by 98 per cent. We have gone the extra mile—in fact, tens of thousands of miles—to seek peace on the negotiating front. We have offered a cease-fire, a total withdrawal of all American forces, an exchange of all prisoners of war, internationally-supervised free elections with participation by the Communists both in the elections and in their supervision. There are three things we have not and will not do: We will never abandon our prisoners of war. We will not join our enemies in imposing a Communist government on our allies—the 17 million people of South Vietnam. We will not stain the honor of the United States.

Accepting the Republican Presidential nomination, Miami Beach, Aug. 23/ Los Angeles Times, 8-24:(1)22.

I realize that many wonder why we insist on an honorable peace in Vietnam. From a political standpoint, they suggest that, since I was not in office when over a half-million American men were sent to Vietnam, I should end the war by agreeing to impose a Communist government on the people of South Vietnam and blame the catastrophe on my predecessors. This might be good politics. But it would be disastrous to the cause of peace in the world. If at this time we betray our allies, it will discourage our friends around the world and encourage our enemies to engage in aggression. In danger areas like the Middle East, small nations who rely on the friendship and support of the United States would be in deadly jeopardy. To our friends and allies in Europe, Asia, the Mid-east and Latin America, I say that America will continue its great bipartisan tradition—to stand by our friends and never to desert them.

Accepting the Republican Presidential nomination, Miami Beach, Aug. 23/ Los Angeles Times, 8-24:(1)22.

(On his 1968 Presidential campaign promise to end the war): I think there are those who have faulted this Administration on its efforts to seek peace; but those who fault it, I would respectfully suggest, are ones that would have the United States seek peace at the cost of surrender, dishonor and the destruction of the ability of the United States to conduct foreign policy in a responsible way. That I did not pledge in 1968. I do not pledge it now.

News conference, San Clemente, Calif., Aug. 29/ The Washington Post, 8-30:(A)16.

(On the U.S. bombing and mining of North Vietnam): There are those who say that the bombing and mining serve no useful purpose . . . I will only say that the bombing and mining was essential to turn around what was a potentially disastrous situation in South Vietnam. The back of the enemy offensive has been broken; they hold no provincial capitals now at all. This could not have been accomplished without the mining and the bombing; and the mining and the bombing will continue, of course, until we get some agreements on the negotiating front.

News conference, Washington, Oct. 5/ The Washington Post, 10-6:(A)10.

(Addressing the families of U.S. prisoners of war and missing-in-action): I know it's been a long, long vigil. I know how much you suffer. I know how much your children suffer. You've never been away from my thoughts. You've never been away from my prayers. There's nothing I want more than to bring your loved ones home. I will never let you down.

Before National League of Families of American Prisoners and Missing in Southeast Asia, Washington, Oct. 16/ Los Angeles Herald-Examiner, 10-16:(A)2.

At a time when a small minority has tried to glorify the few who have refused to serve (draft dodgers and deserters), it is more important than ever that we honor the millions who have loyally stood by their country when the challenge to freedom called for service. To them, and to their parents, wives and loved ones, I promise that, as long as I am President, America will not turn her back on those who served. We are not going to make a mockery of their sacrifice by surrendering to the enemy, or by offering amnesty to draft dodgers and deserters. The two and one-half million who chose to serve America in Vietnam have paid a price for their choice. The few hundred who chose to desert America must pay a price for their choice.

Veterans Day radio address, Camp David, Md., Oct. 22/ Los Angeles Herald-Examiner, 10-23:(A)8.

Jean-Christophe Oeberg
Swedish Ambassador to North Vietnam

(On U.S. bombing in North Vietnam): The Americans are expending enormous resources on . . . destroying small workshops, small bridges, small railway stations, everything. The biggest worry at the moment is the dams. The Red River has already begun to rise, and it reaches its highest point in July and August. The Americans are aiming at the dams and dikes. If the river swells to the same level as last year, there will be an immense catastrophe . . . Everyone, diplomats included, must react as human beings. Diplomat or not, I do not intend to watch what is happening in silence.

Interview, Stockholm/ The Washington Post, 6-29:(A)17.

David Packard
Former Deputy Secretary of Defense of the United States

When I think of the young men and women risking their lives in Southeast Asia, and then of (the) spoiled young elitists on our college campuses demonstrating against President Nixon's efforts to resist blatant aggression, I am sickened. And even those students who only circulate petitions—like the one to cut off all supplies to our men who are in Vietnam—are not much better. They hurt our troops' morale and encourage the North Vietnamese to continue their aggression.

At Military Affairs Luncheon of Greater San Francisco Chamber of Commerce, May 18/ San Francisco Examiner, 5-19:5.

Olof Palme
Prime Minister of Sweden

(On U.S. mining of North Vietnamese ports): How many people must die, how many illusions must be shattered, how great must the destruction be, before the United States realizes that negotiations aiming to guarantee the independence of the Vietnamese people is the only way to peace?

Television broadcast, Stockholm, May 9/ The New York Times, 5-10:20.

Paul VI
Pope

(Addressing the parties involved in the Indochina war): You, who are responsible for the fate of those areas, give proof of wisdom and magnanimity capable of putting human life and dignity above any other entreat. We are echoing the groans of so many innocent victims. We make ours the voice of a population exhausted by slaughter and ruin. We raise the cry of civil humanity, believing in justice and love that must inspire relations between men and nations, to entreat those who can and must discuss and decide—enough!

Vatican City, July 9/ The New York Times, 7-10:5.

Charles H. Percy
United States Senator, R–Ill.

I feel the American people want to get out (of Vietnam)—lock, stock and barrel—and they want to get out by a definite date. They want to see it ahead of them, and they really feel that, if they're (the South Vietnamese) ever going to hack it alone over there, this is the time they've got to do it. We've done enough. We've done all anyone reasonably can be expected (to) in an area that is not at all vital to our national security or vital interests. And I think I am really expressing the feeling of the American people . . .

At Senate Foreign Relations Committee hearing, Washington, April 17/ U.S. News & World Report, 5-1:62.

Tran Nguon Phieu
Minister of Social Welfare of South Vietnam

Fifteen thousand Communists were killed in Quangtri just to put their flag there. Nine thousand of our troops were killed to put our flag back. I have been there to see. The sole result has been that the town is completely destroyed and no one lives there. Isn't that stupid? Isn't it?

Interview, Saigon/ The New York Times, 11-3:13.

Douglas Pike
American editor; Authority on Vietnamese Communist affairs

The Vietnamese are going to be killing each other in large numbers for political reasons long after we Americans are gone.

The Dallas Times Herald, 6-22:(C)30.

William J. Porter
United States Ambassador to Paris peace talks

(Addressing the Communist delegations): Unfortunately, there is no "give" in your position, no readiness on your side to listen to anything except what you call a "positive response" to your ultimatums, meaning a complete acceptance of everything you propose . . . The absurdity of this attitude, in the light of your moral, military and political failures, is apparent to all who look at the Vietnam problem in detail. Among those who do, as you know, are an increasing number of young men of North Vietnam who are beginning to weigh the failure of your policies and their cost . . . In matters governed by international convention—I refer specifically to prisoners of war—you prefer the status of outlaws rather than abiding by the convention you signed. You reject our efforts here, and the efforts of others elsewhere, to persuade you to live up to your legal obligations. You pursue the vain hope that you can use the prisoners in your hands to extract political and military advantage, that you can achieve your goals by exerting a particulary abhorrent form of blackmail. Only your most hardened professional apologists continue to excuse your conduct in that domain . . . Indeed, you have acted in a manner which has made a great many people wonder whether you would dishonor any additional commitments you might make in the future as readily as you have dishonored those you have made in the past . . . As you know, (U.S.) President Nixon, at the request of the Congress, has declared next week as a week of national concern for our men held prisoner by you and your associates. It would be a mockery of our concern for them were we to sit in this room with you and listen to more of your blackmail and distortions to the effect that the prisoner-of-war issue is an "imaginary problem." Therefore, our side does not agree to a meeting next week. As for meetings in the weeks that follow, we believe it would be preferable to await some sign from you that you are disposed to engage in meaningful exchanges on the various points raised in your and our proposals . . .

At Paris peace talks, March 23/ The Washington Post, 3-26:(B)6.

(Addressing the Communist delegations): . . . while you were demanding a return to this table to "continue the work" for peace, what have you done on the ground in South Vietnam? You continue your massive invasion in the most flagrant violation of the 1954 Geneva accords and the 1968 understandings. You have committed additional North Vietnamese troops to the battle. You have shelled and rocketed population centers such as Quangtri, Kontum and Anloc. Your divisions are marauding and killing helpless refugees throughout South Vietnam—a process you describe as assisting the South Vietnamese people to determine their own future. After we had agreed to resume these plenaries in response to your insistence, you—with cynical duplicity—stepped up the level of your all-out military aggression.

At Paris peace talks, May 4/ The New York Times, 5-5:20.

William Proxmire
United States Senator, D–Wis.

(Addressing U.S. Secretary of State William Rogers): . . . if we are going to go in with a bombing that is greater in North Vietnam than our planes dropped on all the countries throughout World War II; if we are going to put the greatest Navy in the world at the disposal of South Vietnam against little North Vietnam; if we are going to have the greatest Air Force in the world engage in the kind of tremendous activity it is; then I don't know how you can say that whatever military progress is being made here is being made as a result of Vietnamization . . . it is the air support and the naval support, that are the strongest military force in the world, against a fifth-rate military power which has perhaps one per cent or less of the military strength that we have. That is what is working here, that is what is effected; it is not the South Vietnamese. I don't know how any fair-minded person can say the South Vietnamese can fight and die and win as compared to the North Vietnamese. They have not done it. They have not showed even that they believe in their government.

At Senate Foreign Operations Subcommittee hearing, Washington, May 15/ The New York Times, 6-10:27.

Edwin O. Reischauer
Professor, Harvard University; Former United States Ambassador to Japan

I do not believe that North Vietnam would have waged its (current) offensive if a definite date had been set for the withdrawal of American troops from South Vietnam. It was either that, or perhaps the North is afraid that the Vietnamization program is working out and that they would find the South Vietnamese too strong once the Americans finally do leave. The third possibility is that the North Vietnamese were afraid that some sort of deal would be made between the Americans and the Russians or the Chinese. They may have thought they had to assert their independence to show that no agreement could be reached behind their backs.

Parade, 5-21:15.

Elliot L. Richardson
Secretary of Health, Education and Welfare of the United States

The consistency of the response to President Nixon's actions (mining North Vietnamese ports and increased bombing) in the wake of the North Vietnamese invasion (of South Vietnam) was really quite remarkable. South Vietnam was on the verge of defeat, the critics charged. Others said the chances of the President's going to Moscow were less than 50-50; or that a major confrontation with the Soviet Union was likely; or that it was a desperate gamble by a desperate—some editorialists even suggested deranged—man. These were the lines of argument established by many media and figures within minutes of the President's address to the nation on Vietnam (May 8, announcing the bombing and mining), and they continued to dominate television and newspaper analyses for the next several days. And yet, as I speak today, these analyses have been proved by events to be wrong—absolutely wrong. South Vietnam has not only not collapsed, but its troops are battling back aggressively. The President not only went to Moscow, but his meeting there was a triumph. Finally, the military confrontation that we were told to look for—the World War III of which Senator (George) McGovern and innumerable media pundits warned of—has not occurred either. Despite gross errors of prediction and punditry, not a whisper of regret has been uttered by one of President Nixon's major media or political critics. They do not feel the slightest need to say, for once, that they were wrong; that their statements about the President's actions were excessive; that they misjudged the reaction of the Soviet Union; that, in retrospect, what the President did was right and responsible and, at least at this point in time, that it has brought closer the day when the Vietnam war will at last be over.

Before California Republican League, Millbrae, Calif., June 3/ San Francisco Examiner & Chronicle, 6-4:(A)21.

William P. Rogers
Secretary of State of the United States

It's not the Saigon regime that we're supporting. We're supporting the idea that the people of South Vietnam should decide themselves their future. That's the reason we're there to begin with. Now, if we at this stage said we didn't care, (that) we're perfectly prepared to have the Communists take over the government of South Vietnam—and then it would mean eventually Laos and Cambodia, too, obviously—then our whole effort would have been for naught. We have fought this war—a long, tragic, difficult war for the United States—with very good intentions. We don't want any territory. We don't want a permanent presence there. We just want to work out a solution so the people in South Vietnam can determine their future. And if the South Vietnamese people want a Communist government, we have said that's acceptable to us. But we're not going to, at this stage, just pull up stakes and get out and say to the Communists, "You go ahead and take it over; we're sorry about this whole thing."

TV-radio interview/
"Face the Nation,"
Columbia Broadcasting System, 2-6.

(On the U.S. bombing of North Vietnam in response to the North's current offensive in South Vietnam): . . . for a long time the North Vietnamese have been able to peddle —to sell—a cruel hoax to a segment of the American people that somehow the war in Vietnam was a civil uprising. Now it is quite clear—and I don't believe anyone can deny it—that this is a major invasion, offensive action by the North Vietnamese in South Vietnam. It comes at a time when its purpose is to disrupt the (U.S.) withdrawal program, to endanger American lives—the lives of Americans who are still in South Vietnam—and the enemy has committed outside of North Vietnam 12 of its 13 combat divisions. So we think it's essential to conduct the attacks that the President (Nixon) has ordered to be conducted against military targets wherever he decides to make these attacks to protect American lives, to permit the withdrawals to continue and to give South Vietnamese forces a chance to defend themselves. He's taken that action. And he intends to continue to take whatever action is necessary to achieve those purposes.

Before Senate Foreign Relations
Committee, Washington, April 17/
The New York Times, 4-18:19.

. . . an immediate withdrawal of American forces (from Vietnam) would be ridiculous. It probably would result in a bloodbath. There are 17 million people in South Vietnam. If the United States did an about-face after all these years of supporting South Vietnam—if that occurred, I think there would be a major bloodbath in South Vietnam. What its form, composition and so forth would be, I, of course, can't be sure. But there's no doubt in my mind it would be a terrible massacre. Secondly, I think it would destabilize that whole area. There are other nations in that area that we have treaty commitments with that have been negotiated and ratified over a period of a great number of years. And it's not a partisan matter in any sense of the word: These treaties have received bipartisan support. If we suddenly withdrew, not only would we have a major bloodbath in South Vietnam, but I think it would be destabilizing in areas like Korea and Japan and the Philippines and other countries in that area. So I think it would be a major disaster; it would be a mistake of major proportions, in my opinion . . .

Before Senate Foreign Relations
Committee, Washington, April 17/
U.S. News & World Report, 5-1:59.

(On current increased U.S. bombing and the mining of North Vietnam): . . . if somebody is trying to break into your house and you try to push him out the window, are you escalating it? We are in this situation; the other side escalated it (by way of its current offensive in South Vietnam) . . . What we are trying to do is take a defensive measure to prevent that escalation from proceeding. It is as simple as that. The decisions the President (Nixon) made were based on the fact that this escalation occurred and he advised the other side before that happened that if they did escalate, if they attempted to take advantage of our position as we were withdrawing our troops, then he would take the necesaary action and he did that. But he did it because *they* escalated the war, not the United States. And it seems to me that everytime an American talks about this he should say that to himself; he should say the escalation resulted from what the enemy did, not what the United States did.

Before Senate Foreign Operations Subcommittee, Washington, May 15/ The New York Times, 6-10:27.

(On UN Secretary General Kurt Waldheim's suggestion that U.S. planes are bombing dikes in North Vietnam): I have asked (U.S. UN) Ambassador (George) Bush to seek an early appointment with the Secretary General, again to point out that the information that he has received concerning alleged deliberate bombing to damage the dikes in North Vietnam is false . . . Furthermore, I have asked Ambassador Bush to inform the Secretary General that these allegations are part of a carefully-planned campaign by the North Vietnamese and their supporters to give worldwide circulation to this falsehood. The Secretary General in his press conference today said that, "It is always my interest in using quiet diplomacy to be helpful." We cannot consider helpful any public statements giving further currency to these reports.

Washington, July 24/ The New York Times, 7-25:1.

(On former U.S. Attorney General Ramsey Clark's trip to North Vietnam and his anti-U.S.-Vietnam-policy statements broadcast on Radio Hanoi): I am frank to say that I was shocked . . . To hear the voice of a former Attorney General, a man involved in sending 500,000 men to Vietnam . . . to hear him on Radio Hanoi, to me was contemptible. Imagine going to a nation we are at war with, taking their version and broadcasting it back on the enemy radio, while our men are losing their lives . . . to me is beyond belief. I would think the American people would be shocked.

News conference, Washington, Aug. 11/ Los Angeles Times, 8-12:(1)11.

(On Democratic Vice-Presidential nominee R. Sargent Shriver's assertion, when he was Ambassador to Paris in early 1969, that the U.S. missed an opportunity for peace when the North Vietnamese signaled they were ready for serious negotiations): I have checked this morning to find out whether he (Shriver) made any such reference, while he was Ambassador in Paris, to such a proposal, whether he made any recommendations of any kind on the matter, whether he spoke to anybody at any time while he was in office, or subsequent to that . . . And so far I have not been able to find anything. I have checked with (then U.S. peace negotiator) Henry Cabot Lodge, who was there, and certainly Mr. Shriver didn't say anything to him . . . I have asked all the members of the negotiating team that I was able to reach, and they all said nothing like that ever happened. I checked the speeches that Mr. Shriver made, his press conferences, all the telegrams he sent in to the (State) Department, including the no-distribution telegrams, and he never made any references to anything of this kind at all . . . Certainly, if the President of the United States is sitting with peace in his lap, as Mr. Shriver says, and Mr. Shriver knows that peace is in his lap, he could pick up the phone and call me, or call the President, or talk to Cabot Lodge or the other negotiators and say, "My God, peace is in the President's lap" . . . He could pick up the phone any time and say, "Bill, this is Sarge Shriver. The President has a historic opportunity for peace. Peace is in his lap. Why don't you do something about it?" And I would have said, "Sarge, what is it? Please tell me quick."

News conference, Washington, Aug. 12/ The Washington Post, 8-12:(A)7.

Walt W. Rostow
Former Special Assistant to the President of the United States

(On whether it was worthwhile for the U.S. to get involved in the Vietnam war): Certainly yes. My answer is precise. The cost of war is great; I remember John Kennedy told me this in 1961. I told him to consider the cost of the alternative: What would have happened in the United States had we not helped South Vietnam, and what would have happened in the world? The alternative—and Kennedy and (Lyndon) Johnson were also convinced of this—was nuclear war, and certainly a more vast war than the one that was being undertaken.

Interview, Ostuni, Italy/ San Francisco Examiner, 8-24:4.

Dean Rusk
Former Secretary of State of the United States

(On former U.S. Attorney General Ramsey Clark's visit to North Vietnam and his charges of deliberate U.S. bombing of civilian areas and flood dikes): I have no doubt that there have been some unintended victims of the bombing in the North. But if the United States had set out intentionally to destroy civilians in the North or to bomb the dikes in the first place, there would not have been a Hanoi for Ramsey Clark to visit. It would have been wiped off the face of the earth. And if we had been intending to destroy dikes, vast areas of North Vietnam would be a lake—it would be flooded.

Television interview, Aug. 15/ San Francisco Examiner, 8-16:5.

Raoul Salan
Former Commander-in-Chief, French forces in Indochina

(North Vietnamese Defense Minister Vo Nguyen Giap) would like to prove that Vietnamization (in South Vietnam) cannot succeed, demonstrate that there is only one army, that of the North. I know it well. It is the best infantry in the world, better than that of the Germans at Verdun. But Giap cannot prove that Vietnamization is a failure. I believe that it has succeeded in part. It has been said: "Everything is going to crumble (in South Vietnam)." But everything has not crumbled. The lads of the South are fighting. Under the deluge of the (North Vietnamese) attack across the DMZ, they fight it out in order to avoid demolition. But they are not surpassed by the enemy. Giap thought that the people would rise up and help. There are around 200,000 refugees. If they had remained and had welcomed the North Vietnamese with open arms, saying "Long live Giap! Long live Ho Chi Minh!" surely everything would be different.

Interview/ The New York Times, 5-19:33.

John G. Schmitz
United States Representative, I—Calif.; American Party Presidential nominee

(U.S. President) Richard Nixon and (Senator) George McGovern are two sides of the same coin on the war. One (McGovern) wants to surrender right away; the other (Nixon) wants to surrender on the installment plan.

Campaigning in Virginia for the Presidential election, Sept. 5/ Los Angeles Herald-Examiner, 9-6:(A)3.

(U.S. President) Richard Nixon makes a so-called peace and trade mission to Moscow. If I were still on active duty, I would be flying over North Vietnam being shot at by very highly-computerized, sophisticated surface-to-air missiles. I would be a loyal Marine, but I would take a dim view of the fact that between flights I would read in the paper that my Commander-in-Chief is in Moscow on a so-called peace and trade mission trading computerized technology to the manufacturer of those computerized surface-to-air missiles so that they can more efficiently kill me in a no-win war. Let's put it this way: We are building airplanes to go to North Vietnam to shoot up trucks on the Ho Chi Minh trail, trucks which were built in factories which were built by Americans. The A. J. Bryant Company of Detroit built the ZIL factory, the Ford Motor Company built the Gorki factory, and right now we are building the largest truck factory in the world on the Kama River—36 square miles—which will turn out more trucks in one year than all the American factories combined in one year. Why? We build the planes to shoot up the trucks and build the factories that

(JOHN G. SCHMITZ)

build the trucks. That is the immorality of the war.

Interview, Washington/ Human Events, 10-21:20.

Maurice Schumann
Foreign Minister of France

(Criticizing U.S. policy in Indochina): War operations, far from being scaled down, have been enlarged into Laos and Cambodia. Even the bombing of North Vietnam has started again. All this means that people in Vietnam, Laos and Cambodia are still being killed, still being wounded and still being made captives. The destruction is continuing. If this is what is meant by "Vietnamization," then, frankly, I don't like it.

News conference, Tokyo, Jan. 18/ Los Angeles Times, 1-19:(1)21.

Hugh Scott
United States Senator, R–Pa.

You can't still a critic who is determined not to be satisfied whatever you do. But the President (Nixon) certainly has blunted criticism on this issue (the war) with remarkable success. He has left his Democratic opponents virtually topless, without any of the glamour which that implies. Let's take it step by step: The critics have said, "Set a date for withdrawal of American forces." It turns out that the President offered to do that long ago. Hanoi can have a date certain any time it is willing to agree to return our prisoners of war and accept a cease-fire. (Former Senator) Eugene McCarthy says the Nixon plan won't work, because we must have a government in South Vietnam that is acceptable. Well, acceptable to whom? He can only mean Hanoi. Senator George McGovern says that we could get American prisoners of war out if we would set a definite timetable for withdrawal. But the recorded tapes of conversation between U.S. emissaries and the North Vietnamese reveal that the furthest Hanoi has ever gone is: "If you will totally withdraw, we will talk about the modalities of the release of prisoners." Teddy (Senator Edward) Kennedy said on the day following the President's broadcast of his peace plan: "So long as we try to condition our withdrawal on things like free elections, a cease-fire, or any of the other trappings disclosed last night, reasonable as they may seem, we shall be pursuing the same blind alley." I didn't know that Senator Kennedy regarded free elections as something to be scorned, in our country or in any other country. I didn't know that a cease-fire was a "trapping." These Senators–I call them the Presidential Senators–now try to make this point: The U.S. has withdrawn so much of its forces that it is too weak to get a good settlement from Hanoi. But they have advocated withdrawal. They are trying to have it both ways.

Interview/ U.S. News & World Report, 2-28:34.

R. Sargent Shriver
United States Democratic Vice-Presidential nominee

I think that to insist . . . that the (South Vietnamese President) Thieu government stay in power in Saigon was to insist upon us winning the war, because the war concerns the political future of South Vietnam. Therefore, what we have done for a number of years is to give General Thieu and his government veto power over our foreign policy. I am not in favor of that. I think we should make our own foreign policy and not let our foreign policy be written for us by a military general of a relatively small nation in Southeast Asia.

TV-radio interview, Washington/ "Meet the Press," National Broadcasting Company, 8-13.

Norodom Sihanouk
Exiled former Chief of State of Cambodia

. . . what does the Cambodian–be he Communist or not–wish? He wants independence for his country and then neutrality. Even my (Cambodia's) Communists want independence; they do not want to become the puppets of China, or of the Soviet Union, or of Vietnam. Of course, it is possible that after liberation the Communists will try to eliminate from power the other forces, as happened to Masaryk in Czechoslovakia. Obviously, I can't predict what the Communists will do after liberation; but until now they have assured me that they will respect our other parties.

Interview, Peking/ The New York Times Magazine, 1-23:9.

As for us Cambodians, we demand the total, immediate and unconditional withdrawal of all American forces from Indochina. The Americans must leave us alone to settle our own problems among ourselves. If there are right-wing and left-wing Indochinese who wish to fight it out among themselves, that is our business and nobody else's. We want to be left alone to settle our own problems.

Interview, Peking/ The New York Times Magazine, 1-23:27.

Robert L. F. Sikes
United States Representative, D–Fla.

I find it very difficult to believe the secret negotiations for peace between the United States and North Vietnam have included commitments for reparations, under the name of reconstruction–but apparently this is the case. This is a shocking development. We are under no obligation to rebuild North Vietnam. The damage which they have sustained they have brought on themselves. They should be required to pay reparations to us for the suffering and cost they caused us as a result of the war. And they should be paying reparations to the nations of Indochina for the destruction wrought by the Communist forces in their efforts to overturn the governments of other nations. Instead of paying reparations or providing reconstruction to the North Vietnamese, I am certain it would be more satisfying to the Congress and to our nation to provide additional benefits to American servicemen of the conflict and to their families, particularly to the families of the dead, to the wounded, and to the families of those missing in action. I strongly urge that the nonsense about reparations, by whatever name, to North Vietnam be dropped now.

Human Events, 2-12:15.

Souvanna Phouma
Premier of Laos

. . . the Laotian problem is tied to the Vietnam problem. North Vietnam must withdraw its troops from Laos. That is an important question for us. We hope that a cease-fire in Vietnam will mean the end of the use of Laos as a transit point for North Vietnamese troops.

Interview, United Nations, N.Y., Oct. 26/ The New York Times, 10-27:20.

Prince Souvanouvong
Leader of the Pathet Lao (Laotian Communists)

We must bear in mind that the U.S. imperialists and their henchmen are as stubborn and crafty as ever. Unless they are defeated on the battlefield, they will not renounce their aggressive scheme. So the only way to obtain genuine peace and independence for the fatherland is to persist in our nationwide struggle till complete victory.

The Washington Post, 7-15:(A)12.

Benjamin Spock
American physician and author

The Vietnam war is not slightly illegal or slightly aggressive. It's one of the dirtiest wars of all time. It's given me a different perspective on American history. It's not a defense war, but part of our desire to dominate the world, militarily and economically . . . In fact, it's convinced me that stopping the war and ending American imperialism are not enough. We've got to change the system

(BENJAMIN SPOCK)

to allow people to regain control of the country which belongs to them.

At University of Vermont/ The New York Times Magazine, 6-4:58.

John C. Stennis
United States Senator, D–Miss.

I know that the American people want to get out of the war. I want to get out; every other Senator here does. But if we scratch beneath the surface of the American people, we will find that they do not want to be driven out. They do not want, like a whipped dog, to have to leave the scrap he has been into. We are facing a tragic situation. The American people do not want all our sacrifices and loss of life to go down the drain . . . The thing over there in South Vietnam (the current Communist offensive) gets worse and worse. Battles are lost one after the other. I think that the American people will have to go through a period of travail and bereavement and disappointment and evaluation such as this generation has never had to do before.

Before the Senate, Washington/ The National Observer, 5-13:4.

Robert Taft, Jr.
United States Senator, R–Ohio

At the present time there are more than 500 young Americans in jail in this country as draft resisters. There are about 3,900 who are under indictment and may face jail. We estimate that there may be as many as 70,000 in exile or in a fugitive status as resisters of the draft. Many of these acted from bad judgment; in their conscience they thought they were right, perhaps. Some may have not acted from such good motives. Some may have had strong convictions against the course of their country in the Vietnam war. I think the time has now come, however, with the phasing out of that war, to raise the question whether it isn't in the national interest to provide a way in which these men can become productive citizens in our society again. We have a long tradition in America of amnesty, and I wonder if we can't be big enough, and strong enough, and a magnanimous enough country to face up to this tradition again . . . I believe that a qualified amnesty offer would be neither out of remorse nor out of sympathy for these men, but rather in the national interest, a practical solution to what should be a great national concern; a solution that, hopefully, would do something to unite these men with their native land. It could do something, I think, too–and this is awfully important–to regain the confidence of millions of young Americans who have disagreed with their country on the course that it's followed in the Vietnam war, but who have nevertheless loved it.

Television broadcast/"Comment!" National Broadcasting Company, 2-20.

Maxwell D. Taylor
General, United States Army (Ret.); Former U.S. Ambassador to South Vietnam

If President Nixon's program is carried out, we will have accomplished the national purpose we set in 1954: establishing conditions under which South Vietnam will be able to choose its own government and not have a Communist one imposed on it by North Vietnam. We may well have paid too much for reaching this goal, but at least we will have accomplished what we set out to do. Secondly, we will have destroyed the myth of invincibility of the "war of national liberation." Moscow, Peking and Hanoi all thought they had found in it a cheap and easy way to overthrow weak foreign governments without formal involvement. They could deny being a party, and the cost of such a war fought largely by guerrillas would be low. South Vietnam was to be the testing ground for this technique. So what happened? Even if we quit today–walked away –the price the North has paid thus far certainly does not suggest that "wars of national liberation" are cheap. It hasn't been cheap for Hanoi; it has been terribly expensive. I would say destroying this Communist myth is a plus for us and our friends.

Interview, Washington/ U.S. News & World Report, 11-27:24.

Edward Teller
American physicist

The war would be over except for one factor—(U.S. Democratic Presidential nominee Senator) George McGovern. If McGovern should be elected and acts as he says he will, the consequences would be disastrous. If we pull out of Vietnam, no country will ever want Americans as allies. No country will ever trust us.

At Berkeley (Calif.) Common Club, Aug. 18/The Dallas Times Herald, 8-20:(A)29.

Nguyen Van Thieu
President of South Vietnam

I propose democratic elections in which the National Liberation Front and the Viet Cong can take part as long as they promise to give up their violent acts. A new election for President and Vice President of South Vietnam will be organized and supervised by an independent organization representative of all the factions of South Vietnam, including the NLF. All factions will be able to take part in the elections and put forth candidates. Vice President (Tran Van) Huong and I will resign and the Speaker of the Senate will take charge of the country in the meantime. This election will be observed by international parties, and will take place within six months after an agreement is reached.

Radio address, Saigon, Jan. 26/ Los Angeles Times, 1-26:(1)24.

If South Vietnam folds, all of Southeast Asia folds. Vietnam is the test. Thailand and the Philippines say that if South Vietnam cannot defend itself against the Communists, no one else in this area can do so. If the Communists gain control of South Vietnam, they will have the richest and the best army in Southeast Asia, and I mean the armies of both North Vietnam and South Vietnam together. (With that) every state in Southeast Asia will fall. The key is Vietnam.

Interview, Saigon, March 18/ San Francisco Examiner & Chronicle, 3-19:(A)8.

(On the current North Vietnamese offensive in South Vietnam): The North Vietnamese aggressors do not recognize it yet, but they have failed before the political awakening and the immortal force of the South Vietnamese. They have not reached any of the military and political results they had planned, and they have suffered heavy losses before the heroic resistance of the South Vietnamese Army. They will fail just as they failed after the 1968 Tet offensive; and finally they will fail after 17 years of war.

April 23/ Los Angeles Herald-Examiner, 5-3:(A)4.

If our ally, the United States, did this (bombing North Vietnam) for six or seven months, I am sure the Communists would accept a cease-fire throughout Indochina with international guarantees . . . If we want to end this war, we must continue to destroy all of North Vietnam's military installations and economic power. Then the North Vietnamese people will revolt against their government . . . If we stop bombing, North Vietnam will continue to infiltrate men and supplies into South Vietnam, and the war will never end.

At National Defense College graduation ceremonies, Saigon, Aug. 1/ The Washington Post, 8-2:(A)14.

I have never denied independence and democracy. As President of South Vietnam, I have always observed democracy. However, if I (may speak as) a citizen, I must complain that our government has allowed us to enjoy too much democracy too soon. This is like—if you will excuse me for my comparison—a small baby that is given an overdose of medicine or like a weak person who takes up physical exercise so that his health cannot endure. I have always respected the people's democratic rights and freedoms as basically outlined in our Constitution. However, these rights and freedoms must be properly practiced, such as simultaneously respecting the Constitution and responding to the demands of our nation.

Quinhon, South Vietnam, Aug. 11/ The New York Times, 9-7:2.

Every freedom must be recognized to the extent consistent with the situation of our nation. If our country were a secure, peaceful and prosperous nation, like the United States, all our democratic rights and freedoms could be fully observed without any trouble at all. But our country is still on the path of development, with the Communists blocking our way and interfering with all our activities. We can find the Communists everywhere—under our beds, under our ancestors' altar, behind our backs and even among our ranks.

Quinhon, South Vietnam, Aug. 11/ The New York Times, 9-25:16.

The Communists have only one dogma: We must follow them or die. There is no half way. There is no neutrality. If we concede territory to the Communists, we will lose it and the people. If we agree to a coalition government, our 17 million people will be forced to follow the Communists. If we adopt neutrality—Communist-style neutrality—this means that we will tie our own hands and let the Communists eat us. And if we allow the Communists to operate openly in South Vietnam, we will lose the country.

Quinhon, South Vietnam, Aug. 11/ The New York Times, 9-25:16.

With the experiences gained by a great number of our combatants, cadres and compatriots through sorrow, mourning, tears, sweat, blood and bones for one-fourth of a century, and in the face of the stubbornness and treachery of our enemy—the Communist aggressors—who have not for the first time but have countless times brazenly carried out aggressive acts and who will carry them out again, I wish to present to you gentlemen and to the nation the following points coming from the bottom of my heart: No one understands the Communists more clearly than we do, and no one has more or as many sorrowful experiences with the Communists than we. No one will bear the responsibility and admit the fault before our national history and children and grandchildren for us if this country is lost. No one can more firmly guarantee that South Vietnam will not fall to the Communists' hands than we at present. Therefore, we must: first, not let ourselves be rocked to sleep, and never forget annexation and that, for the Communists, only they themselves have the right to survive; second, understand that national concord, national unity and elimination of hatred do not mean generosity, sleep or allowing the Communists to rule the roost and presenting them with opportunities for annexing this country and eliminating our people; finally, understand that, in the face of the loss or survival of our country and the 17 million Southern people, there can be no stand which may be called firm and there can be only one stand, which is the stand of loss or no loss of the country.

Before National Assembly, Saigon, Oct. 2/ The Washington Post, 10-31:(A)18.

The Viet Cong speak of controlling two-thirds of the South Vietnamese populace. If they really do, I challenge them to accept free elections; and of course we are ready to accept the results of such an election. I have always advocated that any settlement must be discussed between North and South Vietnamese governments, and the National Liberation Front (Viet Cong) has no right to stick its nose into our business.

Broadcast address, Saigon, Oct. 24/ The New York Times, 10-25:17.

(On what he would do if the Communists broke a cease-fire): If they fire pistols, we will respond with rifles. If they shoot rifles, we will respond with machine guns. If they fire machine guns, we will respond with bombs. If they violate it (a truce), once, I will fight them 10 times.

Broadcast address, Saigon, Oct. 24/
U.S. News & World Report, 11-6:14.

The Communists have claimed that I am an impediment to peace. This is not true, because I have already said that I, as an individual, will be ready to step down when a guaranteed peace has been restored. Only then shall I make a personal sacrifice for the compatriots. But as a President, I will not give in to the Communists before a guaranteed peace is achieved. Our peace and cease-fire stand remains unchanged. We are not afraid of peace and a cease-fire. We must happily welcome a just peace and a serious cease-fire, because the sooner peace comes, the less our compatriots will suffer . . . We do not avoid a cease-fire. We are unafraid of a cease-fire; but it must be a serious cease-fire. The North Vietnamese Communist troops must go home to North Vietnam, not just withdraw to Laos and Cambodia, from which they could renew their attacks against South Vietnam . . .

Broadcast address, Saigon, Oct. 24/
The Washington Post, 10-25:(A)19.

(On a cease-fire proposal and peace treaty nearing agreement between the U.S. and North Vietnam): We (South Vietnam) have not agreed on anything yet, and yet the Communists boasted that there will be a cease-fire and are preparing for it. We are not afraid of a cease-fire and the peace. I am sure it will come. But it only will come when I personally sign the treaty for a cease-fire and peace. The Communists can use 10 hands and 10 legs to sign treaties; but without my signature, it means there has been no agreement by the people. It will be invalid in South Vietnam. I am not an obstacle to peace. I reflect the will of the Vietnamese people.

Before pro-government legislators,
Saigon, Oct. 27/
Los Angeles Herald-Examiner, 10-27:(A)1.

Le Duc Tho
Member, North Vietnamese Politburo;
Chief North Vietnam negotiator
at Paris peace talks

We do not want in any way to impose a Communist regime on South Vietnam as (U.S. President) Nixon has invented. But our people are also determined not to permit the American Administration to establish under its control there a puppet power.

Paris, April 30/
The Dallas Times Herald, 5-1:(A)3.

Contrary to (U.S. President) Nixon's statements, we have never demanded a surrender from the United States; we have never had intention to humiliate anyone. We only demand that the United States side negotiate seriously to settle the Vietnam problem on the basis of respect for the Vietnam people's fundamental national rights provided for by the 1954 Geneva agreements. Hitherto in history, there are two ways to end wars: either one party inflicts a total defeat on the other and forces it to surrender, or the two belligerent parties negotiate to seek a reasonable and logical solution to the benefit of both parties. We have chosen the second course; that is the best way to end the war and to restore peace in Vietnam, and also an honorable way for the United States to get out of Vietnam. That is the reason why we have perseveringly participated in the negotiations for the past four years at the Paris conference on Vietnam at private meetings with the United States side. During these four years, Mr. Nixon has missed many opportunities to peacefully settle the Vietnam problem.

News conference, Paris, May 12/
The New York Times, 5-13:8.

(On the U.S. mining of North Vietnamese ports): The Vietnamese have skillful hands. As soon as the Americans drop the mines, we remove them. They drop them again. We take them out again. We have been receiving supplies over roads on which the Americans have dropped millions of tons of bombs—all to no avail.

News conference, Paris, May 23/ Los Angeles Times, 5-24:(1)12.

Xuan Thuy
North Vietnamese Ambassador to Paris peace talks

If the (U.S.) Nixon Administration really wants to disengage from the Vietnam war and to rapidly repatriate all American servicemen, in combat or in captivity, (then it should) give up aggression, stop the "Vietnamization" of the war, pull out from South Vietnam all the troops . . . stop backing the Nguyen Van Thieu bellicose puppet group (in South Vietnam).

At Paris peace talks, Jan. 6/ The New York Times, 1-7:1.

How can a big, powerful country like the United States "surrender" to a small country like Vietnam? All we want the United States to do is get out and stop interfering where it has no legitimate business. That is not "surrender."

Interview, Paris, Feb. 5/ The New York Times, 2-6:(1)3.

It is not we who use the prisoners (of war) as pawns. It is (U.S. President) Nixon who uses the prisoners as pawns in the political aims. But we should wonder why Mr. Nixon still uses the political problems for his aims. Why does he not make a statement: "Now we stop any commitments to the Saigon Administration; we will stop any support to the Saigon Administration; and we will no longer maintain this Administration." And then the Vietnamese problems will be very rapidly settled—both military questions and political questions. And then all prisoners, all American servicemen, will go home.

TV-radio interview/"Face the Nation," Columbia Broadcasting System, 2-6.

John G. Tower
United States Senator, R–Tex.

I cannot agree that those men who left their friends to suffer the hardships of Vietnam without them (by evading the draft in the U.S.) are deserving of forgiveness. These men have violated the law, and if they have found refuge in foreign lands, they have not yet been tried or punished. Some contend that to be exiled from one's homeland is punishment enough. But those who have chosen this course have done so of their own will. It is hard for me to believe that they love their country more than those who have remained within it. Those who have chosen self-exile as an alternative to military service have placed their own moral judgment above loyalty to their country. I shall not support efforts to return these men to the United States free from prosecution. If they wish to return, they should be allowed to do so; but they should remain subject to prosecution.

Human Events, 8-5:23.

Stanislaw Trepczynski
President, United Nations General Assembly

(Criticizing renewed U.S. bombing in North Vietnam): A horrible war continues to be waged against a small nation fighting for its survival. Now that peace in Indochina is possible and feasible, a new escalation of this war, so inhuman in all its aspects, jeopardizes the future of detente and carries the grave risk of increased tensions in international life.

At United Nations, N.Y., Dec. 19/ Los Angeles Times, 12-20:(1)5.

Hoang Tung
Editor, "Nhan Dan," Hanoi

(The situation in South Vietnam would be ideal if) we, the Vietnamese, could smash everything—the United States and Saigon troops and foreign mercenaries. But we are quite realistic, and we know to do that would take a much longer time. If it were up to me, I would like to see the whole of Vietnam unified and building socialism. But we are realists. We know that in South Vietnam there are certain other forces; not only Thieu and Ky, but other people. The Communists and people who are doing the resistance work must find a way to live with other people. Only in this way can we be in conformity with reality.

Interview, Hanoi/
The New York Times, 3-29:10.

John W. Vogt, Jr.
General, United States Air Force; Air Force Southeast Asia Commander

(On U.S. Indochina bombing policy): We have never gone in to hit a village where it is not absolutely necessary to do it; never when it was known to have civilians in it. We have very strict rules against hitting occupied areas; in fact, we don't do it. Even in some areas where we are asked to put in air because the enemy is there, if my FAC (forward air control) planes look in there and report back that there are civilians in it, that air does not go in. We will not deliberately put civilians in jeopardy.

The Washington Post, 12-10:(A)26.

Kurt Waldheim
Secretary General of the United Nations

This (the UN) is an organization for peace and for security in the world, and it is our duty to offer our good offices whether the parties concerned like it or not. The day will come when they will criticize us again about the war in Vietnam. But then they will not be able to say that we did not do anything. We offered our good offices.

Before UN employees, New York, April 27/
Los Angeles Times, 5-1:(2)8.

Through private unofficial channels . . . we were informed that the dikes (in North Vietnam) are being bombed (by U.S. planes); and we were informed also that, even in cases where the dikes are not directly bombed, the nearby bombing causes cracking of the dams and that in this way the result is the same as if the dikes were bombed directly . . . If these allegations are correct, it would lead to disaster in the area because it would mean that the whole plain would be flooded and thousands and thousands of people would die. This, I think, has to be avoided.

News conference, July 24/
San Francisco Examiner, 7-25:5.

George C. Wallace
Governor of Alabama

We should never have got bogged down in the war in Vietnam. We used to say years ago, "Win it or get out." If you can't win it, don't stay over there. People are not going to put up with it; they're too impatient in this country–not like the Orientals who can go 10 years and think it's a year.

Interview, Washington, Feb. 23/
The Washington Post, 3-5:(D)4.

William C. Westmoreland
General and Chief of Staff, United States Army; Former Allied Commander in Vietnam

This whole war is a war of endurance and a war of will. It is going to boil down to a matter of who can outlast whom . . . I think this war will carry on until one side feels it is exhausted, that it is spending precious natural resources with no prospect of victory, at which time there will be an accommodation, which may take several years. The side who has the stamina, or rather the will and the stamina, is going to be the side that is eventually going to prevail in Indochina . . .

Interview, Washington/
Los Angeles Times, 1-20:(2)7.

The Army has carried the major burden (of U.S. fighting in Vietnam), taking the majority of the casualties. By virtue of this fact, we have perhaps been the focal point of emotional abuse, more so than other services. The six and one-half years have put

(WILLIAM C. WESTMORELAND)

great stress and strains on the Army as an institution. We are now in a transition period in view of the fact that we are winding down our participation in the war in Vietnam. But the basic disease that has infected the Army is the extreme personnel turnover or turbulence within our ranks.

Interview, Washington/ The Dallas Times Herald, 4-16:(A)47.

We (have) learned that in fighting an undeclared war, there is no censorship of the news. The battlefield is going to be covered by the media to an extent unprecedented in the past. And this has involved a public-relations dimension which was rather new. In fact, it added another dimension to war. If it had been a declared war, perhaps it would have been different. We have learned that a limited war involving limited objectives and fought with limited means—a war in which military forces are not used to achieve victory in the traditional manner—is probably destined to be a long war; and a long war is going to try the patience of our people—which, indeed, this war has done. This is the first war ever covered by television, where the horrors of war and some of the extremes on the battlefield have been piped into the living room and into the bedroom. This dramatic coverage of the war has apparently had a marked psychological impact on our people. All of these are facts of life and lessons that we have learned from the Vietnam war.

Interview, Washington/ U.S. News & World Report, 6-19:62.

Samuel W. Yorty
Mayor of Los Angeles

(Supporting President Nixon's decision to bomb North Vietnam in response to the North's offensive in South Vietnam): The doomsayer doves, who too often sound exactly like the voice of Hanoi, should now give patriotism a higher priority than politics . . . It is time to leave carping criticism and fear-peddling to the subversives and their dupes, while the rest of us support the President in his effort to avert a disaster in Southeast Asia. If permitted to happen, (such a disaster) could trigger more bold Communist aggression in other areas . . . I suppose it is too much to expect politicians, seeking the radical left-wing vote, to actually back the President's new initiative, but one would hope they would at least hold their tongues.

News conference, Los Angeles, April 16/ Los Angeles Herald-Examiner, 4-17:(A)4.

Charles W. Yost
Former United States Ambassador/ Permanent Representative to the United Nations

If Americans are under the illusion that cease-fire really means the end of the war, that if the Communists violate it they must be punished, and that if no one else will do the punishing we must, we will soon find ourselves back in the war and up to our necks once again.

San Francisco Examiner & Chronicle, 12-24:(This World)2.

Ronald L. Ziegler
Press Secretary to the President of the United States

There are still some critics today who will not accept the facts of reality of the (Vietnam) peace proposal which the President (Nixon) has put forth. They insist on making statements and drawing conclusions based on what I refer to as unrealities and fantasy. I believe very deeply that peace in the world is too important for partisanship. Now is not the time to play politics with peace. Now is the time that the recognized leadership in the Congress of the United States and the states of the nation should unite together with the American people behind what is a reasonable and a just plan for peace.

Before Texas United Press International Editors Association, Houston, Jan. 29/ The Dallas Times Herald, 1-30:(A)28.

(On reports that U.S. planes have been deliberately bombing North Vietnamese dikes): It is obvious the North Vietnamese are attempting through their normal propaganda to claim that we are purposefully bombing dams and dikes. Every year there is some flooding in Vietnam. We have a policy: There is no targeting of dikes and dams in Vietnam.

July 20/
The New York Times, 7-21:2.

Europe

Spiro T. Agnew
Vice President of the United States

(On U.S. policy toward Greece): I think the present government of Greece is doing the kind of job that is apparently approved by the people of Greece; and how I feel about the system of government, whether it suits me, is immaterial. Foreign policy is a matter of balances and checks and power distribution in the world, and the United States has certain security and economic interests. We have friends, and we have people who have not been friendly. We try to ameliorate the situation as far as the people who have been hostile is concerned, but we would like to hold onto our friends. The Greeks have voted with the United States in the United Nations consistently.

TV-radio interview, Burbank, Calif./ "Meet the Press," National Broadcasting Company, 8-27.

L. J. Andolsek
Commissioner, Civil Service Commission of the United States

(Referring to his Yugoslav descent): We say in Yugoslavia that there are six republics, six nationalities, three alphabets, three religions, and 20 million people, all with their own independent opinion.

Washington, Jan. 7/ The Washington Post, 1-8:(E)3.

Vladimir Ashkenazy
Pianist

You in the West are so naive in thinking that Russia is improving, that Russia is getting more civilized, thinking more along the lines of the West. That's not true, I am perfectly convinced. Russia's primary object will remain the same: to make the world Communist, however they disguise their behavior by various appearances. You should always remember that their ultimate objective is not to become friends, but to subdue.

Interview, New York/ The New York Times, 1-23:(2)28.

Evangelos Averoff-Tossizza
Former Foreign Minister of Greece

In the minds of the Greeks, the (current George Papadopoulos) regime is American, created by the Americans and supported by the Americans. Everybody tells me that the Americans have only to lift a finger to bring them down.

Interview/ The New York Times, 2-6:(1)26.

Anthony Barber
Chancellor of the Exchequer of the United Kingdom

(On the new British tax cuts and business incentives): We now have a rare opportunity to secure a sustained and a faster rate of economic expansion over a considerable period of years. And indeed, a prolonged period of expansion is exactly what British industry so desperately needs to provide the foundation and the confidence for ambitious and forward-looking modernization. If we are to take full advantage of the enlarged Common Market which will be opening up for us in less than a year, one of our foremost tasks must be to improve our competitiveness as a trading nation. A major part of our strategy must therefore be to (im)prove the climate in which industry can have confidence to re-equip and expand.

Before House of Commons, London, March 21/ Los Angeles Times, 3-22:(1)18.

Alphonzo Bell
United States Representative, R–Calif.

My trip to Russia convinced me that it is quite possible to live happily and successfully as a Jew within the Soviet system, if religion and cultural heritage are abandoned. But now I believe it is impossible for Jews to live happily in Russia if they wish to practice their religion and maintain their cultural traditions . . . The cultural genocide which the Soviets are presently imposing on Jews, the severe restrictions which they are placing on the emigration of Jews to Israel . . . suggest that the government of the Soviet Union still has a way to go before becoming a free, just and fully-civilized nation.

News conference, Tel Aviv, Jan. 16/ Los Angeles Times, 1-17:(1)5.

William Blackie
Former chairman, Caterpillar Tractor Company (United States)

The creation of the (European) Common Market has been favored by the United States largely on political grounds–if the countries of Europe could tie themselves together in effective harmony, incorporating more than just a customs union, it would reduce the tensions and minimize the prospects of further wars. I believe that hope is being achieved in part, though there always is a danger that the European community could become a bloc, looking inward to itself rather than outward to a constructive place in world affairs. In my opinion, that is not happening.

Interview/ Nation's Business, August:42.

Willy Brandt
Chancellor of West Germany

(Criticizing opposition to his policy of detente with Eastern Europe and his good-will treaties with Moscow and Warsaw): The foreign policy of the government is not the simplest way, but it is the only well-prepared way to bring German policy into harmony with prevailing international tendencies . . . Nothing can stop me from continuing to work persistently for peace at home and abroad. By saying "no" to the treaties, the opposition and its arguments have run head-long into a stone wall.

Before the Bundestag (lower house of Parliament), Bonn, April 26/ The Washington Post, 4-27:(A)30.

In this phase of change, America's presence in Europe is more necessary than ever. I trust that those who carry responsibility in this country (the U.S.) will not refuse to appreciate this. American-European partnership is indispensable if America does not want to neglect its own interests and if our Europe is to forge itself into a productive system instead of again becoming a volcanic terrain of crisis, anxiety and confusion.

At celebration of the 25th anniversary of the Marshall Plan, Harvard University (United States) June 5/ The New York Times, 6-6:1.

Great leaders derive from chaos–like war or racking crises. And it is a good thing that we do not have chaos in our part of the world nowadays. This doesn't, of course, preclude the existence of leaders with great influence. It doesn't mean that everything must move toward mediocrity.

Interview, Bonn/ The New York Times, 11-19:(4)11.

Leonid I. Brezhnev
General Secretary, Communist Party of the Soviet Union

We have stated before, and confirm now, (that) an improvement of relations between the U.S.S.R. and the U.S. is possible. More than that, it is desirable; but of course, not at the expense of some third countries or peoples, not to the detriment of their lawful rights and interests . . . We are fully aware of the importance of the state of Soviet-American relations for the life of the people of both countries as well as for the entire international situation, for its further development in the direction of lasting peace or in the direction of growing military danger.

At Soviet Trade Unions Congress, Moscow, March 20/ Los Angeles Times, 3-21:(1)18.

(Criticizing West Germany for not yet ratifying its treaties with Moscow and Warsaw): The Federal Republic of (West) Germany is now faced with a choice that will determine the fate of its people and the attitudes of other states toward it for many years to come. In the final analysis, it is a choice between a policy of peace and a policy of war.

Before Russian Trade Union Congress/ Time, 4-3:31.

The policy of peaceful coexistence between states with differing systems permits maintaining and developing normal relations with the capitalist nations and resolutions of questions in dispute by peaceful means. But let no one confuse our persistence and consistency in this question with pacifism, with nonresistance to that evil which the imperialist aggressors bear to the peoples . . . The peaceableness of Soviet foreign policy is inseparable from readiness and resolution to deliver an appropriate rebuff to any aggressor.

Los Angeles Herald-Examiner, 5-21:(A)12.

You know, the problems of the day don't stop spinning in my head at night. And there are quite a few problems in a country as vast as ours. When the people in the south are demanding summer clothes, you still have to supply the northerners with fur boots. There are the big things and the small. There are joys and sorrows. Everything comes straight to us, and we must consider, discuss and find solutions. Foreign policy—that, too, makes for some work. We want peace throughout the universe, but not everyone agrees with us.

Interview/ The New York Times Magazine, 5-21:23.

(Admonishing the Soviet people to work harder to improve the lagging Soviet economy): The best-laid plans will not be fulfilled unless those who toil at machine tools or in the field, research institutes or in the service sector, put their heart and soul into their work. The energy of highly-organized labor, multiplied by love for one's country, is capable of working miracles. That is how it was during the years of the first five-year plans, during the Great Patriotic War and in the years of postwar reconstruction, years filled with the heroism and enthusiasm of the masses.

At celebration of 50th anniversary of the formation of the Soviet Union, Moscow, Dec. 21/ The New York Times, 12-24:(1)2.

Manlio Brosio
Former Secretary General, North Atlantic Treaty Organization

. . . nobody in the West dreams of using military power either to attack or to blackmail or to pressure Russia. Even when the U.S. had clear-cut military superiority over Russia, especially in the nuclear field, it never used that superiority in order to force the Russians into decisions they did not like—about the German problem, for instance. So, if the Russians keep improving their forces, it is not only for defense. It is because they want to reach complete equality with the United States and, if possible, superiority. They want to keep and widen their standing as a great, global world power, and to be able not only to defend their interests but, if need be, to impose them.

Interview, Turin, Italy/ U.S. News & World Report, 8-28:45.

It would be disastrous, and a piece of folly, to withdraw a substantial number of American troops (from Europe) until the Europeans have created some kind of collective force that would be equally effective. And even then there should remain, certainly over the next decade, an American force capable of making a substantial contribution to the defense of Europe, if the Alliance is to preserve its meaning and its effectiveness . . . European forces are not strong enough to resist an attack, even temporarily, without the help of American forces, so that the presence of the American military deterrent and American participation in the defense of Europe in case of aggression is necessary. And, given the reduced credibility of the strategic deterrent, the withdrawal of American troops would reduce the political and psychological effectiveness of the American guarantee of Europe's defense—and this would have inevitable and adverse political and psychological consequences.

Interview, Turin, Italy/
U.S. News & World Report, 8-28:47.

Alastair Buchan
Commandant, British Royal College of Defense; Former director, International Institute for Strategic Studies

Twenty years ago, the Western allies really did own the Mediterranean in the sense that almost every state within it was either a colonial possession, an ally or a Western base. Today, a decade after the crises of decolonization, Western dominance is gone and it is legitimate to be gloomy about the future.

U.S. News & World Report, 3-20:38.

Panayotis Canellopoulos
Former Premier of Greece; Leader, Greek National Radical Union Party

I don't believe the United States was responsible for the coup (of 1967 installing George Papadopoulos as Greek Premier), but 99 per cent of the Greeks do.

Interview/
The New York Times, 2-6:(1)26.

(If U.S. Secretary of State William Rogers' forthcoming trip to Greece is not accompanied by a change of attitude by the U.S. against the Greek regime), the Greek people will consider Mr. Rogers' visit not as a friendly gesture toward Greece but as an act of courtesy toward a regime which has deprived it of its liberties, and as an encouragement for further violation of the principles which made the Fourth of July—the day that Mr. Rogers selected to come to our country—a great anniversary for all peoples throughout the world who love liberty.

July 3/
The New York Times, 7-4:2.

George Colley
Minister of Finance of the Republic of Ireland

(On the possibility of Ireland's entry into the European Common Market): Membership will, if we seize its opportunities, give the Irish economy the biggest boost we have ever experienced. It will open a whole new world of opportunity to our young people; it will broaden our social, economic and cultural horizons; and it will have a deep and far-reaching impact on the psychological, educational and social outlook of all our people.

The Christian Science Monitor, 5-5:6.

Robert Conquest
Former British diplomat; Authority on the Soviet Union

. . . if you look at their (the Soviet's) military forces and their arms production, it's obvious they have built up far greater capabilities than are compatible with a reasonably peaceful policy toward the rest of the world. The Russians talk about wanting to strengthen their economy; and one of the extraordinary things about all this is that their economy isn't capable of supporting the current and immense level of forces they maintain. The military effort shakes the economy terrifically. The Russians know this, but they keep on turning out more and more arms. And that raises the question: What are they going to do with all of this accumulated power? The arms are there and mustn't be wasted. They don't want to provoke a nuclear war, but they have to do

(ROBERT CONQUEST)

something. So they lean on the West; they use their arms as pawns on the chessboard of world power. The U.S. and the West have arms, but they don't want to fight. All they can do is say, "Don't push us too hard." So, if you have a crisis in Iran or anywhere else along the Soviet border, you might have a choice between sending in forces to fight or letting the Russians have their way.

Interview/
U.S. News & World Report, 5-22:33.

I think Rosa Luxemburg, one of the early German Communists, put her finger on it when she said: "If you're not allowed to hear anything except your own voice, your intellect starts degenerating." That's what has happened in Russia. These people, these leaders are all products—a sort of ectoplasm—of the Party apparatus. They are a very narrow lot, and their horizons are extraordinarily limited. They've had no real experience in dealing with foreign countries. (Former Soviet Premier Nikita) Khrushchev may not have been the most brilliant statesman in the world, but he had been at the heights of power for 20 or 30 years and he had relatively broad views. The current generation of leaders has none of that. (Party General Secretary Leonid) Brezhnev and his sort are the constrained, quiet, dull, move-slowly-if-at-all types. The logic of their position and the momentum of their power push them continually in dangerous directions, while their efforts toward a detente, which is as much in their real interest as in ours, have—so far anyway—been pettifogging, spasmodic and generally inadequate. These little men in the Kremlin seem to suffer from political constipation. But this small-mindedness goes with surly devotion to an obsolete ideology, sullen delusions of grandeur, and—most important of all—a vast and dangerous weaponry.

Interview/
U.S. News & World Report, 5-22:34.

Constantine II
Exiled King of Greece

(On his policies if he returned to Greece): As a modern King, I shall neither have nor do I want executive power to impose my ideas on anyone. But when, with the help of God, I shall return to my beloved people, I will listen and I will learn from those who have studied the wisdom of the past and the sciences of the future.

Verona, Italy, Oct. 14/
The Dallas Times Herald, 10-15:(A)3.

Robert Cooper
Chairman,
Alliance Party of Northern Ireland

What internment (of suspected trouble-makers by the government) did was consolidate the mass of Catholic opinion into a united movement with the IRA, and Catholics who had no dealings with the IRA found themselves involved or sympathetic. It was highly emotional, because in the past it was the method used by the Unionist governments solely against the Catholics. It was, in fact, the beginning of the end for (former Northern Irish Prime Minister) Brian Faulkner. It was his last throw. He told the British that this was the only answer to terrorism, and the British accepted this. When it became clear that internment wasn't the answer, the British took over.

The New York Times, 8-10:3.

Earl of Cromer
British Ambassador to
the United States

We (in NATO) cannot afford to be complacent . . . it is only 10 years since (former Soviet Premier Nikita) Khrushchev threatened to take over Berlin by force, only 3½ years since (Soviet Communist Party Secretary Leonid) Brezhnev took over Czechoslovakia by force. The proportion of Soviet GNP devoted to defense expenditure has continued to rise steadily . . . While we are faced with a growing Soviet military might, it would be foolhardy indeed to relax our own defenses.

News conference, Los Angeles, Jan. 19/
Los Angeles Times, 1-20:(2)4.

Bernadette Devlin
Member of British Parliament from Northern Ireland

(Referring to the killing of 13 civilians by British troops in Londonderry): Both the provisional and official wings of the IRA have said they will each kill 13 (British) paratroops in vengeance for those who died on Sunday. That is 26 coffins coming home to England—and I won't shed a tear for any one of them.

News conference, London, Jan. 31/
The Dallas Times Herald, 2-1:(A)1.

Milovan Djilas
Author; Former Vice President of Yugoslavia

(On the possibility of Yugoslavia's return to a strict centralist system): The youth is alienated and unresponsive to the old revolutionary slogans; and the new bourgeoisie does not want the clock turned back. Life is simply marching in another direction. (President) Tito will talk and talk, but in the end he will strike a balanced middle way.

Newsweek, 1-17:37.

Alec Douglas-Home
Foreign Secretary of the United Kingdom

(Regarding Malta's terms for allowing Britain to retain its base on the island): To allow ourselves to be bid up and up in price for military advantages which, in modern conditions, do not apply is quite simply not on.

Auchterarder, Scotland, Jan. 7/
The New York Times, 1-8:2.

(On the desire of Gibraltar to remain under British rule): One of the strange things of life in the modern world . . . is that there are some people who like to be colonies of Great Britain.

News conference, Madrid, Feb. 29/
The New York Times, 3-1:7.

Charles K. Duncan
Admiral, United States Navy; Commander, NATO navies in the North Atlantic

NATO's ability to control the sea has been taken for granted—but it cannot be taken for granted any longer. Control of the entire North Atlantic, as was done in World War II, is simply no longer a viable strategic operation, faced as we are with the Soviet maritime capability.

The Dallas Times Herald, 5-23:(A)3.

Elizabeth II
Queen of England

(Referring to Britain and France): We may drive on different sides of the road, but we are going the same way.

At state banquet,
Versailles, France, May 15/
The New York Times, 5-16:43.

Nihat Erim
Prime Minister of Turkey

The question of allowing or not the Soviets to maintain a base in Cyprus can only be discussed and decided upon by a constitutional Cypriot government in accordance with the provisions of the internationally-guaranteed Cyprus Constitution on foreign and defense-policy matters. However, it may be said that, if such a hypothetical development takes place, the already precarious power balance in the eastern Mediterranean will be still more precarious.

Interview, Ankara/
U.S. News & World Report, 3-27:93.

Brian Faulkner
Prime Minister of Northern Ireland

(Concerning anti-government violence in Northern Ireland): Internment is a measure that's repugnant to me, but it's a policy that we must carry out. The people who are saying that internment must be ended do not say what should be put in its place to end violence. And we've got to end the violence by whatever means are open to us.

Interview, Belfast, Jan. 19/
The New York Times, 1-20:6.

(On the violence in Northern Ireland): All political leaders of our community must decide very soon—for time is not unlimited—whether to dig still deeper trenches for a long and bloody struggle, or whether to show some real courage and generosity. But I warn again: We are not to be coerced, and we will never surrender our destiny into the hands of the gunman or those who seek to profit from his activities.

At Stormont (Parliament),
Belfast, Feb. 8/
The New York Times, 2-9:3.

(Arguing against reunification of Northern Ireland with the Republic of Ireland): Our history, our tradition, our economic interests link us firmly with Great Britain. We see it as an absurdity in the modern world to cast off from a powerful and outward-looking community to join our destinies with a weak and inward-looking one. What we see of the Irish Republic we do not like. The whole ethos of the Republican state, the structure of its Constitution and of its laws—these things are repugnant to us.

At Stormont (Parliament),
Belfast, Feb. 8/
The New York Times, 2-9:3.

(On the assumption of direct rule of Northern Ireland by Britain): I told him (British Prime Minister Edward Heath) that it would be widely construed as an acceptance of totally baseless criticism of our stewardship; that it would be seen by the IRA and others as a first and major step on the road to a terrorist victory.

Before Stormont (Parliament),
Belfast, March 24/
San Francisco Examiner, 3-24:1.

(On the takeover of direct control of Northern Ireland by Britain): We feel our endeavors to provide a just government for Ulster have been betrayed from London. We share the resentment you feel, and we understand the bewilderment of the people of Ulster . . . The government of Ulster is about to pass, temporarily at least, into other hands. We stood firm and we stood together. We did what we believed to be right.

Addressing the public,
Belfast, March 28/
The New York Times, 3-29:9.

Vic Feather
General secretary,
British Trades Union Congress

(On the fact that no written constitution rules Britain): We are not a law-abiding people; we are a decently-behaved people.

The Washington Post, 4-22:(A)12.

Andrew J. Goodpaster
General, United States Army;
Supreme Allied Commander/Europe

Despite all the talk of detente and accommodation, the last few years have been marked by a continuing and disturbing growth in Russian military strength. The Soviets may be talking more quietly just now, but they are carrying a big stick—one which is in fact getting bigger . . . In 1972 we face on the one hand the prospect of continuing negotiations with their accompanying aura of euphoria and wishful thinking; and on the other hand growing Soviet forces—the strongest military power the world has ever seen—and a Soviet leadership ready and willing to use that power.

Heidelberg, West Germany, Nov. 8/
The Dallas Times Herald, 11-9:(A)4.

Andrei A. Grechko
Minister of Defense of the Soviet Union

Thanks to the principled and flexible foreign policy of the Soviet Union and other socialist states, as well as to the vigorous activities of progressive forces of the world, some relaxation of tension has been achieved of late. However, aggressive imperialist forces are still active in the world. They stubbornly resist a relaxation of international tension and any peace-loving actions by the Soviet Union and other socialist countries, wage a shameful war in Indochina, prevent the settlement of the Middle East crisis, heat up and unleash armed conflicts. The Communist Party and the Soviet government are making proper conclusions from this and are taking necessary steps toward the further strengthening of the country's defense capacity.

On 55th anniversary of Bolshevik Revolution, Moscow, Nov. 7/ Los Angeles Herald-Examiner, 11-7:(A)15.

William Hamilton
Member of British Parliament

If I had the chance to debate the monarchy on television with Prince Philip (Queen Elizabeth's husband), I would ask him how he justifies the money Parliament gives him and his family. I would tell him that we encourage them to breed like rabbits. The hereditary principle in the monarchy is less selective than a stud farm; there you can at least choose your stock. In a hereditary monarchy, we have to take what comes along . . . I don't think there's any hope of the monarchy disappearing in the immediate future. They have a very excellent public relations officer in Prince Philip, who is full of glittering repartee; he is very good at it. I think there is going to be an upsurge among the common people when they see how badly this question of royal wealth is handled and how they refuse to discuss their enormous private wealth. The ordinary people are going to react, and in 20 to 30 years I see the end of the monarchy—or in 50 years at most.

Before Foreign Press Association, London, Jan. 26/ Los Angeles Times, 1-27:(1)22.

Edward Heath
Prime Minister of the United Kingdom

(There) must be a Europe which is strong and confident within itself, a Europe in which we shall be working for the progressive relaxation and elimination of tension between East and West, a Europe alive to its great responsibilities in the common struggle of humanity for a better life. This ceremony (Britain's entry into the Common Market) marks an end and also a beginning: an end to divisions which have stricken Europe for centuries, a beginning of another stage in the construction of a new and a greater united Europe.

Brussels, Jan. 22/ The New York Times, 1-23:(1)2.

The people in Northern Ireland are different in type and religion from the south (the Republic of Ireland). There is no historical or logical justification for saying that it must be one country; you might as well say Spain ought to absorb Portugal . . .

Interview, London, Feb. 25/ The New York Times, 2-27:(1)2.

(On the assumption of direct rule of Northern Ireland by Britain): We must make a completely fresh start . . . if we are to break out of the vicious circle of violence and yet more violence . . . Now is your (Northern Irish people's) chance; a chance for fairness; a chance for prosperity; and above all a chance for peace; a chance at last to bring the bombings and killings to an end.

Broadcast address to the nation, March 24/The Washington Post, 3-25:(A)1.

Let us be quite clear about the role of the British government as the sovereign

(EDWARD HEATH)

power in Northern Ireland. We as a government can, and must, provide the framework for an orderly and peaceful future. But it is only a framework, and it is the people of Northern Ireland alone who can decide to make use of it. We as a government can give an assurance that the status of Northern Ireland as part of the United Kingdom will not be altered except by consent. This solemn assurance I repeat today. We as a government can provide the economic help which is needed to repair the damage done by violence and to enable the people of Northern Ireland to use their talents to the full. This help we have given and will continue to give. We as a government can work to bring together the different groups in Northern Ireland to decide how the future administration of the province should be ordered. This too we are doing. And, meanwhile, the security forces continue to do everything within their power to keep violence in check . . . But those who suppose that the government or the Army or the other security forces can by some sudden move or change of tactics bring violence to an end are living in an unreal world. In the present situation I ask the people of Northern Ireland themselves to join in the campaign against violence. I ask them, despite their weariness, to find the determination to say to the men of violence: "We reject your methods, and so long as you use these methods we reject you. So long as you use these methods we will do our utmost to expose and defeat you." I know that all of us in the government feel deep personal sympathy for the sufferings of many thousands of people in Northern Ireland. I believe that this sympathy is shared by everyone in this country. But the British government and the British people have a right to ask the people of Northern Ireland to assert themselves against the men of violence—to assert themselves in their towns, in their streets, in their families, to frustrate their tactics, to refuse them sanctuary, to unite in order to defeat intimidation. This act of assertion will require real courage. But the alternative is to allow men of violence to continue to trample underfoot the daily life of the province and its future. This act of assertion against violence is essential if the people of Northern Ireland are to bring their own destiny within their own control.

The Christian Science Monitor, 8-2:20.

The Community (European Common Market) is not, it must not be, simply a mercantile arrangement designed to profit its individual members. It is a means of harnessing the experience and the enterprise of our separate nations into an entity that will occupy a place in the world that corresponds with our heritage.

At Common Market summit meeting, Paris, Oct. 19/ San Francisco Examiner, 10-19:1.

(The enemies of Northern Ireland) are those who think they can achieve their muddled aims by atrocity and murder. The provisionals (provisional IRA) allege that they kill and maim to bring about a united Ireland; but they only deepen the division in Irish society, and because of this they are further from their aim than ever before. The Protestant extremists say they want to protect their own people and preserve their institutions; but all they do is strengthen the IRA and make a mockery of loyalty to the Crown.

Before political and business leaders, Holywood, Northern Ireland, Nov. 16/ The New York Times, 11-17:5.

Martin J. Hillenbrand
Assistant Secretary for European Affairs, Department of State of the United States

Just as the peace of Europe is crucial to the peace of the world, peace in the Mediterranean is crucial to stability in Europe . . . Any significant weakening of the U.S. posture in the area would create a dangerous kind of invitation to Soviet risk-taking and adventurism.

U.S. News & World Report, 3-20:39.

Patrick J. Hillery
Foreign Minister of the Republic of Ireland

(Referring to the Unionist Party of Northern Ireland which wants Ulster to remain a British province): The deepest concerns of the Unionist community in Ireland will have to be, and can be, met by an eventual accommodation with the national majority—by negotiation and on terms acceptable to both. And the deepest concerns and desires of the Unionist community in Ireland cannot be met any other way—certainly not by coercion or by the intercommunal violence which threatens all Irishmen with common ruin.

At United Nations, N.Y., Oct. 10/ The New York Times, 10-11:6.

Erich Honecker
First Secretary, Communist Party of East Germany

Things are simply like this: Between the socialist (East) German Democratic Republic and the imperialist (West) German Federal Republic there is no unity and can be no unity. That is as clear as the fact that the rain falls to the earth and does not flow up to the clouds.

Before East German troops, Prora, East Germany/ The Washington Post, 1-7:(A)20.

(On the possibility of future reunification of East and West Germany): As far as I can see, this question does not arise at all. The G.D.R. (East Germany) will continue to develop on a socialist basis as an inseparable part of the socialist community. On the other hand, not only the present Bonn (West German) government but its opposition stresses the need for basing West German relations on the Western Alliance. We think that on this issue history has already made the decision. And we think this is an advantage to the world—to see two independent sovereign states on German soil.

Interview, Berlin, Nov. 22/ The New York Times, 11-23:14.

Huang Hua
Communist Chinese Ambassador to the United Nations

(Referring to the Soviet Union): The aggressive designs of the social imperialists know no bounds. Today they can bully Pakistan—tomorrow other nations of the subcontinent. Today they're infiltrating into the Mediterranean and the Indian Ocean—tomorrow the Pacific and the Atlantic. With honey in the mouth and a dagger in the heart, they have committed aggression and subversion in Africa and the Middle East. Some of their schemes have already been revealed, and others are now being revealed.

At United Nations, N.Y., Aug. 25/ Los Angeles Times, 8-26:(1)15.

Hubert H. Humphrey
United States Senator, D–Minn.

The Russians do not want to start a war, but they don't have to. India now seems to be within their influence, and they have boxed in the (Communist) Chinese, with India in the underbelly of Asia. Russia wants a neutralized Vietnam. They then can turn their attention to the Mediterranean. Europe could not be secure if North Africa went Communist.

Interview, Los Angeles, May 23/ Los Angeles Herald-Examiner, 5-24:(A)5.

I am concerned about the cost of our (U.S.) involvement or of our commitment to Europe; but I am more concerned about what would happen to any commitment in Western Europe or to our own security if we unilaterally, all by ourself, without any regard to what the Soviet Union and its allies would do, if we made large-scale reductions of American forces. Therefore, my position has been, yes, let us seek to reduce those forces, but let us do it through negotiation, tough negotiation, just exactly as we were able to do on the antiballistic missile system. We have proven . . . that when we stick with it, when we persevere, when we don't back off, when we have the will and the strength, that we can negotiate reductions in

(HUBERT H. HUMPHREY)

arms, we can make agreements with the Soviet Union, we can do many things that lend themselves to the pursuit of peace.

TV-radio interview, Washington/ "Meet the Press," National Broadcasting Company, 7-9.

Gustav Husak
First Secretary, Communist Party of Czechoslovakia

Over the past year, we can say we have performed a good deal of honest work in the political and social consolidation of our socialist society, in the dynamic development of our economy and in the strengthening and increase of the standard of living of our people . . . (But) we do not succumb to cheap self-satisfaction or self-praise over the results achieved.

At May Day rally, Prague, May 1/ The Washington Post, 5-2:(C)2.

Jacob K. Javits
United States Senator, R–N.Y.

The Soviet Union has almost a paranoic fear of Germany; and the presence of United States troops in Europe tends, notwithstanding what they may say, to give them a sense of reassurance that they will not have to face a super-nationalistic Germany at any time and, therefore, that they do not have to pursue as aggressive a policy toward Germany as they would otherwise feel they have to pursue.

News conference, Bonn, West Germany, Jan. 5/ The New York Times, 1-6:17.

. . . the strictly security-and-defense aspects of NATO as a military defense organization are now subject to great doubt, especially by the youth of Europe and the youth of America. NATO has a bad name as strictly a defense organization because young people feel that to talk in terms of an attack by the Soviet Union on Western Europe, circa 1972, is just unrealistic; they just don't believe the Russians have any such design, and they believe if the Russians took Europe, they might suffer the fate of Hitler, and that the Russians have a little bit more prudence than that.

Interview, Rome/ San Francisco Examiner, 1-6:20.

David M. Kennedy
United States Ambassador/Permanent Representative to the North Atlantic Treaty Organization

(On drastic U.S. troop reductions in Europe): This would be very badly taken by our European allies and very widely appreciated by the Russians. I don't think a few troops either way would make a great deal of difference, but we must keep strong in this period as we move into the (European security) conference with Russia. Very large changes would be unthinkable and would have a very serious effect on the alliance. We cannot permit it to happen. The time to move downward is when we get some sort of agreement.

Interview, Brussels, July 10/ Los Angeles Herald-Examiner, 7-10:(A)5.

Edward M. Kennedy
United States Senator, D–Mass.

We (the U.S.) sent the aircraft-carrier *Enterprise* to the Indian Ocean last December, and we intervened in other ways to try to tilt the balance between India and Pakistan, nations with whom we have had long and friendly ties. But by some cruel irony, today we are unwilling even to make our good offices available to mediate a crisis over Ulster (Northern Ireland) that involves two of our closest friends, Britain and Ireland.

Before House Foreign Affairs Subcommittee on Europe, Washington, Feb. 28/ The Dallas Times Herald, 2-28:(A)8.

Henry A. Kissinger
Assistant to the President of the United States for National Security Affairs

Although we do not expect it (the Soviet

Union violating understandings and agreements reached during the just-concluded U.S.-Soviet summit meeting in Moscow), we are leaving open the possibility that we can go back to where we were in our relations with the Soviet Union. We are not letting down our guard; but we are leaving with a very positive attitude. We are not trying to be sentimental. Looking at all the dangers, all the things that can go wrong, we nevertheless believe it may have turned the page in our relationship.

News conference en route to Iran from the Soviet Union, May 30/ The New York Times, 5-31:8.

We have, of course, always considered our relationships with Europe a cardinal aspect of American policy and the cornerstone of the whole structure of peace . . . (President Nixon's conviction is) that, whatever progress we (are) making in our dealings with other nations, similar and preferably greater progress has to be made in European-American relationships. We are now at the end of the period in which military security alone could be the cement of Western relationships.

News conference, Washington, Sept. 16/ The Washington Post, 12-13:(A)6.

Jacques Kosciusko-Morizet
French Ambassador to the United States

At a time when Russians and Americans agree on their strategic problems, the defense of Western Europe increasingly requires Europeans to do their share in the common effort. France has understood this for a long time. Alone, without help, without access to secrets, she decided to make the technological effort needed to develop a deterrent system which was indispensable for her own defense, for her own independence, and also valuable for the protection of peace and liberty in Europe. This defense system is now in the final stages of completion . . . Those who have visited the battlefields of France will understand why in our nuclear age we have developed our own responsibility, on our own authority, the only defense capable of deterring an aggressor—that is, the atomic weapon. I cited this defense effort because it demonstrates both our will to survive as a nation and our concern with helping to construct a strong Western Europe, an independent Europe which, to use the words of the President of the Republic, will cease to be a pawn and become a link . . . We hope that this Europe, which we want to bring along with us in the task of cooperation with the Third World, will follow our example and also be a link between East and West. And of course, we think that it must first of all, like us, reaffirm and strengthen its traditional friendship with the United States.

July 14/ The Washington Post, 7-27:(A)18.

Alexei N. Kosygin
Premier of the Soviet Union

How effective the agreements and understandings reached (during the current U.S.-Soviet summit meeting) are translated into life and serve peace will be, of course, of great importance. Any agreement, any treaty only leaves a trace in history when its proclaimed principles and intentions become the content of the practical activities of states. So may the agreements we reached be just such agreements.

Toasting U.S. President Nixon at state dinner during U.S.-Soviet summit meeting, Moscow, May 26/ The New York Times, 5-27:9.

Jens Otto Krag
Premier of Denmark

(On why some Danes may vote against Denmark's entry into the Common Market): There is . . . the feeling that this is a very good society here in Denmark, perhaps a better one than in the rest of Europe, and some people will vote "no" to preserve the present state of things. But they don't realize that Europe is changing—whether Denmark agrees or not. The only alternative for us is having some influence on events by

(JENS OTTO KRAG)

participating or having no influence and being shut out in the cold.

Interview, Lyngby, Denmark, Sept. 28/ The New York Times, 9-29:22.

Bruno Kreisky
Chancellor of Austria

(My aim is the) total liquidation of poverty by the installation of the modern welfare state. It must be done in a systematic way, with a restructuring of the economy and the re-creation of our scientific life to take advantage of the vast new opportunities opened up by science and research. We have to jump faster over the barriers created by the old conservatism in our universities. We have to do much more in our health services, for we still are behind Sweden, Denmark and Holland in average age, and our child mortality is too high.

Interview, Vienna/ The Christian Science Monitor, 1-15:7.

Europe is today a continent without war. We have reached a certain degree of detente, and therefore the time is ripe to see whether there are chances for furthering progress. Conferences can lead to some results in Europe only because here the problems involved are not as complicated as in other continents. There are so many questions to discuss, and nothing will happen. You see, if somewhere there is a war or a warlike situation, you need decisions, you need a certain speed. But in Europe things are not in a situation where you need immediate decisions.

Interview, Vienna/ Los Angeles Times, 11-19:(K)1.

Melvin R. Laird
Secretary of Defense of the United States

We cannot eliminate overnight the profound differences that separate us (the U.S. and the Soviet Union). We and the Soviets are now and will remain for some time, if not adversaries, then at least political-military opponents with different global strategies. The true question confronting us is not whether it is possible to have instant revolution in our relations with the Soviet Union. The question instead is whether we can manage our relationship so that we resolve what can be resolved and control what cannot.

Before Cincinnati Council on World Affairs, March 10/ The Washington Post, 3-11:(A)3.

Christopher Layton
British representative to European Common Market Executive Commission

We (Britain) lost our world role and we want to belong to Europe. The British government is really keen about Europe. I believe it is firmly committed, after the great political battle we just went through (for British entry into the Common Market), to make the community work and to get something out of it. For the last six years, the Commission has been frustrated in what it has been trying to do. The people here feel depressed and frustrated. Everybody is waiting for us (the British), and we've been waiting too and doing a lot of thinking. If there is a new input of energy, this could be important in shaping things to come. We're given the great chance to be the catalysts in the process.

Interview, Brussels/ The New York Times, 1-21:51.

Irving Lehrman
President, Synagogue Council of America

. . . it is clear that the majority of Soviet Jews wish to remain in the Soviet Union as loyal citizens of that country. However, they demand the basic right to develop those religious institutions which will assure their religious survival. It is the denial of this right, and not a desire to aggravate the cold war, that has made the situation of Soviet Jews an international issue.

April 27/
The New York Times, 4-28:2.

Joseph Luns
Secretary General, North Atlantic Treaty Organization

. . . there is as yet in Europe no central political power or common will. We may regret this . . . but it is wishful thinking to expect Europe to become unified and to develop overnight that common political will on which defense . . . historically depends.

Before National Press Club, Washington, Feb. 1/
The Washington Post, 2-2:(A)13.

The Soviet Union has been conducting a generation-long campaign to ease the U.S. out of Western Europe and to induce feelings of neutralism among Europeans. The Russians probably want, for the time being, to arrive at a *modus vivendi* in Europe. But they would also like to promote neutralism by reassuring everyone—particularly American public opinion—that it is now safe to begin phasing U.S. troops out of Europe . . . The Russians' first objective is a U.S. withdrawal. And if we can believe their own Party resolutions, their next objective is Soviet supremacy in Europe. This does not mean a classic invasion of Western Europe. But if Russia becomes the paramount military power in Europe, which would automatically become the case if U.S. troops went home, it does not require much imagination to see how a militarily-weakened West Europe would opt for neutralism—in political jargon, "Finlandization"—and be gradually compelled to do Russia's bidding.

Interview/Newsweek, 7-10:42.

The present system of security based on cooperation between North America and Europe has insured an unprecedented period of peace, and it must be maintained. We cannot accept that it be replaced by what the other side chooses to call an all-European security system. Such a system, pursued systematically by the Soviet Union, would mean the exclusion of our American and Canadian friends from the continent and lead, I am convinced, to the slow but certain substitution of the *pax atlantica* by an essentially different *pax russica.* Let us not forget that, in spite of the current abundance of negotiations, the Soviets and their Warsaw Pact allies continue to assemble, exercise and modernize the mightiest military force the world has ever seen. The Soviet armed forces constitute a concentration of military power that goes far beyond reasonable requirements for national security or defense of her borders. It is difficult to reconcile this situation with the Soviet Union's professed desire for detente; but it remains a fact we cannot ignore.

At NATO meeting, Istanbul/
Los Angeles Herald-Examiner, 10-13:(A)8.

Jack Lynch
Prime Minister of the Republic of Ireland

We do not intend to go to war (over Northern Ireland), but the activities of British soldiers could lead to a war situation . . . We have not sought support from Communist countries, but naturally we will have to consider the situation if we cannot get support from normally friendly countries.

News conference, Dublin, Feb. 4/
Los Angeles Times, 2-5:(1)16.

(Referring to those responsible for terrorist bombings in Northern Ireland): These inhuman people seem incapable to comprehend that no ideal (such as the reunification of Ireland) justifies such wanton and indiscriminate killing. It is a sad reflection on us all that it is not just one killing after another, or one bombing after another, but the scales of such bombings that shock our conscience.

Before Fianna Fail Party, Mullingar, Ireland, March 5/
The Washington Post, 3-6:(A)16.

(JACK LYNCH)

British takeover of the provincial administration in Northern Ireland is a step toward a united Ireland. It should help dissolve barriers—personal and economic—between the North and South, although it could take a long time . . . I believe that the only answer to the problems we face as a nation, North and South, is an Ireland united by agreement, in independence; an Ireland in a close and friendly relationship with Britain; an Ireland which will be a member with Britain of the enlarged European Communities.

Interview/
Los Angeles Herald-Examiner, 5-10:(A)6.

(On the approval by the voters of Ireland's entry into the European Common Market): This is a demonstration of the political realism of the Irish people. It shows there is a spirit of enterprise and idealism in our country. I am proud to have the honor of leading our people as they take their place in this community of free people.

May 11/
The New York Times, 5-12:3.

(On the just-concluded vote in Ireland to disestablish the Roman Catholic Church from its special position and thus allay some of the fears of predominantly-Protestant Northern Ireland about reunification): The decisive vote shows that there is a growing disposition for change among the people in this part of Ireland. The results will strengthen the hand of all, in North and South, who are working for peace and reconciliation among all the people of Ireland . . . That message rings out loud and clear for all to hear and understand.

San Francisco Examiner & Chronicle,
12-17:(This World)21.

Malcolm Mackintosh
Consultant, International Institute for Strategic Studies, London; Authority on Soviet Affairs

The Soviet Union sees nothing in its relationship with the United States which should, in its own eyes, weaken its right and, indeed, its duty to expand its power wherever it can—without leading to a military confrontation with the United States or NATO. It feels itself entirely free to go on strengthening the Warsaw Pact, expanding its position in the Mediterranean, expanding its influence in the Middle East and continuing its assistance to North Vietnam. I see no sign out of this summit (meeting between U.S. President Nixon and Soviet leaders in Moscow) which could suggest that the Soviet Union feels that it has got to pull in its horns or slacken in anything . . . In the sense the Soviet government has no intention of going to war, we are in a generation of peace. In the sense that the Soviet Union has negotiated as an equal with the United States, we are in an era of negotation. But these phrases should not conceal the true nature of Soviet foreign policy, which still operates on a largely opportunistic basis—to gain whatever political influence it can find anywhere in the world. It would be more accurate to say that we are in the middle of a period in which the Soviet Union, in its new-found strength as a superpower, follows a generally expansionist policy—particularly vis-a-vis areas like the Mediterranean, the Middle East and the Indian subcontinent.

Interview, London/
U.S. News & World Report, 6-12:71.

Sean MacStiofain
Chief of staff, Provisional Irish Republican Army in Northern Ireland

(On Britain's takeover of direct rule of Northern Ireland): Our operations will continue until there is a complete withdrawal of British troops from the streets of Northern Ireland. (Direct London rule) will make it clear to the Irish people who the real enemy is.

Belfast, March 24/
The Dallas Times Herald, 3-24:(A)1.

Any speculation on a truce in Northern Ireland is complete rot. Peace shall only be restored when the three points (withdrawal of British troops from Ulster, total amnesty for all political prisoners, the right of Irishmen to decide their own future) issued by us March 10 are accepted by the British government. Until then, we fight.

Belfast, March 25/
San Francisco Examiner, 3-25:1.

Makarios III
President of Cyprus

(Referring to Greece's attempts to gain more influence in Cypriot affairs): There may be various plans behind the scenes to impose political ideas on the Greek Cypriot population contrary to the people's will. But all these plans will fail. There is no power able to bend the resistance of the Greek Cypriot people.

Nicosia, Feb. 15/
Los Angeles Herald-Examiner, 2-16:(A)4.

Franco Maria Malfatti
President, European
Common Market Commission

Our edifice (the Common Market) is not, and cannot be, built for trade alone . . . We (must) operate with all our strength and with an unflinching will to achieve the economic integration and political unification of our countries . . . Divided, we will be no more than spectators on the fringe of history.

At signing of treaty bringing Britain, Norway, Denmark and Ireland into the Common Market, Brussels, Jan. 22/
The Washington Post, 1-23:(A)1.

Andre Malraux
Author; Former Minister of
State for Culture of France

The capital fact of our times is the death of Europe, and this cannot be avoided by any foreseeable revolutionary trend. When I was 20 years old, the United States was approximately in the position of Japan today in terms of world importance. It was not yet a superpower. Europe was at the heart of things, and the superpower was the British Empire. But now all the dominating forces in today's world are foreign to Europe. The greatest power is the United States, and then, next in line, there is the Soviet Union. Europe has virtually disappeared as a factor, and it took astonishingly little time for this change to come about. Two centuries ago, the United States was not even a nation; now it is a colossus.

Interview, Paris/
The New York Times, 1-21:47.

Sicco L. Mansholt
President, European
Common Market Commission

If Europe can reach production without pollution, then we must do it. If others do not choose slower expansion in order to preserve the quality of life, then there will be conflict. I don't want Europe to be protectionist, but I think Europe must protect itself—not against others, but to force others to go in similar directions.

News conference/
Time, 4-10:29.

Reginald Maudling
Home Secretary of the
United Kingdom

. . . the fact is that Northern Ireland is part of the United Kingdom, and the Army of the United Kingdom is always and will always be available to maintain law and order in any part of the United Kingdom . . . No doubt, people who believe in a united Ireland are sincere and perfectly entitled to believe in it. But what no one is entitled to do is to impose it by force, brutality and terror and murder.

Before Radio Industries Club, London, Feb. 29/
Los Angeles Herald-Examiner, 3-1:(A)5.

Kevin McCorry
Chairman, Civil Rights Association of Northern Ireland

The impact of internment (of suspected trouble-makers by the government) divided —and is still dividing—the North of Ireland as never before. It was clearly the last death-act of the Unionist government and spelled that government's end forever . . . unless internment is going to end quickly, the minority (Catholic) population will never have any faith in the good intentions of the British. Internment's got to end before any progress is made.

The New York Times, 8-10:3.

George S. McGovern
United States Senator, D–S.D.; Democratic Presidential nominee

The American commitment to the defense of Western Europe is simply a fact that is beyond discussion. The United States would never allow Europe to be overrun by armed aggression; I don't see how anyone can have the least doubt about that.

Interview/ The New York Times, 8-12:22.

For the sake of a dubious short-term military interest, we (the U.S.) have helped to perpetuate Portugal's colonial rule in Africa. We have helped to consolidate Portugal's dictatorial power over its own people; and in the process we have forfeited our good name and image as the protector of the rights of man. Although the Senate is challenging President Nixon's unilateral agreement with Portugal for the lease of naval and air-base rights in the Azores, it is clear that Portugal will still receive at least $400 million in credits which its war-strained economy greatly needs. This is not aid to benefit the people of poverty-stricken Portugal. This is aid to continue the Portuguese government's colonial rule in Africa. I am in favor of humanitarian aid to the Portuguese people; but the United States must not and cannot continue to involve itself in the illegitimate, immoral and reckless adventures of a military dictatorship.

Oct. 2/ The Washington Post, 10-3:(A)10.

We no longer need to maintain 319,000 American troops in Europe to deter aggression, 27 years after the Second World War. But the way we reduce our forces—and share burdens more equally—is critical to the future of the Alliance (NATO) and to European security. The key to force reductions on the side of the Warsaw Pact does not lie in the number of American troops stationed in the West; rather it lies in the cohesion, cooperation and common purpose of the Western Alliance. If we make some force reductions, yet strengthen these attitudes and practices, then there is nothing the Soviet Union can do to weaken us or our allies, or to reduce our security.

Campaigning for the forthcoming Presidential election, Cleveland/ U.S. News & World Report, 10-23:99.

Richard M. Nixon
President of the United States

On balance . . . I have concluded that Soviet willingness to take positive steps toward peace in the past year makes a meeting at the highest level timely, particularly in arms limitation and economic cooperation. That is why, for the first time, a President of the United States will visit Moscow. I will go to that meeting in May with no naive illusions but with some reasonable expectations. Our relations with the Soviet Union were helped by the fact that our two nations have had long-established communication. Because we deeply understood what our real differences were, we could move to negotiate them.

Radio address, Washington, Feb. 9/ The Washington Post, 2-10:(A)13.

. . . we (the U.S. and Soviet Union) do not just meet in an atmosphere of good will, which I know we shall have; we do not just meet to conclude agreements, which I hope we shall conclude. We meet to begin a new age in the relationship between our two great and powerful nations . . . Our two peoples learned to admire each other when we joined together to defeat a common enemy in a time of war (World War II). We learned to respect each other as adversaries in a time of tension after the war. Let us now learn to work with each other in a time of peace. Let us remember, as we begin to lift the burden of armed confrontation from both our peoples, we shall lift the hopes for peace of all the peoples of the world. Never before have two peoples had a greater challenge or a greater goal. Let us be worthy of the hopes of the Soviet people, the American people and all the people on this earth as we work together toward the goal of a peaceful world.

Toast at dinner during U.S.-Soviet summit meeting, Moscow, May 22/ The Washington Post, 5-23:(A)19.

Ian Paisley
Member of Northern Irish Parliament

If the sectarian Constitution of the 26 counties (of the Republic of Ireland) was scrapped and if it was seen that the Catholic hierarchy did not have an improper influence on political affairs, then Northern (Ireland) policy would take a new and more favorable view of the prospect of a united Ireland.

Interview/ The New York Times, 1-8:29.

Let us make no mistake about it. There is a war on in Northern Ireland. The objective of the Irish Republican Army is for a united Ireland. Let no MP here think there is any weakening in the determination of the Ulster people to refuse any deals with the south (the Republic of) Ireland. A united Ireland is definitely out.

Before House of Commons, London, Feb. 1/ The New York Times, 2-2:4.

Complete integration (of Northern Ireland) with the United Kingdom—there lies the best way for all in Northern Ireland, Catholic and Protestant alike. I have only one aim. It is to save the union. If I could achieve that, it would represent the pinnacle of everything I want and hope for.

The New York Times, 4-2:(1)3.

George Papadopoulos
Premier of Greece

There is no hard-and-fast formula of government applicable to all peoples and to all countries. Greece today is an oasis in a strife-torn, problem-ridden world precisely because she is governed in a manner absolutely geared to her national needs.

Broadcast address, April 20/ The New York Times, 4-22:8.

It is true that we have not set a date for the return of representative rule (in Greece). But we will do this when we have fulfilled our duties and obligations to the nation in full knowledge of our responsibilities and consequences.

Broadcast address, Athens, Dec. 16/ The Dallas Times Herald, 12-17:(A)3.

Stylianos Patakos
Deputy Premier of Greece

(On criticisms that his government does not allow elections): Foreigners are so much more anxious about this sort of fun than the Greek people are. The Greek people say, "For heaven's sake, don't start all over again." They want to rest up a bit . . . Would you prefer the fun of elections or would you prefer to concentrate on building your house and doing your work and living happily with your family? Would you rather sit in a coffeehouse and argue over whom to vote for or discuss with your friends day-to-day life? Do you know how many Greeks were killed in arguments before every election? How many families suffered hunger because, after each election, the winners threw the losers out of their jobs? . . . Would the Greek people like to see it again? Why do you insist on reminding us of such stories?

Interview, Athens, Jan. 21/ The New York Times, 1-22:3.

Peter G. Peterson
Secretary of Commerce of the United States

Peter the Great, who founded this magnificent Russian city (Leningrad), thus opened for Russia the window to Europe. We must do everything to ensure that the winds of peace and mutual understanding should blow through this window in both directions.

At luncheon in his honor, Leningrad/ Los Angeles Times, 7-24:(1)19.

Val Peterson
United States Ambassador to Finland

Central to a peaceful world is a peaceful Europe. This is the lesson we all have learned from two world wars. And from that experience Americans have learned yet another lesson: Europe's security is indivisible from our own.

At European Security Conference preparatory meeting, Helsinki, Dec. 4/ Los Angeles Herald-Examiner, 12-5:(A)20.

Nikolai V. Podgorny
President of the Soviet Union

The Soviet Union, together with the countries of the socialist community and all other peace forces, comes out consistently in defense of peace, for the deliverance of the present and future generations from the threat of war, from the disasters of a nuclear conflict and for the elimination of hotbeds of war. We stand for a radical turn toward relaxation of existing tensions in all continents of the world, for freeing the peoples from the heavy arms burden, for a peaceful political settlement of problems through negotiation and with due account taken of the aspirations and will of the peoples and their inalienable right to decide their destinies themselves without interference and pressure from outside.

At dinner during U.S.-Soviet summit meeting, Moscow, May 22/ The Washington Post, 5-23:(A)19.

Georges Pompidou
President of France

(Calling for a French referendum on Britain's entry into the Common Market): The adherence of Britain goes beyond the simple notion of an enlargement of the Common Market. It is a new Europe which is being created and which is going to affirm itself and on which the future of the European peoples will depend—and thus that of all Frenchmen in the political, economic, social and human areas. That is why I declare to you and to all the French people that the enlargement of the community must be ratified by all Frenchmen and Frenchwomen. It is my duty, and it is fundamentally democratic, to ask the French people who elected me to pronounce itself directly on our policy in relation to Europe.

News conference, Paris, March 16/ Los Angeles Times, 3-17:(1)8.

Our (Common Market countries) links with this great country (the U.S.), the world's foremost economic power, with which eight of our countries are united within the Atlantic Alliance, are so close that it would be absurd to conceive of a Europe constructed in opposition to it. But the very closeness of these links requires that Europe affirm its individual personality with regard to the United States. Western Europe, liberated from Nazi armies thanks to the essential contribution of American soldiers, reconstructed with American aid, having looked for its security in the American alliance, having hitherto accepted American currency as the main element of its monetary reserves, must not and cannot sever its links with the United States.

At Common Market summit meeting, Paris, Oct. 19/ The Washington Post, 10-20:(A)12.

Muammar el Qaddafi
Premier of Libya

When we give weapons to the Irish revolutionaries (in Northern Ireland), it is not to kill innocent children but to gain the freedom of enslaved people. We are doing this because Britain has done much worse to the Arab nation, because Britain surrendered Palestine to the Jews and the Persian Gulf islands to Iran.

Tripoli, Libya, June 11/ Los Angeles Herald-Examiner, 6-12:(A)4.

Horacio Rivero, Jr.
Admiral, United States Navy; Commander, NATO forces in southern Europe

It is clear that the Soviets have one aim (in the Mediterranean), and the aim is to achieve such an overwhelming degree of superiority in all aspects of military strength that our countries could be intimidated and could be forced to submit to their political demands. Our improvements, substantial as they have been, have not matched the efforts made by the potential aggressors.

At ceremony relinquishing his command, Naples, Italy, May 31/ The Washington Post, 6-1:(A)11.

William P. Rogers
Secretary of State of the United States

In 1971, the Soviet Union demonstrated . . . restraint in the negotiations over Berlin. The over-all level of worldwide U.S.-Soviet tensions also continued to diminish. I cannot say, however, that the Soviet Union exercised great restraint in South Asia . . . It was not helpful in promoting peace in Indochina, and its record in the Middle East was at best mixed. Our relations will not be harmonious, therefore, until further evolution in Soviet thinking overcomes its temptation to exploit explosive situations for national advantage.

News conference, Washington, March 7/ The New York Times, 3-8:13.

Because of our long and close relationship with the people of Greece, we would, of course, like to see their Constitution speedily implemented and their parliamentary system reinstituted. Some critics of our (friendly) policy toward Greece have urged us to denounce the government of an allied country because it has failed to implement its Constitution in a manner and at a pace they think desirable. Others would use the alliance as a means of pressure. As good friends and allies, we can urge other governments to take certain steps. I do not believe that we should threaten retaliation or use coercive methods to insist that another government conduct its internal affairs in a manner to coincide with our views. Such a policy violates the concept of sovereignty and independence, and in my opinion would not be effective or in our best interests.

Before Order of Hellenic Educational and Progressive Association, Atlanta, Aug. 24/ The New York Times, 8-25:3.

Giuseppe Saragat
Former President of Italy

Where Communism has attained power, expenditures for bureaucracy, for the army, for the party apparatus, for propaganda become crushing. There remains little money in those countries for the social reforms that the workers want or for salaries. Despite the colossal resources of the Soviet Union, the standard of living in that country is the lowest among all industrial nations.

The New York Times, 4-29:3.

J. Robert Schaetzel
Former United States Ambassador to the European Communities

There has been a steady deterioration of relations between the United States and Europe for a variety of reasons, and we are both to blame. The United States has been preoccupied with other issues, notably (Communist) China, Russia and Vietnam, and there has been a tendency to take Europe for granted. There is an equal level of blame on the Europeans. They have taken the United States for granted. They have been almost totally concerned with their own affairs in the most egocentric manner, and

(J. ROBERT SCHAETZEL)

they have been insensitive to American problems.

Interview, Washington/ The Washington Post, 10-28:(A)7.

Eric Sevareid
News commentator, Columbia Broadcasting System (United States)

Politically, (the U.S. and Soviet) systems are far apart. But in terms of popular culture, architecture, gadgetry, even song and dance, it is the West that has won the world. Most of the world, including Russia, just imitates the bad as well as the good in Western life. There is still a curious inferiority complex among the Soviets, constant talk about catching up with the U.S. So they are bending every muscle to catch up with us in cars, skyscrapers, asphalt, pollution, crowding, and jangled nerve ends. Since they imitate, it is necessary that they insist they are wholly different. The so-called workers' and peasants' state is really run by a giant and privileged bureaucracy; it just grows, like our own. There, as here, the bureaucracy is the one collective that cannot stop or diminish what it is doing unless forced to from the outside.

News commentary, May 23/ The Christian Science Monitor, 6-1:16.

Alexander I. Solzhenitsyn
Russian author

In general in our country, we seem to bait people not with arguments, but with the most primitive labels, the coarsest names, and also the simplest, designed, as they say, to arouse the fury of the masses. In the '20s, it was "counter-revolutionary"; in the '30s, "enemy of the people"; since the '40s, "traitor to the country."

Interview, Moscow, March 30/ The Washington Post, 4-3:(A)16.

Alex Springer
West German publisher

. . . the Soviet Union's Western policy has not altered one iota in its aims since the war (World War II). That aim has always been: consolidation of military conquest in Eastern Europe, Sovietization of all Germany and hegemony over Europe . . . The Eastern ambition to rule is served up to the Germans today in cheap demagogics as a peace policy. But for the Soviets, I believe, it is a policy for preparing the conquest of the rest of Europe. To me, therefore, the *Ostpolitik* of the present (West) German government implies a deadly danger for our country and our people; and I consider it at the same time a menace to Europe as well as to the entire free world . . . The immediate objective of the East clearly remains one way or another to overcome the "enemy," which means the West Germans. Why do they want this? Because Communism can only exist unchallenged in East Germany once democracy is eliminated from the Federal Republic in West Germany. Otherwise, its magnetic attraction for the 17 million Germans under the red yoke will persist. That is why it is so important for the Soviet imperial league to banish from the edge of its fortifications the permanent temptation of freedom. That is why Berlin is such a disturbing factor to them and so important to the West. This objective is being pursued by the East in various ways. One is directed to political capitulation by the West. Important landmarks in this are the (West German) treaties of Moscow and Warsaw.

Before German Atlantic Society, Stuttgart/ The New York Times, 5-16:41.

Lubomir Strougal
Premier of Czechoslovakia

We evaluate the state of our country with great satisfaction. This society is living, and living in satisfaction. People have work. People have perspectives and have social surety. For three years, there has been a stability in the cost of living. In fact, we can speak of a mild reduction in living costs. The money earned by a man last year has greater value this year.

Interview, Prague, Dec. 14/
The Washington Post, 12-16:(A)8.

Mikhail A. Suslov
Member, Politburo, Communist Party of the Soviet Union

(On the recently-signed U.S.-Soviet arms-control agreements): Everyone must understand that the Soviet Union, proceeding from its own security interests, will attentively watch attempts of certain forces in the U.S.A. to distort the spirit and letter of the treaty and interim agreement, and will take into consideration in its policy all changes that may appear in the position of the American side . . . The effectiveness and viability of any agreement depend first of all on the unswerving fulfillment by the sides of the commitments they assumed. This is especially important in the case of agreements that are the first major step in the direction of limiting strategic arms. The fulfillment by the sides of the obligations under the treaty and interim agreement, their observance of the principle of equal security of the sides, and impermissibility of unilateral military advantages will be the decisive factor for successful progress in further strategic arms limitation talks.

Before joint meeting of foreign affairs commissions of the Supreme Soviet, Moscow, Aug. 23/
The New York Times, 8-24:6.

Stanislaw Trepczynski
President, United Nations General Assembly

The situation in Europe has developed in such a way that it is a political anachronism not to recognize both (East and West) Germanys at the same level. International agreements have been signed by the four great powers and between the two German countries where they have been recognized as equal partners. So I see no point in keeping the situation as it now is. Only the political struggle has prevented the GDR (East Germany) from being admitted to all international bodies including the UN. Reality is not being recognized.

News conference, United Nations, N.Y., Sept. 19/
The Christian Science Monitor, 9-22:6.

Arthur K. Watson
United States Ambassador to France

(On the possibility of economic strife between the U.S. and Europe): We are so interdependent that the idea of some kind of confrontation is like a Siamese twin biting his brother.

Farewell speech on leaving the Ambassadorship, Paris/
The New York Times, 10-25:52.

William Whitelaw
British Secretary of State for Northern Ireland

I am trying my best to move as fast as I can to create a new climate in which men and women of goodwill get together with me to work out the answer (to Northern Ireland's problems). I have to persuade, cajole, encourage people who, though not without goodwill, are lacking in trust. Though I have repeatedly pledged that the British government will not let them down, many find it hard to believe. They cannot accept that what I say, I mean.

News conference/
The New York Times, 5-21:(4)4.

I have set myself to make use of every possible approach—diplomatic, blunt, direct, polite—to persuade as many people as possible to join hands with me in making Northern Ireland a place where the man who wants to draw attention to his point of view doesn't have to depend on a loaded gun or a bomb for the purpose. The situation is not just about law and order. It is not simply a question of meeting a force of which we cannot approve with a greater force of which we can approve. If history is to pass judgment on the work we are trying to do now,

(WILLIAM WHITELAW)

then please God let it not be, "They took the easy way out—the way to short-term peace and long-term disaster."

London/
The New York Times, 6-22:39.

(Addressing the Northern Irish people): You all know that Her Majesty's government have tried very hard indeed—very hard—to bring peace to this province during the past four months. You also know that a small group of very determined killers are bent on preventing it. They showed by their cruel and callous actions yesterday (a rash of bombings) that, quite without warning, they were prepared to kill, maim and destroy to get their own way. The Provisional IRA will be hard-pressed to find an Irishman who will believe that the means they employed in Belfast and Londonderry yesterday were justified. Could any political objective justify it? All of you must realize that the British Army is here to protect ordinary people's lives and property and must go after the killers, the bomb-makers and the fanatics who mastermind them . . . The time has come when everyone—the churches, the politicians, the trade-union leaders, the housewives, the schoolteachers—must speak out. They must condemn the Provisional IRA, which is fast dragging this community to total ruin.

TV-radio address,
Belfast, July 22/
The New York Times, 7-23:(1)3.

The more the Catholic minority is pleased, the more the Protestant majority is angry. As a result, Britain is caught in a cleft stick. But if 85 per cent of this population is happy to live together, 15 per cent is not; and that includes the extremists of both sides. The moderates are vanishing just as they should speak out. But they don't; and they have no leaders in sight.

San Francisco Examiner & Chronicle, 7-23:
(This World)28.

The British government has repeatedly stated that there would be no unification of Ireland unless the majority in Northern Ireland wanted it. And the campaign of violence of the past few years has set such a prospect back years. My judgment is that when we have such a plebiscite, we may find that quite a lot of the (Catholic) minority community will opt for staying in the United Kingdom. I don't think you can tell yet, but I wouldn't be at all surprised.

Interview/Newsweek, 8-14:32.

Harold Wilson
Leader, British Labor Party;
Former Prime Minister of the
United Kingdom

. . . there can be no future, no military solution (to the Northern Ireland conflict) without a political solution. I believe increasingly there can be no political solution without a united Ireland, with proper safeguards for the Ulster majority, at the end of the road. Our responsibility . . . is to do all in our power to ensure that that history is not written in blood.

Before British Parliament, London/
The New York Times, 2-6:(4)1.

I am deeply disturbed at the growing symptoms of nastiness and ugliness in our society, quite apart from the evil and violence in Northern Ireland . . . Britain has led the world in the civilized conduct of its affairs. It would be a tragedy if we were now to forsake that lead and join in the rough and tumble.

The Dallas Times Herald, 2-28:(B)7.

(On French President Georges Pompidou's attitude toward British entry into the Common Market): I do not believe . . . that President Pompidou wanted Britain in or the enlargement of the (European Economic) Community at all. I do believe he decided that a further veto would endanger the Community and could end the unique benefits France derived from the Community.

At Socialist International Congress,
Vienna/The Washington Post,
6-29:(A)30.

The Middle East

Houari Boumedienne
President of Algeria

(On Egypt's ouster of Russian military personnel): Personally, I hope, of course, that this is in fact the beginning of a major shift and that, apart from the change in the Middle East, we can also look back on this some day as part of the process of neutralizing the Mediterranean. We don't need foreign fleets here. I don't see any advantage to us in having either the American or the Soviet fleets in the Mediterranean. There is certainly no economic reason for it. It has no political interest for us. It presents us with no advantage in either our internal or regional security. The only strategic aspect it has is global. And there will be no war started over this question. A war would come only if the United States or the Soviet Union felt itself directly menaced on its own territory.

Interview, Algiers/
The New York Times, 7-28:29.

Leonid I. Brezhnev
General Secretary,
Communist Party of the Soviet Union

The danger implicit in the tense situation in the Middle East is increasing. The stubborn refusal by Israel to withdraw from the Arab lands she has seized and the incessant provocations by the Israeli military against the Arab states exacerbate the situation, threatening an outbreak of hostilities. The Arab countries have convincingly demonstrated their readiness to reach a political settlement to the conflict and to establish a stable and durable peace in the Middle East. Israel, aided and abetted by the U.S.A., stubbornly clings to its aggressive policy of annexation. This, however, cannot continue forever. Sober-minded politicians cannot expect that the Arab states will tolerate the occupation of their territories. The Arab world today is not what it used to be several years ago. The progressive regimes have been consolidated. Cooperation between the Arab states is being promoted. And the defensive capacity of the Arab states has been greatly strengthened. All these are long-term factors and, in the final count, they will determine the correlation of forces in the Middle East.

At Soviet Trade Unions Congress,
Moscow, March 20/
Vital Speeches, 4-15:391.

George Bush
United States Ambassador/Permanent
Representative to the United Nations

(On recent Arab terrorist violence at Lod Airport in Israel and at the Olympic Games in Munich): Those who preach violence and employ it as a matter of policy always suffer its consequences, for violence always begets violence. The crimes that were carried out at Lod and at Munich cannot but breed tragedy for their perpetrators and for those who defend them. States which harbor and give succor to terrorists cannot then claim sanctuary for themselves . . . We believe each member of the (UN Security) Council–indeed of the entire international community–should make it unmistakably clear that acts of terror and violence practiced against innocent people as a matter of policy are unacceptable in a civilized world. Each of us has a responsibility to make clear that those who practice such acts, or aid and abet them in any way, are the ones deserving a censure and condemnation. Only then will we begin to eliminate this scourge from the earth, and with it the acts of counter-violence to which history inevitably proves it gives rise.

At United Nations, N.Y., Sept. 10/
The New York Times, 9-11:10.

Chiao Kuan-hua
Deputy Foreign Minister of, and chief United Nations General Assembly delegate from, the People's Republic of (Communist) China

The present situation of "no war, no peace" in the Middle East is solely created by the two superpowers (the U.S. and the Soviet Union) for their respective interests. Taking advantage of this situation, they are using Arab countries' territories and sovereignty and the Palestinian people's right to existence as stakes to strike political deals. The United States is openly supporting the aggression by Israeli Zionism. The other superpower claims to "support and assist" the Arab people in their struggle against aggression. Has it supported and assisted them? It has indeed sold them no small amount of weapons. But strangely, the weapons supplied are not allowed to be used. Is this not asking people to buy scrap iron? Moreover, it demands privileges and bases, and even attempts to subvert their government. What kind of "friend" is this? It is more dangerous than an open enemy.

At United Nations, N.Y., Oct. 3/
The New York Times, 10-4:4.

Moshe Dayan
Minister of Defense of Israel

The Egyptians could prevent another war if they asked the Israelis to sit down at a table with them and talk. It would not be easy to come to agreement. It would not be easy, even, to agree what to talk about. But the main thing is to stop the drift to war, and to do that we must start to talk. It is no good passing resolutions in the United Nations. The best thing is for the two countries to meet face to face. By all means, let there be a third party present; let there be mediators . . . (But) it is no good trying to deal indirectly with the Jews and the Arabs by resolutions in the United Nations or committees which come between. The Jews and the Arabs must ultimately deal directly with each other.

Interview, Zahala, Israel/
Los Angeles Times, 1-23:(H)3.

I take (Egyptian) President Sadat very seriously. A few months, perhaps a few weeks, remain in which political negotiation is possible. If we are not negotiating soon, I agree with President Sadat there will be war. It may not be a war started by order of President Sadat; that makes no difference. Great wars have started in small ways. The powder is lying around; and a little match can ignite it . . .

Interview, Zahala, Israel/
Los Angeles Times, 1-23:(H)3.

The United States wants to reach an agreement (on the Middle East) with the Soviet Union; and, therefore, we should be worried. An agreement between the United States and the Soviet Union, even if it is not a forced solution, could not be of a kind we would be happy with.

Television interview, Feb. 11/
Los Angeles Herald-Examiner, 2-12:(A)4.

Abba Eban
Foreign Minister of Israel

(Criticizing Lebanon's hospitality toward Arab guerrilla groups): It is Beirut where the terrorists are at home, where they conduct their vitriolic propaganda and produce their forged passports . . . It is in Beirut where the murders are being planned and where the murderers are being trained and sent out into the world.

The Christian Science Monitor, 6-2:3.

We've been five years on the cease-fire lines (after the Arab-Israeli war of 1967) for the simple reason that the cease-fire lines cannot be changed except to be replaced by a freely-negotiated peace. If there is a freely-negotiated peace in five weeks, the cease-fire lines will last five weeks. If it takes the Arabs five or 10 years, then the cease-fire lines will last as long as that. What we want to see maturing is a willingness on the part of Egypt not only to accept the principle of a peace agreement, but also to draw the conclusions that emanate from that principle that, if they want an agreement, they will have to negotiate.

Interview, Tel Aviv, June 5/ Los Angeles Herald-Examiner, 6-5:(A)4.

The (Arab) terrorist movement . . . constitutes an obstacle to negotiation and therefore we ought to try to get the obstacle out of the way if we want to move on to our ultimate aim of negotiation . . . One of the expressions of (the Arab) refusal to negotiate is the open encouragement they give to terrorist movements . . . The responsibility for the absence of negotiations is exclusively an Arab one—in theory by refusing to negotiate and in practice by . . . going on with this killing and murder.

News conference, Washington, Sept. 22/ The Washington Post, 9-23:(A)18.

The deadlock on the overall settlement (of final Israeli territorial boundaries) arises from the fact that Egypt has so far refused to begin negotiation unless its position on the final outcome is conceded in advance. There is no valid precedent for such a demand. Negotiation creates the final result; the final result does not create negotiation.

At United Nations, N.Y., Sept. 28/ The New York Times, 9-29:13

Nihat Erim
Prime Minister of Turkey

If Turkey collapses, all the Near and Middle East would collapse . . . Greece couldn't stay independent. We consider ourselves as the vanguard of the Western world and the key to security of (the) Mediterranean and Europe.

Interview/ The Washington Post, 2-12:(A)10.

Parliamentary democracy, with all its processes, institutions and ramifications and constitutional guarantees, continues in Turkey. Our goal is to make Turkey safe for democracy.

Interview, Ankara/ The New York Times, 3-18:6.

Israel Galili
Minister Without Portfolio of Israel

(On the recent terrorist attack at Tel Aviv's Lod Airport in which 25 people were killed): The bloodshed showed up once more the true image of the Palestinian terrorists. The real aim of this brutal terror campaign is the establishment of a Palestinian state on the ruins of the Jewish state. It is a fallacy to believe that terror can undermine Israel. Its blows may hurt, but there is no contradiction between today's deep sorrow and the confidence we are entitled to feel toward future tests.

At businessmen's meeting, Tel Aviv, June 2/ The New York Times, 6-3:3.

(On West Germany's release of Arab terrorists, arrested for the killing of Israeli Olympic athletes in Munich, because of demands by Arab hijackers holding a German airliner and its passengers): This surrender to the threat of the Black September terrorists is a terrible deed from every respect. It is an act that could not be condoned, in whatever country it might have occurred . . . It is astonishing that no real attempt was made to thwart the Arab terrorists in their acts. To give in to them is dangerous in the international context . . . and certainly cannot be forgiven from the Jewish and Israeli viewpoint . . . The surrender of the German authorities in this instance will provide considerable encouragement to Arab (terrorists) in the wake of their crime against our sportsmen at the Olympic Games. This method of terror cannot possibly be overcome by so spectacular a surrender to the terrorists.

Oct. 29/ Los Angeles Times, 10-30:(1)1,9.

Andrei A. Grechko
Minister of Defense of the Soviet Union

(On Egypt's ousting of Soviet military advisers): At present, the Soviet military personnel have fulfilled their functions. Taking this into account, and after an ap-

(ANDREI A. GRECHKO)

propriate exchange of views between the sides, it was recognized as expedient to return to the Soviet Union the military personnel which has been sent to Egypt for a limited period.

Moscow, July 23/
Los Angeles Times, 7-24:(1)4.

Tewfik al Hakim
Egyptian author

These days, countries like Egypt think in terms of achieving a certain standard of living or quality of life. We want to make ourselves over in the image of the developed countries. But it isn't enough to do this. Egypt has to find its own personality again. It can borrow ideas or material things from others as you borrow a garment. But it has to seek its own body and soul to put inside the wrappings. We have to learn to be ourselves and resist extreme swings, whether to left or to right.

Interview, Cairo/
The Christian Science Monitor, 3-22:15.

Gustav Heinemann
President of West Germany

(On the Arab terrorist killing of 11 members of the Israeli Olympic team in Munich): Helpless we stand before a truly despicable crime. Eleven days ago in this stadium, on this same spot, I opened the 20th Olympic Games in Munich. They began as truly happy games in the true Olympic spirit. They continued as such until this shadow of darkness passed over us. The responsibility lies with the countries who do not put a stop to these (Arab terrorist) activities. In the name of the Federal Republic of Germany, I appeal to the people of the world to overcome hatred.

At memorial services, Olympic
Stadium, Munich, Sept. 6/
San Francisco Examiner, 9-6:61.

Arthur Hertzberg
President, American Jewish Congress

Our (Jewish) children come by their passion to improve the world from the tradition we have taught them—or should have taught them—that American Jewry will not become a "colony" of Israel. We insist on the right to criticize Israel when criticism is needed, even if that criticism is likely to be exploited by Israel's enemies.

At American Jewish Congress annual
American-Israeli dialogue, Jerusalem/
The New York Times, 8-6:(1)13.

Shafik el Hout
Leader, Palestine Liberation Organization

(On Arab terrorism, such as the attack on Lydda (Lod) Airport in Tel Aviv and the killing of members of the Israeli Olympic team in Munich earlier in the year): We have to shock the West out of its guilty conscience about the Jews, and into recognizing the plight of the Palestinian people. That's why Lydda and Munich were such tactical successes. They showed we were prepared to die for our cause . . . Remember that girl hijacker at Lydda who gave up a hand grenade to her Israeli captors? She could have blown the plane up, but she didn't. I'd have given her a medal for being a good human being, but I'd have kicked her out of the commando movement for being a lousy revolutionary . . . I used to believe that ends should be achieved by good means. But doors are being closed to us everywhere now. The Palestinians are a tired people. I don't remember a single peaceful day. We long for peace. Sometimes I feel I want to explode. But most of the time I just want to live—like everyone else. I want the sympathy of the West, but I want its respect first. I want my nationality recognized. They can call me a Palestinian terrorist if they want; that's some recognition. And I'll go on fighting the people (Israelis) who're occupying my country.

Interview, Beirut/
The Washington Post, 10-15:(B)3.

Hussein I
King of Jordan

In regard to sovereignty and the recognition that there is an Arab part of the city (Jerusalem), a Palestinian part so to speak, this is a must; but following that, we are open-minded to anything and everything that would make Jerusalem the meeting place of all. Jerusalem after all is a unique city. Some may say that people of the Jewish faith should have Jerusalem as the Moslems have Mecca and the Christians have Rome; but I believe that Jerusalem belongs to Abraham, Jesus and Mohammed, and this is the only city that does. Its history has been a tragic and sad one. Once and for all it must be the meeting place of all believers in God, under conditions of peace.

TV-radio interview, Washington/ "Meet the Press," National Broadcasting Company, 4-2.

(On his opposition to war with Israel): I will never be drawn into anything unless one and one make two. Any move that Jordan makes in the future, so long as I am in a position of responsibility, whether political or military or in any other sphere, will only be taken after deep study and after we are sure it is the right course. So if going to war is futile, we will not go to war. Armed struggle is the last result that could be adopted.

Interview, Palm Beach, Fla./ The Washington Post, 4-17:(A)2.

Henry M. Jackson
United States Senator, D–Wash.

We need to recognize that the central problem in the Middle East is the Soviet drive for hegemony; and the maintenance of a high level of tension between Israel and the Arab states is the primary vehicle by which Russia seeks to accomplish this objective.

At Senate Armed Services Committee hearing, Washington/ Human Events, 4-15:10.

Jacob K. Javits
United States Senator, R–N.Y.

. . . the idea that Israel is going to take a guarantee (of help from the UN or other countries in event of war) is out of date completely. After the demonstration of (U.S.) President Johnson's inability to put together even a small naval force to protect the Straits of Tiran in 1967, I doubt that Israel is going to take any guarantee, or that she should. I think you have got to expect a high measure of self-reliance and what she calls secure and defensible boundaries. Now, the argument is made that, since you can shoot with artillery five to 10 miles, and 30 to 200 miles, what difference is a line on the ground? The answer of the Israelis to that is that you cannot have guerrillas infiltrating your borders, destroying the inside of your country.

Interview, Rome/ San Francisco Examiner, 1-7:52.

Mansour Rashid Kekhia
Foreign Minister of Libya

The American commitment to support Zionism is very deep, very strong—so much so that it is not easy to change it . . . Once we have finally despaired of any change in the American position, we will identify the American presence in our country with Zionist interests. Up to now, this situation has not been clear to Americans. Their interests are protected in the Arab countries. Most of the Arab oil is in the hands of Americans. So many Americans laugh at us. They take it for granted that the Arabs are by nature anti-Communist and that we shall not really fight Americans—no matter what they do to help our enemies. But things are changing. A new generation is coming. Maybe the "Vietnamization" of the region will be the right answer to the American commitment to support Israeli aggression.

Interview, Tripoli/ The Christian Science Monitor, 8-31:8.

Edward M. Kennedy
United States Senator, D–Mass.

Despite her national character and strength . . . Israel remains a beleaguered country . . . Our government should . . . permit the sale of jets to Israel in sufficient numbers to help maintain her defensive capacity and the maintenance of a military balance vis-a-vis her Arab neighbors (and) should also exercise more flexibility and generosity in responding to Israel's economic needs.

The National Observer, 5-6:16.

I believe that, short of our own self-preservation as a nation, there can be no greater goal of American foreign policy than the preservation of Israel.

At fund-raising dinner for Jerusalem's Hebrew University, Beverly Hills, Calif., Dec. 11/ Los Angeles Times, 12-12:(1)24.

Abdul Halim Khaddam
Foreign Minister of Syria

(On criticism of Arab terrorism): Until recently, many of the heads of delegations and the delegates now gathered in this Assembly were described by imperialists as terrorists. The voices which define and exploit the term "terrorism" today are the same voices which labelled the freedom leaders in Africa, Asia and Latin America "terrorists." As we move back in history, we ask ourselves were not (Thomas) Jefferson and (Benjamin) Franklin and (George) Washington in their time leaders and commanders of terrorism in the view of the ruling colonial power? Were not the heroes resisting Nazi and Fascist occupation in Europe terrorists in the eyes of the Nazi and Fascist leaders?

At United Nations, N.Y., Oct. 9/ San Francisco Examiner, 10-10:47.

Abdalah Khani
Deputy Foreign Minister of Syria

There can be no question of resumption of diplomatic relations or even trade relations with the U.S. The delivery of more Phantoms (fighter planes) to Israel—even though the U.S. admits that the balance of power is in favor of Israel—has one sole aim: to encourage Israel to commit more aggressions.

The New York Times, 2-1:3.

John Law
Mideast correspondent, "U.S. News & World Report"

(Arab terrorists) are trying to focus world attention on the fact that there is a Palestinian problem that hasn't been solved. I emphasize the word "attention" for a reason: These people realize they lose world sympathy by acts of terror, but they don't really care for world sympathy. What they're striving for is to make the world realize that they are the people who were moved out of their homeland by the Israelis when Israel became a sovereign state in 1948. They feel that they ought to be able to get their land and their homes back. They are bitter and very desperate men who feel that they have a real cause—and nothing to lose. They are, in many cases, college-educated men. These are people who believe that what they are doing is right, even though it is vicious.

Interview/ U.S. News & World Report, 9-18:21.

John V. Lindsay
Mayor of New York

Israel asks not for one single American soldier, but for 80 jets as safeguards for her freedom. But our leaders are not sure. I am sure. Those planes should be sold today to reaffirm our unity, to make good this nation's pledge, to secure the peace of Israel and to secure the peace of the Western community.

Before Zionist Organization of America, Miami Beach, Jan. 9/ The Dallas Times Herald, 1-10:(A)9.

Yakov A. Malik
Soviet Ambassador/Permanent Representative to the United Nations

The easing of international tensions is not

to their (Israel's) interests, an easing which has followed international agreements. They clearly want to sabotage the relaxation of tensions because they are getting fabulous assistance from Zionist circles abroad.

At United Nations, N.Y., June 23/ Los Angeles Times, 6-24:(1)3.

George S. McGovern
United States Senator, D–S.D.

(On why he supports Israel while at the same time urging U.S. pullout from South Vietnam): The government in Saigon is a corrupt dictatorship which long ago lost the support of its people . . . Israel is a democratic nation, whose elected leadership has as firm a support among its people as any government in the world. Vietnam is an internal struggle. Israel is protecting itself against the threat of armed aggression from hostile outside powers.

Campaigning for the Democratic Presidential nomination, Los Angeles, May 28/ San Francisco Examiner, 5-29:8.

(On whether U.S. troops should be sent to Israel to help defend it in an emergency): I don't see any point (in) doing a lot of saber-rattling. I do think we need to make it clear we are going to meet the legitimate request Israel would make, such as jet aircraft. They don't need American troops; they need the tools for their own defense. Of course, if there's a major Soviet invasion of the Middle East, we would have to do what is necessary to meet it . . . I don't think that's going to happen.

Television interview, Los Angeles/ "Issues and Answers," American Broadcasting Company, 6-4.

George S. McGovern
United States Senator, D–S.D.; Democratic Presidential nominee

I invite comparison between myself and my opponent (U.S. President Nixon) on the subject of Israel as far back as anyone would like to trace our records. My commitment to Israel is a moral commitment that began with my entry into public life in 1957, the first year I was in Congress. In contrast, the (Nixon) Administration's commitment has been an instrument largely of power politics that really began with the Soviet military build-up in the Mediterranean. I was not the President who imposed the long and dangerous delay in the shipment of Phantom jets and other vital arms to Israel. I was not part of an Administration that voted with the Soviet-Arab bloc to condemn Israel five times in the United Nations over the last four years . . . It was not I who tried to impose a big-power settlement on the Middle East. And while the present Administration has consistently sought to tie American aid to Israel with appropriations for the Vietnam war, I have argued that any hint at all of similarity between our disastrous involvement in Indochina and our responsibilities in the Middle East was a sadly and dangerously mistaken comparison.

Before New York Board of Rabbis, Aug. 30/ The New York Times, 8-31:24.

(On the Arab terrorist killing of 11 Israeli Olympic athletes in Munich): We must place the responsibility and we must be honest and clear—the blame lies with two Arab governments: Egypt and Lebanon . . . I urge the President (Nixon of the U.S.) to demand . . . that Egypt shall root out these international outlaws who seek to impose the peace of the grave on a whole region of the world and on innocent people from every part of the world. All of civilized society was a casualty of this invasion of the Olympic camp.

Before Southern California Board of Rabbis, Los Angeles, Sept. 6/ Los Angeles Herald-Examiner, 9-6:(A)3.

Giuseppe Medici
Foreign Minister of Italy

Italy is essentially a Mediterranean country and therefore everything that happens in this sea concerns it closely. The consequence in grave concern over the Arab-Israeli

(GIUSEPPE MEDICI)

conflict, which, quite apart from anything else, by the resultant prolonged closure of the Suez Canal, has caused considerable economic damage to the Mediterranean countries and to Italy. Rapid economic and social development for all peoples bordering on this sea can only be achieved on the basis of a just and lasting peace in the Middle East.

Interview, Rome/
San Francisco Examiner, 8-30:38.

Golda Meir
Prime Minister of Israel

. . . one basic article in Israel's policy is that the borders of June 4, 1967, cannot be re-established in the peace agreement (with the Arabs). There must be changes in the border. We want changes in borders, on all our borders, for security's sake. So our policy is, we want to negotiate peace treaties with our neighbors on secure, agreed and recognized borders . . . fixed frontiers which must have two elements: one, a deterrent for further wars and further attacks, and two, if they are not deterrent enough and some day some Arab leader will want to try it again, we should be able to defend our borders with as few casualties as possible. This is all of our policy in a nutshell.

Interview, Jerusalem, Jan. 28/
The New York Times, 1-30:(1)2.

We have never said that there is anything which the other (Arab) side cannot put on the (negotiating) table. If Jordan comes and puts Jerusalem on the table, we won't get up and say, no, now we go home. But Israel has taken a definite position that Jerusalem will not be divided again and is a part of Israel and is the capital of Israel.

Interview, Jerusalem, Jan. 28/
The New York Times, 1-30:(1)2.

If (Egyptian President Anwar) Sadat had the courage to move toward peace with us six months ago, his position would be far better today. He does not have the strength for war, and for this he indeed deserves praise. But now the question is whether he will draw the conclusion to make peace; (and) for that, too, a great deal of courage is needed.

Radio interview, Jan. 29/
San Francisco Examiner, 1-29:1.

(On the terrorist attack at Tel Aviv's Lod Airport which killed 25 people): It is no secret that Beirut is openly enabling the centers of the (Arab) terrorist organizations to reside in its midst. There they plot; from there instructors set out to various countries; and from there come the broadcasts of their great successes. Can it be possible that governments, that aviation companies, should acquiesce in this? Is it at all conceivable that a state which harbors and abets the plotting of such crimes, where the terrorists are free to plot, to set out and return safely with impunity, that on the soil of such a country foreign planes will continue to land?

Before the Knesset (Parliament),
Jerusalem, May 31/
The New York Times, 6-1:1.

. . . I think the Arabs—and especially (President Anwar) Sadat in Egypt—have come to see that they cannot destroy Israel. They know that, if they would try to defeat us, the result would be exactly the same as in '67: They would lose. Of course, deep down inside I don't believe Sadat has changed his mind about what he would like to do. He would still destroy Israel if he could. He says so openly. In fact, his latest statements are not only anti-Israel, but are openly and viciously anti-Semitic. Yet, even with this talk, Sadat knows that, sooner or later, he must come to terms with us—that he must negotiate a settlement. I would even go so far as to say that Egypt perhaps needs peace more than we do. For us, peace is a luxury that we have learned to live without; we can manage; we are developing even with our heavy defense burden. But Egypt is a country of terrible poverty; and to escape this condition they must have peace. Indeed, this is one of my reasons for optimism. I simply cannot believe that 30 million Egyptians will be content to put off development, and waste all their efforts in a futile war, just for the glory of Sadat and the Egyptian leadership.

Interview/Parade, 6-4:12.

. . . we feel very lucky that the basic relationship between Israel and the U.S. has always been one of friendship and support. We do not ask the U.S. to send soldiers and fight battles for us as Egypt asked of the Soviet Union. And we never will. You know that there are several thousand Russians in Egypt flying planes, operating the missiles and so on . . . All *we* ask for are the means to defend ourselves; and we are grateful that the U.S. has always supported us in this way.

Interview/Parade, 6-4:13.

(Calling on Egypt to start negotiations with Israel to end their conflict): We have not declared permanent borders; we have not drawn up an ultimate map; we have not demanded prior commitments on matters which must be clarified by means of negotiations. We do not intend to perpetuate the cease-fire lines between us, or to freeze the existing situation. Let us sit down together to discuss the peace settlements. Let us search for a way to break the deadlock, lest war be renewed between us. This appeal of ours does not stem from weakness, nor out of any desire to take advantage of an embarrassing situation (Egypt's ouster of Soviet military personnel), but rather out of a deep awareness of the need for peace, of the advantages of peace and the preferability of negotiation over any other alternative.

Before the Knesset (Parliament), Jerusalem, July 26/ The New York Times, 7-27:12.

This afternoon a group of our pilots went across the border (into Syria and Lebanon) to try to get rid of some of the Fatah (Arab guerrilla organization) centers. Those terrorists who killed at (the Olympic Games in) Munich, those who attacked a Sabena Airlines plane at Lod (Tel Aviv) Airport and the Japanese who struck at Lod—all of them were trained in Lebanon and Syria. This is not what we would like to send our sons to do. But we have to live; and in order to live, we have to make the Fatah conscious of the fact that Jewish blood cannot be spilled without terrorist blood being spilled as well.

Before Mizrachi Women's Organization of America, Jerusalem, Oct. 15/ The New York Times, 10-16:16.

I doubt if I will live long enough to see an Arab leader who wants peace with Israel. The stronger we are, the more impossible it is to hurt us and the nearer we are to peace. That's why Israel seems so intransigent, so obstinate. People say we have fallen in love with the (Israeli-occupied Arab) territories and love to have hundreds of Arabs working for us. Nonsense.

Before conference of American women, Jerusalem, Oct. 22/ San Francisco Examiner, 10-23:2.

Richard M. Nixon
President of the United States

I think the Soviet leaders realize that it is in the interests of the Soviet Union and the United States to have a live-and-let-live attitude toward the Mideast. The United States is not going to allow Israel and our interests in the Mideast to go down the drain, to be overrun. The Soviets, for their reasons, are going to stand firm in standing by their new allies, the Egyptians. Both the United States and the Soviet Union, therefore, are destined to play a role in the Mideast. We are there and we're going to stay, the Sixth Fleet being our major weapons system. The Soviet Union is in the Mideast, and it will maintain its influence there. What we must do is to find a way to respect each other's interests without allowing the age-old hatreds between those nations to draw us into conflict against our will.

Interview/ The Reader's Digest, February:66.

Mohammad Reza Pahlavi
Shah of Iran

The history of our country is always one of up and down, up and down, up and down. Under great kings, we have reached the summit of glory. Under weaker kings, we have been beaten by nobodies. I don't want that to happen again.

San Francisco Examiner, 9-11:36.

Muammar el Qaddafi
Premier of Libya

What have the Russians done for the Arabs? The cease-fire with Israel must end and the battle must begin. Why doesn't the battle begin? Because the Russians prefer, and profit from, the present state of no-peace, no-war. The Russians talk of all the weapons they are giving us (the Arabs), but it is propaganda. When (Soviet Defense Minister) Marshall Grechko visited Cairo in May, he brought a new long-range supersonic MIG-23 with him, as if to pretend that this type of aircraft would be delivered to Egypt. But he took it back with him to Moscow and left us nothing.

The New York Times Magazine, 8-6:39.

Yitzhak Rabin
Israeli Ambassador to the United States

(Indicating preference for U.S. President Nixon to be re-elected this year): We have to differentiate between aid in the form of action and aid in the form of words. While we appreciate support in the form of words we are getting from one camp (of U.S. Presidential candidates), we must prefer support in the form of deeds we are getting from the other (Nixon) camp.

Radio interview, Washington/
The Washington Post, 6-11:(A)1.

William P. Rogers
Secretary of State of the United States

The no-peace/no-war situation which prevails now in the Middle East does not and will not serve the interest of anyone in the area. Certainly, a stable, just and durable peace agreement based on (United Nations) Security Council Resolution 242 continues to be the objective of the United States. But this cannot be achieved without the beginning of a genuine negotiating process between the parties concerned (Israel and the Arab nations). No settlement imposed from the outside could long endure. Negotiation is not capitulation. Negotiating activity among long-standing antagonists across the world is presently occurring. Why should the Middle East be an exception? When North Korea can talk with South Korea, when East Germans can talk with West Germans, when Indians and Pakistanis can meet in the immediate aftermath of war and prior to the withdrawal of troops—then surely the Middle East should be no exception to the general rule that differences should be reconciled through an active dialogue between the parties concerned.

At United Nations, N.Y., Sept. 25/
Vital Speeches, 11-1:35.

Anwar el Sadat
President of Egypt

I simply cannot understand why—despite the fact that your (U.S.) government said only a few weeks before that the balance of power was overwhelmingly in Israel's favor—you went ahead and suddenly increased Israel's air force by one-third. It is this escalation that wrecked the political solution . . . The U.S. has now swung all its weight behind Israel. You are trying to compensate for your setback on the (Indian) subcontinent . . . America has become a hopeless case, especially in an election year with so many candidates dependent as they are on Jewish financing.

Interview/Newsweek, 3-6:47.

War (with Israel) is inevitable. We cannot liberate our land without a war . . . I will never throw you into a war just to show the world that we are doing something. We will enter the war with full preparation and clear objectives.

At Egyptian air base, March 30/
The New York Times, 4-1:2.

I promise you we shall observe the next anniversary of the Prophet's birthday by celebrating not only the liberation of our land but also the conquering of Israel's arrogance and humiliating them . . . We are preparing for the battle with patience and silence until the hour to resume war comes. And it will not be far off. Israel should know that it will pay two-fold this time.

Celebrating the Prophet Mohammed's birthday, Cairo, April 25/ The Dallas Times Herald, 4-26:(A)3.

I am ready to sacrifice a million men for the battle (against Israel), and Israel should be prepared to sacrifice a million or more . . . In the next battle, liberation of our land will not be enough. We must smash Israel's arrogance which has continued for 23 years.

May Day address, Alexandria, May 1/ Los Angeles Times, 5-2:(1)17.

(Explaining his country's ouster of Soviet military personnel): Throughout our battles, which started against the British occupation and American attempts to contain the Egyptian revolutionary nationalist forces, our foreign policy was based fundamentally on the improvement and promotion of our relations with the Soviet Union, particularly after 1967. This was so because our arch enemy, Israel, was being consolidated fully by the United States, while the Soviet Union stood by our side in all fields, militarily, politically and economically . . . There were differences at times in our points of view; but I was always under the impression that these were normal differences. This was so because the Soviet Union, as a major power, has an international role to play which we cannot ignore and has its own strategy. But a part of our territory is under occupation (by Israel), and our basic target is to eradicate the traces of aggression. We believe, because of Israeli intransigence and continuous American support, these traces would not be removed except through a decisive battle. The Sudan abortive coup took place in July last year, and our relations were affected; but I flew to Moscow in October and explained the situation and ended the differences. There were also differences in my earlier visit in March over the question of arms, its types and delivery dates . . . (The Soviet-Egyptian friendship treaty should have supplied Egypt with) certain types of arms necessary for the battle in view of the timetable which I had mapped out to consider 1971 as a decisive year for the battle. These arms did not arrive on the agreed dates, and that is what made me say then we need to re-evaluate our position . . . I have made clear our refusal of the following three points: our refusal to limit arms deals at this stage, as Israel has piles of arms and was persisting on the occupation of our territory; our rejection of any deal to continue the state of no peace and no war, because this means an Israeli victory in the long run; and no concessions of any part of Arab territories . . . After fully reviewing the situation in all its aspects and in full appreciation of the huge Soviet aid to us, I found it appropriate to adopt the following measures: 1) Terminate the mission of Soviet advisers and military experts, who came at our request, as of yesterday to be replaced by our sons in the armed forces; 2) All military equipment and installations built after June, 1967, are to be manned by the Egyptian armed forces and become the property of Egypt; and 3) Invite a Soviet-Egyptian meeting, at a high level to be agreed upon, to hold consultations to decide on the next phase of operation.

July 18/ The New York Times, 7-20:14.

(The United States has suggested) that direct negotiations (between Israel and Egypt) should be the means for solving the crisis. What does this mean? At a time when my land is occupied by Israel and direct negotiations are being imposed on me, how can I sit down at the table with Israel while it is occupying my country? It would mean direct surrender.

Before Arab Socialist Union Central Committee, Cairo, July 24/ The New York Times, 7-25:10.

(ANWAR EL SADAT)

When (U.S. President) Nixon gives Israel $70 million for the settlement of new refugees from Russia, and when the U.S. Senate, a day or two before, votes another $300 million for Israel, I tell other Arab leaders that the U.S. is getting a lot of money from its investments and revenue in the Arab world. All I can tell you is that U.S. interests will shortly become part of the battle for the recovery of our (Israeli-occupied) land. An oil boycott is feasible but it's a very complex problem. We are not in a hurry on the oil front. We are not hysterical and there is no need for hysteria. But I can assure you that U.S. interests in the Middle East are in for a long hot autumn; and if Mr. Nixon thinks he is going to have a quiet time in the area as he is running for re-election, he has another surprise coming.

Interview/Newsweek, 8-7:29.

. . . all I am asking for is our own land (now occupied by Israel). There should be no reward for aggression. I have offered to fulfill all our obligations under the United Nations resolution of November, 1967. This means the recognition of Israel's territorial integrity and political independence. It means freedom of navigation. It means everything short of exchanging ambassadors when they give up Arab lands they conquered in 1967. My sincerity as a man of peace cannot be questioned. We have no designs whatever on Israel; that's more than impartial observers can say about their designs on Egypt. How have the Israelis responded? By refusing to move. We have seen one pretext invoked after another for staying where they are. If they are prepared to carry out their obligations under the United Nations resolution, as I am prepared to carry out ours, then we will have real peace.

Interview/Newsweek, 8-7:30.

The way American politicians compete to please Israel has become a comedy, perhaps a tragedy. The time has come for the Arabs to make America pay for this mad support of Israel, and pay dearly. The time has come for us to hit, and hit at the heart, unless America extricates itself from this semi-imperialist satellite attitude to Israel.

Before People's Assembly (Parliament), Cairo, Oct. 15/ The New York Times, 10-16:15.

(On why he expelled Soviet military personnel from Egypt earlier in the year): (Another war with Israel was inevitable and) the Russian military presence would render a big strategic service to Israel when the battle begins. Israel would then say that it was fighting the Russians, not the Arabs, and would thus win over the Americans and even European public opinion. This meant that the Russians had become a burden on us . . . Another point I wanted to make in removing the Russian military presence in Egypt was to make the leaders of the Kremlin understand that their strategy in the area cannot be fulfilled at our expense.

Interview, Cairo/ Time, 10-16:36.

I declare it here with the loudest voice and the fullest responsibility, that the door to battle (with Israel) is the door of the future, and that there is no other path . . . We shall fight our way through fire and storm, sacrifice our blood for honor and our sweat for freedom, and place our banners where they should be placed. We shall fight . . . we shall fight . . . we shall fight . . . until God gives us victory.

Before Parliament, Cairo, Dec. 28/ San Francisco Examiner, 12-29:5.

Saeb Salam
Premier of Lebanon

(On recent clashes between Palestinian guerrillas and Lebanese government forces): We are eager to help our brothers, the fedayeen, and to provide them with all assistance. But he who violates law and order (in Lebanon) must be brought to justice. I will not go easy in the application of the law. Everyone responsible must be made to account for his responsibility, regardless of who he may be.

Radio address, Jan. 1/ The New York Times, 1-2:(1)2.

Joseph J. Sisco
Assistant Secretary for Near Eastern and South Asian Affairs, Department of State of the United States

There is a special relationship that does exist between the United States and Israel; I won't deny that. But we also have our differences with the Israelis. Our interests go beyond any one country in the Middle East. Our interests are not served by the no-war, no-peace situation that exists in the area. The Soviets have gained from this. Our interests are best served by a political settlement (between the Arabs and Israel) that brings about stability. And the only way to get a political settlement is to try and meet the legitimate concerns of both sides.

Interview, Washington/ The National Observer, 2-26:7.

Yosef Tekoah
Israeli Ambassador to the United Nations

(Appealing to Communist China for support in Israel's conflict with the Arab states): In the dawn of recorded history, there had been two nations in Asia—China in the East and Israel in the West. China knows that history did not begin with the Arab efforts to oust the Israelis from the Middle East. The people of China will recognize Israel's fundamental rights of peace and coexistence.

At United Nations, N.Y., June 23/ The New York Times, 6-25:(1)14.

(On Israeli attacks in Lebanon in reprisal for Lebanon-based Arab terrorist attacks in Israel): It is the duty of the Lebanese government to insure that its territory is not used as a springboard for aggression against a neighboring state. When Lebanon repudiates that obligation, it leaves Israel no alternative but to act in self-defense.

At United Nations, N.Y., June 23/ Los Angeles Times, 6-24:(1)3.

Mohammed el Zayyat
Minister of State for Information of Egypt

We desire peace and friendship with all, and are eager to have good relations with the United States, China, Japan, the Soviet Union, the United Kingdom and everyone else. But we are not on the Russian team and do not want to be on the American or any other team.

News conference, Cairo, July 22/ The Washington Post, 7-23:(A)1.

The United Nations

Ole Algard
Norwegian Representative to the United Nations

Right now, the UN is used primarily as a forum for national politics—not as a forum for real internationalism . . . Thus the goals of the United Nations are limited by what the member states will allow the UN to accomplish. After all, right now, the UN is not a supranational power. It is only a co-operative of nations.

The New York Times, 6-10:2.

Khalid Ali
Counselor, Pakistani Mission to the United Nations

In a world in which a masterpiece like the "Pieta" is attacked by a man with a hammer, isn't it better for people to work together (at the UN) to shape a peaceful and better world no matter how slow and frustrating the task, no matter how slow the progress? In a world where so many people are at war with each other, isn't it better for people here (at the UN) to worry about the placement of commas in documents aimed at keeping the peace rather than to contribute to the battle? It may be painfully slow moving forward here, but at least we are moving forward. At least we are going in the right direction.

The New York Times, 6-10:2.

George Bush
United States Ambassador/Permanent Representative to the United Nations

(On Communist China's admission to the UN): Peking is represented by strong, upright and able men with whom we will agree some of the time and disagree a lot of the time. But the very fact that there are these opinion exchanges in the full glare of world publicity is a good thing for the world and for this organization . . . In spite of my immense disappointment at the expulsion of Nationalist China, I think the UN is a more realistic manifestation of the world as it is with Peking in it. It could have been even more so if Nationalist China had remained.

Interview, Washington/ The Dallas Times Herald, 1-28:(A)4.

. . . my theory of representation is that I should be an advocate for the foreign policy of the U.S. government. That doesn't mean I have to surrender my judgment. That doesn't mean I don't have some differences of emphasis. But if, out of conviction, I can't support a policy, if I don't believe in a policy, then I think the U.S. is ill-served (at the UN) by having me as Ambassador. No matter what the question is, I must, out of conviction—and I emphasize out of conviction—reflect the views of the (U.S.) Administration. If I can't do that, clearly the only thing to do is to get out. I should not be dragging my feet.

Interview, New York/ San Francisco Examiner, 10-9:5.

We (at the UN) recognize that it can't instantly solve these problems (the India-Pakistan war, Vietnam, etc.), and some people don't. Some people think if you don't want to turn over your foreign policy to the UN in its entirety, then you're not a UN believer. This kind of super-idealism has hurt the UN in this country because there has been an over-expectation, an over-promise. In some of the areas where you go, the people that are supposed to be supporting the UN are kind of damaging it because they have such an unpragmatic view . . .

Interview, New York/ San Francisco Examiner, 10-9:5.

Samuel De Palma
Assistant Secretary for International Organization Affairs, Department of State of the United States

The mood of frustration and disenchantment which has developed in recent years because of the United Nations' shortcomings in political and security matters is now aggravated by skepticism about its managerial effectiveness in economic and social areas. On the one hand, it is less and less used in political crises—except to score propaganda points and administer relief. On the other, the effectiveness of its acknowledged role as an instrument for organizing technical and economic cooperation and services to developing countries is also being questioned.

Before American Assembly/ The New York Times, 6-11:(4)3.

William L. Dickinson
United States Representative, R–Ala.

I think we need to realize what the UN is: It is a debating society. That Tower of Babel on the East River in New York is a fine forum to get together and to discuss world problems; but so far as its doing anything really worthwhile, like stopping the war in the Mideast, it has been of no avail.

May 18/Quote, 7-2:15.

Arthur J. Goldberg
Former United States Ambassador/ Permanent Representative to the United Nations

Without vigorous support by the United States, the United Nations cannot long endure. Never, since its creation in 1945, has the United Nations been so downgraded as an important component of American foreign policy as it is today under the present (Nixon) Administration . . . It is neither seemly nor in our national interest for the United States, a principal architect of the United Nations, to undermine its foundations, and this we are now doing. Our nation derived its great influence in the world not only from great physical power but also from the fact that our basic law and our national outlook are premised on the equality and dignity of all men. The way to peace in this turbulent age is to keep that national vision and to extend it to the international sphere; to work with all our might for the strengthening of the UN as the structure of law and enduring peace. For though the United Nations alone cannot assure world peace, there can be no peace without it.

At seminar of American Assembly on the United States and the United Nations, Harriman, N.Y., April 13/ The New York Times, 4-14:15.

John V. Lindsay
Mayor of New York

The victories of (former UN Secretary General) U Thant were the battles that were not fought—the silent guns and tranquil borders. His were the quiet accomplishments of peace.

At ceremony awarding Mr. Thant the New York City Medal of Honor/ The Christian Science Monitor, 2-14:4.

Yahya Mahmassani
First Secretary, Lebanese Mission to the United Nations

Your first year at the United Nations, you watch and learn. It is all new and it is all terribly confusing. The second year, things start to come into focus and you start to produce and be constructive. The third year, you reach the peak of your productivity. You know the tricks and the ropes of diplomacy here. You feel a sense of accomplishment at the things that you are able to bring to fruition. The fourth year, things start going downhill. It is a story repeated over and over again—endlessly. Disappointment sets in, disillusionment. A resolution is passed and you find yourself thinking: one

(YAHYA MAHMASSANI)

more resolution, and one more resolution that means nothing.

The New York Times, 6-10:2.

Yakov A. Malik
Soviet Ambassador/Permanent Representative to the United Nations

(On a U.S. request that its contribution to the UN budget be reduced): This request is absolutely unjustified, unfounded and unacceptable. The proposal is a direct challenge to the only possible method of assessing contributions to the United Nations budget—the ability to pay.

At United Nations, N.Y., Dec. 13/ Los Angeles Times, 12-14:(1)1.

Michael Manley
Prime Minister of Jamaica

. . . this Assembly has become known as a place where torrents of words that burn with urgency and truth fall upon deaf ears—ears that are closed by the narrowest considerations of national self-interest. The continuing inability of the United Nations to mediate situations of international crisis and reduce the inequalities between nations does not reflect any lack of desire or skill among the staff of this organization or its various agencies. The inadequacies of the United Nations precisely reflect the misplaced priorities of its member nations—and especially of the most powerful and wealthy ones among them.

Addressing the General Assembly, United Nations, N.Y., Oct. 2/ Vital Speeches, 11-15:75.

Gale W. McGee
United States Senator, D–Wyo.; Member, U.S. delegation to United Nations General Assembly

. . . one of the reasons I think we're in trouble in the UN—in this country (the U.S.) at least—is the over-expectation. Whenever something goes wrong in the world, somebody like (U.S. Senators) Bill Fulbright or Mike Mansfield, who ought to know better, says let the UN do it. It was never equipped to do that. And yet our people somehow still have this strange notion that, if everything's going all right, somebody else did it; if something falls apart, the United Nations failed again.

Interview/ Los Angeles Times, 11-9:(7)4.

George S. McGovern
United States Senator, D–S.D.; Democratic Presidential nominee

It is fashionable to dismiss the United Nations as outdated because it has not always been successful. But every human institution is subject to at least occasional failures, as we have learned so painfully in Southeast Asia. The true test of any institution is whether it still serves an important purpose . . . If we are ready to submit disputes to the UN, we can slowly and gradually revive its capacity for the discussion and resolution of threats to the peace. And to those who say that this capacity is limited, I reply: "What could be more limited than the unilateralism of our (U.S.) policy in Vietnam, which delayed peace so long?"

At Gonzaga University, Oct. 28/ The New York Times, 10-29:(1)49.

Richard M. Nixon
President of the United States

We have reached the point at which it is no service to the idea of the United Nations and no contribution to its future to blink at its limitations . . . We believe that the time has come for a large dose of realism and candor in the United States policy toward the United Nations.

The New York Times, 6-11:(4)3.

Brian E. Urquhart
Assistant Secretary General of the United Nations

Three-fourths of the time (in the UN) you achieve nothing; but every once in a while it works just enough to make it worthwhile going on with it.

The Washington Post, 5-11:(H)1.

Kurt Waldheim
Secretary General
of the United Nations

I am not a man who apathetically sticks his head in the sand. Naturally, I realize the Secretary General must know his limits. But within the framework of these limitations, he can and must be as active as possible.

Interview/
The Washington Post, 1-4:(A)10.

The problem is that international crises are taken to the Security Council rather late. The patient is brought to the doctor too late, when he is almost dead, and then when the Security Council is not able to do something about him, still the Security Council is made responsible for the failure.

Interview, United Nations, N.Y.,
Jan. 6/
Los Angeles Times, 1-7:(1)15.

. . . we all know that people are disappointed with the achievements of the United Nations. But I think people have expected too much right from the beginning . . . They thought it was a world government with executive power, and it isn't so. We have no executive power. We are not a world government. We can only convince governments to cooperate, and we can do, I think, a lot through quiet diplomacy.

TV-radio interview, New York/
"Meet the Press,"
National Broadcasting Company, 1-9.

(The UN has not yet succeeded) in making world opinion a living force in international cooperation or in giving the peoples of the world their rightful influence in world affairs. We have so far, except on rare occasions, failed to strike the imagination of the man in the street and thus gain the basic support which will be required if we are to face effectively the enormous problems which confront us.

At dedication of Conference Center
of the School of International Affairs,
Columbia University, March 28/
The New York Times, 3-29:2.

I don't criticize my predecessors. Trygve Lie, the first Secretary General, said this is the most impossible job on earth. The most recent, U Thant, did his best; I have the highest regard for him, and he made a great contribution. But each man must use his own approach to these matters. That is what I am doing.

The New York Times, 3-29:41.

Believe me, if there were no United Nations it would be necessary to invent them. Whether we like them or not, they are a necessity. You know, there was a famous Czech historian who wrote of the Austrian Empire: "If Austria didn't exist, it would have to be created. Otherwise, there would be a vacuum in the Danubian basin." So it is today with the Republic of Austria. It is a necessity. It fills a vacuum between East and West. And the same is true of the United Nations. They fill that vacuum between East and West. If they did not exist, they would have to be created. They are a necessity of our time.

Interview, United Nations, N.Y./
The New York Times, 6-10:2.

Whether it is (the Arab terrorist killing of 11 Israeli Olympic team members in) Munich or whether it is the abduction of a diplomat or any other innocent man or woman, we (the UN) have the duty to do something against it . . . In the United Nations, we are always confronted with this problem—either we do something, in which case we may be criticized for trying and not succeeding, or we do nothing, in which case we are criticized because we did not try. We have to take the risk.

News conference,
United Nations, N.Y., Sept. 12/
Los Angeles Times, 9-13:(1)5.

(KURT WALDHEIM)

I am confident that the UN has a future, because there is no alternative, believe me. Even with all the bilateral diplomacy, which is quite in order—and I have certainly nothing against it—this alone is not enough in this age. You need multilateral cooperation; and the best forum for this is the UN.

The Christian Science Monitor, 9-18:7.

The public in the United States is disappointed by the achievements of the United Nations. They look around the world and see all the conflicts and wars—in Vietnam, in the Middle East, in Northern Ireland, in India and Pakistan—and they ask, why can't the UN solve them? And if they can't solve them, *all* of them, they say, who needs the UN? What Americans sometimes forget is that, since the UN was created in San Francisco in 1945, it has accomplished a great deal, not only in preventing some conflicts from breaking out—which means the public never heard about them—and resolving certain conflicts once they did break out, but also we have done some very important things in the field of social and economic development throughout the world. And we have done these things with not so much money: The American citizen pays each year about the price of a package of cigarettes to support the UN budget—not so much, is it? Personally, I believe that if the American people were more aware of this, there would be far greater appreciation here for the UN. We wouldn't be having quite the same criticism as we are now receiving in this country.

Interview, United Nations, N.Y./ Parade, 10-22:4.

Mohammed el Zayyat
Foreign Minister of Egypt

The United Nations is passing through a grave crisis. Its inability to act effectively whenever international peace and security is endangered has been eroding confidence in its effectiveness. Thus, its authority, credibility and relevance are today at stake.

At United Nations, N.Y., Nov. 29/ Los Angeles Herald-Examiner, 11-29:(A)2.

War and Peace

Robert Anderson
President, North American Rockwell Corporation

I believe global unity in communications, travel and trade—the free movement of trade and industry, following in the footsteps of millions of people who are walking and driving and flying unhindered past national boundaries—is one of the greatest passports to peace and prosperity this world has ever known . . . it's difficult to punch in the nose a man with whom you've just had a friendly lunch.

At WEMA/WESCON meeting, Los Angeles, Sept. 19/ Vital Speeches, 10-15:7.

Chiao Kuan-hua
Deputy Foreign Minister of, and chief United Nations General Assembly delegate from, the People's Republic of (Communist) China

People condemn war and consider it a barbarous way of settling disputes among mankind. But we are soberly aware that war is inevitable so long as society is divided into classes and the exploitation of man by man still exists.

At United Nations, N.Y., Oct. 3/ The New York Times, 10-4:1.

Chou En-lai
Premier of the People's Republic of (Communist) China

The superpowers (the U.S. and Soviet Union) have not ceased their expansion and aggression against other countries, and the international situation is far from truly relaxed. What calls for attention is the fact that, while mouthing disarmament and the strengthening of the international security, in reality they are continuing to step up arms expansion and war preparations. The agreements they reached not long ago on the so-called limitation of strategic nuclear weapons were by no means a step toward curbing the arms race as they boasted, but marked the beginning of a new stage of their arms race. The fact is that the ink on the agreements was hardly dry before one announced an increase of billions of dollars for military expenditure and the other hastened to test new-type weapons, clamoring for seizing nuclear superiority. Disarmament is out of the question, let alone international peace and security, in the circumstances when the superpowers continue to intensify their arms expansion and war preparations.

At banquet for visiting Yemen delegation, Peking, July 17/ Los Angeles Herald-Examiner, 7-18:(A)4.

Indira Gandhi
Prime Minister of India

India realizes war is a bad thing; but there are times when not accepting the challenge of war amounts to cowardice and non-fulfillment of duty.

At Congress Party rally, New Delhi, Jan. 2/ Los Angeles Times, 1-3:(1)9.

Norman E. Kirk
Prime Minister-elect of New Zealand

My belief is that peace is an unnatural state of affairs. Violence is primitive and natural. People have got to create and then maintain peace.

Interview, Christchurch, New Zealand, Nov. 26/ Los Angeles Times, 11-27:(1)19.

Henry A. Kissinger
Assistant to the President of the United States for National Security Affairs

(On the new arms agreements between the U.S. and the Soviet Union): The President (Nixon) . . . has stressed that it is inappropriate to pose the question in terms of victory or defeat. In an agreement of this kind, either both sides win or both sides lose. This will either be a serious attempt to turn the world away from time-worn practices of jockeying for power, or there will be endless, wasteful and purposeless competition in the acquisition of armaments.

Before members of Congress, Washington, June 15/ U.S. News & World Report, 7-3:58.

Melvin R. Laird
Secretary of Defense of the United States

If NATO maintains a realistic concept of what is needed for peace, there will be peace. If the West deludes itself as to what is necessary for defense, the frightful cost of that decision will be war.

News conference, Brussels, Dec. 6/ The New York Times, 12-7:2.

George S. McGovern
United States Senator, D–S.D.; Democratic Presidential nominee

If I have any influence at all over the course of events in the next few years, there is one thing I want to do. I want to make it possible for children to live a full life before they die . . . for a little girl named Kim in Vietnam to be loved—not to be burned by the flames of napalm. I say peace now, but not just now—but peace always for all the people of this world. I say peace on a planet—peace from those who have no right to take life from other people on this planet . . .

Campaigning for the Presidential election, Los Angeles, Sept. 5/ Los Angeles Times, 9-6:(1)32.

Richard M. Nixon
President of the United States

Many think I'm somewhat naive when I talk about a generation of peace. Many think it's purely political. But we all must set great goals and then try to achieve them. Woodrow Wilson talked about the war to save the world for democracy; H. G. Wells said that World War I was the war to end wars; and those were great goals. But having said this, my feeling today is that we are entering the period when the danger of world conflict, of world war, has been very substantially reduced. There is a genuine possibility for a generation of Americans to be free from a major war.

Interview/ The Reader's Digest, February:61.

. . . each nation of the world must renounce the use of force, the use of aggression against other nations. We must also recognize another proposition, and that is that a great responsibility particularly rests upon the great powers, that every great power must follow the principle that it should not encourage, directly or indirectly, any other nation to use force or armed aggression against its neighbor.

At signing of convention outlawing biological weapons, Washington, April 10/ The New York Times, 4-11:17.

Neither the limitation of arms nor the declaration of peaceful purposes will bring peace if, directly or indirectly, the aggressive use of existing weapons is encouraged. And great powers cannot avoid responsibility for the aggressive actions of those to whom they give the means for embarking on such actions. The great powers must use their influence to halt aggression and not to encourage it.

Before Canadian Parliament, Ottawa, April 14/ Los Angeles Times, 4-15:(1)18.

As we look at the prospects for peace, we see that we have made significant progress at reducing the possible sources of direct conflict between us (the U.S. and the Soviet Union). But history tells us that great nations have often been dragged into war without intending it by conflicts between smaller nations. As great powers, we can and should use our influence to prevent this from happening. Our goal should be to discourage aggression in other parts of the world—and particularly among those smaller nations that look to us for leadership and example. With great power goes great responsibility. When a man walks with a giant tread, he must be careful where he sets his feet. There can be true peace only when the weak are as safe as the strong.

Broadcast address, Moscow, May 28/ The New York Times, 5-29:3.

We have the opportunity in our time to be the peacemakers of the world, because the world trusts and respects us, and because the world knows that we will use our power only to defend freedom, never to destroy it; only to keep the peace, never to break it. A strong America is not the enemy of peace. It is the guardian of peace.

Accepting the Republican Presidential nomination, Miami Beach, Aug. 23/ Los Angeles Times, 8-24:(1)24.

(Signing a Congressional resolution approving the U.S.-Soviet arms agreement): This is not an agreement which ends a war. This is not an agreement which guarantees there will be no war. What it is is the beginning of a process that is enormously important—to limit now, and we hope later reduce, the burden of arms, and thereby reduce the danger of war.

Washington, Sept. 30/ San Francisco Examiner & Chronicle, 10-1:(A)2.

It is clear that we will not in our lifetimes have a world free of danger. Anyone who reads history knows that danger has always been a part of the common lot of mankind. Anyone who knows the world today knows that nations have not all been suddenly overtaken by some new and unprecedented wave of pure good-will and benign intentions. But we can lessen the danger. We can contain it. We can forge a network of relationships and of interdependencies that restrain aggression and take the profit out of war. We cannot make all nations the same . . . but we can establish conditions in which they will be more likely to live in peace with one another.

The Dallas Times Herald, 11-12:(L)1.

Paul VI
Pope

We must base peace on justice if we want it to be true, stable and beneficial. Whoever seeks peace on other bases—power, violence, wealth, suppression of civil rights, oppression of just liberties—does not construct a human and authentic peace.

Vatican City, Jan. 1/ San Francisco Examiner, 1-1:22.

Peace is civilization's highest good. It does not come of itself. It does not stay of itself. It comes from great efforts and great plans.

Rome, Jan. 1/ Los Angeles Herald-Examiner, 1-2:(A)5.

(The arms race) is an epidemic phenomenon. No people now seems able to escape its contagion . . . Every country shares in it—great powers and medium ones and even the weak nations or those of the so-called Third World . . . The realization of peace demands—and attempts to attain this are already being carried out with courageous and wise initiatives—that the opposite road be followed: that of progressive disarmament.

Vatican City, Jan. 10/ Los Angeles Herald-Examiner, 1-11:(A)11.

The psychology of humanity is falling back on pessimistic convictions about the impossibility of peace; that is, that only force and conflict can maintain it.

Vatican City, July 2/ Los Angeles Herald-Examiner, 7-3:(A)4.

Nikolai V. Podgorny
President of the Soviet Union

(During 1971, progress was made) in generally changing the international situation in favor of peace. At the same time, we clearly understand that those who favor military adventures have not laid down their arms; that on the path toward stronger peace, there are many difficulties and obstacles.

New Year's broadcast address, Moscow, Jan. 1/ The New York Times, 1-2:(1)46.

Ronald Reagan
Governor of California

Our generation has known war four times. Our love of peace has not been learned from books, but has been born of sorrow—the sorrow of farewell to father, son and brother, and oh so many friends.

At American Legion California convention, San Jose, June 22/ San Francisco Examiner, 6-23:14.

All of us denounce war; all of us consider it man's greatest stupidity. And yet wars happen, and they involve the most passionate lovers of peace . . .

At National Guard convention, San Francisco, Sept. 14/ San Francisco Examiner, 9-15:9.

Carlos P. Romulo
Foreign Secretary of the Philippines

Isn't it about time that the great powers, unable to attack one another directly without mortal danger to themselves, ceased to practice wars by proxy, using the Third World as a cockpit for their persisting ambitions for regional or global hegemony?

At United Nations, N.Y., Oct. 9/ The New York Times, 10-10:3.

Hugh Scott
United States Senator, R–Pa.

I believe today that . . . containment of Communism is not the answer. What the answer is, is to recognize that the world has many systems—socialism as in Yugoslavia, national socialism, Communism, small-country systems, big-country systems, democracy—and all of these systems have got to get together if people aren't going to destroy themselves on the battlefield or in a nuclear holocaust.

San Francisco Examiner & Chronicle, 9-3:(This World)2.

Eric Sevareid
News commentator, Columbia Broadcasting System

. . . the official conviction seems to be (that) the two superpowers (the U.S. and the Soviet Union) can consciously arrange the world's peace. But Germany and Japan grow immensely strong economically; Europe inches toward a kind of unity; (Communist) China is a going and growing concern; the explosive Mideast lives by its own dynamics; India dominates the subcontinent; and everywhere popular, antiestablishment movements are moving.

News commentary, May 23/ The Christian Science Monitor, 6-1:16.

Pierre Elliott Trudeau
Prime Minister of Canada

I think the world has been changing more—certainly in relations between individual countries—in the past couple of years than at any time since the end of World War II. I think the initiatives by the United States toward the Soviet Union and People's Republic of (Communist) China are indications of that change. The success in the strategic arms limitation talks (SALT), the success in the ratification of the four-power treaty over Berlin, the treaties negotiated between West Germany and Poland and the Soviet Union—I think all these represent a turning away from the cold-war period. Now there is a greater realization that peace and progress must come through communication and understanding, and that you can't have that as long as people turn their backs on other people.

Interview, Ottawa/
U.S. News & World Report, 7-3:35.

Kurt Waldheim
Secretary General
of the United Nations

The fact that there has been no world war for 27 years in the most populous and more rapidly changing human society the world has ever seen can be no damper on our impatience and concern with bleeding and unsolved conflicts. While welcoming the smiles, we must also eliminate the tears.

Quote, 8-6:121.

We live today in an era where peace is maintained mainly through the deterrent of weapons of mass destruction; a peace built on fear. The existence of these frightening weapons seriously jeopardizes world peace, and this makes it all the more important that we should devote ourselves to reduce and finally eliminate the wasteful armaments race.

At banquet in his honor,
Peking, Aug. 12/
The New York Times, 8-13:(1)9.

PART THREE

General

The Arts

Amyas Ames
Chairman, Lincoln Center for the Performing Arts, New York; Chairman, Partnership for the Arts

Last year (in the U.S.) we saw a single pressure group, the highway lobby, take away almost $24 billion in tax money, while Federal support for the arts was only the equivalent of about two miles of super highway or one major traffic circle—and that money had to be spread across the entire country . . . we must ask the leaders in government to do for the arts in the 1970s what was done for the sciences in the 1950s and 1960s. We must tell our political leaders that, as a great people, we can no longer allow the anemia of inflation to sap the vitality and, at times, the very life of the arts.

Before National Association of Schools of Music, Minneapolis/ The Dallas Times Herald, 11-24:(C)11.

Robert O. Anderson
Chairman, Atlantic Richfield Corporation; Chairman, Business Committee for the Arts

I believe business will do for the arts as much as it succeeded in doing for higher education since World War II—and will do it in as short a period of time.

The New York Times, 1-10:43.

George Balanchine
Director, New York City Ballet

. . . art is beyond words, beyond science, beyond mathematics, beyond everything else. Most people want things to be concrete or they're not interested. Talking about art is like talking about how wonderful good wine is. You can't really describe it.

Interview/ The Dallas Times Herald, 6-25:(H)3.

Saul Bellow
Author

The ruling class in this country (the U.S.) has produced remarkably few poets and novelists; and considering its immense wealth, it has been incredibly stingy . . . Its contribution to culture—except in the way of money contributed to universities and research institutes—has been negligible . . . it is felt that culture is not something strong, but something weak; not a male power that takes the initiative, but a lady power that gives ground. This suspicion of weakness, I think, accounts for the anti-intellectualism of so many intellectuals, their primitivism, their heedless redskin wildness, their extremism.

At Chicago Public Library's Centennial Series/The National Observer, 11-11:20.

Ingmar Bergman
Motion picture director

. . . I regard art as insignificant. Art has lost the influence it formerly had as a molder of opinion. A hundred years ago, a novel could spark off a revolution; nowadays, other media have assumed significance as molders of opinion. So you can say that art possibly has significance for these new molders of opinion. Possibly. I myself don't think so. But I think the most important thing one can do is to learn how one functions oneself, and perhaps give other people certain ideas as to how they function; and in this way, just to a very small degree—just to a microscopic degree, perhaps—help to raise the general level of cognition in man, I repeat, to a microscopic degree.

Interview/ The Washington Post, 10-29:(L)1.

John Brademas
United States Representative, D–Ind.

Museums have arrived at the point where they can no longer preserve and exhibit our matchless national treasure without substantial national aid. What is particularly striking about the increased attendance of American museums is the extent to which there has been a rise in demand for their services as educational institutions. This continually-increasing museum attendance is of vast benefit to all Americans. Yet for individual museums—museums of all shapes, sizes and purposes—it means sharply-heightened costs. More trained staff, guards, guides, acquisitions, exhibits, maintenance, buildings, insurance—all of these are necessary. No one suggests that the Federal government should now assume the burden of supporting American museums. But it is obvious that, to the extent that museums are providing an educational service benefiting everyone, they should be considered eligible for public support.

Los Angeles/
Los Angeles Times, 8-31:(4)2.

John Canaday
Art critic, "The New York Times"

I think it's (1972) been a pretty healthy year in painting and sculpture, but not a terribly exciting year. It was a year when extreme avant-garde movements got the final black eye, having reduced themselves to such boredom, rather than absurdity, that the public was no longer interested in them . . . I think it was a time of settling down in the arts that was altogether a very good thing. You could show anything in the galleries this year, from the wildest abstraction to your own self stark naked—which people did—and I think get a much more considered reaction to it from critics than you've been able to in the past. Anything went, by which I mean not anything extreme, but just anything—conservative, extreme or what not. I call that healthy.

Panel discussion, New York/
The New York Times, 12-26:44.

Robert Carr
Home Secretary of the United Kingdom

Pornography is a form of pollution. It is a commercial assault on the proper reticences, qualities and standards of everyday life.

San Francisco Examiner, 10-23:32.

John Coolidge
Former director, Fogg Art Museum, Harvard University

. . . the established art museums of the Northeast no longer give high priority to collecting. The truth is that many curators—fully supported by their trustees—have stopped collecting in favor of shopping for masterpieces . . . But man's view of himself, his fellows, his past, his present, his future, changes constantly and fundamentally. The function of collecting works of art is to reflect and to stimulate this creative change. The museum which stops collecting in favor of shopping stops thinking about the issues which matter most, and what is worse, can no longer effectively help those who do think about such things.

The New York Times, 3-19:(2)21.

Norman Corwin
Author

Art is not a refuge from life. Each artist in history communicated something cherishable to all who had eyes or all . . . who had ears. One may ask whether Charles Dickens did not have a greater influence on his time than the scientists of his day; whether George Gershwin did not give more of lasting felicitous value to the whole world than color television.

At University of Judaism
Author-Artist Luncheon, Los Angeles/
Los Angeles Herald-Examiner, 7-4:(B)1.

Charles C. Cunningham
Director, Art Institute of Chicago

The museum is no longer a cloistered hall. It's becoming more and more involved—and rightly so—with social problems, ecology and so forth. But the increasing workload puts tremendous pressure on the director and the staff. It used to be that the director was first an art historian and then an administrator. Now we're dealing with all sorts of other things and—only 10 per cent art.

Telephone interview, Chicago/
The New York Times, 1-24:21.

Giorgio de Chirico
Painter

I like New York best from the air. I can't see modern art from up there.

Interview, New York/
The New York Times, 1-21:26.

. . . painting is not a question of style but of the quality of materials. It was the quality of Titian's painting that interested—the technique, the emulsions he used . . . People see painting as an image, a photo—and don't understand the brushwork, the techniques, behind it . . . the decadence of modern painting began with the decadence of materials . . .

Interview, New York/
The New York Times, 1-23:(2)24.

The world lives by legends! I never had anything to do with the surrealists! My paintings have nothing to do with surrealism! Yet I am called over and over again the father of surrealism. It is mad. The world prefers the legend to the truth.

Interview, New York/
Newsweek, 1-31:60.

Jose de Rivera
Sculptor

My notion is that the primary function of an artist is the creation and production of work. And the second function is showing it. I don't belong to any particular period or school; my job is to make work and then project the experience I have.

New York/
The New York Times, 5-16:48.

Hugues de Varine-Bohan
Director,
International Council of Museums

(America's) museums have deficits. You don't find deficit museums in Europe. You find starving museums.

Interview, Paris/
The New York Times, 5-30:1.

Arthur Fiedler
Conductor, Boston Pops Orchestra

I think we're on a terrible culture binge in this country. We're trying to stuff culture down people's throats. You can't. It has to be done gradually. The snobs talk Stravinsky, John Cage and so forth. They don't know it, they don't like it, they don't understand it. A lot of this music *I*, as a professional musician, have great difficulty understanding.

Interview, Syracuse, N.Y./
The New York Times, 4-2:(2)32.

Armand Hammer
Chairman,
Occidental Petroleum Corporation

(On art collecting): Pictures are more than just collecting. You are connecting yourself with something that really is immortal, something that has survived all these centuries. You are preserving something for posterity.

Los Angeles Herald-Examiner,
1-9:(California Living)10.

Claude Levi-Strauss
Anthropologist

I have nothing against art; but all the same, it's a pretty dull and narrow affair compared with a worldview in which all of nature (speaks) to man.

Interview/
The New York Times, 1-21:47.

Ross Martin
Actor

The arts are really the last bastion of individual identity in a culture which increasingly reduces the individual to a number or a statistic.

At symposium before arts-oriented students, Los Angeles/ Los Angeles Times, 3-23:(4)14.

John O. Pastore
United States Senator, D–R.I.

(Media morality) means that everyone responsible for the creation and presentation of a television program, a movie, or publication of a book ought to be guided by one fundamental standard—"should the audience or readers be better human beings for having seen or read what I am offering?" . . . Our society, in order to be free and vital, must have a sound moral base. That does not mean my individual moral code, or yours, or anyone else's should be the order of the day. Rather, fundamental concepts of decency which are common to us all must prevail. (The true source of our national history) will be our literature, our television and our moving pictures, because the media reflects our lives, our personal dramas and our values. An understanding of these matters will be the key to knowing just what sort of a society and just what sort of people we were . . . It is far more rewarding to challenge the media to be great than to warn it of excesses. If we insist on the very best, and by example inculcate the same values and expectations in our young, there will be no place in our society for those who would offer us less.

At Morality in Media dinner, New York, Nov. 13/ Daily Variety, 11-14:1,11.

Georges Pompidou
President of France

(On government aid and influence in the arts): I believe the essential role of the state is to give the means, which is buying, ordering, contributing study and research centers, organizing and facilitating exhibitions. What else would there be, unless one wanted to create an "official art."

Interview/ The New York Times, 11-5:(1)5.

Chaim Potok
Author

Art as we understand it is really the product of secular humanism. Art in the service of *anything* is not art at all. Art must be at the service of the artist, period—asserting himself, refusing to submerge himself within a total group.

Interview, Philadelphia/ The National Observer, 5-20:23.

Man Ray
Artist

The name—that's what people are interested in. If it's signed, it's you; and if it's not signed, it isn't worth a damn.

Paris/ The Washington Post, 2-26:(E)4.

Edward G. Robinson
Actor

Art is surcease from sorrow; it makes your life livable.

Interview, Los Angeles/ The Dallas Times Herald, 11-2:(E)10.

Norman Rockwell
Painter

(Regarding his paintings): Sentimental trash? Maybe. Maybe as I grew up and found that the world wasn't the perfectly pleasant place I had thought it to be, I unconsciously decided that, even if it wasn't an ideal world, it should be and so painted only the ideal aspects of it—pictures in which there were no drunken slatterns or self-centered mothers . . . only foxy grandpas who played baseball with the kids and boys who fished from logs and got up circuses in the backyard.

The Washington Post, 5-27:(B)4.

William Saroyan
Author

The making of anything really worth making calls for an isolation. Isolation and necessity for intense concentration over a long period of time make the artist almost anti-social . . . The loneliness is no desperate, abject loneliness, but a kind of majestic loneliness—a kinship with larger things. They may be isolated, but they're not alone.

Interview, Fresno, Calif./ Los Angeles Times, 3-1:(2)5.

Isaac Bashevis Singer
Author

Folklore is the very basis of literature and of all art. It is the address, the roots, of art.

Interview, San Francisco, May 2/ San Francisco Examiner, 5-3:9.

Fashion

Nicole Alphand
Director, Pierre Cardin, Paris

You have to adapt clothes to the way you are living. That's what real elegance is . . . To be elegant is not to have a good dress, but good shoes and a good bag and hair that is coiffured and good makeup. It is possible to be well-dressed without spending a lot of money. Of course, you have to have some.

Interview, Paris/
The Washington Post, 1-10:(B)3.

Geoffrey Beene
Fashion designer

I feel a little apprehensive and cautious about the fashion mood of the moment. And (last week's) Paris (openings) didn't help. Despite *Women's Wear Daily's* raves—they're almost obliged to give good reviews in return for first peeks—there were no rumblings of anything great happening. The collections were not so much bad as they were "vanilla."

Interview, Beverly Hills, Calif./
Los Angeles Times, 2-4:(4)2.

Mr. Blackwell
Fashion designer

(Advocating the return to traditional fashions): We'd better have a dinner dress. We'd better have a cocktail dress. We'd better have an evening dress. We'd better have a respectable lunch dress. It's all that's going to save the industry.

Los Angeles Times, 4-17:(4)1.

Bill Blass
Fashion designer

The word "wearable" isn't a fashion obscenity any more. We're returning to sanity. It's chic to look pretty and trim and well put together. Extremes are out, if ever they were in. After the ethnics and the costumes and the midis of the '60s, designers are making the kinds of clothes women want. After all, who wants to be "amused" by fashion?

San Francisco, Jan. 31/
San Francisco Examiner, 2-1:21.

Seventh Avenue is changing radically. Designers, as owners of their own businesses, are no longer hidden in the back room. Competition is greater as the designer emerges as a businessman. You can be more daring.

Interview, Dallas, Feb. 7/
The Dallas Times Herald, 2-8:(A)13.

In the fashion revolution of the '60s, we were afraid not to seem "with it." We lost sight of the fact that we had customers over 20. But by the end of the decade it was rapidly brought home to us how ridiculous women looked in their daughters' clothes.

Newsweek, 8-21:53.

Pierre Cardin
Fashion designer

Within 20 years, we will all be stark naked. The streets will be climatized and, if they are not, we'll wear something, a belt or a necklace, which will climatize our body heat individually.

Quote, 1-9:25.

(Saying he is through creating styles for the exclusive use of the privileged): Good taste should walk in the streets, on the bodies of anonymous women.

Sao Paulo, Brazil/
The Washington Post, 5-27:(A)12.

When you have a creative spirit, you can design a chair as well as a handbag. Nothing should limit the imagination. I have become commercial, but I don't think commercially. I don't prostitute myself, but I want to be bought . . . I have become a public phenomonon—like Charlie Chaplin or Brigitte Bardot. In fact, if it were not for the simplicity of my background, I would have come to Paris to dance, act or be in films.

Interview/Newsweek, 7-24:72.

Oleg Cassini
Fashion designer

There is a small group of designers who are creating for the elite—that's an obsolete market. We're going through social revolution, a fashion revolution—a reactionary movement. I don't want to be a designer for the rich. I'm interested in the girl who up to now has been in jeans. This is my theory: If your customer comes to you in a Rolls-Royce, you go home in the subway. But if she comes to you in the subway, you may go home in the Rolls-Royce.

Interview, New York/ "W": a Fairchild publication, 7-28:5.

Walter Cronkite
News commentator, Columbia Broadcasting System

(On being named one of the nation's ten best-dressed men by the Fashion Foundation of America): So far as I know, this distinction was earned entirely by straightening my tie and putting on a jacket before the TV camera turns on every night. Probably I could have broadcast for years without pants on, and the Fashion Foundation wouldn't have been a bit the wiser.

The Dallas Times Herald, 1-7:(A)3.

Lilly Dache
Fashion designer

Women's hats are in fashion today, but I personally will never make them again. Women's fashion is so very simple today and there is such imaginative hair styles, a woman only needs a little stocking-cap for the wind.

Interview, Los Angeles/ Los Angeles Herald-Examiner, 10-29:(E)1.

Zsa Zsa Gabor
Actress

I'll always stay glamorous. I'll buy the prettiest dresses. I'll look as good as I can. Glamor's gone out of the whole world. Today if a man puts on a black tie and goes out somewhere, he has to make excuses for himself. If I go into Maxim's and find I'm the only woman with a beautiful coat on, should I feel guilty? I don't need to. I'm right. They're wrong.

Interview, London/ San Francisco Examiner & Chronicle, 4-30:(Datebook)7.

Rudi Gernreich
Fashion designer

. . . fashion has become completely dead. *Haute couture* is offensive; it is not acceptable in today's society. It was only for the elite, only for a tiny group of people, who then were aped by the public all over the world. Today, the general public couldn't care less about what even Jacqueline Onassis wears. Fashion as it stood for centuries just cannot work today, because the public is too aware of what it stands for: aristocracy. And aristocracy has no legitimacy now. Clothes are no longer status.

Interview, Los Angeles/ Los Angeles Times, 1-30:(West)16.

Halston (Roy Halston Frowick)
Fashion designer

You are only as good as the people you dress. If fashionable people come to you and you help them, then you are the fashionable designer. Fashion comes from fashionable people.

Newsweek, 8-21:48.

Edith Head
Fashion designer

We've suddenly gone out of "costume" into "clothes." It's no longer amusing to look like a rummage sale, to look quaint, funky. "Sure" clothes are back. It's a return to civilization.

Daily Variety, 3-13:6.

Alla Levashova
Soviet fashion authority

Women's fashions reflect at present their independence, business capacity and freedom to determine their own tastes. Women allow themselves to wear pantsuits even in the evening, rejecting traditional festive dresses.

Los Angeles Times, 3-24:(1)19.

Don Loper
Fashion designer

There is nothing more important for the successful business or professional man than to appear well groomed, in keeping with his station in life, while taking into account personal preferences. Being tastefully and appropriately dressed is one of the best investments any man can make.

Los Angeles Times, 5-17:(6)4.

Norman Norell
Fashion designer

There used to be more of them (chic women). They used to keep the dressmakers busy. Back in the twenties, the well-dressed woman wore one thing in the morning, changed to something else in the afternoon, put on a third dress to go tea dancing and changed again for dinner. Now that's all finished. If you make two changes it's a lot. You can call it deterioration or just putting things in their proper places. Why, women had casts made of their hands so their gloves could fit perfectly. Now they don't wear any gloves at all. Of course, fashion is getting less important. Maybe it's getting where it should be.

Interview, New York/
The New York Times Magazine, 10-15:88.

Ken O'Keefe
Fashion director,
Men's Fashion Association of America

(On the diminishing of flamboyance in men's fashions): The peacock isn't dead. He's just stopped screaming.

The Washington Post, 2-5:(C)1.

Yves Saint Laurent
Fashion designer

(On the current rejection of fashion fads and the return to classics in fashion): (The return to classics is) the pursuit of a style which is not an aggression against the inner personality of women, but which helps them to emphasize or discover their own. It's a personal effort in style and elegance, a fashion one does not adopt as an armsuit but where everything is subtle, feminine, refined . . . A groomed elegance . . . that is thoroughly classical, pure, balanced . . . thus eternal.

Paris/
The Washington Post, 5-25:(C)4.

I used to go out in the streets and like what the girls were wearing . . . and maybe get an inspiration from it. Not any more. What started to be humanistic, relaxed and free has become vulgar, way out and mixed up. Maybe because I am not young any more, but I do not want changes, rather a continuity . . .

San Francisco Examiner, 9-7:22.

Couture is necessary and must be preserved because it is the last day of the craftsman. If a woman is rich, she must support the couture. Maybe it is not a law, but it is her duty. Luxury is necessary in each metier. The rich woman must preserve the luxury. If the rich woman does not do this, the couture will die. *C'est dommage.* Rich women will be responsible for the decline of this *art extraordinaire.*

Interview, New York/
The Washington Post, 11-26:(F)3.

Once, we needed to have changes in fashion, new looks and new disguises. But now it is ridiculous to think that clothes must change, that hemlines must change, that women want pants this season and not the next. Everything in fashion is settled. Women will change their clothes, but always within the ideas that we have now developed.

Interview, New York/ The Washington Post, 11-26:(F)3.

Vidal Sassoon
Hair stylist

Hair is the sex symbol of the '70s. In fact, hair or the lack of it is another word for sex appeal. It's the only substance on the human form that you can mold, play with, make shapes with and develop to suit a person's individual personality—outside of cosmetic surgery. My philosophy about hair is that it should be an individual expression of a person's basic nature and shaped to conform with his bone structure. You really don't need to spend that much money to make a great personal statement with hair. Obviously, you can grow hair for free; and all you need to do is grow it in the right places and have it shaped every now and again. You can't do the same things in fashions without buying very expensive clothes. And besides, clothes are an old sex symbol. Today, hair is another name for sex.

Interview, Beverly Hills, Calif./ Los Angeles Times, 5-28:(West)29.

John Weitz
Fashion designer

Eccentricity (in men's fashions) is only acceptable when one is successful. Can you imagine a board chairman trying to explain foul business results to stockholders when he is wearing a Fu Manchu mustache and a velveteen suit? The stockholders can only conclude he is more concerned with himself than the business. Until he has good news to report, he'd better look like a board chairman.

The National Observer, 1-19:1.

Journalism

Elie Abel
Dean, Columbia University
Graduate School of Journalism

(Criticizing the government's opposition to news and public affairs programming on public TV): A public television system that is prohibited from examining the people's concerns by law, or administrative edict, or plain cowardice, is a system without brain or heart. That kind of system is not worth a single dollar of public money. I would rather see it abolished.

Before Senate Constitutional Rights Subcommittee, Washington, Feb. 17/ The Washington Post, 2-18:(A)11.

Spiro T. Agnew
Vice President of the United States

I believe it's absolutely necessary to have (a) free press in the United States. The one thing that distresses me is there is a trend for interpretive reporting something midway between an editorial statement and a factual story. Reporting should be separate and distinct. The written press has basically held to that. Television and radio tend to allow opinion journalism not separated from the facts.

Before California Scholastic Press Association, Culver City, March 21/ Los Angeles Times, 3-22:(1)26.

. . . experience forewarns that we Republicans have to earn our victories the hard way. They're not served up by a fawning claque of correspondents, columnists and commentators who compare ideological notes in Georgetown parlors, Manhattan studios and aboard campaign planes. The preponderant number of those who shape the policies of the major national vehicles of news information in this country have been opposed from the beginning—in some cases hydrophobically opposed—to the Nixon Administration. However, it is Middle America and not Media America that makes the crucial decision on the first Tuesday after the first Monday in November in every fourth year.

At Republican fund-raising dinner, Manchester, N.H., July 13/ Los Angeles Herald-Examiner, 7-14:(A)13.

There is a place for the press and government to co-exist with respect to each other and yet to maintain that vital and delicate adversary relationship that is so vital to the maintenance and preservation of a free society . . . I hope that those in the media who from time to time are called to account for what I think is bias, or perhaps an inadvertant oversight or omission that is misleading the public in their right to obtain full information—it will be understood to be in good faith, not to be rancorous or bitter.

Before National Newspaper Association, Portland, Ore., July 22/ San Francisco Examiner, 7-24:17.

The way reporting is done today, a thesis is (unintentionally) established—the story behind the news—and a search is made for the facts that will assist in bearing out that thesis.

TV-radio interview, Los Angeles/ "Meet the Press," National Broadcasting Company, 8-27.

Jack Anderson
Political columnist

I was brought up with a deep sense of duty and a sense of outrage, and I think that the public office is a public trust, and I think that those who abuse it should be called on the carpet. There's no one to do it. Who's going to investigate the Justice Department?—the Justice Department? Who's going to investigate an Attorney General?—their subordinates? Who's going to investigate the FBI chief?—the FBI? And for that matter, who's going to investigate the President and (National Security Affairs Adviser) Henry Kissinger? You see? It has to be the press. And we (he and his associates) have the inclination to do it, and the motivation to do it, and, I believe, the staff to do it . . . It's a sacred duty.

Television interview/ "Behind the Lines," WNET-TV, New York, 3-26.

People in power get too puffed up with their own importance, too swollen with hot air, because they're treated with such deference and they're granted as many privileges as Roman emperors. I consider it my function to be a needle to deflate the windbags, to let the hot air out.

The New York Times Magazine, 8-13:77.

(On courts which require journalists to reveal their news sources): They shut off news at the source. They order newsmen to tell their source or go to prison. So far, the reporters have chosen prison. They know (that), if there were no sources, the government would report to you only what it wanted you to know.

Cranston, R.I., Dec. 17/ The Sacramento (Calif.) Bee, 12-19:(A)4.

Melvin Belli
Lawyer

(U.S. President) Nixon would do anything to get re-elected. The reason he doesn't do some of the more outrageous things is because he's afraid of the press. And when he's afraid of the press, he's afraid of the people. I think the press is the greatest weapon we have in a democracy because it reports the open jury trial. Once you get too much government censorship of the press, guys like Nixon will just do what they damn well please. There's more stuff hidden in Washington now than ever before in history. All the more reason for a strong, free press.

Interview, San Francisco/ Los Angeles Times, 4-9:(West)39.

Herbert Block (Herblock)
Political cartoonist, "The Washington Post"

I don't think *all* politicians are a bunch of finks; but our (journalists') job is mostly to criticize, to talk about the things that are wrong. Any President has hundreds of public-relations men . . . PR men in the White House, the Pentagon, the State Department. Their job is to say, "Boy, everything is just great." Never is heard a discouraging word. Our job is to counter that—especially in cartooning. It involves a certain lack of reverence for public officials. I like to think of myself as the kid in the story about the emperor's new clothes, the guy who shout's "Hey, that guy's naked." You know, the Presidential office has become such an elevated thing. (President) Nixon has made more appearances on TV, but never once did he say, "Boy, did I botch it." When he botches it, our job is to say that he botched it.

Interview, New York/ "W": a Fairchild publication, 10-20:9.

Daniel J. Boorstin
Director, National Museum of History and Technology of the United States

I think the inability of our newspapers, radio and television to limit the reinforcement and repetition of sensational events is serious—it comes close to being a national disaster. For about two decades, television especially has been preoccupied with reinforcing the violent, the dissident, the discontinuous, the destructive elements in American life. There have been very few programs and techniques developed for dramatizing what people have been able to do together. Instead, "controversial" has come to mean the "kook" who gets the center of the stage on talk shows in a way never possible before . . . I don't suggest that the press and television give up their critical role. That's very important. But I think they should give more of their attention to exploring the achievements that justify our society and its inhibitions. Unless they do that, the weight will go increasingly on the side of destruction, dissent and discontinuity. It will depreciate more and more the gifts of tradition and civilization which are enormous and which are greater in the United States today than they have ever been anywhere before. We have the instruments to interpret these gifts, but somehow the key people have neither the will nor the concern to do the job.

Interview/
U.S. News & World Report, 5-29:20.

David Brinkley
News commentator,
National Broadcasting Company

When politicians and the press are quarelling with each other, that is their natural state. That is what they ought to do, and it is in the best interest of the American people. If, over the last generation, the politicians and bureaucrats in Washington have made such a mess of things with the press keeping some kind of watch over them, what would they have done with nobody watching? And without the press, there is nobody—nobody to watch over them, nobody at all. When politicians and the press begin making sweet and loving remarks about each other, that will be the time for the American people to be concerned; because it will mean the press had given up its right and natural job of watching the politicians and gone to bed with them . . .

Before University of Southern California Journalism Alumni Association/
The National Observer, 12-2:13.

Helen Gurley Brown
Editor, "Cosmopolitan" magazine

One doesn't know whether anybody can save *Life* (magazine). I think *Life's* problem—and they do have one—is doing everything like they always did it. And the fact is, you don't have to be the magazine you always were. You can throw all that out and start with a different format or start with a drastically-changed format. You can do anything. All the management cares about, or should care about, is staying in business. It's better to have a changed magazine than to have no magazine.

Interview/
The Washington Post, 1-4:(B)2.

Patrick J. Buchanan
Special Assistant
to the President of the United States

(Criticizing the awarding of Pulitzer Prizes to columnist Jack Anderson and *The New York Times* for publishing classified government documents): What kind of lesson is that, really, for young journalists right now? What's he (the journalist) told to do? What he's told to do, in effect, is—if you can get hold of some secret documents, if you can seduce some miserable government employee to give you a National Security Council memorandum and then you run it in your column, you can get the Pulitzer Prize.

Television interview,
Washington, May 5/
Los Angeles Times, 5-6:(1)2.

If there were only three printing presses left in the whole United States, then the people who owned and ran those presses couldn't simply print only those things they wanted to print and refuse to print the points of view they disagreed with. Otherwise, the whole basis of your democratic system would be undermined. You would have then to have the government require the printing presses to print all points of view—conservative, liberal, whatever. This is what these (TV) networks have got. They've got control of essentially three giant complexes which enable individuals to send comment at an instant's notice into 100 million homes. And there are only three of them, and so they have obligations that, say, *The New Republic* doesn't have. Those obligations have been written in law, and one of them is to be balanced and fair in their coverage. I think it would be a disastrous situation if a group of individuals who happen to get control of this CBS conglomerate, for example, could determine without any restrictions whatsoever precisely what came into your homes in the way of news and information.

Interview, Washington/ The New York Times Magazine, 8-20:93.

Art Buchwald
Newspaper columnist

A few years ago, Paul Douglas, the former Senator from Illinois, said an interesting thing to me. He said that in each generation it seems as though the American people give a license to only one or two comedians or writers to make fun of politics and politicians. He mentioned Finley Peter Dunne, for instance, and Will Rogers; and he said that he thought that I had the license. And when you've got the license, you can get away with murder—be praised for writing things that another writer might be stoned in the streets for having written. Of course, I've been told that men in high government circles don't take me seriously; and so, I don't take them seriously, either.

Interview/ The New York Times Magazine, 1-2:11.

Alastair Burnet
Editor, "The Economist," London

Politicians and journalists have a peculiar dependence on, and contempt for, each other.

Quote, 3-5:217.

John Chancellor
News commentator, National Broadcasting Company

Ike (Dwight D. Eisenhower) was the last (U.S.) President to believe that the press is a part of American society, the Fourth Estate. Jack Kennedy didn't like what we did, but he enjoyed the battle. (Lyndon) Johnson and his people got very uncomfortable about TV . . . and L.B.J. wasn't very good at it. (Richard) Nixon is very good on TV. But he and his advisers think it's a contest. They view the world as checkerboarded with adversary contests: the press, TV, Vietnam, the Soviet Union, the Middle East. They never think of our function as ameliorative.

Los Angeles/ Los Angeles Times, 6-9:(4)19.

Otis Chandler
Publisher, "Los Angeles Times"

. . . I don't think it's possible to have an impartial press, because human beings write the news and there's no such thing as "complete objectivity"—beauty is in the eyes of the beholder. We try, to the best of our ability, to do an honest job of reporting the news.

Panel discussion, Stanford University/ Los Angeles Times, 4-9:(D)3.

Harold Clancy
Publisher, "Boston Herald Traveler"

(On closing of his newspaper): The loss of a newspaper strikes those associated with it more like a loss of a child.

Boston, June 17/ San Francisco Examiner & Chronicle, 6-18:(A)27.

John B. Connally, Jr.
Secretary of the Treasury of the United States

I'm not asking the media to be cheerleaders of the nation; but it is only fair that when you report the crises to do so in perspective and also consider the needs of the country. We (in government) talk too much . . . you (the press) write too much.

Before National Press Club, Washington/ San Francisco Examiner, 5-17:34.

Norman Cousins
Editor, "World" magazine

In the final analysis, a magazine is not born. It's reborn, every issue.

Interview, New York/
The New York Times, 6-22:48.

Alan Cranston
United States Senator, D–Calif.

(Supporting the press' privilege to withhold from Congress or any Federal court or agency information, or the source of information, procured for publication or broadcast): We already recognize the absoluteness of other confidentiality privileges. We have an absolute lawyer-client privilege; an absolute priest-penitent privilege. Nobody talks about making an exception for murder in the lawyer-client privilege . . . Why should some people believe there must be such exceptions in the case of a privilege for the press—which is really privilege for the people, all the people?

Testifying on behalf
of his press-privilege bill/
San Francisco Examiner & Chronicle,
11-26:(Sunday Punch)1.

Walter Cronkite
News commentator,
Columbia Broadcasting System

People who depend solely on television for their news are not going to be adequately informed on any subject. We can introduce some of the issues in a fashion that will have greater impact and teach people more (basically) about the candidates and the issues, perhaps, than any other medium. But that's a one-time (thing). For depth and understanding of the issues, you've got to go to the other media.

Interview/
The Washington Post, 8-27:(Potomac)21.

Ralph Davidson
Publisher, "Time" magazine

The question of objectivity (in journalism) always arises when you run across somebody who disagrees with what you've said. If we had chosen to put, say, (Senator Paul N.) "Pete" McCloskey on the cover of *Time* just before the New Hampshire primary, some would have accused us of trying to influence the public; others would have praised us for featuring a refreshing new face. Everyone would have had something to say about our objectivity.

Panel discussion, Stanford University/
Los Angeles Times, 4-9:(D)3.

Edith Efron
Television journalist

After carefully studying television coverage of the (Vietnam) war, racial conflict, the Presidential race and the "New Left" of 1968 (for her book, *The News Twisters*), I discovered a liberal pattern developing, because news from the opposite poles was omitted altogether. It is not what the reporter emphasizes, but what he leaves out that creates the biased pattern . . . If the viewer sneezed once, he could easily have missed the pro-war coverage in 1968.

Before Public Affairs Luncheon Club,
Dallas, April 17/
The Dallas Times Herald, 4-18:(A)19.

John D. Ehrlichman
Assistant to the President of the
United States for Domestic Affairs

We look at the media as a very important guardian of rights. I think every American has the right and expectation to do that. If the nature of fact reporting in the media has changed in the last 10 years, then I think every American has to be alert to that, and I think every journalist has to be alert to it, and he has to figure out whether that is really the direction in which he wants to see his profession run. I am concerned about objectivity and accuracy and reliability in the media as an individual, much less as a part of the Administration. We don't ask for favorable reporting (toward the Nixon Administration). All we ask for is a fair shake and an objective report of the facts.

TV-radio interview, Washington/ "Meet the Press," National Broadcasting Company, 5-7.

(On why President Nixon has few news conferences): He doesn't get very good questions at a press conference, frankly. He goes in there for a half hour and gets a lot of flabby and fairly dumb questions and it doesn't really elucidate very much. I've seen him many times come off one of those things and go back and say, "Isn't it extraordinary how poor the quality of the questions are?"

Los Angeles/ The Christian Science Monitor, 6-17:12.

Sam J. Ervin, Jr.
United States Senator, D–N.C.

I think freedom of the press can be endangered in several ways. The objective of freedom of the press is to make certain that we have an informed electorate, because an informed electorate is necessary to make our institutions of government function properly. Now, that purpose can be frustrated in several ways. One way is that you have all of these public-relations employees of the Federal government who are employed to make the actions of the Executive Branch appear in their best light. And newspapermen are like some members of Congress: They have today's work to do, and the quicker they can do it the better for them—or so they think. So they accept these government handouts. And these government handouts, in many cases, deceive the people about what their government is doing or how efficiently their government is operating. I think that is a threat to the freedom of the press. Then another threat to the freedom of the press is that a lot of people in public office confer honors on members of the press. And I think that creates a sort of unholy alliance that tends to deny people the right to know what their government is doing. Then, of course, you can have freedom of the press threatened not only by favors but by implied threats, and that's particularly true in the broadcast media. The printed word is not quite as susceptible to coercive practices to control it as the broadcast media, because anybody can set up a newspaper if he's got the finances. But nobody can operate anything in the broadcast field without first getting a license from the Federal Communications Commission; and the FCC has authority, under certain circumstances, to revoke licenses or deny their renewal if it doesn't fully approve of the broadcasts. I think that is a Damoclean sword that hangs over the broadcast media all the time.

Interview/ U.S. News & World Report, 3-6:42.

Several developments and incidents over the past few years raise serious questions about the present (Nixon) Administration's understanding of the principles embodied in the First Amendment's guarantee of freedom of the press . . . There is always a temptation for high government officials to seek to undermine the capacity of the press to criticize government policies and leaders. Expanding government control over broadcasting, government's attempt to prevent publication of the "Pentagon Papers," unexplained governmental investigations of newsmen and proposals to increase dramatically postal rates for second- and third-class mail remind us that the present Administration has not resisted such temptation.

Oct. 19/ The New York Times, 10-21:41.

Reuven Frank
President,
National Broadcasting Company News

Very often people who are saying we (in the news media) are biased are really saying we are not biased—not biased in their favor. They have a point of view and we left it out or we didn't make it for them. Then, according to their standards, we are putting across someone else's point of view, which on examination we very often are not. But in a broader sense we are biased; we are

(REUVEN FRANK)

people, we are all human. But I don't remember any case where there was any implication that anyone did something intentionally to make a point, to change society or to make somebody look bad. That may have been the effect. But if so, he was reasoning within his human limitations, which was to boil down information, to be interesting, to get it across and to get to the next story before it became a bore.

Interview/
Los Angeles Times, 6-14:(2)7.

To me the Fairness Doctrine, and equal time, and the right of reply, and the (Federal Communications) Commissioners and the judges, the good ones and bad ones, the sympathetic and hostile ones, the conservative ones and liberal ones, the Congressmen and their new bills, the Executive assistants and their new schemes, are all one lump. They are the government in news, the government in my business. I began on a newspaper. There I learned the government had no business in my business. I am still in the same business, but now it's "okay" for the government to interfere. It is not easy to understand or to follow. If the government should not be in news, it should not be in television news.

At Conference on Electronic Journalism,
Warrenton, Va., June 22/
Vital Speeches, 8-1:632.

Max Frankel
News correspondent,
"The New York Times"

I am amazed by the degree to which reporters do not allow (their preferences) in politics to influence their choice of stories or the way they write them. No politician will believe this, and so I never even try to persuade them . . . Newsmen are certainly as good at being impartial as lawyers are in a courtroom, or as cops on the corner who get spit at and still try to treat everybody fairly . . .

Interview/
The Washington Post, 8-20:(Potomac)16.

John W. Gardner
National chairman, Common Cause

(On the need for freedom of the press): Information is power, and secrecy is the most convenient means of keeping that power out of the hands of citizens.

The Fresno (Calif.) Bee, 12-25:(A)22.

Barry M. Goldwater
United States Senator, R–Ariz.

It has long been my contention that if anything happens in this country to damage what we call the freedom of the press, it will come about through raw partisanship and gross irresponsibility on the part of some segments of the press itself. This is a concept which is seldom heard and which many members of the so-called "Fourth Estate" reject as ridiculous. They would have you believe that the only threat to press freedom in this country is raised by political figures or government officials who have the temerity to criticize the press and point out mistakes made by the news media as well as ideological preferences shown by some segments of that media . . . My point here today is that these have been a rough few weeks for press credibility and certainly not because of anything done by politicians or government officials. The violence done to the credibility of the press—and consequently the threat arising to freedom of the press—were occasioned by the fact that the American Newspaper Guild, for the first time in 40 years, jumped into politics by endorsing the Democratic candidate for President (George McGovern) before the Republicans even held their convention. In addition to the action of the Guild leadership against the wishes of hundreds of its dues-paying members, there is the example of this year's Pulitzer Prize-winner for journalism (columnist Jack Anderson) getting caught in a deliberate effort to smear the ex-Democratic nominee for Vice President (Thomas Eagleton) and being forced to apologize publicly. Of course, in this case public interest made it impossible for Anderson to get away with this bit of character assassination . . . I repeat my assertion that, if freedom of the press suffers any major setbacks in this day and age, it will be as a result of actions taken by some members of the press itself—actions such as the Guild endorsement of a political candidate and the Anderson broadcast.

Human Events, 8-19:15.

Julian Goodman
President,
National Broadcasting Company

(On government censorship of broadcasting news): There is no censorship in the accepted definition. Nobody is telling anybody else what can or cannot be broadcast. Yet a form of censorship does exist—a censorship after the fact. The peril to the American public is that, with time, it can become self-censorship, before the fact, inducing caution and blandness. The theoretical advantages of assuring fairness (in news coverage)—even if they exist—are certainly not worth the weakening effect on the independence of the press—the strongest instrument democracy has.

At Great Issues Forum, University of Southern California, Oct. 11/ Daily Variety, 10-12:5.

Katharine Graham
Publisher, "The Washington Post"

When the press is intimidated and circumscribed in its capacity to report and inform and enlighten, it is the public that loses in the end by losing its capacity to participate in a self-governing society.

San Francisco Examiner & Chronicle, 11-26:(This World)2.

There has been a good deal of evidence of an intensified campaign to undermine public confidence in those segments of the news media which are thought to be hostile to the (Nixon) Administration; to inhibit the functioning of the press; to sport with something that responsible public officials ought to be the first to uphold—the free flow of communications between the government and the governed. To this chorus I would add the Administration's support of efforts on the part of state and Federal attorneys to entangle professional newsmen in the law-enforcement process of summoning them before grand juries and asking them to reveal confidential sources and information obtained in confidence. While respecting the Supreme Court's judgment, our own view is that confidentiality is the essence of news gathering. We could hardly operate entirely on the basis of information provided by sources who are prepared to have themselves publicly identified.

Before Commonwealth Club, San Francisco/ The Sacramento (Calif.) Bee, 12-3:(P)4.

L. Patrick Gray III
Acting Director,
Federal Bureau of Investigation of the United States

It seems to me the strength of this country depends on a free press, reporting responsibly. And the prism through which some journalists have been looking has been stained. We need more objective, factual reporting, rather than subjective, factual reporting.

San Francisco Examiner & Chronicle, 6-25:(This World)2.

Tashoma Haile-Mariam
President,
Supreme Imperial Court of Ethiopia

Protection of the press must not be absolute. A free press must have freedom, but in some cases there may be abuses. My view is that the press must have privileges granted so they can do their work, but I feel it should not be absolute freedom.

News conference, Los Angeles/ Los Angeles Times, 12-11:(2)2.

T. George Harris
Editor,
"Psychology Today" magazine

. . . the "specialty" magazine argument is really talking about the difference (between) a vital link with your reader and a purely symbolic link . . . it's a connection among people who've got some real interest in a common literature, who simply use the magazine as a part of a broader community relationship . . . That's what a big magazine is, too, but it forgot it . . . What a general magazine has become has been sort of like the sermons on Sunday where the editorial staff gets its time to preach at people about their superior knowledge on something. It's no longer a searcher's community where the editors are fascinated in going after and finding out about something . . . and passing it along for other people who might be interested, too. There is a fundamental difference between an editor who edits something to tell people a little bit of his knowledge and an editor who tries damned hard to find out something because he's interested in it and, in the process, shares it.

The Washington Post, 1-4:(B)1.

John Hart
News commentator,
Columbia Broadcasting System

People shouldn't assume they know what's going on just because they've watched a TV news program. We perform the function of responsible gossips, and shouldn't pretend that we do more. We cannot give a balanced picture. But we can deal fairly with the fragments of news we do have time to convey.

Interview, New York/
TV Guide, 3-25:14.

Andrew Heiskell
Chairman, Time, Inc.

During my professional life in publishing, the U.S. has had six Presidents—men of varying temperament and political philosophy. They have had only one characteristic and belief in common. Each thought that the press should have treated him more favorably, and each did all in his power to secure such treatment.

At Hofstra University commencement,
Hempstead, N.Y./
The Wall Street Journal, 2-16:10.

William H. Hornby
Executive editor, "Denver Post"

I've been a little disturbed lately that a growing number of people are surrendering to the view that there is no such thing as objectivity (in reporting news). I recognize the human element . . . but the news media in this country has struggled through a painful history to establish a reputation that it strives for a fair, balanced and impartial presentation of the news. To come so readily to the statement that there is no such thing as objectivity strikes me as a bit dangerous.

Panel discussion, Stanford University/
Los Angeles Times, 4-9:(D)3.

Douglas Kiker
News correspondent,
National Broadcasting Company

Politicians and political reporters in this town (Washington) live like two animals in the same cage. They have learned to live together. They growl at each other, and occasionally they'll take a swipe at each other or get into a real tangle. But they've always coexisted, because they must, under a very scrupulously-observed, unwritten set of rules.

Interview, Washington/
The Washington Post, 8-20:(Potomac)15.

Melvin R. Laird
Secretary of Defense
of the United States

We need not apologize for the adversary relationships of the government and press. Instead, we should praise it and preserve it. And as we go about our Constitutional business of being adversaries, we should avoid becoming antagonists.

At dedication of the Pentagon's "Correspondents Corridor," Washington, Nov. 21/ The Washington Post, 11-22:(A)3.

Peter Lisagor
Washington bureau chief, "The Chicago Daily News"

The media all too often are viewed (by the Nixon Administration) with suspicion and hostility; not as vehicles for disseminating information but as adversaries waiting to ambush them. The cast of mind at the White House is distinctly one of "We'll tell you what's going on when we damn well please."

The New York Times, 4-19:9.

William Loeb
Publisher, Manchester (N.H.) "Union Leader"

The tragedy of the newspaper business today is that it's too gray, not enough black and white, no emotional involvement. Sooner or later, people will stop reading them.

Time, 1-31:38.

Elmer W. Lower
President, American Broadcasting Company News

I've been asked many times what I think the effect on ABC News has been from the original attack and the subsequent attacks (on broadcast news) by (Vice President Spiro) Agnew, and the only thing I can detect is that our editors and producers and writers may ask themselves a second time, "Well, is my presentation of this completely fair?" Fairness in a newsman I don't find a vice, but I hope it hasn't been intimidating any of them, and if it has been, I'm not aware of it . . . I can't object to any politician complaining if he thinks he's been hurt. I don't contend that all media, even broadcasting, or even ABC News, is perfect. If a man has a legitimate complaint, I'll listen to him. I'm not trying to set myself up on a pedestal where I say any time Agnew criticizes us that's like attacking motherhood . . . I honestly think he may have spoken too often on the subject, but that's only my guess. There are still many people who agree with him; I get letters from them.

Interview, Los Angeles, May 1/ The Hollywood Reporter, 5-2:9.

George S. McGovern
United States Senator, D–S.D.; Democratic Presidential nominee

What I think has happened is that the Nixon-Agnew intimidation of the (TV) networks has worked to the point where every Republican who pops off is given equal time with me. That's not what equal time means. I don't think the President (Nixon) ought to be allowed to sit there in the White House and have these lackeys of his running around the country getting equal time with me every day . . . I think what I object to, the one thing that galls me when I occasionally get to a hotel room and watch the evening news, I see the networks give a minute or a minute and a half to report on what I've said that day and then some second-string bureaucrat from the Republican side gets equal time. It's not fair. My opponent is not (Defense Secretary Melvin) Laird; it's not the head of the Wage and Price Board; it's not the Secretary of Agriculture.

News conference, Seattle, Sept. 25/ Los Angeles Times, 9-26:(1)18.

This (Nixon) Administration has tried to bully the press into docile submission. It has launched a deliberate, sustained campaign to discredit newspapers and broadcasters. It has misused Federal law-enforcement officers to investigate the personal lives of reporters. And for the first time in our history, we have seen the government attempt to prevent—and then to punish—the publication of critical facts, not because it harmed the country but because it embarrassed the government. This Administration seeks to replace a press corps with a cheering section —with a propaganda machine that is in

(GEORGE S. McGOVERN)

league with the government, to be used by the government, to tell the people what the government wants them to hear.

At Conference of United Press International Editors and Publishers, Washington, Oct. 2/ Los Angeles Herald-Examiner, 10-3:(A)13.

Marshall McLuhan
Professor of English, University of Toronto

I do believe that news coverage causes most of the harm in the world. The Vietnam war would not have lasted long had there been no coverage of it. I don't think the United States could go on fighting without coverage. (Airplane) hijacking would never exist without coverage. It's part of a show business. The news media, by means of coverage, turns the villain into a hero. It's the public participation in the hero-villain ritual. In Canada, where the media isn't so influential, the rebels of Quebec don't get coverage any more. Some of the trials are going on right now, but there's no mention of it.

Interview, Toronto/ San Francisco Examiner & Chronicle, 8-20:(This World)34.

Harold R. Medina
Senior Circuit Judge, United States Court of Appeals for the 2nd Circuit

Some people may think that the leaders of the free press would perhaps accomplish more if their claims of Constitutional right were less expansive. I do not agree with this. I say it is their duty to fight like tigers right down to the line and not give an inch. This is the way our freedoms have been preserved in the past and it is the way they will be preserved in the future.

The Sacramento (Calif.) Bee, 12-15:(A)21.

Bill Monroe
Washington editor, "Today" show, National Broadcasting Company, Television

I have no atrocity story to tell about outright government censorship (of the press). I have never seen it happen. Perhaps it never has. But I know that what might be called indirect or unintended government censorship has happened . . . We do know there are stations that don't do investigative reporting. There are stations that confine their documentaries to safe subjects. There are stations that do editorialize but don't say anything. There are stations that do outspoken editorials but are scared to endorse candidates. My opinion is that much of this kind of caution, probably most of it, is due to a deep feeling that boldness equals trouble with government; blandness equals peace.

Before Senate Constitutional Rights Subcommittee, Washington, Feb. 16/ The Washington Post, 2-17:(A)4.

Bill Moyers
Former Press Secretary to the President of the United States

The "backgrounder" (press briefing) permits the press and the government to sleep together, even to procreate, without getting married or having to accept the responsibility for any offspring. It's the public on whose doorstep orphans of deceptive information and misleading allegations are left.

Plainview (Tex.) Daily Herald, 2-27:(A)6.

Edmund S. Muskie
United States Senator, D–Maine

I think there ought to be regular (Presidential) press conferences. I don't have hard and fast opinions on how often; I think they ought to be not less frequent than once a month and more if possible . . . I've always found "backgrounders" (press briefings), in my political experience up to now, useful; and yet there are things about them that I don't like. I find that, all too often, backgrounders result in a distorted view of what has been discussed in the public print rather than a more enlightened or understanding view. I don't know how to resolve that dilemma, because obviously it must be easier, especially in national security matters, foreign policy matters, to permit a President the informality and the freedom of an off-the-record discussion. I don't have a formula for that one.

Interview/
The Washington Post, 2-27:(C)4.

Jack Nessel
Managing editor, "New York" magazine

(Saying objectivity is impossible in journalism): Perhaps we should strive toward the Kingdom of Heaven; but when it comes to reporting the news, original sin gets built into the act! Communication is the filtering of phenomena through sensibilities, and besides, sometimes the facts are biased themselves.

Panel discussion, Stanford University/
Los Angeles Times, 4-9:(D)3.

Richard M. Nixon
President of the United States

In looking over the transcripts of various press conferences, I have not seen many soft-balls; and I don't want any, because it is only the hard-ball that you can hit or strike out on.

News conference, Washington, June 22/
The Washington Post, 6-23:(A)9.

We (his Administration) want to have good relations with the press. We expect to. When people talk about numbers of (Presidential) press conferences, though, I respectfully suggest that you go back and look over this year. It was my view that it would not have been in the best interest of the country to have held press conferences during periods of delicate negotiations. Whenever I find that we are engaged in very sensitive negotiations where it wouldn't be useful to have a press conference, I won't have one. Where we are not, I will.

Interview, Nov. 5/
San Francisco Examiner, 11-9:57.

Newbold Noyes
Editor,
"The Washington Evening Star-News"

This group (the Nixon Administration) is a little more up-tight about the press than at any time since I've been a journalist. And in the second (Nixon) term, this may be a little more so, what with their new confidence. But I don't think Nixon wants to destroy press freedom. He couldn't do it even if he wanted to . . . We are as potent a force as exists in this society; and when we exert our force, we can overcome any force, such as government.

Before Sigma Delta Chi, Dallas, Nov. 16/
The Washington Post, 11-17:(A)5.

Lawrence F. O'Brien
Chairman,
Democratic National Committee

In denying the Democratic Party's request for broadcast time to respond to recent network appearances by President Nixon, the executives of NBC and CBS have simply defaulted on their public trust to insure a full, vigorous and fair national discussion—by both major political parties—of the critical issues in this election year. It is difficult to avoid the conclusion that the major networks have capitulated to President Nixon and the Republican majority on the Federal Communications Commission, led by FCC Chairman Dean Burch, the former Chairman of the Republican National Committee.

Washington, Jan. 7/
Los Angeles Times, 1-8:(1)5.

Everett C. Parker
Chairman, broadcasting and film commission,
National Council of the Churches of Christ

Suppression of news by our economic masters—by giant communications conglomerates—looms as a menace to our freedoms equal to suppression by a governmental big brother.

Before Senate Constitutional Rights
Subcommittee, Washington/
Variety, 2-23:40.

Ronald Reagan
Governor of California

I have heard some broadcasters suggest that you should not mix management and news. Well, let me disagree. If there is some bias in TV—and there is, in too many cases—it may be because management does not make its voice heard. If someone down the line is slanting things, you are not being neutral simply because you keep hands off . . . The inflection of the announcer's voice, the arched eyebrows, the skeptical expression—all those can and have injected an element of bias in television news.

At National Broadcasting Company TV affiliates convention, Los Angeles, May 4/ Los Angeles Times, 5-5:(1)3.

A free press is one of this country's major strengths. And the right to protect his sources of information is fundamental to a newsman in meeting his full responsibility to the public he serves.

At signing of bill permitting reporters to refuse to disclose news sources to grand juries, Sacramento, Dec. 28/ San Francisco Examiner, 12-29:24.

J. L. Robertson
Vice Chairman, Federal Reserve Board of the United States

(The concentration of national media ownership in New York) explains, perhaps, why we get the monotonous sameness of opinion from our national news media, much of it very much at odds with the deeply-held views of what I believe to be the great majority of American people.

Before Independent Bankers Association of America, Bal Harbour, Fla., March 15/ The New York Times, 3-16:23.

Nelson A. Rockefeller
Governor of New York

I've enjoyed the benefits of a free press for 14 years as Governor. And let me tell you, reading about one's failings in the daily papers is one of the privileges of high office in this free country of ours. You read stories about what you are supposed to be up to; stories attributed to reliable sources, informed sources and, most of all, unnamed sources. And sometimes you ask yourself, "Who are these anonymous authorities who know so much about me?" But I would far prefer a society where a free press occasionally upsets a public official to a society where public officials could ever upset freedom of the press.

Before Anti-Defamation League, Syracuse, N.Y., Nov. 29/ The New York Times, 11-30:78.

Freedom of the press is a fundamental principle on which this nation was founded. I'm convinced that, if reporters should ever lose the right to protect the confidentiality of their sources, then serious investigative reporting will simply dry up.

Before Anti-Defamation League, Syracuse, N.Y., Nov. 29/ The Washington Post, 12-1:(A)26.

Carl Rowan
Political columnist

Good political reporting requires that you not become too chummy with the people about whom you write. It's pretty hard to drink whiskey and eat food with a man day after day, and then write nasty stories about him when the truth requires that you write something nasty.

Interview/ The Washington Post, 8-20:(Potomac)52.

Morley Safer
News correspondent, Columbia Broadcasting System

This (Nixon) Administration has carefully planted doubt in this country about what we (the press) print or show or say. It has not been a casual, accidental thing, but a carefully-planned program of misinformation. People who practice the big lie cannot stand the smallest truth. Their occasional discomfiture over what we report invites a broadside of sleazy rejoinders . . . The truth? (Vice President Spiro) Agnew and (Deputy Attorney General) Richard Kleindienst and (Defense Secretary) Melvin Laird have done for the truth what the Boston Strangler has done for the door-to-door salesman.

Before Overseas Press Club, New York/Variety, 5-24:31.

Richard S. Salant
President, Columbia Broadcasting System News

. . . (U.S.) Presidents have always been the targets of a critical and often partisan press; and Presidents have struck back in kind; and from (George) Washington on, they have experimented—sometimes subtly, sometimes flagrantly—in news management and news manipulation . . . We who have suffered the slings and arrows of recent Presidents and who have chafed under their news management and news manipulation tend to think that it is all a modern invention—or at least worse than ever before. It is well to remind ourselves that this is not so, and that this seems to be a basic part of the on-going relationships—a built-in tension derived from the conflicting objectives of the Chief Executive on the one hand and the press on the other—with the government's objective being, according to a traditional over-statement, to *conceal*, while the press' objective is to *reveal*.

Before Journalism Foundation of Metropolitan St. Louis and St. Louis Press Club, May 1/ Vital Speeches, 8-15:660.

(On the relationship between the press and government): It's civil war—always . . . George Washington said there was nothing in the papers he could believe except the advertisements. Nothing has changed since then. Nothing.

Interview, Los Angeles/ Los Angeles Times, 5-15:(4)13.

I think government has always had the right to criticize the press. In fact, I think the press has always been subjected to too little systematic criticism . . . But I think government today has a very special problem and dilemma in its criticism of broadcast news it hasn't recognized. As long as the Executive Branch and the Legislative Branch have the power over us they do through licensing, there is more to the game than normal criticism. Suddenly, a good healthy game is changed because one side has the power to chop the other's head off. The fact it hasn't happened isn't important. Even if the sword hanging over your head hasn't fallen, you never know when it might.

Interview/ Los Angeles Times, 6-14:(2)7.

I think one of the greatest mistakes we could make as journalists would be to change our ways so as to avoid controversy. It's the nature of news, especially in this polarized day and age, to cause controversy. We can't start shaping news to avoid it.

Interview/ Los Angeles Times, 6-14:(2)7.

Robert A. Scalapino
Professor of Political Science, University of California

(On the publication in newspapers of classified government documents): The dangerous dance of death now taking place between the media and the government affects every American. If our credibility abroad as a nation is seriously weakened, we all suffer. If our friends determine that we are no longer to be trusted, we are all in greater peril. If decision-making processes within our government are rendered less effective, the President becomes more isolated, and secrecy increases as a result of the government's efforts to protect itself against the theft and publication of documents, we all will be the victims. We live in a free society, and our media are among the most free in the world. But with freedom goes responsibility. It is time for the media to mesh the latter with the former.

San Francisco Examiner & Chronicle, 3-5:(B)2.

Daniel Schorr
News correspondent,
Columbia Broadcasting System

I do not think that many reporters will be directly intimidated (by government criticism and pressure). We are, on the whole, a pretty hardy lot . . . It is our employers who feel the real pressure—especially in the regulated broadcast industry. Anyone concerned about the freedom of the press must be concerned about the climate of suspicion, hostility and nervousness that the (Nixon) Administration has helped to create.

Before Senate Constitutional Rights Subcommittee, Washington/ The Christian Science Monitor, 2-4:5.

Eric Sevareid
News commentator,
Columbia Broadcasting System

(On Nixon Administration criticism of the press as not being objective): They (the Administration) are not interested in objectivity. They are interested in the political fortunes of this Administration, denying all faults and failures, and emphasizing all successes. Who are they to judge objectivity? They're the last people on earth who can do that. For the first time in my life, I've felt angry about this relationship with government. I've had to spend a great deal of my time defending and trying to explain this kind of business . . . I had assumed that most people assumed we were honest folk.

Interview/ The Washington Post, 8-20:(Potomac)16.

Howard Simons
Managing editor,
"The Washington Post"

They (the White House) talk about bias (in news coverage) all the time, but they always forget that each reader has a bias. The blacks say we're pro-white; the whites claim we're pro-black. The hippies say we're pro-Establishment, and the Establishment says we favor the hippies. The Jews say we're pro-Arab, and the Arabs claim we're pro-Jewish. How can you please everybody?

The New York Times Magazine, 8-20:100.

Stanford Smith
President,
American Newspaper Publishers Association

(On proposed newspaper postal rate increases): We are in imminent danger of pricing the daily newspaper beyond the reach of readers on rural routes. The amounts of the pending second-class rates over the next four years are so enormous they will inevitably destroy a large volume of newspaper and magazine readership . . . Readers will undoubtedly be deprived of their daily newspaper because it will become so expensive they no longer can afford to subscribe.

Before House Postal Subcommittee, Washington, June 14/ San Francisco Examiner, 6-15:32.

I. F. Stone
Former publisher,
"I. F. Stone's Bi-Weekly"

(Commenting on his recently-suspended publication): I liked best those issues in which I annoyed the most readers . . . The test of any leadership is the willingness to say things your constituency doesn't want to hear.

San Francisco Examiner & Chronicle, 3-26:(This World)25.

T. N. J. Suharto
President of Indonesia

If pen-wielding soldiers are not careful enough in utilizing their weapons, they will cause wounds not only on the skin but down to the heart of those attacked. Therefore, the press should exercise self-restraint and self-correction.

Before Indonesian Press Council, Jakarta/The New York Times, 4-9:(1)12.

Arthur Ochs Sulzberger
President and publisher,
"The New York Times"

(On his newspaper's publication last year of secret Pentagon papers on U.S. involvement in Vietnam): (Some people have asked us), "Who are you to decide what ought to be secret and not secret—to put your own judgment over that of a properly-elected government entrusted with the national security?" The answer is that either we, acting as responsibly as we knew how, had to decide, or the government had to decide. If the decision had been left with the government, there would have been no publication. Indeed, if such decisions were generally left to the government, much that is published would not be. We would not be a newspaper; we would be the Happy Hour.

At Montclair (N.J.) State College commencement, May 29/ The New York Times, 5-30:10.

There is nothing wrong with anyone inside the (U.S. Federal) Administration—or outside, for that matter—speaking out vigorously when they think that our facts are wrong or our opinions wrong-headed. Debate—boisterous debate—is the lifeblood of a free society (and) we make no claim to infallibility. (But when the criticism) is accompanied by vague hints that the press may be regulated if we don't mend our ways—when it comes from an Administration (Nixon's) that has undertaken prior restraint, subpoenas and investigations of reporters—then it is bound to sound ominous to us.

At Montclair (N.J.) State College commencement, May 29/ The New York Times, 5-30:10.

N. Eldon Tanner
President, Church of Jesus Christ of Latter-day Saints (Mormon)

Our news media today seems to be interested mainly in controversial subjects or someone who is being attacked; and regardless of the 99 good things one may do, it is the one weakness or error that is emphasized and heralded to the world. We are too prone to listen to and accept and repeat such adverse criticism, such maliciously spoken or printed words, without stopping to realize the harm we may be doing to some noble person.

At Mormon Church world conference, Salt Lake City, April 8/ The Washington Post, 4-9:(A)10.

Helen Thomas
White House correspondent, United Press International

There is no other format (than the press) to make a President accountable for his actions. It behooves reporters at the White House, I believe, to be the watchdogs at the Tower of Freedom. We are the only public line of communication between the President and the people; and when he holds so few press conferences as Nixon has—only six this year—the people are short-changed.

At Dallas Times Herald Woman's Forum, Dallas, Sept. 13/ The Dallas Times Herald, 9-13:(A)1.

Morris K. Udall
United States Representative, D–Ariz.

Many magazines of small circulation—those with 250,000 circulation per issue or less—will have a difficult time surviving in the coming years. One major reason is surely the increased cost of postal services. The mails have become our highway for ideas. Our country and our complicated, many-faceted society is tied together through the spreading of information. This applies not only to the mass-circulation magazines but also to the smaller publication(s) of churches, labor unions, colleges and scores of other organizations and professional groups. There is no reason for making the cost of using the mails so prohibitive that the commerce of ideas and information is reduced to a trickle.

Quote, 10-29:420.

Garrick Utley
News commentator,
National Broadcasting Company

As television gets bigger and more expensive, the public may develop a tendency to prefer slick (TV news) productions—entertainment, really. Television must realize that, faced with a choice between the good shot—the good gimmick—and the fact, it has to be the fact every time.

Before Sigma Delta Chi, Dallas, Nov. 16/ The Dallas Times Herald, 11-17:(A)10.

Lionel Van Deerlin
United States Representative, D–Calif.

Eighteen states . . . now have statutes for shielding newsmen's sources from official probers. It is illogical to deny similar protection at the Federal level, particularly in view of the insensitivity in certain quarters of both the Executive Branch and Congress to the needs of a free and untrammelled press.

The Sacramento (Calif.) Bee, 12-4:(A)22.

Lowell P. Weicker, Jr.
United States Senator, R–Conn.

(On his proposed bill which would limit the authority of courts and grand juries to force journalists to reveal their news sources): This legislation is not a "newsman's privilege" law—though that's what it may be called by some—because it's not for newsmen; it's for you—the American public. We do not need to protect newsmen. Rather, we must protect a Constitutional right we all have in the free flow of news. If newsmen are forced to reveal their sources, there is every danger that some of those sources will dry up. That will infringe upon your right to hear the full story. That is what we are protecting. We are protecting a Constitutional right, not somebody's privilege.

Before Association of Life Insurance Counsel, New York, Dec. 12/ The New York Times, 12-13:28.

Clay T. Whitehead
Director, White House Office of Telecommunications Policy, Washington

There is a real question as to whether public television, particularly the national Federally-funded part of public television, should be carrying public affairs, news commentary and that kind of thing—for several reasons. One is the fact that the commercial networks, by and large, do quite a good job in that area. Public television is designed to be an alternative, to provide programming that isn't available on commercial television. So you could raise the legitimate question as to should there be as much public affairs, as much news and commentary, as they apparently plan to do . . . When you're talking about using Federal funds to support a journalism activity, it's always going to be the subject of scrutiny. The Congress will always be watching it very closely. The press will always be watching it very closely. It just invites a lot of political attention.

Variety, 1-19:39.

The reason we proposed abolishing the Fairness Doctrine (for broadcasting) was not that we felt fairness was not important—because, of course, we do—but rather that the Fairness Doctrine, as it has come to be administered, is so confusing, so chaotic and so highly detailed and complex that it really is not a doctrine at all. Nobody knows what it means, no one knows how it would apply in various cases. I think it is safe to say it intimidates the broadcaster, who is constantly worried what Washington is going to do if he opens his mouth about anything or puts anyone on his television station. In short, it's just not producing the intended result of the broad, over-all fairness that we want to get. So we proposed that we (don't) do away with the fairness obligation of the broadcaster, but, rather than enforce it on a case-by-case, day-by-day basis here in Washington, that we enforce it as originally intended—at the time we renew the broadcaster's license. In his coverage of controversial affairs, has he been fair in covering all sides of all the important issues in his community? So . . . it was a proposal to get rid of this very complex doctrine as it has come to be applied and move to a more sensible way of enforcing the fundamental fairness obligation.

Interview/
The Washington Post, 3-5:(A)3.

There is *no* area where (broadcast) management responsibility is more important than news. The station owners and managers cannot abdicate responsibility for news judgments. When a reporter or disk jockey slips in or passes over information in order to line his pocket, that's plugola, and management would take quick corrective action. But men also stress or suppress information in accordance with their beliefs. Will station licensees or network executives also take action against this ideological plugola? Just as a newspaper publisher has responsibilities for the wire-service copy that appears in his newspapers, so television station owners and managers must have full responsibility for what goes out over the public's airwaves, no matter what the origin of the program. There should be no place in broadcasting for the "rip and read" ethic of journalism. Just as publishers and editors have professional responsibility for the news they print, stations and licensees have final responsibility for news balance, whether the information comes from their own newsroom or from a distant network. The old refrain that "we had nothing to do with that report, and could do nothing about it" is an evasion of responsibility and unacceptable as a defense.

Before Sigma Delta Chi,
Indianapolis, Dec. 18/
The New York Times, 12-31:(2)14.

The First Amendment's guarantee of a free press was not supposed to create a privileged class of men called journalists, who are immune from criticism by government or restraint by publishers and editors. To the contrary, the working journalist, if he follows a professional code of ethics, gives up the right to present his personal point of view when he is on the job.

Before Sigma Delta Chi,
Indianapolis, Dec. 18/
The Washington Post, 12-19:(A)9.

For four years, broadcasters have been telling this (Nixon) Administration that, if they had more freedom and stability, they would use it to carry out their responsibilities. We have to believe this; for if broadcasters were simply masking their greed and actually seeking a so-called "license to steal," the country would have to give up on the idea of private-enterprise broadcasting. Some are urging just that. But this Administration remains unshaken in its support of the principles of freedom and responsibility in a private-enterprise broadcasting system. But we are equally unshaken in our belief that broadcasters must do more to exercise the responsibility of private enterprise that is the prerequisite of freedom. Since broadcasters' success in meeting their responsibility will be measured at license-renewal time, they must demonstrate it across the board. They can no longer accept network standards of taste, violence and decency in programming. If the programs or commercials glorify the use of drugs; if the programs are violent or sadistic; if the commercials are false or misleading, or simply instrusive and obnoxious, the stations must jump on the networks rather than wince as the Congress and the FCC are forced to do . . .

Before Sigma Delta Chi,
Indianapolis, Dec. 18/
The New York Times, 12-31:(2)13.

Tom Wicker
Political columnist

(On objectivity in journalism): We're only as able as any other person to rise above our likes and dislikes. The question is: should we? If the press universally regards the President as unlikable and not a particularly trustworthy individual, should we pretend to

(TOM WICKER)

the American people that he is? There is some bias . . . (but) I think that's a good deal less dangerous to the American people than the steps you'd have to take to eliminate the bias.

Interview/
The Washington Post, 8-20:(Potomac)17.

Nick B. Williams
Former editor and executive vice president, "Los Angeles Times"

I thought and still believe that the publication of the "Pentagon Papers" (secret documents on U.S. involvement in Vietnam printed in 1971 by several newspapers) was a mistake, both from the point of national policy and from the point of professional journalism. But . . . the mistake in this one instance was not so calamitous that the prior injunctive process should have been invoked.

Walter R. Humphrey memorial lecture, Texas Christian University, March 16/
The Dallas Times Herald, 3-17:(A)16.

A free and resolute press has become the target of powerful forces determined to weaken or destroy its Constitutional mission. A weak press, a timid press, a subservient press, can indeed be useful to those who cannot stomach a free and independent press, and most of all do not want a strong press. For them, the press—if an instrument of propaganda, their own special propaganda—is a valuable tool.

Walter R. Humphrey memorial lecture, Texas Christian University, March 16/
The Dallas Times Herald, 3-17:(A)16.

Herman Wouk
Author

(Arguing against an increase in U.S. second-class postage rates for magazines): The small periodicals are the primary, often the only, means of publishing a vast quantity of writing by authors, scholars, scientists, historians, economists, engineers, agronomists, social scientists and others. The periodical is the only means of bringing this material to the public. Much of the best contemporary literature—poetry, fiction, criticism and scholarly work—is published in the very magazines that will be the earliest victims of the scheduled second-class rate increases. These journals are meagerly financed and are sustained only by the generosity of staffs and contributors who work without compensation . . . An annual appropriation to maintain the present second-class rates would not be using public funds to help large, profitable corporations increase their profits. Certainly, the periodicals with circulations of less than 500,000 and advertising content ranging from ground zero to 50 per cent, operating for years at little or no profit, have demonstrated that they do not use the second-class mails to reap heavy profits at the public's expense. Rather, their record reflects a dedication to the public interest which deserves more than condolences on their impending demise. There are only limited opportunities for Congress to spend money to support the First Amendment. Government support often means government control—and that is anathema to freedom of expression. But the second-class mails offer that rare opportunity for Congress to take positive action to implement the First Amendment.

Before House Subcommittee on Postal Service, Washington/
The New York Times, 6-22:39.

Isaac Asimov
Author

I'm a compulsive writer. People sometimes ask me what I do for relaxation. My answer is: "What I'm doing now." If I didn't make my living writing, I'd write for nothing. And it's been that way ever since I began making up stories as a boy.

Interview/ San Francisco Examiner & Chronicle, 9-3:(This World)28.

W. H. Auden
Poet

I always have two things in my head; I always have a theme and the form. The form looks for the theme, theme looks for the form; and when they come together, you're able to write.

Interview, New York/ The New York Times, 2-7:34.

Simon Michael Bessie
President, Atheneum Publishers

The book that is successful in the market-place is immensely successful—either in its own sales or in its book-club or paperback sales—and earns a great deal of money, before taxes. The book that fails, fails. The middling book that used to provide a possible career for a writer—the good writer, the man whose book might sell 20,000, 30,000 or 40,000 copies and out of which the man would make enough to live modestly—I think that kind of thing has become much more difficult and rarer.

Panel discussion, New York, April 6/ The New York Times, 4-10:41.

Anthony Burgess
British author

American writers are lucky. There's more money available here, and writers can always go on campus and get a sinecure while they're writing. That's totally impossible in England. The primary audience is here . . . the big things are coming out of America; English novelists can't write "big" any longer.

Interview, New York/ Publishers' Weekly, 1-31:182.

Truman Capote
Author

My theory about publishing a book is that everything—the reviews, the interviews and everything else—has to happen within two weeks of publication. If it's scattered, it's not going to work. But if it all comes together simultaneously, you'll spin right up the list . . . You use your God-given brain (to do it). It takes about six months of organization. You just sort of time it right. I can't explain it. There's a pattern—thought out by me. When *In Cold Blood* came out, I was on the covers of three magazines simultaneously—*Newsweek, Life and Saturday Review*—and I had a lead review in every Sunday book supplement across the country. That's a parlay that has never been beaten and never will be.

Interview/Esquire, November:187.

Susan Chitty
British author

The only modern novels that have excited me recently have been American. Modern English writers are poor on the whole; not because they intrinsically lack talent, but be-

(SUSAN CHITTY)

cause they're writing against a background so limp and cotton-woolly. Whatever you say about America, it's not that. It's stimulating and horrible, and maybe one needs that to react against.

San Francisco Examiner, 2-8:28.

Agatha Christie
Author

I probably could write the same book again and again, and nobody would notice.

Quote, 4-2:313.

Michael Crichton
Author

It always amuses me to write about things of which I haven't any idea, and make them sound like I know what I'm talking about. Conan Doyle had a knack for making a story totally believable even though the details were invented; the stories almost shifted into the realm of nonfiction in the reader's eye. He once said: "It has always seemed to me that, as long as you produce your dramatic effect, accuracy of details matters little. I have never striven for it . . . What matter, if I hold my readers?" I like that.

Interview/ The Washington Post, 5-21:(Book World)2.

Len Deighton
Author

Every morning when I get up, I never can believe that all I have to do is write a book. I feel terribly lucky . . . When I write now, I've got a pace. But when I began *Ipcress File*, I didn't know a thing. I never could have begun it if I'd known how long 70,000 words really is.

Interview/ Los Angeles Times, 1-9:(Calendar):10.

Will Durant
Author, Historian

Ariel (his wife) and I are children of the libraries. They are the home and refuge of our heritage. All that is good in our history is gathered in libraries. At this moment, Plato is down there at the library waiting for us. So is Aristotle. Spinoza is there and so is Keats. Shelley and Byron and Sam Johnson are there waiting to tell us their magnificent stories. All you have to do is walk in the library door and the great company open their arms to you. They are so happy to see you that they come out with you into the street and to your home. And they do what hardly any friend will—they are silent when you wish to think.

Interview, Los Angeles/ Modern Maturity, Aug.-Sept.:25.

Janet Flanner
Writer

I've worked hard and had a good life. I have an enormous respect for work. I think work is good stuff. I fiddle over my writing as if it were embroidery.

Interview/ The Washington Post, 7-2:(F)5.

R. Buckminster Fuller
Engineer, Author, Designer

Generally speaking, the most disappointing reading I do is when I read books by people who quite clearly are mixed up and don't know what they're talking about—particularly when they say things in awkward ways and are ill-informed. There's a great deal of blasphemous writing today which admits to being shocking; and it shocks, all right. But I don't spend much time on it. I'd say there is no negative reading experience for me. If a book is very bad, it actually causes me to do some very good thinking as to how it happened.

Interview/The Washington Post, 6-11:(Book World)2.

Yekaterina A. Furtseva
Minister of Culture of the Soviet Union

(On why books of Soviet author Alexander Solzhenitsyn have not been published in the Soviet Union): He is not opposed to any particular person in this country. He is opposed against our entire society, and that is why we treat him the way we do. In fact, he has raised his hand against the very dignity of the Soviet people; and since we publish books not from private capital but from the people's money, why should we spend the people's money on someone who is against the people?

News conference, Moscow, May 24/ The New York Times, 5-25:13.

Paul Gallico
Writer

I'm a writer. When I fill out a customs form, I say writer, not author. I hate the word author. I'm a professional writer, and I'll write you a novel, a short story, a bit of doggerel, a screenplay, an article. Whatever comes into the purlieu of my professional life I'll do—some things better, some worse, but I'll do it professionally.

Interview, London/ Los Angeles Times, 9-3:(Calendar)10.

Theodor Geisel (Dr. Seuss)
Author

Dr. Zhivago by Boris Pasternak was my worst reading experience. I couldn't get beyond page 13. I had the same trouble with Tolstoy's *War and Peace*, so there must be something amiss between me and long Russian novels. Over the years, I must have tried *War and Peace* 35 times. I think the author has a responsibility to the reader to make it possible for him to understand what the writer is saying, and the two authors I've mentioned just haven't found my wavelength.

Interview/The Washington Post, 5-7:(Book World)2.

Karl R. Gierow
Permanent secretary,
Swedish Academy of Literature

It is not the smallest German miracle that, after such years of destitution, a new generation of writers, thinkers and researchers was ready so soon to shoulder their country's and their own essential task in the spiritual life of our time. The renewal of German literature . . . is not an experiment with form—a drowning man scorns the butterfly stroke. Instead, it is a rebirth out of annihilation, a resurrection, a culture which, ravaged by icy nights and condemned to extinction, sends up new shoots, blossoms and matures to the joy of us all. Such was the kind of work Alfred Nobel wished his prize to reward.

Announcing the award of the Nobel Literature Prize to German writer Heinrich Boll, Stockholm, Oct. 19/ The Fresno (Calif.) Bee, 10-19:(A)8.

Clifford Irving
Author of a fraudulent biography
of industrialist Howard Hughes

It may sound naive, but we (he, his wife and his associate) never thought that what we were doing was a crime. Now that we know, we see there was never anyone as dumb and naive as we were.

Interview, Westport, Conn./ The Washington Post, 4-4:(B)3.

William Jovanovich
Chairman,
Harcourt, Brace, Jovanovich, publishers

I, as a student of 19th-century literature, have great affection and attachment to the novel; but I'm perfectly prepared to face the fact that I may be one of the people presiding over its demise. In fact, the novel has lost some of its utilitarian function. We ought to face that. It no longer is a source of information in the way that it once was, and it no longer is a source of finding out how the rich live or the poor live. It's no longer a means of discovering class differences. And I think maybe the boom may be boomier and the bust may be bustier, but the fact is that the novel hasn't got as much going for it today as it had 20 years ago. I can say "alas," but you know, it's like the

(WILLIAM JOVANOVICH)

famous remark, "Who is the greatest writer in French?—Victor Hugo, alas." There it is.

Panel discussion, New York, April 6/The New York Times, 4-10:41.

Elia Kazan
Author; Motion picture and stage director

I didn't start to write until I was in my mid-50s. I'm 62 now and I have a lot more books in my head. I started to write because I wanted to say exactly what I felt. No matter whose play or film you direct, you must try to interpret that writer's view of life. But the playwright's story and his experience are not mine. His point of view is not my point of view. So, toward the end of my life, I decided to put things down exactly as I see them. When I speak for myself, I get a tremendous sense of liberation. In other words, writing has been by far the most rewarding of my creative experiences.

Interview, San Francisco/ San Francisco Examiner, 2-25:27.

(Writing) a book is a hypnotic thing. With me it's all-absorbing, and I can't think of anything else. It's an attractive way of life. When a book is done, you hold it in your hand and say, "There's a piece of me," and that's great. It just might be the best piece of me.

Interview, New York/ The Dallas Times Herald, 4-4:(D)5.

Emily Kimbrough
Author

The only time I ever met Somerset Maugham, I sat next to him at a lunch. His autobiography had just come out and he was charming that day. I felt emboldened to ask him a question: "You say you always do your writing regularly every day from 9 to half past 1. I don't mean to be presumptuous, but does it happen sometimes that the words don't come, the sentences don't shape themselves?" Mr. Maugham smiled and said, "That, my dear, I consider the average day."

Interview, San Francisco/ San Francisco Examiner, 11-16:26.

Ross Macdonald (Ken Millar)
Author

The things that a man puts in his books are not necessarily the same things he puts in conversation. You tend to talk about the things you just learned; but the things you put in your books are generally things you learned ten years ago and are trying to unlearn or forget. The bedrock of fiction is laid down long ago, and it's very difficult to change it.

Interview, Santa Barbara, Calif./ Esquire, June:188.

Alistair MacLean
Author

I just tell a story very quickly, without delving too deeply into how people think and what their motivations are. It is quite true—and I make no bones about this—that I do tend to use the same set-ups, the same situations, the same characters. They're all more or less a repeat of each other. But I'm clever: I change the locations and I change the names.

Interview, London/ Los Angeles Times, 12-17:(Calendar)34.

Archibald MacLeish
Poet, Playwright

If you commit yourself to the art of poetry, you commit yourself to the task of learning how to see, using words as elements of sight and their sounds as prisms. And to see means to see something worth all the agony of learning how to see. What frightens me about the poetry that I see nowadays is that so much of it is bitterly and brutally and agonizingly hostile and destructive. But search it in vain for the discovery of any reason for the attack! Why attack unless you're defending something worthwhile?

Interview, Conway, Mass./ The New York Times, 5-7:(1)79.

John Macrae
President,
E. P. Dutton, publishers

. . . it's increasingly difficult, I think, to get a so-called quality novel, or even a quality book of nonfiction outside of the new journalism, which in itself might replace the novel. And I think this is a reflection of the culture. I don't want to say that the culture is anti-intellectual now, but the experimental novel is difficult. I even find that the scholarly book—not yet a college text because it's only the leading edge of some idea—has very little chance of market now. And in many cases, the better it is in terms of being an original contribution, the harder it is for such a book to find a market. And I guess that's what bothers us, and it plagues one and disappoints one.

Panel discussion, New York, April 6/The New York Times, 4-10:41.

Helen Meyer
President,
Dell Publishing Company, Inc.

I think paperbacks are going to grow to greater heights than ever before, in all areas. First of all, the population is increasing, and people are reading more. I think with the advent of paperbacks, where you can buy a book at any corner drugstore or newsstand or supermarket or variety store, people are really exposed to books. Thirty years ago, either you bought a high-priced hardcover book or you went to the library, and not too many people went to the library. I think that's the greatest contribution to education—paperback books. We were criticized at the very beginning for the type of cover we did—actually, today it would be child's play as far as sex is concerned—but what it did do was to bring people to the newsstand, and it made readers out of them. To me, that's the important thing—read anything, but read!

Interview/ Publishers' Weekly, 3-6:26.

Henry Miller
Author

. . . there are writers, and there are writers. The only writers I respect are those who have put themselves completely into their work. Not those who use their skillful hands to do something—this isn't writing, in my opinion. A man who can dash off a book, let's say—and say it's a good novel, a best seller, even of some value—but it isn't representative completely of him, of his personality, then there's something wrong there. This man is a fraud in a way, to me. All he put into his book was his skill. I prefer a man who is unskillful, who is an awkward writer, but who has something to say, who is dealing himself one time on every page—that's what the writer is, I think. Of course, that kind of thinking about the writer only applies to modern times. In the past, that wasn't so. I wouldn't say that about Dante, Homer, Goethe, Shakespeare, I don't think so. I can feel in them a certain detachment. I've never been drawn to the classics for this reason. The writing is always too professional, too skillful . . . the breakthroughs have occurred with rare men who spoke in their own voices.

Interview, Los Angeles/ Los Angeles Times, 1-23:(West)20.

James Mills
Author

(On writing fiction as opposed to nonfiction): You can't imagine how liberating it is to be free to lie! Nonfiction can be terribly frustrating, because you can't force things to happen when you need them. Now if something decisive needs to happen or needs to get said, I can make it happen, I can put it in the mouths of the characters. It permits a kind of control I always longed for in nonfiction.

Interview, Washington/ The Washington Post, 10-12:(L)7.

Ezra Pound
Poet

Part of literature seems to spring from hate, but its vitality is not in the hatred.

Interview, Venice, Italy/ The New York Times Magazine, 1-9:59.

Robert L. Radnitz
Motion picture producer-director

Show me a child's book an adult won't pick up and enjoy and I'll show you a book a child won't pick up and enjoy.

Interview, Los Angeles/ San Francisco Examiner & Chronicle, 4-16:(Datebook)18.

Harold Robbins
Author

. . . that's what I am: a writer. That's what I'm about. The day I put that blank piece of paper in the typewriter and took it out as the first page of *Never Love a Stranger*, I knew I didn't want to be anything else. I looked at it and said: "This is how I want to spend all my life. It's easy. I've always been looking for an easy way to do it. This is a cinch." I never had writer's block, sweaty palms or anything—I just sit and write. When I sit down at that damn typewriter, I don't care what goes on in the room around me. I don't have to be alone. All I have to be is "on." It's the only time I'm doing something for myself. In everything else I do, I'm always doing something that involves the consideration of other people. The only time I'm completely selfish is when I write a book. Because that's all me. I'm the only person I have to satisfy, and I'm the only person I try to satisfy, the only person I care about. It's what's in that personal world that I want to get down.

Interview, Los Angeles/ Los Angeles Times, 6-18:(West)16.

There is something about the literary establishment which I never was really aware of, but Philip Roth made a very good point; he said: "They loved me until I became successful." The lovely thing about critics is when they have a big target, they belt 'em. Because it's more fun. It seems to be very fashionable to take a slug at me, or at anyone that sells. This makes a reviewer feel important. I look at it like this: People know what's important. People will read my books who have never read a critic. And there are people who will read the critics who say the book stinks, and then those people will read it to see why, and they'll be ashamed that they are illiterate enough to like it. You'll see a difference between a professional reviewer, the real literary critic, and the invitational critic. In a lot of those nonprofessional reviews, 90 per cent of the review is about me, not about the book. They'll lambast everything—the way I live, the money I spend, my women, all the books I've written; and then in the last paragraph they'll get to the book I've written.

Interview, Los Angeles/ Los Angeles Times, 6-18:(West)19.

William Saroyan
Author

. . . I like all my books. Once in a while, I get them out and read them. That was one of the reasons I first decided to become a writer, don't you know—so I'd have something decent to read.

Interview, Fresno, Calif./ The New York Times Book Review, 4-2:16.

Erich Segal
Author

If one makes money in steel or oil, everyone respects him. When, instead, he does it with a book, it's as if he had sold his soul to the devil.

San Francisco Examiner & Chronicle, 4-23:(This World)2.

Isaac Bashevis Singer
Author

Strange though this may sound, a genuine writer of fiction must pay more attention to what he must *not* say than to what he may express in his work. He must set himself limits. Outsiders may think that such an author is retreating or regressing. But like the chess game of today, the game of literature consists more in avoiding pitfalls than in creating literary spectaculars. The task of avoiding cliches, factual as well as verbal, is well nigh impossible. For however much one human being may be different from another, people have a great deal in common and, given certain situations, will react in the same manner. What the writer must be careful about is not to create the kind of situation that would call for cliches.

Television broadcast/"Comment!" National Broadcasting Company, 6-18.

All great writers are ethnic . . . The great writers confined themselves to the places and people they knew best, and didn't try to teach lessons in sociology, psychology or philosophy, but simply tried to tell a real story connected with a time and a place. The 19th-century writers didn't set out with a mission or a message; they set out to write a story. The message came out anyhow.

Interview/The Washington Post, 6-25:(Book World)3.

Alexander I. Solzhenitsyn
Soviet author

(On the hostile attitude of the Soviet government toward his writing): A kind of forbidden, contaminated zone has been created around my family. You Westerners cannot imagine my situation. I live in my own country; I write a novel about Russia. But it is as hard for me to gather material as it would be if I were writing about Polynesia.

Interview, Moscow/ The New York Times, 4-3:1.

Mickey Spillane
Author

I am not an author. I'm a writer, an entertainer. My stories are antidotes for the anxieties of the world today. I don't write to see my name on the cover of some jerky literary book. The only place I want to see my name is on a check. When I write a book, I first think of the surprise ending and work backwards, building it up like a joke. I don't make a lot of corrections on copy; I sit down and write it and never look at it again . . . don't call me an author; I'm a writer. The difference is that writers make money. An author is a guy who spends two or three years writing a book that nobody's going to buy. That's two or three years out of the guy's life. You know what he gets. His ego gets smashed, and then he's no good for anything else. That's an author.

Interview, Washington/ The Washington Post, 6-8:(B)14.

P. L. Travers
Author

No matter what reviewers and critics may say, I never write for children. If I write for anybody, it's for grownups. How can I know what a child would like; how could I possibly tell? When I was a child I loved a book I found in my father's library called *Twelve Deathbed Scenes.* It fascinated me. Surely that writer had no idea he was writing for children. And so I don't feel equipped to say, "This is a book for children"; I can only feel grateful that they read it.

Interview, New York/ The National Observer, 6-10:22.

Kurt Vonnegut, Jr.
Author

I don't consider myself a science-fiction writer; that's just a literary ghetto area writers want to be in. I'm just a novelist. The thing is, in writing, that there are ground rules, and one that is hard to break is the idea you can't be a serious novelist and include technology. The serious-minded writers have ignored technology because they don't know much about it. But you can't leave machinery out any more. I don't see how you can write a novel now when the sounds

(KURT VONNEGUT, JR.)

of machinery are in your ears constantly.

Interview, New York/ San Francisco Examiner, 1-11:23.

Irving Wallace
Author

I write because I love to write. It's my consuming passion. After I sold *The Chapman Report* to the movies, some of my friends said, "You'll never write another book because now you don't have to." And I told them, "You're dead wrong." I'd been grinding out screenplays for years and hating every minute of it. Now I knew that money was going to give me the freedom to write and write and write. Write books. Write exactly what I wanted. The hungry writer writes what he's told so he can eat. One of my favorite writers, Somerset Maugham, said, "Writing is an adventure of the soul." Every time I start a new novel it's a grand adventure. Needless to say, I can't wait to begin again.

Interview, New York/ Publishers' Weekly, 1-3:23.

I think a novel should be about something, dammit, besides yourself. I like a big theme. I like to write about something I don't know about. I knew nothing about religion when I started *The Word* . . . I'm a great believer in story-telling, something that involves you in other people's lives. Novels should be about "something," and they should be told in terms of people. Too few writers are doing that. It comes down to a childlike thing. It's like when I used to tell my 16-year-old daughter stories when she was young. She always wanted to know what happened next. That's the key.

Interview, San Francisco/ San Francisco Examiner & Chronicle, 5-28:(This World)33.

Yevgeny Yevtushenko
Soviet Poet

. . . Americans don't read any literature. And you have no poet who speaks for America. You have no new Walt Whitman. You need an American Yevtushenko.

Interview, Trenton, N.J., Jan. 23/ San Francisco Examiner, 1-24:4.

I never mix poetry with journalism; but I began to work as a journalist with a newspaper. I like newspapers—some of them I hate, of course—but I like to publish my poems in newspapers, because (it) seems to me it is the duty of the poet to write about topical things. The duty. Of course, it's (a) big danger if a poet will write *only* about topical problems. It seems to me (the) duty of (the) poet—the principal duty—is to be inside topical problems but at (the) same time to work for immortality—for eternity. It's very difficult.

Interview/ The New York Times, 2-6:(2)1.

I make salad like I write poetry: I put everything in. In salad—onions, lettuce, cucumber, oil, grapefruit juice. In poetry—classical styles, folk styles, sad things, happy things. But in both poetry and salads I have one rule: Everything must be fresh.

Interview, New York, April 6/ The New York Times, 4-7:31.

Medicine and Health

Bella S. Abzug
United States Representative, D–N.Y.

(Introducing a bill to legalize abortion): The power to decide what will occur inside a woman's body has for too long been in the hands of males who have never been pregnant, have never suffered childbirth, have never been disemboweled and left to die by back-alley abortionists. (My bill) would guarantee women the freedom to choose for themselves whether they wish to have children and end forever the humiliation of not controlling their own bodies.

Los Angeles Times, 5-3:(1)2.

Spiro T. Agnew
Vice President of the United States

In a sense, all adult Americans–and, in part, teachers–must share in the blame for drug addiction among teenagers. We have been too indifferent. We have been too lazy. We have been too permissive. A large share of the blame must also rest on some of those in the news and entertainment fields who, in the past, intentionally or otherwise, have glorified drug use. For while each teacher or parent can reach only a handful of youngsters, the nation's communications media reach and sway and mold the life patterns of tens of millions. Instead of denouncing narcotics usage as the last pitiful refuge of a flawed or confused human being, they have excused it as an inescapable outlet for young people trying to cope with our complex world and have thus rationalized experimentation and usage. Instead of stressing the agony and humiliation of the drug addict, they have persisted in describing the so-called benefits.

At Midwest district convention, American Association for Health, Physical Education and Recreation, Indianapolis, March 10/ Los Angeles Herald-Examiner, 3-12:(A)1.

Aaron M. Altschul
Professor of Community Medicine and International Health, Georgetown University

Affluent malnutrition, as a disease of entire societies or large segments of societies, is a relatively new phenomenon in history. In general, as societies become more affluent and they change their eating habits, the proportion of obesity increases, as does the incidence of diabetes, coronary artery disease, hypertension and other diseases. Evidence of a cause-and-effect relationship between diet and changes in the disease pattern is not available and, clearly, these diseases are of multiple etiology. Yet the question worth pondering is whether a point may be reached in people's diet patterns where continuation of the effects of affluence is such as to decrease the value of the diet. The curve of improvement in health with increased expenditure on food does not level off but possibly declines past such a point.

Before American Chemical Society, Philadelphia/ The Dallas Times Herald, 3-20:26.

Christiaan Barnard
Surgeon; Pioneer in heart-transplant surgery

The big thing today is, stop heart transplants until you know more about the problem of rejection. Yet, nobody says stop operating on cancer of the stomach until you know more about cancer.

Interview, New York/ Los Angeles Times, 5-7:(A)5.

Birch Bayh
United States Senator, D–Ind.

Barbiturate dependency and addiction has been described as more dangerous than amphetamine dependency and more widespread and physically destructive than heroin addiction. Barbiturate abuse is not a phenomenon restricted to the street culture of multiple drug abusers. It reaches into many areas of American life affecting such diverse groups as grammar-school, high-school and college students, industrial workers, middle-class partygoers and residents of our ghettos and barrios.

At Senate Juvenile Delinquency Subcommittee hearing, Washington, June 12/The Dallas Times Herald, 6-12:(A)7.

Melvin Belli
Lawyer

Out of about 3,600 criminal and civil lawsuits in our office right now, we have maybe 100 malpractice suits pending. I don't call that "going after doctors," though. If I've put the fear of God in some of the unqualified men in medicine, I'm delighted. I didn't personally invent malpractice—it is the result of irresponsible bums practicing medicine who really don't know what they're doing and leave human wrecks around. I hear complaints from some doctors that the fear of malpractice suits is forcing them to overdiagnose, overtreat and overprotect their patients. What kind of doctors are these? I'll tell you: They're incompetents. They ought to have their licenses pulled and be sent back to medical school. Doctors who responsibly practice good medicine—and that's the majority of them—don't worry about malpractice suits, and they certainly have nothing to fear from me.

Interview, San Francisco/ Los Angeles Times, 4-9:(West)38.

George M. Briggs
Professor of Nutrition, University of California

I have said it many times before, and I will say it again: Our national eating habits are terrible . . . The costs to society to undernourished mothers and their sickly infants; physically and mentally inferior children; absenteeism in the working force and school children; the great loss of life from cardiovascular disease and hypertension; the costs of dental decay, alcoholism and diseases of diabetes, obesity, digestive disturbances, osteoporosis, can be attributed in part to poor nutrition.

Before Senate Hunger Committee, Washington, Dec. 5/ Los Angeles Times, 12-6:(1)21.

Robert C. Byrd
United States Senator, D–W.Va.

For a long time, we shrugged our shoulders and comforted ourselves with the belief that drug addiction was confined to the ghettos and to the psychopathics in our society. But now that the curtain has been lifted we have been shocked to find that the children of middle America, the children of well-respected and industrious parents in every stratum of our culture, are frighteningly into the so-called "drug scene" . . . I, of course, do not equate the dangers of aspirin with those of heroin. Nor do I equate pills for sleeping, pills for staying awake, pills for relaxing or pills for "rarin' to go," pills for minor physical discomfort or pills for real or imagined psychic discomfort, with hallucinogenic pills or powers. Nor do the saturation advertisers of proprietary drugs include heroin, hashish, cocaine or LSD in their multimillion-dollar advertising budgets or urge their use on television or in the print media. But what they do—and this, in my opinion, is a deep, deep danger to the future well-being of this great nation of ours—is teach our young people, graphically and powerfully, that success and happiness in life lie not in internal mastery of oneself, based on self-discipline and strength of character, but in a variety of external stimulants. The drug culture that has found its flowering in American society can be pieced together out of hundreds of thousands of advertisements and television commercials. It is the advertising that mounts so graphically, so compellingly, the message that, by merely unscrewing the cap of a pill bottle, our youth can turn rain into sunshine, gloom to joy, depression to euphoria and normal everyday doubts into glowing uncaring confidence.

Before Retail Druggists' Association, Chicago/The Wall Street Journal, 11-29:18.

Frank D. Campion
Director of communications, American Medical Association

Polls by Lou Harris and other people have shown that when people are asked what they think of "organized medicine"—which they automatically translate into the AMA—there is a generally unfavorable reaction, sometimes as high as 80 per cent. But a curious thing happens when you ask them what they think of their own doctors. You get a reverse reaction, with about 80 per cent saying things like, "My own doctor is a great guy." The individual doctor, it seems, enjoys very high favorability.

Los Angeles Times, 1-17:(3)11.

Morris E. Chafetz
Director, National Institute on Alcohol Abuse and Alcoholism of the United States

It is my contention that alcoholism is America's largest untreated illness. We are attempting to reach the entire American public—those who choose to drink and those who do not, as well as the young people who are experimenting with alcoholic beverages. We are not telling people to drink or not to drink; that is a personal, private decision. What we are saying is that if one chooses to drink, he has a responsibility not to destroy himself or society.

Los Angeles Times, 2-19:(1)3.

Frank Church
United States Senator, D–Idaho

When all is said and done, Medicare pays for only 42 per cent of all health costs of the elderly. One of the startling points made by the Senate Committee on Aging is that older Americans are paying in 1972 almost as much in out-of-pocket medical expenses as they were before Medicare became law in 1965. They are paying more than twice as much in out-of-pocket payments than persons under 65.

Before the Senate, Washington, May 31/ Quote, 7-23:83.

Robert D. Conn
Chairman, Department of Medicine, Southern Illinois University

Too many doctors assume the responsibility on themselves when the patient isn't doing very well. Medicine can determine what good health is and develop a mechanism for achieving it, but the responsibility is the patient's . . . Somehow, we've created the (idea that the) doctor is responsible for every little ill. Doctors have fostered this by offering pills for everything. So the public has grown to expect the doctor to be responsible for them when they should be responsible for themselves.

Interview, Los Angeles/ Los Angeles Times, 11-14:(2)1.

Jean F. Crum
President, California Medical Association

. . . it seems clear that our health-care problems cannot magically be eliminated simply by adding billions of dollars to public-sector spending. We must recognize that medical care alone cannot solve all of our health-related problems. Environmental health, inadequate general health education, automobile and home accidents, poor housing, sanitation and nutrition, alcoholism and drug abuse, suicide, homicide and other violent crimes also are important factors. What we need is not more dollars but better ways to use them; programs which are goal-oriented and which concentrate on achieving very specific, carefully defined objectives. In the long run, this approach may well prove the only workable way to eliminate deficiencies in American health care.

Before Commonwealth Club health problems committee, San Francisco, June 27/ San Francisco Examiner, 6-28:60.

Charles C. Edwards
Commissioner,
Food and Drug Administration
of the United States

Because self-medication is essential to the nation's health-care system, it is imperative that the over-the-counter drugs be safe and effective and have fully-informative labeling. The FDA is concerned that many present formulations do not have the claimed effect, have inadequate instructions for effective use by the consumer or are promoted in deceptive and indefensible ways.

The National Observer, 1-15:9.

(On criticism of the FDA for delaying U.S. marketing of medications available abroad): This is a straw man, and like Dorothy's scarecrow in the Land of Oz, is largely witless. It is built on the false assumption that, because a drug is marketed somewhere else, it ought to be available to Americans. The clamor about foreign products is increased by some professionals who do not know the science of the issue and by some patients harboring a desperate hope that Product X may be the miracle cure they are waiting for. Fifteen hundred new drug products were marketed in one foreign country in 1970, and it is reported that 90 per cent of these could not be prescribed in the United States. But which country's drug laws would you choose for your family?

Before Pharmaceutical Manufacturers Association, Boca Raton, Fla., April 28/ The Washington Post, 4-29:(A)7.

Roger O. Egeberg
Special Assistant Secretary for Health Policy, Department of Health, Education and Welfare of the United States

If heroin were cut off from the thousands of addicts in the United States, most of them would get hooked on something else. We've got to start focusing on the addict rather than the agent who addicts him. It's not a short-term goal, but it's the basic untouched one. Explanations and statistics about why people take drugs are at present superficial and incomplete. When you say that somebody is on narcotics because he is bored or frustrated or afraid of the future, you are at the same place they were centuries back when they condemned wells. They knew people were getting sick and from where, but they didn't know about bacteria.

Before World Health Organization, Paris/Parade, 8-6:5.

The Soviets and the (Communist) Chinese know where to go to get into the health-care system. Americans do not. One of the important things they have is a point of entry into the health-care system. If you live in the U.S. and if you're new to a community —or if you are poor—this is a worrisome problem. How do you know where to go to get help? . . . In a rural area in the U.S.S.R., for instance, there is something called a "point" manned by a kind of general practitioner, aides and a midwife. The Soviets have found they can care for about 70 per cent of patients' problems right there. There is radio communication with a medical center, and there is a plane to provide transportation in an emergency or to take the patient to a diagnostic center . . . We have a lot to learn in this country. We are making some progress in community health centers like the one in Watts (Calif.). But in general, what we've done is only a piss in the ocean. And you can quote me.

Interview, San Francisco, Oct. 16/ San Francisco Examiner, 10-17:20.

Richard Feinbloom
Assistant Professor of Pediatrics,
Harvard Medical School

It is hypocritical to deplore youth for using illegal drugs when we parents have often bought the same drug with a prescription and may be heavily dependent on it. Isn't the military inconsistent as it tests urine for heroin addiction while it offers amphetamines routinely to keep troops alert and responsive? Doesn't the pharmacist err when he faults adolescents for escaping into a blur or unreality while he offers packaged relief from nervous tension? The unpleasant reality is that the doctor, the pharmacist, the government, the media, indeed all of us, have become "legal pushers."

Television broadcast/"Comment!" National Broadcasting Company, 9-10.

Otto E. Guttentag
Professor Emeritus of Medical Philosophy, University of California, San Francisco

Doctors have always practiced euthanasia. To me it seems that death comes as a friend, not an enemy. Most doctors wouldn't object to not connecting a patient to a machine that would keep him alive, if he were going to be a vegetable for the rest of his life and if he requested it. But if it is legalized, then individual doctors will abdicate their personal responsibility. Why would a (hospital) committee's decision be better than mine? It's a problem of simple humanity, one that a doctor should not be afraid to deal with.

San Francisco Examiner & Chronicle, 3-5:(Sunday Scene)2.

Charles A. Hoffman
President, American Medical Association

Almost daily there are new infringements on the way we (doctors) practice; intrusions by government and other third parties. Almost daily there are attacks on our methods of practice, on our methods of payment, even on our motives and life-styles. And always there hangs over us the looming specter of a massive government health program.

Inaugural address, San Francisco/ Time, 7-3:34.

I've concluded (from a trip abroad) that there is no perfect health-care system. We keep talking about a health-care crisis in this country (the U.S.), but I was not so sure this was so. After the trip, which I went on with an open mind, I'm convinced we don't. All the systems have problems.

New York, Aug. 11/ The New York Times, 8-12:8.

Lawrence J. Hogan
United States Representative, R–Md.

The trend toward casual, unthinking acceptance of abortion is nearly as scandalous as the act of abortion itself, which is the destruction of a helpless unborn human being. The people who argue that an abortion is just another operation such as a tonsilectomy have either overlooked or ignored the scientific and medical facts and the frightening ramifications of abortion.

Quote, 4-2:315.

Harold E. Hughes
United States Senator, D–Iowa

Marijuana is not physically or, except in remote instances, even psychologically, damaging. During World War II in Africa, I smoked marijuana and it had absolutely no effect on me.

TV-radio interview/ "Meet the Press," National Broadcasting Company, 4-9.

Howard Hughes
Industrialist

. . . there is nothing that interests me more than medical research and the quest for better living facilities and better health and better medical standards, not only in the United States but throughout the world. This, to me, is where we should be concentrating our greatest efforts. In fact, possibly, I might say that I feel it could be more important than some of the space activity.

Telephone news conference, Bahamas, Jan. 7/ The New York Times, 1-10:22.

Hubert H. Humphrey
United States Senator, D–Minn.

I think a drug pusher is a murderer on the installment plan.

The Dallas Times Herald, 5-23:(A)18.

John E. Ingersoll
Director, Bureau of Narcotics and Dangerous Drugs, Department of Justice of the United States

(To control the drug problem) everyone involved in illicit drugs needs specialized attention: the supplier, because business is so lucrative prison won't make any difference—when he gets out, he'll go back to selling; the addict, because he is hopelessly ill and because he transmits his disease to others. Education is no panacea; merely knowing about drugs is not going to deter people. The medical profession theoretically has the greatest knowledge of drugs and their potential dangers, yet it is believed that 1 to 2 per cent of the physicians in this country are drug addicts. If you try to tell teen-agers these days they should not take drugs because they are going to be harmful, that is not going to stop them . . . We have to create an attitude of intolerance to drug traffic and drug abuse in this country, because law enforcement can't solve the basic societal problems. But I think we've reached the crest of the tide on this problem. The results are beginning to show . . . This problem can be reduced to a tolerable irritant, which is what it was before the 1960s; it was not an epidemic, or surge, as now. If we can't have this problem licked by 1976, I will turn in my badge and go teach school or something. '76 (the 200th birthday of the U.S.) would be a fitting year to have the scourge out of our system.

Interview, Washington/ Los Angeles Times, 5-16:(2)7.

There is a growing awareness that a portion of our addict population has got to be brought into some kind of institutional or in-patient program. A large number of addicts will not come forward for any voluntary treatment. Some people have to be coerced into doing what is good for them. I'm not just talking about locking people up. When the addict is ready for release, he must be supervised closely, given counseling and perhaps even moved into a new environment. All this would be expensive. But it would be a lot less than what narcotics are costing this country now.

U.S. News & World Report, 9-11:77.

From sunrise to closing benediction in the late evening, the American public is bombarded on radio and television by catchy little jingles, cute sketches and somber warnings, offering drugs and medicines to cure most little symptoms of real or imagined illness—or to provide escape from reality. The average medicine cabinet gives testimony to the success of this mass-media campaign. And the rows of bottles and vials of pills and tablets are a sad commentary on a society that once was noted for its ability to endure hardship in seeking its destiny. This has been a campaign that has encouraged the American public to develop a "take something" syndrome that invites people to accept and even seek relief through the use of chemicals and drugs from even the least discomfort.

Before National Association of Retail Druggists, Chicago, Oct. 4/San Francisco Examiner, 10-4:7.

Jacob K. Javits
United States Senator, R–N.Y.

We have an absolutely phenomenal, absolutely shocking increase in venereal disease cases in the United States. With approximately 650,000 new cases reported in the United States in 1971, it is estimated by the U.S. Public Health Service that there are really about 2 million, because people tend not to report cases of venereal disease.

Before the Senate, Washington, Feb. 17/ Quote, 4-2:328.

Amos Johnson
Former president, American Academy of Family Physicians

I have seen old people in a reasonably healthy condition who, when put away in the isolation of custodial care facilities, totally lose interest in life. They refuse to communicate, refuse to eat, become totally bedridden, waste away and die. This is a disease process called "isolation" and should be so registered on the death certificate.

San Francisco Examiner & Chronicle, 4-30:(This World)2.

Nicholas Johnson
Commissioner,
Federal Communications Commission of the United States

Because the average American home has a television set running six hours a day and because so much of television is devoted, in some manner, to the promotion or sanctioning of stimulants and depressants, the increasing use of those and other drugs in this country could easily have been predicted. In short, television, its advertising agencies and their corporate clients are preying upon both our minds and our bodies—and those of defenseless children—to promote atheistic corporate greed, whatever the social cost. Okay; what do we do about it? What can be done? Both the television industry and America's drug manufacturers are tough opponents of anyone trying to enhance the public interest . . . I have in the past made several proposals to my colleagues on the Federal Communications Commission, proposals which I believe would go far toward stemming the rising tide of national drug reliance. My first choice would be rules which would ban all broadcast advertising of over-the-counter drugs—particularly analgesics and mood-altering drugs. As a political compromise, rules could require that any over-the-counter drug advertising be cleared with the Federal Drug Administration and the Federal Trade Commission prior to broadcast. At least advertising in programs viewed significantly by children should be of an institutional rather than a product nature. We could require that advertising be informative and factual. Finally, in the absence of any such rules, we could at least extend the Fairness Doctrine so that product advertising would be rebutted by counter ads informing viewers of the adverse consequences of consuming the products at all. However, none of these proposals has been found acceptable by the FCC. My colleagues have unanimously rejected even the proposal to open a proceeding to consider these and other suggestions.

At National Council of Churches of Christ hearings on drug advertising, Washington/ The New York Times, 12-10:(3)15.

Vernon E. Jordan, Jr.
Executive director,
National Urban League

A basic change in the (U.S.) health-care system that keeps poor people sick and afflicted is crucial. For of what use are job opportunities if people are too ill to accept them; of what use are Social Security increases when life expectancy for black men is below age 65; and how can educational programs help those youngsters who do not survive to school age? America may indeed be number one, as many say; but in the health of its population, and especially of its poor, it is far down on the list of the world's countries.

Quote, 12-3:539.

John W. Kauffman
Chairman-elect,
American Hospital Association

In the past, when health care was medical care, it was only appropriate that the AMA should have the loudest voice. But where is the AMA today, when the cries of a health-care crisis grow ever louder and shriller, when people are clamoring for out-patient services, lower costs, health education and mental-health care? I'll tell you where they are—where they've been all along—under the umbrella—representing the physician and physician interests.

Before United Hospital Association, Los Angeles, Nov. 8/ Los Angeles Times, 11-9:(2)2.

Edward M. Kennedy
United States Senator, D–Mass.

I want every man, woman and child in America to be covered at any time and for

(EDWARD M. KENNEDY)

any illness by health insurance at a price he can afford. When they rush you to the hospital in an emergency, I want them to meet you at the door and ask how sick you are—not just how much health insurance you have. I want every citizen to receive the same high quality of health care that anyone else receives. No one should be given second-class health care because he is old or poor or black. I want a system that pays doctors and hospitals to keep the people healthy instead of a system whose profits depend on illness. The sicker you get the richer the system gets, and that's not the way it ought to be. I want a health system that has enough doctors and facilities to meet the need. I want a system that encourages doctors to practice their profession in every community in America, not just the high-rise office buildings on Park Avenue or Beverly Hills.

Before Student American Medical Association, Los Angeles, April 29/ Los Angeles Times, 4-30:(C)3.

I believe in maintaining the free-enterprise system in this country and in American medicine. I would like to see even more variety and competition in the health-care system between different forms of care—solo practice, pre-paid groups, medical foundations or any other way that is efficient and beneficial to the patients and doctors, too. I believe we can create a unique American health-care system that will preserve free enterprise for the doctors, and still offer your patients the financial support and adequate care they need.

Before American Academy of Family Physicians, New York, Sept. 27/The New York Times, 9-28:21.

Richard G. Kleindienst
Deputy Attorney General, and Attorney General-designate, of the United States

(Arguing against legalization of marijuana): You do not maintain the strong fabric of society if youth is permitted to have a substance by which they can remove themselves from the reality around them.

At confirmation hearing before Senate Judiciary Committee, Washington/ Feb. 22/The New York Times, 2-23:26.

George L. Maddox
Professor of Medical Sociology, Duke University

If medicine is vulnerable, it's not so much because doctors behave differently than other people as it is that we expect leadership from them. Is it not agreed that people in nursing homes need care? The medical profession should be asking how we can get it to them. Why doesn't the county medical society make a survey of its nursing homes and announce publicly that it will find a way to take care of these people? If you're going to play the leadership game, you've got to lead.

The New York Times, 4-23:(4)7.

Sanford A. Marcus
President, Union of American Physicians

(On the rapidly expanding unionism of doctors): We're not just a bunch of rich doctors merely trying to get richer. We're trying to prevent the regimentation and nationalization stemming from socio-economic changes in medicine from reducing the doctor to the functionary level of the postman and schoolteacher.

Interview/ The New York Times, 6-18:(1)1.

Robert Q. Marston
Director, National Institutes of Health of the United States

Since the end of World War II, we doctors have had a complete change in our concept of what can be done to save lives and to make them better. If the pace of medical research keeps up, our prospects for successful prevention of diseases—or intervention in the course of disease—will keep pace.

U.S. News & World Report, 1-17:54.

George S. McGovern
United States Senator, D–S.D.

Where marijuana is concerned, my personal view is that we simply don't have enough medical evidence to conclude that it is harmless. If that evidence does come, I would still support prohibition on its use by young people. (But it is a) mistake to commit marijuana offenders, most of whom are youthful experimenters, to the penitentiary.

The Washington Post, 5-6:(A)6.

George S. McGovern
United States Senator, D–S.D.;
Democratic Presidential nominee

(Abortion) is a deeply personal question with many people, a deeply religious and moral question. As a candidate for President, my position has been that the Federal government should not intervene in any way on the question of abortion. From the beginning, this is one of those issues that has always been within the province of the states. The laws vary from state to state on this very difficult question. As far as I'm concerned, both as a candidate and if I become President, I intend no action in this field. I'm going to leave that where it is now.

Campaigning for the forthcoming Presidential election, Providence, R.I., Aug. 11/The Washington Post, 8-12:(A)4.

Wilbur D. Mills
United States Representative, D–Ark.

We (the U.S.) imported last year about the same number of medical graduates that we produced here at home . . . Yet U.S. medical schools turned down 13,000 qualified American applicants . . . because of lack of space. Somehow we have gotten our priorities badly out of balance.

Before American Society of Internal Medicine, Atlantic City, N.J./ The Dallas Times Herald, 4-16:(A)12.

Gaylord Nelson
United States Senator, D–Wis.

We are being chemically medicated against our will and cheated of food value by low-nutrition foods. Food additives are big business. The chemical and drug industries have joined the food industry in a food-industrial complex that the FDA is supposed to regulate. The result is a proliferation of food chemicals that are unnecessary, many of them untested, some of them dangerous and most of them poorly monitored, at best.

Washington/ San Francisco Examiner, 2-15:41.

Richard M. Nixon
President of the United States

I consider abortion an unacceptable form of population control. In my judgment, unrestricted abortion policies would demean human life . . . I do not support the unrestricted distribution of family-planning services and devices to minors . . . I have a basic faith that the American people themselves will make sound judgments regarding family size and frequency of births, judgments that are conducive both to the public interest and to personal family goals.

Los Angeles Times, 5-28:(D)3.

Any government whose leaders participate in or protect the activities of those who contribute to our drug problem should know that the President of the United States is required by statute to suspend all American economic and military assistance to such a regime. I shall not hesitate to comply with that law. I consider keeping dangerous drugs out of the United States just as important as keeping armed enemy forces from landing in the United States. (Those who operate the global heroin trade are) the slave traders of our time . . . they are traffickers in living death. They must be hunted to the end of the earth. They must be left no base in any nation for their operations. They must be permitted not a single hiding place or refuge from justice anywhere in the world. We are living in an age when there are times a great nation must engage in a limited war. I have rejected that principle in declaring total war against dangerous drugs. Our goal is the unconditional surrender of the merchants of death who traffic in heroin. Our goal is that of total banishment of drug abuse from American life.

At International Narcotics Control Conference, Washington, Sept. 18/ The Washington Post, 9-19:(A)1.

Perhaps the fight against cancer can help to teach the world that, despite immense differences between cultures and values and political systems, nations must work together to meet their common needs. Like drug abuse, like (airliner) hijacking, like terrorism, cancer is an international menace. We must confront it with an international alliance.

At National Cancer Conference, Los Angeles/ Los Angeles Herald-Examiner, 9-28:(A)1.

J. C. Nunnally
Professor of Psychology, Vanderbilt University

You tell somebody you have a history of mental illness or that you're mentally ill and you're in trouble. They will watch and discern characteristics of illness where there actually are none. They will note the occasional drinking bout, the silly expressions, the little eccentricities we all have, and they will conclude these are signs of sickness, when, of course, they aren't. The public is in the dark. It regards emotional illness as a mysterious, embarrassing thing.

The National Observer, 8-5:4.

Elliott Osserman
Professor of Medicine, College of Physicians and Surgeons, Columbia University

. . . the public is equating NASA's success in reaching the moon with the government's present plan to conquer cancer by 1976. The public says, "We went to the moon with money," and apparently it expects similar spectacular results in quick cancer cures because the government has pledged $1.6 billion to fight the disease . . . However, just as NASA was back in 1959, medical research is on a plateau of research trying to work up a mathematical base to use as the launching ramp for the first real shot against cancer. Enormous progress has been made in the last five years. We are learning how the body operates to combat cancer. We have learned there are common patterns between widely-separated cancers such as leukemia, breast and bowel cancer. A cancer virus theory has been advanced but not proven. We are in what I call the "search" stage—the step ahead of laboratory and clinical research—all of which must be successful before development of a cure . . . Advances in cancer knowledge are being made daily; but as far as the public is concerned, it is in much the same situation it was 10 years ago while waiting for its first manned landing on the moon. It now must wait for the proper combinations of knowledge on the nature of cancer before a cure is produced.

Interview, Baylor University Medical Center/ The Dallas Times Herald, 3-16:(A)22.

Nicholar Petrakis
Associate director, Hooper Foundation, University of California Medical Center

(Arguing against legalized euthanasia): I just wouldn't want to be the executioner. I wouldn't want a (hospital) "euthanasia committee" to tell me what to do. And there's a discrepancy in this whole euthanasia issue. Most dying patients simply do not want to die. They don't want to give up. If euthanasia becomes the norm, what's to prevent families from advocating euthanasia in the case of a rich relative when they might benefit?

San Francisco Examiner & Chronicle, 3-5:(Sunday Scene)2.

Frank J. Rauscher, Jr.
Director,
National Cancer Institute

In 1973, we expect 645,000 new cases of cancer, and nearly 350,000 deaths from cancer. If present trends are allowed to continue, by the year 2000 A.D. we'll have 1.2 million new cases of cancer in the U.S. alone, with about 500,000 deaths. Our job is to make sure these trends don't continue. I think we can succeed, because of the treatment breakthroughs and also because of what I foresee as even more effective means of preventing cancer, especially in getting information to the patient as soon as possible. I hope that in the next five to 10 years, 90 per cent of our program will center on that problem. We would like to be put out of business by success, just as we have been by research on polio and other diseases.

Interview, Washington/
U.S. News & World Report, 12-4:42.

Ronald Reagan
Governor of California

I am opposed (to the legalization of marijuana). And I am opposed because the score is not in yet (on the medical effects of its use). The thing I think most people don't realize about legalization of marijuana is that 14 companies have already registered trade names for marijuana cigarettes. Once you make them legal, you're going to see billboards, and packs in the vending machines. Since marijuana is smoked for effect—not for the taste, as cigarettes—how are they going to advertise? What are they going to say—"Fly higher with ours"?

Before members of Boys State,
Sacramento, June 22/
San Francisco Examiner, 6-23:19.

The socialization of medicine has not only failed to solve health-care problems where it has been tried, but it has been the first step in socializing the political and economic system of the country. You cannot socialize the doctor without eventually socializing the patients.

Before American College of Surgeons,
San Francisco, Oct. 5/
Los Angeles, 10-6:(2)4.

Nelson A. Rockefeller
Governor of New York

(On why he is vetoing a bill which would have repealed the state's permissive abortion law): I do not believe it right for one group to impose its vision of morality on an entire society. Neither is it just or practical for the state to attempt to dictate the innermost personal beliefs and conduct of its citizens.

Plainview (Tex.) Daily Herald, 7-16:(A)6.

David Rosenthal
Psychologist,
National Institute of Mental Health
of the United States

Almost no family in the nation is entirely free of mental disorders . . . Indeed, it may very well be that the so-called "normal" person, with respect to mental health, does not represent a norm at all, but rather an ideal—relatively rare—that most of us would like to achieve.

Before National Academy of Sciences,
Washington, April 24/
The Dallas Times Herald, 4-24:(A)13.

Raymond P. Shafer
Chairman, National Commission on
Marijuana and Drug Abuse
of the United States

We unanimously agree that marijuana use is not a desirable behavior, and we agree that society should discourage its use. Nevertheless, we feel that, placed in proper perspective with other social problems, citizens should not be criminalized or jailed merely for private possession or use.

Washington, March 22/
The Washington Post, 3-23:(A)7.

We generally discuss drug abuse in terms of elimination. It may be that the misuse of drugs

(RAYMOND P. SHAFER)

is not subject to total elimination. Therefore, it might be useful to regard drug abuse as we do unemployment, making a judgment that social policy should aim to keep drug abuse to an irreducible minimum.

Scottsdale, Ariz./
The Christian Science Monitor, 4-15:12.

Thomas Shaffer
Dean, University of Notre Dame
Law School

(Advocating the release from mental institutions of any patients who wish to leave): If a kookie citizen wants to be kookie, he has a right to be kookie. He has a right not to be electrified, or mutilated, or coerced, or badgered and manipulated into being like everybody else. And no doctor or policeman, spouse, parent, child, neighbor or busybody has any right to do him out of his kookiness . . . Even if they were dangerous, one might wonder why bizarre people should be locked up when the more devious and more dangerous among us are not locked up. Commitment to a mental institution is a life sentence to a place that is probably worse than prison. The sentence is passed with nothing even remotely resembling due process of law.

At American Health Congress,
Chicago, Aug. 10/
Los Angeles Times, 8-11:(1)5.

Michael R. Sonnenreich
Executive Director, National Commission
on Marijuana and Drug Abuse
of the United States

Most people don't know anything about marijuana. Some 49 per cent of the population believes that marijuana is physically addictive. It is not. And 41 per cent believe it causes death. It does not. There is no proof that there is any relationship between smoking marijuana and crime . . . About 2 per cent of the marijuana-smoking population is psychologically dependent upon it. But it does not constitute a health problem. It just isn't the menace it is characterized to be.

At American Bar Association discussion on
drug offenses and decriminalization,
San Francisco, Aug. 14/
San Francisco Examiner, 8-15:8.

Jesse L. Steinfeld
Surgeon General of the
United States

People do a number of things which they know are not in their best interests. Smoking is one of these. Drinking alcohol to excess is another. People don't eat the right foods. Our major successes are when the American citizen is largely passive. When we purify his water supplies, when we make certain that sewage is taken care of, make certain milk is pasteurized, when we develop a vaccine and provide it to our citizens, then we're quite successful. When the citizen must take an active role, we're far less successful. But even with the continued smoking, there are about 29 or 30 million Americans who have given up the habit.

Interview, Washington/
Los Angeles Times, 3-23:(8)2.

The use of marijuana is still quite sporadic and relatively minimal in terms of what it might be if it were legalized. We would probably not know for quite a few years what the effects on some segments of our population would be. I agree with the statements that the criminal penalty should be eliminated for mere use of marijuana and one should restrict penalties to those who are perhaps pushing it into the hands and mouths of our youth. But particularly, we do need much more research. While there's a good bit of evidence showing that it does not appear to be particularly harmful, there are some caveats certainly and there may be areas in which it will have effects . . . I think what we're doing is recognizing some of the actual facts about modern American society as well as recognizing what potential problems might occur if we take precipitate action in legalizing this substance which may have widespread harmful effects and about which we still do not know enough to take this latter action.

Interview, Washington/
Los Angeles Times, 3-23:(8)2,3.

Tom Szasz
Psychiatrist

Psychiatry has struggled to take morals out of the treatment of those they call mentally ill. They say there are no guilty or innocent people, even in courts of law—only sick or well people. Modern psychiatry dehumanizes man by denying the possibility of personal responsibility.

San Francisco Examiner & Chronicle, 10-1:(Sunday Scene)6.

Gerald J. Thain
Assistant Director for National Advertising, Bureau of Consumer Protection, Federal Trade Commission of the United States

Much of today's over-the-counter drug advertising . . . is restricting knowledge, sowing confusion and preventing, rather than helping, the free competition necessary to serve the consumer . . . Not only are over-the-counter drugs huckstered more intensively than soaps and detergents, but the overconsumption of drugs also poses direct dangers to the consumer's health as well as to his pocketbook . . . The hundreds of thousands of hospital admissions every year, resulting from adverse reactions to over-the-counter drugs, belie any casual belief in the absolute safety of (these) drugs.

April 27/
San Francisco Examiner & Chronicle, 5-21:(A)8.

Walter R. Tkach
Personal physician to the President of the United States

(Acupuncture is) something we had better learn about and make use of clinically as a possible whole new kind of anesthetic that would be free of the dangers of what we call "systemic traumas" from the anesthetics we presently use.

Interview, Washington, April 11/
Los Angeles Times, 4-12:(1)1.

Arthur K. Watson
United States Ambassador to France

(On the international effort to crack down on drugs and narcotics trade): The biggest cops-and-robbers game in history is going on around Marseilles . . . A year ago I would have had to speak of hopes. Now it is of figures. All of Europe has declared war on drugs.

Before Council of French-American Societies, New York, April 5/
The New York Times, 4-6:10.

Louis J. West
Chairman, Department of Psychiatry, University of California, Los Angeles

It is my belief that a percentage of regular (marijuana) users—I don't know what percentage and I don't know how to identify them in advance—will be adversely affected in terms of mental health by continued use of the drug.

Interview/
The Dallas Times Herald, 1-16:(F)5.

Paul Dudley White
Physician

We've got to start with the child at birth to change his way of life so he'll no longer be dependent on the automobile, on rich food or smoking.

San Francisco Examiner, 6-23:36.

The Performing Arts

MOTION PICTURES

Jack Albertson
Actor

There's always been an advantage to playing character roles. You can work into your dotage . . . The leading men come and go, but the character actors are around forever.

Interview, Los Angeles/ Los Angeles Herald-Examiner, 8-18:(B)6.

Samuel Z. Arkoff
Chairman, American International Pictures

There's no point in making "cerebral" pictures. The word is "motion pictures," and that says it right there. Motion is what it is all about. You've got to make pictures that move, and they have to move people. If you are going to make them for the thought process, they may be good, but you'll never be able to keep asses in a theatre seat. Having ideas must be secondary to having motion. It's a *motion* picture.

At University of Southern California/ The Hollywood Reporter, 3-8:15.

You fly by the seat of your pants in this business. So far we've (at AIP) been lucky. We've guessed what the audience wanted. Too many movie-makers make their pictures for their peers—for the Beverly Hills circuit instead of for an audience. We don't allow that kind of narcissism in our films. We use name stars even less than most studios. We always have. Now it's that way nearly everywhere. With a few exceptions, stars don't make films. It's the other way around: Films make stars. Look at Peter Fonda, Dennis Hopper and Jack Nicholson. We sensed their talent first, we used them first, and our films did a lot for them.

Interview, Los Angeles/ Los Angeles Times, 3-19:(Calendar)18.

Richard Attenborough
Actor, Director

(On how directors should deal with actors): The last important thing is to tell them how to say the lines. The most important thing is to cast them well and then let them try it their way; don't restrict them. Actors are bloody scared. So you accept their fear and grant them confidence. The actor relaxes and he dares. Without daring you get a restricted performance.

Interview, Los Angeles/ Los Angeles Times, 12-12:(4)1.

Brigitte Bardot
Actress

It is very hard to be happy in life for anybody. I suppose people with everyday worries—about money, children, bills, promotion—must think it is easy and lovely being a film star. But it isn't easy; it isn't lovely at all. Everybody can see you; everybody knows what you are doing—when you change lovers, when you have fights, if you have a spot on your nose. Stardom is a house without shades. And if you have no private life, it is impossible to be really happy. There is a French proverb: To live happy, live hidden. Where can Brigitte Bardot hide?

Interview/ Los Angeles Times, 4-9:(Calendar)1.

Alan Bates
Actor

You can't base your life on the star system. You can't even base one job on it. It's as transitory as that. I mean, whoever might appear today to be the biggest star in the world can make a film tomorrow which nobody will go and see. It doesn't mean anything, stardom. You can't finally bank on it.

Interview, New York/ The New York Times, 10-29:(2)3.

Elmer Bernstein
Composer; Board member, American Academy of Motion Picture Arts and Sciences

The Academy Award is not the Nobel Prize. Charisma plays a part in the vote. It's a mixture of knowledge and sentimentality and love and glamour. The "Oscar" is the most coveted film award, but it is not the definitive opinion of what's best in pictures. It is the definitive opinion of what 3,000 members thought was best.

Interview, Los Angeles/ The New York Times, 5-3:36.

Peter Bogdanovich
Director

I have a perverse antagonism to the "new" movie. My instinct is to reject all those modern techniques . . . The big problem for a director today is to get back to that spirit of innocence, directness and simplicity.

Interview/ The New York Times, 1-23:(2)11.

Marlon Brando
Actor

Most movies are rehearsals. They're improvisations. You're supposed to appear on the set with all your trappings and your doodads in character, and you haven't the slightest idea of who you are and what you're supposed to do, and usually, about the last third of the picture, you kind of get the idea of what you're doing. If you were to do the same thing in the theatre, it would be ridiculous. But that doesn't happen in films—you just walk in and do the first scene, and the only rehearsal you've had is in your mind when you're sitting in the bathtub or driving down to the post office or something. It's always a guessing game. Sometimes you think you're doing badly and it turns out to be good . . . and sometimes it really does turn out to be pretty awful. It's mostly hunt and poke. You really don't know half the time what you want to do. You make it up as you go along.

Newsweek, 3-13:57.

We all carry in us the seeds of any character that we might play. We all entertain the full spectrum of human emotions. Acting in general is something most people think they're incapable of, but they do it from morning to night. Acting is the guy who returns from some out-of-town wingding with some bimbo and tells his wife, "Oh, I had a terrible time." He's acting. In fact, the subtlest acting I've ever seen in my life is by ordinary people trying to show that they feel something that they don't, or trying to hide something. It's something everybody learns at an early age. I think anybody can act. I never really understand why anybody would want to use actors. I guess they're used because they've become household pets.

Newsweek, 3-13:58.

Charles Bronson
Actor

I prefer working in Europe, where the subject matter for films is more varied (than in the U.S.). Producers over there are interested in the international market, and so am I. The American film industry is nationalistic. The critics are nationalistic, too. Producers make films only for Americans. But the American public gets so much entertainment on television that they're calloused. If a movie comes along that is kookie or twisted, they'll rush to it. Otherwise, they stay home.

Interview, Los Angeles/ The Dallas Times Herald, 7-14:(C)10.

Richard Brooks
Director

I think any kind of picture can get people back into the cinema if it's made well.

(RICHARD BROOKS)

But I don't subscribe to the old studio thinking that you can make a picture to please everyone. You have too many selective groups in the world for that . . . Most people go to the cinema in order *not* to be taught anything. They want to forget their problems, their taxes, their bills, the fact they can't get a girl; just for two hours they're willing to pay $3 to get out of the world for a while. "Give me the hero I'd like to dream about, even if I know I can't get him"—that's what they want. And I want to give it to them.

Interview, Los Angeles/ San Francisco Examiner & Chronicle, 1-9:(Datebook)7.

Horst Buchholz
Actor

The film industries are coming back in Italy, in France, in England. Not in Germany. It's unfortunate that the Germans aren't able to produce films of quality. A few years ago, a producer made millions on a picture called *Helga*, and ever since then the Germans have concentrated in pornography. It is sad.

Los Angeles Herald-Examiner, 5-28:(E)4.

Carol Burnett
Actress, Comedienne

. . . I understand why movie people get ulcers. In television, if you blow one, there's always next week. Doing a movie is like being pregnant: You've got that terrible long wait to see if it's ugly. And if it's ugly, it'll rise to haunt you late at night on television. I know; I've got one that haunts me.

Interview, Los Angeles/ Los Angeles Times, 12-28:(4)19.

Michael Caine
Actor

I go by the "masterpiece method" of rating (films). When they say it's a great film, I know I'll be asleep for 10 minutes. When they say it's a masterpiece, I know I'll be asleep for 20 minutes. And when they say it's the greatest picture since the war . . . I know I'll still be asleep when the credits come on.

Interview, Beverly Hills, Calif./ Los Angeles Times, 4-2:(Calendar)9.

I don't think of acting as fun. It takes so much effort to do well that when I have done it well I have no energy left to enjoy it.

Interview, London/ San Francisco Examiner, 8-19:9.

Vincent Canby
Film critic, "The New York Times"

One of the problems . . . is that movies are a business; and the best way to make it in business is to have some sort of reputation, which you only get having done something. And Hollywood is very reluctant to take a chance. The American film industry—and it is an industry and not an art primarily—is in a very sick state. Films are losing more money today than I think they ever have before. And the way that the industry and the major film companies are handling this is to spend less, meaning they'll lose less. But it sort of cuts down the chances, too, of exciting things happening.

Panel discussion, New York/ The New York Times, 12-26:44.

Frank Capra
Former director

Film is a wonderful art form that hasn't even been scratched yet. It is the one art form that has been created in our lifetime—by D. W. Griffith when he made *The Birth of a Nation*. But the great films are yet to be made.

At U.S.A. Film Festival, Dallas, March 19/ The Dallas Times Herald, 3-20:(B)7.

Charles Chaplin
Former actor-director

I'm delighted at the resurgence of interest in my old films. Those were some damn good pictures I did, the best I've seen! I surprised myself. I wouldn't change a thing in them. I never was interested in pornography and obscenity or anything like that. I think it's boring—especially at my age! But I have to tell you, I never thought anything about that little fellow I created. I went into this business for money. Art sort of grew out of it.

News conference, London/ San Francisco Examiner & Chronicle, 2-6:(Datebook)14.

Claudette Colbert
Former actress

It shocks me, yes, really shocks me, to see stark naked bodies on the screen. I can't see the point of it; it's not sexy, there's no suspense—just naked bodies thrashing around. I think if someone had asked me to take my clothes off back in the '30s, I'd still be running. But then, they didn't do such things in my day. This is the permissive society. Perhaps if I'd been born in this age, I'd think differently. It's difficult to say. After all, in the '30s I never wore a bikini, but I do now.

At Teheran International Film Festival, Iran/ The Hollywood Reporter, 5-3:5.

Jackie Cooper
Actor

. . . I wouldn't want any of my kids to be a child star. Why not? I'll tell you. It's a bad background for any kid. It's a terrible start to life. Most of us have a frightful record. We end up in mental institutions, or as alcoholics, or dead before our time. I did all right. They liked me and gave me more work. I got a bicycle and a pat on the head everywhere I went. I got my first car when I was 14. But this is the trap, you see. It's all the adulation, all the bicycles and the rewards for good behavior that make you go wrong. It's not really work you're doing. You don't feel responsible for anything. If you take a child prodigy, work him through the formative years and reward him constantly, what happens? As he grows up he takes it all for granted, as automatic. And then one day, all of a sudden there's no one around to tell you what to do or pat you on the head. And you feel guilty. You think: I'm not a good boy. You don't get anyone's arm around you—and by then you need an arm around you. You've been spoiled all your pampered life, and you need to feel wanted and loved. So in seeking people's esteem, you blow your chances of finding real affection. Then you pull back. You say: "Why should I be nice?" The frustration leads to a wish for escape. You get into booze or drugs. And then you're on the downhill run. I've seen it happen to friends of mine who were child actors with me. It's tragic. But for many of us, it's inevitable. I guess I've been lucky to keep my feet on the ground.

Interview, Los Angeles/ San Francisco Examiner & Chronicle, 4-2:(Datebook)4.

George Cukor
Director

Do people still think of a director as some wild-eyed man with a megaphone stuck in his mouth? There are an awful lot of misconceptions about what a director does and what the hell he is. A film is always a matter of collaboration; and if the actor is an intelligent person, no one is top dog. No one has to butter the other one up. The studios have never been able to afford temperament. They still can't. And that's the way it should be.

Interview, Madrid/ Los Angeles Times, 7-23:(Calendar)26.

Roald Dahl
Author, Screenwriter

What flabbergasts me is that directing a film is the only trade where a man can make the most infernal hash of something, lose a company its profits, and still get another job right away. No wonder the film industry's gone to pot. The director's job isn't the survival of the fittest today. It's the survival of the idiots!

Interview, Great Missenden, England/ San Francisco Examiner & Chronicle, 5-28:(Datebook)4.

Len Deighton
Author, Screenwriter

As a screenwriter, I discovered one of the best ways to gain a little control is to make an agreement with the actors that each of them could cross out any words of his he felt was unnecessary but could not challenge anyone else's. Needless to say, not one word (is) cut out.

Interview/ Los Angeles Times, 1-9:(Calendar)10.

Vittorio De Sica
Director

When I make a picture, I love all the characters, their vices and their defects. My work is human work. There is always an excuse, even for the criminal. Humanity is a very deep mystery.

Interview/Newsweek, 1-10:58.

Kirk Douglas
Actor

. . . there's more to acting than mink coats, Cadillacs and showing all your sparkling teeth. They (audiences) see the picture put together, and they don't realize what goes on behind the scenes. And that's right, isn't it? They must never see the effort. They're not supposed to. Everyone should look at you and think, "Jesus! *I* could do what that son-of-a-bitch is doing . . ."

Interview, Hamburg/ San Francisco Examiner & Chronicle, 5-7:(Datebook)11.

Blake Edwards
Director

(Criticizing conglomerates that have taken over motion picture companies): These are people in oil, for example. You can bet they don't hire oil experts to dig—and then tell them where and how. Yet they'll get into a business they know nothing about and do precisely that. It's sick. It's irresponsible. It's what puts studios in jeopardy.

The New York Times, 4-19:36.

Robert Evans
Executive vice president in charge of production, Paramount Pictures Corporation

The only message we want (in films) is entertainment. The only education we want to give is to get people to the boxoffice to buy tickets. A movie is still a magnet even though the habit of going to the movies is gone. Our films contain a linear story line, and people won't have to go to psychiatrists to get an explanation.

News conference, Los Angeles/ Los Angeles Times, 2-22:(4)7.

Freddie Fields
President, Creative Management Associates (artists' representatives)

The star system is an absolute. That's the whole psychological basis of the (film) business. If one is on the way out, there's another on the way up. Saying the star system is dead is like saying that brand names don't mean anything any more. Let's face it: A great Steve McQueen movie will gross more than a great movie without Steve McQueen. And a bad movie with McQueen will still gross more money than a bad movie without McQueen.

Interview, New York/ "W": a Fairchild publication, 12-15:7.

Peter Finch
Actor

(On his current "Oscar" nomination): I don't have a dirty feeling about awards. (But) the work comes first. If somebody gives you a prize, it's very thrilling. Then you put the prize on the bookshelf and get back to work.

Interview, London/ Los Angeles Times, 3-19:(Calendar)1.

Actors are a group apart, I could almost say a nationality apart. Among ourselves we speak a secret tongue. We have enormous rapport that transcends nationality and political differences.

Interview, Los Angeles/ Los Angeles Herald-Examiner, 4-2:(F)3.

(On the unpredictability of the public's taste in films): The public, bless their hearts, have confounded the studios once again. When *Easy Rider* came along, the eternal Philistines who run this business felt that's what the public wanted. And it was pretty rough for a while as all those sad imitations failed to make it. Then Ross (Hunter) came along with *Airport*. Art has many handwritings.

Interview, Burbank, Calif./ The Dallas Times Herald, 7-30:(K)1.

Bryan Forbes
Director

Everybody today is anxious to diversify and the (film) industry has changed hands. We have a new bunch of executives, and their first love is not necessarily pictures. I think one of the tragedies of our industry . . . is (that) its history in the last two decades has been a combination of greed and incompetence in many areas. There's no dearth of talent, but I think there is an almost suicidal neglect of the people who pay money—the audience . . . What holds the industry steady is hiking the movie prices. But it's getting to cost too much to go to the cinema. We're a luxury industry, and if we neglect the patron, the results are going to be all too serious . . . In recent years, with the exception of Disney, most everybody has neglected a segment of the audience. We've lost the middle-aged man with three kids and a house that is mortgaged. If he does have the money to take them to the cinema, what's he going to take them to? Reissues? Why do we neglect that audience totally?

Interview, Los Angeles/ The Hollywood Reporter, 8-3:5.

Mike Frankovich
Producer

Making movies is like anything else. You have to have training and experience, the right background. Many kids, for example, want to be newspaper editors overnight. I had an interesting experience recently when I spoke at Cornell University. One young fellow said he didn't think young people were getting the opportunities they should in the film business . . . I asked him how old he was. He said 22. And I asked him if he would like for a 22-year-old doctor to operate on his sister if she had an attack of appendicitis. That brought a big laugh. I was trying to make the point that there is no substitute or short cuts to training and experience. You need that along with creative talent to make movies.

Interview, Los Angeles/ The Dallas Times Herald, 1-2:(E)1.

William Friedkin
Director

I don't have a philosophy (to express in films) that is of any interest, even to me. I'm just trying to do stuff that I think works. I take each scene and think of it in terms of a member of the audience. I try to recreate those times when I was a kid, and enraptured by films. I don't have that any more when I go to the movies. I can't think of two or three pictures in the last five years that have let me get totally caught up in the experience.

Interview, New York/ The New York Times, 8-27:(2)9.

Christopher George
Actor

I got to a point where I just didn't want to act any more. I felt ashamed to be an actor after listening to all those cliches about acting being boring, repetitious and lacking in true meaning. Even some of the biggies—you (know) who they are; I don't want to name names—come on with heavy dialogue against their own profession . . . I love acting; I was afraid to say that for awhile. People in this industry that are negative say

(CHRISTOPHER GEORGE)

it's just pretending for a living. But what's wrong with pretending?

Interview, Los Angeles/ The Hollywood Reporter, 2-16:10.

Elliott Gould
Actor

I can't believe that (producer) Ross Hunter can spend $11 million, or whatever it is costing him, to make *Lost Horizon*! You could make six real films for that. Real films are films that are alive—not with costumes and sets.

Interview, Malibu, Calif./ The Dallas Times Herald, 8-6:(F)1.

Princess Grace (Grace Kelly)
Princess of Monaco; Former actress

. . . I don't like the lack of taste or lack of humor in some of the films made now that are otherwise interesting. Have you noticed that some of the pictures that are called comedies have absolutely no humor at all?

Interview, Monaco/ The Christian Science Monitor, 1-18:(B)13.

Alec Guinness
Actor

I think one of the tragedies of advancing age for an actor is that his power of observation decreases. Young people observe more sharply, more instinctively. I certainly did. In my formative years, I used to observe, not very generously, but very sharply. I would observe snidely, cruelly, but with enormous precision. Now I have to make a very big effort to deliberately observe so that things stay in my memory. My whole feeling about acting is that you must observe, absorb and forget. Because when you come to an actual performance, you don't want to know the sources of what you think is your imagination. Well, I've spent maybe 20 years of my life living off the dividends of an initial investment—the investment being very sharp and close observation. Of course, I'm not putting this out as the gospel truth. I just put it out as something *I* believe in.

Interview, London/ The New York Times, 9-10:(2)34.

Gene Hackman
Actor; 1971 Academy Award winner for best actor

I would think there may be some revamping of the Academy (Awards) in the next few years. So many actors that I've talked to have had the feeling that it's a disservice in general to pit actors against each other—because we are all different. It is unfair, in some way, to put (an actor) in a musical against people who are in a straight drama. I really don't even know if it's honorable to pit actors against each other in any way . . . Maybe the nominations would be enough without the big award at the end.

Interview, Long Beach, Calif./ The Hollywood Reporter, 4-17:1.

Richard Harris
Actor

I've heard movie-makers say that people are getting tired of violence, sadism, perversion; that they want something more gentle, like *Love Story*. *Love Story* was a flash in the pan. They saw it, they cried, and they ran right back to *The French Connection* and *A Clockwork Orange*, right back to the violence. Movie-makers are kidding themselves if they think we are drifting back into a romantic era in films. People just want to taste romance, and then spit it out.

Interview, Los Angeles/ Los Angeles Times, 4-8:(2)5.

Alfred Hitchcock
Director

Style seems to have gone out of style. Content is everything now. All one reads about a film is the content. It's as if an art critic, on viewing a Picasso still-life of, say, a platter of apples, devoted his entire discussion to whether the apples were sweet or sour or pulpy or juicy . . .

Interview, Los Angeles/ Los Angeles Times, 2-27:(TV Times)2.

The art of film is the art of cutting, arranging a montage of images to produce an emotional effect. When you break this effect, you destroy any reason for the film. It's like a nightmare. When a nightmare is so vivid it seems real, you have a profound emotional experience. I try to make film so vivid it is real to you and a profound emotional experience.

Interview, Los Angeles/ San Francisco Examiner & Chronicle, 3-5:(Datebook)11.

When an actor comes to me and wants to discuss his character, I say, "It's in the script." If he says, "But what is my motivation?" I say, "Your salary."

Interview, New York/ The New York Times, 6-18:(2)13.

There is a difference between mystery and suspense. Mystery is withholding information from the audience. But suspense is giving them information, otherwise they'd never get anxious without your telling them. If you show a bomb blasting a room, you get 10 seconds of shock; but if you tell the audience there's going to be a bomb blast, you get 10 minutes of suspense. Suspense comes from knowledge.

Interview, New York/ The Christian Science Monitor, 7-13:5.

Dennis Hopper
Actor, Director

Movies as mass entertainment in theatres will be nonexistent by the year 2000, if not sooner. People just don't care about the romanticism and fantasy of the Hollywood film any more. They'd rather see sports events or news programs—on-the-spot occurrences on television.

Quote, 6-11:553.

Ross Hunter
Producer

I am not only a movie producer, I am a movie fan. To this day, I still get a thrill out of meeting a movie star for the first time. The movie has always been an influence on our lives. For example, my father always made a pot of coffee, then poured a cup through the grounds because Norma Shearer did it in the movies. I guess I sound like a real old-fashioned square, but I still think the movies should be made for the family. I made 45 films for the family; 43 of them made good profits. In my pictures, Adam and Eve don't inspire the costumes, but I'm 100 per cent for realism—real sables, real diamonds, real glamour. In my pictures, the kitchen sink features Venetian tile and no dirty dishes.

Before Art Museum Costume Council, Los Angeles/ Los Angeles Herald-Examiner, 1-20(A)14.

Leo Jaffe
President, Columbia Pictures Industries

According to government statistics, motion picture attendance has dropped from a weekly average of 40,000,000 in 1958 to a weekly average of 16,000,000 in 1971 . . . This drop is even more dramatic than it appears, since there has been a population explosion during these years. We (in motion pictures) are not getting our share of the entertainment dollar, which has increased during this period but is being expended on other forms of leisure-time entertainment. A sorry but true statistic . . . We cannot be particularly proud of many of the pictures shown on motion picture screens around the country. In recent years, many mistakes were made and our integrity and responsibility to society questioned. The few great pictures of taste and quality, unfortunately, were not in sufficient number to overcome the damage created. The critics of our business are not completely wrong . . . On the other hand, our industry has many virtues; and little or nothing is being done by us jointly to let the public know we are, for the greater part, a responsible group of people. We must demonstrate that we are capable of restoring confidence in our audiences. This can be accomplished by a succession of pictures that have entertainment rather than carnal values. Great discipline must be exercised to achieve this goal. Quality product doesn't mean images surrounded by green fences in white houses. It means honesty of performance, good taste, an awareness of the requirements of our audiences. The theatregoer also expects us to deliver what our advertising promises, what our rating code indicates, and at prices they can afford.

Accepting Pioneer of the Year award of Motion Picture Pioneers Foundation, New York, Nov. 15/ Variety, 11-22:6.

Howard W. Koch
Producer

(On the decline in motion picture attendance): I don't think we were making pictures people wanted to see. I think we're beginning to get back on the track now. We seem to be moving back toward the old forms. *The French Connection* is *The Maltese Falcon* of these times; *The Godfather* is *Little Caesar* brought up to date. What should teach us something is that these movies are doing tremendous business at the box office, while the permissive and sex films are dying.

Interview, Los Angeles/ San Francisco Examiner & Chronicle, 4-9:(Datebook)17.

Stanley Kubrick
Director

In terms of working with actors, a director's job more closely resembles that of a novelist than of a Svengali. One assumes that one hires actors who are great virtuosos. It is too late to start running an acting class in front of the cameras; and essentially, what the director must do is to provide the right ideas for the scene, the right adverb, the right adjective. The director must always be the arbiter of esthetic taste. The questions always arise: Is it believable? Is it interesting? Is it appropriate? Only the director can decide this.

Interview, Borehamwood, England/ The New York Times, 1-4:26.

The things I enjoy most about making a film are the cinematic aspects of the film—the writing of the script and the editing of the film afterward. The actual shooting of the film is a freakish kind of environment for creating a work of art, and it would be like a novelist or a composer who decided to do his work in the middle of a furniture factory.

Interview, Borehamwood, England/ The New York Times, 1-4:26.

A film is made to be seen by the public. In order for this to be done, the public must be made aware of its existence. When you decide to see a film, you do not turn on the radio or the television, hoping to find it advertised; you look in the newspaper. There is no adequate substitute for newspaper advertising in informing the public of a film's existence and its whereabouts. If a newspaper denies some films of which it does not approve the right to advertise (such as some newspapers have done with X-rated films), while allowing competing films to purchase as much advertising space as they like, then the newspaper is effectively suppressing the film it does not like. For all practical purposes, a film is banned when the public is prevented from knowing of its existence or whereabouts. To start to ban films—or books, or plays, or any medium of free expression—on the grounds of offensiveness is to take the first step on a course that history shows has ended in a suppression of many other liberties.

The Hollywood Reporter, 4-12:6.

Claude Lelouch
Director

My idea of (movie) Westerns is that they should never be taken seriously. They interest me because that is how I view them. Westerns are only for children. Since I like children and feel I am a child, I like them. Directors who have made only Western films are not important. I will have to make a Western myself to prove I am not important.

Interview, Dallas, Oct. 25/
The Dallas Times Herald, 10-26:(F)10.

Jack Lemmon
Actor

. . . fewer films (are) produced. Those that are made are made too important. It's very difficult to work knowing that dark cloud is overhead. The fun has gone out of it, especially comedy. Something has happened to the product; the bubble of joy, madness, whatever you want to call it, isn't there any more; and that kind of feeling can sap you.

Interview, New York/
The New York Times, 1-16:(2)15.

Joseph E. Levine
Producer

I'm beating the drums for the picture business. I believe in it. I'd advise any young man to be a maker of film. I think the future is great . . . I see a whole new business. The independents—guys you never heard of—will take over. The (major) companies will be the distributors. There's a lot of money for pictures from strange places. Some big corporations are diversifying. Then you have cassette pictures. A producer will have a world premiere of a picture on CATV. People will pay $2 to see it. He will get off the hook the first night.

Interview, New York/
San Francisco Examiner, 2-14:35.

Goffredo Lombardo
President, Titanus Films of Italy

I would say that Italian cinema is nonconformist in the intelligence and courage displayed in confronting social reality. With the exception of those attempting to imitate big box-office hits, our cinema is rarely cut to strictly commercial patterns. Almost every film is a prototype in itself, and most relate to the reality of Italian life.

Interview, Rome/
Daily Variety, 4-21:2.

Joseph L. Mankiewicz
Screenwriter, Director

In the censorship days, you were driven to ingenuity and indirection. These are the days of frontal nudity and frontal meanings. Lubitsch, who was my mentor, could show more honest-to-God sexuality by having a beautiful girl go up to a door and open it, or not open it, than any of the wide-screen genitalia. Copulation has become what we used to call action; it's replaced mixing the martini or lighting the cigarette . . . I don't think audiences listen (to) the screen now. They come to stare.

Interview, London/
Los Angeles Times, 8-20:(Calendar)20.

Lee Marvin
Actor

There's too damn much violence on screen. I don't go for it . . . I know man is a violent animal—if he were not, the roses would have taken over long ago—but some people are going too far on the screen. It's bad enough in real life, for God's sake.

Interview, Los Angeles/
San Francisco Examiner, 2-1:25.

Roddy McDowall
Actor

I'd love to direct again, but there's a very peculiar market for films today. There are far fewer films being made, so the opportunities are fewer. People rise and fall with much greater rapidity—directors as well as actors. If you have one great success, everyone thinks you have the answer. If you have a flop, you may never get another chance. But all directors—even the great ones—have made a certain number of dogs. In order to

(RODDY McDOWALL)

be good you also have to be bad. That was one of the great things about live TV—you got a chance to fail a lot. That kind of opportunity just doesn't exist any more.

Interview/Los Angeles Times, 12-10:(Calendar)43.

Walter Mirisch
President, Mirisch Production Company

A motion picture has to be the development of an artistic inspiration. Someone gives birth to a story, an idea or what have you. If it's the thing that captures public interest, they'll come, and they are coming. There are films today which are doing great. The economic problems in the industry spring into being from those which fail to capture the public's excitement and do so poorly. The difference between the lows and highs of public interest—how they do at the box office—is sharper than ever. There isn't the median norm that existed when film-going was habitual.

Interview/Los Angeles Herald-Examiner, 4-9:(California Living)12.

Robert Mitchum
Actor

This business has robbed me of my initiative. It's so easy to do. There are only two hard things about it—wiping off the makeup at the end of the day and putting on and pulling off your boots while you're making a Western. I think I'd like ditch-digging just as well. You just take a shovel and do as you please.

Interview, New York/ The Dallas Times Herald, 8-27:(H)6.

Yves Montand
Actor

I don't want to make any more movies in the (United) States, because American directors have had a French-actor stereotype on the brain for 20 years. They want a man to play the part of an idiotic French lover, and they want a Frenchwoman to be a "putain"—a slut. They want the French actor to play second fiddle to the American actress. If she happens to be Marilyn Monroe, that's fine. Anyway, you can do that kind of thing once, twice, maybe three times, but not more. I've had it.

Interview, New York/ "W": a Fairchild publication, 12-29:16.

David Niven
Actor

I don't know how young actors do it today. Take Clark Gable—"the king" at MGM. They surrounded Gable with a team of highly-intelligent writers, whose sole job was to find and polish the perfect vehicles for Gable's talent. For 15 years I was with Goldwyn. His publicists pushed his product—me. People might say Niven hits his wife and drinks the bath water—but they didn't say, "Who is he?" It was gorgeous in those days. Nobody cared too much. Now the competition to get a movie even started is quite awful. The old days are completely gone, and I don't think they'll ever come back.

Interview, New York/ Los Angeles Herald-Examiner, 2-19:(B)9.

There's no such thing as a movie audience any more. The audience has been brainwashed by television. I don't mean that unkindly or brutally. But they see 40 or 50 dramas a week on television, so for them there are no new plots. Even a good movie is something they can see on the box in nine months.

Interview, New York/ The Dallas Times Herald, 7-16:(K)3.

Peter O'Toole
Actor

There is too much violence in the world—Ireland, Vietnam—without having it on the screen all the time. There is also too much sex (in films). I have bawled and brawled my way around and I am no prude; but sex is something to be enjoyed, not sniggered over or gaped at.

San Francisco Examiner, 6-30:36.

Otto Preminger
Producer, Director

When I make a film, I get very involved. I don't take credit for the writing, but a director should direct the writing. That, to me, is the director's first job, directing the writer. Then, you direct the cast.

Interview, Dallas/
The Dallas Times Herald, 1-23:(G)1.

Vincent Price
Actor

This is the way films should be—fun all the way through. The wonderful thing about those old horror movies I did with Boris Karloff, Peter Lorre and Basil Rathbone was the way we'd all sit around and scream among ourselves as we planned how we'd give the audience their kicks.

Interview, London/
San Francisco Examiner & Chronicle, 1-30:(Datebook)9.

Martin Rackin
Producer

You have to watch these directors. When I produce a film, I'm never more than 10 feet from the camera. I don't direct it, but I want to be there to make a correction if I see something being done wrong. A lot of these directors are clowns; but they think they're creative. You can't let them do what they want. They'll just spend all your money and turn out some garbage movie. Who needs that? Life is too short to waste time pampering some of these idiots.

Interview, San Francisco/
San Francisco Examiner & Chronicle, 7-23:(Datebook)2.

Oliver Reed
Actor

Have you ever thought what we (actors) go through? At 7:30 in the morning I can be told to scream or cry or jump or make love, or call somebody "Darling" and kiss their naked flesh.

Interview, Salisbury, England/
San Francisco Examiner & Chronicle, 6-18:(Datebook)6.

Jean Renoir
Former director

The camera is a little bit like the knife of a surgeon. It opens the meat and reveals the heart. But if there is no heart, you find nothing and you know that the actor is no good.

San Francisco Examiner & Chronicle, 3-5:(Datebook)21.

The film industry wants perfection. Perfection is really extremely boring. But they sacrifice anything for perfection: They sacrifice the meaning of the story; they sacrifice even the performance of the actors for technical perfection. It would be better to start with directors who have something to say. But today most directors have nothing to say. It doesn't matter (today) if you say nothing as long as you say it perfectly.

Interview, Beverly Hills, Calif./
Los Angeles Times, 4-16:(West)32.

Roberto Rossellini
Director

I think that cinema in its narrative form has run its course. It is passe; at least it is for me. I find more fascination in talking about industry, about the atom, than a narration of some kind of a half-neurotic story. I think there is a great deal to say, but not in the way in which it is said. That kind of a movie is dead.

Interview, Rome/
Los Angeles Times, 2-6:(Calendar)38.

Albert Ruddy
Producer

All countries love American films. The U.S. government should give careful consideration to sustain the health of the motion picture business, because not only does it bring in hard currencies like yen and deutsche marks, but it also gives the world a chance to see the U.S. in a far more favorable light than shown by a lot of local news people in these various countries . . . We do two things in the motion picture business: We are economically and absolutely necessary

(ALBERT RUDDY)

to the overall trade program; we create a vivid and much more realistic image of the American to foreign audiences.

Los Angeles/ The Hollywood Reporter, 9-7:13.

Ken Russell
Director

They tell us the public wants family films back. I did *The Boy Friend* and nobody came to see it. What the public wants is sex and violence.

San Francisco Examiner & Chronicle, 10-8:(This World)2.

Rosalind Russell
Actress

The movie business has to get back into the hands of the filmmakers—not those parking-lot owners and meatpackers and conglomerates and whatever. To make good pictures, you have to really feel film, you have to taste it. You love film, you breathe it, and you claw it onto the screen.

Interview, Washington/ The Washington Post, 12-2:(B)7.

Fouad Said
President, Cinemobile Systems

(Criticizing Hollywood film studios): There's no other industry anywhere, and certainly not the filmmakers in Europe, that still uses 30-year-old factories, machinery and work methods. No wonder young filmmakers are deserting Hollywood studios when they find 1931 cameras used, along with equally-old lights; when plywood is laboriously laid down with hammer and nails for dolly tracks; and other old equipment and methods eat up hours every day on the sound stages. It's about time Hollywood moved into the space age along with the rest of American industry . . .

Panel discussion at University of Southern California Film Conference/The Hollywood Reporter, 4-12:7.

Franklin J. Schaffner
Director

Anything is better than censorship. Motion pictures are an art form; and when anyone censors art, it is the worst kind of trouble to be in.

Interview, Los Angeles/ The Hollywood Reporter, 2-4:23.

John Schlesinger
Director

I loathe the trend to violence for its own sake in films. This is more dangerous and censorable than anything sexual. Violence is dwelt on and exploited in a most disgusting way.

Interview, Los Angeles/ The Hollywood Reporter, 1-25:10.

George C. Scott
Actor

I'm not happy being an actor. I never have been happy being an actor. Hell, no . . . I mean, this is an unhappy business. This is not a happy business. I've met some magnificent people in this business; I've been all over the world because of this business. But that doesn't make it a happy way of life. It's not like living in the wilderness, on the great plains of Canada, or raising wheat in Kansas, where you can be your own boss, enjoy nature, have a family, et cetera . . . (But) it's the only thing I can do. I can't make a living any other way.

Interview/Life, 9-22:77.

Stirling Silliphant
Screenwriter, Producer

The motion picture and TV industries are in a current state of revolution and evolution. You might even say they are in a state of shambles. But rather than letting this repress you, it should and must encourage you, because there are no more big studio gates to be closed in your face. It has become as it was in the beginning: the golden time for the independent artist.

At symposium before arts-oriented students, Los Angeles/Los Angeles Times, 3-23:(4)14.

Rod Steiger
Actor

Business—that's all they ever talk about (in Hollywood). There are three times when I refuse to discuss business: while I'm eating, while I'm drinking and while I'm making love. But that doesn't stop them out here. You're just about to reach for the salt when someone says: "About this script"—and your whole goddamn dinner is ruined.

Interview, Malibu, Calif./ San Francisco Examiner, 2-9:29.

Andrew Stone
Director, Producer, Writer

You've got four different types of audience today: Raw pornography, for those who like raw pornography. Then the *Carnal Knowledge* group. Very few of these two will pay a nickel to see a film like *The Great Waltz*, or Disney. Then comes the avant-garde group of young people. And finally you've got the big audience, the general public, who like *Song of Norway* and Disney and that kind of entertainment. We also get a problem with critics. These days you just can't get one critic embracing the whole range of those four groups. The only ones qualified to criticize should be out of the audience group for whom we are making the picture . . .

Interview, Salzburg, Austria/ San Francisco Examiner & Chronicle, 6-25:(Datebook)10.

Barbra Streisand
Actress

(On news items about temperamental actors): How can they report things like that? It just proves that they don't know what this business is really all about. No one who is a bitch to the people she or he works with gets to the top. There's too much cooperative effort, too many people involved in that kind of success. And even if someone like that did make it, he wouldn't last very long, because no one would work with him. The unfortunate thing is that millions of people who don't know the industry read and listen to that nonsense and believe it.

Interview, Los Angeles/ Los Angeles Times, 3-5:(Calendar)10.

Gordon Stulberg
President,
20th Century-Fox Film Corporation

The spectacle is gone. No company can afford to spend many millions on a single picture any more. There will be no more spectacles—unless the film economy changes by adding new markets.

San Francisco Examiner, 2-10:32.

Elizabeth Taylor
Actress

I'm terribly worried about our industry because it seems so bloody disorganized. For my next picture, the money's being put up by a perfume maker. For my last, it came from a manufacturer of trailers.

Interview, Budapest/Life, 2-25:58.

Ernest Tidyman
Screenwriter

The mechanics of the (film) industry seem so structured as to be detrimental or negative to the story and more positive toward the business elements. When production companies focus on the business end as opposed to the story, you have *schlock*. . . When you concentrate on story, you invariably heighten your chances of success. I think the major companies as well as the independents have come to discover in many cases they bought a story they were attracted to, but when it came around to the point of delivery, they got something else.

Interview, Los Angeles, March 22/Daily Variety, 3-23:8.

Francois Truffaut
Director

My films are just to tell what I feel about love, not to push people one way or another . . . I'd never make a political film. When you make a political film, it means telling

(FRANCOIS TRUFFAUT)

people the direction they must take. I hate that. Political films don't provide a constructive alternative; they are simply critical. Love is one of the real sentiments of human beings. To love is to be constructive.

*London/
San Francisco Examiner, 5-24:44.*

Jack Valenti
*President,
Motion Picture Association of America*

Those raw, crude films of nudity and sexuality which sullied the screen are definitely on the way out . . . some have called this trend "square," contrasting it to the so-called "realism" of the recent past. If so, I concur with movie critic Pauline Kael who says, "Square can be beautiful, too."

Before National Association of Theatre Owners of Texas, Dallas, Feb. 1/Daily Variety, 2-2:16.

I have special tastes in movies, although I claim no special expertise. I remember the first time I met Darryl Zanuck, the fabled producer. I told him I thought one of his finest films was *Wilson*, back in 1945. Zanuck smiled, as they say, wryly. "It was a financial bomb," he said. Thus, my taste does not guarantee box office success. The kinds of films I like best are history, suspense in the Hitchcockian manner, classic and modern novels brought to the screen, and political films like *The Best Man* and *Seven Days in May*. My favorite movies? *Becket, Young Mr. Lincoln, A Man for All Seasons, Cromwell, The King and I* and those splendid movies produced by Sam Spiegel—*Lawrence of Arabia, The Bridge on the River Kwai* and *African Queen*. I am not cheered by unrelieved dreariness and depression, the kind of films that beat at me with bleak admonitions.

Family Weekly, 3-12:10.

King Vidor
Director

When I was a young kid in Texas at the beginning of the century, I used to hate movies. I hated their phoniness, their fakiness, the makeup which used to mask the actors' expressions, their dreadful unreal acting with overdone pantomime gestures. People find them laughable today. I found them laughable *then*. I felt drama would be more vital if you could believe events were really happening while you were looking at them. I wanted to focus on small, important things. I decided in my teens to make pictures which would make people feel they were reliving their day-to-day lives through the characters.

*Interview, Paso Robles, Calif./
The New York Times, 9-3:(2)7.*

Eli Wallach
Actor

An actor today has to be like a man walking across pieces of an ice field. He has to keep one step ahead of sinking. He's got to be able to go from theatre to film to TV, regardless of personal satisfaction. The equation seems to be: The worthwhile things you will do at a sacrifice; the junk you'll get well paid for.

*Interview, New York/
Los Angeles Times, 6-16:(4)27.*

Raoul Walsh
Director

(The film industry is) in a pretty serious state, particularly in Hollywood. It seems they have got away from entertainment and into shock. And there are no more Coopers, Gables, Flynns, Bogarts. Actors and actresses used to come dressed up for interviews; now they show up in a sweat shirt and a jockstrap!

*Interview/Los Angeles Times,
1-30:(Calendar)25.*

Andy Warhol
Producer-director; Painter

Art (painting) isn't "now." It's ephemeral; it hangs on a wall. Movies are three-dimensional. They're now and tangible—like a painting with sound.

Interview, Los Angeles/ Los Angeles Times, 10-29:(Calendar)15.

John Wayne
Actor

The movie medium is still the best and cheapest entertainment in the world; but somewhere along the line some producers forgot about entertainment. In all my films I try never to forget people are seeing me for relaxation and to enjoy. If there is a message, I try to keep it positive and simple and decent. I like them to go away smiling, and that's why I say the good guys should win.

News conference, Durango, Mex./ The Dallas Times Herald, 8-31:(C)9.

Robert Weitman
Producer

You can go back as far as you like, where basic entertainment obtains, and you will find those pictures made money. That is my credo: Give the public entertainment for entertainment's sake. You can't lose.

Interview, New York, Feb. 15/ The Hollywood Reporter, 2-16:11.

Roy B. White
President, National Association of Theatre Owners

We have been through the dark ages of chaos and confusion for the past three years. Producers, exhibitors and distributors became confused and frightened . . . Our values dimmed and became fuzzy. The result was chaos and fear. We didn't know what (kinds of films) to make, let alone what to play in our theatres. Is it any wonder that the public also became confused? The vast movie-hungry public, after several experimentations with the so-called youth-oriented films, reacted only to absolutes . . . to known quantities like *Love Story*, *Patton*, *Airport* and James Bond.

At Show-A-Rama 15 convention, Kansas City/ The Hollywood Reporter, 3-3:1.

(Arguing against censorship): We can and must do more to combat the hysteria being created by self-appointed mind-keepers who assume a God-given right to determine what everyone can read, see and do. This hysteria is being fanned and nurtured by the political fact that this is an election year . . . I deplore these (permissive) types of films, but I shall defend with all my vigor a producer's right to make what he wants to make, your right to exhibit what you want to exhibit and a consenting adult public's right to watch what they want to see without interference from someone else who happens to disagree with your taste and mine. Let's not stand by and watch book-burnings and witch hunts. It has been said that, if ever our freedoms are lost, it will not be because our enemy was so strong but because we ourselves were so lazy that we preferred to play at piety rather than work at responsibility.

At Midwestern N.A.T.O. convention, Columbus, Ohio/Variety, 3-29:36.

Billy Wilder
Producer, Director, Writer

The great agony in filmmaking is that you don't have any try-outs in Boston or New Haven. Once it's filmed, it's too late. Nor do I believe the stories about redoing a picture in the cutting room. It's got to be there; it's got to play. Sometimes as you go along, the picture seems to taste good and you get the feeling that it's all going to jell. But the worst feeling for a director is to be two-thirds through a movie and then feel it beginning to curdle. You're not like a painter, able to toss out the canvas and start over. You're painting on a canvas that has cost from $1-to-$8 million and you can't throw it away. Pictures cost so much today, and the number of box office successes is so few,

(BILLY WILDER)

that it is an enormous gamble to make a movie. Not only money is involved: You've invested a year of your life and energies. It can be heartbreaking.

Interview, Rome/
Los Angeles Times, 4-30:(Calendar)21.

I am making something very daring in today's market: A romantic comedy. I am betting that dirty movies will kill themselves off pretty soon. I mean, how far can they go to shock people nowadays? Producers have tried every mutation in the way of sex: man and woman, man and man, woman and woman, brother and sister. God knows what will come next–girl and sardine?

Interview, Sorrento, Italy/
Los Angeles Herald-Examiner, 5-28:(E)3.

Shelley Winters
Actress

Everybody asks me why I work so much, why I make so many movies. Well, I work because I like to work. I don't understand actors who don't act. What's with all this opening up of fried chicken stands and antique shops that everybody's going in for now? I think that's demeaning to the acting profession. I mean, what would people think if Picasso opened a taco stand?

Interview, Los Angeles/
Los Angeles Herald-Examiner, 5-14:(F)4.

Frank Yablans
President,
Paramount Pictures Corporation

Yes, there'll be pay-TV and CATV, but the primary market (for motion pictures) will always be theatres. There's something about the excitement of 2,000 people sitting in a theatre laughing rather than sitting at home watching it on TV.

Interview, New York/
San Francisco Examiner, 4-8:33.

Michael York
Actor

I don't pay much attention to reviews. Critics are so rarely helpful or constructive. Most of them write just to make jokes or points of style, and their meanings get lost in the verbiage.

Interview, New York/
San Francisco Examiner & Chronicle,
3-12:(Datebook)5.

MUSIC

Martina Arroyo
Opera singer

If people think a kind of magic happens on stage, they ought to know that what they're seeing is a lot of work. To me, "charisma" is just a fancy word for rehearsals. And if I catch you using the word "effortless" about me, I'll laugh in your face. Maria Callas was the classic example of what I'm after. She worked for hours; but when she came out on the stage, you felt not only that you were hearing the words for the first time, but that she was singing them for the first time–neither of which was so. Every miracle that was known as a "Callas miracle" was a well-rehearsed miracle.

Interview/
The New York Times Magazine, 5-14:32.

Vladimir Ashkenazy
Pianist

I want to get to the core, to achieve the simplicity combined with inner energy that is inherent in great music like Beethoven's and Mozart's, to have absolute honesty, to understand what they mean by such few notes and not try to introduce a meaning which isn't there. I don't want music to be pretty; I want it to be true. I want to say I detest those artists who degrade their appearances–where they are supposed to communicate something important–into light entertainment. Of course, it's nice to think that life is champagne, but is it really? If life is champagne, it isn't worth living. One hears so many performances that are attractive on the surface, but they don't say what music should say.

Interview, New York/
The New York Times, 1-23:(2)15.

Burt Bacharach
Composer

I hate composing. Well, I don't love it. Writing songs is hard, difficult and painful.

Interview, Los Angeles/
San Francisco Examiner, 4-7:19.

Tony Bennett
Singer

Jazz has lost some of its appeal, because it's become a little too intellectual and abstract. It's too "in," and that's wrong. A performer is supposed to entertain the audience, not instruct. You're supposed to please people. There's no mystery to good music. If it's beautiful, everybody understands it. Just the way it happens with a good painting. Luckily, we've now gone through the age of the amateur, when all you needed was a freaky gimmick and a lot of noise, and we're going back to the pros–the guys and gals who really know what music's all about.

Interview/
San Francisco Examiner & Chronicle, 10-15:(Datebook)20.

Irving Berlin
Composer

(On his inability to read music and play piano more extensively): . . . once, many years ago, I tried to learn to read music and play the piano. I gave it four or five days, playing exercises, but I wasn't a very good student. I gave it up because I realized that I could write two or three songs in that time.

Interview, Dec. 25/
The Washington Post, 12-26:(C)9.

Leonard Bernstein
Composer, Conductor

I can't think of a composer—at least a composer I love—in the history of music who wasn't, to one degree or another, eclectic. All composers are, and no composer can be thought of as existing without the composers who preceded him. You cannot think of Stravinsky, for example, without thinking of Scriabin, Rimsky-Korsakov and Tchaikovsky—not to mention Debussy, not to mention Pergolesi, Mozart, Beethoven, Bach and a few hundred others. Stravinsky is a kind of paradigm of eclecticism. I suppose when the critics hurl the epithet at me, they mean something worse than "eclectic." They mean derivative, in the sense that I have somehow consciously gone and stolen or plagiarized music or music style from other people, which is, of course, a thing that I'm not capable of doing . . . But I proudly accept the epithet "eclectic," because that puts me right smack in the grandest company of all, which is Stravinsky, Beethoven and everybody else.

Interview/
The New York Times, 6-11:(2)15.

Rudolf Bing
Former general manager,
Metropolitan Opera, New York

Our (opera's) public is limited compared to baseball. But in 18 of my 22 years (at the Met) we played to 97% of capacity in a 4,000-seat house. In the last four years, with the economy down and people frightened to go out at night, we're down to 90 or 93%. That's still not so bad.

Interview/
The Hollywood Reporter, 4-28:23.

The Met has several hundred seats which don't cost as much as a pornographic movie. I know; I passed one the other day and it cost $5. That was too much for me. At the Met for that you can get Birgit Nilsson taking off the seven veils in *Salome.*

Interview, New York/Newsweek, 5-1:68.

Pierre Boulez
Musical director,
New York Philharmonic Orchestra

The dilemma of music is the dilemma of our civilization. We have to fight the past to survive.

Quote, 3-5:228.

Don Burrows
Australian musician

Jazz is not a What; it's a How. If it was a What, you could teach 'em a What; but you can't teach 'em a How.

New York/
The New York Times, 7-8:13.

Sarah Caldwell
Director, Opera Company of Boston

There are cities that have big, beautiful auditoriums with nothing to go into them. Here, we have a city bursting with artistic activity and no place to put it. With no real opera house in town, we play where we can. People sometimes raise their eyebrows about our surroundings. But I remember that, when Tanglewood started, some ladies complained to Serge Koussevitsky that the Boston Symphony shouldn't be playing under a tent. He replied: "Madame, the tent is where the priests were." I do think, though, it's high time that Boston built some better temples.

The National Observer, 2-19:28.

Maria Callas
Opera singer

To be an opera singer, you have to be an actor or an actress. You have to be a good musician. You have to look well onstage and off; there is no excuse for being 30 pounds overweight. And you must have nerve. I tell my students to think. Before they sing a phrase, they must have the expression—the thought behind the music—on their faces, so the public will see it first. I tell them to put more poetry behind their voices. I try to teach them humbleness toward music.

Interview, New York/Time, 2-21:57.

Aaron Copland
Composer

To a composer, music is a kind of language. It's true that the sound of music is pleasant in itself; at any rate, to those people who are lucky enough to be sensitive to it. But more importantly, behind those sounds is a language of the emotions. The composer has it in his power to make music speak of many things–tender things, harsh things; lively or sleepy-making moods; consoling or challenging sounds. After all, even the dullest listener can tell the difference between a march and a lullaby. But on a more sophisticated level, the composer is able to evoke a sense of the grandiose, of the satirical, or a deeply-felt emotion. Whatever it may be, the composer uses the language of music to say something; not something that you can translate into words necessarily, but something that constitutes essentialized emotions that are seized and shaped into meaningful form. Now, to do that convincingly in an extended composition lasting over half an hour or more, and to evoke those sounds from an orchestra of a hundred men playing many different instruments, can certainly be considered one of the grander achievements of the human mind.

Television broadcast/"Comment!" National Broadcasting Company, 3-12.

"Duke" Ellington
Musician

There's nothing (for him but music). That's it. That's the thing I do. I play every night. I write music every day or whenever it comes into my head. My bang is not money. My bang is music–the reaction to, the exposure to, the anticipation of and the fruits of hearing.

The New York Times, 5-1:29.

I don't understand this craze to know how everything works. People want to know how I do it, or they say they want to get behind the scenes. Why should the audience ever be behind the scenes? All it does is pull the petals off the creative flower.

San Francisco Examiner & Chronicle, 7-16:(This World)2.

Arthur Fiedler
Conductor, Boston Pops Orchestra

There was a period in my life, when I first started, that I thought of going into the very serious side of conducting. Then I felt that, well, there are trials and tribulations. You go to a town and you have a second- or third-rate orchestra, or there's a faction that likes you and a faction that hates you. In Boston, I had the advantage of a marvelous orchestra at the tip of my fingers. I don't know; I just chose. I always said, if I'm going into this type of music (pops), I want to do it as well as I can. I also felt that much of this music needed somebody to love and caress it, to fondle and perform it–not to look down their noses at it like a dirty thing. This has kept me alive musically.

Interview, Syracuse, N.Y./ The New York Times, 4-2:(2)32.

Rudolf Friml
Composer

(On the modern musical comedy): Crooning and drums have replaced the beautiful arias, duets and finale of the operetta. It is all a bunch of high-paid rubbish. Writers do not write from the heart but for cash.

Interview, Los Angeles/ San Francisco Examiner & Chronicle, 7-9:(Datebook)4.

Nicolai Gedda
Opera singer

A (opera) singer today has to know more than a singer 50 years ago. No conductor has rehearsal time any more to sit and work with an unmusical singer. It costs too much money. A conductor like Karajan wants singers who are not only utterly prepared musically, but who know how to walk on stage and who have a conception of a role. I think that Stanislavsky also changed things for opera singers. Today, we ought to have

(NICOLAI GEDDA)

an idea of history. If we do a character from the Renaissance, we should know about the period. A singer should have imagination. We just can't be dummies any more. Nobody can afford us.

Interview, New York/ The New York Times, 12-10:(2)19.

I personally have the attitude that, if I'm not in perfect shape, or at least 95 per cent good shape, I cancel (the performance). I always remember that the public pays money to come and hear me. They have the right to expect my best or even better. I have that responsibility. You know, there are many singers who take this profession as a kind of sport, who say, "I am never sick. I can't be sick. If I have a cold, I'll show them." That is wrong. Singing is not athletics.

Interview, New York/ The New York Times, 12-10:(2)19.

Goeran Gentele
General manager-designate, Metropolitan Opera, New York

A lot of our productions . . . are falling apart. If we could share the cost with Chicago or San Francisco—or Seattle or Santa Fe—we could use the savings for other new productions. Wherever there are first-rate productions, the Met should hire them, or exchange for them. We must get off our high horse.

Interview/Newsweek, 3-27:76.

Stanley M. Gortikov
President, Recording Industry Association of America

(On charges that contemporary music promotes use of drugs): (If I were in the Commission's place, I too would be) wondering whether music is a catalyst for drug use. (But) I say overwhelmingly not. Music reflects and mirrors a society more than it molds and directs that society.

At National Commission on Marijuana and Drug Abuse hearings, Los Angeles, April 12/Daily Variety, 4-13:1.

Jascha Heifetz
Violinist

Sometimes I have played five, six, seven encores; sometimes I have played none. When I play none, I simply say, "I have given you all I can." Encores are simply a matter of judging yourself and the audience. Sometimes *you* have had enough; sometimes *they* have had enough. But if you're fresh and they're fresh, then you give them more.

Interview, Los Angeles/ The Dallas Times Herald, 11-21:(C)7.

Bronislaw Kaper
Composer

There are no shortcuts in music; you have to be serious about it . . . whatever I do is directed toward music—all my friendships, all my passions, all my existing, from driving a car to listening and smelling. I cannot imagine that I could exist without music. Every day I should pray to Mozart.

At symposium before arts-oriented students, Los Angeles/Los Angeles Times, 3-23:(4)14.

Stan Kenton
Musician

Music is communication. The instrument is an extension of the individual.

Kansas City/ The Dallas Times Herald, 4-6:(B)7.

Istvan Kertesz
Orchestra conductor

The age of the old-school dictator conductor is over. I like to think of myself as the 81st player—80 players, and the conductor as just another musician.

Interview, Los Angeles/ Los Angeles Times, 2-3:(4)14.

James Levine
Principal conductor, Metropolitan Opera, New York

. . . I find myself totally disinterested in the question nowadays of technical proficiency, which literally seems to be the basis for evaluating an orchestra's performance up one side and down the other. You can read the words of composers from Bach to Stravinsky, and what you find them screaming into the night about is not the technical execution but the conception, the balance, the spirit, the purpose, what was supposed to be conveyed. To read Berlioz on this subject is so eye-opening, you can't believe it. He performed in situations so primitive they would curl your hair today. We must now have 15 to 20 orchestras in this country which Berlioz would have thought were a dream technically. But where is the piece? It gets lost.

Interview, New York/ The New York Times, 3-12:(2)25.

Guy Lombardo
Orchestra leader

Country music is the best music being played today. Country music has always been good. It's gone by a lot of names, but it's the same music; and it's still popular because it's good music.

Quote, 4-30:410.

Bruno Maderna
Composer, Conductor

(In Europe) the orchestra players all look stern; but in America, you can read the musicians' faces at once. If an orchestra doesn't like you, it's important to know that immediately. Here, all the musicians want to help you make music. I compare European orchestras with a frigid woman—you have to work too hard to get results.

Interview, New York/ The New York Times, 1-9:(2)30.

Henry Mancini
Composer, Conductor

It used to take six months for a record to make it (in sales). Now it's six weeks; and if it doesn't happen then, they write it off as a tax loss. Everybody's so geared to instant success, if a record doesn't happen instantly, people say, "let's go on; the hell with it."

Interview, Los Angeles/ Daily Variety, 3-23:10.

Zubin Mehta
Musical director, Los Angeles Philharmonic Orchestra

I've often been asked to speak more at my concerts. But I think half the audience comes to listen to their favorite music and the other half has a little bit of the adventurous spirit. I don't think they want to be taught all the time. Maybe we should do the same program a second night. Yes, I've been talking about doing a Thursday night when we'd play, say, a Mahler symphony, and then on Friday night we'd explain it. There could be people who would want to come hack and relearn and rethink it.

Interview, Los Angeles/ The Christian Science Monitor, 1-5:11.

Yehudi Menuhin
Violinist

I still call myself a violinist. But I do love conducting; it offers so much scope; it makes me feel the violin is expanding into a great instrument with all sorts of sounds at its call. There's the fun at rehearsal; there's the joy of spreading out through the orchestral repertoire . . . Everyone, of course, has his style. Conducting is like a signature; one cannot really imitate another. A very concise style will work for one man, while an expansive style—allied with clarity—will get good results for another.

Interview, San Francisco/ San Francisco Examiner, 1-7:34.

Gerry Mulligan
Jazz musician

There have been many valuable innovations (in music), but the tendency is to overwork them. The electronic thing, for instance—too much concentration on electric piano to the exclusion of the real piano; I can hear endless numbers of electric-piano players who all sound alike, but put the same players on a regular piano and their individual qualities will show. To my jaded middle-aged ears, a lot of rock groups, too, are indistinguishable; you hear the same rhythm patterns again and again. You find far more individual kinds of approaches in the folk-rock area, which is producing some brilliant songs and performances . . . There are too many groups nowadays that you can't actually hear; you just feel them . . . It's really non-music, and that's a drag. I regret the demand for that kind of thing as much as I regret the fact that people are willing to supply it. They've turned the chaos of our present-day society into a vast commercial enterprise.

Interview/
San Francisco Examiner & Chronicle,
5-21:(Datebook)6.

Guiomar Novaes
Pianist

Pianos are very capricious, as human beings are. Each day they talk in a different way. They are very sensitive creatures. They feel humidity, cold, moving around, drafts. They don't like to travel, and feel tired exactly as we do. Once I played in the Midwest. There was a terrible snowstorm all day long. When we got to the hall, the piano was absolutely soundless. We put blankets and lights on him to warm him up. Even so, at the performance it was no good at all. The show must go on; but, poor thing, with that hoarse throat, what could he say?

Interview, New York/
The New York Times, 12-2:42.

Ewald B. Nyquist
New York State Commissioner of Education

In terms of contemporary communication, there is little doubt that folk music is one of the most influential factors in determining the values of today's youth. Although the family and the school instill values, these values are frequently rejected when youth reaches adolescence and begins to look upon his early training as a kind of rigid indoctrination. Today, many young people turn to the lessons of folk-rock, and, without pressure or compulsion, they memorize and virtually worship the ideas communicated through the lyrics and the singers. To motivate children, to turn them on, music must be socially relevant to their lives.

Before New York State Council of
Administrators of Music Education/
Quote, 2-20:178.

Seiji Ozawa
Conductor,
San Francisco Symphony Orchestra

Music is a very pure thing. You get it through your ears, and it goes direct to your heart. You don't have to understand it; it is a natural thing. It comes from God to bring joy to people.

Interview, San Francisco/
The Dallas Times Herald, 3-13:(A)15.

Rosa Ponselle
Opera singer

It's the jet age. The young (opera) singers today are launched before they learn. They sing in one place and then rush to sing somewhere else. The important thing is what they want. Do they want to make money fast or do they want to leave something for posterity? Plus a great voice, which they must have, they have to have common sense; they have to respect the voice.

Interview/
The Washington Post, 1-23:(G)3.

Jerome Robbins
Choreographer

One of the things that appeals to me tremendously about (Igor) Stravinsky's music is what I call the motor. There is always a pulse, a tremendous motor going that is attractive to dance to. It almost carries you, takes you along with it. It's almost irresistible. I always feel there is architecture and strength, there is no fat on his work. It is not bulging over his girdle. It is absolutely lean, as essential as it can be. And it's never sentimental, though it's moving.

Interview/Time, 7-3:46.

Richard Rodgers
Composer

(His greatest satisfaction from his music career): The unexpected moments, like driving up the parkway late at night, all alone, and hearing a tune that came from my head. It comes as such a surprise, a shock almost, and it's the most profound feeling I've ever had in my life. Aren't I lucky that, though I never know when it will happen, it's recurred again and again?

Interview, New York/
The Washington Post, 7-16:(G)5.

Artur Rubinstein
Pianist

I'm glad to have admirers; but I don't always share their admiration. Sometimes a concert is a lesson for the next time.

Interview, Buffalo, N.Y./
The New York Times, 1-28:24.

Winthrop Sargent
Music critic

I think music is dead, because I don't think any important music is being written today. It was in Schoenberg's and Stravinsky's generation that the decline set in. Bela Bartok is a musical personality of some stature, but Stravinsky is the Rimsky-Korsakov of his generation. I am willing to bet that in the 21st century Stravinsky won't be played very much. You have to have a tradition. You can't tear it all to pieces and expect to produce anything important. Composers from Mozart to Richard Strauss changed the language slightly, but it still remained the same language.

Interview/Time, 1-10:64.

Renata Scotto
Opera singer

In opera, the singer comes before everything. The prima donna is prima. The conductor must be a good accompanist, but the singer must be first. Many times I have had discussions, sometimes fights, and always I win. Last year in Italy I was singing *Traviata*, and I had a conductor—aaah, terrible! He don't understand me, and he don't want to accompany me. At a rehearsal, he want one tempo and he say, "You must come with me." I scream, "No, maestro; *you* must come with *me!*" Then I stop the rehearsal and go to my dressing room. He follow, and I scream, "*I don't want to sing with you any more*! You don't understand what I feel!" In the performance, he followed me, but with no communication, by force. It was the first and last time I sing with that conductor.

Interview, New York/
The New York Times, 11-19:(2)15.

Beverly Sills
Opera singer

They'll kill me for saying this at the conservatories, but if I were advising a teen-age girl of today how to become a singer, I'd say: Don't go to a conservatory. Get a private teacher and, as soon as you can, get out on a stage and perform. It doesn't really matter what stage. If you can get a job in the chorus of a Broadway show, fine. The important thing, I have found, is to perform, to be before an audience; nothing can substitute for that.

The National Observer, 3-25:27.

As soon as I walk into the theatre, I'm somebody else. I'm Manon, or Lucia, or whoever it happens to be. Even if, God for-

(BEVERLY SILLS)

bid, I'm not getting the message to the audience, *I'm* getting the message.

Time, 3-27:92.

Janos Starker
Cellist

I consider myself a professional and don't allow myself the luxury of playing badly if, for example, I don't feel well. I sometimes smile at colleagues of mine—big people in the field—who play a miserable performance and people say, "Oh, it wasn't a good night. Let's hear him next time." I hope that if I play 10 concerts, a couple are higher than the others. But every time I'm on stage and people come and make an effort to hear me, they, to put it in an ordinary way, should be given their money's worth. They come to honor me, and I should deliver.

Interview, Bloomington, Ind./ The New York Times, 10-15:(2)17.

Leopold Stokowski
Orchestra conductor

A great composer gives his whole life to composing. To understand all the instruments in the orchestra takes a whole lifetime of study. The composer must either compose or study the instruments, because all the instruments in the orchestra have different characteristics. That is what a conductor should do, though it takes all his life. Sometimes the composer writes something which the instrument can't play. Then the instrument and the player, they argue.

Interview, New York/ The Washington Post, 3-12:(K)10.

Dimitri Tiomkin
Composer

I'm not arguing for tradition; it's not necessary to have tradition. But a lot of electronic noise will never replace a symphony nor a small chamber orchestra. Rock is great and I like hillbilly; but overlaying rhythms, which isn't really new, doesn't necessarily end up as music . . . Form is the principal thing in music . . . Music isn't a fashion . . . Picasso and Chagall won't be out in 90 years; yet after 60 years good music is supposed to be out?

Interview, Los Angeles/Daily Variety, 3-8:6.

Gottfried Von Einem
Composer

A composer must feel that his music is directed toward people and isn't just marks on paper. Sociological problems lie behind his concepts. He should not compose in wretched isolation, making conversation only with himself. He must close the gap between his vision and society.

At University of California, Berkeley/ San Francisco Examiner & Chronicle, 11-12:(Sunday Scene)16.

THE STAGE

Lauren Bacall
Actress

(On show business): Tough business. You're constantly having to prove yourself. An actor's life is dependent on the whim of producers, directors, authors. It has nothing to do with talent. An actor's earning years may be very few–10 if he's lucky, 20 if he's very lucky. And that's not consecutive. It's nothing you can depend on. You can be out of work, as I have been, for two, three years at a time. I've had to scrounge. You have a name, but that doesn't mean you get parts. You're just stuck with it. You can be the most brilliant performer in the world. It has nothing to do with anything.

Interview, San Francisco/
Los Angeles Times, 4-23:(Calendar)28.

George Balanchine
Director, New York City Ballet

Ballet is a peculiar art. It's visual, but it's not for the brain. It's not logical, but we have our own logic. Who could I explain it to?

Interview, New York/
The New York Times, 6-16:35.

Clive Barnes
Drama critic, "The New York Times"

Broadway has been in a period of reassessment. It's in a period of questioning its own viability. What we are doing, I think, is moving to the same situation that London is in–we are moving toward what is fundamentally an institutional theatre. By institutional theatre, I mean a theatre that is fundamentally nonprofit-making; that is, it takes as its purpose to provide theatre rather than to make money. Traditionally, the American theatre, unlike most of the world theatre, has been the realm of the entrepreneur, the people who went into it for a buck. But it's questionable now whether the old buccaneering producers can survive and stay alive. It is possible that the subsidized theatre, the nonprofit theatre, the institutional theatre, is going to become the norm.

Panel discussion, New York/
The New York Times, 12-26:44.

Richard Barr
Producer; President,
League of New York Theatres

Do I find many plays I want to produce? No. One trouble is that the writers all seem to think they have to be unmistakably relevant to some question of the day. By the time these get written, the questions have disappeared. To be good, a play must have a basic theme that exists apart from a current question. This demands authenticity of characters whose stories remain above fashions or styles.

Interview, Washington/
The Washington Post, 11-12:(K)4.

Ralph Bellamy
Actor

Too many of the actors and playwrights have turned introspective. We reflect the times in the theatre, and this is the most confused time in decades. Writers use the theatre in an effort to find themselves. But the problems of plays should be about other people rather than the writers. And too many actors are concerned about why their father married their mother.

Interview/
Los Angeles Herald-Examiner, 12-10:(E)2.

Ingrid Bergman
Actress

The Italians don't care so much for the theatre, because what they see on the stage is so much better done at home.

At National Press Club, Washington/ The New York Times, 3-18:21.

Rudolf Bing
General manager, Metropolitan Opera, New York

In theatre, there is an absolutely unalterable relation: Every economic decision reflects itself artistically, and every artistic decision reflects itself economically.

At New York University Theatre Management and Production seminar/ The New York Times, 2-4:13.

Robert Bolt
Playwright

(Playwriting is) more like quarrying. You hammer and chisel and fit and alter. It's like plain hard work an awful lot of the time. And every now and then there's something marvelous—moments of inspiration that come right out of the depths of your integrated self.

Interview, New York/ The New York Times, 1-20:50.

Richard Chamberlain
Actor

It really takes a day's preparation to go on every night (and do Shakespeare), to have control of yourself instead of klutzing and stumbling around, sagging and panting. You can't do Shakespeare on pure emotion.

Interview, Washington/ The National Observer, 5-27:20.

Paddy Chayefsky
Playwright

Today, there is no audience for theatre. A writer should be socially necessary. And right now, whether you're talking about on-Broadway or off-Broadway, that's not what the producers are looking for. They want "entertainment," whatever that may mean. There is no audience today for really serious theatre. The intellectual elite are now all filmgoers.

Interview, Beverly Hills, Calif./ Los Angeles Times, 3-26:(Calendar)12.

Marc Connelly
Playwright

(Today's) writers for the theatre, to my mind, are more concerned with exposure than dramaturgy. Shock value seems terribly important to young playwrights. I think our mechanisms have gone through some kind of contortions. In the theatre, the stimuli used to be 85 per cent personal, 15 per cent mechanical. Now it's become the reverse. Perhaps because of the movies, we're so habituated to mechanical stimuli that the theatre spends more time on that than on the personal chemistry that makes theatre special.

Interview, New York/ "W": a Fairchild publication, 11-17:12.

John Cranko
Director-choreographer, Stuttgart Ballet

People, especially the New York and London critics, are always asking me, "Why on earth do you stay there (in Stuttgart)?" Actually, I enjoy living here very much, and I think the company does, too. It's pleasant, it's restful and everyone is wonderful to us. Besides, here I have a theatre, a company, a first-rate physical plant—all the continuity that a choreographer dreams of. And I have complete artistic freedom with the absolute minimum of outside nonsense. In the United States, I'd be spending all my time with boards of trustees and drinking tea with the ladies who contribute the money to the "Friends of the Ballet." Here I have to answer only to the director of the state theatre . . . and, through him, to the state culture minister. Why would I want to go looking for headaches?

Interview, Stuttgart, West Germany/ The Washington Post, 1-30:(G)7.

Zelda Fichandler
Producing director,
Arena Stage, Washington

It is a sad fact that new plays by established American playwrights have all too few productions in America. Too many theatre producers and directors are caught up with the young playwright–part of our youth culture in general–and ignore the work of our established playwrights in their middle years. And some of our established American playwrights have not caught up with history, being somewhat blinded by the glare of all those Broadway lights. But those flaws are correctible.

Accepting the Margo Jones Award/
The Washington Post, 5-21:(G)5.

Henry Fonda
Actor

The commercial theatre today–Broadway, that is–is an expense-account theatre. It isn't for the people.

Telephone interview, Chicago/
Los Angeles Herald-Examiner, 3-12:(G)1.

Margot Fonteyn
Ballerina

. . . I can't begin to tell you what goes through my mind when I dance. All I can say is that hundreds of little bits and pieces all put together pass through my mind–hundreds of different thoughts, feelings, worries, emotions, images–hundreds of things. Of course, that's only what I *think* happens; because, really, one has no idea. I have no systems for propelling myself onto the stage. I simply go on. If I began thinking and analyzing about the way I dance, then perhaps I wouldn't be able to do it. I simply use my resources. I try to make a contribution. That's really all there is. Remember, in the dance, everyone is different. Everyone must find a way of being themselves on the stage which, I suppose, is a very difficult thing to do. It took me a very long time to come to know myself as a dancer. I suppose it came from being on the stage a lot of years–of dancing many roles, of observing others, of receiving help.

Interview, New York/
The New York Times, 5-28:(2)10.

John Gielgud
Actor

I don't think actors need to be intellectual at all . . . Certainly I have never been. I have a reputation for it because I have been in so many intelligent plays; but I've also done a great deal of rubbish. I try to tell young actors not to criticize the material too much. You can learn a great deal about the technique and skill of acting from playing a cheap farce. The most important thing is to be flexible, to sit in on the early rehearsals and absorb the mood and style of the play and to have a clear understanding with the director and the other players of what sort of play it is. You don't need to go to libraries and museums and read masses of things. What you need, above all, is a good instinct.

Interview, Beverly Hills, Calif./
Los Angeles Times, 2-6:(Calendar)30.

Here in America, you build enormous theatres and have no programs or companies prepared to fill them. In England, the big cities have their own repertory companies, which give each city a sense of pride in its own theatre . . . Expenses are so high in America that the pleasure of the middle-sized theatre is not possible. Of course, our (British) subsidies give us the opportunity to play all sizes of theatres without worry about money. I've heard that the Kennedy Theatre (in Washington) is putting on a tiny commercial play that I wouldn't think they'd deign to produce. It was to be such a high-brow theatre; now they're shoving anything they can get into it. We used to have business managers who really had power, great impressarios like Sol Hurok, who took time to see that the play was their own taste. The sense of pride has been lost.

Interview, New York/
"W": a Fairchild publication, 11-17:9.

Brendan Gill
Drama critic,
"The New Yorker" magazine

(A playwright) purporting to relate facts must not tamper with the evidence; must not scramble reality and make-believe; must not introduce convenient fictions for the sake of good dramatic effect or a so-called "higher" truth; must not take advantage of his audience in order to outwit them as a polemicist.

At panel discussion sponsored by the Drama Desk, New York, Jan. 3/ The New York Times, 1-4:28.

Max Gordon
Producer

(The famine on Broadway is attributable to) economics and the loss of younger audiences to films and the absence of great playwrights like O'Neill, Anderson, Sherwood, Kingsley, Elmer Rice and so forth. Can you imagine how bad things are? The only successful show last season was *Sleuth*, a British import.

Interview, San Francisco, Feb. 9/ San Francisco Examiner, 2-10:33.

Buddy Hackett
Comedian

. . . Lee J. Cobb was here the other night and told me how much he admires and envies the guy who can walk out on a nightclub stage; how lucky I was to be able to do it and what a great art it is. Until a couple of years ago, I never thought of saloon artists that way. I always thought there was something else more important in show business, that saloons were just a way station on the road to something better. Now I know it's the freest way for a comedian to express himself. It's such a pure art form . . . no props, no scenery; just one guy trying to make people laugh.

Interview, Las Vegas, Nev./ Los Angeles Herald-Examiner, 6-4:(F)6.

Richard Harris
Actor

I go to the West End and Broadway and it's all so dull. Literally dull. Nothing going on. Oh, there are two or three good things in London, but I don't care how good they are—the people sitting out front are bored . . . They laugh a little; but they are all Greyhound Tours or Block Bookings.

Interview, Los Angeles/ Los Angeles Times, 4-8:(2)5.

To me, the theatre has become a museum—all the emotion is gone. Actors like Sir Ralph Richardson and (Sir Laurence) Olivier are now just spouting mothballs. The smell of old age hangs heavily in the theatre today. The excitement that once existed with the audience is dead, and I'm sorry to see its passing.

Interview, Dallas/ The Dallas Times Herald, 7-23:(K)1.

Helen Hayes
Actress

I think there are two things which have kept me going as an actress all these years—inquisitiveness and enthusiasm. To start with, I love acting, actors and the theatre. Without that, everything would be meaningless. Second, I've always been curious about people and events. No matter how long you are in the theatre, this curiosity stays with you. It is the mark of a genuine actor as against someone who is just passing through. It helps you to keep learning, to find something new to bring to a part. Without curiosity, an actor would stagnate.

The Washington Post, 3-19:(TV Channels)5.

Arthur Hill
Actor

I value the writer's work more than the director's. I respect the writer more than the director. The play's the thing; if that's wrong, nothing will be right. Sometimes, when a play's no good, people tell you they're going just to see someone's performance. I feel sad about that. I'm bleeding for that actor.

Interview, Los Angeles/ Los Angeles Herald-Examiner, 2-22:(B)2.

When I was working on Broadway and commuting to White Plains, I was the first man out of the theatre and running for that last train. The only night I stayed in was opening night. When I was a very young actor, older actors used to say to me, "You're never going to make it if you don't stick around more. You have to go out and have drinks with producers and agents and writers and backers." I used to think to myself, "Drinks? For what?" How's that going to help me if I go to an audition and I can't act? And if I have to live like that to get parts, I'm not going to be happy with my life, anyway.

Interview, New York/ San Francisco Examiner & Chronicle, 6-4:(Datebook)16.

Christopher Isherwood
Author, Playwright

. . . when I write for the stage I immediately become bold and want broad effects. My instinct is, if there's music, it ought to be louder! It's rather like painting with a broom.

Interview, Los Angeles/ San Francisco Examiner & Chronicle, 5-21:(Datebook)7.

Glynis Johns
Actress

Let's go back to a bit of romance. That's what theatre means. It's entertaining. There's so much drabness about. People have a lot of problems in their lives . . . I get so fed up with the lack of romance in entertainment. I like to see everybody (in plays) very rich, very pretty and very happy, and I like it to end happily—even all the servants happy because they are well paid. I like to wear attractive clothes. That's what theatre means—entertainment.

Interview, Boston/ The Christian Science Monitor, 6-3:6.

Arthur Laurents
Playwright

. . . if you analyze the plays of any honest, serious playwright, you'd see that basically he is saying the same thing, again and again, in various ways. His overriding viewpoint will come out whether he likes it or not.

Interview/ San Francisco Examiner & Chronicle, 5-28:(Datebook)16.

Sam Levene
Actor

If you don't have a stage, you're out of business. There's no continuity in the theatre. No matter how long you run, you have to close.

Interview, New York/ The New York Times, 12-28:38.

Siobhan McKenna
Actress

The American policy is that success must follow success. That's why the American actors have such a horror of flops, which we (in Ireland) don't have. I've never been horrified by one, although I've learned a great deal from them.

Interview/ Los Angeles Times, 1-23:(Calendar)28.

Ray Milland
Actor

To me, the stage is sheer hell. I do it to see if I can lick it. The boredom is incredible—night after night, the same people saying the same words. Some actors . . . will always pick up the pencil as they say a certain word, or light a cigarette on another line. Some nights when I got bored, I would move the pencil, and they would complain to the stagehands. They couldn't function if the pencil wasn't in the same place every night. God, can you imagine?

Interview, St. Jean-Cap Ferrat, France/ The New York Times, 6-25:(2)11.

Arthur Miller
Playwright

New York City fell apart. How can you expect a theatre to exist in a jungle like that? There is no community, or even a facsimile of one. There isn't even enough community to safeguard a pedestrian. So how can you expect a theatre to go on there? Look. The middle class has always supported the theatre. And the middle class has fled New York City. But when you say, "Therefore, the theatre is dead," it isn't so. Not true. Is Macy's dead? What's happened to Macy's? They went to the suburbs. Is the wholesale and retail clothing business dead? No. They simply registered the change in population. So what we've been living through, really, is a transformation in population. It comes to New York to make its money, and it gets out as fast as it can. And New York is stuck with a theatre district and purely extraneous crap, such as negotiations with unions and real-estate people, that were formed in an entirely different social era. But that doesn't mean the form of the theatre is dead. Not at all . . . I think it's going to come back. Maybe not tomorrow or next year, but I have the feeling—not the feeling, the knowledge—that the day will come when theatre again will surmount everything for the simple reason that it is an irreducible simplicity. It's a man up there facing other men. Somehow or other, this always has to be possible. It takes less means than anything else we have, including painting. You don't need a machine. You don't need lenses. You don't need lights. You need a board and an actor. That's all you need; you don't need anything else—except a certain amount of quiet, which is sometimes difficult to find.

Interview, Roxbury, Conn./
The New York Times Magazine, 2-13:36.

Rudolf Nureyev
Ballet dancer

It may sound corny, but for me dancing is martyrdom. That is what I truly feel. The greatest reward is self-satisfaction, and the audience can make you feel that you deserve that self-satisfaction. That is their contribution; it is their part of the performance.

San Francisco Examiner & Chronicle,
6-11:(Sunday Punch)2.

Joseph Papp
Producer, New York Public Theatre

We must pay attention to American writers, otherwise they will die on the vine. We have the most exciting writers in drama in the world, and I'm not merely being chauvinistic about that fact.

At meeting of the Drama Desk,
New York, Feb. 7/Variety, 2-9:78.

John Patrick
Playwright

. . . I am convinced Broadway no longer is the arbiter of the American theatrical tastes. The New York critic has become jaded; and why not? He sees maybe three or four shows a week; and anyone who sees that many shows in a week simply can't maintain a perspective.

Quote, 4-2:314.

Jan Peerce
Opera singer

I hate to sound like a rebel, but this (his starring role in the Broadway musical *Fiddler on the Roof*) is even more rewarding than opera. Here you're playing not only for the music but also for the character of a complete person. You live it; you don't act it. It's so real that, every night, you're just not going to make exactly the same moves. You expect somebody on your left and you find them on your right. That's wonderful.

Interview, New York/
The Dallas Times Herald, 1-9:(C)8.

Harold Prince
Producer, Director

Because of labor, because of cost, all classical, audacious, experimental theatre will have to be subsidized in one way or another. That's all there is to it. And you know what? So will musicals like *Company* and *Follies*. There will be money only for things that are commercially viable–something that can play a long time and for which the figures on paper make sense; only the lightest kind of entertainment. Of my 155 investors, three are very wealthy, and the rest are wardrobe mistresses, associates, friends. When they put $1,000 in a show they want to get it back, and profit for it. They're not patrons of the arts; they're *investors*. Once you accept the fact that subsidy is possible in commercial theatre, you also open up a possibility that doesn't exist in noncommercial theatre: that of profit. If someone had subsidized *Fiddler (on the Roof)*, it would have earned that organization so much money it could have subsidized 50 other shows! Think of it.

Interview, Beverly Hills, Calif./ Los Angeles Times, 7-16:(Calendar)41.

Anthony Shaffer
Playwright

I rebel totally against the notion such work (writing thrillers) is always less than serious. It's part of a good writer's armory to know that suspense on any level is going to make an audience shut up and pay attention.

Interview, New York/ The Dallas Times Herald, 1-9:(C)8.

. . . I prefer going to the theatre in London (rather than New York). You can make up your mind to go 20 minutes before the curtain and have no trouble getting a ticket. That's why the theatres there are full.

Interview, San Francisco/ San Francisco Examiner & Chronicle, 4-9:(Datebook)3.

Edward Villella
Ballet dancer

(Dancers are) probably more highly-trained, more highly-disciplined (than athletes). The technique is very intense. Every movement has to be exact. It's not like an athlete chasing a fly ball; he goes his own way; he just has to get there. In ballet, you don't just hang a hand out. And on top of everything else, you have to be an artist. (Baseball player) Hank Aaron can hit 46 home runs, and he doesn't have to point his toes, he doesn't have to wear tights or have a well-turned calf; it's okay if his stomach sags a bit.

Interview, Washington/ The Dallas Times Herald, 3-26:(H)2.

Tennessee Williams
Playwright

I have no complaints about the theatre. It has given me my life. It has deprived me of some things also. I gave up my life to write.

San Francisco Examiner, 7-19:34.

Shelley Winters
Actress

There is no Broadway theatre. Broadway is Neil Simon comedies, musicals and British imports, and that's it.

The New York Times, 3-7:44.

TELEVISION AND RADIO

Elie Abel
Dean,
Columbia University Graduate School of Journalism

(Advocating public television in the U.S. free from government control and interference): I happen to believe in competition. I am persuaded that the best way to raise standards in commercial broadcasting is to offer the viewers an alternative. That seems to me a wiser course than to place our hope in tougher FCC regulations . . . in Britain—as in Germany, Japan and other countries—public television offers the viewer a balanced diet of programming, quite apart from news and public affairs, that is in my judgment superior to the day-by-day programming available on either commercial or public television in the United States. Most Americans, I would agree, do not know what they are missing.

Before Senate Constitutional Rights Subcommittee, Washington, Feb.17/ The Hollywood Reporter, 2-18:1.

Julie Andrews
Actress

If you hear someone tell you that television is not the most difficult medium of all, the hardest of the performing arts to perform, you are talking to someone who has never done television.

Interview, Los Angeles/ San Francisco Examiner & Chronicle, 10-15:(Datebook)21.

David Attenborough
Director of television programs,
British Broadcasting Corporation

It seems to me that television's job is not to report the average, but to report the significant. It is particularly important to us in this country (Britain) to report the significant in the United States—partly because we are so close, but partly because . . . what is happening today in the United States is going to happen in five years' time in this country. I don't know whether it's true or not, but we do reflect a great deal of what happens in the United States. Certainly, if you look over the past few years, many of the things that have happened—the student movement, the drug situation—both of these were seen earlier in the United States than here. Hippies, the love generation—I knew about them first from reports from America. Of course we report racial troubles. Of course we report student troubles. Of course we report Vietnam. But if that's all we reported, then you would have a real cause for complaint. But what do we see of America? What we see overwhelmingly is *Apollo*. We've devoted a tremendous amount of time to *Apollo* (space) flights and Houston, and we've gained knowledge of the way Americans indulge in badinage and small talk but organize themselves technologically. Last night we had a program on the 6th Fleet. It seemed to me to demonstrate America's concern and responsibility and how much money you are spending on NATO. We also see a great deal of America on the fringes—things like *The Mary Tyler Moore Show* represent a certain aspiration in the American character. So does *Ironside*. All these things together form an amalgam.

Interview/TV Guide, 1-29:33.

Lucille Ball
Actress

I've been in television 20 years, and there have been many changes. Some of you remember that one of my early shows was about going to the hospital to give birth to my son . . . Well, that was a good show; it was human and it was funny. But we received many letters denouncing us for being obscene. Some folks thought it was in bad taste to show a pregnant woman on television. Today, they not only show you pregnant women on television—but they show how they got that way.

TV Guide, 1-8:10.

Richard Boone
Actor

(On television actors who denigrate the medium): I know people who go around saying things like, "You know, I'm doing this crap for the money, but my heart's really elsewhere, where the art is." Well, that's a crock. When you get into the marketplace—and television is the marketplace—that's when you should do your best work.

Interview/ The New York Times, 12-10:(2)23.

Johnny Carson
Television talk-show host

Is it television's obligation to educate the American public? I don't think you can educate people with television; you need a classroom experience. Unfortunately, television is a commercial medium, and anyone who doesn't understand that is idiotic. Television is constantly bludgeoned, but who is to decide what to do? The idea of television, as I understand it, is to reach as many people as possible. That's one measure of success. Or is it to reach a manner of critical success, to do prison reform and other relevant things? If you do that, you're not going to reach the people. David Frost did that, and for some reason he doesn't seem to be on any more.

Interview, Burbank, Calif./ San Francisco Examiner, 9-23:36.

John Cassavetes
Motion picture director

I don't think you can do serious work in television; too many obstacles—networks and sponsors and agencies—all looking over your shoulder. Listen, as bad as the major movie studios are—and they are as bad as they could possibly be—they are still infinitely more creative than television, much more receptive to ideas and experimentation.

Interview, Los Angeles/ San Francisco Examiner & Chronicle, 7-23:(Datebook)7-TV.

Mike Connors
Actor

. . . an audience prefers to see you (the actor) as yourself; especially in TV. In films, you can project other images, because nine times out of ten an audience has come to see a picture and not a personality. But in TV they turn to *your* show, and you damn well better be you—or you're going to lose your audience fast.

Interview, Los Angeles/ San Francisco Examiner & Chronicle, 7-23:(Datebook)17.

Arthur Conte
Director-general, French national radio-television network

I have two feelings about the new job (as director-general): humility—my mission isn't candy—and ambition—to make our television a big and beautiful thing. In my constituency (as a member of Parliament), the fireman told me television was like a canteen: One knows in advance what there will be to eat. Our problem will be to change TV's dishes. There are subjects that interest a larger public, such as playing cards, such as gardening.

News conference/ The New York Times, 7-22:2.

Michael H. Dann
Vice president, Children's Television Workshop; Former vice president in charge of programming, Columbia Broadcasting System Television

If you look back through the history of commercial broadcasting and its presidents—and I worked for 15 of them—the toll it

(MICHAEL H. DANN)

took upon them was tremendous. It made the old movie moguls look absolutely amateurish. But always part of it came—I see now that I've left it—because you really weren't getting any satisfaction. A farmer can come in from the field perspiring and exhausted; he looks out the window and the wheat's pretty high; he feels very good. I've always felt that those of us in commercial broadcasting, after working so hard, were always a little bit leary about turning on the set.

Interview, New York/ The Christian Science Monitor, 6-23:15.

Olivia de Havilland
Actress

The TV business is soul-crushing, talent-destroying and human-being destroying. Those (TV) men in their black towers don't know what they are doing. It's (TV) slave labor and there's no elegance left in anybody. They have no taste.

San Francisco Examiner, 4-20:40.

Dino De Laurentiis
Motion picture producer

Our (Italian) films can make a handsome profit in Italy alone. Why? Because we have not been stupid, as the American producers have. Over here (in Italy) we allow movies to be shown on television only on Monday, Tuesday and Wednesday nights. The rest of television is so bad that people want to go out of their homes for entertainment. But in America people can get good entertainment at home. Once, when I was in New York, I counted 110 important movies on TV during a single week.

Los Angeles Herald-Examiner, 5-28:(E)4.

James E. Duffy
President, American Broadcasting Company Television

The broadcast medium—radio and television—has allowed itself to become a pawn that has been pushed around all too freely by powerful pressures . . . Pressures on broadcasters with regard to program content and editorial judgment are familiar ones. But the pressures that threaten license renewals . . . or what can or cannot be advertised over the airwaves . . . strike at the foundations of our industry, seriously threatening its stability . . . Our American system of broadcasting remains, despite its critics, the most varied, balanced, representative and responsive in the world. Let us begin to be more vigilant—and more militant—in our defense of it.

Before Rocky Mountain Broadcasters Association, Sun Valley, Idaho/ Variety, 8-16:36.

Edith Efron
Television journalist

(Arguing against government regulation of what is broadcast on U.S. television): (What is needed is) a free-enterprise pay system, in which each producer of intellectual and artistic commodities is absolutely sheltered by the First Amendment freedom of speech and press guarantees; in which each individual consumer purchases only the products which please him and leaves alone those with tastes and views alien to his. All this country has gotten from government intervention into this realm is the stupidest, most restricted and most venal medium of communications in the world.

Before Senate Constitutional Rights Subcommittee, Washington/ Los Angeles Times, 2-4:(4)16.

Norman Felton
Producer

Television does not reflect truth. On the *Dr. Kildare* series, we were asked by NBC to get the approval and seal of the AMA. This meant that we submitted scripts for approval to the AMA. Although the organization gave us technical help, it goes without saying that we did not present an accurate picture of the practice of medicine, or the difficulties many people had in obtaining adequate medical care . . . The network's censorship extended from preventing us from tackling whole subjects to a myriad of smaller items, such as making us take out any reference to "breast" or use of the word in a film concerned with mastectomy. Control of ideas exists down to the present in series such as *Marcus Welby, M.D.* and *Medical Center.*

The New York Times, 3-12:(2)1.

Fred W. Friendly
Professor of Journalism, Columbia University; Former president, Columbia Broadcasting System News

(Any newspaper) will get more of an audience out of its comic strips or its amusement section or its sports than it will out of news in depth. But even the worst newspapers don't end up running nothing but comic strips. Commercial television has become not just a mass medium but the massest medium. It wants to have the largest possible audience all the time. Think of that: *the largest audience all the time* . . . Commercial broadcasters—and I hear more and more of them talking this way—have made TV so into a projection booth, a grind house in a movie theatre, running old movies, entertainment, going after the largest possible audience, that there's no room for anything else.

Interview, New York/
The Christian Science Monitor, 6-9:15.

David Frost
Television interviewer

If you go to a movie, you know exactly what you're going to see. You know who's in it and what it's about and you're going specifically to see that picture. TV can afford to be more unpredictable, and it should be. I like the fact that people can switch on my show and not know if they're going to see Richard and Elizabeth (Burton) or Spiro Agnew. Or suddenly I'll have a whole audience of 8-year-olds; or a whole program on the Tony Award winners.

Interview, Los Angeles/
Los Angeles Times, 4-15:(2)8.

John Furia, Jr.
Television writer

We (writers) are constantly pre-censored, because we know that if we were to attempt to write stories involving any side of a controversial issue, the thing would not be acceptable (to the networks). None of the lead characters has any flaws, and that's an aspect of reality I certainly think needs redressing.

Panel discussion, Los Angeles/
San Francisco Examiner & Chronicle, 4-16:(Sunday Scene)14.

Julian Goodman
President,
National Broadcasting Company

. . . we must be freer than we have been from the restrictions and shackles of those who want to reshape broadcasting by government action, to serve their own theories and concepts. The public is our real ally, and we can gain its support by broadcast leadership that does not quake at a threat from those in power. We must fight for freedom from government bondage created by those who seek to impose their own social philosophies on the vast and growing audience that has a legitimate, long-term interest in a free system of broadcasting.

Before International Radio and Television Society, New York, March 9/
Variety, 3-15:56.

Billy Graham
Evangelist

I will tell you with the utmost sincerity that I believe your industry (broadcasting), for the most part, can be peopled with men and women of integrity, character and conscience. I say this despite the brickbat which broadcasting draws from some self-styled critics who chastise it for falling short of perfection. We're living in an imperfect world, and American radio and television have performed with great honor and credibility.

Before National Association of Broadcasters, Chicago, April 11/
The Hollywood Reporter, 4-12:9.

William G. Harley
President,
National Association
of Educational Broadcasters

One problem in national programming (in public broadcasting) is never going to get easier—that is public affairs. It will be better done, it will be more professional. But the central problem will remain: Broadcasting that deals with controversial issues—no matter how skillfully and responsibly handled—will always provoke controversy . . . It will never be easy; but then again, it will be worth it if public broadcasting can become a major means for the people's participation in the conduct of their affairs.

Variety, 4-12:31.

George A. Heinemann
Vice president in charge of children's programs, National Broadcasting Company Television

. . . we're in the entertainment business; we're not here to teach children that two and two are four. Too many people think of television as a social implement; but we never designed it as a social implement. We designed it for entertainment. Yet people keep telling us: You have to carry my message, you have to carry my message.

Interview, New York/
Los Angeles Times, 5-31:(4)1.

Ben Hooks
Commissioner-designate,
Federal Communications Commission
of the United States

(On his being the first black to serve on the FCC): I keep in mind that the communications media . . . are for all people, not just blacks. But in many large cities, blacks make up about 50 per cent of the population, and they deserve their share of media exposure and local programming. I don't want to have any official influence on television programming at this time. But my job gives me a platform. I do not intend at this stage to blackmail, bribe or threaten. Educate is the word. But if that fails, then I will use any means necessary at my disposal to make sure they (communications media) serve the interests of all the public.

Interview, Memphis/
Los Angeles Times, 7-2:(A)3.

Norman Jewison
Motion picture director

Why did all of us leave (television)—me, Arthur Miller, Arthur Penn, John Frankenheimer, Franklin Schaffner, Stirling Silliphant, Paddy Chayefsky? We left because television in America sold out to the advertising industry; because the selling of cars or underarm deodorant became more important than the program.

Interview/
Los Angeles Times, 1-9:(Calendar)11.

Lyndon B. Johnson
Former President of the United States

We are standing on the edge of a communications explosion, a revolution. Technology already in hand makes it possible for a home television set to double as a newspaper, providing not only news but printouts of stocks and sports results—and even comics. Home video tapes may soon give viewers a choice of thousands of movie titles at any time of the day or night. Home television may also give the housewife the capability of doing all of her shopping without ever leaving home—and checking with the bank to make sure she hasn't overdrawn in the process.

At dedication of new studios of KPRC-TV,
Houston/Variety, 3-29:2.

Nicholas Johnson
Commissioner,
Federal Communications Commission
of the United States

Cable television could prove to be a technology that revolutionizes our whole communications system. It is not simply a giant antenna that will provide subscribers with television stations from out of town. It is a technology which can provide unlimited access to television by providing anywhere from 20 to 100 or more channels . . . Garden clubs could put on programs for their members; there would be programs for older people, students, farmers and housewives; not the plastic kinds of programs we now have, but programs that capture our interest and imagination because they serve real needs.

At University of Iowa/
The Hollywood Reporter, 2-25:1,6.

To the extent it fails to contribute to the debate or provide information (of use to consumers), television has failed us. To the extent it provides harmful information, television is killing us . . . For a medium that is so powerful, to abuse its power is sad. For a medium that is statutorily required to operate in the public interest, it is close to criminal. Television affects you, as consumers, because it is the foremost enemy of intelligent consumerism.

Before New York Consumer Assembly,
March 4/The New York Times, 3-5:(1)58.

(Referring to violence on television) (Broadcasters have) molested the minds of our nation's children to serve the cause of corporate profit. (TV) executives, whom one would assume to be rich beyond their wildest dreams of avarice, each year seek even more in salaries, expense accounts and stock options. They found they could become richer still if they would only take a whole nation of children and train them to be more violent. Accordingly, they set about doing it.

Before Senate Subcommittee
on Communications, Washington,
March 22/The Hollywood Reporter, 3-23:1.

When you realize that television has such an enormous impact upon our behavior patterns and that it is the advertising industry, in conjunction with its corporate clients, which has been given unchecked power to dictate what an entire nation will be permitted to watch on the tube, you have begun to comprehend the problem of broadcasting in our society.

At National Council of Churches of Christ
hearings on drug advertising, Washington/
The New York Times, 12-10:(3)15.

Jerzy Kosinski
Author

In the little world of television, all is solved within its magic 30 minutes. In spite of the commercials, the wounded hero either rises or quickly dies, lovers marry or divorce . . . villains kill or are killed, addicts cured, justice usually wins, and war ends. All problems are solved again this week, as they were last and will be next week. Life on TV must be visual. This means single-faceted, revealed in a simple speech and through the obvious gesture. No matter how deep the mystery, the TV camera penetrates it. Parents leave their children in front of the TV as babysitter, because many feel that it is infinitely safer to watch the Sesame world of television than to walk in the world outside their home. But is it? Unlike television, the child grows older. One day it walks out of the TV room. Against his expectations, he's finally put in a classroom full of other children. A child who has been trained to control the little world, by changing the channels when he didn't like it, and was accustomed to maintaining the same distance between himself and the world televised for his amusement, is naturally threatened by the presence of people he cannot control. Others push him around, make faces at him, encroach. There is nothing he can do to stop them. He begins to feel that this real world unjustly limits him; it offers no channels to turn to.

Television broadcast/"Comment!"
National Broadcasting Company, 9-3.

Norman Lear
Writer, Producer

Somewhere, some time ago, someone coined the fiction that the mentality of the American motion picture patron averages between 12 and 13 years of age. This fiction has been accepted as truth and this "truth"

(NORMAN LEAR)

extended to the American public as a whole —it dictates what Americans will wear and drive and listen to, etc., etc. . . . It is time, I feel, to take a new direction in television. There is nothing to lose and everything to gain. The American public is the final arbiter anyway, and it tells us very quickly what it likes and does not like. What it will be allowed to see, however, is another matter, and there the writer deserves the right to express life as he sees it.

Before Senate Constitutional Rights Subcommittee, Washington, Feb. 8/ The Hollywood Reporter, 2-9:6.

Sam Levenson
Writer, Humorist

People have no patience with humor (any more). You get a man on TV who's telling a joke, and if he's not getting a laugh before 10 seconds, people think it's deadly. Will Rogers in his day could stand and think that long, without saying a word. Today a performer has to get a yak every four seconds to be in tempo. This is not really a humorists' era. It's a gag-writers' era. It's flash humor—instant laughs.

Interview, New York/ San Francisco Examiner, 10-14:9.

Jerry Lewis
Motion picture actor-director

Television has been one of the most destructive forces in our society. Ask me about violence, and I'll tell you television has caused it . . . And television has made everything *commonplace.* When Cary Grant used to walk down a street in New York, the city was on fire with excitement. Nowadays, it wouldn't mean a thing. You've got to have dreams. Television destroys dreams; it makes everything real.

Interview, Reno, Nev./ The New York Times, 7-30:(2)18.

Marshall McLuhan
Professor of English, University of Toronto

TV is a psychedelic trip. It goes right through the viewer—like an X-ray. It's not like a movie projected on a screen; it's not. It projects its pictures inside you; the rays are sent not on the screen but to you. And so, the TV viewer, unconsciously, is on a psychedelic trip. That's why television is addictive and acts like a tranquilizer. I am a firm believer that television contributed to the drug problem, because in itself television is a form of drug addiction. The kids get addicted to it very early, and so they are more given to other forms of addiction. TV is the modern Pied Piper. He took the kids away. That's television.

Interview, Toronto/ San Francisco Examiner & Chronicle, 8-20:(This World)34.

Margaret Mead
Anthropologist

Television brings life into a dead room, like light, fire and water. A TV set is like an open window on a village street. A great many people leave the television set on with the sound off, and for them, I suppose, it's like having a window on the world. And what would these same people see if they looked out their real window? Nothing but an endless procession of automobiles.

Interview, New York/ Publishers' Weekly, 12-11:10.

John M. Murphy
United States Representative, D–N.Y.

(Advocating increased Federal regulation of TV-radio networks): The portrayal of violence (on television) is one of the easiest ways to attract an audience—and most important of all, it sells soap. And as long as we in Congress give them the option of "doing better," or making money, I am afraid they will choose the latter course.

Washington, June 8/ San Francisco Examiner, 6-8:7.

Richard M. Powell
Television writer

We're feeding pap and mythology to the public, and we have become their entire culture. They watch television. They don't read books; they don't read magazines as a whole; they don't read newspapers. They watch television. And what they think of life is a reflection of what they see on television—and it's a lie . . . This is the sin of television; and the sin can be laid directly at the doors of the networks.

Panel discussion, Los Angeles/
San Francisco Examiner & Chronicle,
4-16:(Sunday Scene)14.

Robert L. Radnitz
Motion picture producer-director

Television is now where movies were 10 years ago. All they know is "don't" and "can't" and "won't." Negatives. I heard network executives give me exactly the same arguments major studio executives were giving me 10 years ago. It was like the playback of a tape.

Interview, Los Angeles/
San Francisco Examiner & Chronicle,
4-16:(Datebook)18.

Elton H. Rule
President,
American Broadcasting Companies

(Arguing for easier TV-radio license-renewal requirements): We believe that a broadcaster who has demonstrated good faith through actions and accomplishments deserves to know that he has earned the right to stay in business. The standard of performance should be performance itself, and performance should guarantee continuation.

Before California Broadcasters Association,
Palm Springs, Jan. 27/
Los Angeles Times, 1-28:(4)15.

Thomas W. Sarnoff
Executive vice president,
National Broadcasting Company

I believe CATV should have a chance to succeed or fail in the marketplace. It could be an important supplementary service in television, and we're not going to declare war on them. We're in favor of growth, but not in favor of taking it away from free television. Cable will not hamper commercial television because it is not geared as the national medium that some cable people like to believe. It will be more useful in the local, more specialized types of services.

Interview, Beverly Hills, Calif.,
Feb. 26/The Hollywood Reporter, 2-28:9.

Rod Serling
Writer

. . . much too rarely on the (TV) screen comes something sensitive, meaningful, probing, adult and carefully and selectively wrought . . . Shows that leave a residual thought—a memory, if you will, of something that has touched or moved or made you think or made you smile or made you weep—but something that produces a memory of an event. But let it be notated that memories in television are collectors' items—*suis generis*—one of a kind. It is a dismal fact that almost everything that passes through the tube is monumentally forgettable . . . If I were mystically and omnisciently put into the position of a network executive and given the impossible job of balancing programming, quite obviously all of television cannot be *Hallmark (Hall of Fame).* Also, quite obviously, there has to be the situation comedy, the private eye, the frontier sheriff, the variety show. There is an audience for all of this and a sizable one. But the word here is "balance." There should be at least one *Hallmark* for every five Roy Rogers. And if this were the case, this mass medium would be much better by even this limited ratio.

Before Chicago Advertising Club
and Chicago Broadcast Ad Club/
Variety, 11-22:53.

Barry Shear
Producer, Director

TV is an experimental ground to try out ideas that maybe someday you can use in a

(BARRY SHEAR)

feature (film). If you experiment in a $2,000,000 feature and it bombs, you're in trouble. If you do it in a half-hour on TV, it's not as big a loss. There's no difference in shooting for TV or movies except limitations on time and money. TV is the training camp.

Daily Variety, 9-5:3.

Phil Silvers
Actor

I'm against the talk show on television . . . I'm old fashioned, I guess, but I believe a wall should be preserved between an actor and his audience.

Quote, 7-16:50.

Clare Simpson
Vice president of daytime television programming, National Broadcasting Company

Character is the key in daytime drama. At night you can dazzle the viewers with plot. In daytime serials, you can't have a lot of plot, but you must have three story-lines going at one time—one that is peaking, one that is rising and one that is just emerging.

San Francisco Examiner, 4-3:21.

Jesse L. Steinfeld
Surgeon General of the United States

(On a report by the Scientific Advisory Committee on Television and Social Behavior): Certainly my interpretation is that there is a causative relationship between televised violence and subsequent anti-social behavior, and that the evidence is strong enough that it requires some action on the part of responsible authorities—the TV industry, the government, the citizens . . . I think there is a place for violence when it is appropriate. But I think it would be a very bland world and unreal if we banned violence from the TV screens and had our children really living in what would be a never-never land, at least when they watched television. So I wouldn't propose that . . . I think whatever is done should be done in a cooperative way with (the TV) industry working with the government, voluntary groups and citizen groups. I would hope that this is the way. But it does seem to me that so far we have not been successful—that is, the industry has not really reduced the level of violence on television and the industry has not come up with a large number of programs designed to induce pro-social behavior in children.

Before Senate Subcommittee on Communications, Washington, March 21/ U.S. News & World Report, 4-17:92,95.

Leslie Stevens
Producer

(Criticizing TV programming): It doesn't matter what mask the hero wears—whether he's Matt Dillon or Perry Mason or Marcus Welby. It's the same shootout on a dusty Western street or in a courtroom or in a lab or operating room with the doctor shooting it out with the germs. There are other solutions to life than shootouts, but you'll never see them in prime time.

Interview, Los Angeles/ Los Angeles Times, 11-27:(4)22.

Samuel S. Stratton
United States Representative, D–N.Y.

If private operation of the television industry is to continue, it must be exercised at every level—owners, advertisers, programmers and directors—constructively and with restraint. Most of all, there must be recognition on the part of all concerned that, just like public service, there is a duty not merely to respond, to please or to amuse, but also to educate and to lead.

Before National Association of Television Program Executives/ Human Events, 4-1:13.

John Wayne
Actor

Television is like a bad cold you can't throw off, like an addiction. Once you start looking, you can't stop. Many a time, Pilar (his wife) and I swear we aren't going to watch the tube; we're going to really get to sleep early. And I say let's watch the 10 o'clock news and, hell, we don't turn it off; and next thing you know, a white screen is staring at us and we've been watching for five hours. TV's like eating peanuts; you can't eat just one. I don't know if I love it or hate it—but there sure has never been any form of entertainment so . . . so . . . available to the human race with so little effort since they invented marital sex. The worst part of it has been, I think, the adverse effect on family life. It kills off family conversation. And it's hard to get your children to read books. I became a confirmed reader when I was growing up in Glendale. I've loved reading all my life. Now I've got this daughter, Aissa, a very bright young lady—but it's a hard job to get her to read. Television's just too easy.

TV Guide, 11-4:30.

Sylvester L. (Pat) Weaver
Former president,
National Broadcasting Company Television

There's something . . . that bothers me: the death of *live* television. Except in actual events, it's disappeared. They've squeezed the juice out of the medium . . . everything is canned . . . immediacy has disappeared. That's terrible. Excitement, immediacy and the feeling of NOW was important.

Interview/TV Guide, 4-29:7.

Clay T. Whitehead
Director,
White House Office
of Telecommunications Policy, Washington

The FCC is a quasi-judicial regulatory agency, responsible to the Congress, not to the President. It tends to make policy the way the courts make policy—by retrospective case history rather than conscious future planning.

Los Angeles Times, 1-2:(F)1.

Personal Profiles

Lauren Bacall
Actress

Men have preconceived ideas about me. They take one look at me and think I can take care of myself. Nobody bothers to wonder whether I've got the same frailties as other women. Well, I have. I'm not a wildly-secure female. Every time I walk into a room I pray to God somebody will talk to me, that I won't be left on my own. What I need is somebody to take care of me. But where to find him? Where?

Interview, Chicago/ San Francisco Examiner, 3-6:26.

Russell Baker
Newspaper columnist

I'm basically a guy with a yearning for the past, a time when things were better . . . It's probably a sign of the hardening of the arteries, this yearning for boyhood—the kind of thing I dislike when I hear it from other people.

Interview/Publishers' Weekly, 1-24:29.

George Balanchine
Director, New York City Ballet

I don't have vacations; I don't need them. For me, a vacation is to get up at 7 in the morning instead of at 6. *That* would be a vacation . . . for me, it's better to work in the morning. If you're a writer, yes, then maybe night is good—you sit down, have a drink and write; the brain can work then. I have no brain. I have a body, and the body works in the morning.

Interview, Washington/ The Washington Post, 8-30:(E)3.

Brigitte Bardot
Actress

In my way of living, I've always been extremely honest; I've always believed blindly in people I've met. In a certain way, I am the one who is forever being seduced because I trust others.

San Francisco Examiner & Chronicle, 1-9:(This World)2.

Time will destroy me one day, as it destroys everything. But no one else will ever be Bardot. I am the only Bardot, and my species is unique.

Interview/Time, 11-20:50.

Rudolf Bing
General manager, Metropolitan Opera, New York

I'm mild and mellow and old—none of which applies to prima donnas, certainly not the ones I've known.

The New York Times, 4-23:(1)65.

Raymond Burr
Actor

. . . I hate sitting down. I'm not a good sitter. I've got two positions: vertical and horizontal. Anything in between is too darned uncomfortable. To be honest, I really like lying down on the floor.

Interview, London/ San Francisco Examiner & Chronicle, 4-16:(Datebook)13.

Art Carney
Actor

I don't know if I'm more serious than other people. I'm not ON all the time, you know, as far as being funny at home or at parties. I tend to be more of an introvert, I think, and I think my extrovert qualities come out in my work . . . when I go home (after doing a play) I'm a doll. I get everything out on stage; I don't need to go to a doctor. Yeah, I'm a serious guy, I guess.

Interview, New York/
Los Angeles Times, 10-15:(Calendar)32.

Oleg Cassini
Fashion designer

I think I'm physically attractive—due in part to genes, in some part to will. I have a true power to communicate at certain levels with people. I'm an original thinker. I'm very learned—more than I appear to be. I am courageous and honest. I have some bad points, too. At times I'm vain and impudent . . . I'm unable to bend, and I can be belligerent. I am a vital person who can create jealousy. There are three kinds of wealth—monetary, physical and social wealth. I have the kind of wealth that many other people don't have—I am pleasing to the opposite sex. I have an affinity to the world of women. That makes me a dangerous element in the world of men.

Interview, New York/
"W": a Fairchild publication, 7-28:5.

Perry Como
Singer

I'm supposed to be the most relaxed guy in the world. Don't you believe it! I'm not now; I never was. When I had my television show, I used to work seven days a week to make the show as good as possible. I felt I owed it to myself and the audience. I never relaxed. That was just part of the act.

Interview, Palm Beach, Fla./
Family Weekly, 7-2:10.

Colin Davis
Musical director,
Royal Opera, London

I'm not the maestro type, throwing scores at people or eating the telephone. I'm a perfectly ordinary bloke who happens to be musical director of the Royal Opera. Of course, I have to play the role of the chap who is never flustered, always self-confident. But when I wake up in the night, I find there are pieces of my fingers all over the pillow.

Time, 1-3:55.

Doris Day
Actress

Whatever I am is what I came in with. I've had no acting or singing lessons, no training. What you see on the screen is me. I'm not a business. I don't want to sit around and be a big movie star and eat chocolates while 14 servants clean the house. I don't know where the Goody Two Shoes image got started. I'm the image created by my parents, and whatever people think is their problem. So I like ice cream better than scotch; sue me . . . and if people think I'm square, then terrific! I do like old-fashioned values in a world that looks pretty much to me as though it's falling apart . . .

Interview, Los Angeles/
The Washington Post, 1-16:(H)2.

John D. Ehrlichman
Assistant to the President
of the United States for Domestic
Affairs

I think most of the President's (Nixon) biographers have made something of his poker-playing abilities . . . and I think they are well advised to do it. A poker player obviously doesn't telegraph what he is going to do in advance, and he has to be cool. He can't have emotional ups and downs. I think the President was as good a poker player as he was because of his emotional makeup. He is not an individual who reacts emotionally to what somebody else does. He is coolest when he is under fire; and I think, using the poker analogy from my own observation, he is a man who very seldom is called when he doesn't have the cards in his hand. He doesn't run a bluff.

TV-radio interview, Washington/
"Meet the Press,"
National Broadcasting Company, 5-7.

Arthur Fiedler
Conductor, Boston Pops Orchestra

Something is driving me, but I don't know what it is. I have that kind of nature. I just can't sit and twiddle my thumbs. I don't enjoy vacations because I don't know what to do with myself. I don't want to lie on the beach and get sunburned; I've tried that. If I hear a band concert or a fire engine, I go. I don't like to unwind too much either because it's hard for me to get back into the run again. I don't know what I would do if I retired. I'd probably just be hanging around waiting to go to the dentist or the doctor or the undertaker. I might for a while enjoy a *dolce far niente*, taking it easy; I'd like to test it out sometimes. Yet I'm scared to do it.

Interview, Syracuse, N.Y./
The New York Times, 4-2:(2)13.

Geraldine Fitzgerald
Actress

It's great to experiment and to take risks, even to fail. I've had a great deal of failure. I've learned it doesn't kill you. I've learned from failure, a great deal; and one thing I've learned is not to fear it, at least not unduly. I've had a lot of good days, and a lot of bad . . . I love to wake up in the morning looking forward to doing and experimenting and risking. I'm delighted with it all. And I'm going to do as many things as I can and risk it all as often as I can.

Interview, Washington/
The Washington Post, 1-7:(B)8.

Rudolf Friml
Composer

I'm a lucky guy. I'm always in contact with God. Everything comes easy. Beautiful melodies, ideas and great peace of mind are mine.

Interview, Los Angeles/
San Francisco Examiner & Chronicle, 7-9:(Datebook)4.

R. Buckminster Fuller
Engineer, Author, Designer

If there's anything important about me . . . it is that I am quite an average individual. In fact, I am not too convinced even of that. I may be a little below average.

The Christian Science Monitor, 3-22:9.

Ruth Gordon
Actress

I think I'm a most unusual and talented person. As you can see, I gave up modesty a long time ago; it's as outmoded as good taste.

Interview, San Francisco, Jan. 3/
San Francisco Examiner, 1-4:26.

Robert Goulet
Singer

If I had my life to live over again, I would probably study, read feverishly, develop a vocabulary and become a writer. It's the only thing in the world to do, the only thing that lasts—the written word. My performances will be forgotten soon after I'm dead.

Interview, New York/
Family Weekly, 2-27:12.

Buddy Hackett
Comedian

I really like being alone. I love the public collectively but not individually. If I had a chance to do it over again, I'd find another way to make money without being famous. I don't like being famous. I wish I had a different face to wear after the show. I kinda like my face, but I wish it wouldn't be noticed so much.

Interview, Las Vegas, Nev./
Los Angeles Herald-Examiner, 6-4:(F)6.

Florence Henderson
Actress, Singer

That nice-girl image used to bother me, because I felt it would limit me. I worried that I would be type-cast in sweet ingenuish parts for the rest of my life. I don't think I'm all that nice or all that sweet. Ask my kids! . . . once in my life—just once—I'd love to play a bitch. I'd be a wonderful bitch.

Interview/
San Francisco Examiner & Chronicle, 3-26:(Datebook)8.

J. Edgar Hoover
Director,
Federal Bureau of Investigation of the United States

I have a philosophy: You are honored by your friends, and you are distinguished by your enemies. I have been very distinguished.

Before House Appropriations Committee, Washington, March 2/
The Dallas Times Herald, 4-30:(A)38.

Tom Jones
Singer

Every time I'm asked what the women go crazy over (about him), I don't know what to say. I don't know why they react that way. I think each one sees something different. Yes, I suppose it's sex appeal; but I can't explain it. You'd have to ask them. No, it hasn't made me conceited. I think that's something you are or you're not, whether or not you have a reason. Success has nothing to do with it. In fact, as I see it, the bigger people are, the nicer they are.

Interview/Family Weekly, 1-23:10.

Jean-Claude Killy
Skier

For years, I dreamed of being champion. When it happened, I thought everything would change. Nothing changed. I was the same as before. It is like catching a ghost; you put out your hand and there is nothing there. In the winter, I am a hero and they mob me on the streets. In the summer, when the snow is gone, everyone forgets about me. Soon it will be summer all year long, yes?

San Francisco Examiner & Chronicle, 1-9:(C)6.

Henry A. Kissinger
Assistant to the President of the United States for National Security Affairs

You know, with my recent reputation of being a swinger, I'll bet all those women who went out with me before are still wondering what they missed.

At 20th anniversary party for NBC-TV's "Today Show," Washington, Jan. 27/
The Washington Post, 1-29:(C)2.

. . . I've always acted alone. Americans admire that enormously. Americans admire the cowboy leading the caravan alone astride his horse, the cowboy entering a village or city alone on his horse—without even a pistol . . . Not necessarily brave, this cowboy doesn't need courage. It's enough that he is alone . . . This romantic, surprising character suits me, because being alone has always been part of my style or of my technique if you prefer. Independence, too . . . and finally, conviction . . .

Interview, Washington, Nov. 4/
The Christian Science Monitor, 12-29:9.

Stanley Kubrick
Motion picture director

Telling me to take a vacation from filmmaking is like telling a child to take a vacation from playing.

Interview/Newsweek, 1-3:30.

Janet Leigh
Actress

I'm not sure if I'm really naive in the true sense of the word. I know so much more about the world and the various sorts of people in it than I once did. For sure I'm no Pollyanna. But even now I go into relationships with people openly and trustingly. People have got to prove to me they're bad before I'll be angry with them. I've never said to myself, "Somebody's going to steal this scene away from me," or "What does this guy want from me?" I'm vulnerable, susceptible to pain. Because if there's one thing I know for sure, it's impossible to ever ex-

(JANET LEIGH)

perience the highs of life if you've never experienced the lows.

Interview, Beverly Hills, Calif./ Los Angeles Herald-Examiner, 6-25:(F)4.

Groucho Marx
Comedian

. . . the worst thing about being as old as I am is that I can never insult anyone. It's very frustrating, because everyone always thinks I'm kidding.

Interview, Beverly Hills, Calif./ Los Angeles Times, 2-13:(West)5.

George Meany
President, American Federation of Labor-Congress of Industrial Organizations

Every time I see my name in the papers, it's "George Meany, the 77-year-old president." I don't know why they insist on saying I'm only 77. I'm doing my damnest to get older.

The New York Times Magazine, 1-23:41.

Henry Miller
Author

The world in general is only captivated by those books in which I relate my sexual experiences. And that's one side of me. And then another person comes along and he says, "Haven't you always been interested in the Orient? Don't you talk of going to India and Tibet? . . ." There are many different points of view about me. Well, they're all equally true. But the physical side, the lecherous, so to speak—that's the one that they're all interested in.

Interview, Los Angeles/ Los Angeles Times, 1-23:(West)18.

Liza Minnelli
Actress

(People) expect temper tantrums from me and I am so disappointing, never having any, that I feel like making up some. I'm turning out to be the drag of the century.

Interview/ San Francisco Examiner, 2-29:35.

Robert Mitchum
Actor

I don't want to go on anything or get into anything. What I most want is to get out of things. People ask me what I do when I'm not working. The answer is: Nothing. I don't go to movies or plays or anywhere. I don't like to be entertained. I just want to do nothing. What's so bad about that?

Interview, San Francisco, June 29/ San Francisco Examiner, 6-30:28.

Richard M. Nixon
President of the United States

My strong point is not rhetoric; it isn't showmanship; it isn't big promises—those things that create the glamour and the excitement that people call charisma and warmth. My strong point, if I have a strong point, is performance. I always do more than I say. I always produce more than I promise.

Television interview, Washington/ Columbia Broadcasting System, 1-2.

Jacqueline Onassis
Former wife of the late President of the United States John F. Kennedy

. . . I have always tried to remain true to myself . . . I am today what I was yesterday and, with luck, what I will be tomorrow.

Interview, Teheran, Iran/ Los Angeles Times, 5-25:(1)2.

. . . I am a very shy person. People take my diffidence for arrogance and my withdrawal from publicity as a sign of my supposedly looking down on the rest of mankind.

Interview, Teheran, Iran/ Parade, 7-16:5.

Mary Pickford
Former actress

I have no regrets about quitting (films) when I did (in 1933). My heart was breaking when I walked off the set for the last time. But I wanted to quit when I still looked young and people still wanted to see me. I made up my mind to step into the wings while the audience was still applauding.

Telephone interview, Beverly Hills, Calif./ Los Angeles Herald-Examiner, 4-2:(F)6.

Vincent Price
Actor

I don't consider myself a villain. I'm a nice fellow, a good father, a wonderful husband, and I pick up litter.

Quote, 3-5:218.

Tony Randall
Actor

My perfect day might go something like this: Up early; take my singing lesson; work out at the gym; stroll down to 57th to see what's new at the galleries; stopping off for lunch at Grenouille—no, I don't care what I order as long as it's French. Go home; make love; and have an early supper—that's so we have plenty of time to get to the opera: Verdi's *Otello* would be nice, with McCracken and Milnes . . . To make it absolutely perfect, I'd be allowed to restage the third act.

Interview/TV Guide, 9-2:17.

Don Rickles
Comedian

Am I happy? Hell, yes, I'm happy. Because I got good friends. I don't have an entourage; I have people—family and friends who have been with me a long time . . . I do what I do and I'm successful at it so I can pay my bills and do what I want in life. But without friends, it wouldn't be worth anything. What the hell is there in life if you're alone?

Interview, Las Vegas, Nev./ Los Angeles Times, 6-18:(West)11.

David Rockefeller
Chairman, Chase Manhattan Bank, New York

If I come across a rare beetle on my world travels, I grab it. I have them all around the house among my art collection. My wife's a very-long-suffering woman because she doesn't like creepy-crawlies.

San Francisco Examiner, 4-6:30.

Artur Rubinstein
Pianist

I think my life has been extremely interesting. I think it's one of the most interesting lives I know.

Interview, London/ The Dallas Times Herald, 8-30:(G)7.

William Saroyan
Author

A few years back, I realized I was in the downward part of my path through life. I understood I'd stopped growing . . . and started to die. After I got over the initial shock of being subject to the same laws as everybody else, I learned to appreciate the changes that came over my life. Even the isolation was okay, because it put me in touch with issues I hadn't considered before. I used to look at the world with a decorative eye; but I've found that, as I grow older, I can afford a blunter stare at things. Now I live out of what you might call intelligence rather than sensibility. Intelligence makes for integration and I need that now. You could say I'm the same as always but different.

Interview, Fresno, Calif./ The New York Times Book Review, 4-2:3.

Fulton J. Sheen
Former Roman Catholic Bishop of Rochester, N.Y.

I pray that I will drop dead before I am 80. I don't want to live to 100. Beyond 80, I will not be working at full capacity . . . Suicide is taking your own life; I am asking the good Lord to do it.

Houston/The New York Times, 2-29:41.

Boris Spassky
World chess champion

Unlike (U.S. chess champion Bobby) Fischer, I did not set out to be world champion. I like to play chess for fun, not fame. My idea of a pleasant evening is to share some good food and wine with friends and play chess.

Interview, Moscow/ The Washington Post, 9-2:(A)5.

Leopold Stokowski
Orechestra conductor

For me there are two great things in life, and they are friendship and music.

Plainview (Tex.) Daily Herald, 5-9:6.

Barbra Streisand
Actress

. . . I'm a very dull person. Very simple. Very ordinary. I like to stay at home, keep to myself and my real friends. To me, the whole idea of being a "star" is a pain. For some people, it's fine. Sophia Loren is a star; being a star is her whole life. And that's fine, for her. Me, I run away from that sort of thing. I don't want it or need it. The only part of it that interests me is my work.

Interview, Los Angeles/ Los Angeles Times, 3-5:(Calendar)11.

Lowell Thomas
Explorer, Journalist

Looking back from 80 years, I'd say it was rather silly to try to do so many things—except it's been so much fun! Maybe the reason I've enjoyed it is it hasn't given me time to think. You're only unhappy when you have time to think. Mine has been a world of adventure, a world of work. It's been a night-and-day thing.

Interview, New York, April 6/ Los Angeles Times, 4-7:(1-A)2.

Arnold Toynbee
Historian

What keeps me going is curiosity. I am longing to discover things about the past as well as look into the future, and I care about what happens. That is what does it—curiosity and caring.

San Francisco Examiner, 3-27:38.

Lee Trevino
Golfer

I'm going to play as much as I can, as hard as I can, win all I can by the time I'm 40. Then I'm going to go home to El Paso and just sit and count my money. I'm going to have it stacked around the house in bales—not just bundles. And I'm just going to sit there and count it and grin. I ain't going to be out here trying to hack it around and beat the hungry kids. And I sure as hell ain't going to be a pro at some club somewhere and stand around sweating and saying, "Yes, Mr. Moneybags" and "No, Mrs. Fat Thing," and listen to them yell: "I don't like my starting time" or "What's wrong with this cart?" or "Boy, I need some help on my swing." Not for me. That's why I'm piling it up while I can. That's why I play so many tournaments.

Muirfield, Scotland/ Los Angeles Times, 7-12:(3)1.

Irving Wallace
Author

It's not important to me to be a celebrity or be recognized. I'm very gregarious and find it all very exhilarating, but it's not an ego trip. I will not become a character-performer . . . Well, some of it is very nice; it's very good to get the best seat on the plane. But I keep asking myself: do I behave differently? I have a feeling of my own worth. I never care to use my powers. I'm conscious of the role of other people in my relationships. How can you write novels about people if you don't stay in touch, if you don't know anything about the fellow who works in a shoe store or a garage. I make a great effort to be in touch. But I know at the same time that I am removed.

Interview, San Francisco/ San Francisco Examiner & Chronicle, 5-28:(This World)33.

Barbara Walters
Television commentator, "Today" Show, National Broadcasting Company

I'm not beautiful, slick, and I don't have all the answers. I don't think I've broken new paths. I'm not the girl next door; but the girl next door's not the girl next door any more, either. I don't have a movie star's life; I'm not that glamorous. My child lies on the floor and cries when I want her to be charming, and my husband comes home from work unshaven.

Interview, New York/ The Washington Post, 1-30:(E)1.

Raquel Welch
Actress

(What she likes): Hearing my two children laughing or reading to me; Japanese food and white wine; browsing in record shops; the sound of the water and the palm trees in a particular cove at Acapulco; the smell of kitchens and of freshly-baked pastry; playing I Ching, a Chinese philosophy game; sailing with my father; wearing skirts and dresses that make me feel sensual; plum, eggplant and burnt-rose colors; people who are not too set in their thinking; and good-looking, funny, sexy men who are intelligent but don't try to rap you over the head with what they know.

Interview, New York/ The Dallas Times Herald, 8-5:(A)7.

Franco Zeffirelli
Motion picture director

I love to do things around the house, like moving the furniture. That's when I get my best ideas.

San Francisco Examiner & Chronicle, 8-27:(Datebook)12.

Philosophy

Morris B. Abram
Former president, Brandies University

As a trial lawyer I have seen man at periods of crisis—as a plaintiff, defendant, witness—in cases involving high stakes in money, reputation, liberty and family relationships. My conclusion, after 25 years of law practice, is that most men are not as good as they pretend to be nor as bad as their enemies paint them. Nobility and depravity, courage and fear, truth and mendacity, love and hate, generosity and cupidity are often incorporated in a single person regardless of sex, race, creed or nationality. No man is always truthful, especially to himself; and no man lies all the time, even to himself.

At Emory University commencement/ The Wall Street Journal, 8-2:8.

Spiro T. Agnew
Vice President of the United States

The fundamental principles of morality have not changed through the centuries. Their unshakable logic provides the framework that separates man from animal—an awareness of a higher motivation than the drive of the loins on the stomach, a curb on envy, greed and hatred. I suggest that much of what is in the "new morality" is not morality at all, but just a cheap, easy rationale for doing whatever you damn well please, wherever and however you want to do it. It is an excuse for giving in to every temptation and for avoiding every duty and responsibility.

Accepting Father-of-the-Year award, New York, May 25/ Los Angeles Herald-Examiner, 5-25:(A)15.

John J. Akar
Former Ambassador to the United States from Sierra Leone

To suppress truth, and to search for truth, constitutes the fundamental difference between a dictatorship and a democracy.

At Boy Scout banquet, San Francisco/ San Francisco Examiner, 2-10:42.

W. H. Auden
Poet

It's very important to be one's age. You get ideas you have to turn down—"I'm sorry, no longer; I'm sorry, not yet." With age you feel more certain who you are . . . You know the kinds of things you're interested in, and what you want to do and what you don't want to do. I always knew what I had to do next.

Interview, New York/ The New York Times, 2-7:34.

Brigitte Bardot
Actress

What is happiness? I believe in moments of happiness. If happiness existed 24 hours a day, how could one recognize and appreciate it? I'm happy with little pockets of happiness here and there.

Interview/Quote, 12-24.

Stringfellow Barr
Historian

True dialogue requires me to listen harder and more imaginatively, to assume that what appears to be nonsense may be unfamiliar and fresh truth.

The Sacramento (Calif.) Bee, 12-23:(A)12.

Saul Bellow
Author

It is the deep conviction of vast numbers of individuals that they have no proper story. Their personal experience of storeylessness, and hence of valuelessness, is very great. Dramatic resolutions are lacking . . . flights, captivities, wilderness campaigns, the founding of colonies, explorations, the adventures which for centuries were made possible by an expanding world—all these are absent. Nevertheless, people still conceive of themselves as *actors* and as *characters.* They are prepared, but they are not called into action. They feel like unemployed extras; they stand ready and have nothing to do but bear passive, humiliating witness to the greater significance of the new man-made world.

Frank Nelson Doubleday lecture at National Museum of History and Technology, Washington/The Washington Post, 11-19:(B)1.

Lloyd M. Bentsen
United States Senator, D–Tex.

(On why he left a successful business life to come to the Senate): I think that people are a little bit like ivy—they ought to be repotted once in a while.

The Wall Street Journal, 2-14:10.

Robert L. Bernstein
President, Random House publishers; Chairman, Association of American Publishers

It is extraordinary that, at a time when we are concerned about ecology and nuclear explosions, we as a world have not fully realized that the hardest climate to keep pure is a climate where an idea can be born and grow.

Plainview (Tex.) Daily Herald, 6-18:(A)4.

Daniel Bovet
Nobel Prize-winning biochemist

The great catastrophe of our society is that it does not welcome a great number of temperaments. Whence the student unrest. My father used to say that people think more of their children's feet than of their brains since they pick their shoes according to the size of their feet but send them all to the same school.

Interview, Rome/The New York Times, 4-11:6.

Leonid I. Brezhnev
General Secretary, Communist Party of the Soviet Union

A person's behavior in everyday life is not only his personal concern. Free time is not a time free from responsibility to society.

Quote, 5-28:509.

William E. Brock III
United States Senator, R–Tenn.

History remains the touchstone for progress. It is the deterrent to past mistakes and the encouragement to forge ahead. If we are to succeed as individuals or as a nation, we must heed the lessons of prior experience and honor the sacrifices made for us by those who have gone before.

Quote, 4-30:417.

Niven Busch
Author

I don't know that (life) has to have a meaning. The mystique of life is like a beautiful woman. She doesn't have to carry a message to capture one's interest.

Interview, San Francisco/San Francisco Examiner & Chronicle, 7-16:(Sunday Scene)1.

Earl L. Butz
Secretary of Agriculture of the United States

We have just gone through a decade in which the youth of America have spoken out fiercely about the wrongs of society, the sores of society and the unfulfilled dreams of society. But they have been a little *too much* like the patriot Thomas Paine—who spoke out fiercely against tyranny—and *not enough* like Thomas Jefferson—who put forth his efforts in forging a new nation and mak-

(EARL L. BUTZ)

ing it work. It boils down to this: Progress comes only from work, not purity of heart or ballads or sit-ins. The great progress of society has not been won by breaking windows or stopping traffic or outshouting authority. Nothing will replace work and effort and discipline and sacrifice—the things from which progress is made.

At National 4-H Conference, Washington/ The National Observer, 5-13:17.

Johnny Cash
Singer

Years ago, I used to think success would be having all the money I needed for everything; but that's sure not it. I thought maybe success would be everyone knowing me; but that's not success, not now certainly. It might be in some people's eyes, but it's not in mine. Now I know success is being able to lie down and go to sleep at night without your conscience bothering you. Success is having a fine, close relationship with your wife, being happy at home, living in a good spiritual atmosphere. It's feeling good about yourself and feeling close to your God.

Interview, Nashville, Tenn./ San Francisco Examiner & Chronicle, 5-28:(Datebook)21.

Terence Cardinal Cooke
Roman Catholic Archbishop of New York

One of the dangers of a technological society is a tendency to adopt a limited view of man, to see man only for what he does or produces and to overlook the source of man's dignity, the fact that he is made in the image of God and that from the moment of conception he is worthy of the full support of the human family of which he is a member.

At National Conference of Catholic Bishops, Atlanta, April 13/Los Angeles Times, 4-14:(1)25.

Jacques-Yves Cousteau
Oceanographer

The fascinating thing on this planet is that, despite all the talk about over-specialization, to a person who's interested it's much easier to know everything going on in the world today than it was for Leonardo da Vinci. This is a time of super Leonardos.

Interview/ The New York Times Magazine, 9-10:89.

Will Durant
Author, Historian

In these modern times, too little stress is put upon character, too much on intellect. History warns of the danger of sharpening our wits while weakening our restraints. When I was a young man, I used to talk about the bondage of tradition. But now, as an older man, I distrust the fetishness of novelty. We exaggerate the value of newness in both ideas and things. It is much easier to be original than wise. We would do well to remember that the customs, traditions, conventions and creeds of mankind are the harvest of trial and error. History demonstrates that it is unlikely that any individual, even the cleverest, can come up within one lifetime to such a breadth of knowledge and understanding as to sit in sound judgment on ancient ways. Sophistication is disagreeably shallow, for it indicates cleverness about the part, but ignorance of the whole.

Interview, Los Angeles/ Modern Maturity, Aug.-Sept.:24.

After hunger, sex is the strongest instinct and the greatest problem. Nature is so infatuated with continuing the species that it dolls up women with beauty and gives men treasure for the chase. But sex becomes such a fire and a flame in the blood that it can burn up the whole personality, which should be a hierarchy of harmony and desires. Today's society has overstimulated the sexual impulse. Where our ancestors played down the sex instinct, knowing that it was strong enough without encouragement, we have blown it up with a thousand forms of incitation, advertisement and display. Then we have armed sex with the doctrine that inhibition is dangerous. History shows that inhibition—the control of impulse—is the first principle of civilization.

Interview, Los Angeles/ Modern Maturity, Aug.-Sept.:25.

Luis Echeverria (Alvarez)
President of Mexico

The negligence of the great powers with respect to the less powerful countries has brought about a new division of the world. We are witnessing class division in international society. The world power centers are making the major decisions of our time. The joint action of the countries of the so-called Third World has become necessary vis-a-vis the oligarchical trend that prevails internationally.

Before Organization of American States, Washington, June 16/ San Francisco Examiner & Chronicle, 6-25:(This World)8.

Elizabeth II
Queen of England

If I am asked today what I think about family life after 25 years of marriage, I can reply with equal simplicity and conviction. I am for it.

On her 25th wedding anniversary, London, Nov. 20/Newsweek, 12-4:55.

Luis A. Ferre
Governor of Puerto Rico

. . . the world you are entering upon graduation is a world which needs basic changes in its structures, viewpoints and goals. It has excellent tools to work with: creative capitalism, democracy, science and technology. It also has rich values: compassion, love and respect for human life and dignity. The latter must become the goals of the former if humanity is to survive. This is the challenge to the young people of today. They must probe new ways to obtain this purpose, amongst which is the turning of valueless utilitarian capitalism into value-rich altruistic capitalism. Capitalism should become a means and not an end. Its goal, within our free society, should be the efficient production of wealth to satisfy the material needs of man, distributed with a deep sense of social justice, in order to give life spiritual richness. The old dictum, the greatest good for the greatest number, should become the greatest good for everybody.

At graduation exercises, University of Pittsburgh Graduate School of Business, Aug. 4/Vital Speeches, 10-1:748.

Glenn Ford
Actor

Like a time-tested friend, a garden is as ready to rejoice with you as to comfort you . . . Its green welcome has never failed to lift my spirits and restore my peace.

Interview, Los Angeles/ The Christian Science Monitor, 2-15:17.

Henry Ford II
Chairman, Ford Motor Company

The old hard-nosed idea that there is only one game to play in world affairs—a dog-eat-dog struggle for dominion over people and geography and resources—is being pushed aside by deeper concerns. The overriding world problems today are survival problems: nuclear armaments, population explosion, food production and distribution, runaway urbanization, environmental pollution and ecological imbalance. In a world divided, hostile and fearful, failure to deal with these problems realistically could lead to a series of deepening crisis and bring all mankind to the brink of disaster. The realistic alternative to power conflicts is to work for a better-ordered world in which we can each trade peacefully with one another to the mutual benefit of all, without fear, without wars and with a growing sense of a common human destiny. I think there is at least a good chance that we can start moving in these directions, not because we are suddenly wiser, but because the extreme penalties for

(HENRY FORD II)

not doing so have to be obvious to everyone.

Before Montreal Chamber of Commerce, March 14/The Washington Post, 5-21:(B)6.

Indira Gandhi
Prime Minister of India

I do not believe in luck. Luck comes only to those who have the character to attract it and who have the character to hold it. It is not something that by chance flutters in through the window. You have to work jolly hard.

San Francisco Examiner & Chronicle, 1-9:(This World)2.

All the "isms" of the modern age—even those which in theory disown the private profit principle—assume that man's cardinal interest is acquisition. Yet we see that, however much man hankers after material goods, they can never give him full satisfaction. The feeling is growing that we should reorder our priorities and move away from the single-dimensional view of growth . . . which seems to have given a higher place to things rather than to persons, and which has increased our wants rather than our enjoyments.

At United Nations Conference on the Human Environment, Stockholm, June 14/ The Washington Post, 6-15:(A)22.

John Gielgud
Actor

I've always been lucky in my friends because I've been surrounded by rather critical people who've been inclined to make fun of me, a certain amount of which I think is awfully good for you. And I think the danger of being flattered, if you are lucky enough to be successful, is to have too many admiring friends, an entourage who are always at your beck and call.

Interview/ Los Angeles Times, 8-13:(Calendar)27.

Edmund A. Gullion
Dean,
Fletcher School of Law and Diplomacy,
Tufts University

You get kind of tired of being on one side of the generational war. I often think that, if the new generation has opportunities, it is precisely because *ours* . . . did its duty; and, for that reason, the world is much more secure . . . We were wrenched through the iron gates of life.

Los Angeles Times, 2-27:(G)6.

Haile Selassie
Emperor of Ethiopia

Throughout history, it has been the inaction of those who could have acted, the indifference of those who should have known better, the silence of the voice of justice when it mattered most, that has made it possible for evil to triumph.

At United Nations Security Council meeting, Addis Ababa, Ethiopia, Jan. 28/The New York Times, 1-29:3.

Fred L. Hartley
President, Union Oil Company

When I was raised, I never had a period in my life when I didn't know where my next meal was coming from. But I certainly remember plenty of times when I didn't know where my next suit was coming from. Don't theorize that everybody who's poverty-stricken and poor is in misery. Some of the happiest people I know are poor. But they're not poor by their definition; they're not poor by mine. Hell, they have more freedom than I have. I've got a lot of perfunctory things I have to do. I have to go out to three dinners a year and hand out 30-year watches. I actually enjoy doing it. It's a great opportunity for me to meet these people—even if it's just for the moment of shaking hands or looking at them; seeing the pleasure on their faces, (knowing) that I'm just a human being, they're just a human being, and there's no difference between us, not a damn bit. What you've got to realize is that the world's work has got to be done. Each of us, on all levels of society, has got to do our share of the dirty work. And the dirty work can take many forms. And that's the same with everything you do.

Interview, Los Angeles/ Los Angeles Times, 2-20:(West)30.

Carl F. H. Henry
Christian theologian;
Editor-at-large, "Christianity Today"

(Criticizing the New Left youth counter-culture): It is no service to man and society to extend even further the modern revolt against reason. We must not allow a new generation to smash the larger significance of truth as if, in the name of human values, one could lynch the laws of logic, corral the law of contradiction, commit to confinement the claims of coherence—for that is simply another road to cultural suicide and to the sure forfeiture of all the values one could hope to preserve.

At Loma Linda (Calif.) University, Jan. 9/Los Angeles Times, 1-15:(1)29.

Bruce Herschensohn
Former Director,
Motion Picture and Television Service,
United States Information Agency

The word "propaganda" is sometimes given an evil connotation. But the word is not evil, unless used for evil purposes. We believe almost everyone, everywhere is a propagandist. Every store owner or employee who speaks of his job with satisfaction is a propagandist. Everyone who shows slides of his last trip is a propagandist. Every blinking sign on a street, every newspaper headline, even television performers who sell their talents along with Coca-Cola, are propagandists.

Interview, Washington/ The Hollywood Reporter, 4-7:3.

Lewis B. Hershey
Former Director, Selective Service System
of the United States

I figure you can't be very smart if you're an optimist. If you're smart, you're an intellectual, so you can figure out that everything has gone to hell. And if you can figure that out, you can't be very optimistic.

Before Downtown Optimist Club, Indianapolis/The National Observer, 12-16:18.

Julius J. Hoffman
Judge, United States District Court
for the Northern District of Illinois

. . . I dislike very much being introduced as a person of unflinching integrity, as though a man is entitled to a (gold) star for not stealing. I don't think anyone should be given any credit for being honest.

Interview, Chicago/ The Washington Post, 5-28:(M)8.

If you don't have love in a household, it ain't no household. In a home it's the most important thing in the world; it really is. The more simple you are about defining love, the better off you are. People who have never been loved are pretty dull. I've had the same love for 44 years, come September. I think I have the affection of a lot of people; and by the same token it runs the other way.

"W": a Fairchild publication, 7-14:23.

Paul G. Hoffman
Administrator,
United Nations Development Program

All countries tend to make better use of their physical resources than of their human resources. It is hard to conceive of a nation neglecting its diamonds or overlooking its petroleum deposits. Yet human potentials of an immeasurably greater worth are wasted, and frequently for the most unreasonable of reasons.

Interview/Time, 1-17:31.

William Holden
Actor

When I was a little boy, I thought life was made up of two parts: youth and old age. As I got older, I added a middle part

(WILLIAM HOLDEN)

called work. Then I came around to thinking there were four divisions, because middle age was in there, too. And now, at 53—well, now I kind of hate to think about dividing it into any more pieces!

Interview, Los Angeles/ Family Weekly, 7-9:20.

Irving Howe
Author, Historian, Critic

The obligation to defend and extend freedom in its simplest and most fundamental aspects is the sacred task of the intellectual—the one task he must not compromise even when his posture seems intractable, or unreasonable, or hopeless, or even when it means standing alone against fashionable shiboleths like revolution and the Third World.

At University of Texas symposium, Austin/The New York Times, 4-10:11.

Burl Ives
Actor, Singer

When I was a young man, I pictured success as I saw it in magazines. I saw a red-brick house, a car, a dog and a lady. Well, I got the house, the car and the dog. And I got the lady. But it wasn't like the picture. Life is never like the picture. Man has a vivid imagination—his achievements can never match his dreams. And like everything else, the dream changes.

Interview/Family Weekly, 6-4:24.

Donald M. Kendall
Chairman, PepsiCo, Inc.

Roughly speaking, adulthood covers that span of years between Clearasil and Geritol.

At Western Kentucky University commencement/Quote, 8-6:123.

Graham Kerr
Television chef ("The Galloping Gourmet")

Sex and eating are closely connected impulses, and there is a strong link between sex and cooking. Good cooking is the pursuit, like good sex, of other people's pleasure.

San Francisco Examiner, 12-6:40.

Theodore W. Kheel
Lawyer; Labor mediator

(On the process of mediation): The most important thing is getting each side to see what the other side's problems are—to cut through and illuminate these problems. The thing I always tell people to remember is the famous quotation of the poet Robert Burns. He said, "See yourself as others see you." That's what I believe anyone in a dispute should do—see himself as the other person sees him. When you get someone to look at the situation from the opposing viewpoint, you help create the circumstances for finding a basis of agreement.

Family Weekly, 1-23:20.

Jean-Claude Killy
Skier

I've been asked the million-dollar question many times: How much money do I make? I'm like a friend of mine. He says all he knows is how much he spends, not how much he makes.

San Francisco Examiner, 1-21:56.

Hal P. Kirby
Director,
Dallas Museum of Natural History

There is nothing to indicate that man is the climax species of this world. Man has been here for only about 3 million years. The earth has been spinning for something like 6 billion years!

Before Dallas Natural Science Association, March 22/ The Dallas Times Herald, 3-23:(A)12.

Henry A. Kissinger
Assistant to the President of the United States for National Security Affairs

Throughout our history, we have believed that effort was its own reward. Partly because so much has been achieved here in America, we have tended to suppose that every problem must have a solution and that good intentions should somehow guarantee good results . . . Our generation is the first to have found that the road is endless, that in traveling it we will find not Utopia, but our own selves. The realization of our essential loneliness accounts for so much of the frustration and rage of our time.

Before Washington Press Club/ San Francisco Examiner, 1-31:30.

John H. Knowles
President, Rockefeller Foundation

The great disjunction of the times, as we press toward equalization of access to vital services for all, and do this largely through taxation, is how are we simultaneously going to keep the idea in individuals' heads that they, individually, are going to make a difference? This is the major issue as numbers expand and there is a press toward the beneficent state. So we have the grand conflict between freedom, individualism, self-determination versus liberalism or equality, social justice, the good of the whole. Both are virtuous; but a healthy balance between them has never been more difficult to define and maintain.

Interview/Time, 7-17:71.

Stanley Kubrick
Motion picture director

One of the most dangerous fallacies which has influenced a great deal of political and philosophical thinking is that man is essentially good, and that it is society which makes him bad. Rousseau transferred original sin from man to society, and this view has importantly contributed to what I believe has become a crucially incorrect premise on which to base moral and political philosophy.

Interview, Borehamwood, England The New York Times, 1-4:26.

Jerry Lewis
Actor, Comedian

(On his kind of humor): It's not a sophisticated humor. On the contrary, it's based on the ability to enjoy something in its simplest form. Americans are always wondering whether they should laugh if someone gets a pie in the face, if it will demean their character. Europeans don't think about things like that; they just laugh. In other words, I may not get the best table at the Pavillon, but I am the king of the automat.

News conference, Washington, Aug. 30/ The Washington Post, 8-31:(B)3.

Sol M. Linowitz
Lawyer; Former United States Ambassador to the Organization of American States

We have the know-how to do almost anything. The real question is do we have the know-what and know-why.

At University of Texas symposium, Austin/The New York Times, 4-10:11.

George Cabot Lodge
Professor, Harvard Business School

The right to property is not very important any more. What difference is there whether you and I own our houses or rent them? . . . If I don't own a stick of property, what difference does it make? The issue isn't Marxist. I am not questioning the right of people to own property. The question is: What is the use, the necessity, the importance of it? In 17th-century England, John Locke brought forth the idea that private property was the essential guarantor of individual rights. If you have your little piece of land, it gives you political and economic independence. That idea is gone. In today's urbanized, complex society, few people have a chance to own the kind of property that would guarantee them political independence and economic freedom. Owning a house, a car, a TV set, a share of General Motors stock no longer gives you the special rights or guarantees that Locke had in mind. The important thing now is the right to income, the right to health care and the like—the right to survival.

Interview, Cambridge, Mass./ Los Angeles Times, 12-15:(2)7.

William S. Lowe
President, Chamber of Commerce of the United States

To me, a successful man is one who takes those capabilities with which he is endowed at birth and those which he acquires during his lifetime and uses them the nearest to the maximum of his ability to benefit the social and economic structure in which he lives.

Interview, Mexico, Mo./ Nation's Business, May:49.

Myrna Loy
Actress

I don't know why everyone is so infatuated with the past. I'm not interested in "then"; I'm interested in "now," not in the '30s or the '40s. And now we're trying to bring back the '50s, the dreariest decade of them all. The past looks better once it's over, of course; but I think those of us who actually lived through those decades should try to remember what difficult times they often were. There must be something terribly wrong with today to make so many people yearn for the past. But the danger in escaping to the past is that we'll never move forward because we'll be too busy dwelling on the imagined glories of earlier decades.

Interview, Los Angeles/ Los Angeles Herald-Examiner, 8-13:(G)1.

Clare Boothe Luce
Former American diplomat and playwright

. . . it's going to be the whole institution of marriage that will change. It's going to be a contractual marriage. I can see in the future that there will be several contracts: the two-year contract, the four-year contract, the six-year contract. The terms of these contracts would be that, at the end of that time, if the couple wished to part, it would be with no yelling or screaming, no court action. If there were children, the contract would automatically be extended until the youngest was in school. Whichever party would be more able to care for the children would do so. There would be an actual financial contract; it would be renewable if they chose. I think a lot of marriages would hold together much longer; if each party saw the thing ending, he would either hasten to the end if he didn't want to renew it, or if he did want to renew it, he would make an extra effort to keep the thing together. Contracts could be worked out that would avoid all the phoniness, the falsehoods, the hypocrisy of the divorce mill.

Interview, Honolulu/ The Washington Post, 7-23:(E)6.

Louis B. Lundborg
Former chairman, Bank of America

To me, the essentials of leadership are: a clear sense of direction in knowing where you're going, and enough confidence in yourself so that others will feel your confidence. This is important because people tend to trust and follow people who know where they're going. Most leaders also are able to convey to their followers a feeling that they —the followers—can be a part of this movement. Being able to convince people of a sense of participation is one of the high arts of leadership.

Interview, San Francisco/ Nation's Business, June:50.

Archibald MacLeish
Poet, Playwright

The important thing is to live a life out to its conclusion since, although life seems to be going around like a merry-go-round, everything changes as you go around. The completely familiar world an old man finds himself looking at isn't really familiar at all. It has a different light from a different direction; there are different relations of light and dark.

Interview, Conway, Mass./ The New York Times, 5-7:(1)79.

Timothy Manning
Roman Catholic Archbishop of Los Angeles

Take all the crises of the day and they have their origin in family life—the breakup of homes, divorce, the questions of abortion and contraception, care of the aged. The basic virtues a youngster needs—respect for authority, docility, a cleanness of approach to life, even the concept of patriotism—stand or fall by the family relationship.

Interview/
The New York Times, 1-23:(1)49.

I think we all gravitate toward selfishness, all of us. And I think if you knew me inside, you probably would find it so, too. Because we all fundamentally love ourselves, our own ease, our own comfort. I'm no different. I recognize, inside, my being pulled two ways—pulled outward, as it were, by the demands of the situation; pulled inward by the desire for not having to face certain problems, do certain things when it might be far nicer to go off and play golf or something . . .

Interview, Los Angeles/
Los Angeles Times, 3-12:(West)12.

Robert S. McNamara
President,
International Bank for Reconstruction and Development

When the highly privileged are few and the desperately poor are many, and when the gap between them is worsening rather than improving, it is only a question of time before a decisive choice must be made between the political costs of reform and the political risks of rebellion.

The Sacramento (Calif.) Bee, 10-20:(A)22.

Margaret Mead
Anthropologist

In the end, it will be the family way of life that will persevere. The family changes, but it will never disappear. Every attempt to eliminate the family has failed.

Quote, 12-17:577.

Humberto Medeiros
Roman Catholic Archbishop of Boston

The distance between the rich and poor peoples of this world is already enormous and constantly growing greater. A small number of more-wealthy nations, chiefly those of us in the North Atlantic, continue to consume an increasingly disproportionate percentage of the entire world's goods. Our (the U.S.'s) advantages in trade and manufacturing are overwhelming, and our affluence as a rich country seems only to perpetuate the indigence of the poorer nations. Thus, although the human and material interdependence among all nations of the earth grows more evident every day, we find ourselves trapped in a hellish circle of conflicting self-interests that lead to economic injustice and oppression.

At National Mission Animation Conference, Washington/The National Observer, 12-9:10.

Arthur Miller
Playwright

. . . there is no religion that is closer to a man than the one he invents, so I guess you can say in that sense that I'm religious. That is, I think there is a destiny beyond the bread and butter, but it consists for me in creativity. I think there is a spirit that can be killed in a society and in an individual that, for want of a better word, is the life spirit, the creative spirit. This is holy, and it takes great effort, a kind of prayer, to keep it alive and to nurture it. Without it, we might as well not be around; life becomes simply a series of objects and chance relationships, and it gets pretty desiccated.

Interview, New York/
The New York Times, 8-29:22.

Henry Miller
Author

There never was a time when the condition of the world was ideal. We've never had an ideal society. It's always bad. But I think you have to learn to accept it as it is. There's no reason you can't suggest other kinds of worlds, other ways of living; you know, learn to be in it, but not of it. But don't wear yourself out fighting it—which I did in the beginning as a young man. I really thought I could do something to change the world. But I soon found out you

(HENRY MILLER)

don't change the world. You have to learn to live in it. No special group, no particular individual can change the world. I think the world is changed by the aggregate of people in it; by how they live individually. The great changes come by the things they don't do–by their inertia. It's that failure to live up to themselves that creates bad conditions. We always look for some Hitler, some target to blame. They are not the prime causes; the inert mind, the slothful, lazy mind is. There's the quick and the dead, and most of the world is dead.

Interview, Los Angeles/ Los Angeles Times, 1-23:(West)18.

When I die, if you were to say, "What is your last word?" I'd say "Mystery." Everything is more and more mysterious to me; not more and more familiar, but more and more mysterious. I think that scientists would say the same thing. The more and more they get into their particular realm, the more mystified they are. Knowledge is like cutting into a limitless cake–cut a chunk, it's bigger; cut another, the cake is still bigger. That's why knowledge is so relatively unimportant. No one has real knowledge. All you can have is wisdom–wisdom to live; but not knowledge about the universe.

Interview, Los Angeles/ Los Angeles Times, 1-23:(West)23.

Jeanne Moreau
Actress

I think the most important beauty care is for your inside–your mind. It wrinkles very quickly.

San Francisco Examiner, 2-9:36.

Jan Murray
Comedian

I've had a fair amount of success, if you judge success by popularity, money and what not. But when the wheels started turning, the most important thing was work. I don't care who you are–if you have all the money in the world, are mobbed at your car, are popular, given things for nothing–the thing that counts most is still work. Nothing can take its place; because if nobody asks you to sing your song or tell your joke or do your dance or act a role, you're nothing.

Interview, Las Vegas, Nev./ Los Angeles Herald-Examiner, 8-16:(A)16.

Richard M. Nixon
President of the United States

As we look ahead over the coming decades, vast new growth and change are not only certainties, they will be the dominant reality of this world . . . Surveying the certainty of rapid change, we can be like a fallen rider caught in the stirrups–or we can sit high in the saddle, the masters of change, directing it on a course we choose. The secret of mastering change in today's world is to reach back to old and proven principles, and to adapt them with imagination and intelligence to the new realities of a new age.

State of the Union address, Washington, Jan. 20/ The New York Times, 1-21:18.

Among nations–as within nations–the soundest unity is that which respects diversity, and the strongest cohesion is that which rejects coercion.

Before Canadian Parliament, Ottawa, April 14/ The New York Times, 4-15:1.

Jacqueline Onassis
Former wife of the late President of the United States John F. Kennedy

I've come to the conclusion that we must not expect too much from life. We must give to life at least as much as we get from it. At its best, life is not too secure and one must seize every moment as it comes. Every moment one lives is different from the other. The good, the bad, the hardships, the joys, the tragedies, loves and happiness are all interwoven into one indescribable whole that is called life. You cannot separate the good from the bad. And, perhaps, there is no need to do so.

Interview, Teheran, Iran/ Parade, 7-16:5.

John Osborne
Playwright

Life without pain is unsufferable. Life with pain is absolutely necessary. It gives a richer inner life. Without pain, life, instead, becomes trivial and constricted.

Interview, London/ The Washington Post, 5-21:(G)10.

Paul VI
Pope

Every man has his dignity, an inviolable dignity. Woe betide anyone who touches it! It matters not whether he is little or great, poor or rich, white or black. The littler, the poorer, the more suffering, the more defenseless, even the lower a man has fallen, the more he deserves to be assisted, raised up, cared for and honored.

Rome, Jan. 1/ The New York Times, 1-2:(1)12.

Youth today has a stronger tendency than the youth of yesterday to escape from the conventional ways of behavior. They believe themselves almost obliged to withdraw from obedience to the normal ways of family and social life. They prefer to assume an unrestricted and sometimes eccentric attitude, to yield to caprices of strange fashions and to passions that are amoral and antisocial, almost with pleasure in seeing themselves as contesters and subversives . . . They let all know that society as it results from modern evolution does not satisfy or please them.

Palm Sunday sermon before young people, Vatican City, March 26/ Los Angeles Times, 3-27:(1)14.

Ralph W. Phouts
Professor of Economics,
University of North Carolina,
Chapel Hill

Some people who argue that men were happier when they were poorer are arguing in a general sense. That is, they are contending that the bulk of mankind would be happier with a lower standard of living. They are contending that man is happier when he is forced to engage in unending toil merely to stay alive. He is happier if he has little time to enjoy his fellows, if he has no time to think about anything except food, clothing and shelter. The more his human qualities are suppressed by drudgery, the happier he is. His only contemplation should be whether the hard-won turnip crop will last through the winter. If this is the road to happiness then man's highest faculties and noblest emotions should be shunned and abandoned because they bring unhappiness. The human soul becomes God's grim joke.

Phi Beta Kappa Oration at Davidson (N.C.) College, April 27/ Vital Speeches, 11-15:84.

Lewis F. Powell, Jr.
Associate Justice,
Supreme Court of the United States

. . . I was taught and still believe that a sense of honor is necessary to personal self-respect; that duty—recognizing an individual subordination to community welfare—is as important as rights; that loyalty, which is based on the trustworthiness of honorable men, is still a virtue; and that work and self-discipline are as essential to individual happiness as they are to a viable society. Indeed, I still believe in patriotism, not if it is limited to parades and flag-waving, but because worthy national goals and aspirations can be realized only through love of country and a desire to be a responsible citizen.

At American Bar Association prayer breakfast, San Francisco, Aug. 13/U.S. News & World Report, 8-28:42.

It may be that, in our concern with the present and our serious social problems, we are losing a proper perspective of history. History enables one to understand the importance of evolution. It balances the frustration of "how far we have to go" with the satisfaction of "how far we have come." It

(LEWIS F. POWELL, JR.)

teaches us tolerance for the human shortcomings and imperfections which are not uniquely of our generation, but of all time. Indeed, it immortalizes all of us in the sense that we are not seen solely as the product of the present day, but as links in an ageless chain of human struggle and progress.

Quote, 10-8:344.

Simon Ramo
Executive vice president and vice chairman, TRW, Inc.

For some decades, we have had the technological ability to destroy society. Today, we do not have the ability to preclude such a possibility. This is our social immaturity. Of course, a characteristic of intelligent life throughout the universe may be that it reaches a point at which it has the ability to destroy itself and the inability to prevent it and thus destroys itself. Yet such an assumption doesn't help us. We must turn our attention to the possibility that we can mature socially and understand these things. We are socially mature enough to accept the fact that we must stop for traffic lights when we drive our cars. We must give up some of our freedom and restrict our behavior so that society can get along.

Interview, Los Angeles/
Los Angeles Times, 5-21:(West)23.

Ronald Reagan
Governor of California

I don't think it (age) is important. Samuel Colt invented the revolver when he was 20, and Verdi wrote *Falstaff* when he was 80. I'm somewhere in between. There are days when the Legislature is especially busy and I feel older than Verdi—and days when I feel like Colt.

News conference, Miami Beach/
Los Angeles Herald-Examiner, 8-23:(A)1.

James Reston
Vice president and columnist, "The New York Times"

My generation merely had to conquer adversity, while yours has to put up with prosperity—which is much harder.

Before graduating class, Stanford University, June 11/San Francisco Examiner, 6-12:3.

Charles F. Richter
Emeritus Professor of Seismology, California Institute of Technology

I've discovered that civilized man is still a very primitively emotional animal. Despite all the facts you may give people about building construction and cautious behavior during a (earth-) quake, they still react only to panic. I find people worry an awful lot about things of relatively little occurrence that they can't control, but think nothing of roaring onto the freeways carelessly every day where their statistical chances of injury are much higher. Given the choice, I'd worry about the freeway a lot more than an earthquake any day.

Interview/
Los Angeles Times, 2-13:(West)23.

Artur Rubinstein
Pianist

We are given a short, horrible life; no god, no religion ever told us what it is about. What we know is what our senses tell us—flowers, love, poetry, Mozart, Schubert. People think money, success, power are necessary. No! It's so absurdly stupid. I need only one flower in that corner there to be happy.

Interview, Buffalo, N.Y./
The New York Times, 1-28:24.

Donald Rumsfeld
Director, Federal Cost of Living Council; United States Ambassador-designate to the North Atlantic Treaty Organization

Throughout my life I've made some strange judgments, based on the idea that you can't lose if you do something that challenges you—no matter what the appearances. They've usually worked out.

San Francisco Examiner & Chronicle, 12-10:(This World)2.

George C. Scott
Actor

The older you get, the harder you get. People think you mellow when you get older, but I think there's an inclination to become more narrow, more protective. One of the sadnesses of middle age is that you're still feeling the tensions of both ends of the cycle. You don't want to let go, and of course you realize you must. You don't want to be satisfied with the rocking chair, yet you know it's inevitable, if you live. If you don't live—there's no problem.

Interview/Life, 9-22:86.

Fulton J. Sheen
Former Roman Catholic Bishop of Rochester, N.Y.

There is too much talk about war. People need to begin making war with themselves. A man not at war with himself is at war with others.

Dallas/ The Dallas Times Herald, 1-18:(B)22.

B. F. Skinner
Professor of Psychology, Harvard University

Our concept of individual freedom and dignity is standing in the way of progress. We've gotten the world into its present grim situation by allowing people to do as they please. When left alone, it's obvious that people will do what comes naturally—like reproduce and overpopulate the world. So, now, we must begin to control human behavior. We have to redesign the entire system so it makes people behave in better ways—ways that strengthen and perpetuate the culture long after the individual is dead and gone.

Interview, Los Angeles/ Los Angeles Times, 1-10:(4)1.

Joseph B. Soloveitchik
Rabbi, Theologian

Sleeping is a temporary form of death. Awakening every morning is an act of resurrection. The difference between death and sleep is only a question of time.

Before Rabbinical Council of America, Fallsburg, N.Y./ The Washington Post, 6-24:(B)10.

Elke Sommer
Actress

To me, to be wealthy is to have enough. To be *really* wealthy means to have 10 cents more than I need.

Interview/Family Weekly, 7-16:7.

James Stengenga
Professor of Political Science, Purdue University

. . . men seem to fight to possess things they do not need. There seems to be a possessive instinct that engenders conflict. Studies with children have illustrated this irrational possessiveness. A toy which previously neither needed nor wanted is desired and fought over as soon as one child picks it up. And, of course, wealthy men and nations have gone to war for possessions or territory not needed for survival. The drive to possess is so fundamental that it cannot be ignored with impunity.

San Francisco Examiner & Chronicle, 3-12:(This World)26.

Jacques Tati
Actor

Today one is ashamed of being ashamed of things of which he was ashamed yesterday.

San Francisco Examiner & Chronicle, 4-23:(This World)2.

U Thant
Former Secretary General of the United Nations

Too many nations still think in narrow and exclusivist terms and in terms of absolute freedom of action, when the most important lessons of our age are those of human interdependence, mutual respect and

(U THANT)

common approaches to the solving of common problems.

Quote, 9-10:242.

Arnold Toynbee
Historian

(On nationalism): A local state is not a god. It has been treated as a god. People have sacrificed their lives for it. But a local state is really just a public utility, like the gasworks, the electricity grid or the telephone system.

Athens/The New York Times, 7-16:(4)3.

Stanislaw Trepczynski
President,
United Nations General Assembly

In an age of unprecedented development of information media, of tremendous flow of ideas and of artistic achievements, concern for preserving the characteristics peculiar to the different cultures becomes a serious problem for mankind. It is essential that modern man should not lose his individual values. We do not want to see in him an amorphous particle of the mass of humanity. Still less do we want societies and nations to become masses devoid of personality, or all the great values inherent in their distinctive cultures to be lost.

At United Nations, N.Y., Sept. 19/
The New York Times, 9-20:18.

Harry S. Truman
Former President of the United States

I continue (at 88 years of age) to be optimistic about the future. It is only fair to say that I am an optimist by disposition; but my confidence in the future is based more on my reading of history and the evolution of man's works.

Quote, 7-16:49.

Roger Vadim
Motion picture director

I'm for love, but I realize that it's a terribly fragile sentiment that basically doesn't exist and which finishes quickly in any event.

San Francisco Examiner & Chronicle,
6-18:(Datebook)11.

Kurt Vonnegut, Jr.
Author

I think a lot of the discontent people feel now comes from the fact that human beings are not supposed to live in solitude as much as they do or to move around as much as they do. For millions of years, humans lived in stable societies; but now we are fragmented, and it's unbearable. Man was not meant to be that way. Humans are not used to this. So you get the situation where a man and his wife try to be an entire society to each other, with gruesome results. Some people can't stand it; they die; and there's a lot of that going on. The foremost malady of our time is lack of community.

Interview, New York/
San Francisco Examiner, 1-11:23.

Try thinking of this moment, 12:41, as perfectly preserved as a pickled peach . . . I'd like to do myself out of the feeling that time is robbing me. Our whole society is based on that . . . it's terrible when a woman thinks she's losing her beauty because she doesn't look the way she did at 17; it's terrible when a man thinks he's losing his virility when he doesn't feel the way he did at 14. They've still got it. If a woman and a man were married from 1948 to 1969, they didn't "use to" have a marriage—they still have one, it's clearly defined in time. People have such a sense of loss now. At the end of friendship or a love affair—if you hold the present belief in time—everything is lost, we might never have lived; it's like seeing the Milky Way go up (in flames) like a celluloid collar.

Interview, New York/
The Christian Science Monitor, 5-5:4.

George C. Wallace
Governor of Alabama

They say you can't bow your head in school and say, "God is great, God is good.

Dear Lord, we thank you for this food." But you see four-letter words in college newspapers. That's supposed to be progress. Well, the average man calls that degeneracy.

The Washington Post, 5-21:(B)6.

William L. Waller
Governor of Mississippi

Destiny is not a thing to be waited for. It is a thing to be achieved.

Inauguration address, Jackson, Miss., January/ The National Observer, 3-11:20.

W. Allen Wallis
Chancellor, University of Rochester (N.Y.)

(Addressing graduating students): As I compare the world that you enter with the one that I entered when I was graduated from college exactly 40 years ago, I cannot help but be impressed, even awed, by the rosy prospects you face. Almost everything is so much better now than then that I can only envy you. The problems of poverty, war, disease and injustice that you face are so minor compared to those we faced as to seem almost inconsequential. Unfortunately, there is another, less rosy, side of your future. When problems are reduced to manageable proportions, so that their total elimination appears possible, it often turns out that the last remaining problems are the most difficult to solve. Impatience and frustration with the remaining problems grow; and at the same time, boundless new appetites are aroused that generate new problems. The result, as Alexis de Tocqueville said 135 years ago, is that "democratic passions burn most fiercely just when the fuel is least." Your generation faces greater dangers from those fiercely-burning democratic passions than my generation faced from racial intolerance, the great Depression, social inequality, uncontrolled disease, Fascism and Communism and the Second World War. Unless the passions that are burning so fiercely are brought under control, your generation will lose your greatest heritage—the freedom and democracy that we are passing on to you from our forefathers . . .

At University of Rochester commencement/ The Wall Street Journal, 9-5:12.

Lowell P. Weicker, Jr.
United States Senator, R–Conn.

In a democracy, the sound of a snoring populace is marching-music to those who would make political mischief.

Before Association of Life Insurance Counsel, New York, Dec. 12/ The New York Times, 12-13:28.

Elie Wiesel
Author

I believe that never has society been so dehumanized as it is now. Words mean nothing. What is even worse, words of lies come out as words of truth.

San Francisco Examiner & Chronicle, 6-11:(This World)2.

Gordon Wright
Professor of History, Stanford University

(History) is about how humans meet a crisis; how they try to organize themselves and confront problems . . . It's dangerous to look rigidly at history, but at least we can find some guidelines and lessons about what not to do. It's good for students to see how complex problems are and how easy it is to be misled by simplistic solutions. One can understand better how politicians should be judged if one sees in the past how they behaved and been proved sometimes right, sometimes wrong.

Stanford, Calif./ San Francisco Examiner, 12-18:13.

Religion

Brigitte Bardot
Actress

I live outside religion. People lean on religion too much. They use God as an alibi; they are wicked and they confess and they feel good again until the next time. Maybe there is a God, but where or how I don't know. So when things are going bad for me, I don't feel I have the right to ask Him for favors; I would not like to use something or somebody I only half believe in. But look how badly people treat religion. Look at Belfast (Northern Ireland). What kind of religion goes on there? Why kill your neighbor because he prays differently, using different words? Isn't religion supposed to be the highest kind of love? Then where does the blood in the gutters come from? It frightens me. People who are very religious are often so aggressive.

Interview/
Los Angeles Times, 4-9:(Calendar)17.

Eugene Carson Blake
General secretary,
World Council of Churches

Ecumenism has produced improvements in interreligious relationships that no one could have predicted 10 years ago. There is no future for a sectarian Christianity. It must be an ecumenical Christianity.

Before World Council of Churches general board, New York/
June 9/The New York Times, 6-10:35.

I insist that there is no future for sectarian Christianity—including Roman Catholic sectarianism. And there's no future for the sort of establishment-Christianity that sees its role as blessing the government. I don't think Christians will accept either of these directions. They are too intelligent.

Interview/Los Angeles Times, 11-19:(E)6.

Frank J. Bonnike
President,
National Federation of Priests' Councils
(United States)

(Advocating sharing of the ministry by priests and laymen): Jesus never intended to narrow (the) ministry to priests; nor did He ever intend to do what we have done, namely to narrow priests down to highly-educated, middle- and upper-class, white, male celibates.

Before National Federation of Priests' Councils, Denver,
March 13/The New York Times, 3-15:22.

(On the church's commitment to social action): Those in the halls of government may tell us to stick to saving souls; (but) we are here to say to such men that our ministry exists alongside of theirs.

Before National Federation of Priests' Councils, Denver,
March 13/The New York Times, 3-14:22.

Jacques-Yves Cousteau
Oceanographer

I don't believe God created man in His image and that man is the chosen species. But sometimes I look in a microscope and think, there is a God, because I am overcome by the beauty, perfection and complexity we cannot begin to understand. I don't think there is any basis to conclude if life came about by chance or if there is some orientation behind it all. Whether there is a God is *the* problem. What else is important? The second question is if He is interested in us. I can't answer the first, but I can the second: He is not.

Interview/
The New York Times Magazine, 9-10:90.

A. Donald Davies
Episcopal Bishop of Dallas

There are all types of gods today. People are seeking all kinds of religious experiences. Some people have said we have a crisis of faith. I don't believe that. We have a crisis in the manner in which people arrive at their faith, what they want and are really seeking in a faith relationship.

The Dallas Times Herald, 1-3:(A)23.

Francis L. Garrett
Rear Admiral and Chief of Chaplains, United States Navy

The new interest in religion in America, especially among the young, has been reflected in the military and has afforded chaplains important contemporary opportunities for ministry. Whether it is aboard ship, in a hospital ward, in the field with Marines or in a dependent's daily vacation Bible school, Navy chaplains continue to reach out as God's witnesses with prophetic messages as well as with helping hands and understanding hearts to inspire, encourage, comfort and support.

Los Angeles Herald-Examiner, 11-25:(A)7.

Charles F. Golden
United Methodist Bishop

The church is finding its expression more outside the institution, and in other institutions. You have more men in politics quoting Scripture than ministers. The church is getting lost in other things. I see the church wherever there is the governance of God. So you have to define what you mean by the church "losing membership." I think religion today makes more sense to more people, although they may not be identified with the usual religious cliches.

News conference/
Los Angeles Times, 8-26:(1)21.

Jules Harlow
Rabbi; Director of publications, Rabbinical Assembly of America

(Saying prayer is too formal and ceremonially stiff): The problem of petrified prayer is inherent in all liturgy, and acts of worship harden with amazing swiftness into fixed texts, sacred rites and ritual mechanics, which are taken for granted by some and ignored by others.

Interview/
The New York Times, 7-23:(1)48.

Hassan II
King of Morocco

Islam is practical, and not only a contemplative religion. It teaches certain social rules of communal behavior, and lays down a relationship between the government and those it governs.

Interview, Rabat/
The New York Times, 7-26:35.

Hugh M. Hefner
Publisher, "Playboy" magazine

. . . if any kind of spiritual belief makes a man more ethical, more concerned with his fellow man, then I'm in favor of it. But to be in favor of religion for its own sake, to suggest that a blind belief in God automatically makes you a better person is patently preposterous and provably untrue. We've killed more people on this planet because of religious convictions in the last 2,000 years than for any other reason. And they talk about religion as being the great civilizing force . . . I hope that our religion moves to a more humanist level in the future. What we call religion today should have less emphasis on the unknowable things—all the deistic nonsense. I don't know whether there's a God, and nobody else does either. If they want to live their lives according to what they believe is true, fine. But the moment, as is always the case, that they start telling the next guy what to do with his life according to the same edicts, then it's just Fascism under another name.

Interview, Los Angeles/ Los Angeles Times, 2-27:(West)23.

Carl F. H. Henry
Christian theologian;
Editor-at-large, "Christianity Today"

The "Jesus freaks" at least know that Jesus Christ is the way into the supernatural world, but even they have a limited future unless their evangelical faith is theologically informed. Moreover, an authentic Christian witness cannot opt out of the secular milieu.

At Loma Linda (Calif.) University, Jan. 9/Los Angeles Times, 1-15:(1)29.

J. Edgar Hoover
Director,
Federal Bureau of Investigation of the United States

I find a few minutes each day—at home, at the office, while traveling—to meditate and pray. These minutes enable me to gain a perspective about the problems and decisions which each hour come across my desk . . . A man who closes himself off from divine inspiration is a small, narrow man whose decisions will be petty and vindictive.

Interview, Washington, May 1/ San Francisco Examiner & Chronicle, 5-7:(B)7.

Hubert H. Humphrey
United States Senator, D–Minn.

I don't parade my religion—I'm not that good a man, to be frank about it. But service is love . . . If you ask do I believe in the power of prayer—I do. If you ask do I believe in Jesus Christ—I do. If you ask do I live by all these standards—I try. If you ask can any President do less—I think not.

Campaigning for the Democratic Presidential nomination, Albright College, Reading, Pa./ Los Angeles Herald-Examiner, 4-16:(A)7.

Hans Kung
Professor of Theology,
Tubingen (Germany) University

The present Pope (Paul VI) started with probably the greatest credibility the Catholic church has enjoyed in the past 500 years. Now the church's credibility is so low that we cannot imagine how this happened.

Plainview (Tex.) Daily Herald, 4-24:10.

Arnold G. Kuntz
President,
Southern California District,
Lutheran Church-Missouri Synod

Being a Christian is not a solo performance. It is a symphony. One voice crying in the wilderness can never bring it off. It calls for orchestration of hearts and minds.

South Gate, Calif., May 14/ Los Angeles Times, 5-15:(3)14.

Harold Bingham Lee
President,
Church of Jesus Christ of Latter-Day Saints (Mormons)

We know from experience that the religion to which an individual belongs is one of the most important considerations of a happy marriage. We've always said, in effect, that if you plan a marriage to someone outside the church, you'd better count the cost. When the children come along there'll come a contest; and if it results in a quarrel, they might say, "Just let them grow up and make their own choice." In that case, you let children grow up with no choice. The fact is that they will be wholly irreligious. So we try to say, "It will be wise for Catholics to marry Catholics, Methodists to marry Methodists and Mormons to marry Mormons." Therein the safest course.

Interview, Salt Lake City/ Los Angeles Times, 8-21:(1)11.

What is sorely needed is a world-wide movement, with every means possible, to overcome the ignorance to be found among the unfortunate peoples of the earth, where the fundamental principles of right living and self-control and sound economic methods, patterned after our Lord's plan of salvation, are adopted. Our mission is to see that this (Mormon) Church is in the forefront in showing the way . . . we offer a happy, progressive way of life, the Lord's way. No religion on earth can give anything more to the people. We offer them the gospel plan of salvation, help lift them out of poverty and ignorance, encourage them into educational pursuits, and help them band together as brothers and sisters in the gospel of Jesus Christ.

Salt Lake City/ The National Observer, 11-4:6.

Irving Lehrman
President, Synagogue Council of America

We (American Jews) have performed nobly in the areas of rescue and redemption, particularly in our support for the State of Israel, which stands at the spiritual center of Jewish life everywhere, and in our concern for the rights of Soviet Jews. We have been dangerously negligent, however, in developing those indigenous Jewish resources which American Jewry requires for its autonomous existence. We have allowed an erosion of Jewish life in the Diaspora, which must be stopped if there are to be future generations of informed, loyal American Jews on whom Israel and our brethren throughout the world will be able to depend.

The New York Times, 11-26:(1)84.

Lester G. Maddox
Lieutenant Governor, and former Governor, of Georgia

The only hope of America is the fundamentalist church, where the people teach the word of God and not the word of man. Some churches I can't get into—some of these modernist churches; they're trying to get God to adjust to man rather than man to adjust to God.

Time, 8-21:44.

Robert J. Marshall
President, Lutheran Church in America

It seems evident to me that television and radio religion is in the ascendance in contrast to religion that is experienced in a congregation, a local fellowship of people. (Churches must devise a technique for) proclaiming to the public what it means to engage in face-to-face Christian fellowship rather than media-to-face Christian fellowship; what it means to gather as a community of believers around the preaching of the word and administration of the sacrament; and what it means to have a full-time pastor who counsels in depth. What we appear to be settling for in this day of mass media is armchair religion.

Before heads of his denomination's synods, Kansas City/ The Washington Post, 1-29:(C)10.

Charles B. McCoy
Chairman and president, E. I. Du Pont de Nemours and Company

One of the serious problems is the church problem. I am talking about the difficulty of the church trying to adapt itself, trying to figure out what its role is. The church was a tremendously stabilizing influence in Western Europe and this country (the U.S.). Although we have been through cycles in our lifetime—up and down—I don't think it has ever reached the point where it is today. If only anyone could really rewrite the Bible in terms that can be understood by people who are living and growing up today. The way they change the ritual around doesn't help a darn bit; and more clergymen have trouble making sense out of the Biblical story to guys who don't even know what a cow looks like, let alone what it is to take care of one. The Bible has been the backbone of the educational system. Yet I can't cope with imagery in the Bible. I hear it preached once in a while, and I have been over parts of it a number of times. It is pretty hard to put it in terms of automobiles and present life-styles. The trip to the moon and communications—they have kicked the props out from under even some of the most fundamental things. I don't mean that Christianity is out the window. All this is added to the sort of lack of understanding in people's minds as to where they stand.

Interview, Wilmington, Del./ Los Angeles Times, 2-25:(2)7.

Paul VI
Pope

. . . the church, though in herself and essentially aloof from political action, nevertheless claims a place in the civil world. In the first place, because she is made for men and made up of men. By her profession of religious faith, by her healing and sanctifying teaching, and by her upholding of the primacy of spiritual reality, she inculcates in them respect for the rights of each, and the fulfillment of the duties of each for the establishment of an organic and genuine brotherhood. The second and principal reason is that she is called to this mission by the mandate received from her Founder, that of saving man, communicating to him the Word that sets free and the Life that sanctifies, and thus of collaborating in the complete raising up of man. It is therefore obvious that the church also cannot but feel herself obliged to make her own contribution to the realization in the world of peace in justice and justice in peace. And this contribution, as the constitution *Gaudium et Spes* observes, she makes in particular by bringing "light kindled from the Gospel" and placing at mankind's "disposal those saving resources which the church herself, under the guidance of the Holy Spirit, receives from her Founder."

Before Diplomatic Corps, Rome, Jan. 10/Vital Speeches, 2-15:259.

Everything tends to exclude God from thought and customs. Life becomes ever more profane, laicized and secular. The man of today says he is sure that he is sufficient only unto himself, that he can do without God and the celebration of His glory. (But the exclusion of God from everyday life) leaves a great emptiness. The supreme principles of thought and action are lacking. There is an attempt to put man in the place of God.

Vatican City, Dec. 13/ Los Angeles Herald-Examiner, 12-14:(A)18.

David Polish
President,
Central Conference of American Rabbis

(Advocating closer ties between Reform and Conservative branches of American Judaism): The contraction of the world itself, the growing recognition that human salvation lies in the emergence of a world community, the depletion of a Jewish people consumed in a holocaust which made no distinctions between the religious and secularists—all this makes a separatism for its own sake a scandal and a defeat . . . the widest room must be provided for creative relationships among denominations in their common search for meaning and purpose and in their common endeavor to heal the lacerated soul of the Jewish people. If capitalist America and Communist China can play ping-pong, Reform and Conservative Judaism should be able to play chess.

At Central Conference of American Rabbis, Grossinger, N.Y., June 12/ The New York Times, 6-13:14.

Muammar el Qaddafi
Premier of Libya

Islam is a civilization and a pervasive moral structure. It exists to organize all aspects of life and society. More extensive and more general than any other religion, it is a self-generating revolution. It is logical that we adapt it to everything we do.

Interview/ The New York Times Magazine, 2-6:56.

Arthur Michael Ramsey
Archbishop of Canterbury (England)

At the present time, the old Christian institutions are under the weather. While they have carried the Christian faith through the years, they often present a Christianity which seems tired or conventional or formal. And many young people are bypassing the institutional churches and finding an allegiance to Jesus in new, exciting movements which have the name of Jesus as their slogan.

Sermon, New York, Jan. 23/ The New York Times, 1-24:30.

There is a bit of a wish for women priests in England; but I should be anxious not to go too fast for fear of upsetting the cause of Christian unity. I can foresee the day when all Christians might accept the Pope as Presiding Bishop. Perspectives change, and we must give the bag a good shake and see what happens.

New York/Time, 2-7:44.

Robert C. Rusack
Bishop Coadjutor-elect, Los Angeles Episcopal Diocese

Any bishop today must share with Roman Catholics, Orthodox, other Anglicans and Protestant leaders in speaking to injustice, pollution, social and religious crises. The combined Christian voice, as well as those of such other faiths as Judaism, Buddhism, etc., can bring weight to arouse the consciences of men.

Interview, Los Angeles/ Los Angeles Times, 10-28:(1)25.

Frederick Schiotz
Member, central committee, World Council of Churches

The *(Reader's) Digest* has suggested, in one of its two articles on the World Council of Churches, that the council is controlled by the Communists, who use it as a platform. I realize that council delegates often plead for peace and include a dig at the West; but we refer to these as "visa speeches" that these delegates apparently feel obligated to make in order to get home. But the Communists by no means control the council.

San Francisco, Jan. 31/ San Francisco Examiner, 2-1:11.

Alexander I. Solzhenitsyn
Russian author

(Criticizing the Russian Orthodox Church for being a tool of the state): A church dictatorially directed by atheists is a sight not seen in 2,000 years.

Plainview (Tex.) Daily Herald, 4-11:(A)6.

W. McFerrin Stowe
United Methodist Bishop of Dallas

The day of "judgmental" attitudes toward persons who may have broken traditional concepts (of the church) in a variety of ways is passing. The church in all phases is moving toward the value of the individual and the support of persons, whatever their experience or needs.

The Dallas Times Herald, 8-2:(A)21.

Leon-Joseph Cardinal Suenens
Roman Catholic Archbishop of Malines-Brussels; Primate of Belgium

Some stress, some discomfort, some pruning has produced the image of the church today which is different from the image of the church of yesterday. However, with the keen eyes of faith, these changes remain only on the surface without disturbing or negating what is fundamental, vital and essential for continuity. Nevertheless, to perceive this, we need on the one hand a vivacious faith which clings to the living Christ in a personal encounter and a living commitment, and on the other hand a wisdom to separate what is nonessential from that which is essential.

At John Courtney Murray Forum, New York, March 19/ The New York Times, 3-20:7.

I hope that, more and more, the role for women (in the church) is enlarged . . . Perhaps one day it will be possible to have women deaconnesses. I don't think it will be tomorrow morning, but it is a possibility.

San Diego, Calif./
The New York Times, 6-8:36.

Thomas Tschoepe
Roman Catholic Bishop of Dallas

It seems there is a lot more interest in spiritual life, a revival for things of the spirit over material things. I think people are just fed up on the blandness of life. They've been so immersed in the material things, but it hasn't satisfied the spiritual longings.

The Dallas Times Herald, 1-3:(A)23.

Cynthia Wedel
President, National Council of Churches (United States)

I think there's a great revival of religious interest—which is basically a search for purpose in life. I think the "Jesus People" are a sign of concern here, even though so often they give simplistic answers which somebody told them to give—and which crash when confronted with reality. I see in the established churches an increasing number of signs that we "bottomed off" and there may be an upsurge again, if the traditional churches can meet people's needs.

At St. Marks Episcopal Church,
Berkeley, Calif., Jan. 23/
San Francisco Examiner, 1-24:8.

Profound changes have occurred in both the world and the church in the past half-century. Some see ecumenism dying along with all religion. Others believe that Christianity will survive but that any interest in greater unity is gone. We need to remember the same kind of gloomy prophecy is being voiced about democracy, the capitalist system, education, morality and the family. All of these, too, are undergoing a change. And there is a mentality which equates change with destruction. There is abundant evidence of God at work, pulling and pushing mankind toward a very different kind of human society which could be more nearly what God wants it to be. When—thanks to the blessed Pope John XXIII—the Roman Catholic Church entered the ecumenical scene, a whole new chapter in ecumenical understanding began.

Before general board of
National Council of Churches,
Charlotte, N.C./
The New York Times, 2-15:20.

Space • Science • Technology

Bella S. Abzug
United States Representative, D–N.Y.

(Arguing against the proposed space shuttle): We should not allow NASA to continue to drain our economy of its limited resources by shooting billions of dollars worth of hardware into space while our other needs go unmet. Our needs are here at home, with the millions of hungry American children who eat lead-laden paint chips, with our helpless old, with our rat-infested, drug-plagued ghettos . . . with our sewage-filled waterways and polluted skies; not with space searching for rock samples or repairing rockets.

Before House Space Subcommittee, Washington/The National Observer, 5-27:6.

Spiro T. Agnew
Vice President of the United States

I am concerned about the increased activity of this anti-progress campaign—a campaign that seems to be predicated on the philosophy that all technological change is bad, that all industrial growth is bad, that all mechanical devices are bad. This philosophy seems to hold that there is something inherently evil in the notion of man's harnessing and benignly controlling natural forces.

San Francisco Examiner & Chronicle, 7-30:(This World)2.

Robert Anderson
President,
North American Rockwell Corporation

From the very beginning, engineers and scientists have been involved in the building of this nation. As much as any group, they are the spirit of America. It was science and engineering that tied this nation together with the railroads, the automobile and the telephone. It was the airplane, built by science and engineering, that figuratively wiped out any sectional difference in this nation. It was radio that gave it one voice, and television that gave it one image. This is part of technology's contribution to the spirit of America. However, one of the greatest contributions of all happened less than three years ago when science and engineering, in a united effort, gave to this nation the greatest surge of peacetime pride and spirit it had ever known: the landing of men on the moon and their safe return to earth. Surely, the world is changing; the scientists and engineers helped change it for the better. They've earned their place in the American society. They are contributors, both materially and to the spirit that has made this nation number one. Consequently, we're no longer going to listen in silence to sandle-shod nonsense about returning to the bucolic life of 19th-century simplicity. America is an urbanized society, and our job is not to turn the country back to rural simplicity, but to raise it to new high standards of living for everyone. Science and engineering can't cure poverty—but . . . they are the job creators; and there is nothing yet devised that will cure poverty quicker than a job.

Before Institute of Electrical and Electronics Engineers, New York, March 22/ Vital Speeches, 5-1:422.

Neil A. Armstrong
Former American astronaut;
First man to set foot on the moon

It (the *Apollo 11* moon mission in 1969) was the first time in all history that explorers went to a new land without weapons of any sort.

Plainview (Tex.) Daily Herald, 3-6:2.

Eugene A. Cernan
American astronaut

(The forthcoming moon mission of) *Apollo 17* may be the curtain-ringer, the end of the *Apollo* program. But to us, we look at it as just the beginning of a quest for knowledge, mankind's involvement—led by our country—into what we call infinity.

Plainview (Tex.) Daily Herald, 10-16:6.

As I take these last steps from the surface (of the moon) for some time into the future to come, I'd just like to record that America's challenge of today has forged man's destiny of tomorrow. And as we leave the moon and Taurus-Littrow, we leave as we came—and, God willing, we shall return—with peace and hope for all mankind.

Upon entering, on the moon, lunar module "Challenger" of "Apollo 17," last "Apollo" mission, Dec. 14/ The New York Times, 12-15:1.

(Upon just returning from the *Apollo 17* moon-landing mission): I hope people throughout the world can share with us what we have done. We think we have accomplished something and, by golly, we're proud of it. Nothing is impossible in this world when dedicated people are involved. And it's a fundamental law of nature that either you must grow, or you must die. Whether that be an idea, whether that be a man, whether that be a flower or a country. I thank God that our country has chosen to grow.

Aboard U.S.S. Ticonderoga in the South Pacific, Dec. 19/ Los Angeles Times, 12-20:(1)20.

Arthur C. Clarke
Science-fiction writer

One of the problems of the moon is that it's gray. It has been covered with dust for so long. And that's one reason why it's not very visually exciting. And it is so smooth. On Mars there's going to be much more color. There are these enormous canyons—the one they've discovered that's five times as wide as the Grand Canyon and twice as deep and thousands of miles long. Spectacular scenery. And almost certainly I'd say now there's some form of life there. Mars will turn out to be a fascinating and exciting planet. I think once people realize what's up there, there will be a real drive up into space.

Broadcast panel discussion/ The National Observer, 5-6:22.

Norman Corwin
Author

There have been saints among scientists; no question about it. But think of the difference between the sugar cube of Dr. Sabin and the bomb trigger of Dr. Teller; or Einstein's theory of 1905 and the way it was used to ultimately spark Hiroshima in 1945 . . . But the nemesis of man is not science. It is war. The experiment has been to prove new weapons; the guinea pig in the experiment has always been world peace; the white rats in the experiment have always been human beings.

At University of Judaism Author-Artist Luncheon, Los Angeles/ Los Angeles Herald-Examiner, 7-4:(B)1.

Paul R. Ehrlich
Professor of Biology, Stanford University

Science has become thoroughly politicized; indeed, in a sense it always has been. It is high time we (scientists) openly faced up to that fact and became an effective pressure group for survival . . . Adversary forums would do much more than provide careful scrutiny of scientists' claims. They would also call attention to areas of legitimate difference of opinion and interpretation and educate the public about the degree of uncertainty which characterizes much of science. Concerned scientists should not be restricted to saying only what is approved by colleagues, but they must constantly seek broad critical review of their ideas.

Before American Physical Society and American Association of Physics Teachers, San Francisco, Jan. 31/ San Francisco Examiner, 2-1:8.

Luis A. Ferre
Governor of Puerto Rico

Television and other electronic mass media have, during the past two decades, tremendously accelerated communication from the center of society out to the citizen. Now the computer must be used to help speed up communication back in the other direction. If used in this fashion, the computer can become a rehumanizing rather than a dehumanizing influence. Typically, the computer has been superimposed upon top-down bureaucratic hierarchies in an attempt to make them more efficient. Yet the computer is really better suited to improve communication from the bottom up rather than from the top down. The computer can be used to aggregate spontaneous citizen communications in such a manner that patterns of discontent, of frustration, of emerging issues should be detected so that we might have government by anticipation rather than by crisis.

Before American Society of Mechanical Engineers, Washington/ The Wall Street Journal, 1-5:10.

Technology and science are neither good nor bad. They are not value-bearing activities. It is the use that man puts them to which makes them good or bad. We must evaluate their uses from the point of view of their social significance and their ecological impact. We cannot forget that the population of the world today is 3.7 billion people which is three times the population of the year 1850; and certainly it will be 6.5 billion people by the year 2000. Certainly, such an increase in world population needs the help of our present technology to assure its survival, for without present technology, industry could not provide enough food, clothing, housing and other essentials to satisfy its needs.

At graduation exercises, University of Pittsburgh Graduate School of Business, Aug. 1/ Vital Speeches, 10-1:748.

James C. Fletcher
Administrator,
National Aeronautics and Space Administration of the United States

When we achieved the first lunar landing, there was a lot of floundering around on the part of NASA and its advisory groups. What do you do next? It was the hope of many that we would go on to even more impressive accomplishments: lunar bases, space stations and possible manned missions to Mars. It has taken us two or three years to get down to earth.

Interview/ The New York Times, 2-20:49.

(Advocating the proposed space shuttle): We need easy and quick access to space. It seems to me that not only the United States but the free world needs to be in space to respond to anything that might happen there—military, commercial or scientific. It is true we can do that in many ways. But the shuttle is the best we've come up with.

The National Observer, 5-27:6.

At the end of the last decade, when *Apollo 11* occurred and man first set foot on the moon, it gave Americans renewed confidence in themselves. They knew their country could really put together a complex program and do what it says it will do within the price it said it would cost. It's hard to put a tangible value on that because it's an attitude and an emotional feeling. But what makes a country great or not so great depends a lot on whether its people have pride in its achievements.

Interview, Cape Kennedy, Fla./ The Sacramento (Calif.) Bee, 12-3:(C)8.

Edward J. Gurney
United States Senator, R–Fla.

It is absolutely essential for any great nation to have an ongoing program in space research, technology and science. The (space)

(EDWARD J. GURNEY)

shuttle opponents are either blind or don't like space.

The National Observer, 5-27:6.

Karl G. Harr, Jr.
President,
Aerospace Industries Association of America

The Federal government has been the primary sponsor of the basic research, applied research and development that have enabled scientists and technologists to produce the advances in electronics, physics, chemistry and many other fields which have, in turn, generated entire new industries during the twentieth century. Over the last five years, however, the Federal commitment to research and development, when measured in constant dollars, has been decreasing. This downward trend has serious implications, because only the Federal government can afford the lack of immediate return and the massive investment needed to construct such basic research tools as a linear accelerator or a radio telescope.

Before graduate division, Wharton School of Finance and Commerce, University of Pennsylvania/ The New York Times, 1-9:(NES)40.

Julius J. Hoffman
Judge,
United States District Court for the Northern District of Illinois

Much of the rebellion that has occurred in recent years has been attributed to disenchantment with the life that has been shaped by advanced technology. But the problems of our society cannot be solved by wearing of love beads and reversion to the simple life of the pioneer or of Rousseau's *Noble Savage.* The future of the world will be tied inextricably to science, invention and technology. They have the power to destroy mankind—and the power to give it a long, advantageous lease on life. We cannot choose between living in the twentieth century and, say, the eighteenth.

At Illinois Institute of Technology commencement/The New York Times, 1-6:37.

James B. Irwin
American astronaut

(Recalling his flight on *Apollo 15*): The next time I looked down, I could see the southeastern part of the United States—Florida, Cuba, the Bahamas with their clear waters. A couple of hours later, we could see continents, the whole earth in the beauty of color: the brown Sahara, the blue oceans, the white clouds. The earth reminded all of us of a very fragile Christmas-tree ornament, surrounded by the blackness of space.

Los Angeles, Feb. 20/ Los Angeles Times, 2-21:(2)2.

Herman Kahn
Director, Hudson Institute

One of the amazing facts has been that, despite the rapidity of the growth of computing capability, people's ability to try to use computers for things they can't do has grown just as fast. The mystique continues to be ahead of the reality.

At Harvard Club, New York, Nov. 6/ The New York Times, 11-10:58.

Melvin Kranzberg
Director, Graduate Program,
History of Science and Technology,
Case-Western Reserve University

Sociological surveys show that engineers, in general, live in the suburbs, vote Republican and mouth the cliches of conservatism. Yet they have done more for social revolution than political radicals of whatever stature. With wonderful innocence, engineers keep inventing new products, processes, systems and devices which improve, change, upset and confound the social order. They are far quieter, more effective and more insidious than Abbie Hoffman, Jerry Rubin, the Berrigan brothers and Angela Davis put together.

Before Engineers' Public Information Council, Lubbock, Tex., June 21/ Vital Speeches, 9-1:677.

Claude Levi-Strauss
Anthropologist

I do not include myself among those who deem it fashionable to despise scientific knowledge. To me, knowledge appears as the highest goal which man may assign to himself; the only pursuit making life worth living. Nevertheless, there are times when I cannot avoid thinking that science would be more lovable if it had no practical use whatsoever. For, incontrovertible as the fact of technological progress may be, 90 per cent of all its achievements seem only to aim at alleviating the nuisance resulting from the ten per cent which have a positive value. For example, instead of carrying on this maddening race, would it not be wiser to avail ourselves of what progress has already achieved, even if this means slackening its pace, and to use this time to bring our course back to order? Nothing can be achieved without the help of science. Science alone can succeed in stopping the demographic explosion, finding ways to equalize the world's riches, rather than using them up to the advantage of a minority, and discovering processes suitable to give back air and water their lost purity. But science should cease identifying itself with a noxious philosophy which says that man is the master and the sole owner of the earth, as well as of other living beings. And we should learn that progress sometimes consists in looking backward toward these doomed so-called primitive people we anthropologists are studying before it is too late, and who for centuries have placed their wisdom in protecting and keeping safe a sound equilibrium between man and his environment. We, who have created modern science and technological progress, must find means of putting them in tune with the teachings of an age-old morality.

Television broadcast/"Comment!" National Broadcasting Company, 5-14.

In this sad century, in this sad world where we live, with the pressure of population, rapidity of communications, the uniformity of culture, we are closed, like a prison. The *Apollo* shots (of the U.S. space program) open a little window. It is the one experience—vicarious, but we can follow it on TV—the one moment when the prison opens on something other than the world in which we are condemned to live.

Interview/ The New York Times, 12-3:(1)68.

George M. Low
Deputy Administrator, National Aeronautics and Space Administration of the United States

If we don't do something obout the high cost of doing business in space, and do it soon, our nation's space program is in deep trouble. We are on the verge of exciting new discoveries in space science. But we cannot follow through as rapidly as we should because we can't afford it. We see before us many important space applications. But we cannot move out as rapidly as we should because we can't afford it. Most important of all, we may lose our hard-won world-wide leadership in space if we don't find a way to do more for our money.

At joint symposium of National Security Industrial Association and Armed Forces Management Association/ The Washington Post, 8-20:(A)7.

William M. Magruder
Special Consultant to the President of the United States

Technology has been spoiled. Technology has never had to justify itself on the basis of social benefits, a definition of progress or a definition of contribution to quality of life. In our past, the United States has accepted technology as a fundamental in making our country safe, clean, economically prosperous and a happy place in which to live and learn and pursue our own road to happiness. Technology today is being viewed as a danger to our society in some quarters—something that

(WILLIAM M. MAGRUDER)

has polluted our environment, harassed our development toward true social benefits.

Before Salesmanship Club, Dallas, June 1/ The Dallas Times Herald, 6-2:(A)21.

Norman Mailer
Author

. . . the space program has not been a success because this *(Apollo 16)* is the next to the last moon flight. It's shocking that an adventure which I consider as exciting as going to the moon is going to come to an end—and probably won't be started again for another 10 years. I think that the reason is simple. They (astronauts) don't know what to do when they get there. The fact that it's technological is what's wrong with it. It's too exclusively technological. People are sick to death of technology. The technologists themselves are wondering how they can control technology before technology wipes out the earth. So what we're looking for at this time in human history is an enlargement of human consciousness, a rediscovery of spiritual values to which we can adhere because they deepen us. We're looking precisely for excitement and glamor. Glamor is an indispensable element in people's lives. That fact that you have this (space) program which is essentially glamorous—to wit, high adventure—and that this program resolutely determines to become technological and dull is part of the tragedy of the Twentieth Century as far as I'm concerned.

Broadcast panel discussion/ The National Observer, 5-6:22.

Margaret Mead
Anthropologist

We have to credit space exploration with the discovery that there is no meaningful life elsewhere in the solar system. This overcomes the earlier romanticism of other inhabitable places in the solar system. That throws more responsibility on us and on the way we live on earth, for there's nowhere else to go. Without this realization, this community of earth, we might have settled down to plans for endless warfare. But there's a growing feeling that our relationships must change, because there's nowhere else to go.

Interview/ The New York Times, 12-3:68.

Walter F. Mondale
United States Senator, D–Minn.

The Nixon Administration's space shuttle is another example of twisted priorities and colossal waste in Federal spending. This multi-billion dollar manned space extravaganza has enormous hidden costs. It is not essential to our national prestige. And the scientific and practical benefits it promises can be achieved by other existing programs at a fraction of its cost . . . In addition to the exhorbitant cost, there is also the question of what the shuttle will do. The Space Agency argues that it will launch valuable unmanned satellites for communications, weather forecasts, earth observation and scientific exploration. But just one shuttle flight could carry all the unmanned satellites that the Space Agency has launched in the last five years. Thus, NASA is faced with a critical dilemma. Either the shuttle will remain relatively idle—a $40 billion white elephant—or else NASA will be forced to dream up a staggering array of new missions, such as trips to space stations, simply to keep the shuttle busy. The more activity they dream up, the more the program will cost. Given our present projected needs for satellites, the shuttle makes as much sense as building a multi-billion dollar mass transit system in the middle of the Mojave Desert.

Television broadcast/"Comment!" National Broadcasting Company, 2-6.

Harvey Mudd II
Environmentalist

The scientist of the future will have to be politically more sophisticated and courageous than he has been in the past. And he will have to be morally responsible for all applications of technology. He should practice a kind of conscientious objection and refuse to work on weapons development or any project or process which is environmentally or socially harmful. He should blow the whistle from inside when government or industry embark on a project which is irresponsibly risky or destructive. The freeing of the scientific community from its condition of servitude, indebtedness and dependency on the military-industrial arm of the state will be no easy task. A more broadly-educated, less-specialized scientist is part of the answer. A politicized and morally sensitized scientist is also part of the answer.

At Harvey Mudd College commencement, Claremont, Calif./ The National Observer, 7-22:17.

Bruce C. Murray
Professor of Planetary Science, California Institute of Technology

Can't we now spare a tiny fraction of our national energies in exploration and scientific study of the remote and still undisturbed environments of our solar system? We must not let today's disheartening problems of men so erode our optimism, vision and curiosity that we fail to write our chapters in the history of man.

San Francisco Examiner & Chronicle, 3-19:(This World)2.

Richard M. Nixon
President of the United States

In reaching the moon, we demonstrated what miracles American technology is capable of achieving. And now the time has come to move more deliberately toward making full use of that technology here on earth, of harnessing the wonders of science to the service of men.

State of the Union address, Washington, Jan 20/ The New York Times, 1-21:18.

Rocco A. Petrone
Director, "Apollo" program, National Aeronautics and Space Administration of the United States

(On the planned joint space venture between the U.S. and the Soviet Union): Our (U.S.) space program is run in a fish bowl, and they (the Soviets) already know a great deal about our technology. What we will be exchanging are disciplines—their way of operating while in space, and our way. The reason we're going to be successful in it is we're not trying to solve the political problems that face the two countries. Here we both have the same basic objectives—to fly the mission, demonstrate that it will work, and bring our men home safely.

Interview/ U.S. News & World Report, 12-18:19.

Simon Ramo
Executive vice president and vice chairman, TRW, Inc.

. . . the availability of advanced information technology does not have to lead us to a state-controlled economy. Instead, we can use it to reach a higher form of free enterprise. In a "computerized" society, to oversimplify a little, all of the information needed for control—from airplane schedules to pickle distribution—is made available at the right place at the right time. Tens of millions of interconnected electronic devices would be everywhere, picking up, processing and disseminating information. In effect, each citizen would be associated with a "super telephone-TV set" telling him where to be and what to do. But the same system—a national network of computers, communication gear, electronic memory and information input and output consoles—that can tell millions of people exactly what to do, as though they were robots, can just as well ask them to choose a preference from a group of well-presented alternatives. The public in 1990 could tune in on the issues and take part by expressing their reactions electronically in two-way communications—"instant democracy." Information technology could be used to achieve by 1990 a

(SIMON RAMO)

more informed citizenry with an extent of participation in decision-making never imagined in all the previous "pre-technological" history of man.

At White House Conference on the Industrial World Ahead, Washington, Feb. 7/ Vital Speeches, 3-1:314.

Carl Sagan
Astronomer, Cornell University

(On the U.S. *Viking* program of Mars landings): There are those who say that if the *Viking* landers find no life, no signs of fossil life, not even any pre-biological organic chemistry, the results will be of no interest. But that simply is not true; because then we would have the classic scientific situation: two planets (the earth and Mars) more or less like each other; one has life, the other doesn't—why? Two planets—on one of which life arose and the other where it didn't, would be vastly exciting—an experimental planet and a control planet. So if all the biological instruments on *Viking* should give negative results—and if there is no question of ambiguity—I think that would be terrifically interesting. How come here and not there?

San Francisco Examiner & Chronicle, 3-26:(Sunday Punch)4.

Arthur M. Schlesinger, Jr.
Historian

The 20th century will be remembered, when all else about it is forgotten, as the century in which man first burst his terrestrial bonds and began the exploration of space. No one can know where this exploration will finally take us. But the pursuit of knowledge and understanding has been humankind's most abiding quest; and to have confined this quest to our small planet, to have refused the adventure of space, would surely have been a betrayal of man's innermost nature.

Interview/ The New York Times, 12-3:(1)68.

Vladimir A. Shatalov
Soviet astronaut;
Chief of astronaut training

The space flights of the last 10 years showed that space may be very useful to mankind, and that the most valuable uses lie nearest to earth. That's why you must create near-earth satellite laboratories. But first we have to learn how long man can live up there. That's why we are going to go a slow way and with each expedition try to extend the length of stay. This aim is at the core of our program.

Interview, Zvezdny Gorodok, U.S.S.R./ The New York Times, 3-22:20.

Alan B. Shepard
Rear Admiral, United States Navy;
Chief of Astronauts,
National Aeronautics and Space Administration

The question we're asking now is: "Where do we go from here in space?" The answer is that we must put it to use to help the people more directly. Learning about earth resources from space will be very helpful to our country. The environment is one area where this technology can be immediately applied, as well as in navigation, communications and many other fields. People are so blase about turning on the television and watching a news broadcast or a coronation live from halfway around the world, without really realizing that this is possible today because of the space program. That's the kind of technological "fallout" that's necessary for the country to keep making progress; and, of course, that's what the space agency has in mind by increasing the emphasis on earth-related programs.

Interview/ U.S. News & World Report, 4-24:26.

. . . we never really have thought about the (space) program as being one which was exciting and glamorous. I mean, it never has been planned that way. We've always felt that this space program is really just another extension of technology. The technology started with the automobile, the airplane;

and now we see it being expressed in space —not only in the manned flights, but also in the unmanned flights. And I guess perhaps it's encouraging to me . . . to think that we have lost the glamor and excitement of the program. Because, you see, to me that means that it's becoming a way of life, which I think space should be. It's becoming a program which is becoming everyday in our consideration, which is making contributions every day to our way of life. So the fact that it has lost its glamor perhaps is not as disturbing to me as you might think.

Broadcast panel discussion/
The National Observer, 5-6:22.

Roger Sperry
Professor of Psychobiology,
California Institute of Technology

Science, above all other alternatives, constitutes man's best source and hope for finding that urgent new ethic for survival, and also for recovering that lost sense of purpose and meaning . . . Science, as man's number one source of valid information, can be enlisted in the realm of value judgment on the further, simple and straight-forward rationale that an informed judgment is generally better than one that is uninformed or misinformed.

Before American Association for the Advancement of Science, Washington, Dec. 29/
The New York Times, 12-30:8.

Robert H. Steinbacher
Project scientist, "Mariner" program,
National Aeronautics and Space
Administration of the United States

Mars used to be likened to Earth in science fiction, and was compared to the moon after the first pictures from *Mariner 4* in 1965. Now (with *Mariner 9*) we are seeing that Mars has a character all its own. It is not earth-like or moon-like; it is Mars-like.

News conference, Pasadena, Calif./
The New York Times, 6-15:32.

Albert Szent-Gyorgyi
Biologist

The *Apollo* (U.S. space program) flights demand that the word "impossible" be struck from the scientific dictionary. They are the greatest encouragement for the human spirit.

Interview/
The New York Times, 12-3:(1)68.

Olin E. Teague
United States Representative, D–Tex.

Twenty years from now, the country that leads in technology will lead the world.

The Dallas Times Herald, 11-23:(B)2.

Edward Teller
Physicist

It is technology which has made America great. Technology has defeated more evil in our daily lives than we even are apt to remember today. It is technology that has defeated the terrible danger of Hitler. Yet, technology is no longer popular among our young people. Some consider it as a clear evil. Enthusiasm seems to be gone. The consequences are just beginning to appear. In this century, it happened for the first time last year that manufactured imports exceeded manufactured exports (in the U.S.). A good way of life cannot be solved by any financial wizard. If the technological base is lacking, the safety of the United States, the survival of freedom, cannot be guaranteed, without technology. Yet, there are magnificent things that are happening, and can be happening, in technology. Think of the computers—these electronic brains, which can work faster and more reliably than any person, and which can do anything, any intellectual function, if only we can describe that intellectual function accurately, like a condition . . . Now, not everybody needs to work on technology. Not everybody can work on technology. A minority will do. But in a democracy, no subject will flourish unless people participate, unless they understand what it is about, unless they are willing to support it. To learn something about technology, to understand how it can improve our quality of life, is something about which every citizen should know. And there

(EDWARD TELLER)

is one final point. To understand science and technology is real fun. It is one of the most remarkable adventures of our age.

Television broadcast/"Comment!" National Broadcasting Company, 1-30.

Paul Thayer
Chairman, LTV Corporation

To put it bluntly, America's technological growth is stunted. That's bad news for America and I think for the rest of the world . . . There is a strong mood of anxiety, weariness, future shock or perhaps "technological fatigue" operating in the country today, created and successfully exploited by the enemies of technology.

Before Town Hall, Los Angeles/ Los Angeles Times, 6-14:(3)17.

Jesse Werner
Chairman and president, GAF Corporation

. . . technology—which I define as the totality of applied science—when employed to improve the quality of life, is a most important key to the future. Science and technology can provide us with the power to untangle the many knotty problems challenging us today. Let me be quick to point out that they alone will not save us. But without them we simply will not be able to resolve such urgent questions as those concerning environmental life-support systems in ecology, the depletion of material and energy resources, the use of nuclear power, housing and urban planning, mass transit and transportation, overpopulation, world trade, disease control and therapy, new food and agricultural resources and so many others. There are many sociologists who feel that science cannot contribute to the solution of the world's social ills. In fact, some feel that the onrushing developments of science are only adding to our packet of problems . . . But if we examine history critically, we find that the advancement of science has brought with it great social benefits. It has ameliorated suffering, has lengthened our life span by orders of magnitude, has added creature comforts, has added measures of enjoyment to our lives and has spread them not only to the high and mighty, but to the lowly as well. It has provided new standards of life and freedom and independence to the entire populations of entire nations. The Cassandras to the contrary, we must continue to move ahead.

Before Society of Chemical Industry, Oct. 4/Vital Speeches, 11-15:88.

Walter B. Wriston
Chairman,
First National City Corporation

. . . the distrust of science and technology goes back at least to the Greek legend of Prometheus chained to the rock because he brought mankind the benefit of fire. The custom of putting the bearers of scientific truth in jail has happily passed into history in most areas of the world; but the recurring idea that some wise person or group should tell the scientists what to study and, therefore, have them bring forth only those inventions which the ombudsman regards as being in harmony with his own limited knowledge, continues to appeal to some. In political terms, such a concept results in dictatorship and, like all dictatorships, represents a profound distrust of the ability of the other fellow to run his own life. That main problem with all these straight-line projections leading from here to eternity is that they are inevitably based on what is known about today's technology. It never seems to occur to the soothsayers that, as technology has changed in the past, it will continue to change in the future.

At Religion in American Life dinner of the Advertising Council, New York/ The Wall Street Journal, 6-8:12.

Yevgeny Yevtushenko
Russian poet

(On cooperation in space between the U.S. and the Soviet Union): We met at the Elbe (in World War II) and we can meet over the Milky Way.

Cape Kennedy, Fla., April 16/ Los Angeles Times, 4-17:(1)8.

Henry Aaron
Baseball player, Atlanta "Braves"

I don't want to hang around and hear people say, "I remember when they couldn't throw the ball by Aaron. Now they can." I'll know when I should quit . . . When your time is up, you miss the ball you used to hit out. You just nip the ball and go back to the dugout shaking your head and wondering how it happened.

The Christian Science Monitor, 3-15:13.

Spiro T. Agnew
Vice President of the United States

The importance of our competitive ethic lies in the fact that it is only by trial of their abilities—by testing and challenging—can they (young Americans) discover their strengths and, yes, their weaknesses . . . Life is a great competition . . . sports—all sports —is one of the few bits of glue that holds society together . . . I would rather be a failure in the competitive society which is our inheritance than to live in a waveless sea of non-achievers.

Before Touchdown Club, Birmingham, Ala., Jan. 18/ The Washington Post, 1-24:(B)1.

Muhammad Ali (Cassius Clay)
Former Heavyweight Boxing Champion of the World

Boxing is dying because too many blacks are fighting each other. This isn't a matter of racism. It's just that people like to root for their own side. It's human nature, not hatred. The Africans love Dick Tiger and Hogan Bassey. Nino Benvenuti was great for the Italians. The English had Henry Cooper and Randy Turpin, who was black. They drew huge crowds when they fought against men of different countries or different skin. It's like a baseball team. You split up the greatest baseball team in the whole world and have them play each other and they won't draw nothing. But put them against somebody else and they fill the stands. So what the white people need now is white fighters. They need an idol. They need a Jack Dempsey or a Gene Tunney.

Las Vegas, Nev./ Los Angeles Herald-Examiner, 6-16:(C)2.

Dick Allen
Baseball player, Chicago "White Sox"

They write that I'm not a team player, that I force managers to have two sets of rules. Well, I didn't ask them to make two sets of rules. Maybe the problem is their rules . . . I'm getting tired of hearing what a bad influence I am on . . . so-called kids . . . These guys (other players) are not "kids." Baseball is not a game for kids. It is a game for grown men. Professionals. If they're kids, they don't belong in the major leagues. As far as I'm concerned, there's too much emphasis on this Joe College approach. This is a professional sport, not a college sport. These guys have families to feed, and they intend to keep feeding them. They'll come in and do the job they have to do. When the game starts, you pull together as a team; when the game ends, you go your way as an individual.

Interview/ Los Angeles Times, 8-4:(3)10.

I once loved this game. But after being traded four times, I realize that it's nothing but a business. I treat my horses better than the owners treat us. It's a shame they've destroyed my love for the game.

Interview/Newsweek, 8-21:84.

George Allen
Football coach, Washington "Redskins"

In my opinion . . . football is not a game for radicals. We (on the *Redskins*) don't believe in radical offenses and so forth. We're strong for the time-tested virtues like physical conditioning. I like to be called a great conservative . . . Ours is the sound, conservative way. A gambler is a coach who uses a number one draft choice on an untested, inexperienced lineman or receiver from Illinois Normal. A conservative is a man who trades his number one choices for established veterans . . . In my opinion, the odds are against gamblers, innovators and pace-setters in football. Call me a conservative.

Los Angeles Times, 9-22:(3)1.

Phog Allen
Former basketball coach, University of Kansas

. . . basketball was my game, but I don't think it will ever replace football and baseball as the most popular spectator sport. There are not enough players hurt in basketball. Spectators, especially women, like to see people hurt; they say they don't, but they do. Football is brutal; it's just about as bad as boxing. People like that. They don't want their sons to play football, but they go to see other people's sons play it.

Interview, Lawrence, Kan./The Washington Post, 3-23:(D)4.

Lance Alworth
Football player, Dallas "Cowboys"

The most important thing in football is the way you prepare for a game. It's a completely mental game. The more you rehearse mentally, the better you play. Blockers have to be mean, so this year I'm mean. I'm a mean son-of-a-gun . . . I growl at the cat, make faces at the mirror and kick the trash can. Blocking is something you have to make yourself do. Catching is natural; but it isn't natural for a civilized man to run around hitting people. Besides, it hurts.

Interview/The Dallas Times Herald, 1-12:(Super Bowl)12.

Sparky Anderson
Baseball manager, Cincinnati "Reds"

When I remember how, as a youngster, I dreamed of being a big-league ballplayer, then read today about the money some of these players are refusing, it bothers me. And the reason I'm bothered is because I think that when a player accepts the wonderful opportunity offered in the big leagues, and a salary away above that of the average white-collar worker, he takes on a responsibility—a responsibility to maintain an image that kids can look up to. We all know what great imitators kids are. When they see a player with long hair, they want long hair. Whatever they see a big-leaguer do, that's their thing, too. But I often get the feeling today that the people playing baseball have forgotten their obligations—have forgotten what a privilege it is to play up here. I'm sure you get the impression, as I do, that too often players seem far more interested in money than they are in putting out 100 per cent effort on the field. It makes me want to cry.

The Christian Science Monitor, 3-17:14.

The only thing I believe is this: A player does not have to like a manager, and he does not have to respect a manager. All he has to do is obey the rules.

The Dallas Times Herald, 3-22:(B)2.

Most fans think managing is knowing when to bunt, when to flash the steal sign or when to hit behind the runner. Well, it's not. I could let one of my coaches do this for me and chances are he would make the same decisions I would. Actually, managing is two things: communication with your players and knowing how to handle a pitching staff. If you can't get through to your players, you're in the wrong business. And if you don't learn to recognize right away when a pitcher is tired or not himself, then all the runs in the world won't save you.

Interview, Oakland, Calif./The Christian Science Monitor, 10-20:12.

Eddie Arcaro
Former jockey

I don't understand why we haven't had a Triple Crown winner since Citation. It's true there has been an increase in the number of horses being bred, but we still are producing super horses. Native Dancer was one, yet Native Dancer broke down in the (Kentucky) Derby. The demands on a horse aren't as great today as they were when I was riding. For instance, there is a three-week gap between the Derby and Preakness, and there's a month before the Belmont. It used to be that the Preakness came the week after the Derby and the Belmont three weeks after that. It took a lot of horse to meet that schedule.

Interview, New York, March 1/ Los Angeles Times, 3-2:(3)10.

George Archer
Golfer

No (golf) tournament is harder to win than any other. It isn't any harder to win the Masters than the Hartford Open . . . You have to get the breaks to win any tournament.

Augusta, Ga./ The New York Times, 4-5:57.

Les Aspin
United States Representative, D–Wis.

I predict there will be a mass exodus of sports events from home TV and radio to closed-circuit television—where the money is. As they explore the possibilities of closed-circuit TV, the professionals are facing the same choice as a compulsive eater would in choosing between a plain cupcake and a rich, gooey chocolate cake. And anyone who thinks the owners won't go to where the most money is, is just kidding himself.

The Christian Science Monitor, 1-18:(B)10.

Al Attles
Basketball coach, "Golden State Warriors"

True coaching is a teaching process, and the real teaching is done in junior high and high school. Up here (in the professional leagues), it's more or less a matching-up process. We have no time to teach. Most teams play their top seven or eight men. They can't wait for the others to learn. The job is to win today, not teach for tomorrow.

Interview/ The Christian Science Monitor, 2-2:12.

Frank A. Baker
Executive secretary, American Bowling Congress

Other games—without putting the knock on them—are falling into the hands of specialists—the great star, the tall man, the physically overpowering individual. Bowling, conversely, still belongs to the masses . . . as well as its stars. Many games cannot be enjoyed unless they are played well. The hacker doesn't belong on the same golf course with Arnold Palmer; the occasional player doesn't belong on the same tennis court with the pro. In bowling alone, the low-average, recreational-minded participant can be as proficient (on a single roll of the ball) as the most-skilled superstar.

Los Angeles Herald-Examiner, 4-8:(B)5.

Manuel Benitez ("El Cordobes")
Bullfighter

(Announcing his retirement): . . . I used to be an illiterate and have suddenly discovered there are many things in this world I would like to know about . . . I will never again put on the (bullfighter's) suit of lights. Of all the things I want to do, perfecting my English is one of the most important. In this world, if you cannot speak English, you are just a stone . . . One reason why I left bullfighting is that I am no longer the old Cordobes. And if I am no longer as good as I used to be, there is no place for me in the bullring.

Madrid, Feb. 26/ The Washington Post, 2-27:(D)1.

Andre Boniface
French rugby player

I criticize them (American football players) for not running enough with the ball

(ANDRE BONIFACE)

and I think they're in poor physical shape. Most of all, they confirmed what I thought about them—that is that they don't have any imagination. They think too much about their size and look like big machines dressed up in uniforms.

Paris, May 29/
The Dallas Times Herald, 5-30:(B)1.

Lou Brock
Baseball player,
St. Louis "Cardinals"

This is a game of constant adjustment, and that's what keeps me always interested. You have to change just to stay even. The pitchers have a book on you and they know what your tendencies are. What they don't learn on their own they learn through the grapevine, the finest information service in the world. But just as the pitchers have a book on you, so you also have a book on them. The duel never ends.

Interview, St. Petersburg, Fla./
Los Angeles Herald-Examiner, 3-26:(B)2.

Paul Brown
Football coach, Cincinnati "Bengals"

Good football can only be played by good people—those who are nice people inside. I don't know how to define it, but when you meet them, you know them. A clinker can win a game now and then, but they don't win consistently. What success we've had comes from the fact that, over the years, we haven't had many clinkers. It's hard enough to win football games when things are relatively pleasant and stable. It's almost impossible if somebody is stirring things up.

Interview/
The Christian Science Monitor, 11-10:6.

Avery Brundage
President,
International Olympic Committee

The Olympics are not just a competition to see who can run the fastest or throw the farthest. They're not a world championship. They're unique. They're an ideal. They can't be changed by anybody . . . There are two kinds of competitors: those who are interested in sports for sports' sake and the ones interested for financial reasons. Why should the pros want a medal? Let them hold their own world championship if they wish. The Olympics will always remain amateur.

Interview, Santa Barbara, Calif./
The Washington Post, 7-20:(H)7.

. . . I'm disturbed by the way the Olympics keep growing. In a way, I regard the growth of the Olympics as the greatest accomplishment of my presidency, and it's now become the greatest problem. Gigantism is a curse that can turn the Olympics into a damned circus. There have to be cuts made in the summer program, while the winter Olympics should be abandoned in their entirety . . . Winter sports don't belong in the Olympics, and I can't be too emphatic about that. Too few countries in the world engage in winter sports. How many are there—20 or 25? . . . In cutting down on the Olympic program, my solution is to eliminate all sports that lead to professional careers—soccer, football, basketball, cycling, boxing and a few others . . . Of recent years we've been adding new events. We should reverse ourselves and begin cutting down . . . I also am disturbed by the tremendous political pressures that are being applied. They are government pressures and that's where the money comes from. The Rhodesian action (banning Rhodesia from the Olympics because of its internal racial policies) was a disappointment to me because the IOC is supposed to put idealism above expediency. It's going to get worse, too. But if the IOC would stand fast, it could control it.

Interview, Munich, Aug. 25/
The New York Times, 8-26:17.

(On the Arab terrorist killing of 11 members of the Israeli Olympic team in Munich): Every civilized person recoils in horror at the barbarous, criminal (intrusion) of terrorists into the peaceful Olympic precincts. We mourn our Israeli friends, victims of this brutal assault. The Olympic flag and the flags of all the world fly at half mast. Sadly in this imperfect world, the greater and the more important the Olympic Games become, the more they are open to commercial, political and now criminal pressures. The games of the 20th Olympiad have been subjected to two savage attacks. We lost the Rhodesian battle against naked, political blackmail (in which the Rhodesian team was ousted from the games because of its government's racial policies). We have only the strength of a great ideal. I am sure the public will agree that we cannot allow a handful of terrorists to destroy this nucleus of international cooperation and good-will we have in the Olympic movement. The games must go on and we must continue our efforts to keep them clean, pure and honest and try to extend the sportsmanship of the athletic field into other areas. We declare today a day of mourning, and will continue all the events one day later than originally scheduled.

At memorial services, Olympic Stadium, Munich, Sept. 6/ The Washington Post, 9-7:(A)17.

Michael Burke
Owner, New York "Yankees" baseball club

(On the player strike): They talk about getting a 17 per cent increase on their pensions—but I don't hear anyone talk about the fact that their salaries have gone up 30 per cent since 1969. Doesn't that count? We'd like them to have the best plan we can give them—but we have to draw the line somewhere.

April 1/ The New York Times, 4-11:50.

August A. Busch, Jr.
President, St. Louis "Cardinals" baseball club

(On the possibility of a player strike): Few American and National League ball clubs really make any money. I can't speak for other clubs, but, frankly, I wouldn't give a damn if the players went out. I'd vote to let them take a walk . . . I appreciate this could be a considerable blow to other ball clubs who don't have our corporate structure; but I'm afraid that, with the constantly-increasing player demands plus the attempt to rule out the reserve clause, it's getting impossible to operate reasonably.

St. Petersburg, Fla., March 15/ The New York Times, 3-16:66.

Emanuel Celler
United States Representative, D–N.Y.

(On baseball's reserve clause): Baseball, and only baseball of all our professional sports, enjoys antitrust exemption. This inconsistency, the Supreme Court tells us, is to be resolved by Congress . . . The important thing is to once and for all end unwarranted privilege and place all professional sports on equal footing. In the past, the sports monopolists have come before this Subcommittee defending their claimed exemption from the antitrust laws because the health of professional sports is "in the community interest." But when these community-minded gentlemen have left the Halls of Congress, too often their actions have exhibited utter disregard for the communities that support them. Ticket prices skyrocket, television reception is blacked out, greedy threats of franchise moves are made upon municipal officials, teams jump from city to city betraying lifelong supporters.

At House Judiciary Antitrust Subcommittee, Washington/The Washington Post, 8-2:(D)3.

Jack Christiansen
Football coach, Stanford University

These kids realize there's more to life than just football. They aren't 24-hour-a-day football players, and we don't expect them to be. Discipline? Sure, we have discipline. But we believe in two kinds—individual and team. How a player dresses or wears his hair falls under individual discipline. But how he moves when the ball is snapped is team discipline. You need both nowadays if you expect to have a successful program.

Interview, Stanford, Calif./ Los Angeles Times, 9-3:(C)5.

Marlow W. Cook
United States Senator, R–Ky.

(Advocating a Federal sports commission to oversee franchise transfers, TV arrangements, player drafts and contracts, etc.): The first right to be protected is the right of the sports fan to a stable professional sports system—one upon which he can rely and one which he can enjoy. The fans have been the real victims of disputes and controversies. These are the same people who have elevated sports to its lucrative position.

March 30/ Los Angeles Times, 3-31:(3)2.

Howard Cosell
Sports commentator, American Broadcasting Company

Purely and simply, I'm against big-time college sport, at least the way it's conducted in this country. I think big-time college sport is corruptive and hypocritical. When a great university spends a good deal of its time and money—which they almost all do—on the importation of a 6-11½" young man because he can drop a ball through a hoop, it's a distortion of emphasis and values that rebounds to a school's discredit . . . And how can you really blame the young men involved, many of whom are from the ghetto, who are in some cases black, in other cases white, but all of whom are corrupted by the great institutions that entreat them to attend without regard to their pursuit of education or anything else?

Interview/ Los Angeles Herald-Examiner, 4-25:(C)2.

Organized baseball is totally without leadership. The game is in a state of continuing decline; and one reason for this is that it is being run by people with Neanderthal minds.

Quote, 8-6:122.

Joe Cronin
President, American (Baseball) League

The (baseball) reserve clause preserves the absolute integrity of the game, equalizes the competition and gives each club the opportunity to promote its very expensive player development program.

June 20/ San Francisco Examiner, 6-20:53.

Larry Csonka
Football player, Miami "Dolphins"

(On being a running back): Running into the line, you go into a different world. All around you guys are scratching, clawing, beating on each other, feeling pain. There are noises from the crowd and from the linemen; but during that one moment, I never seem to hear them. Then, going back to the huddle, the sound of the pads slamming together will still be in my ears, and I'll listen for the first time. The sensation gives a real insight into the game. It's too bad more people haven't been in there, where football is really played.

Newsweek, 12-4:76.

Howie Dallmar
Basketball coach, Stanford University

The one area of difficulty for any basketball coach is simply that only five players can be in the game at a given time, and any player sitting on the bench feels he should be playing more.

San Francisco Examiner, 3-11:28.

Joseph C. Dey, Jr.
Commissioner, Tournament Players Division, United States Professional Golfers' Association

When communications became instantaneous, endeavors in every field tended to expand. I think a world (golf) tour is a certainty, particularly so if the players continue their posture of independence, as they seem determined to do. With the growing purses, the players can pick their spots—play where and when they want. In a way, of course, the world tour has already started.

The Christian Science Monitor, 1-28:10.

Leo Durocher
Baseball manager, Chicago "Cubs"

You can't talk to players the way you formerly could . . . It's different today. You get kids right out of high school or college boys not used to this kind of language or having anybody rip into them. They know they made mistakes, but they're not used to having anybody tell them about it. So you have to be careful. Why, the club I had in Brooklyn, I could come in after a game and say, "You dumb bleep-bleeper, you sure bleeped up that bleeping play." And the guy would say, "Aw, I bleeped it up." And I'd say, "You sure did, you bleep-bleeper, and don't do it again."

Interview, Chicago/
Los Angeles Times, 6-21:(3)1.

Leo Durocher
Former baseball manager

When I put on a uniform, I was tough and mean. I'd do anything to win a ball game. I didn't care how we won, just as long as we won. I didn't want to know my opponent; I only wanted to beat him. Off the field, I didn't want that image. I didn't want to be known as a tough guy, or somebody always in the middle of controversy. I could never shake the rap. If I went to the bathroom, I'd find somebody looking to punch me. If I crossed the street on the right side, there would have been somebody who said I should have crossed on the left side. It's a way of life I could never avoid . . . You know, when I was managing Brooklyn I'd have to stop at this light each day on the way home. On the corner was a bar, and the guys would always yell, "Hey, Leo, who won?" If I said "Us," they'd say great goin'. If I said "Them," they'd call me a dumb sonofabitch.

Interview, Chicago, July 29/
The Washington Post, 7-30:(E)2.

Francoise Durr
Tennis player

Confidence is 80 per cent of this game. That's why Billie Jean (King) wins so much. She's so confident. She knows she can beat anybody, and she feels she's just not going to lose. I have a little more of that feeling now than I did before, but still not as much as I'd like to have.

Hingham, Mass./
The Christian Science Monitor, 1-28:10.

Sam J. Ervin, Jr.
United States Senator, D–N.C.

Owners of pro (sports) teams have used their freedom from antitrust statutes to exploit players in a condition that amounts to a modern form of peonage—servitude for lifetime at the pleasure of an owner. So far as I am concerned, it doesn't make any difference whether the individual receives 10 cents a day or $100,000 a year—he can still be a peon.

Quote, 10-1:333.

Bill Fallowfield
Secretary,
Rugby Football League of Britain

There's too much emphasis on sheer size in the U.S. The game here is for the small and fast as well as the big and strong. The American way of play isn't open enough for us; too much starting and stopping. Ours is a running and passing game and the emphasis is on keeping the action going. Our spectators would never stand for all those substitutes going off and on; our players would never stand for sitting on the bench.

Leeds, England/
The Dallas Times Herald, 1-30:(D)6.

Charles Feeney
President, National (Baseball) League

The best baseball is being played right now. There never was a time when the quality of the game was higher. There used to be guys like Lefty Grove to bat against. But once you got past him, the other three start-

(CHARLES FEENEY)

ers were awful. Now everyone is bigger, stronger and faster. When the starter tires, some relief pitcher comes on who can throw bullets.

Interview, Phoenix/ San Francisco Examiner, 3-14:55.

Charles O. Finley
Owner, Oakland "Athletics" baseball club

(On the current player strike): All you hear from the players nowadays is gimme, gimme, gimme, and then threat, threat, threat. I'm getting sick and tired of it! . . . I believe that the basis for all our trouble is, first of all, that we have spoiled the players and, secondly, they are being misled by Marvin Miller (executive director of the Players' Association). They've got the best pension in sports, business or industry anywhere. Where in the world can you go and work only four years and start collecting a pension at 45? And they want a 17 per cent increase . . . The players give us (owners) no credit for all the unjustified and astronomical salaries they're getting. They don't think about yesterday—they want to know "what are you going to do for me today?"

Chicago/ Los Angeles Times, 4-5:(3)2.

Bobby Fischer
United States chess champion

(On his upcoming world championship match with Boris Spassky): Spassky is simply not in my class, really. I'm a better player—period. I expect to beat him; he knows I can. It would be nice to be modest, but it would be stupid not to tell the truth. There is only one really immortal player in the world today . . . and it is Fischer!

Los Angeles/ Los Angeles Times, 6-28:(1)28.

Chess is like war on a board. The object is to crush the other man's mind.

The Dallas Times Herald, 9-3:(L)1.

Bobby Fischer
World chess champion

What I really want to do is encourage respect for chess. Chess masters should play under superb conditions and be paid as well as top athletes. Whatever (boxer) Muhammad Ali gets, next time I want more!

Life, 9-15:42.

Emerson Fittipaldi
Auto racing driver

When I get inside my car, it is like being out of this world. All I know is that I am there by myself. If I have any other problems, I have to forget them. It is as if I am part of the car. The wheels are my legs.

The New York Times, 9-10:(5)25.

Bill France, Jr.
President, National Association for Stock Car Racing

For a sport that has to pull itself up by its own boot straps, without the enthusiastic support of the media, without the backing of alumni associations, and paying its own way, we have done all right. Auto racing hasn't yet had to resort to gimmicks to draw people. It depends more on its concept of thrills, on its relation to people who own cars, and its integrity as a sport free of scandal, for its growth.

Talladega, Ala./ The Christian Science Monitor, 5-11:11.

Joe Frazier
Heavyweight Boxing Champion of the World

The name of the game is to win by knocking the guy out. This is what people come to see, not for you to go the distance. They say after a quick KO, "We didn't get our money's worth." But they really came to see you knock the guy out.

Philadelphia/ The Washington Post, 1-4:(D)4.

Am I tired of being the heavyweight champ? I wouldn't say that. In one way, yes, though. Yes, I get tired talking and traveling. I get tired staying in the room. Too much pressure; all the time, pressure. The pressure I'm talking about is like, well . . . having to be what you are all the time. You gotta be nice to everybody. It's impossible. You start getting concerned about doing the right thing and not hurting anybody, hurting their feelings. It bothers you. It bothers your mind. And that's pressure.

Omaha, Neb./
Los Angeles Herald-Examiner, 5-25:(C)4.

Jack Gardner
Former basketball coach,
University of Utah

I am convinced that basketball is developing so rapidly that in only a short time Brazil and other Latin countries will soon compete on an equal basis with the United States, Russia and Yugoslavia. With the great desire and public support I witnessed in Latin America, it is only a matter of time until there is an international league. They need better coaching and some technical refinement, but they are definitely on the way. I hope we are smart enough to take advantage of this opportunity to work with them in this critical area.

Salt Lake City/
The Dallas Times Herald, 1-2:(C)6.

Ed Garvey
Executive director,
National Football League Players Association

We (in football) have the lowest professional sports salaries and a poorer pension plan than baseball, or even hockey. This is in pro football, the sport that (public-opinion analyst) Lou Harris and (NFL commissioner) Pete Rozelle tell us is number one in the hearts of America. It's a gold mine for the owners, most of whom aren't eager to share their fortunes.

Nov. 22/
The Dallas Times Herald, 11-23:(D)1.

Sid Gillman
Former football coach

There's probably no more confining a profession than coaching football. If there's a drawback to coaching, that's it. People think football is a game. It's not. It's a business—12 hours a day, seven days a week. If you don't work at it that way, there's no way you can survive. You can't get ideas on a golf course or sitting around a bar.

Interview, Rancho La Costa, Calif./
The New York Times, 1-23:(5)4.

Arthur J. Goldberg
Lawyer; Former Associate Justice,
Supreme Court of the United States

It is beyond dispute that organized baseball today is business, big business. Its owners are businessmen—or, in some cases, giant corporations selling everything from beer to television time.

Appealing to Supreme Court to reverse a 1922 decision exempting baseball from laws regulating interstate commerce, Washington/
The Dallas Times Herald, 3-21:(A)18.

Jeffrey H. Goldstein
Professor of Psychology,
Temple University

The increasing popularity of football and hockey over baseball suggests to me that people are looking for more excitement and more aggressive kinds of sports. This could be because people are more used to violence in their everyday lives; or it could be that, because people go to the more violent kinds of sports, they are more likely to be violent. Or both.

Philadelphia/
The Washington Post, 8-20:(D)2.

Curt Gowdy
Sports commentator,
National Broadcasting Company

Football lends itself best to TV. It's a big field and yet the action starts off in a narrow sphere, and as the play unfolds you can widen out with your specialized cameras and get it all—the passes, the punts, the runs, the defense. You can cover almost every eventuality on the field. Football was almost built for television. The hardest sport to telecast is

(CURT GOWDY)

baseball. The geography of the game makes it difficult. Basketball . . . relatively easy . . . big ball, few participants. Hockey! Oh, my God! The one thing that has improved hockey for TV is the replay. That way you can see the goals. Without it, you might never see them. Boxing, of course, is two big men in a small area. A breeze.

Interview/TV Guide, 7-15:19.

Donald Grant
Chairman,
New York "Mets" baseball club

(On the just-settled player strike): Everybody recognizes that nobody won.

April 13/
The New York Times, 4-14:1.

Mudcat Grant
Baseball player, Cleveland "Indians"

I'm 37 going on 19. To stay in this business there has to be plenty of "little boy" inside you. I'm a pitcher, a veteran pitcher. I know when I've got my stuff and when I don't; but the man (the manager) still has to come out and take the ball away from me before I'll call it a day. Now, isn't that just like a "little boy"?

Los Angeles Times, 3-18:(3)2.

Bob Griese
Football player, Miami "Dolphins"

There's too much emphasis on winning. You should learn to be a loser, too . . . Life is nothing but a series of victories and defeats, on and off the athletic field. If a kid learns the early lessons of losing, he'll be a better man. If a young boy wins all the time, he takes it for granted and fails to appreciate the accomplishment of victory. When a defeat finally comes along, he can't stomach it. Sometimes he'll even walk away and quit.

The Christian Science Monitor, 7-25:13.

Horace Hayden
Architect; Designer of Louisiana Superdome, New Orleans

(On the ascendancy of modern sports stadiums): The end is already in sight for the old-time, hard-nosed, dyed-in-the-wool sports fan who is willing to tolerate a hard board seat and freeze to death watching a football game in a blizzard or lose five pounds sweating in the mid-summer sun to view a game of baseball.

San Francisco Examiner, 3-23:58.

Louis Harris
Public opinion analyst

One might have bet, 10 years ago, with all the young people rejecting all that they have, that one of the things that might have gone down the drain was spectator sports. It hasn't happened. I guess there is a certain amount of escapism involved. More important, sports is just plain fun. People enjoy sports. It's world-wide, apparently. I took a trip last fall to the Soviet Union and I was staggered that there, every night on TV, they have volleyball, their football (soccer), swimming, basketball finals, etc. I asked a Russian official about it. He said such scheduling was routine. Without getting cosmic about it, I think it's safe to say sports is binding—world-wide.

Interview, New York/
The Washington Post, 6-3:(D)1.

John Holland
Vice president,
Chicago "Cubs" baseball club

Speed always has been an asset (in baseball), but now it has reached a point where it is an absolute must. It is a critical part of the game, because a hard-hit ball takes off like a rocket once it bounds off that solid, slick artificial grass. You need speed offensively and defensively. It takes a faster man to beat out a hit because the ball gets to the infielder quicker. For that same reason, the infielder has to be faster to reach the ball. But where I believe speed has to be stressed most of all, because of these hard artificial surfaces, is in the outfield. You've got to have swifties out there who can cut off the hits into the left-center and right-center alleys and also down the foul lines. Preventing singles from bounding on through for doubles and triples on the Astro-Turf and Tartan-Turf is a key factor when you're playing in those parks. Last season, we didn't have enough speed to do it, and our record on artificial turf bears it out. It wouldn't be stretching the point too much to say that we lost the pennant on those carpeted fields. At least we played so poorly on them that it kept us from making a good run at the flag.

Chicago/The Sporting News, 1-8:34.

Ralph Houk
Baseball manager,
New York "Yankees"

The thing that kills a manager quicker than anything . . . is to have a lead going into the fifth inning and there's rain coming up and you know you have to get three out before the game is official . . . It takes forever. Your pitcher can't throw a strike. Batters just stroll up to the plate. The umpire dusts the plate. I've even had my own catcher go out and talk to the pitcher. Aaaaagh! I've even seen the hitter stop and go back and pick out another bat. We got into one of those in Milwaukee last summer. You wouldn't believe it. The third out alone must have taken at least 12 minutes, and we got it on a screaming line drive that went straight into a glove. Just seconds later, here it came in buckets. We won, but I thought I wouldn't eat again for a week.

Interview, Fort Lauderdale, Fla./
The New York Times, 3-10:27.

Lamar Hunt
President,
Kansas City "Chiefs" football team

In my opinion, coaching is 95 per cent of professional football. Good coaches get good players . . . Pro football is more of a leveler of talent. In college football there is a great difference in personnel between the top and bottom teams. That's not true in pro football, and that's the reason top coaches are so much in demand.

The Christian Science Monitor, 6-9:4.

Ron Johnson
Football player, New York "Giants"

(On being a running back): When you have the football, the show is all yours. You're out there alone, matching quick instincts and wits against tacklers. It's a game within a game and you're determining its destiny. Of course, with everybody's eyes on you, you can look like the goat. But you also have the chance to be the hero. And chances like that don't come along too often in anybody's life.

Newsweek, 12-4:84.

Jim Kensil
Executive director,
National Football League

There's a difference in modern fans, probably due to television. They tend to be total fans rather than hometowners. They still root for the home team, but they follow a lot of them. They're knowledgeable about the (Miami) *Dolphins* and (Dallas) *Cowboys*, for instance, and they care what happens to them in a way that wasn't possible before television.

Los Angeles Times, 1-13:(3)6.

Billy Kidd
Skier

In Europe, skiing is a business and almost a religion. Members of the U.S. (Olympic) team are strictly amateurs. Skiing is the Number 1 sport in Austria, Number 2 sport in France and Number 3 in Switzerland. When a competitor wins a race, he gets a bonus. Success can mean wealth. Our (U.S.) kids get a pat on the back. France puts in $225,000 a year to finance its ski team. In Russia and the other Communist countries competitors are on the national payroll. They live a good life. Our skiers have troub-

(BILLY KIDD)

le getting enough money to train and campaign on the World Cup circuit. It's a matter of difference in our system and attitude.

Sapporo, Japan, Feb. 8/
The Washington Post, 1-9:(E)2.

Billie Jean King
Tennis player

We should encourage (tennis) fans to scream or boo if they like, just like in baseball and football. This sport has had too much stuffiness and protocol. It needs more pizzazz.

Family Weekly, 8-13:14.

George Kolianowski
American chess grandmaster

(On the well-publicized, just-completed world chess championship match won by America's Bobby Fischer): The American people as a whole now at least will recognize chess as something played by people and not just wood being pushed around.

The New York Times, 9-2:34.

Sandy Koufax
Former baseball player,
Los Angeles "Dodgers"

Consistency, I think, is the ultimate goal of every professional athlete. Consistency means having good years—not just one good game.

Interview, Bangor, Maine/
Los Angeles Herald-Examiner, 1-19:(B)1.

Bowie Kuhn
United States Commissioner of Baseball

(On the termination of the player strike): I'm delighted to have this over. I hope we've all learned a lesson. I will work with people in baseball for procedures to prevent this sort of thing in the future. Nobody wants it again—neither the players, the clubs nor the fans. It's inevitable that there will be hard feelings. My job is to hold them to a minimum . . . Who won? Nobody. The players suffered. The clubs suffered. Baseball suffered.

Chicago, April 13/
Los Angeles Times, 4-14:(3)1.

Player development, accomplished by maintaining some 150 minor-league clubs in as many cities, is costing the major-league clubs about $1.5 million apiece, for a total of $35-$40 million a year. It is an enormous drain on the owners. With the exception of hockey, baseball is the only sport which maintains its own player development program. Football, basketball and others are developed in the colleges and universities . . . and it is our hope that baseball, eventually, can enjoy the same break.

Scottsdale, Ariz., Oct. 25/
The Washington Post, 10-26:(D)7.

Tom Landry
Football coach, Dallas "Cowboys"

I believe winning is important. The real danger is when winning becomes the only thing. If you forsake your honesty and integrity to win a football game or championship, it's wrong. To some, victory must be attained at any cost. But there is a cost; and it's your own integrity. I try to win within the rules.

Interview, Dallas, Dec. 8/
The Washington Post, 12-10:(D)3.

Frank Lane
General manager,
Milwaukee "Brewers" baseball club

Professional baseball is the most expensive of the professional sports to operate. It costs between $1 million and $1.5 million a year for a farm system alone. Owning a team isn't the bonanza everyone seems to think. If the baseball strike (earlier this year) had lasted another 10 days or two weeks, I think there would have been three fewer American League clubs.

Interview/
Los Angeles Times, 7-21:(3)10.

Jim Lefebvre
Baseball player, Los Angeles "Dodgers"

(On the current player strike): All I hear from the owners is we're not going to get another red cent; that we can take it or leave it. Then I read the owners say the players are turning it (baseball) into a business. Well, what has it been for the owners for all these years? And when the owners say we don't care about the fans, they're wrong. We love our fans. We're ready to play and we want to play.

April 4/Los Angeles Times, 4-5:(3)3.

Carol Lynley
Actress

Watching professional basketball is a sexy experience . . . I really get kicks from watching those NBA superstars. Actually, basketball is a sort of living *Playboy* magazine in reverse and cleaned up. Football players look like moving mountains. Baseball players look like dear old dad walking down the drive for the Sunday paper in his floppy old bathrobe. But basketball players look like what they are—finely-honed male athletes. Even other men admire a well-built athlete. And with women, there is the added attraction of perfectly natural sex appeal.

Interview/
Los Angeles Herald-Examiner, 4-9:(C)5.

John Mackey
President,
National Football Players' Association

(On the current baseball player strike): It is now abundantly clear that the baseball owners are attempting by every means at their disposal—both legal and illegal—to destroy the Baseball Players' Association. I am shocked by the attitude of the owners who substitute vitriolic attacks on the Association's leadership for honest negotiations. Apparently they believe that they can fool the public by these tactics . . . There is no new money being sought by the players, and yet the baseball owners would like the public to believe that ticket prices will go up if the players are successful. The owners even reject the offer made by the players to submit all issues to neutral binding arbitration. This offer by the players would allow the American public to see baseball while the dispute is settled by the arbitrator. The owners must have something to hide from neutral parties because they have rejected this offer. The owners refuse to negotiate in good faith; refuse to consider outside arbitration; and refuse to allow the American people to see baseball. The conclusion is inescapable that they are intent on destroying the Players' Association.

April 8/
The Dallas Times Herald, 4-9:(C)12.

Mike Mansfield
United States Senator, D–Mont.

In lending itself to displays of violence, of defections, of anarchy, of dispute and dissension and even of madness, the arena of the Olympics has strayed far from its original concept of peace and unity among all men . . . It seems to me that too much emphasis has been placed on gold, silver and bronze medals, on commercialism, on nationalism.

Before the Senate, Washington, Sept. 6/
The Washington Post, 9-7:(A)12.

Tug McGraw
Baseball pitcher, New York "Mets"

Relief pitching is an art, and only the National League recognizes that fact. Specialization is the National League way, the modern way. I'm glad that my league has underlined the importance of a relief pitcher. He's really the 10th man on the team.

Interview, Atlanta, July 25/
Los Angeles Herald-Examiner, 7-26:(D)4.

Marvin Miller
Executive director,
Major League Baseball Players' Association

We hear all about the "high salaries" (of baseball players) every spring; but Hank Aaron probably has been underpaid for more

(MARVIN MILLER)

than 10 years. Wilt Chamberlain of pro basketball's *Lakers* has been making that kind of money (over $100,000 per year) for more than a decade. It's my general conclusion that major league baseball players are not overpaid, and there is strong evidence that they are underpaid. The players are prisoners of the clubs. The club pays them only what the club wants to pay them.

Fort Lauderdale, Fla., March 2/ Los Angeles Times, 3-3:(3)1.

(On claims of baseball clubs losing money): I don't believe any (baseball) club loses money. You'll notice every time a team changes hands it goes for more money. Take the Seattle *Pilots.* They went for $5.6 million originally. A year later, they moved to Milwaukee for $10.6 million. I'd like to have a business where you have a bad year and then can sell for that kind of money.

Palm Springs, Calif., March 22/ Los Angeles Herald-Examiner, 3-22:(B)5.

The point is, while (player) salaries have increased greatly, they have done so in far less proportion than the overall baseball revenue. Television has completely changed the game's economics. This year the owners will receive $41 million from TV. Total salaries are $19 million. The TV revenue almost covers the outlay for salaries and the pension plan without even getting into gate receipts. This is just one fact that wasn't considered by the fans during the (recent player strike), that wasn't really covered by the press. It makes better reading to hear some general manager say, "Marvin Miller is running me out of baseball."

Interview, New York/ Los Angeles Times, 5-3:(3)4.

Ernest Morris
President, Council of New York State Harness Tracks

Off-track betting is essentially a scavenger business. It sells tickets to a show produced and paid for by the horsemen and tracks. It is like a plant pest which feeds on the plant and kills it in the process . . . OTB has produced no revenue for New York City, and the state, the tracks, the horsemen and even the city itself are in the red by millions.

The New York Times, 1-2:(5)8.

Miguel Najdorf
Chess grandmaster

(On U.S. chess champion Bobby Fischer, currently playing Boris Spassky for the world championship in Reykjavik, Iceland): Fischer is interested only in chess. He is a special man. Even his sister, when she came here, had to make an appointment to see him. Always he is working on his chess, and he has refined it like no player before. Always he makes the simple move, the pure move . . . In musical terms, Fischer is a conductor rather than a composer. He directs the pieces, like Stokowski or Toscanini directed the musicians.

Interview, Reykjavik, Iceland, July 27/The New York Times, 7-30:(1)44.

Jack Nicklaus
Golfer

(His theory of golf competition): Over the first three rounds it's medal play—you're playing the course more than anything else, trying to beat the course. Then, somewhere in the final round if you're in contention, it becomes more or less match play and you're playing the man.

The Christian Science Monitor, 5-23:(B)10.

Claude Osteen
Baseball pitcher, Los Angeles "Dodgers"

(On a proposed player trade that would have sent him to another team): I'm not sure which is more insulting—being offered in a trade or having it turned down.

The Sporting News, 1-22:4.

Jesse Owens
Former Olympic track champion

I think this is the personal goal of every boy and girl who participates in the Olympic

Games: It's the end of all the training and the time that you will stand at the starting line, be it swimming, be it basketball or waiting for the bell in boxing or waiting for the gun in 100 meters. These are the kinds of things that stir us, because you think about the number of years you have worked to the point where you are able to stand on that day to represent your nation. Yes, it is nervous tension. It's a nervous, a terrible feeling. You feel, as you stand there, as if your legs can't carry the weight of your body. Your stomach isn't there and your mouth is dry and your hands are wet with perspiration. And you begin to think in terms of all the years that you have worked; in my particular case, the 100 meters, as you look down the field 109 yards and two feet away, and recognizing that, after eight years of hard work, that this is the point that I had reached and that all was going to be over in 10 seconds.

New York/
The New York Times, 7-23:(5)6.

Arnold Palmer
Golfer

I'm going to rest myself. I'm 42 years old. I'm not going to try to birdie the world any more.

Interview, Los Angeles/
The Washington Post, 1-8:(C)1.

Floyd Patterson
Former Heavyweight Boxing Champion of the World

I love boxing. I love training . . . I can't give a reason, outside of the whole experience of 22 years. But what intrigues me is that moment just before the fight, just as the bell rings and the fighters come at each other. The people watching don't know what's going to happen. And I, I don't know what's going to happen, either. That's what intrigues me.

Washington/
The Washington Post, 5-17:(E)1.

(On why he is seeking the championship again): I'm greedy. I want more—not in terms of money but, you know, I'm always trying to do better. I think this is what life is all about—trying to overcome. Why do I want to be champ again? I can't say success —I already have it. But to win the title a third time would be a marvelous thing simply because I'd be breaking my own record (of being two-time heavyweight champion).

Interview, New Paltz, N.Y./
Los Angeles Herald-Examiner, 8-27:(C)7.

Richard Petty
Auto racing driver

Any race driver worth his salt never has a letdown. He can't afford to let down and he can't afford to look ahead to a track or a race he may like better. You also must constantly realize the danger involved and keep your mind alert. The guy who feels he can afford to take it easy occasionally, should get out while he's in one piece.

The Christian Science Monitor, 3-20:13.

Tommy Prothro
Football coach, Los Angeles "Rams"

I don't think a coach can bring his team up. The players have to do it. The more respect a player has for his opponent, the higher he'll be. It's the coach's job to make his players respect the opponent.

Los Angeles Times, 2-14:(3)10.

(On violence in football): As far as football is concerned, there are two better words: aggressiveness and brutality. They come down to the same thing as violence, but they're more specific. Aggressiveness is a big part of football; it's what makes football. But there is no place for brutality.

Interview/
Los Angeles Times, 2-27:(D)1.

John Ralston
Former football coach, Stanford University; Now coach, Denver "Broncos"

I don't judge any boy who comes out for football by the length of his hair. I want to

(JOHN RALSTON)

know more about him as an individual. There was a time when you coached a team; now you coach individuals. There was a time you coached a boy; now you coach a mind.

San Francisco Examiner, 6-29:54.

John Rice
Baseball umpire, American League

(Arguing against women as umpires): For one thing, calling balls and strikes from behind the plate is a dangerous job. In the course of the season, we get nicked quite a few times by fouls, and it's something a man can shake off much easier than a woman. Then there would be the problem of dressing quarters. Where would she shower? Every ball park in the league would have to have a special women's dressing room. Umpiring through the heat of summer and doubleheaders can be physically rugged, with games today running three hours or more. I think they (ladies) would be surprised how demanding the job can be at the professional level, especially in the minors.

The Christian Science Monitor, 2-3:11.

Paul Richards
Vice president and general manager, Atlanta "Braves" baseball club

Let's go into a few facts of life in major league baseball. Say the *Braves* sign five young men, free agents interested in playing professional baseball, and assign them to clubs in our minor-league system . . . Of the five, statistics prove that we're fortunate if just one of them makes it to the parent club. This means that, regardless of what it actually cost us to bring him along as an individual, he becomes a $400,000 investment because of the others who failed. So now he's in the big leagues and what does he want? He wants to become a free agent at the end of his first season. Obviously, if a ball club is going to have all of its players turned loose at the end of the year, there's no point in any long-range expenditure. It would be wasted. So the junking of the reserve clause would mean the end of the farm system and the minor leagues . . . It makes you wonder how many of these men really appreciate the pension security and other benefits baseball has to offer today. They are being ill-advised (to work against the reserve clause) and don't know it . . . Baseball and its players have lived well under the reserve clause for many, many years. Now, all of a sudden, they say it's wrong.

Interview, West Palm Beach, Fla./The Christian Science Monitor, 3-16:11.

Joseph Robbie
Owner, Miami "Dolphins" football team

Every successful football coach is introspective, you know. It's impossible for an extrovert to be a good head coach . . . The distractions to this business you wouldn't believe. And there's only one way to escape them. That's by concentrating on whatever it is you have to do. You simply refuse to be distracted. And introverts concentrate better than extroverts. In fact, an extroverted person can hardly concentrate at all.

Interview, New Orleans/The Dallas Times Herald, 1-16:(C)2.

Jackie Robinson
Former baseball player

(On the current player strike): I congratulate the players. It's high time they stood up in this manner. The owners are going to respect the ballplayers a little more. The average ballplayer doesn't spend more than five or six years in the majors, and they want to get something so their future is secure. The fans will recognize that the ballplayers aren't like people who sit behind a desk. They may make big money for a few years, but Uncle Sam takes a big hunk of that, and then they're out of baseball.

The Washington Post, 4-4:(D)1.

Pete Rozelle
Commissioner, National Football League

I don't have to cater to any (team) owners. I've got a contract that runs for a long,

long time. I have independence. And frankly, a commissioner is much stronger now, in my opinion, than he was when there were 12 clubs; because with 12 clubs, if you've got two or three upset with you over some action you've taken, that's a pretty sizable clique. With 26, we don't have the cliques any more. With that many, you diffuse the pressures that might be exerted by two or three owners.

San Francisco Examiner, 1-5:51.

Legalized gambling on pro sports would dramatically change the character of fan interest in these sports. No longer will sports fans identify their interests with the success or failure of their favorite teams, but with the effect of their team's performance on the winning or losing of bets.

New York, Sept. 28/ The Washington Post, 9-29:(D)6.

Howard J. Samuels
President, New York City Off-Track Betting Corporation

(Advocating government-controlled gambling on sports in order to eliminate organized crime from that area): The only way we are going to reduce and eliminate this illegal gambling activity on such great American sports as baseball, football, basketball and hockey is to establish public institutions to handle and regulate betting on them. It seems to me that, if we can successfully compete with and drive organized crime out of these areas of gambling, we can concern ourselves less with the possibility of these sports being infiltrated by organized crime. If organized crime is making little money on the outcome of these sporting events, why should they be at all interested in affecting the outcome of them?

Before House Select Committee on Crime, Washington, June 7/ The Washington Post, 6-8:(D)1.

George Sauer
Former football player, New York "Jets"

I think as a sport—as sport activity—football can be a very beautiful thing . . . As it is played now, football reinforces the social ethic that aggression and competition is a healthy thing—that that's the way to become a success. That kind of thought has a potential for tragedy.

Interview/ Plainview (Tex.) Daily Herald, 1-26:6.

Tex Schramm
President, Dallas "Cowboys" football team

The key is that football arouses people emotionally. It arouses fans to the point where they get wrapped up in it—actually involved—emotionally. Their leader is the quarterback, and they have to rely on him. But no quarterback is close to perfect. And when a mistake is made, the fans take it personally. They become angry, bitter and hurt—mostly hurt.

Los Angeles Times, 10-17:(3)7.

Rip Sewell
Former baseball player, Pittsburgh "Pirates"

(On the impending baseball players strike): First the players wanted a hamburger, and they (the owners) gave them a hamburger. Then they wanted a filet mignon, and they gave them a filet mignon. Then they wanted the whole damn cow, and now that they got the cow they want a pasture to put him in. You just can't satisfy them (the players), and I have no sympathy for any of them.

The Dallas Times Herald, 4-3:(B)4.

Bill Sharman
Basketball coach, Los Angeles "Lakers"

(Pep talks are) more important in contact sports like football and hockey. Basketball is a game of special skills, and it's probably more important to be relaxed than overtly keyed up.

Los Angeles Times, 2-14:(3)10.

Robert E. Short
Owner,
Texas "Rangers" baseball club

Ticket sales are important, but not the most important piece of income (for ball clubs). This would be radio-TV; here your gross is your net.

Interview/
The Dallas Times Herald, 4-30:(G)1.

(Advocating continuance of the baseball reserve clause): There is a difference between baseball and basketball. I was in both. There's a difference in baseball and football. We (in baseball) look at a kid when he's 18 years old and say he could be a Babe Ruth at 23 or 24, give him an X number of dollars and pay for his apprenticeship. By the time he becomes Babe Ruth—if he does in fact—we kind of think he ought to continue his loyalty to the organization that brought him to that point. In basketball, when you sign someone like Elgin Baylor, everyone knows he's going to be the equivalent of a Babe Ruth in his sport. The same is true in football. The colleges are the farm systems in those sports. Baseball doesn't have that luxury.

June 19/
The New York Times, 6-20:47.

John R. Silber
President, Boston University

The situation in American college football is so ridiculous that any time you speak out on it, it is funny. But I'm not joking. I have recommended to the presidents of the Yankee Conference that we adopt a rule in our conference that coaches be prohibited from engaging in contact with their teams during the playing of the game. It would be highly desirable, in my opinion, to restore the position of quarterback to its former dignity and turn the game over to the students . . . The way coaches call the shots and the way substitutions are made now, things like spirit, conditioning and mental capabilities mean very little. Is there no educational value in the game? I think there is. Let the players learn what to do and then put it into practice.

The New York Times, 9-17:(5)7.

Stan Smith
Tennis player

Confidence and experience in all walks of life are the factors that separate winners from talented people that never quite make it. In tennis, the more confident you are, the more bold you can be in going for the big shot at the crucial time. You have to know in your own mind that you can make the ball do what you want it to. And experience goes right along with that. You have to know how you react in every situation, what you must watch out for, what your opponent is likely to do. Experience tells you what to do; confidence allows you to do it.

Quote, 7-23:93.

Sam Snead
Golfer

A lot of guys on the tour are nice guys, but that's the trouble with them—they're too nice. They'll never win with that attitude. I wouldn't hurt a chicken crossing the road; but if I got a man in trouble on the golf course, I'd kick the hell out of him—I don't care if he's my best friend.

Los Angeles Times, 8-14:(3)2.

Boris Spassky
World chess champion

We (in Russia) take much interest in chess. It is as much the national sport of Russia as baseball in the United States. I would not care to be the man who allows the championship to go to another nation. It would be a serious matter in many ways . . .

The Washington Post, 7-2:(H)4.

Boris Spassky
Former world chess champion

(On his just-completed championship loss to Bobby Fischer): I had so many bad games. I lost my chance to win so many times. I made so many blunders. There is a law in sports: If you have a chance, catch this chance. It's not possible to win if you lose such opportunities . . . Fischer won a good match. I like his fighting spirit. He played very accurately and he showed himself a good technical player. But his understanding of chess is not the best in the world. He is practical but he is not imaginative, not very creative. I am more imaginative in grasping the sense of the position, and I have more experience.

Interview, Reykjavik, Iceland, Sept. 2/ San Francisco Examiner, 9-3:(A)12.

Sam Steiger
United States Representative, R–Ariz.

The last thing I want to be is a destructor of (horse) racing. That's because I really believe in it. The horse business deserves a better reputation than it has. But I think it's clear that the industry hasn't done a good job in policing itself (against crime) . . . racing has a problem it won't face up to.

San Francisco Examiner, 7-20:52.

Jackie Stewart
Auto racing driver

Racing has everything the dreams imagine and the films show. And some of the drivers want to conjure up in the minds of the fans and the women the idea that they are heroes and gladiators—they're no fools. Well, they're not gladiators, but they're not run-of-the-mill guys, either. They've chosen a very difficult road to travel, a road that's exciting and daring. But racing has a lot more. Of course, the drivers go to parties and they attract women. And some of them drink, though few of them drink very much. Basically, we're professionals. You have to be quite mature to be successful in this line of work. You need to have more than just natural driving talent. You have to be a thinker, with an almost computerized mind. If you aren't, you might never live long enough to become a top performer. Motor racing today is just so damned competitive, the technology is so advanced and the stakes so high that there isn't room for dilettantes.

Interview/ Los Angeles Herald-Examiner, 5-21:(C)9.

Harland Svare
Football coach, San Diego "Chargers"

It's personnel that wins, not coaching. You think you can lift a team with your own leadership and coaching, but you can't . . . The function of a football coach is the accumulation, evaluation and training of personnel, and the greatest of these is accumulation.

Interview, San Diego/ Los Angeles Times, 8-11:(3)9.

Cliff Temple
British sports writer

A (sports) journalist is someone who would if he could, but he can't, so he tells those who already can how they should.

Los Angeles Times, 1-26:(3)2.

Duane Thomas
Football player, Dallas "Cowboys"

In professional football, you have to go through channels (if you have a complaint or problem). Everything is channels. It's like playing that little kid game where you whisper a word in somebody's ear and it's passed along down a line. At the end, it comes out differently than the way it started.

Interview, Dallas/ Los Angeles Times, 3-17:(3)7.

Frank Thompson, Jr.
United States Representative, D–N.J.

The relationship between the (baseball) players and the (club) owners has changed rapidly in the past few years. This is because the players realize that professional sports is a multi-million dollar business and are beginning to demand bargaining rights commensurate with their status. As things now stand, the owners have virtual life and death control over the careers of professional athletes.

*March 5/
The Washington Post, 3-6:(D)2.*

Lee Trevino
Golfer

I used to tell jokes and nobody laughed. Now (since becoming a champion golfer), I tell the same jokes and they crack up. Then, I had no car. Now I have five. I used to live in a two-bed trailer. Now I'm building a five-bedroom home. I didn't have a phone then. Now I have an unlisted number. I used to scrape for a living, trying to get people to take lessons. Now everybody wants a lesson. I get $9,000 for an exhibition—$12,000 on a weekend. But you know, I can't teach any better. I've still got the same swing . . . It's all in the mind and the guts. The *opportunity* to play for $150,000 and $200,000 is all you need.

*Interview, St. Louis/
The Sporting News, 1-8:3.*

There are a lot of guys . . . with more (golfing) ability than I have. But I beat them because I've got a better attitude. The only thing you can do is go out and play the best you know how. Don't lose your temper. Don't blow a fuse. When you mess up a shot or get a bad break, shake it off and forget it. Remember, somebody else is pulling the strings.

*Interview, Pebble Beach, Calif., June 18/
Los Angeles Times, 6-19:(3)1.*

Bill Veeck
Former baseball club owner

If you watched the last World Series, which is being acclaimed by many baseball people to be one of the most exciting in history, you may not be too surprised to know that, in reality, the average baseball fan finds nothing very exciting about a 1-0, two-hour game. I, for one, like nothing better than an 11-8 game or something like that. But baseball has refused to take any kind of moves that would add more offense and excitement to the game. On the other hand, every move football has made has been done with the fans in mind, with the accent on opening the game up . . . Frankly, I believe that all sports entrepreneurs—be it baseball, horse racing or anything else—should keep in mind one thing: create an atmosphere of fun. This is the entertainment business, not religion.

*Interview, New York/
San Francisco Examiner & Chronicle, 12-17:(C)8.*

Harry Walker
Baseball manager, Houston "Astros"

I talk to them (his team) as little as I can. The modern player resents authority—he rebels at being told to do this or that. I stay away from the players as much as possible. I am happier this way and I'm sure they are, too . . . If I had 25 who would listen to me, I know I could help them. But there are kids today who won't listen, who don't want help.

Los Angeles Times, 5-24:(3)2.

Earl Warren
Former Chief Justice of the United States

There are two sides of the coin in the question of the relative merits of baseball and football. There is not only the degree of skill and excitement that has been brought into football, but the fact of what they have done to baseball. Baseball has been hurt very largely because of the slowness of the game. It used to be they would play a game of baseball in an hour and 45 minutes. A two-hour game was rather a long game. But now they let the pitcher stand out there and go through a lot of gyrations and pick up the resin bag and pick up his trousers and adjust his hat and a lot of other things, and the game is lasting two or three hours. You add that to the fact that they also play these night games which start at 8 o'clock. People who go can't get to bed before midnight, so people don't go as they used to. We live in an age of action, and people want to see it, particularly in an athletic event. I am just as much a devotee of baseball as football, but I can understand why more people don't go to baseball games.

Interview, Washington/
Los Angeles Times, 12-12:(2)7.

Alex Webster
Football coach, New York "Giants"

(On how he got the *Giants* into line after he became coach): I locked the clubhouse door and said: "I've been a very nice guy and you've taken advantage of me. When I finish talking, I'm going out that door into the corridor and I'm going to beat the stuffings out of anyone who thinks his way is better than mine. I'll take you on one at a time or two at a time. Come on out and fight." After five minutes I went back in and said: "That's what I thought. I'm the toughest guy here. From now on we'll do it my way."

Los Angeles Times, 12-12:(3)2.

Tom Weiskopf
Golfer

I suppose new fans are attracted to our sport because of the glamor of the large paychecks, and that has to be good for me. But I'm out here primarily to try to win, not to try to make a fortune and retire in five years. I hope to be able to play another 20 years. That's what I want to do in life. I enjoy golf. The money's great, but secondary. Besides, if you went around the course on the last day of a tight tournament thinking about what it's going to cost you if you miss a putt, you'd be out of contention before you knew what hit you. When I face a putt, I think about which way it will break, what the grain of the grass is going to do to it, and how hard I need to hit it to get it to the hole—not about how much money it's worth.

Interview, Miami/
The Christian Science Monitor, 3-14:21.

Jerry West
Basketball player, Los Angeles "Lakers"

Among sports fans, there's considerably more interest in an athlete who makes \$100,000 than one who gets \$50,000 . . . They might complain, but they flock to see high-paid athletes play. It's up to us to make the public understand the key fact—that athletes have very short careers. A man making \$100,000 one day is looking for a job the next day. But at \$100,000, he's somebody the world wants to see. Baseball is one of the few sports that understands this and publicizes salaries.

Interview, Los Angeles/
Los Angeles Times, 3-21:(3)1.

Maury Wills
Baseball player, Los Angeles "Dodgers"

Baseball is 100 per cent mental, as far as I'm concerned. And no one is a star, or a superstar, unless he has the right approach. Even Willie Mays or Sandy (Koufax) would have been nothing without the positive, concrete confidence that they *could* be great, that they could do something better than anyone else in the game.

Interview/Family Weekly, 6-25:20.

Pepper Wilson
Former vice president and general manager, Cincinnati "Royals" basketball team

(Criticizing U.S. Senator Sam Ervin's opposition to an ABA-NBA merger): Contrary to what they—Senator Ervin and others—say, pro basketball is on the fringe of bankruptcy. Senator Ervin points out that many of the owners are millionaires; but he didn't point out that they didn't make the money in basketball.

Cincinnati/
The Dallas Times Herald, 5-13:(A)2.

John Wooden
Basketball coach,
University of California, Los Angeles

(On violence in college basketball): Fans, officials, coaches and players are all involved.

(JOHN WOODEN)

But the coach can be the catalyst. I would be very much in favor of a rule that said if the coach got up from the bench even one time—other than at a time out—he'd be run right out of the game. If I got up, I'd expect to go. One coach in our conference this season was up 38 times in a game; I had someone check it for me.

At basketball writers luncheon, Los Angeles, March 27/ Los Angeles Times, 3-28:(3)3.

Phil Woolpert
Athletic director, University of San Diego

It's a shame to see what has happened to amateur basketball as a result of the situation in the pros (professional teams luring college players by offering high salaries) . . . When (Lew) Alcindor went pro, people were amazed at the kind of contract he reportedly got . . . Just one man . . . can make a franchise; and that's worth millions and millions to the team that can get him.

Interview/ Los Angeles Herald-Examiner, 3-5:(C)2.

Tom Yawkey
Owner, Boston "Red Sox" baseball club

There's one phase of this player-management relationship that I simply cannot understand. They (the players) keep wanting more and more—a higher minimum salary, increased pension benefits, more expense money during spring training, more meal money during the season and more traveling money if traded or sold. It just goes on and on, and up and up, with no end in sight. Now I'd like to ask a question. Where do they think all the money is coming from? Do they expect the fans to foot the increased bill? Do they expect us to increase admission prices and risk putting ourselves out of business? . . . I don't think there's an owner in baseball who wouldn't be satisfied to break even financially, or perhaps show a little profit. But if we have to keep passing more and more along to the players, where will it all come from?

Interview, Boston/ The Christian Science Monitor, 6-20:17.

The Indexes

Index to Speakers

A

B

C

D

E

F

G

H

I

J

K

L

M

N

O

P

Q

R

S

T

U

V

W

Y

Z

Index to Subjects

A

B

C

D

E

F

G

H

I

J

K

L

M

N

O

P

T

U

V

W

Y

Z